中国特色汉英分类词典系列

中国社会生活汉英词典

主编 章宜华

商务印书馆
The Commercial Press

图书在版编目(CIP)数据

中国社会生活汉英词典 / 章宜华主编；王倩倩等编写. —北京：商务印书馆，2023
（中国特色汉英分类词典系列）
ISBN 978-7-100-23222-7

Ⅰ.①中… Ⅱ.①章…②王… Ⅲ.①社会生活—中国—词典—汉、英 Ⅳ.① D669-61

中国国家版本馆 CIP 数据核字（2023）第 224950 号

权利保留，侵权必究。

中国特色汉英分类词典系列
中国社会生活汉英词典
章宜华　主编
王倩倩等　编写

商务印书馆出版
（北京王府井大街36号　邮政编码100710）
商务印书馆发行
北京市十月印刷有限公司印刷
ISBN 978-7-100-23222-7

2023年12月第1版　　　开本 880×1230　1/32
2023年12月北京第1次印刷　印张 20

定价：130.00元

主　　　编：章宜华

主 要 编 写：章宜华

编 写 人 员：王倩倩　　　唐舒航　　　崔仲爻　　　何宇艳

部 分 参 编：张凯文　　　吴舒莹　　　陈　珊

特色词整理：廖彩宴　　　徐　浩　　　张　弦　　　范宝仪　　　翟佳慧
　　　　　　廖承敏　　　吴慧敏　　　张梦雨　　　王浩东　　　王欢欢
　　　　　　禹　婷　　　何　贝　　　陈　静　　　谢莉颖　　　胡　博
　　　　　　田盛凯　　　高冠鹏　　　胡　惠　　　刘　思　　　罗丽沙
　　　　　　苏海霞

特色词提取：黎思敏　　　阳豆豆　　　杨雅艺　　　李　玲　　　余文涛
　　　　　　张　慧　　　郑　飞　　　邹婷婷　　　刘　燕　　　朱　垚
　　　　　　程佳琳　　　王彬聪　　　蔡佳良　　　王　丽　　　戴　琴
　　　　　　刘　燕　　　李惠贤　　　贺志桢　　　赵天凤　　　于珊珊
　　　　　　车振卿　　　万芳吁　　　李梅梅　　　宁　萍

语 料 整 理：吴婷婷　　　葛小帅　　　张红岩　　　吴　澄　　　盛　蔚
　　　　　　卢念春　　　王　燕　　　成莉铭　　　何　帆　　　潘良发
　　　　　　刘燕菲　　　葛南南　　　刘梦露　　　吉伟琴　　　翟朗维
　　　　　　蒋佩洁　　　熊　怡　　　刘小芹

医 学 审 校：王晓鹰

英 语 审 校：Fraser Sutherland

本词典得到国家社科基金重点项目（20AYY012）的资助

序

2017年仲秋,商务印书馆英语室主任马浩岚女士来广外调研,在参观词典学研究中心主持的国家社科重点项目"涉华英语语言知识库及应用平台建设研究"的成果时,对涉华英语语料库以及从语料库中提取的中国特色文化词很感兴趣,于是提议在该项目成果的基础上编写《中国特色汉英分类词典》系列。由于我们的前期研究比较扎实,积累的相关语言资源多,很快便得到商务印书馆立项,并纳入了中国出版集团的重点出版规划。

当时之所以申报"涉华英语语言知识库",是因为我们作为高校的外语教师强烈地感受到"涉华英语"或"中国英语"在英语教学、教材编写和词典编纂中的缺位。我国英语学习者众多,仅高校在校学生就有4 000余万人,他们大多学习英语,而英语教学却缺乏原创教材,要么是国外引进,要么是用国外的语言素材编写而成,更缺乏面向中国EFL学习者编写的词典。因此,英语学习主要是域外语言文化的单向输入,即教材、词典和教学内容都来自英美等国家,语言描述的对象和语境都是西方的,教师强调让学生学习地道的英美英语,而学生学到的大多是用英语表达外国事物的技能。然而,绝大多数学生毕业后是立足国内工作的,但却不善于用英语表达本国事物,这直接限制了他们英语能力的发挥。因此,我们想结合"中国英语"(China English)的研究,从语言资源上入手改变目前的这种情况。于是便申报了国家社科基金重点课题,建成了涉华英语语料库和中国特色词英语表达库,以期为英语教学以及教材和词典的编写提供规范的中国特色英语(normative China English),让学生既能较轻松地学会地道的英语,又能够用英语表达国内的事件或事物。同时,这也有利于中国文化的对外传播,向世界阐释中国的作为及其对世界"人类共同体"建设和发展的积极意义,塑造中国的形象。

目前,国内辞书市场上只有几本"汉英新特色词汇(词典)",收词2 000—5 000条,仅提供英语对等词或表达,尚无法满足现实需要。本词典是基于大规模涉华语料库而编写,从中国风土民俗、中国社会生活、中国文史艺术、中国政经法商等四类80多个方面全面收录反映中国文化历史、发展和现实的特色词汇,并从其发展历史、使用语域、英语表达、文化内涵和发生地等多方面进行注释和解释。

由于语料库取自多种渠道,因此一个中国特色词,甚至是专名往往都会有多种表达方式。例如,经典汉语特色词汇由于起源较早,英译形式有拉丁字母拼写、威妥玛式和汉语拼音拼写等,还夹杂着港澳的特殊拼写形式;现代的文化特色词也有音译、直译、意译,以及简译、全译等,构成十分复杂。同一个汉语词在不同时期、不同语料来源往往有不同的表述方法,造成"一对多"的现象普遍存在。这给统一和"规范"带来很大的难度。为此,主持人利用英美访学的机会,对特色词的各种英语表达方法进行了问卷调查,又就前期样稿及中国经典特色词部分书面征求了美国汉学家夏洛特·孙(Charlotte Sun)和教育学专家米汉甫的意见,并请加拿大词典专家弗雷泽·萨瑟兰(Fraser Sutherland)审校了全部的前期词条。在综合各方意见的基础上确定以"尊重历史、立足现实、面向未来,描写为主、适当规范"为总原则进行词典的收词和释义,既要重视历史存在,又考虑了当前的语言现实和今后国际语言传播的趋势。在这个总原则下较好地处理了中国特色词多样化英语表达的问题。

当前,无论是国际文化传播和交流,还是"一带一路"之"五通"(政策沟通、设施联通、贸易畅通、资金融通、民心相通),其关键都是语言交流的畅通;而语言的畅通,主要是要消除中国特色词表达和理解的障碍。但从目前的研究来看,我们外宣中特色词的表达仍比较混乱,有些译法经常会出现错误,造成误解和交流障碍,期望这部系列词典的出版有助于解决这些问题。

  该系列词典收词量大(达4万余条),涉及的语料来源多,同一汉语词所对应的英语表达多种多样,如何取舍和编排,在处理的系统性和规范性等方面仍有较大的改进空间。这当然也涉及一些需要学术探索的内容,也需要辞书学界同仁来共同探讨和研究。

章宜华

广东外语外贸大学词典学研究中心
外国语言学及应用语言学研究中心
2021年12月

前　言

　　《中国特色汉英分类词典》系列主要是基于大型"涉华英语语料库"编写而成的。首先通过专门的分词和提取软件从语料库中提取中国特色词汇的英语表达，然后人工干预识别，确定英语词表；最后由英语翻译成"地道"的汉语，并把汉语确定为词目词。这种方法与先确立汉语词表然后进行翻译的传统做法有很大的不同。"涉华英语语料库"分为两个子库和一个专题库，子库-I为英语母语者书写或翻译的涉华语料，子库-II是中国媒体和出版社出版的中国人用英语写成或翻译的涉华语料。每一子库又分为在线媒体和纸质媒体两部分。在线部分取自具有广泛影响的报纸和刊物，纸质部分取自有关中国历史、文化、经典，以及社会、政治、经济等书籍。这些资料都出自国内外著名出版社，语言质量可信度比较高。专题库的英语语料主要来源于《中国丛报》(Chinese Repository)，是由美部会的传教士裨治文和卫三畏创办和主持编辑，共出版220期1 300余篇文章，其中90%涉及中国当时的语言、地理、自然、风土人情、宗教、文化和社会生活等内容，主要目的一是向西方介绍中国国情，二是做实时报道和评论，故有很多反映中国文化特色的英语表达。

　　三个子库的总文本数为176 605，字符数为5.829亿，单词数为1.18亿词。这种语料库对于提取普通中国特色英语词(China English for general use)是足够了，但对于编写有关多民族的风土民俗、文化遗产、文史艺术和社会文化等方面的词典则显得有些不足。于是，我们便利用人工关键词索引的方法，对词典所涉及各个领域的英语资料进行了广泛的搜集、梳理、筛选和整理，以补充涉华英语语料库的不足。

　　由于语料库取自多种渠道，收词的时间跨度长，语料所反映的特色词英语对应表达多而杂乱。针对这种情况,我们编制了详尽的《中国特色汉英分类词典》编写方案。为了解决好中国特色词中的"一对多"的现象,给读者提供客观、准确和规范的英语表达,编写组在英美相关大学就特色词翻译方法进行了问卷调查,又把相关稿子交给美国爱达荷大学从事中国儒学研究的夏洛特·孙教授和伊利诺伊大学华裔教授米汉甫先生审校,在综合各方意见的基础上确定以"尊重历史、立足现实、面向未来,描写为主、适当规范"为词典编纂的总原则。在此基础上又根据各类特色词的特点拟定了约万字的翻译原则,对各种专用名称、旅游景区和景点、国家物质和非物质文化遗产、政府和组织机构名称和中国菜肴等做了具体规定。

为了确保汉语词目的地道性和"习语性"、英语译文的正确性和易解性,我们首先对从英语翻译过来的汉语词目词进行逐条审核,然后从原文语境中弄清其真实含义后进行审定。在实际操作层面上,取自"涉华英语语料库"的英语表达质量上大多比较可靠,只需稍作调整即可;但后面通过网络在相关网站上收集的专题语料质量上不太可靠,特别是一些旅游景区、文化遗产、传统习俗、风土人情方面的词,大多是汉语拼音组成,或是按字面意思逐字翻译而成,大多不能直接采用,需要通过网络逐条查阅其命名的来源和含义后重新翻译。例如,一些地名或景点的名称含有"山""河""湾""湖""潭""滩""沟""峡""岭""龙""凤"等,对确实与指称相关联的要译出其含义,因为它们反映了地名或景点的基本特征;如果仅是个地名,就按其字面音译。对于一些根据典故和经典诗词名篇命名的景点,要考证其诗文的原文含义,归纳其核心寓意,然后进行翻译,例如承德避暑山庄的72景等分别是康熙和乾隆皇帝命名的,其名如诗,其意如画,要译出其精髓绝非易事,都需要逐条考证其命名过程。对于其他特色词,通常会对一些特色鲜明的词采用音译加注释,或音译/直译加意译的方法。为了考察编写的质量,我们把前期初步编好的两万多词条全部交给英语母语词典专家,加拿大的弗雷泽·萨瑟兰(Fraser Sutherland)进行了审核,最后又请了广外高翻学院的余东、张保红和欧阳俊峰教授对部分经典特色词和国家物质/非物质文化遗产的译名等进行复审。在此基础上,确定了我们整个特色词翻译的质量标准。

《中国特色汉英分类词典》系列共收词4万余条,分为中国风土民俗、中国社会生活、中国文史艺术、中国政经法商四部,每部收词1万左右。具体内容如下:

1)中国风土民俗包括:人文地理(含旅游景区)、动植物、节气、节日、节庆、民族生活(含特有茶、酒、饮食等)、民族乐器、民族音乐/戏曲,体育、运动、风俗、习俗(婚丧嫁娶)等。

2)中国社会生活包括:茶、酒、饮食、炊具、陶瓷、布料、服饰、中医、中药、货币、度量;社会展示、社会教育、社会现象、社会关系、社会生活、社会职业、社会团体以及新兴事物等。

3)中国文史艺术包括:历史朝代、历史人物、历史事件、文化遗产,宗教哲学、理论学说、经典名篇、传统文化、传统习惯表达、语言文学史实,书法艺术、乐器音乐、电影戏曲等。

4)中国政经法商包括:国家体制、社会制度,政治、经济、司法、商业、科技、金融;革命运动、社会变革、武器战争、国家机构团体(政府、事业和服务机构)、政治人物及职业等。

每部词典的内容又分两大部分。普通词条放在词典的正文中,提供语域(使用场合)或性质状态,应用范围信息,特色词的英语表达及其文化、百科、语义和属地等解释,以及必要的参见标注等;系统的、"成建制"条目按不同的类别组织在一起,作为词典的附录。两部分内容均按汉语拼音次序编排。

本词典所依据的涉华英语语料库和知识库的建设始于2013年,广外词典学研究中心研究生自2011级到2021级都不同程度地参与了有关语料搜集和特色词提取等工作,特别是2014级、2016级、2017级、2018级研究生作出了比较突出的贡献。值此词典出版之际对他们的工作表示最诚挚的感谢。本系列词典收词多,语言现象十分复杂,尽管制定了详细的编纂体例和翻译原则,也只是挂一漏万,难以周全;词条种类繁多,统一难度大。况且,学无止境,特色词的文化蕴含深邃博奥,需要不断地追寻探索,不能浅尝辄止。切望广大用户帮助发现问题,以利改进与提高。

章宜华

广东外语外贸大学词典学研究中心

外国语言学及应用语言学研究中心

2021 年 12 月

目　录

凡　例 　　　　　　　　　　　　　　　　　　　　　1

正　文 　　　　　　　　　　　　　　　　　　　1—558

附录一　《牛津英语大词典》中的汉语借词词表　　559

附录二　《韦氏第三版新国际英语词典》
　　　　中的汉语借词词表　　　　　　　　　　579

附录三　坎农版英语中的汉语借词词表　　　　　598

凡　例

一、词目

1. 选词立目

参照语料库频率统计,结合具体需要进行选词。同一概念有多种表达方式时,选取使用最多、最广泛的为词目词;如果有多个变体都常用的,则分别立目;术语、短语、组织机构名一般收其全称,十分常用的简称可收为副条。对于部分搭配能力强、可生成多种短语的表达结构,酌情抽象出核心句式立为词目。

2. 词目词处理

对于典籍等名称保留书名号,对词目词构成成分有特殊含义的按源文保留引号。对于词目的变体或结构相近的词,如果只是局部变化,则用"[　]"注释,表示内容替换,不另立条目,如"浪费公共资产[资金]"等。对于词目词的缩写形式或非局部变化的变体,则另立条目。

3. 排序

词目的排列顺序,以词目词的拼音、声调为主,笔画为辅。同音异调的,按声调顺序排列;同音同调而异形的,按笔画数排列;笔画数相同时,按起笔横、竖、撇、点、折顺序排列。词目词首字相同时,则按第二个字排序,以此类推。词目中的字母、数字或省略号也参加排序;书名号和引号不参加排序。

4. 义项与语义

由于中国特色词大多构词方式比较复杂、语义特殊,不再提供义项划分信息。如,中医　traditional Chinese medicine; doctor of traditional Chinese medicine。

二、语域标签

1. 词典不设置门类词,而是按汉语词目的语言属性和特色词提取的语境设置统一的"域"标注,说明使用范围。

2. 标注内容包括:来源域(不同的民族)、语域(使用场合或领域)、时域(使用的时期)、地域(特定地方或方言)、社会域(不同社会团体/阶层用词)、专业领域(各专业门类用词)等。

3. 域标注用尖括号"〈 〉"表示。如果涉及两个及以上的域名时,均放在同一个括号内,中间用逗号","分隔。

4. 时域的划分只分为两类:〈旧〉〈古〉。

5. 域的标注以"简洁、明快、灵活"为原则,对所指明确的词不再标注域。以服饰为例,词头含有"衣、裙、服、衫"的则不标注域,而"彩帨""蔽膝"则标〈古服饰〉;如果英语表达中有年代注释,也不再注〈古〉,例如:短襦〈服饰〉 short gown (in the Tang Dynasty)。

三、英语释义

1. 由于本词典是基于涉华英美语言语料库编写的,英语对等表达只需反映语言现实,不刻意区分英语和美语拼写方式。

2. 所提供的英语表达(含短语、句式和小句)一律作抽象的词汇单位来处理,除专名和构词本身需要外,一般不加定冠词,起始字母一般不大写,尾部不加句号。

3. 对于"山""河"之类专名,若确与实物相关联则需译出其含义,但对于"单音节专名+通名"构成的专名,需保留其全部专名拼音再加意译通名,如"珠江/Zhujiang River"等。

4. 为了提高词典的参考性和丰富性,适当保留从语料库提取出来的"一对多"英语表达,但一般不超过三个。

5. 在多个英语近义表达中,若只有个别词汇的差异,且形式较长的话,用斜杠"/"并列书写变体,表示可视使用语境相互替代。

6. 对于重要的党政和组织机构的名称,原则优先提供正式文件中使用或约定俗成的英语表达,若有推荐表达则排列在后面。

7. 英语对等词为专名者按语言规则首字母大写,其他如中药名、中医处方名、中餐菜名等,其所有构成成分的实词首字母大写。

8. 景区或景点作为唯一专名者首字母一律大写,但多地都有的景点则当作普通名称处理。

9. 普通名词(如公路、市县、村镇、山川河流等)只有充当某个地方专名的一部分时,才将其首字母大写。当它们单独出现或与专名无关(不指称唯一)时,不大写。

10. 对于带连字符(-)的词,如果两个词都是实词则首字母均需大写,如果前面是词缀或虚词,后面的词小写;姓名的名字中间有连字符的,后面的也小写。

四、英语注释

1. 英语注释分为前注和后注两种,用圆括号"( )"标记。前注说明被释义词英语表达的具体使用场景或适用范围,后注主要提供语义、文化、百科和属地信息等。

2. 前注以"(of …)"形式标注,后注直接放在圆括号内。对于专属景点和景区,注明其所在省的名称(名称中出现省名者不重复加注);大景区内的景点不再加属地注释。

3. 带书名号的词目词,英语表达前注属性(如有必要),后注其作者和年代/年份等。

4. 在英语表达中,音译词后有些会提供拈注,说明其指称意义。

五、参见

1. 对于有某种关联的词目词之间提供参见注释,以汉语形式表达,放在整个词条的结尾处。

2. 对于常用的简称,一般另立词条,提供简称的对等词,并参见全称。

3. 对于同一事物、事件和概念有几种汉语表达,且都十分常用的,可以分立词目,并相互参见,如有主次之分的则只设单向参见。

Numbers

211 工程	Project 211 (the construction projects of about 100 universities and a batch of key disciplines in the 21st century)
21 世纪海上丝绸之路	the 21st-Century Maritime Silk Road
CT 影像	computed tomography imaging
IgM 抗体检测	〈防疫〉IgM antibody test
N95 口罩	〈防疫〉N95 mask/respirator

A

阿里巴巴集团	Alibaba Group
阿是穴	〈中医药〉Ashi acupoint; non-fixed point
阿宗面线	〈饮食〉Ay-Chung Flour-Rice Noodles (Taiwan snack)
艾德莱丝绸	Adlai silk (a speciality of Xinjiang)
艾灸	〈中医药〉moxa-wool moxibustion; moxibustion therapy
艾绒	〈中医药〉(of Latin) Folium Fibra Artemisiae Argyi; Moxa Floss; Mugwort Floss
艾条	〈中医药〉moxa stick
艾条灸	〈中医药〉moxa stick moxibustion; moxibustion with moxa stick
艾窝窝	〈饮食〉Aiwowo; Steamed Rice Cakes with Sweet Stuffing
艾叶	〈中医药〉(of Latin) Folium Artemisiae Argyi; Argy Wormwood Leaf; Mugwort Leaf
艾炷	〈中医药〉moxa cone
艾炷灸	〈中医药〉moxa cone moxibustion; moxibustion with moxa cone
爱国华侨	patriotic overseas Chinese
爱面子	to be concerned with face-saving; to be sensitive about one's reputation
爱鸟周	Bird-Loving Week (from April to the early May)
爱心工程	Loving Care Project
安宫牛黄丸	〈中医药〉Angong Niuhuang Wan; Cow-Bezoar Bolus for Resurrection

安化黑茶	Anhua Dark tea
安化松针	〈茶〉Anhua Pine Needle-Shaped Green tea
安徽菜	〈饮食〉→徽菜
安徽古黟黑茶	Anhui Guyi dark tea; Anhui Ancient Yi tea
安徽毛峰	〈茶〉Anhui Maofeng tea; Anhui Tippy tea
安吉白片	〈茶〉Anji Baipian green tea
安家费	settling-in allowance
安酒	Anjiu liquor (one of the eight famous liquors in Guizhou)
安全返岗	〈防疫〉to return to the post in security
安全有序返乡	〈防疫〉to return home in a safe and orderly manner
安神补心丸	〈中医药〉Anshen Buxin Wan; Sedative and Heart-Invigorating Pill
安神法	〈中医药〉spirit-quieting method; tranquillization method
安神剂	〈中医药〉cerebral sedative; tranquillizing formula
安神胶囊	〈中医药〉Anshen Jiaonang; Spirit-Calming Capsule
安胃片	〈中医药〉Anwei Pian; Stomachache Calming Tablet
安慰奖	consolation prize
安消部经理	fire safety manager
安阳刀	〈币〉Anyang knife (an ancient coin of the Spring and Autumn period and Warring States period)
安臧圜钱	〈币〉Anzang round coin (issued in the Warring States period)
安置房	housing placement; resettlement housing; housing sold to those being relocated
鞍马俑	〈陶瓷〉figurine of horse with saddle
按揭贷款	mortgage loan
按揭购房	to buy a house on mortgage; to mortgage a house
按劳分配	distribution according to one's performance
按压法	〈中医药〉pressure massage; pressure manipulation

案板	〈饮食〉kitchen board
暗红张	〈茶〉dull red leaf
暗裥袋	inverted pleated pocket
暗恋	unrequited love; to fall in love with someone secretly
暗箱操作	black case work
暗杂	〈茶〉dull and mixed
奥密克戎病毒	〈防疫〉Omicron virus

B

八宝冰	〈饮食〉Eight-delicacy Ice; Shaved Ice with Eight Delicacies
八宝菠菜	〈饮食〉Quick-Boiled Spinach Mixed with "Eight Delicacies"
八宝饭	Babao Fan, Eight-Delicacies Rice Pudding (steamed glutinous rice with bean paste, lotus seeds and preserved fruit, etc.)
八宝海茸羹	〈饮食〉Seaweed Soup of Eight Delicacies
八宝鸡	〈饮食〉Steamed Rice-Stuffed-Chicken
八宝酥鸭	〈饮食〉Crispy Duck Stuffed with Eight-Stuffed Delicacies
八段锦	〈武术〉Baduanjin; Eight-Section Brocade Exercise; Exercises in Eight Forms
八风穴	〈中医药〉Bafeng acupoint; Eight-Wind point (EX-LE10)
八纲辨证	〈中医药〉pattern differentiation of eight principles (analysis and identification of pathological conditions are the main process for diagnosis and treatment)
八公山豆腐	〈饮食〉Bagongshan Tofu; Bagongshan Bean Curd
八会穴	〈中医药〉→八脉交会穴
八角茴香	〈中医药〉(of Latin) Fructus Anisi Stellati; Chinese Star Anise
八角巾	octagonal towel
八角莲	〈中医药〉(of Latin) Radix Dysosma versipellis; Dysosma Root

八角帽	octagonal hat
八脉交会穴	〈中医药〉eight confluence points; confluence points of the eight vessels
八抬大轿	large sedan chair carried by eight people; large men-carried sedan chair
八仙酒	eight immortals wine
八仙桌	eight-immortal table; old-fashioned square table for eight people; square table (with a rectangular top, normally with eight seats around it)
八一礼堂	August 1st Auditorium; August 1st Assembly Hall (Tianjin)
八珍煲	〈饮食〉Assorted Meat in Casserole/Clay Pot
八珍发菜扒鸭	〈饮食〉Braised Duck with Assorted Meat and Thread Moss
八珍葫芦鸭	〈饮食〉Gourd-Shaped Duck with Eight-Stuffing; Stuffed Duck Shaped as a Gourd
八珍汤	〈中医药〉Bazhen Tang; Eight-Gem Decoction
八珍益母丸	〈中医药〉Bazhen Yimu Wan; Eight-Gem Leonurus (Motherwort) Pill
八正合剂	〈中医药〉Bazheng Heji; Eight-Correction Mixture
八正散	〈中医药〉Bazheng San; Eight-Correction Powder; Eight Health Restoratives Powder
八字	→生辰八字
巴豆	〈中医药〉(of Latin) Fructus Crotonis; Croton Fruit
巴戟天	〈中医药〉(of Latin) Radix Morindae Officinalis; Morinda Root
巴蜀小炒鸡	〈饮食〉Stir-Fried Chicken with Hot and Green Pepper
扒鸡腿	〈饮食〉Grilled Chicken Drumsticks
扒鸡胸	〈饮食〉Chargrilled Chicken Breast
扒芥香鸡胸	〈饮食〉Grilled Chicken Breast with Mustard Flavor
扒香菇油菜	〈饮食〉Stir-Fried Rape/Vegetables with Savory Mushrooms

扒羊排	〈饮食〉Grilled Lamb Chops
拔罐疗法	〈中医药〉cupping therapy
拔火罐	〈中医药〉cupping cup; cupping glass; cupping therapy
拔丝苹果	〈饮食〉Frittered Apple with Bright Sugar; Crispy Fried Apple Slices with Syrup
拔丝山药	〈饮食〉Chinese Yam in Hot Toffee
拔丝香蕉	〈饮食〉Frittered Banana with Bright Sugar
鲅鱼水饺	〈饮食〉Jiaozi Stuffed with Mackerel; Chinese Mackerel Dumplings
白扒鲍鱼	〈饮食〉Braised Abalone in White Sauce
白扒燕窝	〈饮食〉Braised Bird's Nest with White Sauce
白扒鱼翅	〈饮食〉Braised Shark's Fins in White Gravy
白扒鱼肚	〈饮食〉Braised Fish Maws with White Sauce
白扁豆	〈中医药〉(of Latin) Semen Dalichoris Album; White Hyacinth Bean; Lablab Bean
白彩黑花瓶	〈陶瓷〉white glaze vase with black floral pattern
白彩刻花婴儿戏莲瓷枕	〈陶瓷〉white glaze porcelain pillow with a carved pattern of children playing with lotus
白彩剔花水注	〈陶瓷〉white glaze water dropper with carved floral pattern
白菜豆腐焖酥肉	〈饮食〉Braised Pork Cubes with Tofu and Chinese Cabbage
白菜豆腐汤	〈饮食〉Chinese Cabbage and Tofu Soup
白菜心拌蜇头	〈饮食〉Marinated Jellyfish and Choy Sum
白茶	white tea
白瓷	〈陶瓷〉white porcelain; ceramic whiteware
白瓷长颈瓶	〈陶瓷〉white porcelain long-necked vase
白瓷灯	〈陶瓷〉white porcelain lamp
白瓷盖罐	〈陶瓷〉white porcelain lidded jar
白瓷黑彩侍吏俑	〈陶瓷〉white porcelain figurine of retinue with black ornament
白瓷葫芦壶	〈陶瓷〉white porcelain gourd-shaped ewer

白瓷鸡冠扁壶	〈陶瓷〉white porcelain flask decorated with a cockscomb
白瓷莲座烛台	〈陶瓷〉white porcelain candlestick with lotus-seat
白瓷品茗杯	〈茶〉white porcelain tea-sipping cup
白瓷双螭双联瓶	〈陶瓷〉white porcelain twin-body vase with two dragon-like animals pattern
白瓷贴花高足钵	〈陶瓷〉white glazed stem bowl with applique
白瓷童子壶	〈陶瓷〉white porcelain pot in the shape of a boy
白瓷围棋盘	〈陶瓷〉white porcelain weiqi board
白带丸	〈中医药〉Baidai Wan; Leukorrhea Pill
白豆蔻	〈中医药〉(of Latin) Fructus Ammomi Rotundus; Amomum Cardamom; White Cardamon Fruit
白豆汤	〈饮食〉White Bean Soup
白堕酒	Baiduo liquor
白肺汤	〈饮食〉Pork Lung Soup
白附子	〈中医药〉(of Latin) Rhizoma Typhonii; Giant Typhonium Tuber
白干	〈酒〉white spirit; white liquor
白果煲老鸭	〈饮食〉Stewed Duck with Gingko in Casserole
白果鸡丁	〈饮食〉Stir-Fried Diced Chicken with Gingko
白果仁	〈中医药〉(of Latin) Semen Ginkgo; Ginkgo Seed/Nut
白毫	〈茶〉pekoe
白毫乌龙	〈茶〉White Tipped Oolong
白毫银针	〈茶〉Baihao Silver Needle
白鹤灵芝	〈中医药〉(of Latin) Rhinacanthus Nasutus; Rhinacanthus Twig and Leaf
白鹤香烟	Baihe cigarettes; White Crane cigarettes
白虎汤	〈中医药〉Baihu Tang; Baihu Decoction
白花蛇舌草	〈中医药〉(of Latin) Herba Hedyotis; Hedyotis Diffusa; Hedyotis
白烩鸡翅	〈饮食〉Braised Chicken Wings in White Sauce
白烩小牛肉	〈饮食〉Stewed Diced Beef with Onion and Turnip in White Wine

白椒炒鸡胗	〈饮食〉Stir-Fried Chicken Gizzards with White Pepper
白金龙香烟	Baijinlong cigarettes; White-Golden Dragon cigarettes
白菊花	〈中医药〉(of Latin) Chrysanthemi Flos Albus; White Chrysanthemum Flower
白菌炒蛋	〈饮食〉Scrambled Eggs with Mushrooms
白扣羊肉	〈饮食〉Plain-Boiled Mutton
白灵菇扒鲍片	〈饮食〉Braised Sliced Abalone with Mushrooms
白灵菇炒鸡片	〈饮食〉Stir Fried Chicken Slices with Mushrooms
白灵菇炒牛柳	〈饮食〉Stir-Fried Beef Fillets with Bailing Mushrooms
白灵菇扣鸭掌	〈饮食〉Mushrooms with Duck Webs
白领工人	white-collar worker
白马毛尖	〈茶〉Baima Maojian green tea; Baima Tippy tea
白毛藤	〈中医药〉(of Latin) Herba Solani; Climbing Nightshade
白茅根	〈中医药〉(of Latin) Rhizoma Imperatae; Cogongrass Rhizome
白牡丹茶	white peony tea
白片鸡	〈饮食〉Steamed Sliced Chicken
白切鸡	〈饮食〉Sliced Poached Chicken; Sliced Boiled Chicken with Sauce
白曲领	〈服饰〉white curved lapel
白人刀	〈币〉white knife (issued in the Warring States period)
白人参	〈中医药〉Radix Ginseng Alba; white ginseng
白肉血肠	〈饮食〉White Pork and Blood Large Intestine with Pickled Mustard-Green
白沙液酒	Baishaye liquor
白芍	〈中医药〉(of Latin) Radix Paeoniae Alba; White Peony Root; Root of Herbaceous Peony
白胎	〈陶瓷〉white body

白胎蓝釉菩萨塑像	〈陶瓷〉Buddha statue with white body and blue glaze (Yuan Dynasty)
白陶双系尊	〈陶瓷〉white pottery jar with two ears
白头翁	〈中医药〉(of Latin) Radix Pulsatillae; Chinese Pulsatilla Root
白头翁汤	〈中医药〉Baitouweng Tang; Pulsatilla Chinensis Decoction
白薇	〈中医药〉(of Latin) Radix Cynanchi Atrati; Black-end Swallowwort Root
白鲜皮	〈中医药〉(of Latin) Cortex Dictamni; Densefruit Pittany Root-Bark; Dictamnus Root Bark
白油冬笋	〈饮食〉Stir-Fried Bamboo Shoots with Lard
白釉	〈陶瓷〉white glaze
白釉黑彩诗文枕	〈陶瓷〉white glaze pillow with poem and black floral pattern
白釉黑花缠枝牡丹纹碗	〈陶瓷〉white glaze bowl with interlaced branches and peony pattern in black
白釉黑花凤纹罐	〈陶瓷〉white glaze jar with phoenix pattern in black
白釉黑花孩儿蹴球瓷枕	〈陶瓷〉white glaze porcelain pillow with a pattern of children playing ball in black
白釉黑花花口瓶	〈陶瓷〉white glaze flower-mouthed vase with black floral pattern
白釉黑花龙凤纹大罐	〈陶瓷〉white glaze big jar with dragon and phoenix pattern in black
白釉黑花龙凤纹罐	〈陶瓷〉white glaze jar with dragon and phoenix pattern in black
白釉黑花盘	〈陶瓷〉white glaze tray with black floral pattern
白釉黑花蜻蜓点水瓷枕	〈陶瓷〉white glaze porcelain pillow with a pattern of dragonfly dancing on water in black
白釉黑花四耳瓶	〈陶瓷〉white glaze four-eared vase with black floral pattern
白釉黑花童子垂钓瓷枕	〈陶瓷〉white glaze porcelain pillow with fishing children pattern in black

白釉黑花鱼纹碗	〈陶瓷〉white glaze bowl with black fish pattern
白釉黑花鱼藻纹盆	〈陶瓷〉white glaze plate with fish and water-weed pattern in black
白釉刻花瓶	〈陶瓷〉white glaze vase with carved flower pattern
白釉双兽耳盘口瓶	〈陶瓷〉white glaze double-animal-eared vase with a plate opening (Ming Dynasty)
白釉双鱼壶	〈陶瓷〉white glaze double-fish kettle
白玉藏珍	〈饮食〉Steamed Wax Gourd with Fried Assorted Meat
白玉云螺鸟	〈饮食〉Stir-Fried Sparrow with Tripes and Ham
白玉蒸扇贝	〈饮食〉Steamed Scallops with Tofu
白云石瓷	〈陶瓷〉dolomitic porcelain
白斩鸡	〈饮食〉Boiled Tender Chicken with Soy Sauce
白汁炒鱼唇	〈饮食〉Stir-Fried Fish Lips in Cream Sauce
白汁大乌参	〈饮食〉Stewed Black Sea Cucumbers in White Sauce
白汁干贝	〈饮食〉Stewed Dried Scallops with White Sauce
白汁鳜鱼	〈饮食〉Steamed Mandarin Fish with Cream Sauce
白汁焖鳜鱼	〈饮食〉Stewed Mandarin Fish with White Sauce
白汁焖鱼唇	〈饮食〉Stewed Shark's Lips with White Sauce
白汁牛筋	〈饮食〉Stewed Beef Tendons in White Sauce
白汁熏鲳鱼	〈饮食〉Smoked Pomfret with White Sauce
白芷	〈中医药〉(of Latin) Radix Angelicae Dahuricae; Dahurian Angelica Root
白粥	〈饮食〉Rice Congee; Rice Porridge →大米粥
白术	〈中医药〉(of Latin) Rhizoma Atractylodis Macrocephalae; Largehead Atractylodes Rhizome; Ovate Atractylodes Root
白灼	〈饮食〉to boil; to scald; boiled; scalded →煮
白灼肥牛	〈饮食〉Boiled Beef Slices with Soy Sauce; Poached Beef with Soya Sauce
白灼海螺片	〈饮食〉Scalded Sliced Conch, Scalded Whelk Slices

白灼芥蓝	〈饮食〉Boiled Chinese Broccoli
白灼时蔬	〈饮食〉Boiled Seasonal Vegetables
白灼西兰花	〈饮食〉Boiled Broccoli; Scalded Chinese Broccoli
白灼虾	〈饮食〉Boiled Prawns with Chives and Ginger Sauce
百般拖延	to do everything to procrastinate
百部	〈中医药〉(of Latin) Radix Stemonae; Stemona Root
百草妇炎清栓	〈中医药〉Baicao Fuyanqing Shuan; Baicao Female-Inflammation-Clearing Suppository
百度	Baidu
百度贴吧	Baidu Post Bar
百官冠服	〈古〉official coronet and dressing
百合	〈中医药〉(of Latin) Bulbus Lilii; Lily Bulb
百合炒南瓜	〈饮食〉Stir-Fried Pumpkin with Lily Bulbs
百合固金汤	〈中医药〉Baihe Gujin Tang; Lily Bulb Metal-Securing Decoction
百合髻	〈古〉(of hairstyle) baihe bun; lily chignon
百合虾球	〈饮食〉Stir-Fried Prawn Balls with Lily Bulbs
百花鲍鱼卷	〈饮食〉Steamed Abalone Rolls Stuffed with Minced Shrimp
百花髻	〈古〉(of hairstyle) baihua bun; various flowers topknot
百花酿鲍片	〈饮食〉Steamed Sliced Abalone with Egg Whites
百花酿海参	〈饮食〉Steamed Sea Cucumbers with Minced Shrimps
百花酿蟹钳	〈饮食〉Steamed Crab Claws Stuffed with Minced Shrimp
百会	〈中医药〉Baihui acupoint; Hundred-Convergence point (GV20)
百节鞋	〈白族〉embroidered toe-cocked shoes
百衲衣	monk's robe of patches; monk's robe made of patches →水田衣
百世快递	Best Express

百姓安居乐业	a better life for all the people; to live and work in peace and contentment
百叶包肉	〈饮食〉Bean Curd Sheet Rolls with Minced Pork
百叶结烧肉	〈饮食〉Stewed Pork Cubes and Tofu Skin with Brown Sauce
百褶裙	pleated skirt; accordion-pleated skirt
百褶筒裙	pleated tight/tube skirt
柏子仁	〈中医药〉(of Latin) Semen Platycladi; Chinese Arborvitae Kernel
柏子养心丸	〈中医药〉Baizi Yangxin Wan; Arborvitae Seed Heart-Nourishing Pill
摆花架子	to do sth. for show
摆架子	to put on airs; to show off
摆谱儿	→摆架子
摆设瓷	→陈[摆]设瓷
摆脱贫困	to shake off poverty; to be lift out of poverty
败毒散	〈中医药〉Baidu San; Antiphologistic Powder
败酱草	〈中医药〉(of Latin) Herba Patriniae; Whiteflower Patrinia Herb
拜把兄弟	sworn brothers
拜金女	material girl
拜金主义	money worship
拜年	to pay a New Year visit
拜年网	New Year greeting network
扳倒井酒	Bandaojing liquor
扳指	thumb ring; fingerstall
班门弄斧	to teach one's grandma to suck eggs; to display one's slight skill before an expert
班主任	class adviser; head teacher (a teacher in charge of a class)
斑蝥	〈中医药〉(of Latin) Mylabris; Blister Beetle
搬迁户	relocated unit or household; relocated family
瘢痕灸	〈中医药〉scarring moxibustion; scar-producing moxibustion

板蓝根	〈中医药〉(of Latin) Radix Isatidis; Isatis Root; Indigowoad Root
板蓝根含片	〈中医药〉Banlangen Hanpian; Isatis Sucking Tablet
板蓝根颗粒	〈中医药〉Banlangen Keli; Isatis Root Granule
板栗白菜	〈饮食〉Poached Chinese Cabbage with Chestnut Kernels
板栗红烧肉	〈饮食〉Braised Pork with Chestnut Kernels
板栗焖仔鸡	〈饮食〉Braised Chicken with Chestnut Kernels; Stewed Young Hen with Chestnut Kernels
板栗烧鳝段	〈饮食〉Braised Eel with Chestnut Kernels
板栗香	〈茶〉chestnut-like aroma
板肉焖鹌鹑	〈饮食〉Braised Quail with Bacon
板式楼	slab-type apartment building
板条	〈饮食〉Flat Rice Noodles
板烟	cavendish; pressed tobacco
版纳竹酒	Banna bamboo wine
版税率	royalty rate
版税收入	royalty income
版图设计工程师	layout design engineer
办公室恋情	office romance
办公室文员	office clerk
办公室主任	director of an office; office chief
办公室助理	office assistant
办事处	office; agency
办事处经理	branch office manager
办事员	clerk; office worker
半臂	〈服饰〉half-sleeve garment (short-sleeved or sleeveless tops used from the Qin Dynasty to the Song Dynasty)
半边莲	〈中医药〉(of Latin) Herba Lobeliae Chinensis; Chinese Lobelia Herb
半边天	half the sky (referring to the great power of modern women in the new society)

半吊子	dabbler; smatterer; half-bake man; a person who is not sensible
半发酵茶	semi-fermented tea; partially fermented tea
半干葡萄酒	semi-dry wine
半煎煮鱼	〈饮食〉Braised Yellow Croaker and Dried Mushroom
半口蘑蒸鸡	〈饮食〉Steamed Chicken with Truffles
半两	〈币〉banliang copper coin (issued in the Qin and early Han Dynasty)
半甜葡萄酒	semi-sweet wine
半托	to send kids to the day care; day care for kids
半脱产	partly released from productive labor; partly released from one's regular work
半夏	〈中医药〉(of Latin) Rhizoma Pinelliae; Pinellia Tuber
半夏白术天麻汤	〈中医药〉Banxia Baizhu Tianma Tang; Pinellia Tuber, Atractylodes Macrocephala and Rhizoma Gastrodiae Decoction
半夏厚朴汤	〈中医药〉Banxia Houpu Tang; Pinellia Tuber-Officinal Magnolia Bark Decoction
半夏曲	〈中医药〉(of Latin) Rhizoma Pinelliae Fermentata; Fermented Pinellia
半夏糖浆	〈中医药〉Banxia Tangjiang; Pinellia Tuber Syrup
半夏泻心汤	〈中医药〉Banxia Xiexin Tang; Pinellia Tuber Harmonizing Decoction
半枝莲	〈中医药〉(of Latin) Herba Scutellariae Barbatae; Barbated Skullcup Herb
拌豆腐丝	〈饮食〉Shredded Tofu with Sauce
拌海螺	〈饮食〉Whelks and Cucumber
拌苦菜	〈饮食〉Mixed Bitter Vegetables
拌茄泥	〈饮食〉Mashed Eggplant with Garlic
拌双耳	〈饮食〉Tossed Black and White Fungi
拌爽口海苔	〈饮食〉Sea Moss with Sauce
拌香椿苗	〈饮食〉Chinese Toon with Sauce

邦单	〈藏服〉bangdan; apron trapping (a type of silk fabrics tied at the waist of the Tibetan ethnic group)
帮倒忙	to do a disservice for one's good will; to be more of a hindrance than a help; to try to help but cause more trouble in the process
棒棒鸡	〈饮食〉Chicken Cutlets in Chilli Sauce
棒子面粥	〈饮食〉Corn Porridge; Corn Congee
傍大款	(of a girl) to find a sugar daddy; to be a mistress for a rich man; to lean on a moneybag
包车	to charter a vehicle
包打听	baodating; nosy parker; rubberneck
包二奶	to have a concubine (originally a Cantonese expression)
包工头	head of labor contractor
包购包销	exclusive right to purchase and sell
包机	to charter a plane; a chartered plane
包心外露	〈茶〉heart unenveloped
包扎固定疗法	〈中医药〉bandage-fixing therapy
包装设计师	package designer
包子	〈饮食〉Baozi; Steamed Stuffed Bun; Steamed Bun with Stuffing
胞宫湿热证	〈中医药〉uterine damp-heat pattern; pattern of dampness-heat in uterus
胞宫虚寒证	〈中医药〉pattern of uterine vacuity cold; pattern of deficient cold in womb
煲	〈饮食〉to braise; to stew; braised; stewed
薄饼	〈饮食〉Thin Pancake; Griddle Cake
薄胎瓷	〈陶瓷〉eggshell porcelain; thin china →蛋壳瓷
薄硬	〈茶〉thin and hard
宝顶绿茶	Baoding Green tea
宝丰酒	Baofeng liquor
宝石蓝釉金彩酒杯	〈陶瓷〉sapphire blue glazed wine cup with golden floral pattern

保安部	security department
保安部经理	security manager
保安部主任	security supervisor
保安(部)文员	security clerk
保安(人)员	security personnel; security guard
保持隔离状态	〈防疫〉to stay in isolation
保持基本民生服务不断档	〈防疫〉to ensure the availability of basic public services
保持人身距离	〈防疫〉to enforce/practice physical distancing; to physically distance
保持社交距离	〈防疫〉to enforce/practice social distancing; to socially distance
保兑银行	confirming bank
保和丸	〈中医药〉Baohe Wan; Lenitive Pill; Harmony-Preserving Pill; Pachyma Compound Digestive Tonic Pill
保护价格	protective price
保护伞	protective umbrella
保护消费者合法权益	to protect the legitimate rights and interests of consumers
保健按摩	therapeutic massage
保健部经理	manager of health department
保健操	health exercises
保健茶	healthy tea; herbal tea; tonic tea
保健护士	health nurse
保健灸	〈中医药〉keeping fit moxibustion; health preserving moxibustion
保健(食)品	health-care food; health care products
保健诊所	health care clinic
保靖黄金茶	Baojing Golden tea
保送生	direct admission student; recommended student for (immediate) admission (to school, free from entrance examinations)
保外帮教	to remain out of custody by receiving help from the family or work unit

保险产品开发员	insurance product developer
保险承销商	insurance underwriter
保险代理人	insurance agent
保险理赔员	loss adjuster
保险培训师	insurance trainer
保险索赔	insurance claim
保险协调员	insurance coordinator
保育员	daycare worker; nursery governess
保障生活必需品市场总体稳定	〈防疫〉to maintain an overall balance in the market for daily necessities
保障性住房	indemnificatory housing
保障医疗防护物资供应	〈防疫〉to ensure the supply of medical protective equipment
保证物流畅通	to ensure unimpeded flow of goods and materials
保值利率	index-linked interest rate; inflation-proof interest rate
保住面子	to save face; maintenance of face
报关员资格证书	customs declaration certificate; certificate of customs specialist
报童	〈旧〉newspaper boy
报喜不报忧	to report only the good news but not the bad; to hold back unpleasant information
报销	to apply for reimbursement
鲍参翅肚羹	〈饮食〉Shark's Fin Soup with Shredded Abalone; Shark's Fin Soup Stewed with Minced Seafood
鲍鱼海参	〈饮食〉Braised Sea Cucumbers with Abalone
鲍鱼海珍煲	〈饮食〉Braised Abalone and Seafood in Casserole
鲍鱼红烧肉	〈饮食〉Red-Cooked Pork with Abalone; Braised Pork with Abalone
鲍鱼鸡片汤	〈饮食〉Abalone Soup with Sliced Chicken
鲍鱼芦笋汤	〈饮食〉Abalone Soup with Asparagus
鲍鱼焖鸡翼	〈饮食〉Braised Chicken Wings with Abalone
鲍鱼汤	〈饮食〉Abalone Soup; Soup with Abalone
鲍鱼珍珠鸡	〈饮食〉Steamed Diced Abalone and Chicken with Glutinous Rice

鲍汁北菇鹅掌	〈饮食〉Braised Goose Webs and Savory Mushrooms in Abalone Sauce
鲍汁葱烧海参	〈饮食〉Braised Sea Cucumbers with Scallion in Abalone Sauce
鲍汁鹅肝	〈饮食〉Braised Goose Livers in Abalone Sauce
鲍汁鹅掌扣海参	〈饮食〉Braised Sea Cucumbers and Goose Webs in Abalone Sauce
鲍汁海鲜烩饭	〈饮食〉Rice with Boiled Seafood in Abalone Sauce
鲍汁海鲜面	〈饮食〉Noodles with Seafood in Abalone Sauce
鲍汁花菇烧鹅掌	〈饮食〉Braised Goose Webs and Mushrooms in Abalone Sauce
鲍汁花胶扣海参	〈饮食〉Braised Sea Cucumbers and Fish Maw in Abalone Sauce
鲍汁鸡腿菇	〈饮食〉Braised Mushrooms in Abalone Sauce
鲍汁煎鹅肝	〈饮食〉Pan-Fried Goose Livers in Abalone Sauce
鲍汁扣东坡肉	〈饮食〉Braised Dongpo Pork with Abalone Sauce
鲍汁扣鹅掌	〈饮食〉Braised Goose Webs in Abalone Sauce
鲍汁扣三宝	〈饮食〉Braised Sea Cucumbers, Fish Maw and Mushrooms in Abalone Sauce
鲍汁牛肝菌	〈饮食〉Braised Boletuses in Abalone Sauce
鲍汁扒鲍贝	〈饮食〉Braised Abalone with Abalone Sauce
鲍汁扒裙边	〈饮食〉Braised Soft Turtle Rim with Abalone Sauce
暴发户	upstart; parvenu; noveau riche (persons or households who have suddenly become rich through unscrupulous means or unexpected opportunities)
暴风客热	〈中医药〉acute catarrhal and allergic conjunctivitis; fulminant wind-heat invasion; sudden attack of wind-heat on the eye
暴力拆迁	forced relocation
暴喜伤心	〈中医药〉overwhelming joy impairing heart
曝光	to make a public expose; to lay sth. bare
爆炒	〈饮食〉to quick-fry; quick-fried

爆炒牛肋骨	〈饮食〉Quick-Fried Beef Ribs
爆炒鳝鱼丝	〈饮食〉Quick-Fried Shredded Eel
爆炒腰花	〈饮食〉Quick-Fried Pork Kidneys with Green Onions, Garlic and Ginger
爆冷门	to produce an unexpected winner; a dark horse bobbing up; a bolt from the blue
杯垫	〈茶〉coaster
杯盖	〈茶〉cup cover
杯套	〈茶〉cup sleeve; cup set
杯托	〈茶〉cup saucer
背包袱	to be burdened with sth.; have a mental burden of sth.
背黑锅	to become a scapegoat; to take the blame for others
悲忧伤肺	〈中医药〉melancholy impairing lung
悲则气消	〈中医药〉excessive grief exhausting qi; excessive sorrow leading to qi dispersion
北斗三号全球定位系统	Beidou-3 Global Position System
北斗卫星导航系统	Beidou Navigation Satellite System
北斗系统	Beidou system
北豆根	〈中医药〉(of Latin) Rhizoma Menispermi; Asiatic Moonseed Rhizome; Northern Asarum
北方游牧民族	northern nomadic people
北菇海参煲	〈饮食〉Stewed Black Mushrooms and Sea Cucumbers in Casserole
北菇烩兔丝	〈饮食〉Stewed Shredded Rabbit with Dried Mushroom
北菇扒大鸭	〈饮食〉Braised Duck with Savory Mushrooms and Vegetables
北菇扒菜心	〈饮食〉Stir-Fried Choy Sum and Mushrooms
北菇云腿蒸乳鸽	〈饮食〉Steamed Pigeon with Mushrooms and Ham
北极贝刺身	〈饮食〉Scallops Sashimi; Arctic Pole Shellfish Sashimi

北京奥运会	Beijing Olympic Games; 2008 Beijing Olympics
北京奥运会吉祥物	Beijing Olympic Games mascot; mascot of Beijing Olympics
北京奥运火炬	Beijing Olympic torch
北京奥运火炬传递	Beijing Olympic torch relay
北京奥运开幕式	Beijing Olympics Opening Ceremony
北京奥运体育场	Beijing Olympic Stadium
北京奥运委员会	Beijing Olympics Committee
北京白葡萄酒	Beijing white wine
北京百补养元酒	Beijing multi-nourishing medicated liquor
北京醇	〈酒〉Beijing mellow liquor
北京大兴国际机场	Beijing Daxing International Airport
北京冬奥会	→北京冬季奥运会
北京冬季奥运会	Beijing Winter Olympics; Beijing Winter Olympic Games (in 2022)
北京桂花陈酒	Beijing osmanthus wine
北京国际花港	Beijing International Flower Port
北京国际金融博览会	Beijing International Finance Expo
北京国际马拉松	Beijing International Marathon
北京国际体育电影周	Beijing International Sports Film Week
北京国际投资理财金融博览会	Beijing International Finance & Investment Exhibition
北京国际图书博览会	Beijing International Book Fair
北京红葡萄酒	Beijing red wine
北京花园博览会	Beijing Garden Expo
北京火车站	Beijing Railway Station
北京金博会	→北京国际金融博览会
北京烤鸭	〈饮食〉Beijing Roast Duck
北京南站	Beijing South Railway Station
北京人参蜂王浆	〈中医药〉Beijing Renshen Fengwangjiang; Beijing Ginseng Royal Jelly
北京生啤	Beijing draught beer
北京时间	Beijing time; Beijing standard time
北京首都国际机场	Beijing Capital International Airport

北京四合院	quadrangle dwellings of Beijing; Beijing courtyard house
北京图博会	→北京国际图书博览会
北京王府井大街	Beijing Wangfujing street
北京王府井商圈	Beijing Wangfujing shop district
北京西站	Beijing West Railway Station
北京夏季奥运会	Beijing Summer Olympics; Beijing Summer Olympic Games (in 2008)
北京香山旅游峰会	Beijing Fragrant Hill Tourism Summit
北京香烟	Beijing cigarettes
北京学生自治联合会	Beijing Students Autonomous Federation
北京烟草控制协会	Beijing Tobacco Control Association
北京演出行业协会	Beijing Trade Association for Performances
北京野生动物园	Beijing Wildlife Park
北漂	Beijing drifter; drifter in Beijing; to float around in Beijing
北沙参	〈中医药〉(of Latin) Radix Glehniae; Coastal Glehnia Root
北宋官窑	〈陶瓷〉Northern Song Royal Kiln
北五味子	〈中医药〉(of Latin) Radix Schisandra Chinensis; Northern Schisandra Berry
北细辛	〈中医药〉(of Latin) Asarum heterotropoides; Northern Asarum
贝母	〈中医药〉(of Latin) Bulbus Fritillaria; Fritillary Bulb
贝松扒菜心	〈饮食〉Stir-Fried Choy Sum with Minced Scallop
贝松鱼肚羹	〈饮食〉Minced Scallop Soup with Fish Maw
《备急千金要方》	〈中医药〉*Beiji Qianjin Yao Fang*; *Essential Recipes for Emergent Use*; *Invaluable Formulary for Ready Reference* (by Sun Simiao in the Tang Dynasty)
背甲	〈古〉back armor
背心	〈服饰〉underwaist; sleeveless sweater →比甲
背心裙	jumper skirt; sundress

背俞穴	〈中医药〉Back-Shu acupoint; Back Transport point
被病毒感染	〈防疫〉to be infected by the virus
被动吸烟	passive smoking
被隔离	〈防疫〉to be put into quarantine; to be under quarantine
焙火	〈茶〉to dry over a fire; to bake; to torrefy
褙[背]子	〈服饰〉straight collar robe with opposite lapels and flank slits
贲巴壶	〈陶瓷〉Ben Pakistan pot
本草	〈中医药〉materia medica →草药
《本草纲目》	〈中医药〉*Bencao Gangmu*; *Compendium of Materia Medica* (by Li Shizhen in the Ming Dynasty)
《本草纲目拾遗》	〈中医药〉*Bencao Gangmu Shiyi*; *Supplement to the Compendium of Materia Medica* (by Zhao Xuemin in the Qing Dynasty)
《本草品汇精要》	〈中医药〉*Bencao Pinghui Jingyao*; *Collected Essentials of Species of Materia Medica* (by Liu Wentai et al. in the Ming Dynasty)
《本草拾遗》	〈中医药〉*Bencao Shiyi*; *A Supplement to Materia Medica* (by Chen Cangqi in the Tang Dynasty)
《本草衍义》	〈中医药〉*Bencao Yanyi*; *Elucidation of Materia Medica*; *Augmented Materia Medica* (by Kou Zongshi in the Song Dynasty)
本经配穴法	〈中医药〉acupoint combination of the same meridian; combination/association of the affected channel/meridian
本经取穴	〈中医药〉point selection along the affected channel; point selection along the related meridian
本命年	this animal year; one's year of birth (in regard to the twelve terrestrial branches); recurrent year in the twelve-year cycle
奔小康	to strive for a relatively comfortable life
逼上梁山	to be driven to revolt; to be driven to do sth.

荸荠鸡片	〈饮食〉Stir-Fried Chicken Slices with Water Chestnuts
鼻窦炎口服液	〈中医药〉Bidouyan Koufuye; Nasosinusitis Oral Solution/Liquid
鼻腔填塞疗法	〈中医药〉nose-stuffing therapy
鼻嗅疗法	〈中医药〉smelling therapy
鼻咽清毒颗粒	〈中医药〉Biyan Qingdu Keli; Nose Larynx Toxin-Clearing Granule
鼻烟壶	〈陶瓷〉snuff bottle; snuff box
鼻炎灵片	〈中医药〉Biyanling Pian; Rhinitis Efficacy Tablet
鼻炎片	〈中医药〉Biyan Pian; Rhinitis Tablet
鼻准	〈中医药〉Tip of the Nose; Nasal Apex
比甲	〈服饰〉bijia; sleeveless over-dress (used in the Yuan and Ming Dynasties) →背心
必要的协调预防和控制工作	〈防疫〉necessary coordinated prevention and control efforts
毕婚族	marry-upon-graduation
毕业鉴定	graduation appraisal; graduation appreciation
毕业生分配制度	assignment system for graduates
毕业实习	graduation field work; graduation practice
闭门羹	cold-shoulder treatment; refusal of entrance
荜拨	〈中医药〉(of Latin) Fructus Piperis Longi; Long Pepper
荜澄茄	〈中医药〉(of Latin) Fructus Litseae; Mountain Spicy Fruit
筚篥	〈乐〉(of a wind instrument) bili; bamboo pipe
蓖麻子	〈中医药〉(of Latin) Semen Ricini; Castor Seed
痹病	〈中医药〉arthralgia; impediment disease
碧绿干烧澳带	〈饮食〉Dry-Braised Scallops with Green Vegetables
碧绿桂鱼卷	〈饮食〉Stir-Fried Mandarin Fish Roll with Green Cabbage
碧绿椒麻鱼肚	〈饮食〉Braised Fish Maws and Vegetables with Pepper and Chili

碧绿鲜带子	〈饮食〉Braised Scallops with Green Vegetables
碧绿香肘扣鲍片	〈饮食〉Braised Sliced Abalone with Pork and Vegetables
碧绿原汁鲍鱼	〈饮食〉Braised Abalone with Green Vegetables in Fumet
碧螺春	〈茶〉Biluochun tea; Green Spiral
碧玉细炀器	〈陶瓷〉jasper; jasper ware
碧玉簪	jade hairpin; emerald hairpin
蔽膝	〈古服饰〉knees-cover; knee shield (a large scarf around the front of the clothes used to cover the knees)
避免聚集	〈防疫〉to avoid crowds
避免使某个国家蒙受污名	〈防疫〉to avoid stigmatizing a country
避免使某个特定群体蒙受污名	〈防疫〉to avoid stigmatizing a particular group
避嫌	to avoid doing anything that may arouse suspicion
边防证	frontier pass
边缘科学	borderline (boundary) science; fringe (border) discipline
边缘知识人	marginal intellectuals
边远地区	remote and border areas
边远贫困地区	outlying poverty-stricken areas
编导	(of a play, film, etc.) scenarist; writer and director
编发	braided hair
编辑主任	editorial director
编内职工	permanent staff
编审	review editor; senior editor
煸	〈饮食〉to stir-fry before stewing; stir-fried
蝙蝠袖	batwing sleeve
扁瘪	〈茶〉flat and thin
扁豆炒肉丝	〈饮食〉Stir-Fried Shredded Pork and Green Beans
扁豆肉丝	〈饮食〉Stir-Fried Shredded Pork with French Beans

扁块	〈茶〉flat and round
扁鹊	Bian Que (a famous Chinese physician in the Spring and Autumn period)
扁食	〈饮食〉Bianshi; Dumpling Soup (called wonton in Jiangsu, Fujian)
扁食汤	〈饮食〉Dumpling Soup
扁削	〈茶〉sharp and flat
扁鱼白菜	〈饮食〉Braised Dried Silver Carp with Chinese Cabbage
扁直	〈茶〉flat and straight
弁	〈服饰〉bian (a conical cap worn on ceremonious occasions in ancient times)
弁服	〈古〉bianfu (one of the ancient Chinese imperial robes worn by the emperor in the formal occasions)
变废为宝	to make waste profitable
变相涨价	disguised inflation
变形高足杯	〈陶瓷〉stylized stem cup
变形笠式碗	〈陶瓷〉stylized bamboo-hat bowl
变异毒株	〈防疫〉virus variant
便利店	convenience store
便民服务	convenience service; service for the convenience of customers; handy service for the public
便钱会子	〈币〉huizi bank draft (the most widely used clearing bill in the Song Dynasty)
便衣警察	police in plain clothes
辨病论治	〈中医药〉treatment based on disease differentiation; disease identification as the basis for determining treatment
辨证取穴	〈中医药〉acupoint selection by pattern identification
辩论赛	debate competition
辫线袄	〈服饰〉robe with braid strings (for men in the Yuan Dynasty)

标本兼治	〈中医药〉1〈中医药〉to treat both principal and secondary aspect of disease; to treat both the symptoms and root causes 2 to seek both temporary and permanent solutions; to tackle problems as well as root causes
标准化工程师	standardization engineer
标准普通话	standard mandarin
表寒里热证	〈中医药〉exterior cold and interior heat pattern; pattern of superficies cold and interior heat
表里辨证	〈中医药〉exterior-interior pattern identification; pattern differentiation of superficies and interior
表里俱寒证	〈中医药〉exterior-interior cold pattern; pattern of cold in both superficies and interior
表里俱热证	〈中医药〉exterior-interior heat pattern; pattern of heat in both superficies and interior
表里配穴法	〈中医药〉exterior-interior point combination/association
表里双解	〈中医药〉to resolve both the exterior and interior; to release both the exterior and interior; to expel pathogens from both interior and superficies
表里双解剂	〈中医药〉exterior-interior releasing formula; formula for relieving both superficial and internal disorders
表里同病	〈中医药〉exterior-interior concurrent disease; co-existence of exterior and interior symptoms
表面文章	tokenism; mere show; lip service; surface formality
表热里寒	〈中医药〉exterior heat with interior cold; exterior heat and interior cold
表热里寒证	〈中医药〉exterior heat and interior cold pattern; pattern of superficies heat and interior cold
表实证	〈中医药〉exterior repletion pattern; superficies excess pattern

表邪入里	〈中医药〉exterior pathogens entering the interior; invasion of the exterior pathogenic factors into the interior
表虚证	〈中医药〉exterior vacuity pattern; superficies deficiency pattern
表演赛	demonstration match
鳖甲	〈中医药〉(of Latin) Carapax Trionycis; Turtle Carapace; Turtle Shell
鳖甲煎丸	〈中医药〉Biejia Jian Wan; Turtle Shell Decocted Pill
宾客服务经理	guest service manager
宾客关系经理	guest relation manager
槟榔	〈中医药〉(of Latin) Semen Arecae; Areca Seed
冰花炖血燕	〈饮食〉Stewed Red Bird's Nest with Rock Candy
冰硼散	〈中医药〉Bingpeng San; Borneol and Borax Powder
冰片	〈中医药〉Borneolum Syntheticum; Synthetic Borneol
冰肉椰蓉蛋糕	〈饮食〉Minced Pork Cake Coated with Coconut Mash
冰糖炖银耳	〈饮食〉Braised White Fungi with Crystal Sugar
冰糖葫芦	〈饮食〉a stick of sugar-coated haws; candied haws on a stick; sugar-coated fruit (haws, yam, etc.) on a stick
冰糖甲鱼	〈饮食〉Steamed Turtle in Crystal Sugar Soup
冰糖莲心	〈饮食〉Lotus Seeds with Crystal Sugar Syrup
冰糖莲子银耳羹	〈饮食〉Lotus Seeds and White Fungus in Rock Sugar Soup
冰糖蜜炙火腿	〈饮食〉Stewed Ham with Crystal Sugar
冰糖燕窝	〈饮食〉Bird's Nest in Crystal Sugar
冰糖银耳炖雪梨	〈饮食〉Snow Pear and White Fungus in Rock Sugar Soup
冰糖银耳燕窝	〈饮食〉Stewed Bird's Nest with White Fungi and Rock Candy

冰糖蒸甲鱼	〈饮食〉Steamed Turtle in Rock Sugar Soup
冰心苦瓜	〈饮食〉Bitter Melon Salad
冰镇芥蓝	〈饮食〉Chinese Broccoli with Wasabi
冰镇南瓜茸	〈饮食〉Iced Pumpkin Mash
兵马俑	terra-cotta figures; soldier and horse figures
饼房厨师领班	patissier
病毒爆发	〈防疫〉virus outbreak
病毒变异	〈防疫〉virus variation
病毒的动物宿主	〈防疫〉animal host
病毒分离	〈防疫〉virus isolation
病毒感染者	〈防疫〉virus infected person; virus infestor
病毒监控和隔离措施	〈防疫〉virus monitoring and quarantine measures
病毒蔓延	〈防疫〉spread of the virus
病毒宿主	〈防疫〉virus host
病毒突变	〈防疫〉virus mutation
病毒携带者	〈防疫〉virus carrier
病毒性肺炎	〈防疫〉viral pneumonia
病毒性感冒	〈防疫〉viral influenza
病毒载量	〈防疫〉viral load
病发于阳	〈中医药〉disease arising from yang
病发于阴	〈中医药〉disease arising from yin
病机学说	〈中医药〉theory of pathogenesis; theory of mechanism of disease
病机总纲	〈中医药〉general principle of pathogenesis
病理	〈防疫〉pathology; cause of human disease
病理变化	〈中医药〉pathological changes
病理性骨折	〈中医药〉pathological fracture
病历管理员	medical records clerk
病例随访	〈防疫〉case follow-up
病脉	〈中医药〉abnormal pulse; morbid pulse
病起过用	〈中医药〉overuse causing disease
病色	〈中医药〉sickly complexion; morbid complexion
病色相克	〈中医药〉mutual restriction between disease and complexion

病死率	〈防疫〉fatality rate; death/mortality rate
病位与病性	〈中医药〉location and nature of disease
病因辨证	〈中医药〉pattern differentiation of etiology; disease cause pattern identification
病因学说	〈中医药〉etiology; theory of disease causes
病原体	〈防疫〉pathogen; causative agent
病症的虚实变化	〈中医药〉asthenia and sthenia changes of disease
玻璃品茗杯	glass tea-sipping cup
玻璃同心杯	glass concentric cup
钵	〈陶瓷〉(of a Buddhist monk) earthen bowl; alms bowl; small earthenware basin
菠菜豆腐	〈饮食〉Stewed Tofu with Spinach
菠菜鸡煲	〈饮食〉Boiled Chicken with Spinach
菠萝凉瓜炖鸡汤	〈饮食〉Chicken Soup Simmered with Bitter Melon and Pineapple
菠萝虾球	〈饮食〉Stir-Fried Prawn Balls with Pineapple
菠萝香酥肉	〈饮食〉Sweet and-Sour Pork with Pineapple
播音员	announcer; radio broadcaster
播音指导	broadcast supervisor
帛	〈服饰〉(of generic term) silk (product)
博鳌亚洲论坛	Boao Forum for Asia; BFA
博士生导师	Ph. D. supervisor; doctoral supervisor; doctoral advisor
薄利多销	small profit, large sale volume; small profits but quick turnover
薄荷	〈中医药〉(of Latin) Herba Menthae; Peppermint
簸箕	dustpan; winnowing fan
补短板	to strengthen weak links; to compensate for weakness; to shore up weak spots
补肺阿胶汤	〈中医药〉Bufei Ejiao Tang; Donkey-Hide Gelatin Decoction for Tonifying the Lung
补服	〈古〉bufu; official uniforms of the Ming and Qing Dynasties
补骨脂	〈中医药〉(of Latin) Fructus Psoraleae; Malaytea Scurfpea Fruit

补酒	tonic wine; tonic tincture
补脾益肺	〈中医药〉to invigorate the spleen for benefiting the lung; to supplement the spleen and boost the lung
补脾益气	〈中医药〉to invigorate the spleen and replenish qi; to supplement the spleen and boost qi
补气固脱	〈中医药〉to invigorate qi for relieving desertion; to supplement qi for stemming desertion
补气剂	〈中医药〉qi-tonifying prescription; qi-supplementing formula
补气明目	〈中医药〉to benefit qi for improving eyesight; to supplement qi and brighten the eyes
补气养血	〈中医药〉to benefit/supplement qi and nourish the blood
补肾安胎	〈中医药〉to supplement the kidney and quiet the fetus; to tonify kidney for preventing miscarriage
补肾固齿丸	〈中医药〉Bushen Guchi Wan; Kidney-Supplementing and Tooth-Securing Pill
补肾明目	〈中医药〉to tonify the kidney for improving eyesight; to supplement the kidney and brighten the eyes
补肾强身片	〈中医药〉Bushen Qiangshen Pian; Kidney-Tonifying and Health-Strengthening Tablet
补肾摄精	〈中医药〉to invigorate the kidney for consolidating semen; to supplement the kidney and contain essence
补肾调经	〈中医药〉to invigorate the kidney for regulating menstruation
补肾益脑胶囊	〈中医药〉Bushen Yinao Jiaonang; Kidney-Tonifying and Brain-Enriching Capsule
补肾益寿胶囊	〈中医药〉Bushen Yishou Jiaonang; Kidney-Tonifying and Life-Prolonging Capsule
补习班	tutoring center
补泻手法	〈中医药〉reinforcing and reducing manipulation

补血	〈中医药〉to tonify blood; to replenish blood
补血固脱	〈中医药〉to replenish blood for relieving depletion; to supplement blood to stem desertion
补血剂	〈中医药〉blood-supplementing formula; blood-replenishing potion
补血润燥	〈中医药〉to nourish blood for moistening dryness; to supplement blood and moisten dryness
补血养肝	〈中医药〉to replenish blood and nourish the liver; to supplement blood for nourishing the liver
补血养心	〈中医药〉to replenish blood for nourishing the heart
补阳	〈中医药〉to tonify yang; to reinforce the vital function
补阳剂	〈中医药〉yang-supplementing formula; yang-nourishing prescription
补益法	〈中医药〉invigoration method; therapy for restoration
补益肺气	〈中医药〉to replenish and restore lung-qi; to invigorate the qi of the lung
补益肝脾	〈中医药〉to invigorate the liver and spleen
补益肝气	〈中医药〉to benefit liver-qi; to invigorate liver-qi
补益剂	〈中医药〉supplementing and boosting formula; tonifying and replenishing formula
补益精髓	〈中医药〉to strengthen and nourish marrow and essence
补益脾肾	〈中医药〉to invigorate the spleen and kidney
补益心肺	〈中医药〉to invigorate the heart and lung
补益心气	〈中医药〉to benefit heart-qi; to reinforce functional activities of the heart
补阴剂	〈中医药〉yin-supplementing formula; yin-nourishing prescription
补中益气汤	〈中医药〉Buzhong Yiqi Tang; Decoction for Strengthening Middle Energizer to Nourishing Qi
补中益气丸	〈中医药〉Buzhong Yiqi Wan; Pill for Tonifying Middle-Warmer and Qi

不吃香	to be unpopular; to go out of vogue; to be out of favor
不吃这一套	it is not the way to deal with (us); it doesn't work on (us); not to buy it
不打不成交	no discord, no concord
不打不相识	no discord, no concord; out of blows friendship grows
不良贷款	non-performing loan
不漏一户，不漏一人	〈防疫〉to leave no one unscreened
不买账	not to take it; not to go for it
不明原因肺炎	〈防疫〉pneumonia of unknown etiology/cause
不内外因	〈中医药〉anendoexogenous pathogen; pathogenic factors neither endogenous nor exogenous; cause neither internal nor external
不惹是非	to stay out of trouble; to let sleeping dogs lie
不透明釉	〈陶瓷〉opaque glaze
不夜城	sleepless city; ever-bright city
不折腾	don't do sth. over and over again; to avoid self-inflicted setbacks
不正当竞争	unfair competition
不正之风	unhealthy work style; bad work style; harmful practice
布币［钱］	〈古〉spade coin; spade-shaped money (issued in the Spring and Autumn period and Warring States period) →铲布［币］
布草部领班	uniform and linen captain
布草传送员	linen chute runner
布草房务员	linen room attendant
布草房主管	uniform supervisor
布草分类员	linen chute sorter
布揉	〈茶〉cloth rolling
布纹青瓷双系罐	〈陶瓷〉celadon double-eared jar with fabric striation
步步高升	promoting to a higher position

步行街	pedestrian street
步行天桥	pedestrian overpass
步摇	〈首饰〉buyao; step-shaking hairpin; hair dangling ornament (inlaid with pearl and jade worn by women in ancient times)
部门经理	branch manager; department manager
部委办主任	director of ministry and commission
部长	minister; head of a department
部长助理	assistant minister

C

擦尔瓦	〈彝族〉caerwa; folk cape
擦剂	〈中医药〉liniment; linimentum
才子佳人	gifted scholars and beautiful ladies (in Chinese romances)
财神爷	God of Wealth; God of Fortune
财务报告人	financial reporter; finance reporter
财务部	finance department; accounting department
财务部部长	minister of finance department
财务分析员	financial analyst
财务分析主管	financial analysis supervisor
财务顾问	financial consultant; finance consultant
财务规划师	financial planner; finance planner
财务经理	finance manager; financial manager
财务行政副总裁	vice-president of administration and finance
财务总监	financial controller; chief financial officer; CFO
裁减冗员	to cut down on overstaffing; to lay off redundant staff
采耳师	ear cleaner
采购部经理	purchasing manager
采购代理	purchasing agent
采购专员	procurement specialist
采矿工程师	mining engineer
采青	〈茶〉tea harvesting; to pick the green
彩绸腰带	colored silk waistbelt
彩虹蒸豆腐	〈饮食〉Steamed Tofu with Vegetables
彩绘骑马陶俑	〈陶瓷〉painted pottery equestrian figurines

彩绘陶茧形壶	〈陶瓷〉painted pottery silk-worm shaped jar
彩绘陶乐俑	〈陶瓷〉painted pottery figures of musicians
彩绘陶盆	〈陶瓷〉painted pottery basin
彩绘乐舞杂技陶俑	〈陶瓷〉painted pottery figurines of musicians and acrobats
彩椒炒火鸭柳	〈饮食〉Stir-Fried Roast Duck Fillets with Bell Pepper
彩椒牛柳	〈饮食〉Stir-Fried Beef Fillets with Bell Peppers
彩铃	polyphonic ringtone
彩帨	〈古服饰〉caishui; a long silk ornament (hanging in or tied on the chest or on the left waist in the Qing Dynasty)
彩塑	〈陶瓷〉painted sculpture; colored modelling
彩陶	〈陶瓷〉painted pottery; colored pottery
彩陶器	〈陶瓷〉faience; colored earthenware
彩妆培训师	makeup trainer
踩曲	〈酒〉to knead the raw starter component
菜板	〈饮食〉kitchen board
菜包子	〈饮食〉Steamed Bun with Vegetable Stuffing; Steamed Bun Stuffed with Vegetables
菜炒鲈鱼	〈饮食〉Stir-Fried Perch with Vegetables
菜炒鱼片	〈饮食〉Stir-Fried Fish Slices with Vegetables
菜胆白灵菇	〈饮食〉Braised Mushrooms and Green Vegetables
菜胆蚝油牛肉	〈饮食〉Stir-Fried Sliced Beef and Vegetables with Oyster Sauce
菜胆奶油鸡	〈饮食〉Braised Chicken Mixed with Brussel Sprout and Milk
菜刀	〈饮食〉kitchen knife; cleaver knife; cook chopper
菜豆花	〈饮食〉Braised Tofu with Vegetables
菜干煲猪肺	〈饮食〉Stewed Pork Lung with Dried Vegetables
菜花炒虾丸	〈饮食〉Stir-Fried Jumbo Shrimp Balls with Cauliflower
菜花虾羹	〈饮食〉Shrimp and Broccoli Soup

菜尖牛肉丝	〈饮食〉Stir-Fried Shredded Beef with Mung Bean Sprouts
菜篮子工程	vegetable basket program; non-staple food project
菜鸟	green hand; awkward squad; rookie
菜鸟驿站	Cai Niao Station; Cainiao Courier Station
菜片乳鸽松	〈饮食〉Stir-Fried Minced Pigeon with Sliced Vegetables
菜脯叉烧肠粉	〈饮食〉Steamed Rice Rolls with Pickled Vegetables and Barbecued Pork
菜肉馄饨	〈饮食〉Pork and Vegetable Wonton Soup
菜肉馄饨面	〈饮食〉Noodle Soup with Wonton Stuffed with Pork and Vegetables
菜肉饺子	〈饮食〉Jiaozi/Dumplings Stuffed with Pork and Vegetables
菜头烧板鹅	〈饮食〉Braised Dried Goose and Lettuce in Spicy Sauce
菜心扒牛肉	〈饮食〉Grilled Beef with Shanghai Greens/Choy Sum
菜心扒鱼圆	〈饮食〉Braised Fish Balls with Choy Sum
菜远炒排骨	〈饮食〉Stir-Fried Spare Ribs with Green Vegetables
菜远鸡球	〈饮食〉Stir-Fried Chicken Balls with Vegetable Heart
菜远石斑球	〈饮食〉Stir-Fried Rockfish Balls with Green Vegetables
菜远虾球	〈饮食〉Stir-Fried Prawn/Shrimp Balls with Green Vegetables
参与意识	desire to participate; sense of participation
餐厅经理	restaurant manager
餐厅领班	restaurant captain
餐饮部	food and beverage division/department
餐饮部经理	food and beverage manager
餐饮部长	food and beverage captain
餐饮成本控制员	restaurant cost controller

餐饮服务员	restaurant waiter; restaurant waitress; F & B (Food and Beverage) server
餐饮业	catering industry
餐饮总监	food and beverage director
蚕蛾公补酒	male silkworm moth tonic chiew
蚕丝脱脂棉混纺布料	silk-degreased cotton blended fabric
惨淡经营	to work hard and carefully to keep one's business going
仓储领班	store room captain
仓库主管	warehouse supervisor
苍鹅鼻炎片	〈中医药〉Cang'e Biyan Pian; Blue Swan Rhinitis Tablet
苍耳散	〈中医药〉Cang'er San; Xanthium Powder
苍耳子	〈中医药〉(of Latin) Fructus Xanthii; Siberian Cocklebur Fruit
苍山雪绿	〈茶〉Cangshan Snow Green tea
苍术	〈中医药〉(of Latin) Rhizoma Atractylodis; Chinese Atractylodes; Atractylodes Root
藏而不泻	〈中医药〉storage without excretion
藏精气而不泻	〈中医药〉to store essence without draining
草豆蔻	〈中医药〉(of Latin) Semen Alpiniae Katsumadai; Katsumada Galangal Seed
草根	caogen; grassroots
草根阶层	grassroots level; grassroots class
草根组织	grassroots organization
草菇鸡片汤	〈饮食〉Sliced Chicken Soup with Mushrooms
草菇牛肉肠粉	〈饮食〉Steamed Rice Rolls with Straw Mushrooms and Beef
草菇蒸滑鸡	〈饮食〉Steamed Chicken with Straw Mushrooms
草果	〈中医药〉(of Latin) Fructus Tsaoko; Tsaoko Amomum Fruit; Spicate Hedychium Fruit
草履	straw sandals; straw shoes
草莓族	strawberry generation (who cannot withstand social pressure or hard work like their parents' generation)

草食男	herbivore men; herbivorous males (referring to young people, who often do not take initiative actions in their romantic relationships with females)
草乌	〈中医药〉(of Latin) Radix Aconiti Kusnezoffii; Kusnezoff Monkshood Root; Wild Aconite [Tuber]
草药	〈中医药〉medicinal herbs; herbal drugs →本草
草药产品	〈中医药〉herbal product; herbal medicinal product
草药疗法	〈中医药〉Chinese herbal remedy; Chinese herbal therapy
侧柏叶	〈中医药〉(of Latin) Cacumen Platycladi; Chinese Arborvitae Leaf; Biota Leaf
叉烧包	〈饮食〉Baozi Stuffed with Barbecued Pork
叉烧桂鱼	〈饮食〉Grilled Stuffed Mandarin Fish in Net Lard
叉烧里脊	〈饮食〉Barbecued Pork Fillet Roll; BBQ Pork Tenderloin
叉烧肉	〈饮食〉Roasted Pork Fillets
叉烧酥	〈饮食〉Barbecued Pork Pastry
叉烧无骨排	〈饮食〉Barbecued Boneless Spare Ribs
叉烧杏仁酥	〈饮食〉Barbecued Pork and Almond Shortcake
叉烧野鸭	〈饮食〉Braised Wild Duck
插袋	insert pocket; side pocket; vertical pocket
插杠子	to poke one's nose into someone's businesses
插秧酒	chayang wine; rice transplanting wine
茶杯	teacup
茶杯碟	〈陶瓷〉teacup with saucer
茶博会	tea expo; tea fair; tea abundant meeting
茶布	tea cloth; tea towel
茶产地	tea producing area
茶产业	tea industry
茶车	tea cart
茶船	tea boat; saucer (for holding a teacup)
茶道	teaism; tea ceremony
茶道杯	tea ceremony cup →飘逸杯

茶道六君子	six tea utensils (including tea scoop, tea needle, tea strainer, tea clamp, tea spoon and canister)
茶道内涵	tea lore connotation
茶道素养	tea lore accomplishment
茶道特质	tea lore characteristics
茶底	tea dreg
茶点	refreshment; tea cake; tea and pastry
茶店	tea shop
茶碟	tea plate
茶丁	→苦丁茶
茶拂	tea brush
茶馆	teahouse; tea house
茶壶	teapot; teakettle
茶壶保温炉	teapot warming furnace
茶壶套	tea cozy
茶话会	tea forum; tea party
茶会	tea party; bun-fight
茶剂	〈中医药〉medicinal tea; medicated tea
茶夹	tea clamp →茶道六君子
茶巾	tea cloth; tea towel
茶巾盘	tea towel tray
茶经济	tea economy
茶具	tea service; tea set
茶具袋	tea ware bag
茶历史	tea history
茶漏	tea strainer →茶道六君子
茶罗	tea sieve
茶滤托	tea filter tray; tea filter holder
茶美学	tea aesthetics
茶农业	tea agriculture
茶盘	tea tray; teaboard
茶片	tea siftings
茶品种	tea variety; tea cultivar
茶器	tea utensil; tea ware

茶青	tea leaves; fresh tea leaves
茶师	tea master
茶诗	tea poetry
茶匙	teaspoon; tea spoon →茶道六君子
茶树	(of Latin) Camellia sinensis; tea plant; tea bush
茶树菇炒鹿片	〈饮食〉Stir-Fried Venison Fillet with Tea Tree Mushrooms
茶俗	tea custom
茶汤	tea juice; gruel of millet flour and sugar (traditional snack in Beijing, Tianjin and Shandong)
茶通	→茶针[通]
茶筒	tea canister →茶道六君子
茶托	→茶船
茶碗	tea bowl; teacup
茶文化	tea culture
茶筅座	tea whisk holder
茶香	tea aroma; fragrance of tea
茶香鸡	〈饮食〉Red-Cooked Chicken with Tea Flavor
茶休	tea break; coffee break
茶锈	tea stain
茶叶罐	tea caddy; tea canister
茶医药	tea medicine
茶艺	arts or skills of tea-making; tea art
茶艺表演	tea art performance; to perform tea art
茶艺师	tea art specialist; tea specialist; tea master
茶艺史	tea art history
茶饮料	tea beverage; tea drinks
茶园	tea plantation; tea garden
茶则	tea scoop; tea chooser →茶道六君子
茶渣	tea grounds; tea leaves
茶盏	teacup
茶哲	tea philosophy; philosophy of tea
茶针[通]	tea needle →茶道六君子
茶盅	tea pitcher; Chinese tea cup

茶桌	tea table; teapoy
茶籽油	camellia oil; tea seed oil
搽剂	〈中医药〉liniment; linimentum
差评	negative feedback; negative review; negative comment
差异化精准防控策略	〈防疫〉precise and differentiated epidemic control strategies
拆东墙补西墙	to rob Peter to pay Paul
拆骨鸡	〈饮食〉Boneless Chicken
拆迁补偿费	compensation for demolition
拆迁费	removal expense; relocation compensation
拆迁费用	removal expense
拆迁户	households or units relocated due to building demolition
拆台	to cut the ground from under someone's feet; to pull away a prop; to hinder the progress of sth.
钗	〈首饰〉twin-stick hairpin (formerly worn by women for hair-bun)
钗钿礼衣	chai-dian formal dress (for women with titles in the Tang Dynasty)
差旅费	expenses for business trips
柴葛解肌汤	〈中医药〉Chaige Jieji Tang; Bupleurum and Kudzu Decoction to Release the Muscle Layer
柴沟堡熏肉	〈饮食〉Chaigoubu Smoked Meat with Pepper, Aniseed and Cinnamon
柴胡	〈中医药〉(of Latin) Radix Bupleuri; Chinese Thorowax Root
柴胡口服液	〈中医药〉Chaihu Koufuye; Bupleuri Oral Solution/Liquid
柴胡疏肝散	〈中医药〉Chaihu Shugan San; Bupleurum Liver-Coursing Powder
掺水文凭	diploma obtained by using unfair or unlawful means
掺杂兑假	to mix in fake or inferior components

襜裙	chanqun; flapping apron skirt (worn by women in the Liao and Jin Dynasties)
禅衣	zen garment; monastic robe
缠缚疗法	〈中医药〉binding therapy
缠[裹]足	〈旧〉foot-binding (an outdated habit of women to wrap their feet to make them small)
蝉鬓	(of hairstyle) cicada temple hair; cicada hair on the temple (of a woman)
蝉蜕	〈中医药〉(of Latin) Periostracum Cicadae; Cicada Slough; Cicada Molting
蟾蜍酒	toad wine
蟾酥	〈中医药〉(of Latin) Venenum Bufonis; Toad Venom
产复康颗粒	〈中医药〉Chanfukang Keli; Post-Delivery Recovery Granule
产假	maternity leave
产教融合	〈防疫〉to integrate the resources of enterprises with vocational schools and universities
产科医师	obstetrist; obstetrician
产粮大省	granary province
产品工艺工程师	product process engineer
产品规划工程师	product planning engineer
产权界定	delimitation of property rights
产权收益	income from property
产权转让	transference of title of property
产销对接	〈防疫〉to coordinate production and sales
产销两旺	both production and marketing thrive
产销直接挂钩	to directly link production with marketing
产学研相结合的技术创新体系	the system for technological innovation guided by combining enterprises, universities and research institutes
产业基础雄厚	〈防疫〉solid industrial foundation
产酯酵母	〈酒〉ester forming yeast
铲布[币]	〈古〉spade copper coin (issued in the Spring and Autumn period and Warring States period) →布币[钱]

菖蒲酒	calamus wine (served at Dragon-Boat Festival)
长安钱	〈古〉Chang'an coin
长白山人参炖老鸡	〈饮食〉Stewed Local Chicken with Changbai Gensing
长城干红	〈酒〉Great Wall dry red wine
长耳帻	〈古服饰〉turban-shaped hat with flattened long ears
长冠服	long crown dress (of the Han Dynasty)
长江学者奖励计划	Cheung Kong Scholars Program; Chang Jiang Scholars Program
长毛绒针织物	high pile knitted fabric
长袍	mandarin long gown; one-piece long robe
长期国债	long-term government bonds
长旗袍	long cheongsam
长襦	long gown; long jacket
长沙窑釉下彩鹿纹执壶	〈陶瓷〉Changsha Kiln underglazed ewer with deer pattern
长石瓷	〈陶瓷〉feldspar porcelain; feldspathic porcelain/china
长寿酒	longevity liquor →菊花酒
长寿面	〈饮食〉Birthday Noodles; Longevity Noodles (served on one's birthday for good wishes)
长寿桃	〈饮食〉Longevity Peaches
长袖袍服	robe with long sleeves
长针	〈中医药〉long needle
长征火箭	Long March rocket
长治久安	a long period of stability; prolonged political stability; lasting political stability
肠清茶	〈中医药〉Changqing Cha; Intestine Clearance Tea
肠胃宁胶囊	〈中医药〉Changweining Jiaonang; Intestine-Stomach Tranquilizing Capsule
尝苦头	to drain the cup of bitterness; to taste the bitterness of sth.
常服	routine suit; informal dress

常见并发症状	〈防疫〉common syndrome; symptoms of complications
常山	〈中医药〉(of Latin) Radix Dichroae; Antifeverile Dichroa Root
常务副校长	managing vice president; vice principal
常务理事	standing director; managing director
常用汉字	common Chinese characters
常住人口登记	permanent population register; registration of permanent residents
嫦娥二号	Chang'e-2
嫦娥工程	Chang'e Project →中国探月工程
嫦娥三号登月舱	Chang'e-3 lunar module
嫦娥月球车	Chang'e lunar rover
嫦娥月球探测器	Chang'e lunar orbiter/prober
嫦娥月球着陆器	Chang'e lunar lander
厂家代表	manufacturer's representative
倡议书	initial written proposal
唱独角戏	to play a monodrama
唱对台戏	to put on a rival show (against sb.); to challenge sb. with opposing views
唱高调	mouth high-sounding words; to use high-flown words
唱双簧	to give a two-man comic show; to collaborate with each other in a kind of duet
唱祝酒歌	to sing drinking song; to sing a toasting song
抄手	〈饮食〉Fresh Meat Huntun/Wonton with Sauce
超编人员	exceed personnel; supernumerary
超长潜伏期	〈防疫〉ultra-long incubation period
超负荷运转	overloaded operation
超级传播者	〈防疫〉super spreader
超前教育	superior education
超前消费	pre-mature consumption; excessive consumption
超前意识	superior consciousness
超生孩子	extra children; children outside the state plan

超支户	household/family living perpetually in debt
焯水	〈饮食〉to quick-boil; to quick-scald; quick-boiled; quick scalded
巢元方	Chao Yuanfang (a medical scientist in the Sui Dynasty)
朝[具]服	〈古〉court dress
朝褂	〈服饰〉court gown (female official dress worn in formal occasions in the Qing Dynasty)
朝冠	〈古〉court crown; an official hat with ornamental circlet (worn by ancient officials when going to court)
朝袍	〈服饰〉court robe (for emperors to wear in celebrations and sacrificial activities in the Qing Dynasty)
朝裙	court skirt (for imperial concubines to wear in celebrations and sacrificial activities in the Qing Dynasty)
朝天髻	(of hairstyle) upward bun
朝阳群众	Chaoyang masses/residents; residents of Chaoyang District
朝珠	〈古〉court beads (a string of coral or agate beads worn by court officials in the Qing Dynasty)
潮汕卤水鹅	〈饮食〉Chaoshan Goose in Spiced Soy Sauce
潮汕烧鸡	〈饮食〉Chaoshan Braised Chicken
潮式椒酱肉	〈饮食〉Chaozhou Stir-Fried Pork with Chili Soy Sauce
潮式凉瓜排骨	〈饮食〉Chaozhou Spare Ribs with Bitter Melon
潮州菜	〈饮食〉Chaozhou Cuisine
潮州烧雁鹅	〈饮食〉Chaozhou Roasted Goose
炒	〈饮食〉to stir-fry; to sauté; stir-fried; sautéed
炒白术	〈中医药〉(of Latin) Rhizoma Atractylodis Macrocephlae Preparata; Prepared Ovate Atractylodes; Parched White Atractylodes Rhizome
炒大蛤	〈饮食〉Stir-Fried Fresh Clams

炒大虾片	〈饮食〉Stir-Fried Prawn/Shrimp Slices
炒肝尖	〈饮食〉Stir-Fried Pig Liver with Onion and Carrot
炒桂花干贝	〈饮食〉Stir-Fried Scallops with Osmanthus
炒锅	〈饮食〉(of a cooker) wok; Chinese frying pan
炒海蟹肉	〈饮食〉Stir-Fried Minced Crab Meat
炒河粉	〈饮食〉Stir-Fried Rice Noodles
炒汇	to speculate in foreign currency
炒鸡丁	〈饮食〉Stir-Fried Chicken Cubes; Stir-Fried Diced Chicken
炒鸡肝虾片	〈饮食〉Stir-Fried Prawn Slices with Chicken Liver
炒鸡片	〈饮食〉Stir-Fried Sliced Chicken; Stir-Fried Chicken Slices
炒鸡什	〈饮食〉Stir-Fried Chicken Giblets
炒芥蓝	〈饮食〉Stir-Fried Chinese Broccoli
炒金热	stock-market fever
炒腊肉	〈饮食〉Stir-Fried Cured Pork with Red Pepper and Garlic
炒里脊丝	〈饮食〉Stir-Fried Pork Fillet Shreds
炒里脊丝粉皮	〈饮食〉Stir-Fried Pork Fillet with Starch Sheets
炒料	〈饮食〉stir frying aromatics
炒米粉	〈饮食〉Stir-Fried Rice Vermicelli
炒面	〈饮食〉Chow Mien; Stir-Fried Noodles (with Vegetables)
炒面线	〈饮食〉Stir-Fried Mee Sua; Stir-Fried Rice-Flour Noodles
炒木须[樨]肉	〈饮食〉Moo Shu Pork; Stir-Fried Pork Slices with Eggs and Fungi
炒木须银鱼	〈饮食〉Stir-Fried White Bait with Eggs
炒牛肉片	〈饮食〉Stir-Fried Sliced Beef; Stir-Fried Beef Slices
炒牛肉丝	〈饮食〉Stir-Fried Shredded Beef with Scallions
炒全蟹	〈饮食〉Stir-Fried Hard Shell Crab
炒肉丁	〈饮食〉Stir-Fried Meat Cubes
炒肉片	〈饮食〉Stir-Fried Pork Slices with Onion and Ginger

炒肉丝	〈饮食〉Stir-Fried Shredded Pork with Pepper and Ginger
炒鳝背	〈饮食〉Stir-Fried Eel Back
炒鳝片	〈饮食〉Stir-Fried Eel Slices with Cucumber and Bamboo Shoots
炒鳝丝	〈饮食〉Stir-Fried Shredded Finless Eel
炒勺	(of a cooker) wok spatula; ladle
炒什件	〈饮食〉Stir-Fried Mixed Meat with Bamboo Shoot and Fungus
炒石榴鸡	〈饮食〉Stir-Fried Chicken (in Megranate Shape)
炒时蔬	〈饮食〉Stir-Fried Seasonal Vegetables
炒双脆	〈饮食〉Stir-Fried Kidney with Pork Tripe
炒双冬	〈饮食〉Stir-Fried Dried Mushrooms and Winter Bamboo Shoots
炒素丁	〈饮食〉Stir-Fried Vegetable Dices
炒笋干	〈饮食〉Stir-Fried Dried Bamboo Shoot
炒虾仁	〈饮食〉Stir-Fried Shelled Fresh Shrimps; Stir-Fried Shrimp Meat
炒虾蟹	〈饮食〉Stir-Fried Shrimps and Crab Meat
炒鲜桃仁丝瓜	〈饮食〉Stir-Fried Sponge Gourd and Peach Kernel
炒香干	〈饮食〉Pan-Fired Dried Tofu; Stir-Fried Marinated Beancurd
炒蟹粉	〈饮食〉Stir-Fried Crab Meat and Roes
炒芽菜鸭丝	〈饮食〉Stir-Fried Shredded Duck with Mung Bean Sprouts
炒羊肚	〈饮食〉Stir-Fried Lamb Tripe
炒腰肝	〈饮食〉Stir-Fried Pig Kidney and Liver
炒腰花	〈饮食〉Stir-Fried Pig Kidney; Stir-Fried Sliced Pig Kidney
炒鱿鱼	〈饮食〉Stir-Fried Squid with Onion and Coriander
炒鱿鱼丝	〈饮食〉Stir-Fried Shredded Squids
炒鱼片	〈饮食〉Stir-Fried Fish Slices with Carrots and Green Onions
炒杂菜	〈饮食〉Mixed Green Tender; Mixed Vegetables

炒作	(of news) to hype up; to sensationalize (sth.); media hype
车队队长	team captain; chief driver
车间主管	workshop supervisor
车间主任	workshop manager
车辆购置税	vehicle purchase tax
车奴	car slave; car mortgage slave
车牌摇号	lottery for license plate; license-plate lottery
车前草	〈中医药〉(of Latin) Herba Plantaginis; Plantain Herb
车前子	〈中医药〉(of Latin) Semen Plantaginis; Plantain Seed
扯后腿	to hold (or pull) sb. back; to be a drag on sb.
撤销职务	to annul one's position
抻面	〈饮食〉Hand-Pulled Noodles; Noodles Made by Drawing out the Dough by Hand
臣药	〈中医药〉ministerial drug; associate drug
沉缸酒	chengang liquor (sweet yellow rice wine)
沉香	〈中医药〉(of Latin) Lignum Aquilariae Resinatum; Chinese Eaglewood
沉香香烟	Chenxiang cigarettes; Eaglewood cigarettes
陈醇	〈茶〉stale and mellow
陈缸酒	chengang chiew
陈列陶瓷	〈陶瓷〉porcelain for display
陈年彩坛花雕	〈酒〉Aged Caitan Huadiao Medium Sweet
陈年酒	chen nian chiew; aged wine/liquor
陈年普洱	〈茶〉aged Puer
陈年曲酒	aged fermented liquor
陈皮	〈中医药〉(of Latin) Percarpium Citri Reticulatae; Dried Tangerine/Orange Peel
陈皮炖全鸭	〈饮食〉Stewed Duck with Orange Peel
陈皮红豆沙	〈饮食〉Tangerine-Flavored Red Bean Paste
陈皮鸡	〈饮食〉Tangerine-Flavored Chicken
陈皮牛肉	〈饮食〉Tangerine-Flavored Beef; Beef with Dried Orange Peel

陈皮兔肉	〈饮食〉Tangerine-Flavored Rabbit Meat
陈气	〈茶〉stale odor
陈设瓷	〈陶瓷〉display china; ornamental porcelain
陈[摆]设瓷	〈陶瓷〉display china; porcelain for display; ornamental porcelain
陈氏太极	Chen-style Tai Chi
陈味	〈茶〉stale taste
陈香	〈茶〉stale flavor
晨练	morning exercise
衬布	lining cloth; lapping cloth; interlining
衬里	〈服饰〉liner; interlining; backing
衬衫领	shirt collar
趁热打铁	to make hay while the sun shines; to strike while the iron is hot
蛏肉炒蛋	〈饮食〉Stir-Fried Eggs with Razor Clam Meat
成本部经理	cost control manager
成本管理员	cost controller
成本核算员	cost clerk; cost accounting clerk
成本会计师	cost accountant
成都大熊猫繁殖研究基地	Chengdu Research Base of Giant Panda Breeding (Sichuan)
成都－欧洲铁路服务	Chengdu-Europe railway service
成化斗彩盖罐	〈陶瓷〉lidded jar with strong contrasting colors (Ming Chenghua period)
成化青花人物梅瓶	〈陶瓷〉blue and white plum vase with portraiture pattern (Chenghua period)
成人高考	national higher education exams for self-taught adults
成人夜校	night school for adults
成人中等职业技术教育	adult secondary vocational and technical education
成人中等专科学校	secondary specialized/technical school for adults
诚实守信	to be honest and trustworthy; honesty and trustworthiness

诚信企业	high-integrity enterprise; enterprise of integrity
承浆	〈中医药〉Chengjiang point; Saliva Receptacle; Mandibular Fossa (CV24)
承筋	〈中医药〉Chengjin acupoint; Sinew Support (BL56)
承灵	〈中医药〉Chengling acupoint; Spirit Support (GB18)
承满	〈中医药〉Chengman acupoint; Fullness Support (ST20)
承泣	〈中医药〉Chengqi acupoint; Tear Containers (ST1)
承山	〈中医药〉Chengshan acupoint; Mountain Support (BL57)
城管	city management; urban management officer; urban inspector
城际高速列车	intercity high-speed train
城市低保对象	urban residents entitled to basic living allowances
城市规划师	urban planner; city planner
城市户口	permanent urban residence certificate
城市基础设施建设	city's/urban infrastructure construction
城市美容师	urban environmental worker
城市运动会	municipal athletics meet
城乡低收入居民	low-income residents in both town and country
城乡电网改造	projects for upgrading urban and rural power grids
城乡接合部	rural-urban fringe zone
城乡特殊困难群众	urban and rural residents with special difficulties
城乡消费设施	consumption facilities in both urban and rural areas
城乡信用社	credit cooperatives in both urban and rural areas
城镇规划员	urban & regional planner; town planning officer
城镇居民基本医疗保险	basic medical insurance for urban residents; urban resident basic medical insurance
城镇职工基本医疗保险	basic medical insurance for urban employees/workers
城中村	village inside/in a city; urban village

逞英雄	to play the braggart; to display gallantry
吃白食	to have a free meal; to live off sb.; to eat idly without work
吃饱穿暖	to have enough to eat and wear; to have adequate food and clothing
吃闭门羹	to be given a cold shoulder; to find the door slammed to in one's face
吃豆腐	to flirt with women; to take advantage (of a woman about sth.)
吃干醋	to be jealous without reason; to be green with envy
吃皇粮	to live on salary paid by the state; to live on the government payroll
吃苦果	to swallow a bitter pill; to bear adverse consequences
吃苦在前,享受在后	to be the first to bear hardships and the last to enjoy comforts; to embrace hardships, not material comforts
吃劳保	to live on labor insurance allowance; to live on worker's compensation
吃老本	to live off one's past gains or achievements; to rest/retire/repose on one's laurels; to bask in one's past glory without making further improvement
吃偏饭	to eat better than average meals; to enjoy special privilege or treatment
吃软饭	to live on the favor of a woman; to live off of a rich woman
吃闲饭	to live an idle life; to be a loafer; to be unemployed and without income
吃香	to be very popular; to be in great demand; to be much sought after
吃小亏占大便宜	to lose a little but gain much; to take small losses for the sake of big gains
绤	〈服饰〉chì; fine ko-hemp cloth/fiber; fine linen

驰援武汉	〈防疫〉to race against the clock to assist Wuhan
迟脉	〈中医药〉slow pulse; retarded pulse (less than 60 beats per minute)
尺(脉)	〈中医药〉chi pulse; cubit pulse
尺泽	〈中医药〉Chize acupoint; Cubit Marsh (LU5)
齿痕舌	〈中医药〉teeth-printed/marked tongue; tongue bearing dental impressions
齿痛消炎灵颗粒	〈中医药〉Chitong Xiaoyan Ling Keli; Toothache and Inflammation-Reducing Granule
豉椒炒鸡球	〈饮食〉Stir-Fried Chicken Balls with Chili Bean Sauce
豉椒炒牛肉	〈饮食〉Stir-Fried Beef with Black Bean Sauce
豉椒炒肉蟹	〈饮食〉Stir-Fried Crab with Fermented Soya Bean
豉椒炒鱿	〈饮食〉Stir-Fried Squid with Bell Pepper and Fermented Soy Bean
豉椒鸡	〈饮食〉Stir-Fried Chicken with Black Bean Sauce
豉椒焗龙虾	〈饮食〉Braised Lobster with Peppers and Black Bean Sauce
豉椒鳗鱼丝	〈饮食〉Stir-Fried Shredded Eel with Peppers in Black Bean Sauce
豉椒焖排骨	〈饮食〉Stewed Spareribs with Pepper and Fermented Soya Bean
豉椒鲜鱿	〈饮食〉Stir-Fried Squids with Peppers in Black Bean Sauce
豉椒鲜鱿饭	〈饮食〉Rice with Squid, Peppers and Black Bean Sauce
豉香尖椒炒豆干	〈饮食〉Stir-Fried Dried Tofu with Hot Peppers and Black Bean Sauce
豉香型(风格)	〈酒〉soybean-flavor style
豉油皇乳鸽	〈饮食〉Braised Pigeon with Soy Sauce
豉油皇咸肉	〈饮食〉Steamed Preserved Pork in Black Sauce
豉油牛肉	〈饮食〉Steamed Beef in Black Bean Sauce
豉油乳鸽皇	〈饮食〉Braised Pigeon with Black Bean Sauce
豉油王蒸鲈鱼	〈饮食〉Steamed Perch in Black Bean Sauce

豉油蒸肠粉	〈饮食〉Steamed Rice Rolls with Black Bean Sauce
豉油蒸鲩鱼	〈饮食〉Steamed Grass Carp with Soy Sauce
豉油蒸生鱼	〈饮食〉Steamed Fish with Soy Sauce
豉汁炒大蚬	〈饮食〉Stir-Fried Clams with Black Bean Sauce
豉汁炒鸡球	〈饮食〉Stir-Fried Chicken Balls with Black Bean Sauce
豉汁炒青口	〈饮食〉Stir-Fried Mussels with Black Bean Sauce
豉汁炒三鲜	〈饮食〉Stir-Fried Assorted Seafood with Black Bean Sauce
豉汁豆腐蒸带子	〈饮食〉Steamed Scallops and Tofu in Black Bean Sauce
豉汁炖鹧鸪	〈饮食〉Stewed Partridge with Pickled Bean Juice
豉汁煎焗塘虱	〈饮食〉Pan-Fried Catfish with Black Bean Sauce
豉汁凉瓜	〈饮食〉Bitter Melon with Black Bean Sauce
豉汁凉瓜皮	〈饮食〉Stir-Fried Bitter Melon Peels with Black Bean Sauce
豉汁熘排骨	〈饮食〉Quick-Fried Spareribs with Black Bean Sauce
豉汁牛仔骨	〈饮食〉Steamed Beef Ribs with Black Bean Sauce
豉汁排骨饭	〈饮食〉Rice with Spare Ribs in Black Bean Sauce
豉汁蒸白鳝	〈饮食〉Steamed White Eel with Black Bean Sauce
豉汁蒸多宝鱼	〈饮食〉Steamed Turbot Fish with Black Bean Sauce
豉汁蒸桂花鱼	〈饮食〉Steamed Mandarin Fish with Black Bean Sauce
豉汁蒸九孔	〈饮食〉Steamed Abalone with Black Bean Sauce
豉汁蒸鲈鱼	〈饮食〉Steamed Sea Bass with Black Bean Sauce
豉汁蒸排骨	〈饮食〉Steamed Spare Ribs in Black Bean Sauce
豉汁蒸扇贝	〈饮食〉Steamed Scallops in Shell with Black Bean Sauce
豉汁蒸石斑球	〈饮食〉Steamed Rockfish Balls with Black Bean Sauce
豉汁蒸石斑鱼	〈饮食〉Steamed Garoupa with Black Bean Sauce
豉汁蒸鱼	〈饮食〉Steamed Fish with Black Bean Sauce

赤豆煲鲤	〈饮食〉Red Bean and Carp Potage; Stewed Carp with Red Bean in Casserole
赤脚医生	〈旧〉barefoot doctor (part-time paramedical workers in rural areas)
赤芍	〈中医药〉(of Latin) Radix Paeoniae Rubra; Red Peony Root
赤石脂	〈中医药〉(of Latin) Halloysitum Rubrum; Red Halloysite
《赤水玄珠》	〈中医药〉*Chishui Xuanzhu; Black Pearl from Red River* (by Sun Yikui in the Ming Dynasty)
赤陶	〈陶瓷〉terracotta; red earthenware
赤卫队	〈旧〉Red Guards (county army in Jinggangshan led by the Communist Party of China in the Agrarian Revolutionary War period)
赤小豆	〈中医药〉(of Latin) Semen Phaseoli; Rice Bean
翅尖帽	〈基诺族〉wing tip hat
翅汤浸什菌	〈饮食〉Braised Assorted Mushrooms in Shark's Fin Soup
翅汤青瓜虾球	〈饮食〉Shrimp Balls and Cucumbers in Shark's Fin Soup
瘛脉	〈中医药〉Chimai acupoint; Spasm Vessel; Tugging Vessel (TE18)
冲动性购买	impulse buying; impulse shopping
冲服	〈中医药〉to be administered after dissolved; to take drenched
冲脉	〈中医药〉chong channel; thoroughfare vessel
冲门	〈中医药〉Chongmen acupoint; Rushing Gate (SP12)
冲任不固	〈中医药〉debility unconsolidation of chong and ren channels; insecurity of the thoroughfare and controlling vessels
冲任不固证	〈中医药〉pattern of insecurity of the thoroughfare and controlling vessels

冲任不调证	〈中医药〉pattern of chong and ren channels disharmony; pattern of disharmony of the thoroughfare and controlling vessels
冲洗疗法	〈中医药〉irrigation therapy; douche treatment
舂米画像砖	brick of rice husking scene
虫草炖老鸭	〈饮食〉Stewed Duck with Aweto
虫草清肺胶囊	〈中医药〉Chongcao Qingfei Jiaonang; Cordyceps Lung-Clearing Capsule
虫草鸭块汤	〈饮食〉Diced Duck with Aweto Soup
虫草蒸裙边	〈饮食〉Steamed Turtle Rim with Aweto
《重楼玉钥》	〈中医药〉*Chonglou Yuyao*; *Jade Key to the Secluded Chamber* (by Zheng Meijian in the Qing Dynasty)
重庆火锅	〈饮食〉Chongqing hot pot
《重修政和经史证类备用本草》	〈中医药〉*Chongxiu Zhenghe Jing Shi Zheng Lei Beiyong Bencao*; *Revised Zhenghe Materia Medica for Emergency from Classics and History Documents* (by Tang Shenwei in the Song Dynasty, supplemented by Zhang Cunhui in the Jin Dynasty)
重阳糕	Double-Ninth cake
重阳酒	Chongyang wine
重组蛋白亚单位疫苗	〈防疫〉recombinant protein subunit vaccine
崇宁通宝	〈币〉(of reign title money) coin with characters chongning tongbao (issued in the Northern Song Dynasty)
崇宁元宝	〈币〉(of reign title money) coin with characters chongning yuanbao (issued in the Northern Song Dynasty)
崇洋媚外	to worship things foreign and fawn on foreign countries
崇祯青花花鸟纹缸	〈陶瓷〉blue and white wat with flower and bird pattern (Ming Chongzhen period)
抽气罐	〈中医药〉suction cup
抽气罐法	〈中医药〉suction cupping

绸子	silk fabric; thin and soft silk; tela de seda
筹令	〈酒〉chouling; drinking game rules (to determine the drinker by drawing lots); drinking game verses →雅令
筹资渠道	fundraising channels
臭豆腐	〈饮食〉Stinky Tofu; Smelly Tofu
臭老九	〈旧〉stinking ninth category; stinking old ninth; stinking number nine (an offensive term for intellectuals during the Great Cultural Revolution)
出风头	to show off; to seek the limelight; to attract more attention
出国热	craze for going abroad
出家人	Buddhist or Taoist; monk or nun; ascetic
出境旅行	outbound trip
出境游	outbound tourism; outbound travel
出境(旅)游	outbound travel; outbound tourism
出境游客	outbound tourist; outbound traveler
出门戴口罩	〈防疫〉to wear a mask when going out
出气筒	punching bag; one who serves as a vent to sb.'s anger
出入境防疫	〈防疫〉epidemic prevention at borders
出入平安	safe trip wherever you go
出现疫情扩散的国家和地区	〈防疫〉countries and regions affected by the pandemic
出行高峰	travel rush
出洋相	to make a fool/monkey/show of oneself; to make an exhibition of oneself
出院	〈防疫〉to be discharged from hospital
出针	〈中医药〉needle withdrawal
初发症状	〈防疫〉incipient symptom
初级会计	junior accountant; junior-level accountant
初级职称	primary professional title
除湿通络	〈中医药〉to eliminate dampness and dredge channels

除湿止带	〈中医药〉to eliminate dampness and arrest leucorrhea
除四害	to eliminate the four pests (rats, bedbugs, flies and mosquitoes)
厨房部	kitchen department
厨房主管	kitchen manager; kitchen supervisor
处方法	prescribing method; rules of prescription
处理价格	bargain price; reduced price
处世之道	philosophy of life
储备干部	management trainee; associate trainee
储币待购	save for purchases
处长	division director; head of a department; division chief
川北凉粉	〈饮食〉Sichuan Tossed Bean Jelly with Chili Sauce; Clear Noodles in Chili Sauce
川北牛尾	〈饮食〉Sichuan Braised Oxtail with Chili Sauce
川贝母	〈中医药〉(of Latin) Fritillariae Cirrhosae Bulbus; Tendrilleaf Fritillary Bulb; Sichuan Fritillaria Bulb
川贝枇杷糖浆	〈中医药〉Chuanbei Pipa Tangjiang; Bulbus Fritillariae Syrup
川贝雪梨膏	〈中医药〉Chuanbei Xueli Gao; Sichuan Fritillaria Snow Pear Paste
川菜	〈饮食〉Chuan Cuisine; Sichuan Cuisine
川菜白灵菇皇	〈饮食〉Sichuan Braised Mushrooms with Chili Sauce
川归烧酒虾	〈饮食〉Stewed Shrimps with Liquor and Herbs
川槿皮	〈中医药〉(of Latin) Cortex Hibisci; Rose-of-Sharon Root Bark; Shrubalthea Bark
川楝子	〈中医药〉(of Latin) Fructus Meliae Toosendan; Sichuan Chinaberry Fruit
川木通	〈中医药〉(of Latin) Caulis Clematis Armanoii; Armand Clematis Stem
川牛膝	〈中医药〉(of Latin) Radix Cyathulae; Medicinal Cyathula Root

川式红烧肉	〈饮食〉Sichuan Braised Pork in Black Bean Sauce
川式红烧鱼翅	〈饮食〉Sichuan Braised Shark's Fins in Chili Sauce
川式煎鹅肝	〈饮食〉Sichuan Pan-Fried Goose Livers
川味红汤鸡	〈饮食〉Sichuan Chicken in Hot Spicy Sauce
川味麻辣鸡	〈饮食〉Sichuan Braised Chicken with Hot Spicy Sauce
川味石斑球	〈饮食〉Sichuan Sea Bass Balls
川味小炒	〈饮食〉Sichuan Shredded Pork with Vegetables
川乌	〈中医药〉(of Latin) Radix Aconiti; Common Monkshood Mother Root
川芎	〈中医药〉(of Latin) Rhizoma Ligustici; Szechuan Lovage Rhizome
川芎茶调散	〈中医药〉Chuanxiong Chatiao San; Tea-Blended Chuanxiong Powder; Tea-Blended Sichuan Lovage Rhizome Powder
川汁牛柳	〈饮食〉Sichuan Stir-Fried Beef Fillets with Chili Sauce
穿帮	to let the cat out of the bag; to be caught in a lie
穿山甲	〈中医药〉(of Latin) Squama Manis; Pangolin Scales
穿心莲	〈中医药〉(of Latin) Herba Andrographis; Common Andrographis Herb
穿心莲内酯滴丸	〈中医药〉Chuanxinlian Neizhi Diwan; Andrographis Lactones Dripping Pill
穿心莲片	〈中医药〉Chuanxinlian Pian; Andrographis Tablet
穿新鞋走老路	to wear new shoes to walk on the old path; to change in form but not in content; to put old wine in new wineskins
穿针引线	(of idiom) to get the thread through the eye of the needle; to act as a go-between (middleman)
传播［染］方式	〈防疫〉mode of transmission
传播［染］途径	〈防疫〉route of transmission
传菜主管	food runner supervisor

传化水谷	〈中医药〉transmission and transformation of water and food
传化物而不藏	〈中医药〉to digest and transport food and drink without storing essence
传染病科医生	doctor for infectious diseases
传染方式	→传播[染]方式
传染途径	→传播[染]途径
传染性	〈防疫〉transmissibility; infectivity
传染性疾病	〈防疫〉communicable disease; infectious disease
传染源	〈防疫〉source of infection
传统刺绣大师	traditional embroidery master
传统中国服饰	traditional Chinese clothes; traditional Chinese costume
传销	multi-level marketing; pyramid selling; pyramid schemes
船舶工程师	shipping engineer
船务操作员	shipping operator
船务人员	shipping clerk
串串辣子虾	〈饮食〉Shrimp Kebab with Hot Pepper Sauce
串烧五香肉	〈饮食〉Grilled Pork Brochette with Spice
串香白酒	distilled aromatic liquor
《串雅内编》	〈中医药〉*Chuanya Nei Bian*; *Internal Therapies of Folk Medicine* (by Zhao Xuemin in the Qing Dynasty)
《串雅外编》	〈中医药〉*Chuanya Wai Bian*; *External Therapies of Folk Medicine* (by Zhao Xuemin in the Qing Dynasty)
钏	〈服饰〉traditional wristlet; bracelet
创伤后应激障碍	〈防疫〉post-traumatic stress disorder; PTSD
疮疡补法	〈中医药〉invigorating method for healing of sore and ulcer
疮疡托法	〈中医药〉pustulation promotion of sore and ulcer by strengthening vital qi; method of expelling pathogens by strengthening vital qi
窗口行业	service trade

闯关东	to brave a risky journey to the northeast; to seek a living in the northeast (people from Shandong and Hubei provinces left home to make a living in areas east of the Shanhai Pass)
创建卫生城市	to build an advanced clean city
创客文化	maker culture
创业大赛	venture contest
创业精神	enterprising spirit; pioneering spirit
创意群总监	group creative director; GCD
创意组长	creative group head
创作总监	creative director
吹鼻疗法	〈中医药〉nose-insufflating therapy; nasal insufflation therapy
吹耳疗法	〈中医药〉ear-insufflating therapy; ear insufflation therapy
吹风会	briefing meeting; leaking meeting
吹喉疗法	〈中医药〉larynx-blowing therapy; laryngeal insufflation therapy
吹哨人	〈防疫〉whistle blower; whistleblower
吹药法	〈中医药〉blowing drug method; insufflation therapy
垂挂髻	(of hairstyle) hanging down chignon
垂鬟分肖髻	(of hairstyle) circular chignon with separate twists of hair hanging downwards
垂盆草	〈中医药〉(of Latin) Sedum sarmentosum; Herba Sedi; Stringy Stonecrop Herb
垂直传播	〈防疫〉vertical transmission
春耕备耕	〈防疫〉spring farming and preparation
春菇烧麦	〈饮食〉Steamed Shaomai Stuffed with Mushrooms
春季农业生产	〈防疫〉spring-season agricultural activity
春节	Spring Festival; Chinese New Year
春节假期	Spring Festival holiday
春卷	〈饮食〉Spring Rolls (a thin sheet of dough, rolled with various stuffings and fried)

春蕾计划	Spring Buds Program
春晚	Spring Festival Gala; Chinese New Year Gala
春芽豆腐丝	〈饮食〉Shredded Tofu with Sprouts
春游	spring outing; to have a spring outing; to go for a spring outing
春运	transport service during the Spring Festival; Spring Festival travel rush
春运高峰	Spring Festival peak; lunar-new-year rush
椿根皮	〈中医药〉(of Latin) Cortex Ailanthi; Ailanthus Bark; Toona Root Bark
椿皮	〈中医药〉Cortex Ailanthi; Tree-of-Heaven Ailanthus Bark
纯净水	purified water
莼菜鲈鱼烩	〈饮食〉Stewed Perch with Water Shield Leaves
淳化元宝	〈古币〉(of reign title money) coin with characters chunhua yuanbao (issued in the Northern Song Dynasty)
醇厚	〈酒〉mellow; rich; full-bodied
醇爽	〈茶〉mellow and brisk
醇香酒	mellow wine; mellow liquor
醇正	〈茶〉mellow and normal
瓷博会	→中国景德镇国际陶瓷博览会
瓷都	〈陶瓷〉porcelain metropolis; ceramic metropolis (generally referring to Jingdezhen)
瓷泥	〈陶瓷〉petunse; petuntse/petuntze
瓷漆	〈陶瓷〉enamel paint, enamel
瓷器	〈陶瓷〉china; porcelain; chinaware
瓷器雕	〈陶瓷〉porcelain carving
瓷土	〈陶瓷〉kaolin; porcelain clay; china clay
瓷土加工	〈陶瓷〉kaolin processing
瓷盅	〈陶瓷〉handleless porcelain cup
慈善组织协会	charity organization society
慈展会	→中国公益慈善项目交流展示会
磁[瓷]漆	〈陶瓷〉enamel paint; enamel lacquer

磁悬浮列车	maglev train (magnetically levitated train); magnetic suspension train
磁州窑	〈陶瓷〉Cizhou Kiln
磁州窑白地黑花瓷瓶	〈陶瓷〉Cizhou Kiln white porcelain jar with black floral pattern
磁州窑钓鱼枕	〈陶瓷〉Cizhou Kiln porcelain pillow with fishing pattern
磁州窑三彩刻花花口瓶	〈陶瓷〉Cizhou Kiln Tri-colored vase with carved floral pattern and flower-shaped opening (Northern Song period)
磁朱丸	〈中医药〉Cizhu Wan; Magnetite and Cinnabar Pill
糍粑	〈饮食〉Ciba; Glutinous Rice Cake
刺儿头	a troublesome or difficult person; nitpicker; faultfinder
刺法	〈中医药〉needling method; acupuncture manipulation
刺灸法	〈中医药〉needling and moxibustion method; techniques of acupuncture and moxibustion
刺梨酒	thorn pear wine
刺络拔罐	〈中医药〉pricking-cupping bloodletting; pricking and cupping →刺血拔罐
刺身凉瓜	〈饮食〉Bitter Melon with Wasabi
刺参扣鸭掌	〈饮食〉Braised Duck Webs with Sea Cucumber
刺突蛋白	〈防疫〉spike protein
刺五加	〈中医药〉(of Latin) Acanthopanacis Senticosi; Manyprickle Acanthopanax; Manyprickle Acathopanax Root
刺五加片	〈中医药〉Ciwujia Pian; Acanthopanax Root Tablet
刺血拔罐	〈中医药〉pricking blood with cupping →刺络拔罐
刺血疗法	〈中医药〉blood-pricking therapy
赐赏钱	〈古〉coin with award inscription
葱爆白肉	〈饮食〉Quick-Fried Pork Slices with Scallion
葱爆肥牛	〈饮食〉Stir-Fried Beef with Scallion
葱爆海参条	〈饮食〉Quick-Fried Sea Cucumbers with Scallion

葱爆里脊	〈饮食〉Quick-Fried Pork Fillet Slices with Scallion
葱爆里脊丁	〈饮食〉Quick-Fried Diced Tenderloin with Scallion
葱爆肉丁	〈饮食〉Quick-Fried Pork Dices with Scallion
葱爆肉粉丝	〈饮食〉Stir-Fried Pork Slices and Vermicelli with Scallion
葱爆肉粉条	〈饮食〉Quick-Fried Pork Slices and Vermicelli with Scallion
葱爆羊肉	〈饮食〉Quick-Fried Lamb Slices with Green Scallion
葱爆羊肉丁	〈饮食〉Quick-Fried Mutton Dices
葱煸羊腩	〈饮食〉Stir-Fried Diced Lamb Brisket with Scallion
葱串排骨	〈饮食〉Clustered Pork Chop with Scallion
葱花炒鸡蛋	〈饮食〉Scrambled Eggs with Scallion
葱姜(炒)肉蟹	〈饮食〉Stir-Fried Crab with Ginger and Scallion
葱姜生蚝	〈饮食〉Stir-Fried Oysters with Ginger and Scallion
葱姜油淋鸡	〈饮食〉Chicken with Ginger and Scallion Oil
葱椒炒肉	〈饮食〉Stir-Fried Pork Fillet with Chive and Pepper
葱烤银鳕鱼	〈饮食〉Grilled Codfish with Scallion
葱焙河鲫鱼	〈饮食〉Braised Crucian Carp with Scallion
葱烧海参	〈饮食〉Braised Sea Cucumbers with Scallion
葱烧海参鲍鱼	〈饮食〉Braised Sea Cucumbers and Abalone with Scallion
葱烧海参牛蹄筋	〈饮食〉Braised Sea Cucumbers and Ox Tendon with Scallion
葱烧黑木耳	〈饮食〉Stir-Fried Black Fungi with Scallion
葱烧鳗鱼	〈饮食〉Braised Eel with Scallion
葱烧鱼片	〈饮食〉Braised Sliced Fish with Scallion
葱头牛肉丝	〈饮食〉Stir-Fried Shredded Beef with Onion
葱香荷兰豆	〈饮食〉Stir-Fried Snow Peas with Scallion
葱油白鸡	〈饮食〉Boiled Chicken with Scallion Oil

葱油拌面	〈饮食〉Noodles with Scallion, Oil and Soy Sauce
葱油饼	〈饮食〉Baked Scallion Pancake; Pan-Fried Cake with Sesame Seeds and Scallion
葱油鹅肝	〈饮食〉Goose Liver with Scallion and Chili Oil
葱油荷叶粉蒸鸡	〈饮食〉Steamed Chicken with Rice Flour Wrapped in Lotus Leaves
葱油鸡	〈饮食〉Chicken with Scallion in Hot Oil
葱油煎饼	〈饮食〉Pan-Fried Scallion Pancake; Pan-Fried Pancake with Scallion Oil
葱油泼多宝鱼	〈饮食〉Steamed Turbot with Scallion Oil
葱油泼石斑鱼	〈饮食〉Steamed Rock Cod with Scallion Oil
葱油香露鸡	〈饮食〉Chicken in Gravy with Scallion Oil
聪耳酒	〈中医药〉Cong'er Jiu; Ear-Sharpening Wine
从零开始	to start from scratch
从阳化热	〈中医药〉heat transformed from yang
从阴化寒	〈中医药〉cold transformed from yin
从众行为	behavior of blindly conforming to the norm
凑份子	to club together (to give a gift to sb.); to contribute to the pool
凑热闹	to join in the fun; to add trouble to sb./sth.; to create more trouble
粗扁	〈茶〉coarse and flat
粗瓷	〈陶瓷〉stoneware; coarse porcelain
粗大	〈茶〉coarse and large
粗淡	〈茶〉coarse and plain
粗活	heavy manual work
粗浓	〈茶〉coarse and heavy
粗气	〈茶〉harsh odor
粗实	〈茶〉coarse and bold
粗松	〈茶〉coarse and loose
粗圆	〈茶〉coarse and round
促脉	〈中医药〉abrupt pulse; irregular-rapid pulse; quick pulse
促销经理	→推销经理

促销主管	promotion supervisor
醋椒三片汤	〈饮食〉Three Delicacies Soup with Vinegar and Pepper
醋熘白菜	〈饮食〉Stir-Fried Chinese Cabbage with Vinegar Sauce
醋熘豆芽	〈饮食〉Stir-Fried Bean Sprouts with Vinegar Sauce
醋熘蟹	〈饮食〉Stir-Fried Crabs with Sour Sauce
醋熘子鸡	〈饮食〉Stir-Fried Spring Chicken with Vinegar Sauce
氽	〈饮食〉to quick-boil; to poach; quick-boiled; poached
氽熘鲩鱼	〈饮食〉Poached Grass Carp with Egg Sauce
氽卤面	〈饮食〉Stewed Noodles with Diced Meat in Soup
脆皮春卷	〈饮食〉Crispy Spring Rolls
脆皮豆腐	〈饮食〉Deep-Fried Tofu/Bean Curd
脆皮鹅	〈饮食〉Crisp Skin Goose
脆皮锅酥肉	〈饮食〉Fried Crispy Pork; Deep-Fried Pork Slices
脆皮鸡	〈饮食〉Crispy Chicken; Deep-Fried Chicken with Crisp Skin
脆皮嫩鸡	〈饮食〉Crispy Fried Tender Chicken
脆皮糯米鸡	〈饮食〉Crispy Chicken Stuffed with Glutinous Rice
脆皮乳鸽	〈饮食〉Crispy-Fried Spring Pigeon
脆皮乳猪	〈饮食〉Roasted Crispy Suckling Pig
脆皮三丝卷	〈饮食〉Crispy Rolls of Shredded Pork, Cucumbers and Bamboo Shoots
脆皮鸳鸯鸭	〈饮食〉Two-Colored Crispy Duck Stuffed with Minced Shrimps
脆皮炸子鸡	〈饮食〉Crispy Fried Spring Chicken
脆虾白菜心	〈饮食〉Fried Shrimps with Choy Sum
脆炸桂鱼	〈饮食〉Crispy-Fried Mandarin Fish
脆炸芋头糕	〈饮食〉Fried Taro Cake
翠豆玉米粒	〈饮食〉Stir-Fried Green Peas and Sweetcorn

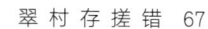

翠华茶	Cuihua Green tea
翠绿釉	→翡翠[翠绿]釉
村支书	village branch secretary
存货控制分析员	inventory control analyst
搓揉法	〈中医药〉kneading manipulation
错峰上下班	〈防疫〉staggered rush hour plan

D

搭错车	to follow a wrong train; to join in a wrong group; to follow a wrong example
搭售	conditional sale; tie-in sale
达标活动	target hitting activities
答谢宴会	return banquet; reciprocal banquet
打白条	to issue IOU (I owe you); illegitimate promissory notes
打包	to use doggy bags to take food home
打车软件	taxi-hailing app; cab-hailing app
打出王牌	to play one's trump card
打翻身仗	to fight to change for the better; to turn the tables; to work hard to bring about an uprising
打工	to work to earn a living; to do some odd jobs; to do a part-time job
打工妹	country girl working in cities
打拐	→打击拐卖儿童妇女犯罪
打好武汉保卫战	〈防疫〉to win the battle against the coronavirus and protect the city of Wuhan
打好新冠肺炎疫情防控全球阻击战	〈防疫〉to fight an all-out global war against COVID-19
打黑	to crack down on evil forces/speculation and profiteering
打击非法捕猎	to crack down on illegal hunting
打击非法投机活动	to strike out at speculation; to crack down on speculation
打击非法移民	to fight against illegal migration

打击拐卖儿童妇女犯罪	to crack down on the abduction of women and children
打击假冒伪劣商品	to crack down on counterfeit goods; to crack down on fake and shoddy products
打击走私	to combat smuggling
打假	→打击假冒伪劣商品
打酱油	to get some soy sauce; to be a bystander
打卡机	punch machine
打开天窗说亮话	(of idiom) to put all one's cards on the table; to speak frankly; let's not mince matters
打卤面	〈饮食〉Noodles with Meat Slices in Thick Gravy; Noodles Served with Thick Gravy
打破传播链	〈防疫〉to break the chains of transmission
打破三铁	to break the Three Irons: iron armchairs (life-time posts), iron rice bowl (life-time employment) and iron wages (guaranteed pay)
打通人流物流堵点	〈防疫〉to smooth travel and logistics channels
打小报告	to secretly report on a colleague; to rat on a fellow worker →告小状
打疫苗	〈防疫〉to get an immune shot; to get vaccinated
打赢疫情防控的人民战争	〈防疫〉to fight and win the battle against the epidemic by mobilizing all resources
打游击	to work in unfixed places; to work as a seasonal laborer
打造人类卫生健康共同体	〈防疫〉to build a global community of health
大败毒胶囊	〈中医药〉Da Baidu Jiaonang; Major Toxicity-Defeating Capsule
大包大揽	belly-worship; to take on all things
大病保险	serious disease insurance
大病统筹	comprehensive arrangement for serious disease; social pooling for catastrophic disease; major disease coordination
大补阴丸	〈中医药〉Da Buyin Wan; Major Yin-Nourishing Pill

大柴胡汤	〈中医药〉Da Chaihu Tang; Major Bupleurum Decoction
大肠寒结	〈中医药〉large intestinal cold bind; cold accumulation of large intestine
大肠热结	〈中医药〉large intestinal heat bind; heat accumulation of large intestine
大肠热结证	〈中医药〉pattern of heat accumulated in large intestine; pattern of large intestinal heat bind
大肠湿热	〈中医药〉dampness-heat in large intestine; large intestinal damp-heat
大肠湿热证	〈中医药〉pattern of dampness-heat in large intestine; pattern of large intestinal damp-heat
大肠俞	〈中医药〉Dachangshu acupoint; Large Intestine Transport (BL25)
大肠液亏	〈中医药〉deficiency of fluid in large intestine; large intestinal fluid insufficiency
大肠主传导	〈中医药〉large intestine governing conveyance
大肠主传化糟粕	〈中医药〉large intestine governing transformation and conveyance of waste
大朝通宝	〈币〉coin with characters dachao tongbao (issued in Mongolian Khanate)
大承气汤	〈中医药〉Da Chengqi Tang; Major Drastic Purgative Decoction
大酬宾	to give a large discount to customers or guests
大出血	massive haemorrhage caused by damaging artery or internal organs; (for figurative use) to make a big markdown; deep price cut
大葱土豆汤	〈饮食〉Potato and Scallion Soup
大跌眼镜	to have people drop glasses; to be greatly surprised by sth. unexpected; jaw dropping
大定风珠(丸)	〈中医药〉Da Dingfeng Zhu Wan; Major Wind-Stabilizing Pill
大额医疗费用补助	subsidy for big amount of medical expenditure
大而全	large and comprehensive; large and all-inclusive

大方	〈中医药〉major formula; major prescription
大方脉	〈中医药〉department of traditional Chinese medicine for adults; great prescription clinic
大腹皮	〈中医药〉(of Latin) Pericarpium Arecae; Areca Peel
大骨空	〈中医药〉Dagukong acupoint; Big Bone Hollow (EX-UE5)
大锅饭	communal pot; meal from a big pot; egalitarian practice of everyone taking food from the same big pot
大赫	〈中医药〉Dahe acupoint; Great Manifestation (KI12)
大横	〈中医药〉Daheng acupoint; Great Horizontal (SP15)
大红袍	〈茶〉Dahongpao; Big Red Robe tea (Wuyi Mountain Rock tea)
大红鹰香烟	Da Hongying cigarettes; Big Kestrel cigarettes
大环境	social, political and economic environment; overall situation
大换血	overall renewal of the membership of an organization; overall change
大黄	〈中医药〉(of Latin) Radix et Rhizoma Rhei; Rheum Officinale Baill
大黄附子汤	〈中医药〉Dahuang Fuzi Tang; Rhubarb and Aconite Decoction
大黄牡丹汤	〈中医药〉Dahuang Mudan Tang; Rhubarb and Moutan Decoction
大黄䗪虫丸	〈中医药〉Dahuang Zhechong Wan; Rhubarb Wingless Cockroach Pill
大活络丹[丸]	〈中医药〉Da Huoluo Dan/Wan; Major Channel-Quickening Elixir/Pill; Large Bolus for Activating Channels and Collaterals
大饥荒	great famine; great hunger

大蓟	〈中医药〉(of Latin) Herba seu Radix Cirsii Japonici; Japanese Thistle Herb/Root
大建中汤	〈中医药〉Dajianzhong Tang; Major Center-Fortifying Decoction
大奖赛	prize-giving competition
大襟衣	Chinese garment with the front lapel on the right
大巨	〈中医药〉Daju acupoint; Gigantic Qi & Blood (ST27)
大开眼界	to broaden one's horizons; to be an eye-opener
大客户经理	key account manager
大孔式货贝	〈币〉coarse-pored cowrie; macroporous cowrie (issued in the Shang Dynasty)
大款	very rich person; tycoon; moneybags; fat cat
大拉皮	〈饮食〉Tossed Mung Clear Noodles with Sauce; Tossed Clear Noodles with Sauce
大良野鸡卷	〈饮食〉Daliang Fried Meat Roll with Pepper Salt
大龄青年	single youth above the normal matrimonial age; overage youth
大流行病	〈防疫〉pandemic; pandemic disease
大陆游客	mainland visitor; mainland traveller; mainland tourist
大路货	staple goods; popular goods of dependable quality
大米绿豆粥	〈饮食〉Rice Porridge with Mung Beans
大米粥	〈饮食〉Rice Porridge; Rice Congee →白粥
大怒伤肝	〈中医药〉rage impairing the liver; great anger damaging the liver
大排档	large stall; food stall; sidewalk snack booth
大齐通宝	〈币〉coin with characters daqi tongbao (issued in the Southern Tang Kingdom)
大前门香烟	Chienmen cigarettes; Front Gate cigarettes
大秦艽汤	〈中医药〉Daqinjiao Tang; Major Gentian Decoction
大青叶	〈中医药〉(of Latin) Folium Isatidis; Dyers Woad Leaf

大曲	〈酒〉daqu; brick shaped wheat starter (for alcoholic fermentation); wheat yeast for making liquor
大曲酒	Daqu liquor; twice fully-fermented liquor
大泉五十	〈币〉coin with characters daquan fifty (issued in the Xin Dynasty)
大人物	great man; big potato; very important person; VIP
大山楂丸	〈中医药〉Dashanzha Wan; Major Crataegus Pill
大绶	〈古〉grand ribbon of jewels
大数据试验区	big data pilot zone
大数据研究	big data research
大蒜干贝	〈饮食〉Steamed Dried Scallops with Garlic
大蒜烧白鳝	〈饮食〉Braised White Eel with Garlic
大蒜鲜菇	〈饮食〉Stir-Fried Fresh Mushrooms with Garlic
大蒜羊仔片	〈饮食〉Stir-Fried Lamb Fillet with Garlic
大堂主理	lobby manager
大头帕	〈侗族〉large headkerchief; large headscarf
大碗茶	stall tea (served in big bowls and sold in stalls)
大腕(儿)	top notch; big shot; (of a performance) key player
大型廉价商店	warehouse store
大熊猫保护	giant panda protection
大[外]袖	〈古〉top sleeve; super sleeve
大学毕业生就业	college graduate employment
大学(生)扩招	college enrollment expansion →高校扩招
大学生创业	university students' innovative undertaking
大学生志愿者	college student volunteer
大学肄业生	undergraduate
大学英语六级	College English Test Band 6 Certificate; CET6
大学英语四级	College English Test Band 4 Certificate; CET4
大血藤	〈中医药〉(of Latin) Caulis Sargentodoxae; Sargentgloryvine Stem
大洋	〈旧〉silver dollar →银元
大义通宝	〈币〉coin with characters dayi tongbao (issued in the late Yuan Dynasty)

大印象减肥茶	〈中医药〉Dayinxiang Jianfei Cha; Dayinxiang Slimming Tea
大鱼际揉法	〈中医药〉thenar kneading manipulation
大枣	〈中医药〉(of Latin) Fructus Jujubae; Chinese Date
大闸蟹	〈饮食〉Chinese Hairy Crabs; Chinese Mitten Crab
大中通宝	〈币〉coin with characters dazhong tongbao (issued in the late Yuan Dynasty)
大众富裕阶层	mass affluent class/stratum
大众民族主义	popular nationalism
大煮干丝	〈饮食〉Braised Shredded Chicken with Ham and Dried Tofu
大杼	〈中医药〉Dazhu acupoint; Great Shuttle Bone (BL11)
大专生	junior college student
大专文凭	associate degree
大专学历教育	associate/junior college education
大椎	〈中医药〉Dazhui acupoint; Great Vertebra (DU14)
大字报	〈旧〉dazibao; big-character poster (in the period of the Great Cultural Revolution)
大做文章	to make a big fuss about sth.; to make a big issue
代沟	generation gap
代培	to be commissioned to train; directional training; to train on contract
带脉	〈中医药〉Daimai acupoint; Girdling Vessel; Belt Vessel (GB26)
带薪产假	paid maternity leave
带薪分流	to assign redundant civil servants to other jobs with original rank and benefits
贷款管理员	loan administrator
贷款利率	lending rate
贷学金	student loan
待岗	to await job assignment; post-waiting
待业人员	job-waiting people
戴高帽	to make compliment; to flatter sb.

戴口罩	〈防疫〉to wear a mask
黛蛤散	〈中医药〉Daige San; Indigo and Clamshell Powder
丹皮	〈中医药〉(of Latin) Cortex Moutan Radicis; Moutan Root Bark
丹七片	〈中医药〉Danqi Pian; Salvia Notoginseng Tablet
丹参	〈中医药〉(of Latin) Radix Salviae Miltiorrhizae; Salvia Root; Danshen Root
丹参注射液	〈中医药〉Danshen Zhushe Ye; Salvia Miltiorrhiza Injection
《丹溪心法》	〈中医药〉*Danxi Xinfa*; *Danxi's Experiential Therapy*; *Danxi's Mastery of Medicine* (by Zhu Zhenheng in the Yuan Dynasty, revised by Cheng Chong in the Ming Dynasty)
丹栀逍遥丸	〈中医药〉Danzhi Xiaoyao Wan; Moutan and Gardenia Free Wanderer Pill
单车共享系统	bike sharing system
单刀髻	(of hairstyle) dandao bun; single knife-shaped chignon
单方	〈中医药〉simple recipe; single drug prescription
单螺髻	(of hairstyle) danluo bun; single spiral-shaped chignon
单面针织物	single jersey; single knit fabric
单旗袍	one layer cheongsam
单嵌线袋	single welt pocket
单亲家庭	single-parent family; single-parent household
单色釉瓷	〈陶瓷〉monochrome-glazed porcelain
单身贵族	single noble; noble bachelor
单手进针法	〈中医药〉single-handed needle insertion; needle-inserting with a single hand
单双号限行	traffic restriction based on odd-and-even license plate
单位	danwei; unit; organization that one works in
箪	dan; rice basket (a bamboo utensil for holding cooked rice)

统	〈服饰〉silk fringe of a coronet; silk ribbon sewn on quilt end
胆经郁热	〈中医药〉stagnated heat of gallbladder channel
胆经郁热证	〈中医药〉pattern of stagnated heat in gallbladder channel
胆囊穴	〈中医药〉Dannang acupoint; Gallbladder acupoint (EM-43)
胆石通胶囊	〈中医药〉Danshitong Jiaonang; Gallstone Opening Capsule
胆舒胶囊	〈中医药〉Danshu Jiaonang; Gallbladder Comfortability Capsule
胆俞	〈中医药〉Danshu acupoint; Gallbladder Transport (BL19)
胆虚不得眠	〈中医药〉insomnia due to gallbladder asthenia
胆虚证	〈中医药〉gallbladder deficiency pattern
胆郁痰扰	〈中医药〉depressed gallbladder with harassing phlegm; stagnated gallbladder qi with disturbing phlegm
胆郁痰扰证	〈中医药〉pattern of depressed gallbladder with harassing phlegm; pattern of stagnated gallbladder qi with disturbing phlegm
但寒不热	〈中医药〉aversion to cold without heat effusion
但热不寒	〈中医药〉heat effusion (fever) without aversion to cold
担	(of unit of weight) dan (equal to 50 kilograms)
担担面	〈饮食〉Noodles with Sesame Paste and Pea Sprouts
淡白舌	〈中医药〉whitish tongue; pale tongue
淡菜煨蹄筋	〈饮食〉Stewed Pork Tendons with Mussel
淡豆豉	〈中医药〉(of Latin) Semen Sojae Preparatum; Fermented Soybean
淡红舌	〈中医药〉pink tongue; pale red tongue
淡渗利湿	〈中医药〉to promote diuresis with drugs of tasteless flavor; to induce diuresis with bland drugs
淡水恶化	freshwater degradation

淡糟香螺片	〈饮食〉Stir-Fried Sliced Sea Whelks with Rice Wine Sauce
淡竹叶	〈中医药〉(of Latin) Herba Lophatheri; Lophatherum Herb
蛋白虫草鸡	〈饮食〉Chicken Cooked with Caterpillar Fungi and Egg Whites
蛋饼	〈饮食〉Egg Cake; Omelette
蛋炒饭	→鸡蛋炒饭
蛋花炒鱼肚	〈饮食〉Stir-Fried Fish Maws with Scrambled Eggs
蛋花汤	〈饮食〉Egg Drop Soup; Egg Soup
蛋黄莲茸酥	〈饮食〉Pastry Puff Stuffed with Lotus Seed Paste and Egg Yolk
蛋黄凉瓜	〈饮食〉Bitter Melon with Egg Yolk
蛋黄明虾	〈饮食〉Stir-Fried Prawns with Egg Yolk
蛋黄狮子头	〈饮食〉Stewed Meat Balls with Preserved Egg Yolks
蛋黄酥	〈饮食〉Egg-Yolk Puff; Egg-Yolk Crispy Pastry
蛋煎猪脑	〈饮食〉Scrambled Eggs with Pig Brains
蛋卷	〈饮食〉Egg Rolls; Omelette
蛋壳瓷	〈陶瓷〉eggshell porcelain; thin china →薄胎瓷
蛋皮鱼卷	〈饮食〉Fish Rolls Stuffed with Preserved Eggs
蛋衣河鳗	〈饮食〉Egg Rolls Stuffed with Eel
膻中	〈中医药〉Danzhong acupoint; Chest Center; Thoracic Center (CV17)
当归	〈中医药〉(of Latin) Radix Angelicae Sinensis; Chinese Angelica
当归补血汤	〈中医药〉Danggui Buxue Tang; Chinese Angelica Blood-Supplementing Decoction
当归酒	〈中医药〉Danggui Jiu; Angelica Sinensis Wine
当归流浸膏	〈中医药〉Danggui Liujin Gao; Chinese Extractum Angelicae Liquidum
当归六黄汤	〈中医药〉Danggui Liuhuang Tang; Chinese Angelica Six Yellows Decoction

当归龙荟丸	〈中医药〉Danggui Longhui Wan; Chinese Angelica, Gentian, and Aloe Pill
当归芦荟丸	〈中医药〉Danggui Luhui Wan; Chinese Angelica and Aloe Pill
当归四逆汤	〈中医药〉Danggui Sini Tang; Chinese Angelica Counterflow Cold Decoction
当归鸭	〈饮食〉Angelica Duck
当归鸭卷	〈饮食〉Duck Rolls with Chinese Angelica
当红演员	red-hot actor; popular actor
当红炸子鸡	〈饮食〉Deep-Fried Spring Chicken with Chili Pepper
当阳峪窑剔刻番莲枕	〈陶瓷〉Dangyangyu Kiln porcelain pillow with carved lotus pattern
党参	〈中医药〉(of Latin) Radix Codonopsis; Codonopsis Root; Pilose Asiabell Root; Dangshen
档案管理员	archivist; filing clerk
档案秘书	secretary-archivist
刀币	〈古〉knife money; knife-shaped money (used in the Spring and Autumn period and Warring States period)
刀豆	〈中医药〉(of Latin) Semen Canavaliae; Jack Bean
刀形半翻髻	→单刀髻
刀形双翻髻	→双刀髻
刀削面	〈饮食〉Sliced Noodles; Shaved Noodles
导赤散	〈中医药〉Daochi San; Red-Abducting Powder
导购	shopping guide
导游资格证书	guide ID card; guide certificate
捣浆糊	to give the runaround; to act restlessly
倒票	to speculate in resale of tickets; speculative re-selling of tickets
倒爷	wheeler-dealer; ticket tout
倒春寒	(of weather) cold spell in later spring; unusual cold spell in an otherwise warm early spring
倒挂销售	to sell at a price lower than the purchasing price

道德绑架	moral coercion; moral kidnapping; moral abduction
道德风尚奖	ethic award
道冠	daoguan; Taoist priest's cap
道光瓷	〈陶瓷〉Daoguang porcelain; porcelain of the Daoguang's reign
道光通宝	〈币〉coin with characters daoguang tongbao (issued in the Qing Dynasty)
道教服饰	Taoist gown; Taoist robe
道巾	Taoist priest's soft hat
道口烧鸡	〈饮食〉Daokou Red-Cooked Chicken
稻芽	〈中医药〉(of Latin) Fructus Oryzae Germinatus; Rice-Grain Sprout
得气	〈中医药〉arrival of qi; obtaining qi; needling sensation (to bring about the desired sensation in acupuncture treatment)
德邦快递	Deppon Express
德尔塔(变异)毒株	〈防疫〉Delta variant
德化陶瓷	〈陶瓷〉Dehua porcelain; Dehua ceramic
德化窑白瓷观音	〈陶瓷〉Dehua Kiln white porcelain Guanyin; white porcelain Goddess of Mercy
德山大曲酒	Deshan Daqu liquor; Deshan twice fully-fermented liquor
德州扒鸡	〈饮食〉Dezhou Braised Chicken
灯火灸	〈中医药〉juncibustion; rush-fire cauterization; burning rush moxibustion
灯笼鸡片	〈饮食〉Stir-Fried Chicken Slices (Shaped as a Lantern); Lantern-Shaped Sliced Chicken
灯笼裤	bloomers; knickerbockers
灯笼青椒酿肉	〈饮食〉Braised Green Pepper Stuffed with Minced Pork
灯笼虾仁	〈饮食〉Stir-Fried Shelled Shrimps (Shaped as a Lantern); Lantern-Shaped Shelled Fresh Shrimps
灯笼袖	lantern sleeve; puff sleeve

灯芯草	〈中医药〉(of Latin) Medulla Junci; Common Rush; Rush Pith
灯芯绒	corduroy fabric; patent velvet
登封窑双虎纹瓷瓶	〈陶瓷〉Dengfeng Kiln porcelain vase with two tigers pattern
登记失业率	registered jobless rate
登月舱	lunar module
等候区	〈防疫〉waiting area
低度酒	low-alcohol liquor; mild wine
低风险地区	〈防疫〉low-risk region
低焦油香烟	low-tar cigarette
低温曲	〈酒〉low temperature brick shaped raw starter
低温陶瓷	〈陶瓷〉low-fired porcelain
低氧血症	〈防疫〉hypoxemia; low blood oxygen
滴鼻剂	〈中医药〉nasal drop; nose drop; naristillae
滴耳剂	〈中医药〉ear drop; auristilla
滴耳疗法	〈中医药〉ear-dripping therapy; eye drop therapy
滴酒法	〈中医药〉alcohol fire method; alcohol fire cupping
滴丸剂	〈中医药〉dripping pill; guttate pill
滴眼剂	〈中医药〉eye drop
滴药法	〈中医药〉dripping method; treatment with medicinal drops
鍉针	〈中医药〉arrowhead needle; spoon needle
鍉针疗法	〈中医药〉arrowhead needle therapy
涤棉混纺	polyester-cotton fabric
涤棉混纺品种	polyester cotton blended variety
涤痰息风	〈中医药〉to clear phlegm for calming endogenous wind
抵押保险员	mortgage underwriter
抵制任何与病毒相关的污名	〈防疫〉to reject any stigma associated with the virus
地丁	〈中医药〉(of Latin) Viola Yedoensis Makino; Chinese Violet
地方保护主义	regional protectionism

地方公务员	local public servant
地枫皮	〈中医药〉(of Latin) Cortex Illicii; Maple Tree Skin
地肤子	〈中医药〉(of Latin) Fructus Kochiae; Belvedere Fruit
地沟油	illegal oil made from kitchen waste; illegal cooking oil; swill-cooked dirty oil
地骨皮	〈中医药〉(of Latin) Cortex Lycii; Chinese Wolfberry Root-Bark
地瓜冰	〈饮食〉Sweet Potato Ice
地瓜烧肉	〈饮食〉Stewed Diced Pork with Sweet Potatoes
地瓜粥	〈饮食〉Sweet Potato Congee
地黄	〈中医药〉(of Latin) Radix Rehmanniae; Rehmannia Root
地黄饮子	〈中医药〉Dihuang Yinzi; Rehmannia Drink
地锦草	〈中医药〉(of Latin) Herba Euphorbiae Humifusae; Creeping Euphorbia
地龙	〈中医药〉Pheretima aspergillum; Pheretima; Earthworm
地陪	local guide; regional guide
地勤人员	(of airlines) ground crew; ground staff
地区专员	prefectural commissioner
地三鲜	〈饮食〉Stir-Fried Potato, Green Pepper and Eggplant
地五会	〈中医药〉Diwuhui acupoint; Earth Fivefold Convergence (GB42)
地榆	〈中医药〉(of Latin) Radix Sanguisorbae; Garden Burnet Root
地榆槐角丸	〈中医药〉Diyu Huaijiao Wan; Sanguisorba and Sophora Fruit Pill
地榆升白片	〈中医药〉Diyu Shengbai Pian; Sanguisorba White-Blood-Cell-Increasing Tablet
地震棚	earthquake shelter-tents (used as emergency shelter after an earthquake)
地质勘测工程师	geological survey engineer

地主	〈旧〉landlord; landowner (who do not work and rely on land rent as their living resource)
第二课堂	second classroom; extracurricular activities; out-of-class activities
第三方支付	third-party payment
第三期临床试验	〈防疫〉Phase III clinical trial
第一入境点	〈防疫〉the first point of entry
滇红	〈茶〉Yunnan black tea
点按法	〈中医药〉point-pressing manipulation
点播节目	phone-in program
点刺法	〈中医药〉swift pricking blood therapy
点对点直达运输服务	〈防疫〉point-to-point transport service
点桃虾球	〈饮食〉Stir-Fried Shrimp Meat Balls with Walnut Kernels
点心	〈饮食〉Dim Sum; Dessert; Light refreshments
点穴法	〈中医药〉finger pointing manipulation
点眼疗法	〈中医药〉eye-dripping therapy
点子公司	consulting company
电工陶瓷	〈陶瓷〉eletro ceramic; electrotechnical porcelain
电话采编员	telephone reporter
电话调查员	tele-interviewer
电话留言机	answering machine
电话销售	telesales; telemarketing
电话销售员	telemarketer; tele-salesperson
电话销售总监	telemarketing director
电老虎	electricity guzzler; big power consumer
电力工程师	electrical power engineer
电力工程证书	certificate in electrical engineering
电脑部经理	computer department manager; IT manager
电脑操作员	computer operator
电脑操作主管	computer operation supervisor
电脑程序员	programmer; computer programmer
电气工程师	electrical engineer
电器维修工程师	maintenance engineer of electrical appliance

电热针	〈中医药〉electrothermic needle; moxibustion with electric warming needles
电商	→线上零售商
电声工程师	electroacoustic engineer
电声技术员	electroacoustic technician
电视导演	television director
电视直销	TV home shopping
电视制片工程师	television production engineer
电视制片人	television producer
电台播音员	radio announcer
电信交换工程师	telecommunication exchange engineer
电信网络工程师	telecommunication network engineer
电信业顾问	telecommunication consultant
电信业经理	telecommunication manager
电影摄制助理	film production assistant
电针疗法	〈中医药〉electro-acupuncture therapy
电针麻醉	〈中医药〉electro-acupuncture anesthesia
电针仪	〈中医药〉electro-acupuncture device; electro-acupuncture therapeutic apparatus
电子宠物	electronic pet
电子工程师	electronic engineer
电子公告牌	Bulletin Board System (BBS)
电子红包	electronic red envelop; digital red envelop
电子货币	electronic currency; electronic money
电子技术员	electronic technician
电子监控系统	electronic monitoring system
电子客票	e-ticket
电子商务	electronic commerce; e-business
电子商务经理	e-business manager; e-commerce manager
电子商务平台	e-commerce platform
电子设备维修员	electronic equipment repairer
电子设计大赛	electronic design contest
电子维修工程师	electronic maintenance engineer
电子维修技师	electronic maintenance technician

电子香烟	electronic cigarette
电子银行	electronic bank
店长	shop manager; store manager
靛青	Chinese indigo; indigo-blue
貂缘披领	〈服饰〉sable-fur edged cape collar
雕母钱	〈古〉hand-carved coin model
雕塑瓷	〈陶瓷〉statuary porcelain
吊	〈古〉(of monetary unit) diao; a string of 1 000 copper coins (used in the Ming and Qing Dynasties)
吊烧乳鸽王	〈饮食〉Roast Superior Pigeonneau
吊胃口	to whet sb.'s appetite; to stimulate sb.'s desire; to tantalize
吊销执照	to revoke one's license
钓鱼工程	angling engineering projects
钓鱼价	very low price (which tempts customers into a trap)
调研员	research analyst
跌打伤痛理疗贴	〈中医药〉Dieda Shangtong Liliao Tie; Plaster for Falling Sprain and Trauma Pain
跌打万花油	〈中医药〉Dieda Wanhua You; Flower-Oil for Traumatic Injury
丁公藤	〈中医药〉(of Latin) Caulis Erycibes; Obtuseleaf Erycibe Stem
丁香	〈中医药〉(of Latin) Flos Caryophylli; Clove; Lilac
丁香柿蒂汤	〈中医药〉Dingxiang Shidi Tang; Clove and Persimmon Decoction
钉子户	dingzihu; "nail" household (person or household who refuses to move and bargains for unreasonably high compensation when the land is requisitioned for a construction project)
顶戴花翎	〈服饰〉official decoration on hat (indicating their ranks in the Qing Dynasty)
顶格处罚	〈防疫〉maximum penalty
顶卡花	〈毛南族〉flowery bamboo hat

顶起半边天	to hold/prop up half the sky
鼎	〈古〉ding; tripod; cauldron (a cooking vessel with two loop handles and three or four legs)
定喘	〈中医药〉Dingchuan acupoint; Panting Stabilizer; Asthma Relieving (EX-B1)
定喘汤	〈中医药〉Dingchuan Tang; Asthma-Reliving Decoction; Panting-Stabilizing Decoction
定点医院	〈防疫〉designated hospital
定调子	to set the tone
定额计酬	quota remuneration
定岗	to determine posts
定胜糕	〈饮食〉Suzhou Dingsheng Cake
定痫丸	〈中医药〉Dingxian Wan; Epilepsy-Calming Pill; Fit-Settling Pill
定向培训	training for specific posts; job-oriented training
定向生	targeted-area student
定向招生	to enroll students who are pre-assigned to specific posts or areas
定心丸	heart-soothing pill; mind relief (sth. capable of setting sb.'s mind at ease)
定窑	〈陶瓷〉Ting Yao; Ding Kiln (one of the five famous kilns in the Song Dynasty)
定窑白瓷暗花瓶	〈陶瓷〉Ding Kiln white porcelain vase with covert floral pattern
定窑白瓷刻花长颈瓶	〈陶瓷〉Ding Kiln white porcelain tall-necked vase with carved floral pattern
定窑白瓷刻花净瓶	〈陶瓷〉Ding Kiln white porcelain holy-water vase with carved floral pattern
定窑白瓷刻花水注	〈陶瓷〉Ding Kiln white porcelain water dropper with carved floral pattern
定窑白瓷桃形纽盖罐	〈陶瓷〉Ding Kiln white porcelain lidded jar with peach-shaped knob
定窑白瓷五足熏炉	〈陶瓷〉Ding Kiln white porcelain five-legged incense burner

定窑白釉刻花龙首净瓶	〈陶瓷〉Ding Kiln white porcelain holy-water vase with dragon-head spout and carved floral pattern
定窑"官"字款白瓷盘	〈陶瓷〉Ding Kiln white porcelain plate marked with "Guan" (official)
定窑孩儿瓷枕	〈陶瓷〉Ding Kiln white porcelain pillow in the form of a boy
定窑印花荷莲双鱼纹盘	〈陶瓷〉Ding Kiln white porcelain plate with printed double-fish pattern
定窑印花云龙盘	〈陶瓷〉Ding Kiln plate with printed cloud and dragon pattern
定志丸	〈中医药〉Dingzhi Wan; Mind-Calming Pill; Mind-Stabilizing Pill
定制服装	custom-made costumes; order-made clothes
丢车保帅	to give up a pawn to save a chariot; to sacrifice sth. minor to save sth. major
丢脸	to lose one's face; to be disgraced
丢面子	→丢脸
东白春芽茶	Dongbai Spring Bud tea
东北大花袄	Northeast grandiflora lammy
东北农家饭	〈饮食〉Northeast Countryside Cuisine
东湖银毫	〈茶〉East Lake Silver Needle
东坡方肉	〈饮食〉Braised Dongpo Pork (with Cinnamon, Scallion and Ginger)
东坡[乌角]巾	〈服饰〉Su Dongpo style kerchief
东坡肘子	〈饮食〉Braised Dongpo Pork Hocks with Brown Sauce
东甜西辣	〈饮食〉sweet eastern cuisine and spicy western cuisine; sweet flavor in the east and spicy in the west
东乡羊肉	〈饮食〉Stewed Dongxiang Mutton with Onion and Cilantro
冬菜扣肉	〈饮食〉Steamed Pork with Preserved Vegetables
冬菜牛肉肠粉	〈饮食〉Steamed Rice Rolls with Beef and Preserved Vegetables

冬菜银鳕鱼	〈饮食〉Steamed Codfish with Preserved Vegetables
冬草花炖海星	〈饮食〉Stewed Starfish with Caterpillar Fungus
冬草花炖鹧鸪	〈饮食〉Stewed Partridge with Aweto
冬朝冠	winter crown (used in the Qing Dynasty)
冬虫夏草	〈中医药〉(of Latin) Cordyceps; Chinese Caterpillar Fungus
冬虫夏草香烟	Dongchong Xiacao cigarettes; Cordyceps Sinensis cigarettes
冬粉	〈饮食〉Green Bean Noodle
冬菇鲍鱼	〈饮食〉Braised Abalone with Black/Dried Mushrooms
冬菇鸡球大包	〈饮食〉Steamed Bun Stuffed with Chicken Balls and Dried Mushrooms
冬菇扒菜心	〈饮食〉Stir-Fried Choy Sum with Dried Mushrooms
冬菇鸭杂汤	〈饮食〉Duck Giblets Soup with Savory Mushrooms
冬菇蒸鸡	〈饮食〉Steamed Chicken with Dried Mushroom
冬菇猪蹄	〈饮食〉Pig Trotters with Mushrooms
冬瓜炖鸭块	〈饮食〉Stewed Duck Cutlets with White Gourd
冬瓜蛤蜊汤	〈饮食〉Clam Soup with White Gourd
冬瓜火腿	〈饮食〉Stewed Sliced Ham with White Gourd
冬瓜皮	〈中医药〉(of Latin) Exocarpium Benincasae; Chinese Waxgourd Peel
冬瓜瑶柱炖田鸡	〈饮食〉Stewed Frog Leg with Scallop and Vegetable Marrow
冬瓜子	〈中医药〉(of Latin) Semen Benincasae; Waxgourd Seed
冬葵果	〈中医药〉(of Latin) Fructus Malvae; Cluster Mallow Fruit
冬葵子	〈中医药〉(of Latin) Semen Abutili; Chingma Abutilon Seed

冬青荷叶洗	〈陶瓷〉greenish blue glazed brush washer in a lotus leaf shape (Qing Qianlong period)
冬笋炒兔片	〈饮食〉Stir-Fried Rabbit Slices with Bamboo Shoots
冬笋炒肉丝	〈饮食〉Stir-Fried Pork Shreds with Bamboo Shoots
冬笋炒鱿鱼	〈饮食〉Stir-Fried Squid with Fresh Bamboo Shoots
冬笋干烧肉	〈饮食〉Dry-Braised Pork with Bamboo Shoots
冬笋烩鸭肝	〈饮食〉Braised Duck Liver with Bamboo Shoots
冬笋鸡片	〈饮食〉Stir-Fried Sliced Chicken with Bamboo Shoots
冬笋牛肉丝	〈饮食〉Stir-Fried Beef Shreds with Bamboo Shoots
冬瑶花胶炖石蛙	〈饮食〉Stewed Frog with Scallop and Fish Maw in Soup
董事会董事	trustee; member of the board of trustees
董事长	(of a business or school) president; board chairman; chairman of the board
董香型（风格）	〈酒〉dong-flavor style
动脉	〈中医药〉artery; tremulous pulse; arteriole
动迁户	household to be relocated; relocating households
动态清零政策	〈防疫〉dynamic zero-COVID policy
动物试验	〈防疫〉animal testing
动物源性病毒	〈防疫〉zoonotic virus
动植物疫病防控	〈防疫〉to prevent and control animal and plant epidemics
动作明星	action (movie) star
冻疮软膏	〈中医药〉Dongchuang Ruangao; Chilblain Curing Cream
冻马蹄糕	〈饮食〉Water Chestnut Jelly (Cake)
侗布	cloth of Dong ethnic group
侗帕	〈侗族〉woman headwear
峒布	〈土家族〉hand-weaved fabric with patterns
洞庭碧螺春	〈茶〉Dongting Biluochun tea; Biluochun tea of the Dongting Lake
斗	〈旧〉(of measuring utensil) dou (equaling to 6.25 kg)

斗笠	douli (a hat protecting people from the rain and sunlight); bamboo split hat; bamboo leaf hat
斗彩	〈陶瓷〉(of chinaware) contending color; clashing color
斗彩暗八仙盘	〈陶瓷〉clashing-colored plate with covert Eight-Immortal symbols (Qing Qianlong period)
斗彩八卦炉	〈陶瓷〉clashing-colored porcelain burner with Eight Trigrams pattern
斗彩缠枝花卉纹碗	〈陶瓷〉clashing-colored bowl with interlaced branches and flowers pattern (Qing Qianlong period)
斗彩瓷盘	〈陶瓷〉clashing-colored porcelain plate
斗彩瓷如意	〈陶瓷〉clashing-colored porcelain ruyi (an auspicious ornament) (Ming Jiajing period)
斗彩番莲纹盘	〈陶瓷〉clashing-colored plate with passiflora pattern (Qing Qianlong period)
斗彩海水龙纹盖罐	〈陶瓷〉clashing-color lidded jar with sea water and dragon pattern (Ming Chenghua period)
斗彩花鸟纹梅瓶	〈陶瓷〉clashing colored plum vase with flower and bird pattern (Qing Kangxi period)
斗彩葡萄杯	〈陶瓷〉clashing-colored porcelain cup with grape pattern
斗彩云龙纹菊芦瓶	〈陶瓷〉clashing-color gourd-shaped vase with dragons and clouds pattern (Qing Qianlong period)
豆瓣大马哈鱼	〈饮食〉Braised Chum Salmons with Bean Paste
豆瓣鳜鱼	〈饮食〉Braised Mandarin Fish with Bean Paste
豆瓣酱鲜鱿	〈饮食〉Stir-Fried Squid with Soy Bean Paste
豆瓣鲈鱼	〈饮食〉Braised Perch in Soy Bean Paste
豆瓣牛肉	〈饮食〉Beef with Chilli Bean Sauce
豆瓣全鱼	〈饮食〉Fried Whole Fish Dressed with Spicy Bean Sauce
豆瓣烧大黄鱼	〈饮食〉Braised Yellow Croaker with Bean Sauce

豆豉	fermented black bean sauce; fermented soya beans
豆豉鹌鹑脯	〈饮食〉Braised Quail Breast with Black Bean Sauce
豆豉炒鸭片	〈饮食〉Stir-Fried Duck Fillets with Fermented Soya Beans
豆豉大龙虾	〈饮食〉Stir-Fried Lobster with Black Bean Sauce
豆豉豆腐	〈饮食〉Stir-Fried Tofu with Black Bean Sauce
豆豉多春鱼	〈饮食〉Braised Shisamo in Black Bean Sauce
豆豉鲫鱼	〈饮食〉Crucian Carp with Black Bean Sauce
豆豉鲮鱼油麦菜	〈饮食〉Stir-Fried Lettuce with Diced Fish and Black Bean Sauce
豆豉芦笋炒鸭柳	〈饮食〉Stir-Fried Sliced Duck with Asparagus in Fermented Soya Beans
豆豉牛柳	〈饮食〉Stir-Fried Beef Fillets with Black Bean Sauce
豆豉牛肉	〈饮食〉Stir-Fried Shredded Beef with Black Bean Sauce
豆豉田鸡腿	〈饮食〉Fried Frog Legs with Fermented Soya Beans
豆豉虾球	〈饮食〉Stir-Fried Prawn Balls with Black Bean Sauce
豆豉猪蹄	〈饮食〉Stewed Pig Trotters with Black Bean Sauce
豆腐菜汤	〈饮食〉Tofu and Vegetable Soup
豆腐草鱼	〈饮食〉Stewed Grass Carp with Bean Curd
豆腐炒蟹肉	〈饮食〉Stir-Fried Minced Crab Meat with Tofu
豆腐干	〈饮食〉Dried Tofu; Dried Bean Curd
豆腐海带汤	〈饮食〉Tofu and Kelp Soup
豆腐脑儿	〈饮食〉Jellied Bean Curd; Uncongealed Tofu
豆腐牛肉	〈饮食〉Tofu and Beef
豆腐片	〈饮食〉Tofu Chips; Beancurd Slices
豆腐乳炒通菜	〈饮食〉Stir-Fried Water Spinach with Preserved Tofu Sauce

豆腐烧肉片	〈饮食〉Stewed Sliced Pork with Bean Curd
豆腐烧鱼	〈饮食〉Stir-Fried Fish with Tofu
豆腐汤	〈饮食〉Tofu Soup; Bean Curd Soup
豆腐虾	〈饮食〉Tofu with Shrimps
豆腐渣工程	jerry-built project; shoddy construction
豆花	〈饮食〉→豆腐脑儿
豆浆	〈饮食〉Soybean Milk
豆酱炒肉蟹	〈饮食〉Stir-Fried Crab Meat with Soy Bean Paste
豆酱炒珍宝蟹	〈饮食〉Stir-Fried Jumbo Crab with Soy Bean Paste
豆卷	〈饮食〉Bean Rolls; Chinese Tacos
豆蔻	〈中医药〉(of Latin) Fructus Amomi Rotundus; Round Cardamom
豆蔻馒头	〈饮食〉Mantou with Round Cardamom
豆蔻年华	(of a girl) age of the cardamom (age of thirteen)
豆苗炒鸡片	〈饮食〉Stir-Fried Sliced Chicken with Pea Sprouts
豆苗大虾	〈饮食〉Stir-Fried Prawns with Pea Sprouts
豆苗枸杞汤	〈饮食〉Pea Sprouts Soup with Chinese Wolfberries
豆苗虾仁	〈饮食〉Stir-Fried Shelled Shrimps with Pea Sprouts
豆苗羊肚菌	〈饮食〉Braised Sponge Mushrooms with Pea Sprouts
豆青釉青花釉里红双耳方瓶	〈陶瓷〉yellowish pea green-glazed amphora square vase with copper red and blue and white pattern (Qing Qianlong period)
豆沙百合酥	〈饮食〉Red Bean Paste and Lily Cake/Pastry
豆沙包	〈饮食〉Baozi Stuffed with Red Bean Paste; Steamed Bun Stuffed with Sweetened Bean Paste
豆沙锅饼	〈饮食〉Red Bean Paste Pancake; Pancake Stuffed with Red Bean Paste
豆沙粽子	〈饮食〉Zongzi Stuffed with Red Bean Paste; Glutinous Rice with Red Bean Paste Wrapped in Bamboo Leaves
豆酥鳕鱼	〈饮食〉Steamed Codfish with Savory Crispy Beans
豆汁儿	〈饮食〉Fermented Soybean Milk

都匀毛尖	〈茶〉Duyun Maojian tea; Duyun Tippy Leaf tea
督脉	〈中医药〉governor vessel; governor channel
督俞	〈中医药〉Dushu acupoint; Governing Transport (BL16)
毒大米	poisonous rice
毒火犯耳证	〈中医药〉pattern of toxic fire invading the ear
毒奶粉丑闻	tainted milk powder scandal; poisonous milk powder scandal
毒枭	drug trafficker
毒性试验	〈防疫〉toxicity testing
独活	〈中医药〉(of Latin) Radix Angelicae Pubescentis; Pubescent Angelica Root
独活寄生汤	〈中医药〉Duhuo Jisheng Tang; Pubescent Angelica and Mistletoe Decoction
独苗	→独生子女
独生子女	the only child in one's family; the only son or daughter
独生子女家庭	one-child family
独生子女证	certificate of one-child; one-child certificate; single child certificate
独阴	〈中医药〉Duyin acupoint; Solitary Yin (EX-LE11)
独资经营	single-investor enterprise; sole proprietorship enterprise; sole investment enterprise
渎职	dereliction of duty
犊鼻	〈中医药〉Dubi acupoint; Nose of Calf (ST35)
杜绝瞒报漏报	to say NO to concealing or underreporting infections
杜康酒	Dukang liquor
杜仲	〈中医药〉(of Latin) Cortex Eucommiae; Eucommia Bark
杜仲茶	〈中医药〉Duzhong Tea; Eucommia Tea
杜仲酒	〈中医药〉Duzhong Jiu; Eucommia Ulmoides Wine
肚兜	〈服饰〉dudou (diamond-shaped undergarment covering the abdomen and chest); stomacher

短袄	lined short coat; lined jacket
短褂	→马[短]褂
短旗袍	short cheongsam
短襦	〈服饰〉short gown (in the Tang Dynasty)
短信	short messages; text messages
断档	severed shelf; to sold out
断码	short in size
缎纹布	satin-back crepe; satin fabric
缎子	(of silk) satin; damask; charmeuse
煅淬	〈中医药〉calcining and quenching
煅炭	〈中医药〉carbonizing by calcining
锻造技师	forging technician
对…不吭一声	not to say a word about sth.; to remain silent about sth.
对…不买账	not to go for …; to think nothing of …
对…来电	to have a vibe going on between …; to fall in love with sb.
对襟	〈服饰〉duijin (a kind of Chinese-style jacket with buttons down the front); symmetrical pieces jacket
对襟棉袄	double breasted cotton padded coat; cotton-padded jacket with buttons down the front
对襟袒胸衫	double breasted shirt; front opening shirt with opposite lapels
对襟衣	Chinese garment with opposite front lapels
对襟装	〈服饰〉double breasted clothes; opposite-lapel jacket; upper garment with opening front (a kind of Chinese-style jacket with buttons down the front)
对口帮扶	assistance through pairing programs
对口味	to suit one's taste
对口支援	〈防疫〉partner assistance; pairing-assistance
对文五铢	→剪边[对文]五铢
对症取穴	〈中医药〉selection of pathocondition acupoint; symptomatic point selection

炖	〈饮食〉to stew; to braise; to simmer; stewed; braised; simmered
炖八宝全鸭	〈饮食〉Stewed Whole Duck with Eight-Stuffing Ingredients; Stewed Whole Duck Stuffed with Eight Kinds of Materials
炖冬菇鸽	〈饮食〉Stewed Pigeon with Dried Mushroom
炖锅	stewpot; saucepan
炖牛肉	〈饮食〉Braised Beef; Stewed Beef
顿服	〈中医药〉to be administered at draught; to take in one single dose; to take medicine at a draft
多彩(的)	〈陶瓷〉(of chinaware) tou-ts'ai; duocai; multi-colored
多重国籍	plural nationality; multiple nationality
多经取穴	〈中医药〉point selection form multiple channels/meridians
多劳多得	more pay for more work
多媒体	multimedia
多媒体工程师	multimedia engineer
多媒体应用设计师	multimedia designer
多渠道灵活就业	〈防疫〉flexible employment through multiple channels
多梳栉经编针织物	multi-bar fabric
多退少补	to refund for any overpayment or a supplemental payment for any deficiency
多维电影	multidimensional movie (3D or 4D etc.)
多种方式扩大产能	〈防疫〉to expand capacity in a variety of ways
多种方式增加产量	〈防疫〉to increase output in a variety of ways
多子多福	(of idiom) the more children/sons, the more blessings
剁椒炒鸡蛋	〈饮食〉Scrambled Eggs with Chopped Chili Pepper
剁椒土豆丝	〈饮食〉Stir-Fried Shredded Potatoes with Chopped Chili Pepper

剁椒娃娃菜	〈饮食〉Stir-Fried Baby Cabbage with Chopped Chili Pepper
剁椒鸭肠	〈饮食〉Duck Intestines with Chili
剁椒鱼头	〈饮食〉Steamed Fish Head with Diced Hot Red Peppers

E

阿胶	〈中医药〉(of Latin) Colla Corii Asini; Donkey-Hide Gelatin
俄勒	〈傈僳族〉e'le; woman headwear decoration (woven with coral, material beads, sea shells and small copper beads)
莪术	〈中医药〉(of Latin) Rhizoma Curcumae; Curcuma Zedoaria; Zedoary
峨眉春语	〈茶〉Emei Spring Bud tea
峨眉毛峰	〈茶〉Emei Maofeng tea; Emei Tippy tea
峨眉雪芽	〈茶〉Emei Xueya tea; Emei Snow Bud tea
峨眉竹叶青	〈茶〉Emei Bamboo-Leaf-Green tea
鹅不食草	〈中医药〉(of Latin) Herba Centipedae; Small Centipeda Herb
额温枪	〈防疫〉forehead thermometer
恶风发热	〈中医药〉fever with aversion to wind; aversion to wind with fever
恶寒发热	〈中医药〉fever with aversion to cold; aversion to cold with fever
恶作剧	practical joke; to play a prank/trick on sb.
遏制疫情蔓延	〈防疫〉to contain the outbreak
恩施玉露	〈茶〉Enshi Yulu tea; Enshi Jade Dew tea
儿茶	〈中医药〉(of Latin) Acacia Catechu; Cutch; Black Catechu
儿科医生	paediatrician; paediatrist
耳背肺	〈中医药〉Lung on Posterior Surface (P2)
耳背肝	〈中医药〉Liver on Posterior Surface (P4)

耳背沟	〈中医药〉Groove on Posterior Surface (PS)
耳背脾	〈中医药〉Spleen on Posterior Surface (P3)
耳背肾	〈中医药〉Kidney on Posterior Surface (P5)
耳背心	〈中医药〉Heart on Posterior Surface (P1)
耳鼻喉科医师	ear-nose-throat (ENT) doctor; otolaryngologist
耳和髎	〈中医药〉Erheliao acupoint; Ear Harmony Bone-Hole (TE22)
耳尖	〈中医药〉Erjian acupoint; Ear Apex (HX6, 7i)
耳聋左慈丸	〈中医药〉Erlong Zuoci Wan; Deafness Left-Benefiting Loadstone Pill
耳门	〈中医药〉Ermen acupoint; Ear Gate (TE21)
耳内流脓	〈中医药〉purulent discharge from the ear; purulent ear discharge
耳穴	〈中医药〉ear acupuncture point
耳压疗法	〈中医药〉ear pressure therapy
耳针疗法	〈中医药〉otopuncture therapy; ear-acupuncture therapy
耳针麻醉	〈中医药〉ear-acupuncture anesthesia
耳中	〈中医药〉Erzhong acupoint; Ear Center (HX1)
二[两]把头	〈发型〉two side bun; two-sided chignon
二百五	stupid person; foolish person
二陈汤	〈中医药〉Erchen Tang; Two Matured Ingredients Decoction
二次创业	to start a new undertaking
二代病例	〈防疫〉the second-generation case
二代身份证	second-generation ID card
二锅头	〈酒〉Erguotou (a strong spirit usually made from sorghum); sorghum spirit
二孩经济	second-child economy
二妙散	〈中医药〉Ermiao San; Two Wondrous Powder
二十八脉	〈中医药〉twenty-eight pulse conditions; twenty-eight pulses
二手房市场	pre-owned/second-hand house market
二维码扫描付款	QR code scanning payment

二线城市	second-tier city
二元户籍	dual household registration; binary urban and rural division census register system

F

发病率	〈防疫〉morbidity; incidence rate
发菜	〈饮食〉Long Thread Moss; Nostoc Flagelliforme
发菜蒸蛋	〈饮食〉Steamed Eggs with Nostoc Flagelliform
发汗解表	〈中医药〉to promote sweating to release the exterior; to relieve exterior syndrome by diaphoresis
发酵周期	fermentation cycle
发热病人	〈防疫〉patient with fever; febrile patient; fever patient
发热门诊	〈防疫〉fever clinic; department for high fever
发散解表	〈中医药〉to relieve exterior syndrome by hidrosis
发烧友	audiophile; enthusiastic fan
发言人	spokesman
罚敬	to make sb. drink as a result of having lost a bet
法半夏	〈中医药〉(of Latin) Rhizoma Pinelliae Preparatum; Processed Pinellia Tuber; Pro Formula Pinellia (Tuber)
法币	〈旧〉legal tender; legal currency (paper currency issued by Kuomintang government from 1935 to 1948)
法［翡］翠釉	〈陶瓷〉kingfisher colored blue glaze
法服	monk's gown; nun's robe
法冠	〈古〉faguan; judicial and censorial officers' hat
法华花鸟罐	〈陶瓷〉enameled jar with flower and bird pattern
法律顾问	legal adviser; legal counsel
法务经理	legal manager; legal officer
发型师	hairdresser; hairstylist

发簪	〈服饰〉hairpin; hair ornament
珐华八卦莲花吉祥语纹抱月壶	〈陶瓷〉Fahua full moon pot with Eight Diagrams, lotus and auspicious words pattern (Ming Jiajing period)
珐华麒麟莲花吉祥语纹盒	〈陶瓷〉Fahua box with Kylin, lotus and auspicious words pattern (Ming Jiajing period)
珐琅	→搪瓷
珐琅彩瓷	〈陶瓷〉colorful enamel porcelain
珐琅彩花鸟纹瓶	〈陶瓷〉enamel vase with colored flower and bird pattern (Qing Qianlong period)
珐琅彩墨竹碗	〈陶瓷〉enamel bowl with color inked bamboo pattern (Qing Yongzheng period)
珐琅彩人物瓶	〈陶瓷〉enamel vase with figural depiction pattern (Qing Qianlong period)
珐琅彩婴戏纹双连瓷瓶	〈陶瓷〉enameled twin-body vase with playing children pattern
珐琅彩婴戏纹双体瓶	〈陶瓷〉enamel twin-body vase with playing children pattern (Qing Qianlong period)
番茄蛋花[鸡蛋]汤	〈饮食〉Tomato and Egg Soup
番茄炖牛腩	〈饮食〉Braised Beef Brisket with Tomato
番茄黄焖鸡块	〈饮食〉Braised Chicken with Tomato
番茄牛肉炒饭	〈饮食〉Stir-Fried Rice with Tomato and Beef
番茄牛肉炒面	〈饮食〉Tomato Beef Chow Mein; Stir-Fried Noodles with Tomato and Beef
番茄浓汤	〈饮食〉Tomato Bisque Soup
番茄松鼠鱼	〈饮食〉Fried Yellow-Fin Tuna Accompanied by Tomato Sauce
番茄虾仁锅巴	〈饮食〉Stir-Fried Shelled Shrimps and Crispy Rice with Tomato Sauce
番茄汁鸡丝炒饭	〈饮食〉Stir-Fried Rice with Shredded Chicken and Tomato Sauce
番泻叶	〈中医药〉(of Latin) Folium Sennae; Senna Leaf
翻刀髻	〈发型〉knife-shaped turning bun

翻老账	to bring up old scores again; to dredge stuff up from the past
翻领	lapel; turndown collar
翻译核对员	translation checker
凡客体	Vancl style (for advertising)
矾红彩五福碗	〈陶瓷〉allite red glazed bowl with five-bat pattern (Qing Qianlong period)
矾红缠枝花卉海水纹折沿盆	〈陶瓷〉allite red folded edge basin with interlaced branches and sea water pattern (Ming Yongle period)
繁体字	complex character; traditional Chinese character
反败为胜	to snatch a victory out of defeat; to turn defeat into victory; to turn the tables (on someone)
反膊衫	〈壮族〉fanbo shirt; shirt with reverse furbelow
反腐剧	anti-corruption TV series
反关脉	〈中医药〉ectopic radial pulse; dorsally located radial artery
反治法	〈中医药〉paradoxical treatment; retrograde treatment
反佐药	〈中医药〉contrary drug; corrigent; paradoxical assistant
返回舱	re-entry module
饭碗	rice bowl (a means of life); a way of making a living
泛油	〈中医药〉extensive diffusion of oil
贩毒集团	drug cartel
方便面	〈饮食〉Instant Noodles; Snack Noodles
方便食品	instant food; convenience food
方舱医院	〈防疫〉temporary treatment center; mobile cabin hospital
方剂学	〈中医药〉prescriptions of Chinese materia medica; pharmacology of traditional Chinese medical formulae
方襟旗袍	cheongsam with square lapel
方领	square collar, square lapel

方领口	square neckline
方位配五行	〈中医药〉correspondence of the directions and five elements
方彝	〈古〉fangyi; wine vessel
方折刀	〈币〉square clasp knife (issued in the Yan State) →磬折刀
方竹笋炖肉	〈饮食〉Braised Pork with Bamboo Shoots
方足布	〈币〉shovel-shaped square spade; square foot spade coin (issued in the Warring States period)
芳香化湿	〈中医药〉to resolve dampness with aroma; to remove dampness by means of aromatics
芳香化浊	〈中医药〉to resolve turbidity with aroma; to eliminate turbid pathogen with aroma
防盗门	burglarproof door; antitheft door
防范跨境输入输出	〈防疫〉to curb cross-border coronavirus spreading
防范区	〈防疫〉precaution zone
防范疫情跨境传播	〈防疫〉to curb the cross-border spread of the epidemic
防风	〈中医药〉(of Latin) Radix Saposhnikoviae; Divaricate Saposhnikovia Root
防风通圣丸	〈中医药〉Fangfeng Tongsheng Wan; Miraculous Pill of Ledebouriella; Saposhnikovia Sage-Inspired Pill
防护服	〈防疫〉protective clothing; protective suit
防己	〈中医药〉(of Latin) Radix Stephaniae Tetrandrae; Mealy Fangji Root
防己黄芪汤	〈中医药〉Fangji Huangqi Tang; Tetrandra and Astragalus Decoction
防控关键阶段	〈防疫〉crucial moment/stage of prevention and control
防控就是责任	〈防疫〉the prevention and control is a responsibility

防控力量向社区下沉	〈防疫〉to empower communities the coronavirus prevention and control
防窃听电话	eavesdropping proof telephone
防身术	personal defense skill
防损员	loss prevention specialist
防伪标志	fake-proof mark; counter-forgery mark
防疫	〈防疫〉epidemic prevention; prevention and control of the virus
防疫管控	〈防疫〉epidemic prevention and control
防疫筛查	〈防疫〉epidemic prevention screening
防疫员	epidemic prevention coordinator
防御外邪入侵	〈中医药〉to prevent the invasion of exogenous pathogenic factor
防止大规模社区传播	〈防疫〉to prevent the wide spread of the coronavirus in communities
防止信息恐慌	〈防疫〉to prevent panic and manage information properly
防止疫情跨境传播	〈防疫〉to prevent the epidemic from spreading across borders
防止疫情扩散蔓延	〈防疫〉to prevent the spread of the epidemic
防芷鼻炎片	〈中医药〉Fangzhi Biyan Pian; Ledebouriella Angelica Rhinitis Tablet
妨害国境卫生检疫罪	〈防疫〉crime of jeopardizing border quarantine security
房产估价师	real estate evaluator
房产权证	property ownership certificate; premises permit
房产项目配套工程师	conveyance system engineer
房虫儿	real estate speculator (jokingly called housing broker)
房地产策划经理	real estate planning manager
房地产策划专员	real estate planning specialist
房地产经纪人	real estate broker; estate agent; property manager
房地产开发经理	real estate development manager
房地产评估师	real estate appraiser

房地产项目招标专员	real estate tender specialist
房地产销售经理	real estate sales manager
房地产销售主管	real estate sales supervisor
房地产中介	real estate agent
房改	housing system reform
房价泡沫	housing price bubble; bubble of real estate price
房劳	〈中医药〉excessive sexual intercourse; exhaustion due to sexual indulgence
房奴	fangnu; house slave; mortgage slave
房事淡漠	〈中医药〉weak libido; asexuality
房屋拆迁	housing demolition and relocation
房屋拆迁单位	relocation house unit
房屋空置率	housing vacancy rate
房屋验收员	building inspector
房务部	room division
房务中心文员	room service clerk
仿成化青花番莲纹盘	〈陶瓷〉Chenghua-styled blue and white plate with passiflora pattern (Qing Qianlong period)
仿古陶瓷	〈陶瓷〉imitation of antique porcelain
仿宣德青花番莲八宝高足碗	〈陶瓷〉Xuande-styled blue and white stem bowl with passiflora and eight treasures pattern (Qing Qianlong period)
仿真应用工程师	simulation application engineer
纺织设计总监	textile design director
放…鸽子	(of idiom) to stand sb. up; to break an appointment with (sb.)
放开货运物流限制	〈防疫〉to lift cargo transport bans
放射性污染	radioactive contamination
放射诊断室	〈防疫〉radiodiagnosis department
放下架子	to get off one's high horse; to throw off one's airs
放心店	trustworthy shop
放心肉	quality-assured meat; safe meat
放血疗法	〈中医药〉blood-letting therapy; phlebotomy therapy
飞沫传播	〈防疫〉droplet transmission

飞天髻	〈古〉(of hairstyle) feitian bun; three-coil-shaped bun
飞仙髻	〈古〉(of hairstyle) feixian bun; two-coil shaped bun
非瘢痕灸	〈中医药〉non-scarring moxibustion
非常规能源	non-conventional energy
非典型肺炎	〈防疫〉atypical pneumonia →严重急性呼吸综合征［非典］
非婚生子女	love child; illegitimate child; child born out wedlock
非劳动收入	income not from work; passive income
非吸烟者	nonsmoker
非再生资源	non-renewable resources
非职务发明	non-service invention
肥儿宝颗粒	〈中医药〉Fei'erbao Keli; Baby's Weight-Increasing Treasure Granule
肥儿丸	〈中医药〉Fei'er Wan; Fattening Baby Pill; Chubby Child Pill
肥猪肉煨甲鱼裙边	〈饮食〉Stewed Calipash and Calipee with Fat Pork
翡翠(玉)	jadite; jadeite jade
翡翠鲍脯麒麟鸡	〈饮食〉Braised Chicken with Sliced Abalone and Ham
翡翠鸡粥	〈饮食〉Jade-Colored Chicken Broth; Chicken Porridge with Vegetables
翡翠烧麦	〈饮食〉Steamed Vegetable Shaomai
翡翠虾球	〈饮食〉Stir-Fried Prawn Balls with Vegetables
翡翠虾仁	〈饮食〉Stir-Fried Shelled Shrimp with Vegetables
翡翠釉	→法［翡］翠釉
翡翠［翠绿］釉	〈陶瓷〉kingfisher blue glaze
肺朝百脉	〈中医药〉pulmonary connection with all vessels; convergence of vessels in the lung
肺脓肿	〈防疫〉lung abscess
肺脾两虚	〈中医药〉deficiency of both lung and spleen; dual deficiency of the lung-spleen
肺气不宣	〈中医药〉failure of lung qi in dispersion; lung qi obstruction

肺气虚	〈中医药〉lung-qi deficiency; deficiency of lung qi
肺气虚证	〈中医药〉lung-qi vacuity pattern; pattern of deficiency of lung-qi
肺气阴两虚证	〈中医药〉pattern of dual vacuity of lung-qi and yin
肺热肠燥证	〈中医药〉pattern of lung heat and intestine-dryness
肺热炽盛证	〈中医药〉intense lung heat pattern; pattern of flaring up of lung heat
肺热血瘀证	〈中医药〉lung heat and blood stasis pattern; pattern of blood stasis due to lung heat
肺热阴虚证	〈中医药〉pattern of yin deficiency/vacuity due to lung heat
肺肾气虚	〈中医药〉lung-kidney qi deficiency; qi deficiency of lung and kidney
肺肾气虚证	〈中医药〉pattern of lung-kidney qi vacuity; pattern of qi deficiency of lung and kidney
肺肾[金水]相生	〈中医药〉mutually promotion of lung and kidney
肺肾阴虚	〈中医药〉yin deficiency of lung and kidney; lung-kidney yin deficiency
肺肾阴虚证	〈中医药〉pattern of lung-kidney yin vacuity; pattern of yin deficiency of lung and kidney
肺俞	〈中医药〉Feishu acupoint; Lung Transport (BL13)
肺司呼吸	〈中医药〉lung controlling breathing
肺为贮痰之器	〈中医药〉lung being reservoir of phlegm
肺纤维化	〈防疫〉idiopathic pulmonary fibrosis
肺炎疫情防控	〈防疫〉prevention and control of the outbreak of pneumonia
肺阴虚	〈中医药〉deficiency of lung yin; lung yin deficiency
肺阴虚证	〈中医药〉lung-yin vacuity pattern; pattern of deficiency of lung-yin
肺主气	〈中医药〉lung governing qi
肺主宣发	〈中医药〉lung governing diffusion

肺主治节	〈中医药〉lung governing management and regulation
废物的循环使用	recycling waste
分	(of monetary unit) fen (equaling to one percent of a yuan); cent
分瓣小帽	〈拉祜族〉fenban cap; petals-sewed cap with colorful fabric strips
分包商	subcontractor
分餐制	individual serving; serving of individual dishes
分服	〈中医药〉to be taken separately; to be administered separately
分红	to share out bonus; to draw extra dividends; to distribute/receive dividends
分红酒	banquet of sharing out bonus
分类指导	〈防疫〉to give sector-specific guidance
分区分级精准防控	〈防疫〉region-specific, multi-level targeted approach to epidemic prevention and control
分区施策	〈防疫〉to apply different policies for different areas
分数线	grade cut-off point; minimum passing score
分髾髻	〈古〉(of hairstyle) fentiao bun; swallow-tail chignon
分销经理	distribution manager; channel manager
分销专员	distribution specialist; channel specialist
汾酒	Fenjiu liquor (distilled in Fenyang, Shanxi)
焚香	to burn incense; to burn joss sticks; thurification
粉彩鹌鹑猎纹天球瓶	〈陶瓷〉famille rose globular vase with quail hunting pattern
粉彩瓷	〈陶瓷〉famille-rose porcelain
粉彩花鸟碗	〈陶瓷〉famille rose bowl with flower and bird pattern (Qing Yongzheng period)
粉彩人物笔筒	〈陶瓷〉brush holder with famille rose decorated with portraiture (Qing Yongzheng period)
粉彩山水带钩	〈陶瓷〉belt hook with famille rose landscape (Qing Qianlong period)

粉彩桃纹盘	〈陶瓷〉plate with famille rose peach pattern (Qing Qianlong period)
粉彩套盒	〈陶瓷〉layered boxes with famille rose decoration (Qing Qianlong period)
粉浆饭	〈饮食〉Slurry Rice Porridge
粉末绿茶	powdered green tea
粉青釉	〈陶瓷〉lavender grey glaze
粉青釉鸡形熏	〈陶瓷〉lavender grey glaze incense burner in the shape of chicken
粉筛	(of a cooker) flour sieve; flour sifter; powder filter
粉丝咖喱蟹煲	〈饮食〉Rice Noodle Curry Crab; Stewed Rice Noodle with Curry Crab
粉丝虾米杂菜煲	〈饮食〉Stewed Vermicelli, Dried Shrimps and Assorted Vegetables in Casserole
粉蒸鸡	〈饮食〉Steamed Chicken Wrapped in Flour
粉蒸牛肉	〈饮食〉Steamed Beef with Glutinous Rice Flour
粉蒸排骨	〈饮食〉Steamed Spareribs with Ground Glutinous Rice
份(子)礼	apportioned gift (usually given at weddings)
份子钱	money given as a wedding gift
粪口传播	〈防疫〉fecal-oral transmission
愤青	young cynic; angry youth; young malcontent (who are dissatisfied with the status quo and eager to change reality)
风池	〈中医药〉Fengchi acupoint; Wind Pool (GB20)
风赤疮痍	〈中医药〉vesiculated dermatitis of eyelid; wind-red sore
风毒证	〈中医药〉wind-toxin pattern
风府	〈中医药〉Fengfu acupoint; Windy House (GV16)
风寒犯头证	〈中医药〉pattern of wind-cold invading the head
风寒感冒	〈中医药〉anemofrigid cold; common cold due to wind-cold
风寒化热证	〈中医药〉pattern of heat transformed from wind-cold

风寒束表证	〈中医药〉pattern of wind-cold fettering the exterior; pattern of exterior tightened by wind-cold
风寒袭鼻证	〈中医药〉pattern of wind-cold assailing the nose
风寒袭肺	〈中医药〉invasion of lung by wind-cold; attack of wind-cold on the lung
风寒袭肺证	〈中医药〉pattern of wind-cold assailing the lung
风火犯齿证	〈中医药〉pattern of wind-fire invading the teeth
风火热毒证	〈中医药〉wind-fire and heat toxin pattern; pattern of wind-fire and heat-toxicity
风帽	hood; cowl-like hat
风门	〈中医药〉Fengmen acupoint; Windy Door/Gate (BL12)
风琴袋	accordion pocket
风热犯鼻证	〈中医药〉pattern of wind-heat invading the nose
风热犯耳证	〈中医药〉pattern of wind-heat encroaching the ear
风热犯肺	〈中医药〉invasion of lung by wind-heat; attack of wind-heat on the lung
风热犯肺证	〈中医药〉pattern of wind-heat invading the lung
风热犯目证	〈中医药〉pattern of wind-heat encroaching the eye
风热犯头证	〈中医药〉pattern of wind-heat invading the head
风热侵喉证	〈中医药〉pattern of wind-heat encroaching the throat
风热袭表证	〈中医药〉pattern of wind-heat attacking superficies/the exterior
风热阻络证	〈中医药〉pattern of wind-heat blocking collaterals/the network vessels
风湿安泰片	〈中医药〉Fengshi Antai Pian; Rheumatism Calming Tablet
风湿犯头证	〈中医药〉pattern of wind-dampness invading the head
风湿关节贴	〈中医药〉Fengshi Guanjie Tie; Rheumatism Plaster

风湿化热证	〈中医药〉pattern of heat transformed from wind-dampness
风湿挟毒证	〈中医药〉pattern of wind-dampness with toxicity
风湿凌目证	〈中医药〉pattern of wind-dampness invading the eyes
风湿马钱片	〈中医药〉Fengshi Maqian Pian; Rheumatism Strychnos Tablet
风湿圣药胶囊	〈中医药〉Fengshi Shengyao Jiaonang; Sacred Rheumatism Capsule
风湿贴	〈中医药〉Fengshi Tie; Rheumatism Plaster
风水师	feng shui master; geomancer; future-teller
风水先生	→风水师
风水相搏证	〈中医药〉pattern of fighting of wind with water
风痰入络证	〈中医药〉pattern of wind-phlegm invading the collaterals/the network vessels
风痰上扰证	〈中医药〉pattern of wind-phlegm invading upward
风痰证	〈中医药〉wind-phlegm pattern
风痛片	〈中医药〉Fengtong Pian; Rheumatalgia Tablet
风为百病之长	〈中医药〉wind being primary pathogen; wind is the leading factor in various diseases
风险防范机制	risk prevention mechanism
风险意识	risk awareness
风邪犯肺	〈中医药〉invasion of the lung by wind pathogen
风易伤阳位	〈中医药〉yang portion of the body susceptible to wind attack
风油精	〈中医药〉Fengyoujing; (Wind) Medicated Oil; Essential Balm
风云四号 A 卫星	Fengyun-4A Satellite
风燥	〈中医药〉wind-dryness
风中经络证	〈中医药〉pattern of channel hit by wind
枫蓼肠胃康片	〈中医药〉Fengliao Changweikang Pian; Intestine Stomach Recovery Tablet
枫香脂	〈中医药〉(of Latin) Resina Liquidambaris; Beautiful Sweetgum Resin

封城	〈防疫〉to lockdown a city; lockdown of a city
封建地主阶级	feudal landlord class
封建礼教	feudal ethic code; feudal ethics
封控区	〈防疫〉lockdown zone
封口费	hush money; sealing fee
封泥	〈古〉lute; sealing clay; mud capping
封髓丹	〈中医药〉Feng Sui Dan; Marrow Storing Pill; Marrow-Sealing Elixir
封锁禁运	blockade and embargo
锋针	〈中医药〉lance needle; sharp-edged needle
蜂毒疗法	〈中医药〉bee-toxin therapy
蜂房	〈中医药〉(of Latin) Nidus Vespae; Honeycomb
蜂蜡	〈中医药〉(of Latin) Cera Flava; Beeswax
凤肝炒鸡片	〈饮食〉Stir-Fried Sliced Chicken with Chicken Livers
凤肝虾仁	〈饮食〉Stir-Fried Shelled Shrimps with Chicken Liver
凤冠	〈服饰〉phoenix coronet (worn by empresses or imperial concubines and also as a bride's head-dress in feudal China)
凤冠霞帔	phoenix coronet with embroidered shawl
凤凰单丛［枞］茶	Fenghuang Dancong tea; Fenghuang unique bush tea
凤凰男	phoenix man (an outstanding man with a humble origin); self-made man
凤凰鱼蓉羹	〈饮食〉Thick Soup of Minced Fish and Egg-White
凤凰玉米羹	〈饮食〉Sweetcorn Soup with Eggs
凤梨酥	〈饮食〉Pineapple Cake; Pineapple Pastry
凤丝仙人掌	〈饮食〉Fried Cactus with Shredded Chicken
凤头丝履	silk shoe with phoenix toe cap
凤尾草	〈中医药〉(of Latin) Herba Pteridis Multifidae; Phoenix-Tail Fern; Chinese Brake Herb
凤尾裙	phoenix-tail skirt (popular in the Qing Dynasty)
凤尾莴笋	〈饮食〉Plain-Fried Lettuce Stems (Shaped as a Phoenix Tail)

凤尾虾丝汤	〈饮食〉Phoenix-Tailed Prawn and Seaweed Soup
凤尾尊	〈陶瓷〉phoenix-tail-shaped vase
凤香型(风格)	〈酒〉feng-flavor style
凤腰鲍鱼	〈饮食〉Stewed Abalone and Chicken Kidneys
凤足炖甲鱼	〈饮食〉Stewed Turtle with Chicken Paws in Soup
凤足炖鹿筋	〈饮食〉Chicken Feet and Deer Sinew in Casserole
奉茶	tea serving
奉茶盘	tea serving tray
奉公守法	to abide social discipline
佛手	〈中医药〉(of Latin) Fructus Citri Sarcodactylis; Finger Citron; Buddha's Hand
佛手花	〈中医药〉(of Latin) Flos Citri Sarcodactylis; Finger Citron Flower; Buddha's Hand Flower
佛跳墙	〈饮食〉Fo Tiaoqiang; Steamed Abalones with Shark's Fins and Fish Maw in Broth
夫妻肺片	〈饮食〉Pork Lungs in Chili Sauce
夫妻相	husband-wife looks
肤痔清软膏	〈中医药〉Fuzhiqing Ruangao; Skin Hemorrhoid Clearing Ointment
麸炒	〈中医药〉stir-frying with bran
麸曲	〈酒〉bran starter; moldy bran →大曲
麸曲酒	bran starter liquor; moldy bran liquor
敷脐疗法	〈中医药〉umbilical compress therapy; umbilicus therapy
敷眼疗法	〈中医药〉eye compress therapy
伏天灸	〈中医药〉moxibustion in dog days/hot summer days
伏邪温病	〈中医药〉epidemic febrile disease caused by incubating pathogens; warm disease caused by incubating pathogens
扶持政策	supportive policy
扶贫	poverty alleviation; poverty relief
扶贫开发	poverty alleviation through development
扶阳退阴	〈中医药〉to strengthen yang to reduce yin; to reinforce yang for abating yin

扶正固本	〈中医药〉to support right and secure the root; to strengthen and consolidate body resistance
扶正解表	〈中医药〉to reinforce the healthy qi to release the exterior; to strengthen body resistance for relieving exterior syndrome
扶正解表剂	〈中医药〉formula for supporting body resistance and relieving superficies; formula for supporting right and resolving the exterior
扶正祛邪	〈中医药〉to reinforce the healthy qi to eliminate the pathogen; to strengthen vital qi for eliminating pathogenic factor
芙蓉炒鸡柳	〈饮食〉Stir-Fried Chicken Fillets in Egg Whites
芙蓉炒蟹肉	〈饮食〉Stir-Fried Crab Meat with Egg Whites
芙蓉干贝	〈饮食〉Stewed Dried Scallops with Egg Whites
芙蓉归云髻	(of hairstyle) hibiscus-shaped bun
芙蓉鳜鱼	〈饮食〉Stir-Fried Mandarin Fish with Egg Whites
芙蓉鸡片	〈饮食〉Stir-Fried Sliced Chicken in Egg Whites
芙蓉肉丝	〈饮食〉Stir-Fried Shredded Pork with Egg Whites
芙蓉王香烟	Furong Wang cigarettes; Cotton Rose King cigarettes
芙蓉蟹斗	〈饮食〉Stir-Fried Crab Meat in Shell
芙蓉鸭腰	〈饮食〉Stewed Duck Kernel with Egg Whites
服务部经理	service manager
服务中心领班	service center captain
服药食忌	〈中医药〉dietary contraindication during medication; food taboo in drug application; dietetic restraint in drug application
服装设计师	apparel stylist; fashion designer
服装设计总监	director of fashion design
茯苓	〈中医药〉(of Latin) Poria; Indian Bread; Tuckahoe
茯苓丸	〈中医药〉Fuling Wan; Poria Pill
浮动工资	floating wages; fluctuating wages
浮动汇率	floating exchange rate
浮动价格	floating price

浮萍	〈中医药〉(of Latin) Herba Spirodelae; Common Ducksmeat Herb
浮小麦	〈中医药〉(of Latin) Fructus Tritici Levis; Immature Wheat
福鼎白茶	Fuding White tea
福建菜	〈饮食〉→闽菜
福建银针	〈茶〉Fujian Silver Needle
福利彩票	welfare lottery
福利分房	welfare-oriented public housing distribution
福利院	welfare house; charity house
福娃	(of Beijing Olympic mascot) Fuwa; Five Friendlies
幞头	〈服饰〉futou hat; soft cloth surrounding the head
辅导员	(political and ideological) instructor; assistant; counsellor
辅料	〈中医药〉adjuvant material
腐乳汁烧肉	〈饮食〉Stewed Pork with Preserved Bean Curd
腐乳猪蹄	〈饮食〉Stewed Pig Trotters with Preserved Tofu
父系家庭层级	patriarchal/patrilineal family hierarchy
父系家庭结构	patriarchal/patrilineal family structure
父系家庭秩序	patriarchal/patrilineal family order
父系社会结构	patriarchal/patrilineal social structure
父系社会秩序	patriarchal/patrilineal social order
父子党	father-son party
付费国产剧	pay-per-view homemade TV drama
负压救护车	〈防疫〉negative pressure ambulance
负债经营	managing with loan; liabilities operation
妇康宝口服液	〈中医药〉Fukangbao Koufuye; Female Health-Protecting Oral Liquid
妇康宁片	〈中医药〉Fukangning Pian; Women's Health and Tranquilness Tablet
妇科调经片	〈中医药〉Fuke Tiaojing Pian; Women's Menses-Regulating Pill
妇科医师	gynaecologist
妇乐冲剂[颗粒]	〈中医药〉Fule Chongji; Gynecopathy-Healing Granule

妇联主席	chairman of women's federation
妇女联合会	women's federation
妇女主任	women's director
《妇人大全良方》	〈中医药〉*Furen Daquan Liangfang*; *Compendium of Effective Prescriptions for Women*; *Complete Effective Prescriptions for Women's Diseases* (by Chen Ziming in the Southern Song Dynasty)
妇炎净胶囊	〈中医药〉Fuyanjing Jiaonang; Female Inflammation Clearing Capsule
妇炎康丸	〈中医药〉Fuyankang Wan; Anti-Female-Infection Pill
妇炎平胶囊	〈中医药〉Fuyanping Jiaonang; Anti-Gynecological Inflammation Capsule
妇幼保健员	maternity and health care assistant
妇幼保健院	maternal and childcare service center; maternal and child health hospital
附加意外险	supplemental accident insurance
附属高中	affiliated high school
附属中学	affiliated middle school; attached middle school
附子	〈中医药〉(of Latin) Radix Aconiti Lateralis Preparata; Aconite; Monkshood
附子理中丸	〈中医药〉Fuzi Lizhong Wan; Aconite Center-Rectifying Pill
阜昌通宝	〈币〉coin with characters fuchang tongbao (issued by the puppet Qi regime in Jin Dynasty)
阜昌重宝	〈币〉coin with characters fuchang zhongbao (issued by the puppet Qi regime in Jin Dynasty)
复读生	return students (reattending classes after failing college entrance examination)
复方	〈中医药〉compound recipe; compound formula; polypharmacy
复方板蓝根颗粒	〈中医药〉Fufang Banlangen Keli; Multiple-Ingredients Isatis Granule
复方草珊瑚含片	〈中医药〉Fufang Caoshanhu Hanpian; Multiple-Ingredients Sarcandra Sucking Tablet

复方川贝止咳糖浆	〈中医药〉Fufang Chuanbei Zhike Tangjiang; Compound Bulbus Fritillariae Cough Syrup
复方川芎胶囊	〈中医药〉Fufang Chuanxiong Jiaonang; Compound Ligusticum Root Capsule
复方丹参滴丸	〈中医药〉Fufang Danshen Diwan; Compound Salvia Miltiorrhiza Dripping Pill; Compound Salvae Dropping Pill
复方丹参口服液	〈中医药〉Fufang Danshen Koufuye; Compound Salvia Miltiorrhiza Compound Oral Liquid
复方丹参片	〈中医药〉Fufang Danshen Pian; Compound Salvia Miltiorrhiza Tablet; Compound Tablet of Red Sage Root
复方丹参注射液	〈中医药〉Compound Salvia Miltiorrhiza Injection; Compound Injection of Red Sage Root
复方胆通胶囊	〈中医药〉Fufang Dantong Jiaonang; Multiple-Ingredients Gall-Opening Capsule
复方胆通片	〈中医药〉Fufang Dantong Pian; Compound Eulektrol/Plecton Tablet
复方阿胶浆	〈中医药〉Fufang Ejiao Jiang; Multi-ingredient Ass Hide Glue Syrup
复方公英片	〈中医药〉Fufang Gongying Pian; Multiple-Ingredients Dandelion Tablet
复方黄连素片	〈中医药〉Fufang Huangliansu Pian; Multiple-Ingredients Coptis Tablet
复方黄芩片	〈中医药〉Fufang Huangqin Pian; Multiple-Ingredients Scutellaria Tablet
复方桔梗止咳片	〈中医药〉Fufang Jiegeng Zhike Pian; Multiple-Ingredients Platycodon Coughing-Relieving Tablet
复方苦木消炎胶囊	〈中医药〉Fufang Kumu Xiaoyan Jiaonang; Multiple-Ingredients Bitter Wood Anti-Inflammation Capsule
复方满山白糖浆	〈中医药〉Fufang Manshanbai Tangjiang; Multiple-Ingredients Rhododendron Syrup

复方青黛丸	〈中医药〉Fufang Qingdai Wan; Compound Pill of Natural Indigo
复方雪参胶囊	〈中医药〉Fufang Xueshen Jiaonang; Multiple-Ingredients Snow Ginseng Capsule
复方珍珠暗疮片	〈中医药〉Fufang Zhenzhu Anchuang Pian; Compound Pearl Acne Tablet
复工人员专列	〈防疫〉special train for returning workers
复合型人才	interdisciplinary talent
复[混]合釉	〈陶瓷〉composite glaze
复襦	〈服饰〉furu; short coat stuffed with silk
复式住宅	duplex apartment; compound apartment
复元活血汤	〈中医药〉Fuyuan Huoxue Tang; Origin-Restorative and Blood-Quickening Decoction
复员	(of armymen) demobilization; to be discharged from active military service
复诊	〈防疫〉subsequent visit
副编审	associate senior editor
副行长	(of a bank) vice president
副会长	vice president
副校长	(of a university) vice president; (of a middle/primary school) vice principal, assistant headmaster
副研究馆员	associate research librarian
副研究员	associate research fellow
副译审	associate senior translator
副院长	(of a court) vice president; (of a university) associate dean, deputy director of the faculty; (of a hospital) deputy director
副主编	associate managing editor; associate editor-in-chief
副主任编辑	associate managing editor
副主任护师	associate senior nurse
副主任记者	associate senior journalist
副主任技师	associate senior medical technologist
副主任药师	associate senior pharmacist/physician

副主任医师	associate chief physician
副总编	deputy chief editor; deputy editor-in-chief
副总裁	vice-president; vice chairman
副总工程师	vice chief engineer
《傅青主女科》	〈中医药〉*Fu Qingzhu's Obstetrics and Gynecology* (by Fu Shan in the Qing Dynasty)
富二代	the second-generation rich; rich second generation; silver-spoon kids
富贵病	maladies of the rich; rich man's disease (which calls for long period expensive diet)
富贵鸡	〈饮食〉Steamed Chicken with Stuffing
富民政策	policy to enrich the people
腹可安片	〈中医药〉Fuke'an Pian; Abdomen-Calming Tablet
腹穴	〈中医药〉Fuxue acupoints; abdominal acupoints (AH8)
腹诊推拿	〈中医药〉massage for abdominal diagnosis
覆盆子	〈中医药〉(of Latin) Fructus Rubi; Palmleaf Raspberry Fruit

G

咖喱串烧生中虾	〈饮食〉Prawn Kebab with Curry Sauce
咖喱豆腐	〈饮食〉Curry Tofu; Curried Bean Curd
咖喱鸡	〈饮食〉Curry Chicken; Curried Chicken
咖喱鸡饭	〈饮食〉Rice with Curry Chicken
咖喱焗肉蟹	〈饮食〉Baked Hard-Shell Crab with Curry Sauce
咖喱焗鲟	〈饮食〉Baked Sturgeon with Curry Sauce
咖喱焗珍宝蟹	〈饮食〉Baked Jumbo Crab with Curry Sauce
咖喱牛肉饭	〈饮食〉Rice with Curry Beef
咖喱牛肉面	〈饮食〉Noodle Soup with Sliced Curry Beef
咖喱牛肉酥盒	〈饮食〉Curry Beef Puff; Crispy Chilli Beef
咖喱肉松煸大豆芽	〈饮食〉Stir-Fried Minced Pork with Bean Sprouts in Curry Sauce
咖喱虾	〈饮食〉Curry Shrimps; Curry Prawns
咖喱蟹煲	〈饮食〉Curry Crabs in Casserole
咖喱鱿鱼	〈饮食〉Fried Squid with Curry Sauce
咖喱鱼扒饭	〈饮食〉Rice with Fish Fillets and Curry Sauce; Rice with Curry Fish Fillets
咖喱蒸牛肚	〈饮食〉Steamed Beef Tripe with Curry
咖喱猪排饭	〈饮食〉Rice with Spare Ribs and Curry Sauce; Rice with Curry Spare Ribs
尕巴	〈维吾尔族〉gaba →四棱小花帽
钙釉	〈陶瓷〉calcareous glaze →石灰釉
盖底釉	〈陶瓷〉cladding glaze
盖面透明釉	〈陶瓷〉transparent-layered glaze; clear overglaze
盖头	→红盖头
盖碗	〈陶瓷〉bowl with fitted cover; lidded bowl

干白葡萄酒	dry white wine
干拌牛舌	〈饮食〉Ox Tongues with Chili Sauce
干贝扒芦笋	〈饮食〉Braised Asparagus with Scallops
干贝炖烧翅	〈饮食〉Stewed Scallops in Shark's Fin Soup; Stewed Shark's Fin in Scallops Soup
干贝芥菜鸡锅	〈饮食〉Chicken Soup with Scallops and Leaf Mustard
干贝萝卜珠	〈饮食〉Braised Chinese Radish Balls with Clam Meat
干贝木樨蛋	〈饮食〉Stir-Fried Eggs with Scallop and Black Fungi
干贝酿虾扇	〈饮食〉Braised Scallop and Shrimps (Shaped as a Fan)
干贝水晶鸡	〈饮食〉Steamed Chicken Breast and Scallop
干贝鲜腐竹草菇	〈饮食〉Braised Dried Scallops with Straw Mushrooms and Fresh Beancurd Sticks
干贝银丝羹	〈饮食〉Dried Scallop and Shredded Tofu Soup
干煸扁豆	〈饮食〉Stir-Fried Hyacinth Beans
干煸黄豆芽	〈饮食〉Stir-Fried Soybean Sprouts
干煸苦瓜	〈饮食〉Stir-Fried Bitter Melon
干煸牛柳丝	〈饮食〉Stir-Fried Shredded Beef Fillets with Chili Sauce
干煸牛肉丝	〈饮食〉Stir-Fried Shredded Beef with Chili Sauce
干煸四季豆	〈饮食〉Stir-Fried Green Beans with Minced Pork
干煸小猪腰	〈饮食〉Dry-Fried Pig Kidney with Onion
干炒	〈饮食〉to dry-fry; dry-fried
干炒牛河	〈饮食〉Stir-Fried Rice Noodles with Beef
干葱豆豉鸡煲	〈饮食〉Stewed Chicken in Scallion and Black Bean Sauce
干豆角回锅肉	〈饮食〉Stir-Fried Spicy Pork with Dried Beans
干锅茶树菇	〈饮食〉Griddle Cooked Tea Tree Mushrooms
干锅黄牛肉	〈饮食〉Griddle Cooked Beef with Wild Mushrooms
干锅鸡	〈饮食〉Stir-Fried Chicken with Pepper in Iron Wok
干锅鸡胗	〈饮食〉Stir-Fried Chicken Gizzards in Iron Wok

干锅排骨鸡	〈饮食〉Griddle Cooked Spare Ribs and Chicken
干锅笋片	〈饮食〉Griddle Cooked Bamboo Shoots
干锅台菇	〈饮食〉Griddle Cooked Mushrooms
干红葡萄酒	dry red wine
干煎带鱼	〈饮食〉Dry-Fried Ribbonfish with Shredded Onion and Ginger
干煎金钱鱼	〈饮食〉Dry-Fried Scatophagus Argus with Tomato Sauce (Shaped as a Coin)
干姜	〈中医药〉(of Latin) Rhizoma Zingiberis; Zingiber; Dried Ginger
干豇豆炖猪蹄	〈饮食〉Braised Pig Trotters with Dried Cowpeas
干椒牛肉饭	〈饮食〉Rice with Beef and Dried Chili
干烤鸡块	〈饮食〉Dry-Braised Chicken
干咳	〈防疫〉dry cough
干烹子鸡	〈饮食〉Fried Spring Chicken with Chive and Sesame Sauce
干烧草鱼	〈饮食〉Dry-Braised Grass Carp with Chili Sauce
干烧大虾	〈饮食〉Dry-Braised Prawn with Ham and Asparagus
干烧冬笋	〈饮食〉Dry-Fried Bamboo Shoots; Pungent Winter Bamboo Shoots
干烧鳜鱼	〈饮食〉Dry-Braised Mandarin Fish with Chili Sauce
干烧鸡	〈饮食〉Dry-Braised Chicken with Chili Sauce
干烧明虾	〈饮食〉Dry-Braised Prawns with Pepper Sauce
干烧牛肉	〈饮食〉Sichuan Dry-Braised Shredded Beef
干烧虾球	〈饮食〉Dry-Braised Prawn Meat; Fried Prawn Meat with Chili Sauce
干烧虾仁	〈饮食〉Dry-Fried Shelled Shrimp with Chili Sauce
干烧鸭丝	〈饮食〉Dry-Fried Duck Shreds; Dry-Fried Shredded Duck
干烧伊面	〈饮食〉Teriyaki Noodles; Braised Yifu Noodles
干洗领班	dry-clean captain
干羊肉野山菌	〈饮食〉Stir-Fried Dried Lamb with Wild Truffles

干炸鸽块	〈饮食〉Dry-Fried Pigeon Pieces with Sweet Paste and Parsley
干炸虾卷	〈饮食〉Deep-Fried Shrimp Rolls with Parsley
干炸虾枣	〈饮食〉Deep-Fried Shrimps (in Date Shape)
干炸羊肉	〈饮食〉Dry-Fried Lamb Breasts with Parsley
干炸鱼条	〈饮食〉Dry-Fried Fish Slices with Eggs
干炸鹧鸪	〈饮食〉Dry-Fried Partridge with Parsley
甘草	〈中医药〉(of Latin) Radix Glycyrrhizae; Liquorice Root
甘丹刀	〈币〉Gandan knife (issued in the Warring States period)
甘居下游	to be resigned to backwardness
甘露消毒丹	〈中医药〉Ganlu Xiaodu Dan; Sweet Dew Toxin-Dispersing/ Dispersing Elixir
甘麦大枣汤	〈中医药〉Ganmai Dazao Tang; Licorice, Wheat, and Jujube Decoction
甘松	〈中医药〉(of Latin) Radix et Rhizoma Nardostachyos; Nardostachys Root
甘遂	〈中医药〉(of Latin) Radix Euphorbiae Kansui; Gansui Root
甘温除热	〈中医药〉to eliminate heat with warmth and sweetness; to relieve fever with sweet and warm-natured drugs →治未病
肝必复软胶囊	〈中医药〉Ganbifu Ruan Jiaonang; Liver-Recovering Soft Capsule
肝胆辨证	〈中医药〉pattern differentiation of liver and gallbladder
肝胆湿热	〈中医药〉dampness-heat of liver and gallbladder; liver-gallbladder dampness-heat
肝胆湿热证	〈中医药〉pattern of dampness-heat of liver and gallbladder
肝胆实火	〈中医药〉excessive fire of liver-gallbladder
肝胆实热	〈中医药〉excessive heat of liver-gallbladder

肝风内动	〈中医药〉up-stirring of the liver; liver wind agitation; internal stirring of the liver wind
肝风内动证	〈中医药〉pattern of liver wind stirring up internally
肝火炽盛证	〈中医药〉pattern of liver fire flaring up
肝火燔耳证	〈中医药〉pattern of liver fire invading the ear
肝火犯肺	〈中医药〉invasion of lung by liver fire
肝火犯肺证	〈中医药〉pattern of liver fire invading the lung
肝火上炎	〈中医药〉up-flammation of liver fire
肝火上炎证	〈中医药〉pattern of liver fire flaming upward
肝经风热	〈中医药〉wind-heat of liver channel; liver channel wind-heat
肝经湿热	〈中医药〉dampness-heat of liver channel; liver channel dampness-heat
肝经湿热证	〈中医药〉pattern of liver channel dampness-heat
肝经郁热	〈中医药〉stagnated heat of liver channel
肝气犯脾	〈中医药〉invasion of spleen by liver-qi
肝气犯胃	〈中医药〉invasion of stomach by liver-qi
肝气横逆	〈中医药〉transverse dysfunction/invasion of liver-qi
肝气上逆	〈中医药〉upward invasion of liver-qi; upward adverse flow of liver-qi
肝气虚	〈中医药〉deficiency of liver-qi; liver-qi deficiency
肝气虚证	〈中医药〉pattern of liver-qi deficiency/vacuity
肝气郁结	〈中医药〉stagnation of liver-qi; liver-qi depression
肝气郁结证	〈中医药〉pattern of liver-qi stagnation/depression
肝肾精血不足	〈中医药〉insufficiency of essence and blood in the liver and kidney
肝肾同源	〈中医药〉homogeny of the liver and kidney
肝肾阴虚	〈中医药〉yin deficiency of the liver and kidney; liver-kidney yin deficiency
肝肾阴虚证	〈中医药〉pattern of liver-kidney yin deficiency/vacuity
肝俞	〈中医药〉Ganshu acupoint; Liver Transport (BL18)
肝泰舒胶囊	〈中医药〉Gantaishu Jiaonang; Liver Calmness Comfortability Capsule

肝旺脾虚	〈中医药〉hyperfunction of the liver and weakness of the spleen
肝胃不和	〈中医药〉liver-stomach disharmony; disharmony between liver and stomach
肝胃不和证	〈中医药〉pattern of incoordination between the liver and stomach
肝血虚	〈中医药〉deficiency of liver-blood; liver-blood deficiency
肝血虚证	〈中医药〉pattern of liver-blood deficiency/vacuity
肝阳化风	〈中医药〉hyperactive liver-yang transformed into wind
肝阳化风证	〈中医药〉pattern of liver yang hyperactivity transformed into wind
肝阳上亢	〈中医药〉liver-yang hyperactivity; hyperactivity of liver-yang
肝阳上亢证	〈中医药〉pattern of ascendant hyperactivity of liver yang
肝阳虚	〈中医药〉deficiency of liver yang; liver yang deficiency
肝阳虚证	〈中医药〉liver-yang vacuity pattern; pattern of liver-yang deficiency
肝胰扒海参	〈饮食〉Braised Sea Cucumbers with Pork Liver and Pancreas
肝阴不足	〈中医药〉insufficiency of liver-yin
肝阴虚	〈中医药〉liver-yin deficiency; deficiency of liver-yin
肝阴虚阳亢证	〈中医药〉pattern of liver-yin deficiency and liver-yang hyperactivity
肝阴虚证	〈中医药〉pattern of liver-yin deficiency/vacuity
肝郁脾虚	〈中医药〉stagnation of liver-qi and spleen deficiency; liver depression and spleen deficiency
肝郁脾虚证	〈中医药〉pattern of liver-qi stagnation and spleen deficiency/vacuity

肝郁血虚证	〈中医药〉pattern of liver-qi stagnation and blood deficiency/vacuity
肝郁血瘀证	〈中医药〉pattern of liver-qi stagnation and blood stasis
肝主筋	〈中医药〉liver governing tendon; liver controlling sinews
肝主升发	〈中医药〉liver governing ascending and dredging; liver governing ascent and effusion
肝主疏泄	〈中医药〉liver controlling conveyance and dispersion
赶超先进	to surpass the advanced
赶时髦	to follow the fashion; to want to be in the swim of things
感冒咳嗽颗粒	〈中医药〉Ganmao Kesou Keli; Common Cold Coughing Granule
感冒清热颗粒	〈中医药〉Ganmao Qingre Keli; Common Cold and Heat-Clearing Granule
感冒止咳颗粒	〈中医药〉Ganmao Zhike Keli; Common Cold and Cough-Suppressing Granule
感冒止咳糖浆	〈中医药〉Ganmao Zhike Tangjiang; Common Cold and Cough-Stopping Syrup
感情投资	emotional investment; investment in human relationships; investment in affection
感染	〈防疫〉to be infected with…
感染病例	〈防疫〉case of infection
感染控制	〈防疫〉infection control
感染控制和流行病学专业人员协会	〈防疫〉Association for Professionals in Infection Control and Epidemiology; APICE
感染性休克	〈防疫〉septic shock
感受寒邪	〈中医药〉to be attacked by pathogenic cold
橄榄瓶	〈陶瓷〉olive-shaped vase
橄仁斑雀片	〈饮食〉Stir-Fried Sliced Sparrow with Olive Kernel
擀面杖	rolling pin; rod for flour food making

肛泰	〈中医药〉Gangtai; Anti-Hemorrhoid Plaster
岗位津贴	post allowance
岗位培训	on-the-job training
岗位责任制	work post responsibility
港币	Hong Kong currency; Hong Kong dollar
杠糟鸡	〈饮食〉Braised Chicken in Red Rice Wine Paste
高保真音乐	hi-fi music
高材生	top student
高传染度毒株	〈防疫〉highly transmissible strain
高传染性新型变异毒株	〈防疫〉highly infectious variant of the new coronavirus
高大上	high-end, magnificent and classy; high-end atmospheric grade
高档中国酒	high-end Chinese liquor; high-end Chinese alcoholic drinks
高等教育贷款	higher education loan
高等教育自学考试	self-study higher education examination
高等师范学校	higher normal school
高顶卷檐毡帽	〈柯尔克孜族〉felt hat with high top and rolled eave
高度重视公共利益	〈防疫〉serious concern for the public good
高端产品	high-end product
高发期	high-incidence season
高分低能	high scores and low abilities; high in score but low in ability
高风险地区	〈防疫〉high-risk region
高富帅	tall, rich and handsome male
高硅质[硅酸质]釉	〈陶瓷〉siliceous glaze
高级法律专家	senior legal expert
高级服务员	senior service staff; senior waiter
高级工程师	senior engineer
高级工艺美术师	senior craft artist
高级顾问	senior consultant; senior adviser
高级管理人员	senior executive

高级国际商务师	senior foreign trader
高级会计师	senior accountant
高级建筑工程师	senior architect
高级教练	senior coach
高级经济师	senior economist
高级经理人员	high-level managerial personnel; senior personnel
高级客房销售经理	senior housekeeping sales manager
高级客户经理	senior customer/account manager
高级美术指导	senior art director
高级秘书	senior secretary
高级农业师	senior agronomist
高级软件工程师	senior software engineer
高级商务师	certified business executive; senior business engineer; high-level economist
高级实习指导教师	senior internship instructor
高级实验师	senior experimentalist
高级兽医师	senior veterinarian
高级统计师	senior statistician
高级物业顾问	senior property advisor
高级销售代表	senior sales representative
高级畜牧师	senior livestock specialist
高级宴会销售经理	senior banquet sales manager
高级业务跟单员	senior merchandiser
高级硬件工程师	senior hardware engineer
高级招标师	senior tenderer
高级职称	senior professional title
高级质量检测工程师	senior quality testing engineer
高级主管	senior supervisor
高技术产业化	to apply high technology to production
高髻	(of hairstyle) high bun; updos
高精尖技术	high-grade, high-precision and advanced technology
高考	Gaokao; National College Entrance Exam; NCEE
高考分数	Gaokao score

高考改革	Gaokao reform
高考经济	Gaokao economy
高考移民	NCEE migrant (referring to students who covertly leave their hometowns and immigrate to other places before the NCEE in order to get bonus points or be in a less competitive environment)
高考制度	College Entrance Examination system; Gaokao system
高考专列	Gaokao charter train
高考状元	Gaokao champion; Gaokao top scorer
高科技板块	high-tech sector
高丽参	〈中医药〉(of Latin) Panax ginseng; Korean Ginseng Root
高良姜	〈中医药〉(of Latin) Rhizoma Alpiniae Offininarum; Lesser Galangal Rhizome
高岭土［石］	〈陶瓷〉kaolin/kaoline; ceramic clay
高岭土化	kaolinization
高铝瓷	〈陶瓷〉high-alumina porcelain
高清晰度电视	high definition TV
高山冠	〈服饰〉alpine crown →通天冠
高手	master hand; past master
高速铁路	high speed railway; high speed train
高汤炖官燕	〈饮食〉Stewed Bird's Nest in Chicken Stock
高汤鸡丝面	〈饮食〉Noodle Soup with Shredded Chicken; Noodles with Shredded Chicken in Soup
高汤鸡丝生翅	〈饮食〉Shark's Fin Soup with Shredded Chicken
高汤水饺	〈饮食〉Jiaozi in Soup; Dumplings in Soup
高汤榨菜肉丝面	〈饮食〉Noodle Soup with Shredded Pork and Preserved Vegetables
高铁	Gaotie; G-series high-speed train →高速铁路
高筒毡靴	high felt boots
高危人群	〈防疫〉high-risk group
高温曲	〈酒〉high temperature brick shaped raw starter
高温陶瓷	〈陶瓷〉high temperature ceramics; refractory china

高温釉	〈陶瓷〉hard glaze; high-melting glaze
高消费	high consumption
高校毕业生就业指导	career/employment guidance for university and college graduates
高校扩招	university enrollment expansion →大学(生)扩招
高校扩招计划	college expansion plan
高效节能	energy-efficient
高新技术产业化	industrial application of new and high technologies
高腰裙	high-waist skirt
高腰襦裙	〈古〉high-waist ru skirt (in the Sui and Tang Dynasties)
高知	high-level intellectual
高质量教育体系	high-quality education system
高致病性禽流感	〈防疫〉highly pathogenic avian influenza (HPAI)
高椎髻	〈古〉(of hairstyle) high-conical bun
羔皮袍	lambskin robe
羔裘服	lambskin coat
膏蟹肉炒饭	〈饮食〉Stir-Fried Rice with Crab Meat
膏药	〈中医药〉medicinal paste; plaster; ointment
搞花架子	to do sth. superficial
缟	〈服饰〉plain white fabric
藁本	〈中医药〉(of Latin) Rhizoma Ligustici; Chinese Lovage
告刁状	to secretly report on sb.; to rat on sb.
告小状	to secretly report on sb.; to rat on sb. →打小报告
锆质瓷	〈陶瓷〉zircon porcelain; zirconia chinaware
疙瘩汤	〈饮食〉Dough Drop Soup with Assorted Vegetable
哥窑	〈陶瓷〉Ge Kiln (one of the five famous kilns in the Song Dynasty)
哥窑贯耳瓶	〈陶瓷〉Ge Kiln vase with two tubular lug-handles
哥窑花浇	〈陶瓷〉Ge Kiln flower watering jug (Ming Chenghua period)
哥窑盘	〈陶瓷〉Ge Kiln plate (Ming Chenghua period)

哥窑青瓷贯耳八方瓶	〈陶瓷〉Ge Kiln octagonal celadon vase with two tubular lug-handles
哥窑青瓷轮花盘	〈陶瓷〉Ge Kiln celadon plate with floral pattern
鸽蛋焖野鸭	〈饮食〉Braised Wild Duck and Pigeon Eggs
歌舞杂技画像砖	brick with portrait of musician, dancer and acrobat
革命老区	old revolutionary base areas
革命气派	revolutionary mettle
革命伤残军人	disabled revolutionary servicemen
《格致余论》	〈中医药〉*Gezhi Yulun*; *Treatise on Inquiring the Properties of Things*; *Further Discourses on the Properties of Things* (by Zhu Zhenheng in the Yuan Dynasty)
蛤蚧	〈中医药〉(of Latin) Gekko Gecko; Gecko
蛤蚧定喘丸	〈中医药〉Gejie Dingchuan Wan; Asthma-Relieving Bolus of Gecko
蛤壳	〈中医药〉(of Latin) Concha Meretricis seu Cyclinae; Clam Shell
蛤蜊汤	〈饮食〉Clam Soup; Clam Chowder
蛤蜊蒸蛋	〈饮食〉Steamed Eggs with Clams
隔空诊疗	〈防疫〉online diagnosis and treatment
隔离	〈防疫〉quarantine
隔离病房	〈防疫〉isolation ward
隔离条例	〈防疫〉quarantine regulations
隔离医院	〈防疫〉isolation hospital
隔离政策	〈防疫〉quarantine policies
隔离治疗	〈防疫〉to receive treatment in isolation
隔离自娱	〈防疫〉quarantine and chill
隔物灸	〈中医药〉indirect moxibustion; sandwiched moxibustion
膈关	〈中医药〉Geguan acupoint; Diaphragm Pass (BL46)
膈俞	〈中医药〉Geshu acupoint; Diaphragm Transport (BL17)

葛布	ko-hemp cloth
葛根	〈中医药〉(of Latin) Radix Puerariae; Kudzuvine Root
葛根芩连汤	〈中医药〉Gegen Qinlian Tang; Pueraria, Scutellaria, and Coptis Decoction
葛根素注射液	〈中医药〉Gegensu Zhusheye; Puerarin Injection
葛根汤	〈中医药〉Gegen Tang; Pueraria Decoction
个人储蓄账户	personal savings account
个人防护设备	〈防疫〉personal protective equipment
个人购房贷款	individual housing loan
个人结算账户	personal clearing account
个人理财计划	personal financing plan
个人所得税	personal income tax
个人信用制度	individual credit rating system
个人演唱会	solo concert
个人质押贷款	personal pledged loan
个税申报	declaration of individual incomes for tax payment
个体经济	private economy
各大菜系	〈饮食〉major styles of cooking
各尽所能	to let each person do his best; from each according to his ability
各色釉彩大瓷瓶	〈陶瓷〉large vase with multi-colored glaze
给…穿小鞋	to secretly make things difficult/hard for sb.; to deliberately put sb. to trouble; to make it hot for sb.
给…开红灯	to give a stop light to
给…开小灶	to give special favor to
给…扣帽子	to put a label on sb./sth.; to put an unwanted/unfavorable label on sb./sth.
给力	gelivable (awesome or amazing); to give power
给面子	to give face; to show respect
给排水工程师	water supply and drainage engineer
根除腐败	to root out corruption; to eliminate corruption
跟团旅游	package tour; group travel

跟着感觉走	to go with the flow; to follow one's heart; to do what one thinks is right
更年安胶囊	〈中医药〉Gengnian'an Jiaonang; Menopause Calmness Capsule
更年安片	〈中医药〉Gengnian'an Pian; Climacteric-Syndrome-Relieving Tablet; Menopause-Quieting Tablet
更年期权利	menopause rights
梗叶连枝	〈茶〉whole flush
工厂安防工程师	plant security engineer
工程部	engineering department
工程顾问	engineering consultant
工程绘图员	project draftsman
工程技术员	engineering technician
工程监理	engineering project supervisor
工程造价师	budgeting specialist; project estimator
工程主管	engineering supervisor
工程总监	chief engineer; engineering director
工[功]夫茶	congou; kung fu tea (a Chinese black tea prepared with care)
工会主席	chairman of trade union; labor union chairman
工龄工资	seniority pay
工商管理硕士	master of business administration; MBA
工薪阶层	salaried person; salaried group
工业陶瓷	〈陶瓷〉industrial ceramics
工艺工程师	process engineer
工艺花茶	artistic scented tea
工艺美术师	craft artist; industrial artist
工艺品设计师	handicraft designer
工艺设计工程师	process design engineer
工艺设计主管	process design supervisor
工艺陶瓷	〈陶瓷〉porcelain for artistic; art and craft ceramics
工资福利管理员	payroll and benefits administrator
工资管理员	payroll administrator

工资结算员	payroll clerk
工资税	payroll tax
工资削减	pay-cut
工资正常增长机制	a mechanism for regular pay increases
工作安置专员	job placement officer
工作创新奖	innovation award; prize for the creative working
工作狂	workaholic
工作午餐	working lunch
公安分局	public security sub-bureau
公车私用	misuse of government cars
公丁香	〈中医药〉(of Latin) Flos Caryophyllata; Lilac Flower; Clove
公房商品化	commercialization of public housing
公费旅游	junket; facility trip; to travel at public expenses
公费医疗	socialized medicine; free medical care/treatment
公共汽车候车亭	bus shelter
公共卫生设施	public health infrastructure
公共文化基础设施	culture-related facilities for public use
公关部	public relation department
公关部经理	public relation manager
公关部主任	public relation supervisor
公关代表	public relation representative
公交老人专车	senior-only bus
公开或变相涨价	to raise prices openly or in disguised forms
公筷	serving chopsticks; extra picking chopsticks
公筷公勺	〈防疫〉serving chopsticks and spoons
公款吃喝	recreational activities using public funds; banquet at public expenses
公路工程师	highway engineer
公路造价师	highway cost estimator
公平定价	arm's length pricing
公平合理	fairness and justifiableness
公平竞争	fair competition
公勺	serving spoon

公卫领班	public area captain
公卫主管	public area supervisor
公务员	public functionary; civil servant
公务员考试	civil service exam; civil servant's exam
公务员录用考试	examination for admission to the civil service; civil service recruitment examination
公务员热	civil servant fever; civil servant frenzy
公休	work recess
公益广告	public-interest ad
公益活动	public benefit activities; charity activity
公益性文化事业	non-profit cultural undertakings
公证财产	to notarize the properties
公证员	notary; greffier; notary public
功法训练	〈中医药〉exercise for practicing tuina
功夫茶	→工[功]夫茶
功夫电影	kung fu movie
功夫红茶	kungfu black tea; unshredded black tea
功夫明星	kung fu star
功劳木	〈中医药〉(of Latin) Caulis Mahoniae; Chinese Mahonia Stem
功劳叶	〈中医药〉(of Latin) Folium Ilex; Chinese Mahonia Leaf
攻补兼施	〈中医药〉to treat with both elimination and reinforcement; tonification and purgation in combination; reinforcement and elimination in combination
攻下法	〈中医药〉purgation method; offensive precipitation
攻下冷积	〈中医药〉to treat coagulated cold by purgation; to dispel cold accumulations by yang-warming drugs
供应链经理	supply chain manager
供应链主管	supply chain supervisor
供应链专员	supply chain specialist

宫保大虾	〈饮食〉Kung Pao Prawns; Sautéed Prawns with Hot Pepper
宫保大虾肉	〈饮食〉Kung Pao Prawn Meat; Sautéed Prawn Meat
宫保豆腐	〈饮食〉Kun Pao Tofu; Quick-Fried Dry Tofu with Chili Sauce
宫保凤尾虾	〈饮食〉Kung Pao Fantail Shrimp; Sautéed Phoenix Tail Prawns
宫保鸡丁	〈饮食〉Kung Pao Diced Chicken; Quick-Fried Diced Chicken with Chili Sauce and Peanuts
宫保鲜带子	〈饮食〉Kung Pao Fresh Scallops; Quick-Fried Scallops in Chilli Sauce
宫爆肉丁	〈饮食〉Stir-Fried Diced Pork with Chili Sauce and Peanuts
宫爆腰花	〈饮食〉Stir-Fried Kidney with Chili and Peanuts
宫瘤宁胶囊	〈中医药〉Gongliuning Jiaonang; Hysteromyoma-Quieting Capsule
宫瘤清胶囊	〈中医药〉Gongliuqing Jiaonang; Uterine Masses Eliminating Capsule
宫扇	court fan; mandarin fan →团扇, 纨扇
宫血宁胶囊	〈中医药〉Gongxuening Jiaonang; Uterine Blood Calmness Capsule
恭喜发财	may you be prosperous; wish you prosperity; (of Cantonese) kung hei fat choy
共同安全	common security
共同富裕	common prosperity; common wealth; shared prosperity
共同利益	common interests
共屯赤金	〈币〉coin with characters gongtun chijin (issued in the Warring States period)
共享车辆	shared vehiclc
共享单车	bicycle sharing; bike sharing; shared bike
共享单车行业	bike-sharing industry
共享空间	shared space

共享汽车	car-sharing; shared car
共享移动服务	to share mobility service
共享治理	shared governance
共享自行车服务	bike-sharing service
共享自行车市场	bike-sharing market
贡菊花	〈中医药〉(of Latin) Chrysanthemum Morifolium Anhuiensis; Anhui Chrysanthemum Flower
贡眉茶	Kung Mee White tea
贡丸汤	〈饮食〉Pork Meat Ball Soup
勾芡	〈饮食〉dressing with starchy sauce
沟通能力	communicational ability
钩藤	〈中医药〉(of Latin) Ramulus Uncariae cum Uncis; Gambir Plant
狗不理包子	〈饮食〉Goubuli Baozi; Goubuli Steamed Stuffed Bun; Go Believe (a famous brand of baozi from Tianjin)
狗脊	〈中医药〉(of Latin) Rhizoma Cibotii; Cibot Rhizome
狗浇尿油饼	〈饮食〉Goujiaoniao Fried Dough Cake (a special wheaten food in Qinghai)
狗皮膏	〈中医药〉Goupi Gao; Dog Skin Plaster
狗腿子	hired thug; lackey; henchman
狗仔队	dog packs; paparazzi (journalists who are hunting the news of celebrities)
枸杞百合西芹	〈饮食〉Stir-Fried Celery and Lily Bulbs with Chinese Wolfberries
枸杞炒肉丝	〈饮食〉Stir-Fried Shredded Pork with Wolfberry
枸杞炖蛤	〈饮食〉Stewed Clam with Chinese Wolfberries
枸杞酒	Chinese wolfberry wine
枸杞凉瓜	〈饮食〉Bitter Gourd with Chinese Wolfberries
枸杞浓汁烩凤筋	〈饮食〉Stewed Chicken Tendons with Chinese Wolfberries
枸杞蒸裙边	〈饮食〉Steamed Turtle Rim in Chinese Wolfberry Soup

枸杞子	〈中医药〉(of Latin) Fructus Lycii; Barbary Wolfberry Fruit
构筑群防群治的严密防线	〈防疫〉to build stringent lines of defense across society
购房承受能力	housing affordability; affordability of house purchase
购买力	purchasing power
购买欲	desire to buy; desire to purchase
购物车	shopping trolley
咕噜鸡	〈饮食〉Sweet and Sour Chicken
咕噜肉	〈饮食〉Gulurou; Stir Fried Pork with Sweet and Sour Sauce
咕噜石斑球	〈饮食〉Sweet and Sour Garoupa Balls
古瓷	〈陶瓷〉ancient porcelain
《古今医统大全》	〈中医药〉Gujin Yitong Daquan; Complete Compendium of Medical Works, Ancient and Modern; Medical Complete Book, Ancient and Modern (by Xu Chunfu in the Ming Dynasty)
古井贡酒	Gujinggong liquor
古良方廿四味润嗓含片	〈中医药〉Guliangfang Niansiwei Runsang Hanpian; Voice-Moistening Sucking Tablet of Twenty Four Ingredients
古陶	〈陶瓷〉ancient pottery
古丈毛尖	〈茶〉Guzhang Maojian tea; Guzhang Tippy tea
谷氨酸钠综合征	〈中医药〉monosodium glutamate symptom complex
谷精草	〈中医药〉(of Latin) Flos Eriocauli; Pipewort Flower
谷芽	〈中医药〉(of Latin) Fructus Setariae Germinatus; Rice-Grain Sprout; Millet Sprout
股票操盘手	stock operator
股票经纪人	stock broker
股长	subsection chief
骨瓷	〈陶瓷〉bone china; fine bone china
骨刺丸	〈中医药〉Guci Wan; Bone Spur Pill

骨刺消痛胶囊	〈中医药〉Guci Xiaotong Jiaonang; Bone-Hyperplasia Pain-Stopping Capsule
骨雕	〈工艺〉bone sculpture; bone carving
骨度折量定位法	〈中医药〉location of points by bone standard; proportional bone measurement
骨筋丸胶囊	〈中医药〉Gujinwan Jiaonang; Capsule for Bones and Sinews
骨碎补	〈中医药〉(of Latin) Rhizoma Drynariae; Fortune's Drynaria Rhizome; Drynaria Root
骨头汤	〈饮食〉Bone Broth; Bone Soup
骨簪	bone hairpin
骨质增生理疗贴	〈中医药〉Guzhi Zengsheng Liliao Tie; Osteohyperplasia Plaster
骨质增生丸	〈中医药〉Guzhi Zengsheng Wan; Hyperosteogeny Pill
鼓励奖	consolation prize
固本咳喘胶囊	〈中医药〉Guben Kechuan Jiaonang; Root-Securing Cough and Panting Capsule
固本益肠片	〈中医药〉Guben Yichang Pian; Root-Securing Intestine-Boosting Tablet
固崩止带剂	〈中医药〉formula for arresting leucorrhea and metrorrhagoia; menorrhagia-leukorrhea stanching prescription
固表止汗	〈中医药〉to secure the exterior to check sweating; to consolidate exterior/superficies for arresting sweating
固表止汗剂	〈中医药〉formula for consolidating superficies and arresting sweating; exterior-strengthening and sweat-reducing prescription
固冲汤	〈中医药〉Guchong Tang; Thoroughfare-Securing Decoction
固冲止带	〈中医药〉to secure the thoroughfare vessel and stanch vaginal discharge; to consolidate Chong Vessel for stopping leucorrhea

固定资产会计	fixed asset accountant
固经丸	〈中医药〉Gujing Wan; Menses-Securing Pill
固经止血	〈中医药〉to consolidate channel for hemostasis; to regulate menstruation to stanch bleeding
固脬止遗	〈中医药〉to strengthen bladder to stop retention failure; to secure the bladder for stopping enuresis
固涩法	〈中医药〉securing and astringing method; astringing method
固涩剂	〈中医药〉astringent prescription; astrigent formula; securing and astringent formula
故障分析工程师	failure analysis engineer
顾渚紫茶	Guzhu Purple Bud tea
瓜蒂散	〈中医药〉Guadi San; Melon Stalk Powder; Muskmelon Pedicel Powder
瓜蒌	〈中医药〉(of Latin) Fructus Trichosanthis; Snakegourd Fruit
瓜蒌壳	〈中医药〉(of Latin) Pericarpium Trichosanthis; Snakegourd Peel
瓜蒌子	〈中医药〉(of Latin) Semen Trichosanthis; Snakegourd Seed
瓜皮绿釉	〈陶瓷〉cucumber green glaze
瓜皮帽	skullcap; melon-shaped hat (resembling the rind of half a watermelon)
刮鼻子	to criticize someone; to reprimand someone; to punish sb. (usually in card games)
刮法	〈中医药〉needle-handle scraping
刮刮卡	(of lottery ticket) scratch card; scratch ticket pattern
刮痧	guasha; holographic meridian scraping therapy; a popular treatment for sunstroke by scraping the patient's neck, chest or back
刮痧疗法	〈中医药〉guasha treatment; scraping therapy; Asian bodywork therapy
挂靠户	an adjunct organization

挂炉烧鸡腿	〈饮食〉Barbecued Chicken Drumsticks
挂面	〈饮食〉Packaged Noodles; Fine Dried Noodles
挂职下放	to transfer to lower units with one's post retained
褂子	guazi; Chinese style unlined jacket
拐点	〈防疫〉turning point
拐卖妇女儿童	women and children trafficking
怪味海参	〈饮食〉Special Flavored Sea Cucumbers
怪味鸡丝	〈饮食〉Special Flavored Shredded Chicken
怪味牛腱	〈饮食〉Special Flavored Beef Shanks
怪味猪手	〈饮食〉Special Flavored Pig Trotters; Braised Spicy Pig Trotters
关闭景点	〈防疫〉to close scenic spot
关闭室内娱乐场所	〈防疫〉to shut down indoor entertainment venues
关冲	〈中医药〉Guanchong acupoint; Pass Flush (TE1)
关金(券)	〈币〉Guanjin Voucher (issued by the Kuomintang Central Bank) →海关金单位兑换券
关门	〈中医药〉Guanmen acupoint; Pass Gate (ST22)
关木通	〈中医药〉(of Latin) Caulis Aristolochiae Manshuriensis; Manchurian Aristolochia Stem
关山云雾	〈茶〉Guanshan Cloud and Mist tea
关系户	closely-related unit; relative family; well-connected individual/group
关系网	network of informal ties; relationship network; closely-knitted guild
关元俞	〈中医药〉Guanyuanshu acupoint; Origin Pass Transport (BL26)
关子	〈币〉→现钱关子
观察室	〈防疫〉observation ward
观潮派	those who take a wait-and-see attitude
观光电梯	sightseeing (tourist) lift
观望派	those who take a wait-and-see attitude
观望态度	wait-and-see attitude/approach
观音堂	→普济禅院
纶巾	〈服饰〉black silk ribbon scarf; silk head dress resembling ridged roof (worn by men in ancient time)

官瓷	〈陶瓷〉official porcelain; mandarin porcelain (in the late Northern Song Dynasty)
官二代	second powerful generation; the second generation of leadership; the officiallings
官方吉祥物	official mascot
官方微博	official microblog
官方微信	official Wechat
官服	〈古〉robe; official costume
官服玉带	〈古〉robe's jade belt
官帽	〈古〉mandarin hat; official hat
官袍	〈旧〉official robe; mandarine robe
官窑	〈陶瓷〉Official Kiln; Imperial Kiln (one of the five famous kilns in the Song Dynasty)
官窑双耳炉	〈陶瓷〉Guan Kiln two-eared incense burner
官窑双耳双环弦纹瓶	〈陶瓷〉Guan Kiln vase with double ear-rings and string pattern (Yuan Dynasty)
官窑弦纹瓷瓶	〈陶瓷〉Guan Kiln porcelain vase with string pattern
官衣	〈服饰〉guanyi; officer dress; dress wore by officers
官庄毛尖	Guanzhuang Maojian tea; Guanzhuang Tippy tea
冠弁	〈服饰〉guanbian (symbolizing coming-of-age); generic term for ancient top hats
冠帽	guan hat
冠心静片	〈中医药〉Guanxinjing Pian; Coronary Heart Quietness Tablet
冠心苏合丸	〈中医药〉Guanxin Suhe Wan; Coronary Storax Pill; Storax Pill for Treating Coronary Heart Disease
冠状病毒	〈防疫〉coronavirus
冠状病毒病人	〈防疫〉coronavirus patient
冠状病毒工作组	〈防疫〉coronavirus study group; CSG
管家部调度员	housekeeping scheduler
管家部文员	housekeeping administrative assistant
管家部主管	housekeeping supervisor

管控区	〈防疫〉control zone
管理会计	management accountant
管理会计师证书	management accounting certificate
管理式保健计划	managed health care program
管理员	(of a library) librarian; (of an institution) administrator
管针进针法	〈中医药〉tube insertion; insertion of needle with tube
灌肠疗法	〈中医药〉enema therapy
灌汤蒸饺	〈饮食〉Steamed Dumplings with Gravy
罐焖大虾	〈饮食〉Braised Prawns in Pot; Pot-Braised Prawns
罐焖鸡	〈饮食〉Braised Chicken in Pot; Pot-Braised Chicken
罐焖牛肉	〈饮食〉Stewed Beef in Casserole
罐焖鸭	〈饮食〉Braised Duck in Pot; Pot-Braised Duck
罐焖鸭丝鱼翅	〈饮食〉Stewed Shredded Duck with Shark's Fins in Casserole
罐焖羊肉	〈饮食〉Braised Mutton in Pot; Pot-Braised Mutton
光瓷	〈陶瓷〉lusterware; luster porcelain
光棍	single male; bachelor
光棍节	Singles' Day (on the 11th November)
光通讯	optical communication; photo-communication
光绪通宝	〈古币〉coin with characters guangxu tongbao (issued in the Qing Dynasty)
光泽釉	〈陶瓷〉bright glaze; glossy glaze
广播节目总监	radio program director
广播制作人	broadcast producer
广场舞	square dance
广场砖	plaza stone; paving tile
广瓷	〈陶瓷〉Canton ware; Canton porcelain
广东菜	〈饮食〉Guangdong Cuisine →粤菜
广东文昌鸡	〈饮食〉Wenchang Sliced Chicken with Chicken Livers and Ham
广泛普及疫情防控知识	〈防疫〉to disseminate information on epidemic prevention and control

广防己	〈中医药〉(of Latin) Radix Aristolochiae Fangchi; Southern Fangchi Root
广告创意经理	advertising creative manager
广告创意主管	advertising creative supervisor
广告客户经理	advertising account manager
广告客户主管	advertising account supervisor
广告客户专员	advertising account specialist
广告客户总监	advertising account director
广告设计经理	advertising design manager
广告设计主管	advertising design supervisor
广告协调员	advertising coordinator
广告撰稿人	advertising copywriter
广藿香	〈中医药〉(of Latin) Herba Pogostemonis; Cablin Patchouli Herb
广金钱草	〈中医药〉(of Latin) Herba Desmodii; Snowbellleaf Tickclover Herb
广[泥]钧釉	〈陶瓷〉Guang Jun glaze
广绫	(of silk) Canton crepe
广绒	Canton flannel
广行派	〈佛〉tradition of vast conduct
广窑	〈陶瓷〉Guang Kiln (in the Song Dynasty); Kwangtung ware
广釉	〈陶瓷〉Canton enamel
广州白云国际机场	Guangzhou Baiyun International Airport
广州红双喜	Red Double Happiness cigarettes (Guangzhou)
归国留学生	returned students
归经	〈中医药〉meridian entry; channel tropism; meridian tropism
归脾汤	〈中医药〉Guipi Tang; Spleen-Restoring Decoction
归脾丸	〈中医药〉Guipi Wan; Spleen-Nourishing Pill
归侨	returned overseas Chinese
归芍调经片	〈中医药〉Guishao Tiaojing Pian; Tangkuei Peony Menstruation-Adjusting Tablet
归真髻	(of hairstyle) guizhen bun →双刀髻

龟板	〈中医药〉(of Latin) Plastrum Testudinis; Tortoise Plastron
龟甲胶	〈中医药〉(of Latin) Colla Carapax et Plastrum Testudinis; Tortoise Plastron Glue
龟龄集胶囊	〈中医药〉Guilingji Jiaonang; Turtle Aging Capsule; Longevity Capsule
龟龄集酒	Guilingji Medicinal Wine
龟鹿补肾丸	〈中医药〉Guilu Bushen Wan; Turtle Deer Kidney-Tonifying Pill
龟鹿二仙胶	〈中医药〉Guilu Erxian Jiao; Tortoise Shell and Deerhorn Two Immortals Glue
龟鹿酒	Guilu Jiu; Tortoise-Deer Medicinal Wine
龟茸酒	Guirong Jiu; Tortoise and Pilose Antler Medicinal Wine
龟山岩绿	〈茶〉Turtle Mountain Rock Green tea
规范民办教育	to standardize non-government funded schools
规范信息发布机制	〈防疫〉to standardize the information release mechanism
硅酸质釉	→高硅质[硅酸质]釉
袿衣	〈古〉guiyi; noble gown; lady's fine dress
轨道工程师	railway engineer
轨道技术员	railway technician
簋	〈旧〉kuei (deep circular vessel with two or four handles, used as a container for grain)
柜台接待人员	front desk receptionist
贵宾体验专员	member engagement specialist
贵定云雾茶	Guiding Cloud and Mist tea
贵妃鸡	〈饮食〉Imperial Concubine Chicken; Chicken Wings and Drumsticks with Brown Sauce
贵州醇	Guizhou mellow liquor
贵州茅台	Kweichow Moutai; Moutai liquor
桂东玲珑茶	Guidong Linglong Green tea
桂附地黄丸	〈中医药〉Guifu Dihuang Wan; Cinnamon and Aconite Rehmannia Pill

桂附理中丸	〈中医药〉Guifu Lizhong Wan; Cinnamon and Aconite Center-Rectifying Pill
桂花茶	osmanthus tea; sweet-scented osmanthus tea
桂花炒干贝	〈饮食〉Stir-Fried Dried Scallops with Osmanthus Sauce
桂花炒肉蟹	〈饮食〉Stir-Fried Crab with Osmanthus Sauce
桂花炒鱼翅	〈饮食〉Stir-Fried Shark's Fins with Crab Meat and Bean Sprouts
桂花炒珍宝蟹	〈饮食〉Stir-Fried Jumbo Crab with Osmanthus Sauce
桂花酒	osmanthus wine
桂花酒酿圆子	〈饮食〉Glutinous Rice Balls in Osmanthus-Flavored Rice Wine
桂花糯米藕	〈饮食〉Steamed Lotus Root Stuffed with Glutinous Rice
桂花山药	〈饮食〉Chinese Yam with Osmanthus Sauce
桂花乌龙	〈茶〉osmanthus Oolong
桂花雪鱼羹	〈饮食〉Codfish Soup with Osmanthus Sauce
桂花鱼翅	〈饮食〉Shark's Fins with Pak Choi (in the shape of fragrans)
桂林毛尖	〈茶〉Guilin Maojian tea; Guilin Tippy tea
桂皮	〈中医药〉(of Latin) Cortex Cinnamomi; Cassia Bark; Chinese Cinnamon
桂皮油	〈中医药〉(of Latin) Oleum Cinnamomi; Chinese Cinnamon Oil
桂平西山茶	Guiping Xishan tea
桂圆肉	〈中医药〉(of Latin) Arillus Longanae; Longan Meat
桂圆童子鸡	〈饮食〉Steamed Spring Chicken with Lungans
桂枝	〈中医药〉(of Latin) Ramulus Cinnamomi; Cassia Twig
桂枝茯苓胶囊	〈中医药〉Guizhi Fuling Jiaonang; Cinnamom Twig and Poria Capsule
桂枝茯苓丸	〈中医药〉Guizhi Fuling Wan; Cinnamon Twig and Poria Pill

桂枝汤	〈中医药〉Guizhi Tang; Cinnamon Twig Decoction
衮冕	〈服饰〉gunmian; robe painted with dragon and coronet (for emperors and superior officials in sacrificial ceremonies)
辊道窑	〈陶瓷〉roller kiln; roller hearth kiln
滚雪球	snowball; (of a plan, problem, etc.) to grow bigger on an increasing rate
棍棒教育	stick parenting (education in the form of beating and scolding the educatee)
锅巴鲍鱼	〈饮食〉Abalone Sauce on Deep-Fried Rice Cake
锅巴海三鲜	〈饮食〉Sizzling Assorted Seafood with Crispy Rice
锅巴海参	〈饮食〉Sea Cucumbers in Crisp Rice; Crisp Rice with Sea Cucumbers
锅巴口蘑汤	〈饮食〉Mushroom Soup with Fried Rice Crust
锅巴虾仁	〈饮食〉Stir-Fried Shelled Shrimps with Crispy Fried Rice Crust
锅烧鸭子	〈饮食〉Steamed and Fried Boneless Duck with Scallions, Sweet Sauce and Pepper Salt
锅烧羊肉	〈饮食〉Braised Mutton with Sweet Paste and Chive
锅烧肘子	〈饮食〉Braised Pork Knuckles in Casserole
锅烧肘子配饼	〈饮食〉Deep-Fried Pork Hocks Served with Pancake
锅塌豆腐	〈饮食〉Tofu Omelet; Fried Tofu with Egg Wrapping
锅贴	〈饮食〉Guotie; Pan-Fried Dumpling; Pot Sticker
锅仔潮菜银鳕鱼	〈饮食〉Stewed Codfish with Salted Vegetables in Chaozhou Style
锅仔潮式凉瓜猪肚	〈饮食〉Stewed Pork Tripe with Bitter Melon in Chaozhou Style
锅仔鸡汤菌	〈饮食〉Stewed Mushrooms in Chicken Soup
锅仔辣汁煮牛筋丸	〈饮食〉Stewed Beef Balls with Chili Sauce in Casserole

锅仔萝卜焖牛腩	〈饮食〉Stewed Beef Brisket with Radish in Casserole
锅仔木瓜浸鱼片	〈饮食〉Braised Sliced Fish with Papaya
锅仔泡椒煮鲈鱼	〈饮食〉Stewed Perch with Marinated Chili
锅仔雪菜鲈鱼	〈饮食〉Stewed Perch with Preserved Vegetable
锅仔药膳乌鸡	〈饮食〉Stewed Black-Boned Chicken with Chinese Herbs
国博	→中国国家博物馆
国产化率	import substitution rate; localization rate of parts and components
国公酒	〈中医药〉Guogong Jiu; Statesman Wine; guogong medical wine
国画家	traditional Chinese painter
国际病毒分类委员会	〈防疫〉International Committee on Taxonomy of Viruses; ICTV
国际电子商务师	certified international e-commerce specialist; CIECS
国际电子商务师职业资格认证	certification of international e-commerce specialist
国际关注的突发公共卫生事件	〈防疫〉public health emergency of international concern; PHEIC
国际漫游流量资费	overseas roaming flow rates
国际贸易单证员证书	certificate of international commercial document clerk
国际商务律师	international business lawyer
国际商务师	foreign trader; international business operator
国际商务谈判师	certificated international professional negotiator
国际卫生条例	〈防疫〉International Health Regulations; IHR
国际物流师	certified international logistics specialist
国际消费者权益日	International Day for Consumers' Rights and Interests; World Consumer Rights Day
国际销售员	international salesperson
国家5A旅游景点	national 5A tourist attraction
国家电网公司	State Grid Corporation of China

国家冬季运动管理中心	National Winter Sports Management Center; China's Winter Sports Administrative Center
国家公共卫生应急管理体系	〈防疫〉national public health emergency management system
国家会议中心	China National Convention Center; CNCC (Beijing)
国家基因库	China National Genebank; CNGB
国家级教练	national-level coach
国家级特殊津贴	special state allowance
国家级卫生城市	state-level hygiene city
国家奖学金	national scholarship
国家京剧院	National Peking Opera Company (Beijing)
国家励志奖学金	national encouragement scholarship
国家普通话水平考试	National Proficiency Test of Putonghua
国家市场监管总局	〈防疫〉State Administration for Market Regulation; SAMR
国家司法考试	national judicial examination
国家外汇储备	state foreign exchange reserves
国家外汇管理局	State Administration of Foreign Exchange; SAFE
国家卫生健康委员会	〈防疫〉National Health Commission; NHC
国家行政编制	government staff status
国家烟草专卖局	State Tobacco Monopoly Bureau
国家药品监督管理局	〈防疫〉National Medical Products Administration; NMPA
国家一级保护	first-grade State protection
国家一级演员	national first-level performer; national class-A actor/actress
国家医疗保障局	〈防疫〉National Healthcare Security Administration; NHSA
国家艺术基金	China National Arts Fund
国家中医药管理局	National Administration of Traditional Chinese Medicine; NATCM
国家助学金	national tuition assistance
国脚	player of the national football team

国窖 1573	〈酒〉Guo Jiao 1573
国库券	treasury bonds
国民生产总值	gross national product; GNP
国民素质	populace's cultivation; national quality
国内生产总值	gross domestic product; GDP
国内游	inbound tourism
国企下岗职工津贴	allowances for workers laid off from state-owned enterprises
国情	national conditions
国庆假期	National Day holiday
国外旅游	overseas travel
国务院联防联控机制	〈防疫〉Joint Prevention and Control Mechanism of the State Council
国有资产流失	loss of state-owned assets
果茶山药	〈饮食〉Chinese Yam with Nectar
果酒	fruit wine
果仁炒鸡丁	〈饮食〉Stir-Fried Diced Chicken with Fruit Kernels
果仁生汁脆皮虾球	〈饮食〉Stir-Fried Prawn Meat with Fruit Kernels and Special Sauce
果香	〈茶〉fruity flavor; aroma
果子狸	〈防疫〉masked palm civet
馃子	→油条
裹足	→缠[裹]足
过渡期	transitional period
过劳死	karoshi; death from overwork
过滤嘴香烟	filter-tipped cigarette
过桥米线	〈饮食〉Cross Bridge Rice Noodles

H

哈达	〈藏族〉khata; hada (a long piece of white silk used as a greeting gift among the Zang and Mongol people)
哈德门香烟	Hatamen cigarettes; Hade Gate cigarettes
蛤蟆油	〈中医药〉(of Latin) Oviductus Ranae; Forest Frog's Oviduct
孩儿脸［美人醉］釉	〈陶瓷〉strawberry red glaze; beauty's flush glaze
海带酥鸡	〈饮食〉Braised Crisp Chicken and Seaweed
海风藤	〈中医药〉(of Latin) Caulis Piperis Kadsurae; Kadsura Pepper Stem
海狗肾	〈中医药〉(of Latin) Callorhini seu Phocae Testis et Penis; Ursine Seals Penis and Testes
海关金单位兑换券	〈币〉Customs Gold Unit Voucher (issued by the Kuomintang Central Bank) →关金(券)
海归	returned overseas Chinese; overseas returnee
海蛤粉	〈中医药〉(of Latin) Amylum Concha Meretricis Seu Cyclinae; Clamshell Power
海皇炒饭	〈饮食〉Stir-Fried Rice with Seafood
海龙	〈中医药〉(of Latin) Syngnathus; Sea Dragon; Pipe-Fish
海马	〈中医药〉(of Latin) Hippocampus; Sea Horse
海鳗鸡骨汤	〈饮食〉Conger Eel and Chicken Soup
海米白菜心	〈饮食〉Stir-Fried Choy Sum with Dried Shrimp
海米珍珠笋	〈饮食〉Fried Pearl-Shaped Bamboo Shoots with Dried Shrimp

海南文昌鸡	〈饮食〉Hainan Steamed Chicken with Coconut Sauce
海茸墨鱼花	〈饮食〉Stir-Fried Diced Cuttlefish and Seaweed
海参鹅掌煲	〈饮食〉Braised Goose Webs with Sea Cucumbers in Casserole
海参过油肉	〈饮食〉Light-Fried Pork with Sea Cucumber
海参扣鹅掌	〈饮食〉Braised Goose Webs with Sea Cucumbers
海参釉	〈陶瓷〉trepang glaze
海棠冬菇	〈饮食〉Braised Dried Mushrooms with Begonia
海棠红釉	〈陶瓷〉begonia red glaze
海淘	cross-border online shopping
海天虾饺皇	〈饮食〉Steamed Jiaozi Stuffed with Shrimp and Fungi
海外华人	ethnic Chinese overseas; overseas Chinese
海味扒鱼翅	〈饮食〉Braised Shark's Fins with Seafood
海虾云吞面	〈饮食〉Noodle Soup with Fresh Shrimp Wonton
海峡两岸关系协会	Association for Relations Across the Taiwan Strait; ARATS
海峡论坛	Straits Forum
海鲜炒面	〈饮食〉Stir-Fried Noodles with Seafood
海鲜春卷	〈饮食〉Seafood Spring Rolls; Spring Rolls Stuffed with Seafood
海鲜脆皮豆腐	〈饮食〉Fried Tofu with Seafood
海鲜大煲翅	〈饮食〉Braised Shark's Fins and Seafood in Casserole
海鲜豆腐	〈饮食〉Braised Tofu with Seafood
海鲜粉丝煲	〈饮食〉Assorted Seafood with Vermicelli in Casserole
海鲜锅饼	〈饮食〉Pan-Fried Pancake with Seafood Stuffing
海鲜馄饨	〈饮食〉Seafood Wonton; Wonton Stuffed with Seafood
海鲜砂锅煲	〈饮食〉Stewed Seafood in Pottery/Clay Pot
海鲜市场	〈防疫〉seafood market
海鲜蔬菜炒面	〈饮食〉Stir-Fried Noodles with Seafood and Vegetables

海鲜汤饺	〈饮食〉Jiaozi Stuffed with Seafood in Soup
海鲜汤面	〈饮食〉Noodle Soup with Seafood; Noodles with Seafood in Soup
海鲜汁扒大虾	〈饮食〉Grilled Prawns with Seafood Sauce
《海药本草》	〈中医药〉*Haiyao Bencao*; *Oversea Materia Medica*; *Herbal Foundation of Overseas Medicines* (by Li Xun in Qianshu of Five Dynasties)
含酒精洗手液	〈防疫〉alcohol-based hand rub/sanitizer
含氯消毒液	〈防疫〉chlorinated disinfectant; chlorine antiseptic
函授大学	correspondence university; correspondence college
函授教育	correspondence education
寒极生热	〈中医药〉heat generation by extreme cold; extreme cold engendering heat
寒凉药物	〈中医药〉(of Latin) cold-natured herbs; herbs of cold and cool nature
寒凝胞宫证	〈中医药〉pattern of cold congealing in the uterus
寒热错杂	〈中医药〉intermingled cold and heat; cold-heat complex
寒热错杂证	〈中医药〉cold-heat complex pattern; pattern of intermingled cold and heat
寒热起伏	〈中医药〉alternative fever and chill
寒热如疟	〈中医药〉malaria-like fever and chill; chill and fever similar to malaria
寒热往来	〈中医药〉alternate attacks/spells of chill and fever
寒热真假	〈中医药〉true-false of cold and heat
寒湿困脾	〈中医药〉impediment of the spleen by cold-dampness; spleen disorder due to cold and dampness
寒湿困脾证	〈中医药〉pattern of cold-damp encumbering the spleen
寒湿证	〈中医药〉cold-dampness pattern

寒湿阻络证	〈中医药〉pattern of cold-dampness blocking the collaterals/the network vessels
寒痰证	〈中医药〉cold-phlegm pattern
寒痰阻肺证	〈中医药〉pattern of cold-phlegm obstructing the lung
寒下剂	〈中医药〉cold cathartic formula; cold purgative formula; cold purgation prescription
寒邪犯胃证	〈中医药〉pattern of cold pathogen attacking the stomach
寒邪郁而化热	〈中医药〉stagnation of pathogenic cold transformed into heat
寒易伤阳	〈中医药〉cold pathogen prone to attack yang; cold tending to injure yang
寒饮停肺证	〈中医药〉pattern of cold fluid stagnating in the lung; pattern of cold rheum retained in the lung
寒滞肝脉证	〈中医药〉pattern of cold accumulated in liver channels
寒滞经脉证	〈中医药〉pattern of cold accumulated in channels
汉代刺绣	embroidery of the Han Dynasty; Han embroidery
汉服	Han clothing; Han costume; traditional clothes of Han nationality
汉家刘氏茶	Han Family Liu's tea
汉水银梭	〈茶〉Han Silver Shuttle Green tea
汉语沉浸式课程	Chinese immersion course
汉语课程	Chinese language course; Chinese course
汉语拼图	Chinese puzzle
汉语四字成语	Chinese four-character idiom
汉语文化圈	Chinese-speaking community
汉字处理软件	Chinese character processing software
旱莲草	〈中医药〉(of Latin) Herba Ecliptae; Eclipta
行长	(of a bank) president; bank president
杭椒炒牛柳	〈饮食〉Stir-Fried Beef Fillets with Hot Green Pepper
杭椒牛柳饭	〈饮食〉Rice with Beef Fillet and Hot Green Pepper

杭椒虾爆鳝	〈饮食〉Stir-Fried Shrimps and Eel with Hot Green Pepper
杭菊花	〈中医药〉(of Latin) Chrysanthemum Morifolium Hangzhouensis; Hangzhou Chrysanthemum Flower
航班机长	airplane captain; captain of the flight
航班熔断	〈防疫〉circuit breaker
航海工程师	marine engineer
航空工程师	aerospace engineer; aeronautical engineer
蒿芩清胆汤	〈中医药〉Haoqin Qingdan Tang; Sweet Wormwood and Scutellaria Gallbladder-Clearing Decoction
薅草酒	〈土家族〉weeding wine
蚝豉炆冬菇	〈饮食〉Stewed Dried Mushrooms with Dried Oysters
蚝皇鲍鱼	〈饮食〉Braised Abalone in Oyster Sauce
蚝皇滑牛肉	〈饮食〉Stir-Fried Sliced Beef with Oyster Sauce
蚝皇扣干鲍	〈饮食〉Braised Dried Abalone in Oyster Sauce
蚝皇鲜竹卷	〈饮食〉Steamed Tofu Sheet Rolls with Oyster Sauce
蚝黄煎银鳕鱼	〈饮食〉Pan-Fried Codfish in Oyster Sauce
蚝油北菇[冬菇]	〈饮食〉Oyster Sauce Mushrooms; Stir-Fried Mushrooms with Oyster Sauce
蚝油叉烧包	〈饮食〉Baozi Stuffed with Barbecued Pork and Oyster Sauce
蚝油炒鸭片	〈饮食〉Stir-Fried Duck Slices with Oyster Sauce
蚝油炒鸭掌	〈饮食〉Stir-Fried Duck Webs with Oyster Sauce
蚝油滑鸡片	〈饮食〉Stir-Fried Sliced Chicken with Oyster Sauce
蚝油烩牛肉	〈饮食〉Braised Beef in Oyster Sauce
蚝油芥蓝	〈饮食〉Stir-Fried Chinese Broccoli with Oyster Sauce
蚝油焖鲍鱼	〈饮食〉Stewed Abalone Slices with Oyster Sauce
蚝油焖鸡	〈饮食〉Stewed Chicken with Oyster Sauce
蚝油焖鱼唇	〈饮食〉Braised Fish Lips with Oyster Oil

蚝油扒芥菜	〈饮食〉Braised Leaf Mustard with Oyster Sauce
蚝油扒时蔬	〈饮食〉Braised Seasonal Vegetables in Oyster Sauce
蚝油扒鸭掌	〈饮食〉Stewed Duck Webs with Oyster Sauce
蚝油扒鱼唇	〈饮食〉Braised Fish Lips with Oyster Sauce
蚝油茄子	〈饮食〉Stir-Fried Eggplant with Oyster Sauce
蚝油肉柳	〈饮食〉Stir-Fried Pork Slices with Oyster Sauce
蚝油生菜	〈饮食〉Stir-Fried Lettuce with Oyster Sauce
蚝油小鲍鱼	〈饮食〉Stir-Fried Awabi with Oyster Sauce
蚝汁鲍鱼片	〈饮食〉Stir-Fried Abalone Slices with Oyster Sauce
蚝汁海参扣鸭掌	〈饮食〉Braised Sea Cucumbers with Duck Webs in Oyster Sauce
毫尖	〈茶〉golden pekoe
毫香	〈茶〉pekoe flavor
毫心肥壮	〈茶〉fat bud
毫针	〈中医药〉filiform needle
毫针刺法	〈中医药〉technique of filiform needle acupuncture
好久不见	(of greeting) long time no see
号脉	〈中医药〉to feel the pulse →切脉
诃子	〈中医药〉(of Latin) Fructus Chebulae; Medicine Terminalia Fruit
合谷	〈中医药〉Hegu acupoint; Union Valleys; Connected Valleys (LI4)
合规专员	compliance officer
合欢花	〈中医药〉(of Latin) Flos Albiziae; Silk Tree Flower
合欢花酒	albizia flower wine
合欢皮	〈中医药〉(of Latin) Cortex Albiziae; Silk Tree Bark
合理引导消费	to guide rational consumption
合同管理员	contract administrator
合同医院	contract clinic; assigned hospital (where people from a given organization or area go for treatment)
合阳	〈中医药〉Heyang acupoint; Confluence of Yang (BL55)

合作医疗站	cooperative medical station
何首乌	〈中医药〉(of Latin) Radix Polygoni Multiflori; Fleece Flower Root
和剂局	〈古〉Welfare Pharmacy; Bureau for Compounding (in the Song Dynasty)
和解表里	〈中医药〉to harmonize and release the exterior and interior; to reconcile exterior/superficies and interior
和解少阳剂	〈中医药〉shaoyang reconciling formula; formula for harmonizing the lesser yang
和气生财	harmony brings wealth; cheek brings success
和天下香烟	Hetianxia cigarettes; Harmonization cigarettes
和胃降逆	〈中医药〉to harmonize the stomach for descending adverse qi; to regulate the stomach for lowering adverse qi
和胃燥湿剂	〈中医药〉stomach-harmonizing dampness-eliminating formula
河道整治	river regulation; dredging waterway
河南烩面	〈饮食〉Henan Braised Noodles
荷包蛋	〈饮食〉Poached Eggs
荷包豆腐干	〈饮食〉Dried Bean Curd Wrapped in Lotus Leaves
荷包栗子鸡	〈饮食〉Steamed Chicken Stuffed with Chestnut Kernels
荷包燕窝白鸽	〈饮食〉Steamed Pigeon Stuffed with Bird's Nest
荷兰豆炒鸽片	〈饮食〉Stir-Fried Pigeon Slices with Holland Bean
荷塘百花藕	〈饮食〉Braised Sliced Lotus Roots
荷塘焖什菌	〈饮食〉Stewed Assorted Mushrooms with Lotus Roots
荷叶	〈中医药〉(of Latin) Folium Nelumbinis; Lotus Leaf
荷叶饼	〈饮食〉Lotus-Leaf-Shaped Pancake
荷叶帽	lotus-leaf-like hat
荷叶米粉蒸肉	〈饮食〉Steamed Pork Dices with Ground Glutinous Rice Wrapped in Lotus Leaves
荷叶蒸鸡	〈饮食〉Steamed Chicken in Lotus Leaf Packets; Steamed Chicken Wrapped in Lotus Leaves

核能工程师	nuclear engineer
核酸检测	〈防疫〉nucleic acid testing; NAT
核桃炒鸡花	〈饮食〉Stir-Fried Chicken Oblique Slices with Walnut Kernels
核桃鸽蛋	〈饮食〉Frittered Stuffed Pigeon Eggs with Walnut Kernels
核桃鸡卷	〈饮食〉Braised Stuffed Chicken Rolls with Walnut Kernels
核桃鸡脯	〈饮食〉Stir-Fried Chicken Breast with Walnut Kernels
核桃酪	〈饮食〉Walnut Kernel Cream; Sweet Walnut Paste
核桃仁	〈中医药〉(of Latin) Semen Juglandis; Walnut Seed
核桃仁炒鸡丁	〈饮食〉Stir-Fried Diced Chicken with Walnut Kernels →鸡丁核桃仁
核桃肉煲牛肉汤	〈饮食〉Beef Soup with Walnut Kernels
核心家庭	nuclear family; core family
核心竞争力	core competitiveness
盉	〈酒〉he; bronze jug-shaped utensil with three or four legs (for warming wine)
盒饭	box lunch; Chinese take-away; packed meal
贺岁片	New Year's film/movie; New Year celebration
褐黑	〈茶〉auburnish black
褐红	〈茶〉auburnish red
褐黄	〈茶〉auburnish yellow
褐衣	〈服饰〉coarse cloth; coarse clothing; homespun cloth
褐釉瓜棱瓷罐	〈陶瓷〉brown-glazed porcelain jar in melon ribbing shape
褐釉刻花瓷瓶	〈陶瓷〉brown-glazed porcelain vase with carved flowers
褐子	〈服饰〉hezi; handwoven coarse cloth (out of twisted wool threads by nomads in northern China)
鹤顶	〈中医药〉Heding acupoint; Crane Top (EX-LE2)
鹤年贡酒	Heniangong health wine

鹤虱	〈中医药〉(of Latin) Fructus Carpesii; Common Carpesium Fruit
黑帮	mafia gang; sinister gang; reactionary gang
黑茶	dark tea
黑车	black taxi (which carries passengers illegally and without a business license); unlicensed taxi
黑瓷	〈陶瓷〉black porcelain
黑店	gangster inn; an inn run by brigands; tourist trap
黑豆煲鱼头汤	〈饮食〉Fish Head Soup with Black Beans
黑褐	〈茶〉black auburn
黑户	unregistered citizen; people without hukou
黑花四系白瓷瓶	〈陶瓷〉white porcelain vase with four ears and black floral pattern
黑椒炒甲鱼	〈饮食〉Stir-Fried Turtle with Black Pepper Sauce
黑椒焗猪手	〈饮食〉Baked Pig Trotters with Black Pepper
黑椒焖鸭胗	〈饮食〉Braised Duck Gizzards with Black Pepper
黑椒牛炒肋骨	〈饮食〉Stir/Pan-Fried Beef Ribs with Black Pepper
黑椒牛柳粒	〈饮食〉Stir-Fried Diced Beef Fillets with Black Pepper
黑椒牛柳条	〈饮食〉Stir-Fried Beef Fillets with Black Pepper
黑椒牛仔骨	〈饮食〉Stir-Fried Beef Ribs with Black Pepper
黑椒鳝球	〈饮食〉Stir-Fried Eel with Black Pepper
黑椒鲜贝	〈饮食〉Stir-Fried Scallops with Black Pepper Sauce
黑椒猪肉饭	〈饮食〉Rice with Pork and Black Pepper
黑米小窝头	〈饮食〉Wotou with Black Rice; Steamed Black Rice Bun
黑啤酒	black beer; bock beer
黑陶(器)	〈陶瓷〉basalt; black pottery
黑心棉	"black heart" cotton; shoddy cotton
黑釉斑点纹瓷拍鼓	〈陶瓷〉black glazed drum with mottled decoration
黑釉彩斑执壶	〈陶瓷〉black-glazed ewer with painted spot
黑釉鸡头瓷壶	〈陶瓷〉black-glazed porcelain pot with rooster-head spout
黑釉树叶纹碗	〈陶瓷〉black-glazed bowl with leaf design/pattern

黑釉四系盘口壶	〈陶瓷〉black-glazed pot with dish-like mouth and four loop handles
黑釉提梁水注	〈陶瓷〉black-glazed water dropper with swing handle
黑芝麻	〈中医药〉(of Latin) Semen Sesami Nigri; Black Sesame
烘干	〈中医药〉drying by baking
弘治青花缠枝莲双兽耳瓶	〈陶瓷〉blue and white vase with twined lotuses pattern and two animal-shaped ears (Ming Hongzhi period)
红茶	black tea
红椿	〈中医药〉(of Latin) Toona Ciliata; Red Cedar
红大戟	〈中医药〉(of Latin) Radix Knoxiae; Knoxia Root
红地开光粉彩山水碗	〈陶瓷〉red glazed bowl with panelled famille rose landscape (Qing Qianlong period)
红豆糕	〈饮食〉Red Bean Cake; Red Bean Pudding
红豆蔻	〈中医药〉(of Latin) Fructus Alpiniae Galangae; Galanga Galangal Fruit
红豆沙圆子	〈饮食〉Glutinous Rice Balls Stuffed with Red Bean Paste
红豆椰汁糕	〈饮食〉Red Bean and Coconut Pulp Cake
红炖海参	〈饮食〉Stewed Sea Cucumbers in Brown Sauce
红炖芥菜	〈饮食〉Stewed Leaf Mustard with Brown Sauce
红炖鹿筋	〈饮食〉Red-Stewed Deer Sinew with Sliced Ham, Mushroom and Magnolia
红炖全参	〈饮食〉Stewed Whole Sea Cucumbers in Brown Sauce
红炖鱼翅	〈饮食〉Stewed Shark's Fins with Soy Sauce
红炖鱼唇	〈饮食〉Stewed Fish Lips in Casserole with Brown Sauce
红炖紫鲍	〈饮食〉Braised Abalone Garnished in Brown Sauce
红盖头	(of wedding) bridal veil; red veil (used to cover the bride's head)
红果山药	〈饮食〉Chinese Yam with Hawthorn

红河香烟	Honghe cigarettes; Red River cigarettes
红褐	〈茶〉reddish auburn
红花	〈中医药〉(of Latin) Flos Carthami; Safflower
红花汁烩海鲜	〈饮食〉Braised Seafood in Saffron Sauce
红花注射液	〈中医药〉Honghua Zhusheye; Carthamus Injection
红黄	〈茶〉reddish yellow
红烩虎皮鸽蛋	〈饮食〉Stewed Boiled and Fried Pigeon Eggs in Brown Sauce
红胶官燕	〈饮食〉Braised Bird's Nest and Seaweed
红金龙香烟	Hong Jinglong cigarettes; Red Golden Dragon cigarettes
红景天	〈中医药〉(of Latin) Herba Rhodiolae; Rhodiola Rosea; Rose-boot
红酒鹌鹑	〈饮食〉Braised Quail in Port Wine
红酒烩鸽脯	〈饮食〉Braised Pigeon Breast in Red Wine
红酒烩牛尾	〈饮食〉Braised Oxtail with Red Wine
红酒烤竹鸡	〈饮食〉Braised Bamboo Partridge in Port Wine
红蓝混合釉	〈陶瓷〉red and blue mixed glaze
红绿彩寿山福海人物纹高足杯	〈陶瓷〉red and green stem cup with long-life-wish and figural depiction pattern (Yuan Dynasty)
红玫瑰葡萄酒	Red Rose Grape wine
红梅香烟	Hongmei cigarettes; Red Plum cigarettes
红焖蝴蝶骨	〈饮食〉Braised Spare Ribs in Brown Sauce
红焖花菇	〈饮食〉Braised Shiitake Mushrooms in Brown Sauce
红焖鸡腰	〈饮食〉Braised Chicken Kidney in Brown Sauce
红焖鹿肉	〈饮食〉Braised Venison with Brown Sauce
红焖牛腩	〈饮食〉Braised Beef Brisket with Soy Sauce
红焖牛肉	〈饮食〉Braised Sliced Beef with Soy Sauce
红焖牛蹄筋	〈饮食〉Braised Beef Tendon with Soy Sauce
红焖牛尾	〈饮食〉Braised Oxtail with Soy Sauce
红焖牛杂	〈饮食〉Braised Beef Offal with Soy Sauce
红焖田鸡腿	〈饮食〉Braised Frog Legs with Brown Sauce

红焖虾球	〈饮食〉Braised Jumbo Shrimps in Brown Sauce
红焖羊排	〈饮食〉Braised Lamb Chops with Carrots and Soy Sauce
红焖羊肉	〈饮食〉Stewed Lamb with Brown Sauce
红焖肘子	〈饮食〉Stewed Pig Hocks in Brown Sauce
红焖珠瓜	〈饮食〉Braised Bitter Gourd and Dried Shrimp with Brown Sauce
红扒鸡	〈饮食〉Braised Chicken in Brown Sauce
红扒鱼翅	〈饮食〉Braised Shark's Fins with Brown Sauce
红扒肘子	〈饮食〉Braised Pork Hocks in Brown Sauce
红排虎皮肘子	〈饮食〉Steamed Pork Hocks in Chive Oil
红芪	〈中医药〉(of Latin) Radix Hedysari; Manyinflorescenced Sweetvetch Root
红旗单位	red-banner unit; advanced unit; advanced (model) establishment
红旗渠香烟	Hongqi Qu cigarettes; Red Flag Canal cigarettes
红曲鸭膀	〈饮食〉Braised Duck Wings with Red Yeast
红色旅游	red tourism; revolutionary tourism
红烧	〈饮食〉stewed with soy sauce; braised in/with brown sauce
红烧白灵菇	〈饮食〉Braised Mushrooms with Vegetables in Brown Sauce
红烧鲍片	〈饮食〉Braised Abalone Slices in Brown Sauce
红烧鲍鱼	〈饮食〉Braised Abalone in Brown Sauce
红烧长江鲥鱼	〈饮食〉Braised Hilsa Herring with Brown Sauce
红烧大虾	〈饮食〉Braised Prawns in Soy Sauce
红烧带鱼	〈饮食〉Braised Hairtail with Brown Sauce
红烧豆腐	〈饮食〉Braised Tofu/Bean Curd in Brown Sauce
红烧鳜鱼	〈饮食〉Braised Mandarin Fish with Soy Sauce
红烧海参	〈饮食〉Braised Sea Cucumbers in Brown Sauce
红烧河鳗	〈饮食〉Braised River Eel with Soy Sauce
红烧鸡块	〈饮食〉Braised Chicken Chips in Brown Sauce
红烧鸡丝翅	〈饮食〉Braised Shark's Fins and Shredded Chicken with Brown Sauce

红烧甲鱼	〈饮食〉Braised Turtle in Brown Sauce
红烧鲤鱼	〈饮食〉Braised Carp with Brown Sauce
红烧鲤鱼头	〈饮食〉Braised Carp Head with Soy Sauce
红烧鲈鱼	〈饮食〉Braised Perch with Brown Sauce
红烧鹿茸血燕	〈饮食〉Red-Braised Bird's Nest with Deer Antler
红烧鹿肉	〈饮食〉Braised Venison with Brown Sauce
红烧鹿尾巴	〈饮食〉Braised Deer's Tail with Brown Sauce
红烧马鞍鳝	〈饮食〉Braised Finless Eel and Pork
红烧鳗鱼	〈饮食〉Braised Sea Eel with Soy Sauce
红烧毛芋头	〈饮食〉Braised Taro in Brown Sauce
红烧南非鲍	〈饮食〉Braised South African Abalone in Brown Sauce
红烧牛腩米粉	〈饮食〉Rice Noodles with Braised Beef Brisket
红烧牛腩汤面	〈饮食〉Noodle Soup with Braised Beef Brisket
红烧牛肉	〈饮食〉Stewed Beef with Brown Sauce
红烧牛肉饭	〈饮食〉Rice with Stewed Beef
红烧牛舌	〈饮食〉Stewed Ox Tongue with Brown Sauce
红烧牛蹄筋	〈饮食〉Stewed Beef Tendons with Brown Sauce
红烧排骨	〈饮食〉Braised Pork Ribs in Brown Sauce
红烧排骨汤面	〈饮食〉Noodle Soup with Red-Braised Spare Ribs
红烧青鱼	〈饮食〉Braised Black Carp with Soy Sauce
红烧全鸭	〈饮食〉Braised Whole Duck in Brown Sauce
红烧日本豆腐	〈饮食〉Braised Japanese Tofu with Vegetables in Brown Sauce
红烧肉	〈饮食〉Braised Pork in Soy Sauce; Braised Pork in Soy Sauce
红烧狮子头	〈饮食〉Stewed Pork Ball in Brown Sauce
红烧石斑鱼	〈饮食〉Braised Garoupa with Brown Sauce
红烧石岐项鸽	〈饮食〉Braised Young Pigeon with Brown Sauce
红烧蹄筋	〈饮食〉Braised Pork Tendons in Soy Sauce
红烧鲜鲍	〈饮食〉Braised Fresh Abalone in Brown Sauce
红烧小黄鱼豆腐	〈饮食〉Braised Small Yellow Croakers and Tofu in Brown Sauce
红烧羊蹄	〈饮食〉Braised Goat Knuckles with Brown Sauce

红烧鱼	〈饮食〉Braised Fish with Soy Sauce
红烧鱼唇	〈饮食〉Braised Fish Lips with Brown Sauce
红烧鱼肚	〈饮食〉Braised Fish Maws with Soy Sauce
红烧肘子	〈饮食〉Braised Pork Knuckles in Brown Sauce
红参	〈中医药〉(of Latin) Radix Ginseng Rubra; Red Ginseng
红参须	〈中医药〉(of Latin) Radix Ginseng Rubra Whiskers; Red Ginseng Tails
红薯金饼	〈饮食〉Fried Sweet Potato Cake
红双喜	(of brand) Double Happiness (a kind of cigarette); red double happiness
红碎茶	broken black tea
红塔山香烟	Hongta Shan cigarettes; Red Pagoda Mountain cigarettes
红汤圆子	〈饮食〉Pork Balls in Tomato Soup
红陶土	〈陶瓷〉red clay; terracotta
红外体温测量仪	〈防疫〉infrared thermometer
红心鸭卷	〈饮食〉Duck Meat Rolls with Duck Yolk
红星二锅头	〈酒〉Red Star Erguotou
红鲟米糕	〈饮食〉Steamed Red Sturgeon with Glutinous Rice
红艳	〈茶〉red brilliant
红腰带	red waistband; red belt
红缨帽	〈古〉red tasseled cap; cap with red tassel (worn by officials in the Qing Dynasty)
红油抄手	〈饮食〉Wonton Soup in Hot and Spicy Sauce
红油肚丝	〈饮食〉Shredded Tripe in Chilli Sauce
红油鸡丁	〈饮食〉Boiled Diced Chicken with Chili Soil
红油牛百叶	〈饮食〉Boiled Beef Tripe with Chili Oil
红油牛筋	〈饮食〉Boiled Beef Tendons with Chili Oil
红油牛头	〈饮食〉Beef Head Meat with Hot Chili Oil
红油水饺	〈饮食〉Boiled Dumplings with Chili Oil
红油虾片	〈饮食〉Boiled Prawn Slices with Chili Oil
红油鸭丁	〈饮食〉Boiled Diced Duck with Chili Oil

红油鸭掌	〈饮食〉	Boiled Duck Webs with Chili Oil
红油鱼肚	〈饮食〉	Boiled Fish Maws with Chili Oil
红油猪肚丝	〈饮食〉	Boiled Shredded Pork Tripe with Chili Oil
红釉	〈陶瓷〉	red glaze
红釉画缸	〈陶瓷〉	red glaze printed vat (Ming Xuande period)
红釉莲瓣瓷洗	〈陶瓷〉	red-glazed writing-brush washer in the shape of lotus petal
红釉僧帽壶	〈陶瓷〉	red glaze pot in the shape of monk's cap (Ming Yongle period)
红糟鸭片	〈饮食〉	Braised Duck Slices with Wine Sauce
红枣甑糕	〈饮食〉	Glutinous Rice with Jujube
红枣蒸南瓜	〈饮食〉	Steamed Pumpkin with Chinese Dates
红柱石	〈陶瓷〉	andalusite; feldspath apyre
宏图鸭	〈饮食〉	Steamed Duck Slices with Sliced Ham, Winter Bamboo Shoots and Mushrooms in Soup (Combination Style)
虹彩釉	〈陶瓷〉	luster glaze
洪武通宝	〈币〉	coin with characters hongwu tongbao (issued in the Ming Dynasty)
鸿运蒸凤爪	〈饮食〉	Steamed Chicken Paws
《喉科指掌》	〈中医药〉	Houke Zhizhang; Guide Book for Laryngology (by Zhang Zongliang in the Qing Dynasty)
喉痛消炎丸	〈中医药〉	Houtong Xiaoyan Pian; Throat Pain Inflammation-Reducing Pill
猴头菇炖竹丝鸡	〈饮食〉	Stewed Chicken with Monkey-Head Mushroom
猴头菇扒鱼唇	〈饮食〉	Braised Fish Lips with Bearded Tooth Mushrooms
猴头蘑扒菜心	〈饮食〉	Braised Choy Sum with Mushrooms
后发酵茶		post-fermented tea
后襟		back part of a Chinese robe or jacket
后门		back door; ways of fraud
后起之秀		up-and-coming star; up-rising star; promising young people

后天之本	〈中医药〉source of acquired constitution; postnatal base of life; acquired base of life
后天之精	〈中医药〉acquired essence; postnatal essence
后真相时代	〈防疫〉post-truth era
厚朴	〈中医药〉(of Latin) Cortex Magnoliae Officinalis; Officinal Magnolia Bark
厚朴花	〈中医药〉(of Latin) Flos Magnoliae Officinalis; Officinal Magnolia Flower
厚朴温中汤	〈中医药〉Houpu Wenzhong Tang; Center-Warming Decoction of Officinal Magnolia; Matgnoliae Officinalis Decoction for Warming Middle Energizer
候气	〈中医药〉awaiting qi; to wait for qi arrival; to wait for the needle sensation
呼叫中心	call center; contact center
呼吸补泻	〈中医药〉respiratory supplementation and drainage; reinforcing-reducing method by respiration
呼吸道	〈防疫〉respiratory tract
呼吸道[系统]疾病	〈防疫〉respiratory disease
呼吸机	〈防疫〉ventilator; respirator
呼吸急促	〈防疫〉shortness of breath; panting
呼吸困难	〈防疫〉dyspnea; respiratory distress; breathing difficulties
呼吸器官	〈防疫〉respiratory organ
呼吸卫生	〈防疫〉respiratory hygiene
呼吸系统	〈防疫〉respiratory system
呼吁采取紧急的行动	〈防疫〉to call for an urgent action
忽悠	to coax; to bamboozle; to sweet-talk
狐臭净	〈中医药〉Huchou Jing; Bromhidrosis Clearing Liquid
狐裘服	fox-fur robe
弧坑釉	〈陶瓷〉crater glaze
胡黄连	〈中医药〉(of Latin) Rhizoma Picrorhizae; Figwortflower Picrorhiza Root
胡椒	〈中医药〉(of Latin) Fructus Piperis Nigri; Pepper Fruit

胡芦巴	〈中医药〉(of Latin) Semen Trigonellae; Fenugreek Seed
胡萝卜炖牛肉	〈饮食〉Braised Beef with Carrots
胡麻子	〈中医药〉(of Latin) Semen Lini; Linseed
胡同	hutong; alleyway →里弄
胡同串子	peddler; hawker
胡子工程	long-drawn-out project (a project which takes so long that young workers become bearded)
壶垫	〈茶〉tea pad
葫芦八宝鸡	〈饮食〉Gourd-Shaped Chicken with Stuffing
葫芦罐	〈陶瓷〉gourd jar; gourd-shaped drinking vessel
葫芦鸭	〈饮食〉Gourd-Shaped Duck Stuffed with Sweet Glutinous Rice
湖北青砖茶	Hubei Green Brick tea
湖沟烧饼	〈饮食〉Hugou Sesame Seed Cake
湖南菜	〈饮食〉→湘菜
槲寄生	〈中医药〉(of Latin) Herba Visci; Chinese Viscum Herb
蝴蝶骨	〈饮食〉Braised Spare Ribs
蝴蝶海参	〈饮食〉Steamed Sea Cucumbers in Butterfly Shape; Butterfly-Shaped Sea Cucumbers
蝴蝶海参羹	〈饮食〉Sea Cucumber Soup
蝴蝶燕窝	〈饮食〉Bird's Nest (Shaped as a Butterfly)
糊辣基围虾	〈饮食〉Stir-Fried Shrimps with Hot Pepper
糊辣子鸡	〈饮食〉Peppered Chicken; Chicken in Hot Sauce
虎斑釉	〈陶瓷〉tiger-skin glaze
虎口三关	〈中医药〉three passes at the tiger-mouth; three passes at the first web space
虎妈	tiger mother (who requires children to work along the path she chooses through all kinds of high-pressure means)
虎皮鸽蛋	〈饮食〉Deep-Fried Boiled Pigeon Eggs in Tiger Skin Color
虎皮烩鸡丁	〈饮食〉Braised Chicken Slices with Bean Curd Sheets

虎皮尖椒	〈饮食〉Pan-Seared Green Chili Pepper
虎杖	〈中医药〉(of Latin) Rhizoma Polygoni Cuspidati; Giant Knotweed Root
琥珀鸽蛋	〈饮食〉Deep-Fried Boiled Pigeon Eggs in Amber Color
琥珀核桃	〈饮食〉Honeyed Walnut Kernels
琥珀花生	〈饮食〉Honeyed Peanuts
琥珀釉	〈陶瓷〉amber glaze
互动广告	interactive advertisement
互动演示	interactive demonstration
互惠互利	reciprocity and mutual benefit
互联网银行	Internet-based bank; Internet bank; e-bank
互通有无	to supply each other's needs
户籍改革	household registry reform; residential system reform
户籍所在地	registered permanent residence
户籍制度	hukou system; household registration system
户口	hukou; household registration; registered permanent residence
户口簿	residence booklet; household registration booklet
户口管理制度	domicile system; residence registration system
户口迁移	hukou relocation; transfer of household registration; residence migration
户主	householder; head of a household; family head
护肝片	〈中医药〉Hugan Pian; Liver-Protecting Tablet
护理部主任	head of the nursing department
护理管理员	nursing administrator
护理者	〈防疫〉carer; caregiver
护理主任	nursing director
护目镜	〈防疫〉goggles; eye protector
护士长	nursing supervisor; head nurse
护腿	〈服饰〉leg armor; leg protector
护腋	〈古〉(of an armor) armpit protector
花瓣袖	petal sleeve

花布	cotton print; figured cloth; multicolor cloth
花布棉袄	cotton-padded jacket of printed cloth
花草茶	herbal tea
花茶	scented tea; flower tea
花钿	〈服饰〉floral-patterned trinket (ornament on the face of women)
花雕酒	Huadiao rice wine; high-grade Shaoxing wine
花雕酒蒸膏蟹	〈饮食〉Steamed Green Crab in Huadiao Rice Wine
花菇素烩	〈饮食〉Stewed Assorted Vegetables with Shiitake Mushrooms
花鼓戏演员	flower-drum opera performer
花果茶	flower and fruit tea
花果山云雾茶	Mount Huaguo Cloud and Mist tea
花红片	〈中医药〉Huahong Pian; Flower Redness Tablet
花髻	〈古〉(of hairstyle) flower-shaped bun
花椒	〈中医药〉(of Latin) Pericarpium Zanthoxyli; Pricklyash Peel
花椒炒鸡球	〈饮食〉Stir-Fried Chicken Balls with Wild Pepper
花椒甲鱼	〈饮食〉Braised Turtle with Sichuan Pepper Corns
花椒炸排骨	〈饮食〉Stir-Fried Pork Chop with Wild Pepper
花卷	〈饮食〉Huajuan; Steamed Roll; Steamed Twisted Roll
花翎	〈服饰〉peacock feather; top hat hualing (a peacock tail feather on the hat to show one's official ranking in the Qing Dynasty)
花露水	floral water; cologne water
花鸟纹花盆	〈陶瓷〉flower pot with flower and bird pattern
花盆底鞋	〈古〉flower-pot-soled shoes; shoes with flower-pot-like sole (used in the Qing Dynasty)
花旗参炖竹丝鸡	〈饮食〉Braised Chicken with Ginseng; Stewed Tender Chicken with Ginseng
花生糕	〈饮食〉Peanut Cake; Peanut Pudding
花生米牛肉汤	〈饮食〉Steamed Beef with Peanuts and Chicken Breast in Soup

花生太湖银鱼	〈饮食〉Braised Taihu Silver Fish with Peanuts
花生汤	〈饮食〉Peanut Soup
花香	〈茶〉flowery flavor
花釉	〈陶瓷〉polychromatic glaze; color glaze; fancy glaze
花招儿	monkey business; trick; sleight of hand; showy movement in wushu
花枝羹	〈饮食〉Squid Thick Soup
花珠冠	〈服饰〉flower bead crown
华顶云雾	〈茶〉Huading Cloud and Mist tea
华景天祛斑胶囊	〈中医药〉Huajingtian Quban Jiaonang; Rhodiola Patch-Removing Capsule
华人商会	Chinese chamber of commerce; Chinese business association
华夏长城赤霞珠	〈酒〉Huaxia Great Wall Cabernet Sauvignon red wine
华夏长城特选	〈酒〉Huaxia Great Wall Selection red wine
华夏风情	(of a model contest) Chinese Kaleidoscope
滑蛋炒牛肉	〈饮食〉Stir-Fried Beef with Scrambled Eggs
滑蛋虾仁	〈饮食〉Stir-Fried Shelled Shrimps with Scrambled Eggs
滑蛋虾仁饭	〈饮食〉Rice with Fried Shrimps and Scrambled Eggs
滑里脊片	〈饮食〉Stir-Fried Tenderloin Slices with Bamboo Shoots
滑熘里脊	〈饮食〉Stir-Fried Tenderloin with Thick Gravy
滑熘里脊片	〈饮食〉Quick-Fried Tenderloin Slices with Sauce
滑熘肉片	〈饮食〉Quick-Fried Sliced Pork with Cream Sauce
滑肉门	〈中医药〉Huaroumen acupoint; Slippery Flesh Gate (ST24)
滑石瓷	〈陶瓷〉steatite porcelain; steatite ceramic
滑子菇扒菜胆	〈饮食〉Braised Green Vegetables with Nameko Mushrooms
化虫丸	〈中医药〉Huachong Wan; Anthelmintic Pill; Worm-Eliminating Pill

化橘红	〈中医药〉(of Latin) Exocarpium Citri Grandis; Pummelo Peel
化脓灸	〈中医药〉scarring moxibustion; blistering moxibustion; festering moxibustion
化湿和中	〈中医药〉to remove dampness for regulating the stomach; to resolve dampness and harmonize the center
化痰开窍	〈中医药〉to resolve phlegm to open the orifices; to eliminate/dissipate phlegm for resuscitation
化痰散结	〈中医药〉to dissipate phlegm and resolve masses
化痰消瘿	〈中医药〉to dissipate phlegm for eliminating goiter
化痰消瘀	〈中医药〉to dissipate phlegm and eliminate blood stasis
化学[理化]瓷	〈陶瓷〉chemical porcelain; laboratory porcelain
化学分析测试员	chemical analyst
化学技能证书	chemical skills certificate
化学检验员	chemistry testing laboratory technician
化痔栓	〈中医药〉Huazhi Shuan; Hemorrhoid-Desolving Suppository
化妆师	cosmetician; make-up artist
华佗	Hua Tuo (145—208, a famous doctor in the late Eastern Han Dynasty)
华佗清咽片	〈中医药〉Huatuo Qingyan Pian; Huatuo Pharynx-Clearing Tablet
华佗再造丸	〈中医药〉Huatuo Zaizao Wan; Huatuo Revival Pill
淮山	〈中医药〉(of Latin) Dioscorea Opposite; Dioscorea Root; Chinese Yam Rhizome
淮山圆肉炖甲鱼	〈饮食〉Braised Turtle with Yam and Longan
淮扬菜	〈饮食〉Huaiyang Cuisine (one of the four traditional Chinese cuisines)
淮阳小饺	〈饮食〉Huaiyang Poached Small Dumpling/Jiaozi
槐花	〈中医药〉(of Latin) Flos Sophorae; Pagodatree Flower

槐花散	〈中医药〉Huaihua San; Sophora Flower Powder
槐角丸	〈中医药〉Huaijiao Wan; Fructus Sophorae Compound Pill; Sophora Fruit Pill
槐米	〈中医药〉(of Latin) Flos Sophorae Immaturus; Pagodatree Flower Bud
环保电池	environment-friendly battery
环保工程师	environmental protection engineer
环境安全健康工程师	Environmental health and safety engineer
环境保护	environment protection
环境工程师	environment engineer; environmental engineer
环境影响评价工程师	environmental impact assessment engineer
环卫工人	environmental sanitation worker
圜[环]钱	〈币〉round coin (in the Warring States period)
鬟髻[结]	(of hairstyle) coiled bun; hair worn in a coil
缓方	〈中医药〉gentle formula/prescription; slow-acting formula
缓缴税款	〈防疫〉deferment of taxes
缓则治其本	〈中医药〉to relieve the primary symptoms in a chronic case
换手率	turnover rate
肓俞	〈中医药〉Huangshu acupoint; Vitals Transport (KI16)
皇宫煎鹿柳	〈饮食〉Stir-Fried Venison with Black Pepper
皇宋通宝	〈古币〉coin with characters huangsong tongbao (issued in the Northern Song Dynasty)
皇窑窑址	〈陶瓷〉site of imperial kiln
黄暗	〈茶〉yellow dull
黄柏	〈中医药〉(of Latin) Cortex Phellodendri; Amur Corktree Bark; Golden Cypress Bark
黄包车	rickshaw; jinrikisha
黄标车	yellow-label car; heavy-polluting vehicle; high-emission vehicle
黄茶	yellow tea
黄道袍	〈古〉yellow Taoist robe

黄地珐琅彩花卉碗	〈陶瓷〉yellow ground enameled bowl with floral pattern (Qing Kangxi period)
黄地绿釉福寿禄花卉纹罐	〈陶瓷〉yellow ground green glaze jar with 福寿禄-characters and flowers pattern (Ming Jiajing period)
黄地青花栀子花卉纹盘	〈陶瓷〉yellow-ground blue and white plate with gardenia floral pattern (Ming Hongzhi period)
黄帝	Huangdi; Yellow Emperor (2717 B.C.—2599 B.C., one of the legendary Chinese sovereigns and culture heroes)
《黄帝内经》	〈中医药〉*Huangdi Neijing*; *Yellow Emperor's Internal Classic*; *Inner Canon of Huangdi*; *Inner Canon of Yellow Emperor* (written in the Warring States period)
《黄帝素问宣明论方》	〈中医药〉*Huangdi Suwen Xuanming Lun Fang*; *Clear Synopsis on Recipes*; *An Elucidation of Formulas of Huangdi's Plain Questions* (by Liu Wansu in the Jin Dynasty)
黄豆煮水鸭	〈饮食〉Stewed Teal with Soya Beans
黄瓜炒鸡丝	〈饮食〉Stir-Fried Chicken Shreds with Cucumber Shreds
黄瓜肉片汤	〈饮食〉Sliced Meat Soup with Cucumber Slices
黄果树香烟	Huangguo Shu cigarettes; Yellow Fruit Tree cigarettes
黄褐	〈茶〉yellowish auburn
黄鹤楼酒	Yellow Crane Tower liquor
黄鹤楼香烟	Huanghe Lou cigarettes; Yellow Crane Tower cigarettes
黄黑	〈茶〉yellowish black
黄花素鸡	〈饮食〉Vegetarian Chicken with Day Lily
黄昏恋	love in the sunset of one's life; late-life love; twilight romance
黄金大排面	〈饮食〉Noodles with Fried Spare Ribs
黄金线路	hot travel route

黄金雪蛤酿蟹盖	〈饮食〉Baked Crab Shell Stuffed with Hasma and Salted Egg Yolk
黄金叶香烟	Huangjingye cigarettes; Golden Leaf cigarettes
黄金玉米	〈饮食〉Stir-Fried Sweetcorn with Salted Egg Yolk
黄金周	golden week; golden week holidays
黄精	〈中医药〉(of Latin) Rhizoma Polygonati; Solomon-seal Rhizome
黄酒	Chinese rice wine; yellow rice/millet wine
黄酒脆皮虾仁	〈饮食〉Crispy Shelled Shrimps with Yellow Rice Wine
黄酒焖全鸭	〈饮食〉Braised Whole Duck in Yellow Rice Wine; Braised Whole Duck in Shaoxing Wine
黄酒鸭	〈饮食〉Braised Duck in Yellow Rice Wine
黄连	〈中医药〉(of Latin) Rhizoma Coptidis; Golden Thread
黄连解毒汤	〈中医药〉Huanglian Jiedu Tang; Coptidis Decoction for Detoxification; Coptis Toxin-Resolving Decoction
黄亮	〈茶〉yellow bright
黄绿	〈茶〉yellowish green
黄绿彩双龙寿字碗	〈陶瓷〉yellow and green bowl with 寿-character and twin-dragon pattern (Qing Qianlong period)
黄绿釉鹦鹉壶	〈陶瓷〉green and yellow glazed parrot-shaped pot
黄马褂	〈古〉yellow (mandarin) jacket (used in the Qing Dynasty)
黄梅天	(of weather) plum rain season; rainy season
黄焖大虾	〈饮食〉Braised Prawns in Brown Sauce
黄焖干鲍	〈饮食〉Braised Dried Abalone in Brown Sauce
黄焖鸡块[翼]	〈饮食〉Braised Chicken Chips/Wings in Brown Sauce
黄焖山珍菌	〈饮食〉Braised Wild Mushrooms in Brown Sauce
黄焖鸭块	〈饮食〉Braised Duck Cubes in Brown Sauce
黄焖鱼翅	〈饮食〉Braised Shark's Fins in Rice Wine Sauce
黄牛党	→票贩子

黄牛票	scalped ticket; speculative resold ticket
黄袍	〈古〉yellow robe; imperial robe
黄芪	〈中医药〉(of Latin) Radix Astragali seu Hedysari; Milkvetch Root
黄芪精	〈中医药〉Huangqi Jing; Astragalus Essence
黄芪颗粒	〈中医药〉Huangqi Keli; Astragalus Granule
黄芪注射液	〈中医药〉Huangqi Zhusheye; Astragalus Injection
黄桥烧饼	〈饮食〉Huangqiao Sesame Cake
黄芩	〈中医药〉(of Latin) Radix Scutellariae; Baical Skullcap Root
黄芩苷	〈中医药〉(of Latin) Scutellaria baicalensis; Baicalin
黄青	〈茶〉yellowish blue
黄山毛峰	〈茶〉Huangshan Maofeng tea; Yellow Mountain Tippy tea
黄山香烟	Mt. Huangshan cigarettes
黄氏响声丸	〈中医药〉Huangshi Xiangsheng Wan; Dr. Huang Loud Voice Pill
黄药子	〈中医药〉(of Latin) Rhizoma Dioscorea Bulbifera; Air Potato
黄油马拉糕	〈饮食〉Steamed Brown Sugar Cake
黄釉瓷尊	〈陶瓷〉yellow-glazed porcelain zun (wine vessel)
黄釉俯首马	〈陶瓷〉yellow glazed horse with bowed head
黄釉红彩缠枝莲纹葫芦瓶	〈陶瓷〉yellow-glazed gourd-shaped vase with red interlaced branches and lotus pattern
黄釉刻花盘	〈陶瓷〉yellow-glazed tray with carved floral pattern
黄釉绿彩莲瓣四系陶壶	〈陶瓷〉yellow-glazed pottery jar with four ears and green lotus-petal pattern
黄釉人物狮子扁壶	〈陶瓷〉yellow-glazed flask with lion and figural depiction pattern
黄釉仙鹤云纹碗	〈陶瓷〉yellow glaze bowl with crane and cloud pattern (Ming Hongzhi period)
黄釉印花扁壶	〈陶瓷〉yellow glaze flask with printed floral pattern (Northern Qi Dynasty)

黄釉鹦鹉形水注	〈陶瓷〉yellow-glazed parrot-shaped water dropper
黄鱼羹	〈饮食〉Yellow Fish Soup; Croaker Thick Soup
黄元米果炒腊肉	〈饮食〉Stir-Fried Preserved Pork with Huangyuan Glutinous Rice Cake
黄竹白毫	〈茶〉Huangzhu (Yellow Bamboo) Pekoe
灰暗	〈茶〉greyish dull
灰白	〈茶〉greyish white
灰褐	〈茶〉greyish auburn
灰黄	〈茶〉greyish yellow
灰领	gray-collar; skilled technicians
灰领工人	gray-collar worker
灰绿	〈茶〉greyish green
灰色经济	grey economy
灰色收入	gray income; off-the-books income; income from moonlighting
灰釉	〈陶瓷〉ash glaze
恢复期血浆治疗	〈防疫〉convalescent plasma therapy
恢复生产生活秩序	〈防疫〉to resume work and normal life
恢复堂食	〈防疫〉to resume dine-in service
徽菜	〈饮食〉Hui Cuisine; Anhui Cuisine
回甘	〈茶〉sweet after taste
回锅辣白肉	〈饮食〉Twice Cooked Fat Pork in Hot Sauce
回锅肉片	〈饮食〉Twice-Cooked Pork Slices in Hot Sauce; Stir-Fried Sliced Pork with Pepper and Chili
回锅羊肉	〈饮食〉Twice-Cooked Mutton with Carrot and Onion, Ginger
《回回药方》	〈中医药〉*Huihui Yaofang*; *Huihui Formularies* (by the end of the Yuan Dynasty)
回扣	(of pejorative) kickback; rebate; sales commission
回流移民	returning emigrant
回头客	returned customer; regular customer; repeat customer
回头率	rate of second glance
回心髻	(of hairstyle) huixin bun; twisted bun on head top

回旋灸	〈中医药〉revolving moxibustion; circling moxibustion
回阳救逆剂	〈中医药〉formula for emergent resuscitation; yang-restoring and counterflow-stemming formula
回阳生肌	〈中医药〉to restore yang and promote granulation
茴香橘核丸	〈中医药〉Huixiang Juhe Wan; Fennel and Tangerine Pip Pill
会标	association's emblem; organization's symbol
会考	unified examination; general examination for students from various schools
会务协调员	event coordinator; conference coordinator
会务主管	conference supervisor; event supervisor
会务主任	conference director; event supervisor
会阳	〈中医药〉Huiyang acupoint; Confluence of Yang (BL35)
会阴	〈中医药〉Huiyin acupoint; Confluence of Yin (CV1)
会长	(of an association or society) president; chairman/chairwoman
会子	〈币〉→便钱会子
会宗	〈中医药〉Huizong acupoint; Convergence of Yang-Qi (TE7)
烩	〈饮食〉to braise; to cook the meat or vegetables in soy and vinegar (with water)
烩滑籽菇	〈饮食〉Braised Mushrooms in Sauce
烩黄鱼羹	〈饮食〉Stewed Yellow Croaker and Eggs Potage
烩鸡丝	〈饮食〉Stewed Shredded Chicken
烩里脊丝	〈饮食〉Braised Tenderloin Shreds with Magnolia Slices and Egg Whites
烩三冬	〈饮食〉Stewed Three Kinds of Vegetables
烩蒜香肚丝	〈饮食〉Braised Shredded Pork Tripe with Mashed Garlic and Sauce
烩虾仁	〈饮食〉Braised Shelled Shrimps with Green Peas
烩鸭丁腐皮	〈饮食〉Braised Diced Duck with Bean Curd Clot

烩鸭舌乌鱼蛋汤	〈饮食〉Duck Tongue and Cuttlefish Roe Soup
烩鸭舌掌	〈饮食〉Stewed Duck Tongue and Webs
烩鸭掌	〈饮食〉Braised Duck Webs with Magnolia Slices and Mushrooms
婚检	→婚前体检
婚介所	→婚姻介绍所
婚恋网站	dating website; match-making website; online dating site
婚前体检	premarital health check-up; prenuptial medical/physical examination
婚前同居	premarital cohabitation; prenuptial cohabitation
婚前协议	premarital agreement; prenuptial agreement
婚丧喜庆	weddings and funerals
婚纱摄影	wedding photo
婚外恋	extramarital love affair
婚宴销售代表	wedding banquet sales representative
婚宴销售主任	wedding banquet sales director
婚姻介绍所	matchmaking agency; marriage service cooperation; matrimonial agency
婚姻状况	marital status
婚姻状况证明	marital status certificate
浑水摸鱼	to fish in troubled water
馄饨	〈饮食〉Wonton; Wonton Soup; Dumpling Soup
馄饨面	〈饮食〉Noodles with Wonton
馄饨汤	〈饮食〉Wonton Soup
馄饨汤面	〈饮食〉Noodle Soup with Wonton; Noodles with Wonton in Soup
混合武术	mixed martial art
混合型卷烟	blended cigarette
混合釉	→复[混]合釉
魂门	〈中医药〉Hunmen acupoint; Soul Gate (BL47)
活期存款	demand deposit; current account
活体农贸市场	〈防疫〉live animal market
活血化瘀	〈中医药〉to activate blood to resolve stasis; to promote blood circulation for removing blood stasis

活血剂	〈中医药〉blood-activating formula; blood-quickening prescription
活血解毒	〈中医药〉to promote blood circulation and detoxication
活血去腐	〈中医药〉to promote blood circulation and eliminate necrosis
活血调经	〈中医药〉to activate blood to regulate menstruation; to promote blood flow/circulation for regulating menstruation
活血通络	〈中医药〉to promote blood circulation for removing obstruction in collaterals
活血止痛	〈中医药〉to activate blood to relieve pain; to regulate blood to alleviate pain
活血止痛胶囊	〈中医药〉Huoxue Zhitong Jiaonang; Blood-Quickening and Pain-Relieving Capsule
活血止痛散	〈中医药〉Huoxue Zhitong San; Blood-Quickening and Pain-Relieving Powder
火爆腰花	〈饮食〉Quick-Fried Pig Kidney with Lettuce, Ginger and Garlic
火罐法	〈中医药〉fire cupping
火锅	〈饮食〉hot pot; chafing-dish
火候	〈饮食〉heat control; optimal fire
火烙疗法	〈中医药〉cauterization therapy
火燎鸭心	〈饮食〉Quick-Fried Duck Hearts
火麻仁	〈中医药〉(of Latin) Fructus Cannabis; Hemp Seed
火腩生蚝煲	〈饮食〉Stewed Belly Pork with Oysters in Clay Pot
火腩塘虱煲	〈饮食〉Stewed Pork and Catfish in Clay Pot
火烧	〈饮食〉Baked Wheaten Cake
火烧泥包鸡	〈饮食〉Roasted Mud-Wrapped Chicken
火神山医院	〈防疫〉Huoshen Shan Hospital (Wuhan)
火腿炒蚕豆	〈饮食〉Stir-Fried Broad Beans with Ham
火腿炒蛋	〈饮食〉Scrambled Eggs with Ham
火腿炒饭	〈饮食〉Stir-Fried Rice with Ham
火腿冬瓜汤	〈饮食〉Ham and Winter Gourd Soup

火腿鸡丝汤	〈饮食〉Shredded Chicken and Ham Soup
火腿甲鱼汤	〈饮食〉Turtle Soup with Ham
火腿酿冬瓜	〈饮食〉Stewed Ham-Stuffed White Gourd
火腿肉丸烧海参	〈饮食〉Braised Sea Cucumbers with Pork Balls and Ham Slices
火鸭芥菜汤	〈饮食〉Sliced Roasted Duck with Leaf Mustard in Soup
火焰红釉	〈陶瓷〉flamboyant red glaze
火针疗法	〈中医药〉fire needle therapy; puncturing point with hot-red needle
和稀泥	to blur the line between right and wrong; to reconcile differences regardless of principles
货到付款	cash on delivery; to pay on delivery
货运铁路网	freight rail network
霍山黄芽	〈茶〉Huoshan Huangya; Huoshan Yellow Bud tea
藿胆丸	〈中医药〉Huodan Wan; Agastache and Pig's Bile Pill
藿香	〈中医药〉(of Latin) Agastache Rugose; Herba Agastachis; Wrinkled Giant Hyssop
藿香祛暑软胶囊	〈中医药〉Huoxiang Qushu Ruan Jiaonang; Agastache Summer-Heat Clearing Soft Capsule
藿香正气胶囊	〈中医药〉Huoxiang Zhengqi Jiaonang; Agasteche Right-Qi Capsule
藿香正气散	〈中医药〉Huoxiang Zhengqi San; Agastache Powder for Restoring Healthy Energy; Agastache and Qi-Righting Powder
藿香正气丸	〈中医药〉Huoxiang Zhengqi Wan; Agastache Right-Qi Pill

J

击打法	〈中医药〉striking manipulation
击鼓说唱俑	drumming rap figurine
机场处置专区	〈防疫〉processing area for inbound passengers at the airport
机场建设费	airport construction fee
机电工程师	mechanical and electrical engineer
机读形式	machine-readable form
机构臃肿	overstaffing in organizations (government)
机会成本	opportunity cost
机器阅卷	machine scoring
机械工程师	mechanical engineer
机要秘书	confidential secretary
鸡包鱼翅	〈饮食〉Braised Chicken Stuffed with Sharks Fins
鸡煲海虎翅	〈饮食〉Braised Tiger Shark's Fins in Chicken Soup
鸡翅鲍鱼片	〈饮食〉Braised Abalone Slices with Chicken Wings
鸡蛋炒饭	〈饮食〉Egg-Fried Rice; Stir-Fried Rice with Eggs
鸡蛋羹	〈饮食〉Steamed Egg Custard
鸡蛋韭菜水饺	〈饮食〉Jiaozi Stuffed with Leek and Egg
鸡蛋碰石头	like an egg striking a rock; to attack sth. stronger than oneself
鸡丁核桃仁	〈饮食〉Stir-Fried Diced Chicken with Walnut Kernels →核桃仁炒鸡丁
鸡冻干贝	〈饮食〉Fricassee Dried Scallops in Chicken Mousse
鸡肝炒蛋	〈饮食〉Scrambled Eggs with Chicken Livers
鸡缸杯	〈陶瓷〉cylinder cup with chicken pattern

鸡骨草	〈中医药〉(of Latin) Herba Abri; Canton Love-Pea Vine
鸡骨酱	〈饮食〉Stir-Fried Chicken with Bean Sauce
鸡冠壶	〈陶瓷〉cock comb-shaped jug
鸡冠花	〈中医药〉(of Latin) Flos Celosiae Cristatae; Cockcomb Flower
鸡脚炖牛腩	〈饮食〉Stewed Beef Brisket with Chicken Paws
鸡块汤	〈饮食〉Diced Chicken Soup; Soup with Diced Chicken
鸡兰鱼翅	〈饮食〉Braised Shark's Fins with Chicken Shreds and Bamboo Shoots
鸡里爆	〈饮食〉Stir-Fried Chicken Fillets and Pork Tripe
鸡粒茨菇饼	〈饮食〉Pancake with Diced Chicken and Mushrooms
鸡粒豌豆	〈饮食〉Stir-Fried Green Peas with Diced Chicken
鸡粒咸鱼茄子煲	〈饮食〉Diced Chicken, Salted Fish and Eggplants in Casserole
鸡熘爆肚	〈饮食〉Quick-Fried Pork Tripe with Chicken
鸡鸣散	〈中医药〉Jiming San; Rooster-Crowing Powder
鸡末粥	〈饮食〉Porridge with Chopped Chicken
鸡内金	〈中医药〉(of Latin) Endothelium Corneum Gigeriae Galli; Gizzard Lining; Chicken's Gizzard-Membrane
鸡皮烩花菜	〈饮食〉Stewed Cauliflower with Chicken Skin
鸡皮釉	〈陶瓷〉fowl-skin glaze
鸡片鲍鱼	〈饮食〉Stir-Fried Abalone with Sliced Chicken
鸡球鲍脯	〈饮食〉Braised Abalone with Chicken Balls
鸡球炒/煎面	〈饮食〉Chow Mein with Chicken Balls; Stir-Fried Noodles with Chicken Balls
鸡茸白菜羹	〈饮食〉Mashed Chicken and Chinese Cabbage Soup
鸡茸炒鲍丝	〈饮食〉Stir-Fried Abalone Shreds with Minced Chicken
鸡茸炒海参	〈饮食〉Stir-Fried Sea Cucumbers with Mashed Chicken

鸡茸豆花	〈饮食〉Braised Minced Chicken with Tofu
鸡茸炖燕窝	〈饮食〉Braised Birds Nest with Minced Chicken
鸡茸黄鱼羹	〈饮食〉Yellow Croaker Potage with Minced Chicken
鸡茸烩豆苗	〈饮食〉Stewed Pea Sprouts with Mashed Chicken
鸡茸烩干贝	〈饮食〉Stewed Dried Scallops with Minced Chicken
鸡茸烩燕窝	〈饮食〉Fricassée Birds Nest with Minced Chicken
鸡茸芦笋	〈饮食〉Asparagus with Mashed Chicken
鸡茸芦笋汤	〈饮食〉Asparagus Soup with Mashed/Minced Chicken
鸡茸蘑菇汤	〈饮食〉Cream of Mushroom with Minced Chicken
鸡茸粟米羹	〈饮食〉Minced Chicken and Corn Soup
鸡茸苋菜	〈饮食〉Stir-Fried Amaranth with Minced Chicken
鸡茸燕窝	〈饮食〉Bird's Nests with Mashed/Minced Chicken
鸡茸鱼翅	〈饮食〉Braised Shark's Fins with Minced Chicken
鸡茸玉米汤	〈饮食〉Corn Soup with Mashed/Minced Chicken
鸡肉炒年糕	〈饮食〉Stir-Fried Rice Cake with Chicken
鸡什[杂]汤	〈饮食〉Chicken Giblets Soup
鸡丝碧螺春	〈饮食〉Sliced Chicken with Biluochun Tea
鸡丝炒饭	〈饮食〉Stir-Fried Rice with Shredded Chicken
鸡丝炒河粉	〈饮食〉Stir-Fried Rice Noodles with Shredded Chicken
鸡丝炒面	〈饮食〉Stir-Fried Noodles with Shredded Chicken
鸡丝春卷	〈饮食〉Spring Rolls Stuffed with Shredded Chicken
鸡丝烩海参	〈饮食〉Stewed Sea Cucumbers with Shredded Chicken
鸡丝烩面	〈饮食〉Stewed Noodles with Chicken Shreds
鸡丝烩鱼翅	〈饮食〉Stewed Shark's Fins with Shredded Chicken
鸡丝烩鱼肚	〈饮食〉Stewed Fish Maws with Shredded Chicken
鸡丝凉面	〈饮食〉Cold Noodles with Chicken Shreds
鸡丝上汤窝面	〈饮食〉Chicken Noodle Soup
鸡丝汤	〈饮食〉Shredded Chicken Soup; Soup with Shredded Chicken
鸡丝汤面	〈饮食〉Noodle Soup with Shredded Chicken
鸡汤	〈饮食〉Chicken Soup; Soup with Chicken

鸡汤面	〈饮食〉Noodles in Chicken Soup
鸡汤泡饭	〈饮食〉Rice in Chicken Soup
鸡汤云吞	〈饮食〉Wonton in Chicken Soup
鸡汤竹笙浸时蔬	〈饮食〉Braised Bamboo Fungi and Vegetables in Chicken Soup
鸡心领口	sweetheart neckline; heart shaped neckline
鸡心碗	〈陶瓷〉bowl with heart-shaped bump on the bottom
鸡血豆腐	〈饮食〉Stewed Tofu with Chicken Blood Curd
鸡血藤	〈中医药〉(of Latin) Caulis Spatholobi; Millettia Root and Stem
鸡腰扒鸽蛋	〈饮食〉Stewed Chicken Kidney with Pigeon Eggs
鸡腰豆腐	〈饮食〉Stewed Tofu/Bean Curd with Chicken Kidney
鸡油鲍鱼蘑菇	〈饮食〉Stir-Fried Abalone and Mushrooms with Chicken Fat
鸡油牛肝菌	〈饮食〉Braised Boletuses with Chicken Oil
鸡油丝瓜	〈饮食〉Stir-Fried Sponge Gourd with Chicken Fat
鸡油四宝	〈饮食〉Four Delicacies in Chicken Fat (Abalone, Asparagus, Pigeon Eggs and Mushroom)
鸡杂汤	→鸡什[杂]汤
鸡汁扒翅	〈饮食〉Braised Shark's Fins with Chicken Gravy
鸡汁鲍鱼鱼翅	〈饮食〉Steamed Abalone with Shark's Fins in Chicken Soup
鸡樽	〈旧〉chicken cup
咭汁鱼片	〈饮食〉Stir-Fried Sliced Fish in Tomato Sauce
积分落户制(度)	point-based household registration system
积少成多	many a little makes a mickle
积压滞销	overstocked commodity (inventory)
笄	(of jewelry) ji; traditional hairpin for hair-bun; hair clasp
基本工资	basic salary; basic wage; base pay
基本公共服务	basic public service
基本公共服务体系	basic public service system

基本公共教育服务	basic public education service
基本公共卫生服务	basic public health service
基本公共养老金	basic public pension
基本国情	fundamental realities of the country
基本人权	fundamental human rights
基本社会服务	basic social service
基本养老保险	basic old-age insurance; basic endowment insurance
基本养老金	basic (retirement) pension; subsistence allowances
基本药物制度	basic drug/medicine system; the system for basic pharmaceuticals
基本医疗	basic medical/health care
基本医疗保健服务	basic medical/health care service
基本医疗保险	basic medical/health insurance
基本医疗服务	basic medical services
基本月租费	basic monthly fee (charges)
基本再生率	〈防疫〉basic reproduction rate
基本住房需求	basic need for housing
基层防控能力	〈防疫〉capacity for prevention and control at the community level
基层工作	grass-roots work
基层监督	grass-roots supervision
基层民主	democracy at the grassroots level; democracy at the local level
基层卫生员	grass-roots health worker; primary health care worker
基层文化建设	primary-level cultural development/undertakings
基层医护人员	grass-roots health care worker; staff in primary level hospital
基层组织	organizations at the grass-roots level; primary-level organization
基础教育	basic education; elementary education
基础设施建设	infrastructure construction; infrastructure development

基础税率	base tariff level
基础釉	〈陶瓷〉parent glaze; parquet varnish
基因结构	〈防疫〉genetic structure
基因水稻	trans-genetic hybrid rice
基因序列	〈防疫〉genetic sequence
基源鉴定	〈中医药〉identification of origin
缉私力量	forces engaged in the fight against smuggling
激发正能量	〈防疫〉to evoke positivity
激光唱片	compact disc; laser record; laser disc
及时分析	〈防疫〉to timely analyze the epidemic
及时回应社会关切	〈防疫〉to provide timely responses to public concerns
及时同国际社会分享信息	〈防疫〉timely sharing of information with the international community
吉金	〈旧〉metal sacrificial vase →青铜器
吉日良辰	auspicious day; a lucky time and day (wedding day)
吉祥带	〈服饰〉lucky ribbon
吉祥如意	everything goes well
吉祥物	mascot; expo mascot
吉语钱	〈古〉coin with auspicious inscription
吉州窑	〈陶瓷〉Jizhou Kiln (built in the late Tang Dynasty, one of the well-preserved ancient famous kiln sites in China)
吉州窑彩绘莲纹炉	〈陶瓷〉Jizhou Kiln incense burner with colored lotus pattern
吉州窑酱色梅枝盏	〈陶瓷〉Jizhou Kiln brown colored bowl-shaped cup with plum branch pattern
极品粥	〈饮食〉Assorted Seafood Congee
极兔速递	Jitu Express Company
即开式奖券	scratch-open ticket; scratch pad
即墨刀	〈币〉Jimo knife (issued in the Qi State)
即墨老酒	Jimo aged liquor
即期消费	immediate consumption

即食火锅	instant hotpot
急方	〈中医药〉urgent formula/prescription; prescription for emergency; drastic prescription; quick-acting formula
急功近利	to be eager for instant success and quick profits
急脉	〈中医药〉Jimai acupoint; Quick Pulse (LR12)
急性呼吸窘迫综合征	〈防疫〉acute respiratory distress syndrome; ARDS
急性子	〈中医药〉(of Latin) Semen Impatientis; Garden Balsam Seed
急则治其标	〈中医药〉to relieve the secondary symptoms in an urgent case
急诊技师	emergency medical technician
急支糖浆	〈中医药〉Jizhi Tangjiang; Acute Bronchitis Syrup
疾病医疗救治体系	〈防疫〉the fully functioning system for emergency medical aid
疾病预防控制机构	〈防疫〉disease prevention and control institution
疾病预防控制体系	〈防疫〉the fully functioning system for disease prevention and control
集成电路设计工程师	integrated circuit design engineer
集成电路验证工程师	integrated circuit verification engineer
集思广益	to draw on collective wisdom and absorb all useful ideas
集体承包	to be contracted to collectives; collective contract
集体观念	collective spirit; sense of community
集体婚礼	collective wedding ceremony; group wedding
集团消费	institutional spending
集中隔离点	〈防疫〉centralized isolation site
集中医疗资源	〈防疫〉to treat the infected in dedicated medical facilities
集中医学观察	〈防疫〉concentrated medical observation
集资办学	to raise money to set up new schools
集资房	houses built with/on the funds collected by the buyers

蒺藜	〈中医药〉(of Latin) Fructus Tribuli; Tribulus Root
籍贯	native place
《济阴纲目》	〈中医药〉*Jiyin Gangmu*; *Synopsis of Treating Women's Diseases*; *Outline for Women's Diseases* (by Wu Zhiwang in the Ming Dynasty)
济阴钱	〈古币〉Jiyin round coin (used in the Warring States period)
脊中	〈中医药〉Jizhong acupoint; Middle of the Spine (GV6)
计划财务部	planning and finance department; finance and accounting division
计划内招生	planned enrollment
计划生育	family planning; birth control
计划生育工作者	family planning worker/staff
计划生育责任制	responsibility system of family planning
计量工程师	measure engineer
计算机辅助教学	computer-assisted instruction; CAI
计算机辅助设计工程师	computer-aided design (CAD) engineer
计算机辅助学习	computer-aided learning; CAL
计算机工程师	computer engineer
计算机化战争	computerized war
计算机绘图员	computer visualizer
计算机软件工程师	computer software engineer
记大过	to record a serious demerit
记名债券	registered bond
记账式国库券	inscribed treasury bond
记账式国债	book-entry T-bond
纪念封	commemorative envelope
技工学校	secondary technical school; technician training school
技术编辑	technical editor; copy-editor
技术产权交易所	technology equity market; technology property right exchange
技术成果商品化	commercialization of technological achievements

技术储备	technological reserve
技术创新	technological innovation
技术发展部经理	manager of technical development department
技术翻译	technical translation; technical translator
技术服务部经理	manager of technical service department
技术服务工程师	technical service engineer
技术服务主管	technical service supervisor
技术改造	technological transformation
技术工人	technician; skilled worker
技术攻关	strive to make technological breakthrough
技术集约企业	technology-intensive enterprise
技术密集产品	technology-intensive product
技术密集型	technology-intensive
技术设计工程师	technical design engineer
技术设计员	technical designer
技术设计主管	technical design supervisor
技术维护工程师	technical maintenance engineer
技术下乡	spread technological knowledge to farmers
技术研发工程师	technical development engineer
技术研发经理	technical development manager
技术研发主管	technical development supervisor
技术依托	technical backstopping
技术有偿转让	transfer of technology with compensation
技术支持工程师	technical support engineer
技术职称	technical title; professional title
技术指导讲师	technical instructor
技术总监	technical director; chief technology officer; CTO
季德胜蛇药片	〈中医药〉Jideshing Sheyao Pian; Jideshing Anti-Venom Tablet; Jideshing Snake Tablet
季节工	seasonal worker; seasonal laborer
季节性调价	seasonal price adjustment
荠菜炒冬笋	〈饮食〉Stir-Fried Winter Bamboo Shoots and Leaf Mustard
荠菜炒鸡片	〈饮食〉Stir-Fried Sliced Chicken with Shepherd's Purse

荠菜鸡丝	〈饮食〉Stir-Fried Shredded Chicken and Shepherd's Purse
荠菜山鸡冬笋片	〈饮食〉Stir-Fried Sliced Pheasant, Shepherd Purse and Bamboo Shoot Slices
荠菜山鸡片	〈饮食〉Stir-Fried Pheasant Slices with Shepherd's Purse
继承税	inheritance tax
继续教育	continuing education
祭服	〈古〉vestment; sacrificial garment; robe worn for a funeral or burial rite
祭红(瓷)	〈陶瓷〉altar red porcelain; sacrificial red porcelain
祭红罗汉碗	〈陶瓷〉sacrificial red glazed luohan bowl (Qing Qianlong period)
祭红釉	〈陶瓷〉sacrificial red glaze
祭蓝玉壶春瓶	〈陶瓷〉sacrificial blue Yuhuchun vase (Qing Qianlong period)
寄售	consignment sale; on consignment; to put up for sale in second-hand shop
绩效考核经理	performance assessment manager
绩效考核主管	performance assessment supervisor
绩效考核专员	performance assessment specialist
霁[祭]蓝釉	〈陶瓷〉sacrificial blue glaze
鲫鱼黄花煲	〈饮食〉Crucian Carp and Day Lily in Casserole
鲫鱼汤	〈饮食〉Gold Carp Soup; Soup with Gold Carp
加彩跪坐女陶俑	〈陶瓷〉colored pottery figurine of a woman sitting on heels
加大力度遏制疫情	〈防疫〉to contain the outbreak through intensified efforts
加饭酒	Chia Fan wine; Jiafan wine (a kind of Shaoxing rice wine)
加工贸易	processing trade; trade involving the processing of supplied raw materials
加快努力	to speed up efforts

加快市场步伐	to accelerate the marketization; to quicken the pace of marketization
加密频道	encoded channel
加强国家间政策协调	〈防疫〉to enhance policy coordination between countries
加强伙伴关系	to strengthen partnerships
加味益母草膏	〈中医药〉Jiawei Yimucao Gao; Supplemented Leonurus Paste
夹板固定疗法	〈中医药〉splint-fixing therapy
夹持进针法	〈中医药〉fingers-squeezed-needle inserting
夹沙肉	〈饮食〉Steamed Pork Slices with Red Bean Paste
夹沙香蕉	〈饮食〉Banana Stuffed with Red Bean Paste
家常饼	〈饮食〉Home-Style Pancake
家常豆腐	〈饮食〉Home-Style Bean Curd; Stir-Fried Bean Curd/Tofu with Sliced Pork and Pepper
家常海参	〈饮食〉Home Style Sea Cucumbers; Home-Made Sea Cucumbers
家常鸡杂饭	〈饮食〉Home-Style Rice with Chicken Giblets
家常皮冻	〈饮食〉Home-Style Pork Skin Aspic
家常臊子海参	〈饮食〉Stir-Fried Sea Cucumbers and Minced Pork with Chili Bean Paste
家常烧蹄筋	〈饮食〉Home-Style Braised Beef Tendon
家常鱼肚	〈饮食〉Home-Style Braised Fish Maws
家电下乡	to bring home appliances the countryside
家护管理员	nursing home manager; residential care officer
家谱	family tree; genealogical tree; family stemma
家谱文化	family tree culture
家庭暴力	domestic violence
家庭出身	family background; family origin; class status of one's family
家庭服务机器人	domestic home service robot; household robot
家庭服务员	family service worker; human services worker
家庭护理	home care; family nursing; home nursing
家庭健康助理	home health assistant

家庭经济困难学生	needy student; financially-troubled student
家庭聚集感染	〈防疫〉clustering infected family
家庭旅馆	family inn; family hotel
家庭美德教育	education of family virtue
家庭内感染	〈防疫〉intra-familial transmission
家庭影院	home theater
家庭装修用品	home improvement products
家庭状况	family status
家乡豆豉鸡	〈饮食〉Native Stir-Fried Chicken with Preserved Bean
家乡鳝鱼	〈饮食〉Stir-Fried Eel with Hot and Green Pepper
家乡小炒肉	〈饮食〉Stir-Fried Pork in Country Style
家长会	parent-teacher conference; parents' meeting
家长式中国家庭	patriarchal Chinese family
家长制作风	patriarchal style
家政服务	household service
家族企业	family firm
袈裟	kasaya; cassock; patchwork outer vestment of a Buddhist monk
嘉禾雁扣	〈饮食〉Roasted Goose Meat with White Gourd and Sleeve-Fish
嘉靖青花云龙纹罐	〈陶瓷〉blue and white jar with cloud and dragon pattern (Ming Jiajing period)
夹袄	lined jacket
夹旗袍	lined cheongsam
夹衣	lined clothes
颊车	〈中医药〉Jiache acupoint; Jawbone Joint (ST6)
甲类传染病	〈防疫〉category A infectious disease
甲型流感病毒	〈防疫〉influenza A virus
甲鱼裙边煨肥猪肉	〈饮食〉Stewed Fat Pork with Calipash and Calipee
甲子	jiazi; a cycle of sixty years
假户口	fake hukou; fake household registration/identity
假冒伪劣产品	counterfeit and shoddy product
假冒伪劣商品	counterfeit and substandard goods
假文凭	fake diplomas

假账	accounting fraud
斝	〈古〉bronze-jia; round-mouthed and three-legged wine vessel
价格波动	price fluctuation
价格操纵	price manipulation; price rigging
价格反弹	price rebound
价格浮动范围	price-float range
价格鉴证师	price appraiser
价格听证会	public price hearing
架火法	〈中医药〉fire throwing method; alcohol fire-separated cupping
假后综合征	post-holiday syndrome
假日经济	holiday economy
尖顶帽	〈仫佬族〉peaked cap; steeple-crown; cap with a visor
尖椒炒肥肠	〈饮食〉Stir-Fried Pork Intestines with Hot Pepper
尖椒炒里脊丝	〈饮食〉Stir-Fried Shredded Pork Tenderloin with Hot Pepper
尖椒香芹牛肉丝	〈饮食〉Stir-Fried Shredded Beef with Hot Pepper and Celery
尖晶石瓷	〈陶瓷〉spinel porcelain
尖领	pointed collar peaked collar
尖首刀	〈币〉sharp knife; sharp-headed knife coin (issued in the pre-Qin period)
尖庄酒	Jianzhuang liquor
尖足布	〈币〉bronze spade coin with acute feet (issued in the Warring States period)
坚持全国一盘棋	〈防疫〉to ensure a coordinated national response
坚定信心	〈防疫〉to strengthen confidence
肩甲	〈古〉shoulder armor
肩井	〈中医药〉Jianjing acupoint; Shoulder Well (GB21)
肩髎	〈中医药〉Jianliao acupoint; Shoulder Crevice (TE14)
肩外俞	〈中医药〉Jianwaishu acupoint; Outer Shoulder Transport (SI14)

肩髃	〈中医药〉Jianyu acupoint; Shoulder Bone (LI15)
肩中俞	〈中医药〉Jianzhongshu acupoint; Middle Shoulder Transport (SI15)
肩周炎痛贴	〈中医药〉Jianzhouyantong Tie; Painful Scapulohumeral Periathritis Plaster
监测体温	〈防疫〉to monitor body temperature
兼香型酒	mixed flavor liquor
兼职教师	part-time teacher
煎	〈饮食〉to pan-fry; to decoct; pan-fried; decocted
煎茶	sencha; steamed green tea
煎蛋	〈饮食〉Pan-Fried Eggs
煎锅	fryer; frying pan
煎金钱酿苦瓜	〈饮食〉Pan-Fried Bitter Gourd Stuffed with Pork (Shaped as a Coin)
煎金钱牛柳	〈饮食〉Pan-Fried Beef Fillets with Fried Potatoes (Shaped as a Coin)
煎明虾	〈饮食〉Pan-Fried Prawns with Shell in Gravy
煎酿鲜茄子	〈饮食〉Pan-Fried Eggplants Stuffed with Pork and Shrimps
煎烹虾仁	〈饮食〉Pan-Fried and Simmered Shelled Shrimps
煎琵琶豆腐	〈饮食〉Pan-Fried Bean Curd; Pan Fried Tofu (Shaped as a Pipa)
煎山鸡丝饼	〈饮食〉Fried Pheasant Shreds Pancake
煎什菜粉果	〈饮食〉Pan-Fried Vegetable Dumplings
煎虾饼	〈饮食〉Pan-Fried Prawn Cutlets; Pan-Fried Shrimp Patties
煎虾丸	〈饮食〉Pan-Fried Shrimp Balls with Sauce
煎香蕉	〈饮食〉Pan-Fried Banana
煎蟹饼	〈饮食〉Fried Crab Meat Pancake
煎蟹盒	〈饮食〉Pan-Fried Crab Meat Stuffed in Crab Shell
煎银鳕鱼	〈饮食〉Pan Fried Codfish Fillet
煎猪柳	〈饮食〉Pan-Fried Pork Fillet with Garlic Sprout and Ginger
茧绸	pongee; soft silk

检测样本	〈防疫〉test sample
检举箱	accusation letter box; box for accusation letters
检验室	〈防疫〉clinical laboratory
检疫所	〈防疫〉quarantine office
检疫羞辱	〈防疫〉quarantine shaming
减肥茶	diet tea; slimming tea
减负	to alleviate burdens on students; to lighten students' study load
减轻农民负担	to reduce farmers' burdens; to lighten the burden on farmers
减少留学人员双向流动	〈防疫〉to reduce the two-way flow of overseas students
减少外出	〈防疫〉to make fewer trips outside
减速玻璃	(of car) decelerating glass
减员增效	to downsize staffs and improve efficiency; to reduce staff for greater efficiency
剪边[对文]五铢	〈币〉five-zhu coin with edge cut (issued in the Eastern Han Dynasty)
剪辑导演	montage director
剪轮五铢	〈币〉five-zhu coin with inner frame cut off (issued in the Western Han Dynasty)
简化通关手续	〈防疫〉to simplify procedures for customs clearance
简明新闻	news in brief
简体字	simplified character; simplified Chinese character
碱石灰釉	〈陶瓷〉alkaline calcareous glaze
碱釉	〈陶瓷〉alkaline glaze
间断窑	〈陶瓷〉periodic kiln; intermittent kiln
间接灸	〈中医药〉→隔物灸
间色裙	skirt with two-color pieces together (popular in the Tang Dynasty)
建德苞茶	Jiande Bud Green tea
建立健全防止返贫机制	〈防疫〉to establish a sound mechanism to prevent any return to poverty; to establish a sound mechanism to prevent any relapse into poverty

建设公债	public bonds for construction
建筑工程师	construction engineer; architectural engineer
建筑工程项目经理	construction project manager
建筑工程验收员	construction project inspector
建筑面积	area of structure; floor area; covered area
荐贤举能	to recommend the virtuous and the able
剑南春酒	Jiannanchun liquor
剑片绿茶	sword-shaped green tea
健康保险	health insurance
健康服务协调员	health service coordinator
健康及意外险	health and casualty insurance
健康俱乐部经理	health club manager
健康码	〈防疫〉health code
健康筛查	〈防疫〉health screening
健康申报	〈防疫〉declaration of health status
健康申报表	〈防疫〉health declaration form
健康丝绸之路	〈防疫〉Silk Road of Health
健美师	fitness instructor
健民咽喉片	〈中医药〉Jianmin Yanhou Pian; People-Strengthening Throat Tablet
健脑补肾丸	〈中医药〉Jiannao Bushen Wan; Brain-Fortifying and Kidney-Tonifying Pill
健脾化湿	〈中医药〉to invigorate spleen for eliminating dampness
健脾利水	〈中医药〉to invigorate spleen for diuresis
健脾驱虫	〈中医药〉to strengthen/invigorate spleen for expelling intestinal parasites
健脾生血颗粒	〈中医药〉Jianpi Shengxue Keli; Spleen-Fortifying and Blood-Supplementing Granule
健身房服务员	gymnasium attendant
健身顾问	fitness consultant
健身教练	fitness trainer; fitness instructor
健身中心	fitness center
健肾生发丸	〈中医药〉Jianshen Shengfa Wan; Kidney-Fortifying and Hair-Growing Pill

健胃消食片	〈中医药〉Jianwei Xiaoshi Pian; Stomach-Fortifying and Food-Digesting Tablet
舰载飞机	carrier-borne aircraft; carrier aircraft
鉴真	Jian Zhen (688—763, an eminent monk and the founder of Japanese Vinaya Sect in the Tang Dynasty)
江米酿鸡	〈饮食〉Chicken with Glutinous Rice Stuffing
江南百花鸡	〈饮食〉Steamed Chicken Skin with Shrimp Paste in South China Style
江山绿牡丹	〈茶〉Jiangshan Green Peony tea
江苏菜	〈饮食〉→苏菜
江小白	〈酒〉Jiangxiaobai liquor
将军肚	general's belly; beer belly; abdominal obesity → 啤酒肚
将军香烟	Jiangjun cigarettes; General cigarettes
将入境航班分流至指定机场	〈防疫〉to redirect inbound flights to designated airports
姜半夏	〈中医药〉(of Latin) Rhizome Pinelliae Preparata; Ginger-Processed Pinellia
姜茶	ginger tea
姜葱霸膏鸡	〈饮食〉Pan-Fried Chicken with Ginger and Scallion
姜葱爆牛肉	〈饮食〉Stir-Fried Sliced Beef with Ginger and Scallion
姜葱炒膏蟹	〈饮食〉Stir-Fried Green Crab with Ginger and Scallion
姜葱炒红花蟹	〈饮食〉Stir-Fried Spotted Sea Crab with Ginger and Scallion
姜葱炒龙虾	〈饮食〉Stir-Fried Lobster with Ginger and Scallion
姜葱炒牛肉	〈饮食〉Stir-Fried Beef with Ginger and Green Scallion
姜葱炒肉蟹	〈饮食〉Stir-Fried Hard-Shell Crab with Ginger and Scallion
姜葱花雕鸡	〈饮食〉Steamed Chicken with Ginger and Scallion

姜葱生蚝	〈饮食〉Stir-Fried Oysters with Ginger and Green Onion
姜葱酥炸生蚝	〈饮食〉Deep-Fried Oysters with Ginger and Scallion
姜葱蒸叶梅子鸭	〈饮食〉Steamed Duck with Ginger, Green Onion and Plum Sauce
姜花	〈中医药〉(of Latin) Hedychium Coronarium; Garland-Flower
姜黄	1〈中医药〉(of Latin) Curcuma Longa 2〈茶〉ginger yellow
姜皮	〈中医药〉(of Latin) Zingiber Officinale; Ginger Skin
姜丝鱼片	〈饮食〉Braised Sliced Fish with Ginger
姜芽炒斑鸠	〈饮食〉Stir-Fried Turtledove with Ginger Sprouts
姜芽鸭片	〈饮食〉Boiled Sliced Duck with Ginger
姜汁炒时蔬	〈饮食〉Stir-Fried Seasonal Vegetables with Ginger Sauce
姜汁鸡	〈饮食〉Steamed Tender Chicken with Ginger Sauce
姜汁螃蟹	〈饮食〉Steamed Fresh Crab with Ginger Sauce
姜汁皮蛋	〈饮食〉Preserved Eggs with Ginger Sauce
姜汁鲜鱿	〈饮食〉Fresh Squid with Ginger Sauce
姜汁鱼片	〈饮食〉Boiled Fish Slices with Ginger Sauce
姜汁蜇皮	〈饮食〉Jellyfish with Ginger Sauce
姜汁制	〈中医药〉stir-frying with ginger juice
豇豆红釉	〈陶瓷〉cowpea/haricot red glaze
僵蚕	〈中医药〉(of Latin) Bombyx Batryticatus; Stiff Silkworm
僵化思想	ossified thinking
讲求实效	to stress practical results; to strive for practical results
讲义气	to remain faithful to friends; to be loyal to one's friends
降低病亡率	〈防疫〉to reduce the fatality rate

降低感染率	〈防疫〉to reduce the infection rate
降气剂	〈中医药〉formula for descending qi; qi-depressing formula
降糖舒丸	〈中医药〉Jiangtangshu Wan; Blood-Sugar Lowering Pill
降香	〈中医药〉(of Latin) Lignum Dalbergiae Odoriferae; Dalbergia Wood; Rosewood
降压片	〈中医药〉Jiangya Pian; Hypertension-Reducing Tablet
降脂减肥片	〈中医药〉Jiangzhi Jianfei Pian; Fat-Reducing Slimming Tablet
降脂灵片	〈中医药〉Jiangzhiling Pian; Fat-Reducing Effective Tablet
降脂排毒胶囊	〈中医药〉Jiangzhi Paidu Jiaonang; Fat-Lowering and Toxin-Expelling Capsule
绛纱袍	〈服饰〉red satin gown; gauze grown in crimson
酱板鸭	〈饮食〉Spicy and Salted Duck with Crystal Sugar, Ginger and Star Anise
酱爆鸡丁	〈饮食〉Quick-Fried Diced Chicken with Soybean Paste
酱爆里脊肉	〈饮食〉Quick-Fried Diced Tenderloin with Soybean Paste
酱爆里脊丝配饼	〈饮食〉Quick-Fried Shredded Pork Fillet in Soybean Paste with Pancake
酱爆龙虾	〈饮食〉Stir-Fried Lobster with Soy Bean Paste
酱爆肉	〈饮食〉Quick-Fried Sliced Pork with Soy Sauce
酱爆肉丁	〈饮食〉Quick-Fried Diced Pork with Soybean Paste
酱爆肉丝	〈饮食〉Quick-Fried Shredded Pork with Soy Sauce
酱爆鸭片	〈饮食〉Stir-Fried Sliced Duck with Soy Sauce
酱炒鸡翼球	〈饮食〉Fried Chicken Wing Balls with Bean Sauce
酱炒腊羊肉	〈饮食〉Stir-Fried Preserved Mutton with Soy Sauce
酱黄瓜	〈饮食〉Pickled Cucumbers with Soy Sauce

酱鸡	〈饮食〉Chicken Seasoned in Brown Sauce
酱鸡腿拉面	〈饮食〉Hand-Pulled Noodles with Marinated Chicken Drumsticks
酱牛肉	〈饮食〉Spiced Beef; Beef Seasoned with Soy Sauce
酱肉	〈饮食〉Braised Pork Seasoned with Soy Sauce
酱肉包	〈饮食〉Steamed Bun Stuffed with Braised Pork in Sauce
酱烧排骨	〈饮食〉Braised Spare Ribs with Brown Sauce
酱烧茄子	〈饮食〉Braised Eggplants in Soy Bean Paste
酱香型（风格）	〈酒〉jiang-flavor style; Maotai-flavor liquor
酱香猪蹄	〈饮食〉Pig Paws Seasoned with Soy Sauce; Braised Pork Trotters in Brown Sauce
酱鸭	〈饮食〉Braised Duck in Brown Sauce
酱鸭翅	〈饮食〉Braised Duck Wings in Brown Sauce
酱野菌炒胭脂蚌	〈饮食〉Stir-Fried Mussels and Mushrooms in Special Sauce
酱油	soy sauce
酱油蟹	〈饮食〉Stir-Fried Crabs with Soy Sauce
酱釉划花瓶	〈陶瓷〉brown glazed vase with incised flower pattern
酱炸里脊丁	〈饮食〉Stir-Fried Diced Pork Fillet with Brown Paste
酱汁活鱼	〈饮食〉Fried Fish with Soy Sauce and Wine
酱汁鸭方	〈饮食〉Boiled Duck Pieces in Sauce
酱肘花	〈饮食〉Braised Sliced Pig Knuckles in Brown Sauce
酱猪手	〈饮食〉Braised Pig Trotters with Brown Sauce
酱猪肘	〈饮食〉Braised Knuckles in Brown Sauce
交杯酒	(of wedding) cross-cupped wine; to drink wedlock toast; to drink the nuptial cup
交叉感染	cross transmission, cross-infection
交会穴	〈中医药〉crossing acupoint; intersection point
交际联	social couplet
交领	〈服饰〉crossed collar; overlapping collar

交领右衽	〈服饰〉cross collar gown or robe with right front lapel
交替搓揉	〈中医药〉alternate rubbing and kneading
交通补助	travel allowance
交通管制员	traffic controller
交钥匙工程	turn-key project
交子	〈币〉jiaozi; paper-money (China's earliest banknotes, issued in the Northern Song Dynasty)
浇一瓢冷水	to throw cold water on; to dampen the enthusiasm of
胶鞋	rubber-soled shoes; rubber overshoes; galoshes
教书育人	to impart knowledge and educate people
椒柏酒	〈中医药〉Jiaobai Jiu; Sichuan Pepper and Biota Tops Wine
椒酱肉	〈饮食〉Mixed Meat with Chili; Minced Pork in Chili Paste
椒麻鹌鹑腿	〈饮食〉Stewed Quail Legs with Pepper and Chili
椒香鳝段	〈饮食〉Stir-Fried Eel with Peppers
椒盐大虾球	〈饮食〉Deep-Fried Prawn Balls with Spiced Salt
椒盐豆腐	〈饮食〉Pan-Fried Tofu with Spiced Salt
椒盐膏蟹	〈饮食〉Stir-Fried Green Crab with Spiced Salt
椒盐鳜鱼	〈饮食〉Fried Mandarin Fish with Spiced Salt
椒盐花卷	〈饮食〉Steamed Twisted Rolls with Salt and Pepper
椒盐黄鱼	〈饮食〉Fried Yellow Croaker with Spiced Salt
椒盐鸡	〈饮食〉Chicken with Spicy Salt
椒盐基围虾	〈饮食〉Deep-Fried Shrimps with Spiced Salt
椒盐焗膏蟹	〈饮食〉Baked Green Crab with Spiced Salt
椒盐焗肉蟹	〈饮食〉Baked Hard-Shell Crab with Spiced Salt
椒盐墨鱼	〈饮食〉Deep-Fried Cuttlefish with Spiced Salt
椒盐牛仔骨	〈饮食〉Stir-Fried Calf Ribs with Spicy Salt
椒盐排骨	〈饮食〉Fried Pork Ribs with Spicy Salt; Crispy Spare Ribs with Spicy Salt
椒盐茄子丁	〈饮食〉Deep-Fried Diced Eggplant with Spiced Salt

椒盐肉排	〈饮食〉Fried Spareribs with Pepper Salt; Spare Ribs with Spicy Salt
椒盐肉蟹	〈饮食〉Stir-Fried Hardshell Crab with Spiced Salt
椒盐头爪	〈饮食〉Deep-Fried Lobster Heads and Claws with Spiced Salt
椒盐虾	〈饮食〉Quick-Fried Prawns with Spiced Salt
椒盐鲜鱿	〈饮食〉Fried Fresh Squid with Spiced Salt
椒盐蟹	〈饮食〉Stir-Fried Crab with Spiced Salt
椒盐鳕鱼	〈饮食〉Deep-Fried Codfish with Spiced Salt
椒盐鱿鱼	〈饮食〉Crispy Squid with Spiced Salt
椒盐炸排条	〈饮食〉Deep-Fried Spare Ribs with Spicy Salt
焦炒鱼片	〈饮食〉Dry-Fried Fish Slices with Bamboo Shoot
焦点访谈	(of a news program) Topics in Focus
焦熘黄鱼片	〈饮食〉Crispy-Fried Yellow Croaker Slices with Distilled Grain Sauce
焦熘鱼片	〈饮食〉Crispy-Fried Fish Slices with Distilled Grain Sauce
焦香	〈茶〉scorch aroma
嚼烟	chewing tobacco
角	(of monetary unit) jiao (equaling to ten percent of a yuan); (in ancient time) military blowing instrument; tripod wine cup
角窝上	〈中医药〉Jiaowoshang acupoint; Superior Triangular Fossa (TF1)
角窝中	〈中医药〉Jiaowozhong acupoint; Middle Triangular Fossa (TF3)
饺子	〈饮食〉Jiaozi; Chinese Dumplings
绞股蓝	〈中医药〉(of Latin) Gynostemma Pentaphyllum; Fiveleaf Gynostemma Herb
绞股蓝茶	Gynostemma pentaphyllum tea
绞股蓝总苷片	〈中医药〉Jiaogulan Zonggan Pian; Gynostemma Total Glucoside Tablet
绞胎纹瓷盘	〈陶瓷〉porcelain tray with twistable glaze
绞缬	→扎染布

铰接[通道]式公共汽车	articulated bus; bendy bus
矫形外科医师	orthopaedic surgeon; orthopaedist
矫形牙医	orthodontist
脚踩[踏]两只船	to have a foot in both camps; to deceive or be unfaithful to (a lover or spouse)
脚踏实地	to be down-to-earth
叫板	to challenge; to pick a quarrel; to throw down the gauntlet
叫花鸡	〈饮食〉Beggar's Chicken; Yellow Mud Roasted Chicken →火烧泥包鸡
叫座	a box-office success; to draw a large audience
轿子	sedan; sedan chair
教导主任	dean of students; dean of studies
教师资格证	teacher certification
教授级高级工程师	professor level senior engineer; professorate senior engineer; professor of engineering
教务处	office of teaching affairs; academic affairs office
教务管理人员	educational administrator
教务主任	dean of studies; registrar
教研组长	head of teaching and research group
教育程度	educational background
教育科学文化卫生委员会	education, science, culture and public health committee
教育乱收费	unauthorized collection of fees by educational institutions
教育质量	quality of education
酵气	〈茶〉ferment odor
阶段性减税降费政策	〈防疫〉phased tax and fee breaks
阶段性就业	periodic employment
阶段性政策	interim policy
阶梯教室	lecture theatre; terrace classroom
接触传播	〈防疫〉contact transmission
接触者追踪	〈防疫〉contact tracing
接受医学观察	〈防疫〉to be under medical observation

揭老底	to reveal the inside story; to dig up sb.'s unsavory past
街道办事处	sub-district office; sub-district administrative office
街道办事处主任	director of sub-district office
街道企业	neighborhood enterprise
街谈巷议	gossip; rumor
街心花园	park at an intersection; garden in the city center
节墨之法化五字刀	Jiemo knife coin with five-characters (issued in the Warring States period)
节能型轿车	energy-efficient car
节日病	holiday excess; holiday ailments
节水龙头	water-saving tap
节育率	rate of contraception
结拜兄弟	sworn brothers; blood brothers
结构工资制	structural wage system
结构失调	structural imbalance
结婚礼服	wedding dress
结晶釉	〈陶瓷〉crystalline glaze
结盟酒	allied banquet
桔梗	〈中医药〉(of Latin) Radix Platycodonis; Platycodon Root
解表法	〈中医药〉superficies/exterior-resolving method
解表剂	〈中医药〉diaphoretic prescription; superficies-resolving formula; exterior-relieving/resolving formula
解表清里剂	〈中医药〉formula for relieving superficies and clearing the interior; exterior-resolving and interior-clearing formula
解表通里剂	〈中医药〉formula for relieving superficies and catharsis; exterior-resolving and interior-freeing formula

解表温里剂	〈中医药〉formula for relieving superficies and warming the interior; interior warming diaphoretic and exterior-relieving prescription
解除隔离	〈防疫〉to release from quarantine; to be out of quarantine; de-isolation
解除肌肉紧张	〈中医药〉to relieve muscular tension
解除痉挛	〈中医药〉to relieve spasm; to alleviate convulsion
解除离鄂通道管控	〈防疫〉to lift outbound transport restrictions on areas in Hubei
解除医学观察	〈防疫〉to be discharged from medical observation
解毒护阴	〈中医药〉to remove toxin/toxicity for safeguarding yin
解毒化癍	〈中医药〉to remove toxicity substance and resolve macula
解毒息风	〈中医药〉to remove toxicity substance and calm endogenous wind
解毒消痈	〈中医药〉to remove toxin/toxicity for eliminating carbuncles
解毒消肿	〈中医药〉to remove toxin/toxicity for reducing the swelling
解肌清热	〈中医药〉to expel pathogenic factors from muscles for clearing heat
解困基金	anti-poverty funds
解郁安神	〈中医药〉to resolve stagnation for tranquilization
解郁安神颗粒	〈中医药〉Jieyu Anshen Keli; Depression-Resolving Spirit-Calming Soluble Preparation
介帻	〈古服饰〉jieze hat (a kerchief wrapping hair with two ears)
戒毒康复中心	drug rehabilitation center
戒毒所	→戒毒康复中心
戒急用忍	to overcome impetuosity and exercise patience; to be patient
戒烟	to quit smoking; to give up smoking; smoking cessation

戒烟灵	〈中医药〉Jieyan Ling; Smoking Session Oral Liquor
戒烟门诊	smoking cessation clinic
芥菜肉片咸蛋汤	〈饮食〉Leaf Mustard and Sliced Meat with Salted Egg Soup
芥菜鸭汤	〈饮食〉Duck Soup with Leaf Mustard
芥蓝扒牛柳	〈饮食〉Stir-Fried Beef Fillets with Chinese Broccoli
芥蓝炒肉	〈饮食〉Stir-Fried Pork with Chinese Broccoli
芥蓝鸡	〈饮食〉Stir-Fried Chicken with Chinese Broccoli
芥蓝牛肉	〈饮食〉Stir-Fried Beef with Chinese Broccoli
芥蓝虾	〈饮食〉Stir-Fried Shrimps with Chinese Broccoli
芥蓝鲜鱿	〈饮食〉Stir-Fried Squid with Chinese Broccoli
芥末木耳	〈饮食〉Black Fungi with Mustard Sauce
芥末虾球	〈饮食〉Deep-Fried Prawn Topped with Mustard
芥末鸭掌	〈饮食〉Boiled Duck Webs with Mustard
芥子	〈中医药〉(of Latin) Semen Sinapis Albae; Mustard Seed
借调	temporarily transfer; secondment
借读生	transient student (whose name is not in the school roll)
借火搭讪	smirting; to smirt
巾帽	kerchief or hat
巾帻	〈古服饰〉Turban-hat; conical cap
斤	(of weight unit) jin (equal to 500g)
金贝	〈币〉golden shell; golden cowrie (used as currency in ancient times, also referring to fortune in general)
金错刀	〈币〉gold-inlaid knife (issued in the Han Dynasty)
金(和)刀	〈古〉gold knife coin (used as currency in ancient times)
金豆芥蓝	〈饮食〉Chinese Broccoli with Soy Beans
金饭碗	golden rice bowl; a well-paid occupation
金沸草	〈中医药〉(of Latin) Herba Inulae; Inula Herb

金刚藤	〈中医药〉(of Latin) Rhizoma Smilacis Bockii; Bock Greenbrier Rhizome
金刚藤软胶囊	〈中医药〉Jingangteng Ruanjiaonang; Bock's Greenbrier Root Soft Capsule
金菇豆腐	〈饮食〉Braised Tofu with Mushrooms
金瓜东坡肉	〈饮食〉Braised Dongpo Pork with Ornamental Gourd
金瓜鲔鱼炒米粉	〈饮食〉Stir-Fried Rice Noodles with Fish and Pumpkin
金贵特曲	〈酒〉Jingui Tequ liquor; Jingui Special Yeast spirit
金果榄	〈中医药〉(of Latin) Radix Tinosporae; Tinospora Root
金花	〈茶〉golden flower
金花头饰	gold flower headdress
金华玉树鸡	〈饮食〉Braised Sanhuang Chicken with Ham and Broccoli; Steamed Chicken with Jinhua-Ham and Vegetables
"金话筒"主持人大赛	Golden Microphone Host Competition
金鸡虎补丸	〈中医药〉Jinji Hubu Wan; Golden Chicken Strongly Tonifying Pill
金鸡奖	Golden Rooster Award
金奖白兰地(酒)	Special Fine Brandy; Gold Prize Brandy
金津	〈中医药〉Jinjin acupoint; Golden Fluid (EX-HN12)
金菌灵胶囊	〈中医药〉Jinjunling Jiaonang; Flammulina Velatipes Capsule
《金匮要略》	〈中医药〉*Jingui Yaolüe*; *Synopsis of Golden Chamber*; *Essential Prescriptions of the Golden Coffer* (by Zhang Zhongjing in the Eastern Han Dynasty)
金蓝领	golden blue collar (workers with high skills)
金铃子散	〈中医药〉Jinlingzi San; Toosendan Powder
金领工人	gold-collar worker
金六福酒	Jinliufu liquor
金门	〈中医药〉Jinmen acupoint; Golden Gate (BL63)

金礞石	〈中医药〉(of Latin) Lapis Micae Aureus; Mica-Schist
金柠乳鸽脯	〈饮食〉Stir-Fried Pigeon Breast in Lemon Sauce
金钱白花蛇	〈中医药〉(of Latin) Bungarus Parvus; Little Multi-banded Krait; Coin-like White-Banded Snake
金钱草	〈中医药〉(of Latin) Herba Lysimachiae; Longhairy Antenoron Herb
金钱鸭卷	〈饮食〉Steamed Shredded Duck Breast, Pork Liver and Ham Stuffed into Tofu Sheet Rolls and Sliced as Coins
金荞麦	〈中医药〉(of Latin) Rhizoma Fagopyri Dibotryis; Golden Buckwheat Rhizome
金融风险管理师	financial risk manager; FRM
金融理财师	associate financial planner; AFP
金融危机	financial crisis
金嗓开音丸	〈中医药〉Jinsang Kaiyin Wan; Golden-Throat Voice-Restoring Pill
金嗓子喉片	〈中医药〉Jinsangzi Houpian; Golden Throat Lozenge
金沙回沙酒	Jinsha Huisha liquor
金沙玉米虾	〈饮食〉Stir-Fried Shrimps with Corn and Salted Egg Yolk
金山翠芽	Jinshan Jade Bud tea
金属釉	〈陶瓷〉metallic glaze
金水翠峰	〈茶〉Jinshui Jade Tip
金水相生	→肺肾[金水]相生
金丝黄釉	〈陶瓷〉gold filament yellow glaze
金丝虾球	〈饮食〉Braised Shrimp Balls with Crispy Potato Shreds
金丝绣	gold thread embroidery
金丝燕窝酒	collocalia nest liquor
金丝枣酒	golden silk jujube wine
金蒜脆鳝球	〈饮食〉Deep-Fried Eel Balls with Garlic
金蒜煎牛籽粒	〈饮食〉Pan-Fried Diced Beef with Crispy Garlic

金锁固精丸	〈中医药〉Jinsuo Gujing Wan; Golden Lock Essence-Securing Pill
金坛雀舌	〈茶〉Jintan Bird's Tongue tea
金汤烩鸡脯	〈饮食〉Braised Chicken Breast in Pumpkin Soup
金星绿釉	〈陶瓷〉aventurine green glaze
金星[砂金]釉	〈陶瓷〉aventurine glaze; goldstone glaze
金叶	gold leaf (laudatory title for tea)
金银花	〈中医药〉(of Latin) Flos Lonicerae; Honeysuckle; Lonicera Flower
金银花茶	honeysuckle tea
金银花含片	〈中医药〉Jinyinhua Hanpian; Lonicera Sucking Tablet
金银花颗粒	〈中医药〉Jinyinhua Keli; Honeysuckle Granule
金银花露	〈中医药〉Jinyinhua Lu; Lonicera Flower Distillate; Aqua Lonicerae Foliae
金银迷你馒头	〈饮食〉Steamed and Deep-Fried Mini Mantou/Bun
金银蒜蒸大花虾	〈饮食〉Steamed Prawns with Garlic
金银提取液	〈中医药〉distilled liquid of honeysuckle flower
金樱子	〈中医药〉(of Latin) Fructus Rosae Laevigatae; Cherokee Rose Fruit
金鹰奖	(of TV series) Golden Eagle Award
金鱼发菜	〈饮食〉Gold-Fish-Shaped Nostoc Flagelliforme
金玉满堂	gold and jade filling the hall; treasures filling the home
金玉石	〈陶瓷〉polished mosaic
金元鲍红烧肉	〈饮食〉Braised Pork and Abalone with Brown Sauce
金圆券	〈币〉gold yuan note (paper money issued by Kuomintang government in 1948)
金簪	gold hairpin; (of Chinese legend) gold hairpin (the magic weapon of the Queen Mother)
金针拨障疗法	〈中医药〉cataractopiesis with metal needle therapy

金针云耳蒸鸡	〈饮食〉Steamed Chicken with Lily Flowers and Fungi
金钟杯	→铃铛杯
金种子酒	Golden Seed wine
津酒	Tianjin liquor; Jinjiu liquor
津枯血燥	〈中医药〉desiccation of liquid and blood dryness
津亏热结证	〈中医药〉pattern of fluid deficiency and accumulated heat
津气亏虚证	〈中医药〉pattern of fluid and qi depletion; pattern of deficiency of fluid-qi
津血同源	〈中医药〉homogeny of fluid and blood
津液不足	〈中医药〉body fluid deficiency; insufficiency of the body fluid
津液代谢平衡	〈中医药〉metabolic balance of the body fluid
津液亏虚证	〈中医药〉pattern of body fluid deficiency; fluid depletion pattern
津液生化匮乏	〈中医药〉scanty production of the body fluid
津液失常	〈中医药〉disturbance of body fluid; body fluid disorder
紧箍咒	inhibiting magic phrase
紧急避孕药	emergency contraception; morning-after pill
紧急服务设施	emergency assistance facility
紧急救治	〈防疫〉emergency treatment
紧急通知	emergency notice; emergency notification
紧急状态	emergency; state of emergency
紧俏产品	commodities in short supply
紧缺人才	urgently-needed professional; short-supplied personnel
紧身的衣服	tight-fitting clothes
紧缩银根	tight money policy; monetary restraint
堇青石瓷	〈陶瓷〉cordierite porcelain
锦灯笼	〈中医药〉(of Latin) Calyx seu Fructus Physalis; Franchet Groundcherry Calyx and Fruit
锦绣糯米鸡	〈饮食〉Steamed Chicken Stuffed with Glutinous Rice

尽力阻止疫情跨境传播	〈防疫〉to minimize cross-border spread
进城务工	to look for jobs in cities
进城务工人员	migrant workers in cities
进城务工人员随迁子女	children of migrant workers in cities; children of rural migrants working in cities
进出口经理	import and export manager
进出口主管	import and export supervisor
进出口总额	total volume of foreign trade
进口联络员	import liaison staff
进修班	class for further studies
进针法	〈中医药〉method of needle insertion; needle insertion method
近部取穴	〈中医药〉neighboring point selection; selection of adjacent point
近海渔业	offshore fishery
劲酒	Jinjiu liquor
晋级考试	promotion test (test given to promote candidates on their knowledge of the relevant subjects); examination for promotion
晋阳刀	〈古币〉Jinyang small knife coin (issued in the Warring States period)
禁渔期	closed fishing seasons; fishing moratorium; fishing ban period
禁止密集聚会	〈防疫〉to ban mass gatherings
禁止面对面就餐	〈防疫〉prohibition of face-to-face dining
禁止吸烟区	smoke-free area
京葱爆炒牛柳	〈饮食〉Stir-Fried Beef Fillets with Scallion
京葱鸡块	〈饮食〉Chicken Pieces with Beijing Scallion; Diced Chicken with Beijng Scallion
京葱明虾	〈饮食〉Stir-Fried Prawn with Beijing Scallion
京葱虾籽烧海参	〈饮食〉Stir-Fried Sea Cucumbers with Shrimp Roe and Scallion
京葱羊肉	〈饮食〉Steamed Sliced Mutton with Beijing Scallion
京葱野鸽	〈饮食〉Braised Rock Pigeon with Beijing Scallion

京大戟	〈中医药〉(of Latin) Radix Euphorbiae Pekinensis; Peking Euphorbia Root
京东物流	Jingdong Logistics
京都上肉排	〈饮食〉Peking Spareribs with Tomato Sauce and Garlic Cloves
京广高速铁路	Beijing-Guangzhou high-speed railway
京广高铁	→京广高速铁路
京广铁路	Beijing-Guangzhou railway
京广线	→京广铁路
京沪高速列车	Beijing-Shanghai high-speed train
京酱龙虾球	〈饮食〉Lobster Balls with Sweet Bean Sauce
京酱肉丝	〈饮食〉Stir-Fried Shredded Pork with Sweet Bean Sauce
京九直通车	Beijing-Kowloon through train
京酒	Jingjiu liquor
京剧	Beijing Opera; Peking Opera
京剧脸谱	Beijing/Peking Opera mask; facial makeup in Beijing Opera
京剧票友	Peking Opera fan/amateur; amateur performer of Peking Opera
京剧人物脸谱	types of facial make-up in Peking Opera
京万红软膏	〈中医药〉Jingwanhong Ruangao; Jingwanhong Ointment
经编针织物	warp-knitted fabric
经典线路	classic travel route
经济承包制	management contract system
经济发展协调员	economic development coordinator
经济繁荣	economic boom; economic prosperity
经济复苏	economic resurgence; economic revival
经济杠杆	economic lever; economic leverage
经济过热	overheated economy; overheated development of the economy
经济开发区	economic development zone
经济社会秩序恢复	〈防疫〉to get the economy and society back to normal

经济适用房	economically affordable house; affordable housing
经济适用墓	affordable grave
经济危机	economic crisis
经济萧条	economic depression; economic slump
经济效益	economic performance; economic returns; economic efficiency
经济研究员	economic researcher
经济专员	economic commissioner; economic attaché
经络	〈中医药〉channels and collaterals; channels and network vessels
经络辨证	〈中医药〉pattern differentiation according to meridians; pattern differentiation of channel theory
经络系统	〈中医药〉system of meridians and collaterals
经络现象	〈中医药〉channel phenomenon; meridian phenomenon
经络学	〈中医药〉science of channels and collaterals; meridian physiotherapy
经络诊断	〈中医药〉meridian diagnostics; channel diagnostics
经络阻滞	〈中医药〉blockage of channel meridians
经脉	〈中医药〉channels; meridians (passages through which vital energy circulates)
经脉循行	〈中医药〉running course of the channels/meridians
《经史证类备急本草》	〈中医药〉*Jingshi Zhenglei Beiji Bencao*; *Classic Classified Materia Medica for Emergency*; *Classified Emergency Materia Medica Based on Historical Classics* (by Tang Shenwei in the Song Dynasty)
经穴	〈中医药〉channel acupoint; meridian acupoint
经营管理不善	mismanagement; poor management; poor operation and management
经营性文化单位	for-profit cultural institution
经营性文艺演出	commercial art and cultural performance

荆芥	〈中医药〉(of Latin) Herba Schizonepetae; Fineleaf Schizonepeta Herb
荆芥穗	〈中医药〉(of Latin) Spica Schizonepetae; Schizonepeta Spike
惊鹄髻	(of hairstyle) jinghu bun; flying-bird-shaped chignon
惊悸不安	〈中医药〉palpitation due to fright
惊恐伤肾	〈中医药〉kidney injury by fright and fear
惊则气乱	〈中医药〉qi turbulence due to fright and fear
精打细算	to make every cent count; to meticulously plan all expenditures; careful calculation and strict budgeting
精简开支	to cut down the outlay; to retrench expenses; retrenchment in expenditure
精密度检查员	precision inspector
精气亏虚证	〈中医药〉pattern of vital essence depletion; depletion pattern
精神病顾问	psychiatric counsellor
精神病医师	psychiatrist; headshrinker
精神食粮	nourishment for the mind; intellectual food
精神文明	cultural and ethical progress
精神文明奖	high morality prize
精神文明先进个人	spiritual advanced individual
精神修养	spiritual health care
精神支柱	spiritual prop; mental support
精陶	〈陶瓷〉fine earthenware; fine pottery
精血同源	〈中医药〉homogeny of essence and blood
精英治国论	theory of elite administration
精制银翘解毒片	〈中医药〉Jingzhi Yinqiao Jiedu Pian; Honeysuckle Forsythia Toxin-Resolving Tablet
精装香烟	hardbound cigarettes
精准对接劳务输出地和输入地	〈防疫〉to accurately connect both ends of labor transfer
精准防治	〈防疫〉targeted measures in the prevention and control of the epidemic

精准施策	〈防疫〉to take targeted measures
精准医疗	precision medicine; personalized medicine; targeted treatments
精子库	sperm bank
井冈翠绿	〈茶〉Jinggang Jade Green tea
井冈山香烟	Mt. Chingkang cigarettes
井穴	〈中医药〉Jing acupoint; well point
颈部穴位	〈中医药〉acupoint on cervical
颈复康颗粒	〈中医药〉Jingfukang Keli; Neck-Recovering Granule
颈椎	〈中医药〉Jingzhui acupoint; Cervical Vertebrae (AH13)
景德镇	Jingdezhen (known as a leading porcelain manufacturing center)
景德镇瓷	〈陶瓷〉Jingdezhen porcelain
景德镇窑	Jingdezhen Kiln
景德镇窑影青瓷像	〈陶瓷〉misty-blue glaze porcelain figure of Jingdezhen Kiln
景观建筑师	landscape architect; landscape designer
景观设计师	landscape designer
景泰蓝	〈陶瓷〉cloisonné enamel; cloisonne ware
景泰青花龙纹梅瓶	〈陶瓷〉blue and white plum vase with dragon pattern (Ming Jingtai period)
景阳冈酒	Jingyang Gang liquor
《景岳全书》	〈中医药〉*Jingyue Quanshu*; *Complete Works of Jingyue*; *Jingyue's Complete Works* (by Zhang Jingyue in the Ming Dynasty)
景芝酒	Jingzhi liquor
警戒水位	warning (water) level; danger level
净石灵胶囊	〈中医药〉Jingshiling Jiaonang; Stone-Dispelling Capsule
胫衣	calf-length split pants; open-seat pants
竞技体育	competitive sports
竞争机制	competitive mechanism

竞争上岗	to take up a job through competition
竞争优势	competitive edge; competitive advantage; advantage in competition
敬老院	home for the aged; seniors' home
敬业奉献	professional devotion and contribution
敬业精神	professional dedication; professional ethics
境外进京人员	〈防疫〉travelers arriving in Beijing from overseas
境外就业	to be employed abroad; overseas employment
境外输入关联病例	〈防疫〉cases resulting from virus carriers traveling from abroad; patients infected by virus carriers traveling from abroad
境外消费	consumption abroad
镜面舌	〈中医药〉mirror-like tongue; mirror tongue
纠结	jiujielity; entanglement; to be entangled with
九重茄子	〈饮食〉Stir-Fried Eggplants with Basil
九重鲜鲍	〈饮食〉Stir-Fried Fresh Abalone with Basil
九刺	〈中医药〉nine needling methods; nine techniques of needling
九宫格火锅	〈饮食〉trellis hot pot; nine-block-box hot pot; nine-grid spicy hot pot
九华膏	〈中医药〉Jiuhua Gao; Jiuhua Plaster
九华毛峰	〈茶〉Jiuhua Maofeng tea; Jiuhua Tippy tea
九江双蒸酒	Jiujiang double distilled liquor
九节菖蒲	〈中医药〉(of Latin) Rhizoma Anemones Altaicae; Altai Anemone Root
九里香	〈中医药〉(of Latin) Folium et Cacumen Murrayae; Murraya Jasminorage
九年制义务教育	nine-year compulsory education
九味羌活汤	〈中医药〉Jiuwei Qianghuo Tang; Nine-Ingredient Notopterygium Decoction
九仙散	〈中医药〉Jiuxian San; Nine Immortals Powder
九香虫	〈中医药〉(of Latin) Aspongopus; Stink-Bug
九酝春酒	Jiuyun Spring liquor
九针	〈中医药〉nine classical needles

九转大肠	〈饮食〉Braised Pork Intestines in Brown Sauce
久仰	(of polite greeting) jiuyang; I've long been looking forward to meeting you; I've heard so much about you
灸法	〈中医药〉moxibustion method
灸剂	〈中医药〉moxibustion formula
灸禁	〈中医药〉moxibustion contraindications
韭菜炒蛋	〈饮食〉Scrambled Eggs with Chinese Chives
韭菜炒豆干	〈饮食〉Stir-Fried Dried Tofu with Chinese Chives
韭菜炒河虾	〈饮食〉Stir-Fried Shrimps with Chinese Chives; Stir-Fried River Prawn with Chinese Chives
韭菜盒(子)	〈饮食〉Leek Turnover; Fried Leek Dumplings
韭菜晶饼	〈饮食〉Steamed Chinese Chives/Leek Pancake
韭菜水饺	〈饮食〉Boiled Jiaozi/Dumplings Stuffed with Chinese Chive
韭菜鲜桃仁	〈饮食〉Fresh Walnut Kernels with Leek
韭菜籽	〈中医药〉(of Latin) Semen Allii Tuberosi; Chinese Leek Seed
韭黄炒肉丝	〈饮食〉Stir-Fried Shredded Pork with Chives
韭黄螺片	〈饮食〉Stir-Fried Sliced Sea Whelks with Hotbed Chives
韭黄山鸡片	〈饮食〉Stir-Fried Pheasant Slices with Leek's Shoots
韭黄鳝片	〈饮食〉Stir-Fried Sliced Eel with Chive
韭黄虾肠粉	〈饮食〉Steamed Rice Rolls Stuffed with Shrimps and Chives
韭王花枝片	〈饮食〉Stir-Fried Cuttlefish with Chive
韭王鸡丝春卷	〈饮食〉Spring Rolls Stuffed with Chicken and Chives
韭王象拔蚌	〈饮食〉Stir-Fried Geoduck Clam with Chive
韭香武昌鱼	〈饮食〉Braised Wuchang Fish with Chinese Chive
酒纯度	liquor purity
酒炖	〈中医药〉to stew with wine
酒鬼酒	Jiugui liquor; Jiugui spirit
酒海	big conservator for liquor storage

酒剂	〈中医药〉wine formula; medicated wine; medicinal wine
酒煎	〈中医药〉to decoct with wine; wine preparation
酒令	drinking game; drinkers' wager game; drinking game verses
酒母	yeast mash; barm
酒酿圆子	〈饮食〉Glutinous Rice Balls in Fermented Rice Wine
酒醅	alcoholic fermentative material; fermented grain
酒肉朋友	fair-weather friend; mercenary friend; brothers in debauchery
酒水部经理	beverage manager
酒体	wine body
酒头	initial distillate
酒尾	last distillate
酒仙	winebibber; brewmaster
酒筵[席]	banquet; feast banquet
酒药	yeast for brewing rice wine or fermenting glutinous rice →小曲酒
酒糟	vinasse; distiller's grains; distillers' solubles
酒蒸	〈中医药〉to steam with wine
酒蒸鸡	〈饮食〉Steamed Chicken with Rice Wine and Dates
酒政	government decree of liquor (related to the brewing, sale and taxation)
酒制	〈中医药〉processing with wine; to process with wine
酒炙	〈中医药〉to stir-fry with wine
酒醉排骨	〈饮食〉Spare Ribs in Wine Sauce
《救荒本草》	〈中医药〉*Jiuhuang Bencao*; *Materia Medica for Relief of Famines*; *Materia Medica for Famines* (by Zhu Xiao et al. in the Ming Dynasty)
救急稀涎散	〈中医药〉Jiuji Xixian San; Emergency Drool-Thinning Powder

救济金	relief fund
救死扶伤	(of idiom) to heal the wounded and rescue the dying
救灾扶贫	to provide disaster relief and help the poor
救助系统通用操作员	GMDSS general operator
救助系统限用操作员	GMDSS restricted operator
就地考察	on-the-spot inspection
就地取材	to obtain materials from local sources; to draw on local resources
就业保险	employment insurance
就业服务	employment service
就业服务中心	job/employment service center
就业高峰年	peak year for college graduates entering the job market
就业机会	job opening; job opportunity; employment opportunity
就业前培训	pre-job training; pre-employment training
就业市场状况	job/employment market condition
就业信息网络	job/employment information networks
就业压力	employment pressure
就业优先政策	pro-employment policy
居家办公	〈防疫〉work from home; WFH
居家隔离	〈防疫〉home quarantine; home isolation
居家养老	home-based care for the aged
居家医学观察	〈防疫〉medical observation at home
居留权	right of residence/abode
居民身份证	resident identification card
居民委员会	resident committee; neighborhood committee
居民消费价格指数	Consumer Price Index; CPI
居民住房建设	residential construction
居住证	residence permit; residential pass
局部取穴	〈中医药〉selection of local point; local point selection
《局方发挥》	〈中医药〉*Jufang Fahui*; *Elaboration of Bureau Prescription*; *Elucidation of Dispensary Formula* (by Zhu Zhenheng in the Yuan Dynasty)

局域网管理员	local area network (LAN) administrator
局域网系统分析员	local area network system analyst; LAN system analyst
菊花	〈中医药〉(of Latin) Flos Chrysanthemi; Chrysanthemun Flower
菊花茶	chrysanthemum tea
菊花酒	chrysanthemum wine
菊花乌龙烩鱼肚	〈饮食〉Stewed Fish Maws with Chrysanthemum and Oolong Tea
菊花心	〈中医药〉Gracilaria Coforvoides; Radial Striations
焗肉排	〈饮食〉Deep-Fried Spare Ribs with Salt and Pepper; Baked Spare Ribs
橘核	〈中医药〉(of Latin) Semen Citri Reticulatae; Tangerine Seed
橘核丸	〈中医药〉Juhe Wan; Tangerine Pip Pill
橘红	〈中医药〉(of Latin) Exocarpium Citri Rubrum; Red Tangerine Peel
橘红颗粒	〈中医药〉Juhong Keli; Cough-Checking Pomelo Granule
橘红丸	〈中医药〉Juhong Wan; Red Tangerine Peel Pill
橘皮油	〈中医药〉Jupi You; Tangerine Peel Oil
橘皮竹茹汤	〈中医药〉Jupi Zhuru Tang; Tangerine Peel and Bamboo Shavings Decoction
橘(皮)釉	〈陶瓷〉orange-peel glaze
橘子汤团羹	〈饮食〉Dumplings with Orange Sauce
莒大[邦]刀	〈币〉judadao; Ju broadsword (a symbol of national stability in the Warring States period)
举报信箱	complaint mailbox
举报中心	informant center
举国机制	〈防疫〉nationwide mechanism
举手表决	vote by show of hands
巨骨	〈中医药〉Jugu acupoint; Great Bone (LI16)
巨阙	〈中医药〉Juque acupoint; Great Sinus (CV14)

巨仁风湿定胶囊	〈中医药〉Juren Fengshiding Jiaonang; Juren Rheumatism-Conquering Capsule
具服	→朝[具]服
聚集性感染	〈防疫〉cluster of infections; Covid-19 cluster
屦	〈古〉straw sandals; hemp and rattan shoes
捐资办学	to denote money for school
蠲痹汤	〈中医药〉Juanbi Tang; Impediment-Alleviating Decoction
卷烟纸	cigarette paper
绢	juan (thin and tough silk); spun silk
绢帛	silk fabrics
绢云母质瓷	〈陶瓷〉sericite porcelain; sericite china
决明降脂片	〈中医药〉Jueming Jiangzhi Pian; Fetid Cassia Fat-Reducing Tablet
决明子	〈中医药〉(of Latin) Semen Cassiae; Cassia Seed
厥阴俞	〈中医药〉Jueyinshu acupoint; Yin Reverting Transport; Yin Equilibrium Transport (BL14)
军便装	military jacket
军嫂	soldier's wife; military spouse
军神	God of War (who directs military operations with miraculous skill and thought)
军训	military training
军训先进个人	advanced individual in military training
君臣佐使	〈中医药〉(the basic principle of prescription composition regarding compatibility and referring to different medicinal roles as) sovereign, minister, assistant, and envoy
君山银针	〈茶〉Junshan Silver Needle tea
君药	〈中医药〉sovereign drug; sovereign medicine (the drug acting as a dominant role in a prescription)
钧瓷	〈陶瓷〉Jun porcelain; Jun chinaware
钧窑	〈陶瓷〉Jun Kiln (one of the five famous kilns in the Song Dynasty)

钧窑冲天耳贴塑炉	〈陶瓷〉Jun Kiln molded furnace with upward ear (Yuan Dynasty)
钧窑瓷	〈陶瓷〉Chün porcelain; Jun Kiln porcelain
钧窑瓷罐	〈陶瓷〉Jun Kiln porcelain jar
钧窑瓷花盆	〈陶瓷〉Jun Kiln ceramic flower pot
钧窑海棠式花盆	〈陶瓷〉Jun kiln Chinese crabapple-shaped flower-pot
钧窑红釉贯耳瓶	〈陶瓷〉Jun Kiln red glaze vase with two tubular lug-handles (Yuan Dynasty)
钧窑双耳炉	〈陶瓷〉Jun Kiln two-eared incense burner
钧窑天青釉八卦纹香炉	〈陶瓷〉Jun Kiln azure-glazed incense burner with Eight Diagrams pattern (Yuan Dynasty)
钧窑香炉	〈陶瓷〉Jun Kiln incense burner
钧(瓷)釉	〈陶瓷〉Jun porcelain glaze
菌花香	〈茶〉arohid flavor
竣工仪式	completion ceremony

K

咖啡厅经理	coffee shop manager
咖啡厅主管	coffee shop supervisor
开氅	〈服饰〉(of traditional Chinese opera) Kaichang robe
开除公职	to discharge sb. from public employment; to take the name off the book; to be discharged from office
开发工程师	development engineer
开发式扶贫	poverty reduction through development projects; development-oriented poverty alleviation/relief
开发新产品	to develop new product
开发总监	chief development officer; CDO
开工不足	enterprises running under their production capacity; to operate/work under capacity
开工典礼	commencement ceremony
开工率	rate of operation; rate of opening capacity
开国纪念币	founding commemorative coin
开后门	to offer advantages to one's friends or relatives by underhand means; under-the-counter deals; to resort to back-stair influence
开户头	to open an account
开架销售	self service (in a store)
开炉钱	〈古〉coin made upon the furnace opening
开门红	to make a good start; to get off on the right foot; an auspicious start
开窍法	〈中医药〉resuscitation-inducing method; orifice-opening method

开窍剂	〈中医药〉formula for resuscitation; resuscitation inducing prescription
开涮	to make sb. the laughing stock; to make a fool of sb.; to poke fun at sb.
开水白菜	〈饮食〉Chinese Cabbage in Soup
开水冲服	〈中医药〉to mix in boiled water for oral taking
开拓前进	to open up new ways forward
开胃消食片	〈中医药〉Kaiwei Xiaoshi Pian; Appetite-Promoting and Food-Digesting Tablet
开小灶	to give special attention/favor
开胸毛衫	bolero sweater
开胸顺气丸	〈中医药〉Kaixiong Shunqi Wan; Digestion-Promoting Pill
开夜车	to work late into the night/overnight; to burn the midnight oil
开元通宝	〈币〉coin with characters kaiyuan tongbao (issued from the early Tang Dynasty to the early Song Dynasty)
开源节流	to increase income and reduce expenditure
开展国际联防联控	〈防疫〉to make a collective response for control and treatment at the international level
开展流行病学调查	〈防疫〉to conduct epidemiological investigation
开足马力	to put into high gear; to go full steam ahead
坎儿井	karez (an irrigation system of wells connected by underground channel in Xinjiang)
坎肩	〈服饰〉waistcoat; sleeveless jacket (usu. padded or lined) →马甲
侃大山	to chat idly; to shoot the breeze; to chew the fat
看心理医生	to see a psychologist
康复治疗	〈中医药〉rehabilitation therapy; rehabilitation treatment
康居工程	comfortable housing project
康乐部	recreation (and entertainment) department
康乐部组长	head of recreation department

康乐主管	recreation center supervisor
抗病毒	〈防疫〉anti-viral
抗病毒口服液	〈中医药〉Kang Bingdu Koufuye; Anti-Virus Oral Liquid
抗病毒药	〈防疫〉antiviral drug
抗病毒治疗	〈防疫〉antiviral therapy
抗低氧血症	〈防疫〉anti-hypoxemia medication
抗感解毒颗粒	〈中医药〉Kanggan Jiedu Keli; Anti-Flu Toxin-Resolving Granule
抗宫炎胶囊	〈中医药〉Kang Gongyan Jiaonang; Uterine Inflammation Preventing Capsule
抗骨增生片	〈中医药〉Kang Guzengsheng Pian; Anti-Osteohyperplasia Tablet
抗骨增生丸	〈中医药〉Kang Guzengsheng Wan; Osteohyperplasia-Curing Pill
抗击肺炎疫情	〈防疫〉to combat the pneumonia outbreak
抗击疫情第一线	〈防疫〉front line of the battle against the epidemic
抗继发感染	〈防疫〉measures to prevent secondary infections
抗脑衰胶囊	〈中医药〉Kang Naoshuai Jiaonang; Anti-Brain-Weakening Capsule
抗生素治疗	〈防疫〉antibiotic therapy
抗体	〈防疫〉antibody
抗体筛查	〈防疫〉antibody screening
抗休克	〈防疫〉anti-shock
抗原检测	〈防疫〉antigen detection; antigen testing
抗战胜利阅兵	Victory Day parade; victory parade of the War of Resistance Against Japanese Aggression
抗震棚	quake-proof shelter
炕	kang (bed-stove in the north of China); heatable brick bed
考古学家	archaeologist
考核标准	criteria of assessment
考勤制度	work attendance checking system

考碗族	stable job seeker; gold-rice-bowl seeker; rice-bowl-test-taking tribe
考研	to take part in the entrance exams for postgraduate schools; to take part in the postgraduate entrance exams
考研热	craze for graduate school
烤臭豆腐	〈饮食〉Grilled Smelly Tofu/Bean Curd
烤羔羊	〈饮食〉Roasted Lamb
烤红薯	〈饮食〉Roasted Sweet Potatoes
烤花揽鳜鱼	〈饮食〉Braised Mandarin Fish
烤鸡	〈饮食〉Roasted Chicken; Grilled Chicken
烤鸡肉串	〈饮食〉Roasted Chicken Kebabs
烤馒头	〈饮食〉Baked Mantou; Baked Bun
烤墨笔鲳鱼	〈饮食〉Baked Rolled Pomfret
烤鲇鱼	〈饮食〉Roasted Fresh Catfish
烤酿鳜鱼	〈饮食〉Baked Stuffed Mandarin Fish
烤牛肉	〈饮食〉Roast Beef; Roasted Beef
烤全羊	〈饮食〉Roasted Whole Lamb; Grilled Whole Lamb
烤肉厨师领班	rotisseur
烤乳猪	〈饮食〉Roasted Suckling Pig with Seasoning Sauce
烤沙茶鸡	〈饮食〉Baked Chicken with Satay Paste in Casserole
烤酥鱼	〈饮食〉Crispy-Baked Crucian Carp
烤香妃鸡球	〈饮食〉Baked Chicken Balls with Egg Whites
烤羊里脊	〈饮食〉Roasted Lamb Tenderloin
烤羊排	〈饮食〉Roasted Mutton Chops
烤羊肉串	〈饮食〉Roasted Mutton Cubes on Skewer
烤羊腿	〈饮食〉Roasted Lamb Leg; Baked Gigot
烤汁茄子	〈饮食〉Roasted Eggplants
靠边站	to be deprived of authority; to be dismissed
科班	Peking Opera school of the old type; old-type opera school; professional training class
科班出身	(a general term) to be a professional by formal education and training

科技发展基金	science and technology development fund
科教兴国	to rejuvenate our country through science, technology and education
科学防治	〈防疫〉science-based prevention and control of the epidemic
科学技术委员会	science and technology commission
科研攻关	to work towards key technological breakthroughs
科研管理人员	scientific research management personnel
蚵仔大肠面线	〈饮食〉Fried Rice Noodles with Pork Intestine and Oyster
蚵仔煎	〈饮食〉Oyster Omelette
颗粒剂	〈中医药〉granule; granule formulation
咳嗽礼仪	〈防疫〉cough etiquette
可比价格	comparable prices
可重复使用口罩	〈防疫〉reusable mask
可靠度工程师	reliability engineer
可乐凤中翼	〈饮食〉Pan-Fried Chicken Wings in Coca-Cola Sauce
可鲁宾釉	〈陶瓷〉columbine glaze
可帕尔塔釉	〈陶瓷〉coperta glaze
可溶性釉	〈陶瓷〉soluble glaze
可视电话	video telephone
可再生资源	regenerative resources
可支配收入	disposable income; discretionary income
可转换债券	convertible bond
渴不欲饮	〈中医药〉thirst without desire to drink
刻花白瓷罐	〈陶瓷〉white porcelain pot with carved floral pattern
恪守职业道德	to observe professional ethics
客房布草员	room linen clerk
客房部	housekeeping department
客房部经理	housekeeping manager
客房服务员	room attendant
客房管家部主任	housekeeping director

客房销售代表	room sales representative
客房销售经理	room sales manager
客房销售文员	room sales clerk
客房销售主任	room sales director
客房中心	housekeeping center
客房总监	director of housekeeping
客服经理	customer service manager
客服主管	customer service supervisor
客服助理	customer service assistant
客服专员	customer service specialist
客服总监	customer service director
客户服务代表	customer service representative
客户服务热线	customer hot line
客户关系经理	customer relation manager
客户关系主管	customer relation supervisor
客户管理助理	assistant customer/account executive
客户经理	account manager; customer manager
客户群总监	group account director
客户专员	account service specialist
客户总监	account director; chief user officer
客家封鸡	〈饮食〉Meizhou Stewed Chicken
客家小炒	〈饮食〉Hakka Stir-Fried Pork and Squid with Dried Turnip and Garlic
客家盐焗鸡	〈饮食〉Hakka Salt Baked Chicken
客流量	volume of commuters; passenger volume
客务主任	guest relation officer
客座教授	guest professor; visiting professor
课件比赛	courseware design contest
课外活动	extracurricular activities
啃老族	parasite single (to live off one's parents); boomerang kid; NEET group (not in Education, Employment or Training)
空杯留香	〈酒〉fragrance remained in the cup; alcoholic aroma-filled glass (referring to high-quality Chinese white liquor)

空巢家庭	empty nest family (where the elderly live alone because their children work in some other place)
空巢老人	empty-nest elderly; empty nester (whose children have left home)
空乘人员	flight attendant
空腹服	〈中医药〉to be administered at an empty stomach; to be taken on an empty stomach
空姐	airline stewardess; female flight attendant
空气污染	air pollution
空气污染物	air pollutant
空嫂	married airline stewardess
空首布	〈币〉head breached spade coin; shovel-shaped coin (issued in the Spring and Autumn period and Warring States period)
空头市场	bear market
空头支票	unconvertible cheque; empty promise; unfulfilled promise
空中教育	education through broadcast media
空中楼阁	castle in the air; mirage; ivory tower
空中小姐	airline stewardess; female flight attendant
空中走廊	air corridor; air lane
孔府家酒	Confucius family/house liquor
孔集烧鸡	〈饮食〉Kongji Pot-Stewed Chicken
孔雀蓝釉	〈陶瓷〉peacock blue glaze
孔雀绿釉	〈陶瓷〉peacock green glaze
孔雀女	peacock woman; silk-stocking lady; pampered urban girl
控烟	tobacco control; smoking control
控烟办公室	tobacco control office
控制传染源	〈防疫〉to control the sources of infection
控制人口流动	〈防疫〉to curb population flow
控制疫情波及范围	〈防疫〉to curb the spread of the disease
控制疫情永远不会太晚	〈防疫〉it is never too late to get the pandemic under control

口服液	〈中医药〉oral liquid
口蘑菜胆	〈饮食〉Stir-Fried Green Vegetables and Mushrooms
口蘑炖鸽子	〈饮食〉Stewed Pigeon with Dried Mushroom
口蘑烩鸡丁	〈饮食〉Braised Diced Chicken with Mushrooms
口蘑鸡块	〈饮食〉Stewed Chicken Pieces with Mushrooms
口蘑煎蛋卷	〈饮食〉Pan-Fried Mushroom Omelettes
口水鸡	〈饮食〉Steamed Chicken with Chili Sauce
口水鸭肠	〈饮食〉Duck Intestines with Chili Sauce
口炎清颗粒	〈中医药〉Kouyanqing Keli; Stomatitis-Clearing Granule
口罩恐惧	〈防疫〉maskaphobia
口子窖酒	Kouzi Cellar liquor
扣肉	〈饮食〉Braised Pork Slices in Soy Sauce
扣碗牛肉	〈饮食〉Steamed Beef with Soy Sauce
苦丁茶	〈中医药〉(of Latin) Folium Llicis Latifoliae; Leaf of Chinese Holly
苦瓜茶	balsam pear tea
苦瓜蛋清羹	〈饮食〉Bitter Melon and Egg White Soup
苦果	bitter fruit (metaphorically referring to something unpleasant as a result of some actions); adverse consequence; harmful consequence
苦楝皮	〈中医药〉(of Latin) Cortex Meliae; Sichuan Chinaberry Bark
苦参	〈中医药〉(of Latin) Radix Sophorae Flavescentis; Lightyellow Sophora Root
苦参栓	〈中医药〉Kushen Shuan; Flavescent Sophora Suppository
苦温燥湿	〈中医药〉dry dampness with bitter-warm; to dispel dampness with bitter- and warm-natured drugs
苦杏仁	〈中医药〉(of Latin) Semen Armeniacae Amarum; Bitter Apricot Seed
库存管理经理	inventory control manager

库平两	〈旧〉(of weight unit) Kuping tael
库依乃克	〈服饰〉(of Uyghur) kuyinaike; shirt
裤褶服	〈古〉kuzhe clothes; jumpsuit; body suit
跨境采购	〈防疫〉cross-border procurement
跨境婚姻	cross-country marriage; marriage of a native with a foreigner
跨境交付	cross border supply
会计部经理	accounting manager
会计从业资格证	certificate of accounting professional
会计证	accounting certificate
会计主管	accounting supervisor
快餐厨师	short-order cook
快餐工	fast food worker
快车线路	express line
快递公司	express company
快递员	courier; expressman
快乐大本营	(of an entertainment show) Happy Camp (Hu'nan TV, 1997—2021)
快乐男声	(of a TV program) Super Boy
快书	quick-patter (rhythmic storytelling accompanied by bamboo or copper clappers)
快速消费品	fast-moving consumer goods; FMCG
快舟火箭	Kuaizhou rocket
筷子	chopsticks
宽边草帽	broad-brimmed straw hat
髋骨	〈中医药〉Kuangu acupoint; Hip Bone (EX-LE1)
款冬花	〈中医药〉(of Latin) Flos Farfarae; Common Coltsfoot Flower
纩袍	〈古〉silk robe (worn by the rich)
矿产勘探工程师	mineral exploration engineer
矿产资源储量评估师	mineral reserve appraiser
矿业权评估师	mining rights appraiser
亏本生意	losing proposition
魁纳克	〈服饰〉(of Uzbek) kuinake; one-piece dress

坤鞋	〈古〉→花盆底鞋
裈甲	〈古〉front crotch armor
焜锅馍馍	〈饮食〉Kun Pot Steamed Bun (a specialty in Qinghai)
扩大国内需求	to expand domestic demand
扩大消费需求	to expand consumer demand
阔边旗袍	cheongsam with wide brim
阔口花瓶	〈陶瓷〉wide-mouthed flower vase

L

垃圾分类	garbage classification; refuse sorting
垃圾债券	junk bond
垃圾综合处理	integrated garbage treatment
拉帮结派	(of idiom) to form cliques and factions; to form a personal-interest clique
拉关系	to try to curry favor with sb.; to build connection; to try to establish a rapport with sb.
拉链工程	zipper project
拉拢	to draw over to one's side; to cozy up to sb.
拉山头	to form a faction
喇叭裤	flare trousers; bell-bottom pants
喇叭袖	flare sleeve; trumpet sleeve
腊八豆炒腊肉	〈饮食〉Stir-Fried Preserved Pork with Fermented Soy Beans
腊八蒜茼蒿	〈饮食〉Crown Daisy with Sweet Garlic
腊八粥	〈饮食〉Laba Porridge; Congee with Fruit Kernels and Dried Fruits (served on the 8th day of the 12th lunar month)
腊肉炒饭	〈饮食〉Stir-Fried Rice with Preserved Pork
腊肉炒香干	〈饮食〉Stir-Fried Preserved Pork with Dried Tofu Slices
腊肉炒香芹	〈饮食〉Stir-Fried Preserved Pork with Celery
腊肉红菜薹	〈饮食〉Stir-Fried Preserved Pork with Red Vegetables
腊肉西芹卤汁面	〈饮食〉Noodles with Preserved Pork and Celery

腊汁肉夹馍	〈饮食〉Cured Meat in Pancakes; Minced Braised Meat in Baked Bun with Sauce
蜡染	wax printing; wax-dyeing
蜡染服装	batik garment; wax-printed clothes
辣白菜炒牛肉	〈饮食〉Stir-Fried Beef with Cabbage and Chili Sauce
辣白菜炒五花肉	〈饮食〉Stir-Fried Pork Belly with Cabbage and Chili Sauce
辣炒蛤蜊	〈饮食〉Stir-Fried Spicy Clams
辣炒墨鱼竹百叶	〈饮食〉Stir-Fried Spicy Cuttlefish and Tofu Sheets
辣黄瓜	〈饮食〉Pickled Cucumber with Chili Sauce
辣黄瓜条	〈饮食〉Pickled Cucumber Strips with Chili Sauce
辣酱油烤鸡腿	〈饮食〉Roasted Chicken Drumsticks in Chili Sauce
辣酱蒸鲜鱿	〈饮食〉Steamed Squid with Chili Sauce
辣椒炒鸡块	〈饮食〉Stir-Fried Chicken Cubes with Green Pepper
辣椒风湿膏	〈中医药〉Lajiao Fengshi Gao; Hot Pepper Rheumatism Plaster
辣椒红釉	〈陶瓷〉paprika glaze; chilli red glaze
辣椒炝时蔬	〈饮食〉Stir-Fried Seasonal Vegetables with Chili Pepper
辣酒煮花蟹	〈饮食〉Boiled Crab with Chili in Liquor
辣味红扒鹿筋	〈饮食〉Spicy-Braised Venison Tendon with Brown Sauce
辣味烩虾	〈饮食〉Braised Prawns in Chili Sauce
辣味烩虾球	〈饮食〉Braised Prawn Balls in Chili Sauce
辣香大鱼头	〈饮食〉Braised Fish Head with Pepper and Peanuts
辣汁串烧鱼	〈饮食〉Fish Kebabs with Chili Sauce
辣汁炸鸡腿	〈饮食〉Deep-Fried Chicken Drumsticks in Hot Sauce
辣子炒鸡丁	〈饮食〉Stir-Fried Diced Chicken with Green Pepper
辣子炒肉	〈饮食〉Stir-Fried Pork with Hot Pepper Sauce

辣子豆腐	〈饮食〉Tofu in Hot Pepper Sauce
辣子干贝	〈饮食〉Stir-Fried Dried Scallops in Hot Pepper Sauce
辣子鳜鱼	〈饮食〉Mandarin Fish with Pickled Cayenne Pepper
辣子牛肉	〈饮食〉Stir-Fried Beef with Hot Pepper Sauce
辣子肉丁	〈饮食〉Stir-Fried Diced Pork with Green Pepper
辣子虾仁	〈饮食〉Stir-Fried Shelled Shrimps with Hot Pepper Sauce
莱菔子	〈中医药〉(of Latin) Semen Raphani; Radish Seed
赖永初酒	Lai Yongchu liquor
兰花鸽蛋	〈饮食〉Orchid-Shaped Pigeon Eggs
兰花双味虾仁	〈饮食〉Stir-Fried Shelled Shrimps with Broccoli of Two Tastes
兰花珍品二锅头	〈酒〉Orchid Treasure Erguotou
兰陵酒	Lanling wine
《兰室秘藏》	〈中医药〉*Lanshi Micang*; *Secret Records of the Orchid Chamber*; *Secret Book of Orchid Chamber* (by Li Gao in the Jin Dynasty)
兰溪毛峰	〈茶〉Lanxi Maofeng tea; Lanxi Tippy tea
兰州牛肉拉面	〈饮食〉Hand-Pulled Noodle Soup with Beef, Lanzhou Style
栏干服	〈布依族〉langan clothes; laced suit of jacket and trousers trimmed with laces
阑尾穴	〈中医药〉Lanwei acupoint; Appendix Point (EX-LE7)
蓝地珐琅彩缠枝花纹瓶	〈陶瓷〉blue ground enamel vase with interlaced branches and floral pattern
蓝地粉彩轧道牡丹纹碗	〈陶瓷〉blue glazed bowl with famille rose peony pattern (Qing Qianlong period)
蓝靛	Chinese indigo
蓝靛印染	〈侗族〉indigo dyeing
蓝领工人	blue-collar worker
蓝印户口	〈旧〉household registration with blue-print (meaning temporary residence)

蓝釉暗刻凤纹玉壶春瓶	〈陶瓷〉blue glaze Yuhuchun vase with covert-engraved phoenix pattern (Yuan Dynasty)
蓝釉暗刻龙纹杯	〈陶瓷〉blue glaze cup with covert-engraved dragon pattern (Ming Chenghua period)
蓝釉暗刻龙纹罐	〈陶瓷〉blue glaze jar with covert-engraved dragon pattern (Yuan Dynasty)
蓝釉白龙纹瓷盘	〈陶瓷〉blue glazed plate with white dragon pattern
蓝釉金彩梅花瓶	〈陶瓷〉blue glaze vase with golden plum blossom pattern
蓝釉青花番莲碗	〈陶瓷〉blue glazed bowl with passiflora pattern (Qing Qianlong period)
襕衫	〈古〉lanshan robe; scholar's clothing (with stitches and round neckline)
榄菜肉菘炒四季豆	〈饮食〉Stir-Fried French Beans with Minced Pork and Kale Borecole
榄菜肉碎炖豆腐	〈饮食〉Stewed Tofu with Olive Pickles and Minced Pork
榄仁炒鱼环	〈饮食〉Stir-Fried Minced Dace with Olive Seeds
榄仁马拉糕	〈饮食〉Steamed Olive Kernel Cake
烂摊子	awful mess; shambles
烂尾楼	unduly completed building project; abandoned and unfinished building
滥发文凭	to issue diplomas recklessly
滥发纸币	excessive issue of bank notes; excessive note issue
郎酒	Langjiu liquor
郎泉酒	Langquan liquor
郎窑红(釉)	〈陶瓷〉Lang Kiln red glaze
郎窑绿釉	〈陶瓷〉Lang Kiln green glaze
郎中	〈古〉a physician trained in herbal medicine; an ancient official title
狼狈不堪	to be in an awkward predicament
朗诵比赛	recital contest

浪子回头	to return to the fold; to turn over a new leaf; return of the prodigal son
捞面	〈饮食〉Lo Mein; Noodles Taken out of the Boiling Water with a Strainer
劳保医疗制度	labor medicare system; medical labor insurance system
劳动保护服	working wear
劳动定额	labor quota
劳动服务公司	labor service company
劳动关系专员	labor relations specialist
劳动合同制	labor contract system
劳动力产权	labor property rights
劳动力的流动性	fluidity of labor
劳动力过剩	labor surplus; manpower surplus
劳动模范	model worker; labor hero (an honorable title conferred on sb. for their excellent achievement)
劳动委员	commissary in charge of physical labor
劳动者素质	quality of the workforce; workers' quality
劳动争议	labor dispute
劳模	→劳动模范
劳务市场	labor market
劳务输出	export of labor services
劳资纠纷	trouble between labor and management; labor dispute
醪糟鸡蛋	〈饮食〉Poached Egg in Fermented Glutinous Rice Wine
老白干香型(风格)	〈酒〉Laobaigan-flavor style
老北京豆酱	〈饮食〉traditional Beijing bean paste
老醋黑木耳	〈饮食〉Black Fungi with Vinegar
老醋泡花生	〈饮食〉Deep-Fried Peanuts Pickled in Vinegar
老醋蜇头	〈饮食〉Jellyfish with Black Vinegar
老大难问题	long-standing problem; big and difficult problem
老刀牌香烟	Laodao cigarettes; Old Sword cigarettes
老鹳草	〈中医药〉(of Latin) Herba Erodii; Herba Geranii; Common Heron's Bill Herb; Wilford Granesbill Herb

老黄牛	willing ox (a person who serves the people wholeheartedly); honest and industrious worker; diligent and conscientious person
老酒菌汤	〈饮食〉Mushroom and Aged Rice Wine Soup
老君丹	〈中医药〉Laojun Dan; Great Sage Bolus
老赖	deadbeat (who tries to avoid paying his debts); debt defaulter
老龄化社会	aging society
老龄事业	cause of aging
老年保险制度	endowment insurance
老年病	age-related disease; aged diseases
老三届	junior and senior high school graduates of 1966—1968; school leavers of 1966—1968
老外	foreigner; layman (who don't know much about a field or industry)
老乡	fellow-townsman; fellow-villager
老烟鬼	chain smoker
老烟枪	heavy smoker
老爷	〈旧〉laoye; master; milord (a bureaucratic appellation or title)
老爷式态度	bureaucratic attitude
老一套	old practice; the same old story; an outmoded method
老油条	wily old bird; old slicker
老有所养	all the people enjoy their rights to old-age care
老中青三结合	combination of the old, the middle-aged and the young in the leadership
老字号	old and famous shop or enterprise; time-honored shop; time-honored brand
勒紧裤腰带	to tighten one's belt (to cut down on spending)
《雷公炮炙论》	〈中医药〉*Leigong Paozhi Lun*; *Lei's Treatise on Processing of Drugs*; *Master Lei's Discourse on Drug Processing* (by Lei Xiao in the Northern and Southern Dynasties)

雷公藤	〈中医药〉(of Latin) Tripterygium Wilfordii; Thunder God Vine
雷公藤片	〈中医药〉Leigongteng Pian; Common Threewingnut Root Tablet; Thunder God Vine Tablet
雷神山医院	〈防疫〉Leishenshan Hospital (in Wuhan)
雷神爷	Lord of Thunder
雷丸	〈中医药〉(of Latin) Omphalia; Thunder Ball
累计病例数	〈防疫〉cumulative number of cases
《类经》	〈中医药〉*Leijing*; *Classified Classic*; *Classified Canon* (an annotation to Inner Canon by Zhang Jingyue in the Ming Dynasty)
冷板凳	cold stool (an indifferent post or a cold reception)
厘	measurement unit name; (of length unit) li (equal to 10 mm); (of weight unit) li (equal to 0.03 gram); (of interest) li (equal to one percent per year)
离退办	office for the affairs of the retired workers
梨皮釉	〈陶瓷〉pear peel glaze
梨子酒	pear wine; pear cider
黎平雀舌	〈茶〉Liping's Bird's Tongue tea
藜蒿炒腊肉	〈饮食〉Stir-Fried Preserved Pork with Artemisia Selengensis
藜芦	〈中医药〉(of Latin) Falsehellebore Root and Rhizome; Veratrum Root
礼宾部	concierge; guest service
礼宾部经理	concierge manager
礼宾部主管	chief concierge
礼服	ceremonial robe; full dress; formal dress
礼壶	〈茶〉ritual pot
礼仪队	reception team; protocol team
礼仪小姐	Miss etiquette; ritual girl; guiding girl
李渡酒	Lidu spirit
李时珍补酒	Li Shizhen tonic liquor
里	li (a unit of length for itinerary about 500m)
里弄	linong; lanes and alleys

理财顾问	financial advisor; financial consultant
理法方药	〈中医药〉principle-method-recipe-medicines
理化瓷	→化学[理化]瓷
理化鉴定	〈中医药〉physical and chemical identification
理疗师	physical therapist; physiotherapist
理气法	〈中医药〉qi-flow rectifying/regulating method
理气和胃	〈中医药〉to regulate qi-flowing for harmonizing stomach; to rectify qi to harmonize the stomach
理气化痰	〈中医药〉to regulate qi-flowing for eliminating phlegm; to rectify qi to resolving phlegm
理气剂	〈中医药〉qi-regulating formula; qi-rectifying prescription
理气健脾	〈中医药〉to regulate qi-flowing for strengthening spleen; to rectify qi and fortify the spleen
理气行滞	〈中医药〉to regulate qi-flowing for activating stagnancy; to rectify qi to move stagnation
理气止痛	〈中医药〉to regulate qi-flowing for relieving pain; to rectify qi to relieve pain
理事长	president; president of a council
理血剂	〈中医药〉blood-regulating formula; blood-rectifying formula
《理瀹骈文》	〈中医药〉*Li Yue Pianwen*; *Topical Remedies in Rhyme*; *Rhymed Discourse for Topical Remedies* (by Wu Shangxian in the Qing Dynasty)
理中汤	〈中医药〉Lizhong Tang; Center-Rectifying Decoction; Ginseng Decoction for Regulating the Middle Energizer
锂辉石釉	〈陶瓷〉spodumene glaze
鲤鱼焙面	〈饮食〉Carp with Noodles in Sweet and Sour Sauce
立体电视	three-dimensional television
利胆排石片	〈中医药〉Lidan Paishi Pian; Gallbladder-Disinhibiting and Stone-Expelling Tablet; Cholagogic and Lithagogue Tablet
利群香烟	Liqun cigarettes

利水渗湿	〈中医药〉to disinhibit water and percolate dampness; to remove dampness and promote urination
利水渗湿剂	〈中医药〉formula for diuresis and diffusing dampness; dampness-clearing and diuresis-promoting formula
荔茸鹅肝卷	〈饮食〉Deep-Fried Goose Liver Rolls with Taro
荔茸锅烧鸡	〈饮食〉Stir-Fried Minced Chicken and Yam Croquette
荔枝鲳鱼	〈饮食〉Crispy-Fried Pomfret with Lichee
荔枝炒牛肉	〈饮食〉Stir-Fried Beef with Litchi
荔枝炒猪蹄	〈饮食〉Stir-Fried Pork Trotters with Lichee
荔枝核	〈中医药〉(of Latin) Semen Litchi; Lychee Seed
栗子黄焖山鸡腿	〈饮食〉Braised Pheasant Drumsticks with Chestnut Kernels
栗子鸡	〈饮食〉Stewed Chicken with Chestnut Kernels
栗子扒白菜	〈饮食〉Braised Chinese Cabbage with Chestnut Kernels
笠式碗	〈陶瓷〉straw-hat bowl
连花清瘟胶囊	〈中医药〉Lianhua Qingwen Jiaonang
连朴饮	〈中医药〉Lianpu Yin; Coptis and Officinal Magnolia Bark Beverage
连钱草	〈中医药〉(of Latin) Herba Glechomae; Longtube Ground Ivy Herb
连翘	〈中医药〉(of Latin) Fructus Forsythiae; Weeping Forsythia Capsule; Forsythia Suspense
连续窑	〈陶瓷〉continuous kiln
连衣裤	union suit; jumpsuits; overalls
连衣裙	woman's dress; one-piece dress
帘子曲	〈酒〉raw starter incubated on bamboo curtain
莲房	〈中医药〉(of Latin) Receptaculum Nelumbinis; Lotus Receptacle
莲花白酒	lotus liquor
莲花豆腐	〈饮食〉Lotus-Shaped Tofu; Stuffed Bean Curd with Minced Shrimps (Shaped as a Lotus Flower)

莲花冠	lotus gown
莲藕辣香鸡球	〈饮食〉Stir-Fried Spicy Chicken Balls with Lotus Roots
莲藕粥	〈饮食〉Lotus-Root Congee
莲蓉皮蛋酥	〈饮食〉Lotus Seed Paste Shortcake with Preserved Eggs
莲蓉酥	〈饮食〉Lotus Seed Puff Pastry; Lotus Seed Paste Cake
莲心茶	lotus plumule tea
莲心青蟹肉羹	〈饮食〉Sea Crab Meat and Lotus Plumule Soup
莲须	〈中医药〉(of Latin) Stamen Nelumbinis; Lotus Stamen
莲子	〈中医药〉(of Latin) Semen Nelumbinis; Lotus Seed; Lotus Fruit
莲子百合红豆沙	〈饮食〉Sweetened Red Bean Paste with Lotus Seeds and Lily Bulbs
莲子红豆沙	〈饮食〉Sweetened Red Bean Paste with Lotus Seeds
莲子碗	〈陶瓷〉lotus seed bowl
莲子心	〈中医药〉(of Latin) Plumula Nelumbinis; Lotus Plumule; Lotus Embryo
莲子鸭羹	〈饮食〉Duck and Lotus Seed Soup
莲子银耳羹	〈饮食〉Lotus Seeds and White Fungus Soup
联防联控	〈防疫〉joint prevention and control efforts
廉泉	〈中医药〉Lianquan acupoint; Tongue Spring (CV23)
廉租房	low-cost rental housing; low-rent house
敛疮止痛	〈中医药〉to heal sore and relieve pain; to cure sores and relieve pain
敛肺止咳	〈中医药〉to constrain the lung to suppress cough; to astringe lung for relieving cough
敛肺止咳剂	〈中医药〉formula for astringing the lung for relieving cough; lung-astringing and cough-stopping prescription

敛阴固表	〈中医药〉to astringe yin and consolidate superficies/exterior
练	〈服饰〉white silk; to boil the raw silk (to make it soft and white)
恋父情结	Electra complex; father complex
恋母情结	Oedipus complex; mother complex
良附丸	〈中医药〉Liangfu Wan; Lesser Galangal and Cyperus Pill; Alpinia-Cyperus Pill
良性循环	virtuous circle
良园枇杷叶膏	〈中医药〉Liangyuan Pipaye Gao; Excellent Garden Loquat Leaf Paste
凉拌八爪鱼	〈饮食〉Marinated Octopuses with Soy Sauce
凉拌豆腐丝	〈饮食〉Shredded Tofu with Soy Sauce
凉拌豆芽菜	〈饮食〉Bean Sprouts with Soy Sauce
凉拌肚丝	〈饮食〉Shredded Tripe with Soy Sauce
凉拌干丝	〈饮食〉Shredded Dried Bean Curd with Soy Sauce
凉拌海带	〈饮食〉Shredded Kelp with Soy Sauce
凉拌海蜇	〈饮食〉Shredded Jellyfish with Soy Sauce
凉拌花螺	〈饮食〉Prepared Sea Whelks in Sauce
凉拌黄瓜	〈饮食〉Prepared Cucumber with Sauce
凉拌鸡丝	〈饮食〉Shredded Chicken with Soy Sauce
凉拌金针菇	〈饮食〉Needle Mushrooms and Vegetables with Soy Sauce
凉拌苦瓜	〈饮食〉Bitter Melons with Soy Sauce
凉拌面	〈饮食〉Cold Noodles with Sauce
凉拌双耳	〈饮食〉Black and White Fungi with Soy Sauce
凉拌爽口海苔	〈饮食〉Seaweed Seasoned with Soy Sauce
凉拌西芹云耳	〈饮食〉Celery and White Fungi with Soy Sauce
凉拌香椿苗	〈饮食〉Chinese Toon with Soy Sauce
凉拌鸭掌	〈饮食〉Duck Webs with Soy Sauce
凉茶	herbal tea; Chinese herbal tea
凉冻燕菜糕	〈饮食〉Water Chestnuts and Pineapple Slices in Jelly
凉粉	〈饮食〉Bean-Starch Noodles; Bean Jelly (made from pea powder and cut into short strips)

凉膈散	〈中医药〉Liangge San; Diaphragm-Cooling Powder
凉瓜炒牛肉	〈饮食〉Stir-Fried Beef with Bitter Melon
凉瓜赤豆煲龙骨	〈饮食〉Stewed Pork Backbone with Bitter Melon and Adzuki Bean
凉瓜排骨煲	〈饮食〉Braised Pork Ribs with Bitter Melon in Casserole
凉瓜炆排骨	〈饮食〉Braised Spare Ribs with Bitter Melon
凉帽	summer (trumpet) hat (in the Qing Dynasty)
凉面	〈饮食〉Liangmian; Cold Noodles with Sesame Sauce (usu. with vegetables and sesame sauce)
凉皮	〈饮食〉cold noodle
凉拼盘	〈饮食〉Assorted Cold Foods; Assorted Appetizers
凉血息风	〈中医药〉to cool blood for calming endogenous wind
粮油关系	〈旧〉grain and oil rationing registration
两	(of weight unit) liang (equal to 50 grams); (of monetary unit) tael (equal to 31.25g)
两岸关系	cross-Straits relations; relations between the two sides of the Taiwan Straits
两把头	→二[两]把头
两吃干炸丸子	〈饮食〉Deep-Fried Meat Balls with Choice of Sauces
两弹一艇	A-bomb, H-bomb and nuclear-powered submarine
两弹一星	two bombs and one satellite; atomic bomb, hydrogen bomb and artificial satellite
两个文明一起抓	to place equal emphasis on material and ethical progress
两面讨好	to hunt with the hounds and run with the hare
两面针	〈中医药〉(of Latin) Radix Zanthoxyli; Shinyleaf Pricklyash Root
两人对饮	(of a poem) two people having a drink together
两虾豆腐	〈饮食〉Braised Tofu with Shrimps and Shrimp Roe

两用领	〈服饰〉convertible collar
两院院士	academicians of the two academies (Chinese Academy of Sciences and Chinese Academy of Engineering)
两周观察期	〈防疫〉two-week observation period
两锱[锱]	〈币〉two zi coin (issued in the middle and late Warring States period)
裲[两]裆	〈古服饰〉ancient waistcoat; sleeveless garment
亮底牌	to show one's hand; to reveal the ins and outs
亮相	to strike a pose on the stage; to state one's view
辽三彩印花海棠式长盘	〈陶瓷〉tri-colored long plate in the shape of begonia with floral pattern (Liao Dynasty period)
列车车长	train conductor
列车乘务员	train attendant
列车司机	train driver
列宁装	Lenin dress; Lenin-style suit (woman's revolutionary dress from 1940s to 1960s)
劣等酒	rotgut; sneaky pete
劣异气	〈茶〉tainted odor
劣异味	〈茶〉tainted taste
烈酒	spirit; strong liquor
猎装	hunting wear; safari jacket
裂纹瓷	〈陶瓷〉crazed china; cracked porcelain
裂纹釉	〈陶瓷〉crackle glaze; glaze with crack pattern
邻里效应	neighborhood effect
临床表现	〈防疫〉clinical picture
临床检验	〈防疫〉clinical laboratory; clinical examination
临床前研究	〈防疫〉preclinical research
临床试验	〈防疫〉clinical trial
临床数据	〈防疫〉clinical data
临床协调员	clinical coordinator
临床研究员	clinical researcher
临床医学家	therapist
临床诊断病例	〈防疫〉clinically diagnosed case

临床症状	〈防疫〉clinical signs and symptoms
临床中医	clinical Chinese medicine
临汝窑胆式瓶	〈陶瓷〉Linru Kiln gall-bladder vase
临汝窑青瓷刻花碗	〈陶瓷〉Linru Kiln celadon bowl with carved flower pattern
临时抱佛脚	(of idiom) to embrace Buddha's feet and pray for help in time of emergency; to make hasty and last-minute efforts
临时本地户口	temporary local hukou
临时户口	temporary hukou
临时户口持有人	temporary hukou holder
临时户口登记	temporary hukou registration
临时居住证	temporary residence certificate/permit
临时医院	〈防疫〉improvised hospital
临睡服	〈中医药〉to be administered before bed time; to be taken before sleeping
《临证指南医案》	〈中医药〉Linzheng Zhinan Yi'an; A Guide to Clinical Practice with Medical Records; A Clinical Guide with Case Histories (by Ye Tianshi in the Qing Dynasty)
淋饭酒	linfan rice wine; drenched rice wine
蔺布	〈币〉Linbu coin (issued in the pre-Qin period)
灵龟八法	〈中医药〉eightfold method of the sacred tortoise; sacred tortoise method
灵活复工	〈防疫〉to apply a flexible approach to the resumption of work
灵丘黄烧饼	〈饮食〉Lingqiu Yellow Sesame Seed Cake
灵蛇髻	(of hairstyle) lingshe bun; snake-like bun
《灵枢经》	〈中医药〉(of Yellow Emperor Internal Classic) Lingshu Jing; Miraculous Pivot; The Magic Pivot (written in the Warring States period, revised by Shi Song in the Song Dynasty)
灵芝	〈中医药〉(of Latin) Ganoderma Lucidum; Glossy Ganoderma

灵芝金银鸭血羹	〈饮食〉Duck Blood, Mushrooms and Tofu Soup
灵芝人参酒	ganoderma ginseng wine
苓桂咳喘宁胶囊	〈中医药〉Linggui Kechuanning Jiaonang; Poria-Cinnamon Coughing and Panting Calming Capsule
苓桂术甘汤	〈中医药〉Linggui Zhugan Tang; Poria, Cinnamon Twig, White Atractylodes, and Licorice Decoction
铃铛杯	〈陶瓷〉bell-shaped cup
凌霄花	〈中医药〉(of Latin) Flos Campsis; Trumpetcreeper Flower
凌虚髻	(of hairstyle) lingxu bun; rising-cloud shaped bun
凌云白茶	Lingyun White tea
凌云髻	(of hairstyle) lingyun bun; high-cloud-shaped bun
菱粉	〈中医药〉(of Latin) Amylum Trapa Bispinosa Roxb; Water Caltrop Starch
菱角烩花菇	〈饮食〉Stewed Shiitake Mushrooms with Water Calthrop
羚角钩藤汤	〈中医药〉Lingjiao Gouteng Tang; Antelope Horn and Uncaria Decoction
羚羊感冒片	〈中医药〉Lingyang Ganmao Pian; Common Cold Tablet
羚羊角	〈中医药〉(of Latin) Cornu Saigae Tataricae; Antelope Horn
羚羊角散	〈中医药〉Lingyang Jiao San; Antelope Horn Powder
绫子	〈服饰〉damask silk; thin satin
绫字	ling (thin but fairly stiff silk); thin satin
零号病人	〈防疫〉patient zero
零就业家庭	zero-employment family/household
零售采购员	retail buyer
零售店经理	retail store manager
零星散发新冠病例	〈防疫〉sporadic coronavirus cases
领头羊	bellwether; leading person or unit
另煎	〈中医药〉to decoct separately
另起炉灶	(of idiom) to set up a separate kitchen; to start all over again; to start from scratch

溜须拍马	to flatter sb.; to apple polish; to fawn on sb.
熘	〈饮食〉to sauté (with starch extract); tender-fry; to quick-fry; tender-fried; quick-fried
熘肚块	〈饮食〉Quick-Fried Pork Tripe Slices
熘肝尖	〈饮食〉Quick-Fried Liver with Distilled Grains Sauce
熘鸡脯	〈饮食〉Quick-Fried Chicken Breast with Thick Gravy
熘菊花肫	〈饮食〉Quick-Fried Chicken Gizzard (Shaped as a Chrysanthemum)
熘青蟹	〈饮食〉Stir-Fried Mud Crab with Sweet and Sour Sauce
熘丸子	〈饮食〉Stir-Fried Meat Balls with Brown Sauce
熘鱼片	〈饮食〉Quick-Fried Fish Slices with Distilled Grain Sauce
《刘涓子鬼遗方》	〈中医药〉*Liu Juanzi Guiyifang*; *Liu Juanzi's Ghost-Bequeathed Prescriptions*; *Liu Juanzi's Remedies Bequeathed by Ghosts* (by Liu Juanzi in the Jin Dynasty and revised by Gong Qingxuan in the Southern Qi)
留罐	〈中医药〉retained cupping; retaining cup; cup retaining
留守儿童	stay-at-home children; left-behind children; left-over children
留守老人	old people left behind; empty nester
留校工作	to work at one's Alma Mater after graduation
留学市场	study-abroad market
留学项目	study-abroad program
留学咨询	consulting on the study abroad
留针	〈中医药〉needle retention; retention of needle
留职停薪	to retain the job but suspend the salary
流动服务	mobile service
流动人口	transient population; floating population
流动售货	mobile vending

流动图书馆	travelling library; bookmobile
流动资产	current assets; liquid assets
流动资金	circulating fund; liquid fund; working fund
流感监测站	influenza monitoring station
流感丸	〈中医药〉Liugan Wan; Influenza Pill
流感疫苗接种	influenza vaccination
流浸膏剂	〈中医药〉liquid extract; fluid extract
流量不清零服务	rollover data services
流水对	streamy couplets
流水账	daybook; day-to-day account; current count
流调	〈防疫〉→流行病学调查
流纹釉	〈陶瓷〉flowing glaze
流行病学	〈防疫〉epidemiology
流行病学史	〈防疫〉historical epidemiology
流行病学调查	〈防疫〉epidemiological investigation
流行款式	fashion; fashionable style
流行文化	pop culture
流转税	(commodity) turnover tax; indirect tax
琉璃瓦	glazed tile
榴莲酥	〈饮食〉Crispy Durian Pastry; Durian Crisp Cake
鎏金铜贝	〈币〉gilded copper shell (issued in the Western Zhou Dynasty)
六堡茶	Liubao tea
六极	〈中医药〉liuji; six exhaustions; six extremities
六经辨证	〈中医药〉six-channel pattern identification; pattern differentiation of the six meridians
六神丸	〈中医药〉Liushen Wan; Six Spirits Pill; Pill of Six Ingredients with Magical Effect
六味地黄丸	〈中医药〉Liuwei Dihuang Wan; Six-Ingredient Rehmannia Pill
六味木香胶囊	〈中医药〉Liuwei Muxiang Jiaonang; Six-Ingredient Sausurean Capsule
六味香连胶囊	〈中医药〉Liuwei Xianglian Pian; Six-Ingredient Saussurea and Coptis Capsule

六一散	〈中医药〉Liuyi San; Six to One Powder
六蒸六酿	〈酒〉to steam and stuff for six times
龙胆	〈中医药〉(of Latin) Radix Gentianae; Chinese Gentian
龙胆草	〈中医药〉(of Latin) Radix Gentianae; Gentian Root
龙胆泻肝胶囊	〈中医药〉Longdan Xiegan Jiaonang; Gentian Liver-Discharging Capsule
龙胆泻肝汤	〈中医药〉Longdan Xiegan Tang; Decoction of Gentian for Purging Liver-Heat; Gentian Liver-Draining Decoction
龙胆泻肝丸	〈中医药〉Longdan Xiegan Wan; Gentian Liver-Discharging Pill
龙的传人	descendants of the Chinese dragon (metaphor for the Chinese nation)
龙凤羹	〈饮食〉Minced Chicken with Fish Soup
龙凤琵琶豆腐	〈饮食〉Steamed Tofu with Eggs, Chicken and Shrimp
龙凤汤	〈饮食〉Chicken and Snake Soup
龙骨	〈中医药〉(of Latin) Os Draconis; Dragon Bone
龙虎人丹	〈中医药〉Longhu Rendan; Dragon-Tiger Brand Heat-Cooling Pill
龙徽赤霞珠	〈酒〉Dragon Seal Cabernet Sauvignon red wine
龙徽干白葡萄酒	Dragon Seal dry white wine
龙徽干红葡萄酒	Dragon Seal dry red wine
龙徽怀来珍藏	〈酒〉Dragon Seal Huailai Reserve
龙徽怀来珍藏干红葡萄酒	Dragon Seal Huailai Reserve dry red wine
龙徽雷司令	〈酒〉Dragon Seal Riesling
龙徽汽酒	Dragon Seal sparkling wine
龙徽莎当妮	〈酒〉Dragon Seal Chardonnay white wine
龙徽庄园干红葡萄酒	Dragon Seal Cru de Dry Red
龙井茶	Loungjing tea; Lung Ching tea; Dragon Well tea
龙井花雕醉鸡	〈饮食〉Huadiao-Wined Chicken with Longjing Tea
龙井金元鲍	〈饮食〉Braised Abalone with Longjing Tea

龙葵	〈中医药〉(of Latin) Solanum Nigrum; Black Nightshade
龙牡壮骨颗粒	〈中医药〉Longmu Zhuanggu Keli; Dragon Oyster Bone-Strengthening Granule
龙袍	dragon robe; imperial robe (the emperor's robe)
龙皮釉	〈陶瓷〉dragon-skin glaze; glaze with dragon pattern
龙泉瓷	〈陶瓷〉Lung-Ch'üan porcelain; Longquan porcelain
龙泉青瓷	〈陶瓷〉Longquan celadon
龙泉青瓷八角刻花十六子双鱼碗	〈陶瓷〉Longquan Kiln celadon octagonal bowl with carved pattern of sixteen children and double fish
龙泉青瓷缠枝牡丹纹碗	〈陶瓷〉Longquan Kiln celadon bowl with interlaced branches and peony pattern
龙泉青瓷琮式瓶	〈陶瓷〉Longquan Kiln celadon vase in the shape of a square column with a round inner
龙泉青瓷高足碗	〈陶瓷〉Longquan Kiln celadon stem bowl
龙泉青瓷鼓钉洗	〈陶瓷〉Longquan Kiln celadon writing-brush washer with drum-nail pattern
龙泉青瓷荷叶形碗	〈陶瓷〉Longquan Kiln celadon bowl in the shape of lotus leaf
龙泉青瓷葫芦瓶	〈陶瓷〉Longquan Kiln gourd-shaped celadon vase
龙泉青瓷菊花荷莲盘	〈陶瓷〉Longquan Kiln celadon plate with chrysanthemum and lotus pattern
龙泉青瓷刻蕉叶纹碗	〈陶瓷〉celadon bowl with engraved palm leaf pattern of Longquan Kiln
龙泉青瓷双凤耳瓶	〈陶瓷〉Longquan Kiln celadon vase with double phoenix-shaped handles
龙泉窑	〈陶瓷〉Lung-ch'üan Kiln; Longquan Kiln (in the early Song Dynasty)
龙泉窑缠枝花卉纹瓶	〈陶瓷〉Longquan Kiln vase with interlaced branches and floral pattern (Ming Dynasty)
龙泉窑瓷壶	〈陶瓷〉Longquan Kiln celadon ewer

龙泉窑雕龙瓷罐	〈陶瓷〉porcelain jar with dragon pattern in relief of Longquan Kiln
龙泉窑花卉纹双耳瓶	〈陶瓷〉Longquan Kiln double eared vase with floral pattern (Ming Dynasty)
龙泉窑花卉纹双兽耳双环盘口瓶	〈陶瓷〉Longquan Kiln double animal eared vase with floral pattern (Ming Dynasty)
龙泉窑花卉弦纹洗	〈陶瓷〉Longquan Kiln writing-brush washer with floral string pattern (Ming Dynasty)
龙泉窑加彩小碗	〈陶瓷〉Longquan Kiln colored bowl
龙泉窑刻花凤尾尊	〈陶瓷〉Longquan Kiln phoenix tail zun with engraved flower pattern (Ming Dynasty)
龙泉窑刻花五管盖罐	〈陶瓷〉Longquan Kiln lidded vase with carved patterns and five upward tubes
龙泉窑青瓷	〈陶瓷〉Lung-ch'üan Celadons; Celadons from Longquan Kilns
龙泉窑青瓷堆塑蟠龙莲瓣盖瓶	〈陶瓷〉Longquan Kiln celadon lidded vase with heaped dragon and lotus petal
龙泉窑双耳蒜头瓶	〈陶瓷〉Longquan Kiln garlic shaped vase with double ears (Ming Dynasty)
龙泉窑双绳耳八卦纹炉	〈陶瓷〉Longquan Kiln double eared furnace with Eight Diagrams pattern (Ming Dynasty)
龙泉窑双兽耳双环福寿字纹瓶	〈陶瓷〉Longquan Kiln double animal eared vase with 福寿-characters pattern (Ming Dynasty)
龙泉窑双兽耳双环瓶	〈陶瓷〉Longquan Kiln vase with double animal ears and rings (Ming Dynasty)
龙泉窑弦纹方尊	〈陶瓷〉Longquan Kiln square zun with string pattern (Ming Dynasty)
龙泉窑舟形水注	〈陶瓷〉(of stationery) Longquan Kiln boat-shaped water dropper
龙头产品	flagship product
龙头老大	leading enterprise; flagship of the industry
龙王爷	Dragon Lord; Dragon King; God of Rain in Chinese mythology
龙虾干烧伊面	〈饮食〉Lobster Teriyaki Noodles

龙虾浓汤	〈饮食〉Lobster Soup; Lobster Broth with Cognac
龙须扒菜心	〈饮食〉Stir-Fried Choy Sum with Asparagus
龙须线面	〈饮食〉Stir-Fried Fine Noodles with Shredded Pork
龙须炸蟹枣	〈饮食〉Deep-Fried Shrimp with Crab Meat
龙岩沉缸酒	Longyan vat-bottom-sunken wine
龙眼	〈中医药〉(of Latin) Dimocarpus Longan Lour; Longan
龙眼风味肠	〈饮食〉Sausage Stuffed with Salty Eggs
龙眼肉	〈中医药〉(of Latin) Arillus Longan; Longan Aril
龙洋	〈币〉dragon-patterned silver coin (issued in the late Qing Dynasty)
龙窑	〈陶瓷〉dragon kiln
龙棕	〈中医药〉(of Latin) Trachycarpus Nana Becc; Longzong
笼冠	〈服饰〉cage crown; ancient Chinese crown ornament
笼裙	long silk skirt
隆中茶	Longzhong Green tea
垄断行业	monopolized industry
楼层领班	floor captain
楼层主管	floor supervisor
楼层组长	floor leader
楼阁	pavilion; tower
楼面管理	floor inspector
楼面经理	service manager; floor manager
镂雕[空]	〈陶瓷〉piercing; hollow engraving
镂孔三彩玻璃釉炉	〈陶瓷〉tri-colored glass glaze burner
漏芦	〈中医药〉(of Latin) Radix Rhaponrici; Uniflower Swisscentaury Root
漏抛	〈陶瓷〉omission from polishing
漏勺	strainer; colander
漏征漏管户	tax dodgers
露马脚	to give oneself away; to let the cat out of the bag; to show the cloven hoof

芦根	〈中医药〉(of Latin) Rhizoma Phragmitis; Reed Rhizome
芦笋鲍鱼	〈饮食〉Stewed Abalone and Asparagus
芦笋(炒)鸡片	〈饮食〉Stir-Fried Chicken Slices with Asparagus
芦笋牛柳	〈饮食〉Stir-Fried Beef Fillets with Green Asparagus
庐山香烟	Mt. Lushan cigarettes
庐山云雾茶	Lushan Cloud and Mist tea
庐州烤鸭	〈饮食〉Luzhou Roast Duck
泸州老窖	〈酒〉Luzhou Old Cellar; Luzhou Laojiao liquor
泸州老窖大曲	〈酒〉Luzhou Laojiao Daqu liquor; Luzhou twice fully-fermented liquor in old cellar
泸州老窖特曲	〈酒〉Luzhou Laojiao Special Yeast/Spirit
卤	〈饮食〉to marinate; to steep (food) in a marinade; marinated; marinade-steeped
卤蛋	〈饮食〉Marinated Egg; Hard Boiled Egg; Spiced Egg
卤鸡杂	〈饮食〉Boiled Chicken Giblets with Spices
卤牛腩	〈饮食〉Marinated Beef Brisket in Spiced Sauce
卤肉饭	〈饮食〉Rice with Stewed Pork; Steamed Rice with Red-Cooked Pork
卤三鲜	〈饮食〉Marinated Three Deliccacies (prawn meat, scallop meat and jellyfish head)
卤水大肠	〈饮食〉Marinated Pork Intestines
卤水豆腐	〈饮食〉Marinated Tofu
卤水鹅头	〈饮食〉Marinated Goose Heads
卤水鹅翼	〈饮食〉Marinated Goose Wings
卤水鹅掌	〈饮食〉Marinated Goose Webs
卤水鹅胗	〈饮食〉Marinated Goose Gizzards
卤水鸡蛋	〈饮食〉Marinated Eggs
卤水金钱肚	〈饮食〉Marinatcd Beef Tripe
卤水牛腱	〈饮食〉Marinated Beef Shanks
卤水牛腩	〈饮食〉Marinated Beef Brisket
卤水牛舌	〈饮食〉Marinated Ox Tongucs

卤水拼盘	〈饮食〉Marinated Meat Combination
卤水鸭膀	〈饮食〉Marinated Duck Wings
卤水鸭肉	〈饮食〉Marinated Duck Meat with Ginger, Garlic and Coriander
卤水鸭舌	〈饮食〉Marinated Duck Tongues
卤水猪舌	〈饮食〉Marinated Pig Tongues
卤香干	〈饮食〉Boiled Bean Cheese with Spices; Spicy Bean Cheese
卤鸭翅	〈饮食〉Boiled Duck Wings with Spices
卤汁	〈饮食〉marinade; gravy; bittern
卤制	〈饮食〉marinating/marinated
卤猪舌	〈饮食〉Marinated Pig Tongue
鲁菜	〈饮食〉Lu Cuisine; Shandong Cuisine
鲁锦	Lu brocade; Shandong brocade →鲁西南织锦
鲁山窑	〈陶瓷〉Lushan Kiln
鲁西南织锦	southwestern Shandong brocade →鲁锦
六安瓜片	〈茶〉Lu'an leaf; Lu'an Guapian tea (one of the ten famous teas in China)
录取分数线	minimum enrollment score; admission score; minimum passing marks for admission
录取通知书	admission notice; letter of admission; enrollment notification
录音师	sound engineer
鹿鞭	〈中医药〉(of Latin) Penis et Testis Cervi; Deer's Testis and Penis
鹿角胶	〈中医药〉(of Latin) Colla Corni Cervi; Deer-Horn Glue
鹿角酒	hartshorn liquor
鹿角霜	〈中医药〉(of Latin) Cornu Cervi Degelatinatum; Degelatined Deer-Horn
鹿茸	〈中医药〉(of Latin) Ccornu Cervi Pantotrichum; Pilose Antler
鹿茸酒	deer antler wine
鹿茸养生翅	〈饮食〉Braised Shark's Fin Soup with Deer Antler

鹿尾汤	〈饮食〉Stewed Deer Tail in Clear Soup
鹿纹瓦当	(of building) eaves tile with deer pattern
鹿衔草	〈中医药〉(of Latin) Herba Pyrolae; Pyrola Herb
路路通	〈中医药〉(of Latin) Fructus Liquidambaris; Beautiful Sweetgum Fruit
鹭香焗生中虾	〈饮食〉Baked Prawns with Mixed Flavor
露顶帻	〈服饰〉luding ze (a kerchief without covering the top head)
露水衣	〈土家族〉dew clothing (wedding dress/gown)
驴打滚	〈饮食〉Lüdagun; Rolling Donkey; Glutinous Rice Rolls Stuffed with Red Bean Paste
驴胶补血颗粒	〈中医药〉Lüjiao Buxue Keli; Ass Hide Glue Blood-Supplementing Granule
驴友	tour pal; traveling companions
旅客列车票价	price of passenger train tickets
旅行代办员	travel agent
旅行顾问	travel consultant
旅行纪录片	travel documentary
旅行结婚	honeymoon trip; wedding vacation; wedding travel
旅行限制	〈防疫〉travel restriction
旅游定点饭店	certified restaurant/hotel for tourism
旅游黄金周	golden week for tourism
旅游热	tourism wave; travel/tourist boom
履	shoes
履袍	〈服饰〉black leather shoes and crimson silk robes (worn by emperors of the Song Dynasty, used for sacrificial ceremony)
履新	to take or assume one's new office or post
律师职业资格证书	lawyer qualification certificate
律师资格考试	bar exam; lawyer qualification exam
律师资格证书	attorney's certificate
绿茶	green tea
绿翠	〈茶〉green jade
绿地粉彩花卉纹大碗	〈陶瓷〉large green glazed bowl with famille rose floral pattern (Qing Qianlong period)

绿地酱色龙纹碗	〈陶瓷〉green ground bowl with dark reddish brown dragon pattern (Ming Chenghua period)
绿地紫龙碗	〈陶瓷〉green ground bowl with purple dragon pattern (Qing Qianlong period)
绿豆糕	〈饮食〉Green Bean Cake; Mung Bean Paste Cake
绿豆粥	〈饮食〉Mung Bean Congee; Green Bean Porridge
绿化工	landscaping worker
绿化运动	afforestation drive
绿化组长	landscaping supervisor
绿黄	〈茶〉greenish yellow
绿色产品	green product
绿色电脑	green computer
绿色急救通道	emergency green path
绿色科技	green science and technology
绿色旅游	green tourism
绿色能源	green energy resource
绿色农业	green agriculture
绿色企业	green enterprise
绿色食品	green food; organic food
绿色通道	green channel; landscaped roadway
绿色野菌汤	〈饮食〉Wild Mushroom Soup
绿婷减肥胶囊	〈中医药〉Lüting Jianfei Jiaonang; Lüting Slimming Capsule
绿艳	〈茶〉brilliant green
绿釉缠枝牡丹纹枕	〈陶瓷〉green-glazed pillow with interlocked branches and peony pattern
绿釉划花凤首瓶	〈陶瓷〉green-glazed phoenix-head vase with carved flower pattern
绿釉净瓶	〈陶瓷〉green-glazed holy-water vase
绿釉刻花凤首瓶	〈陶瓷〉green-glazed vase with phoenix head and carved floral pattern
绿釉六博陶俑	〈陶瓷〉green-glazed pottery figurines of liubo chess game

绿釉三层陶望楼	〈陶瓷〉green-glazed pottery model of three-storied watchtower
绿釉双兽耳炉	〈陶瓷〉green glaze furnace with double animal ears (Ming Dynasty)
绿釉水注	〈陶瓷〉green-glazed water dropper
绿釉陶仓	〈陶瓷〉green-glazed pottery model of storehouse
绿釉陶楼	〈陶瓷〉green-glazed pottery model of towered pavilion
绿釉陶水罐	〈陶瓷〉green-glazed pottery water pot
绿釉贴花凤首瓶	〈陶瓷〉green-glazed vase with phoenix head and applique pattern
绿釉贴花鸡冠壶	〈陶瓷〉green-glazed chicken head shaped pot with applique pattern
滤茶器	tea strainer
卵白釉钵	〈陶瓷〉egg white glaze earthen bowl (Ming Dynasty)
卵白釉凤嘴壶	〈陶瓷〉egg-white glazed pot with phoenix-headed spout (Yuan Dynasty)
卵白釉龙纹梅瓶	〈陶瓷〉egg-white glazed plum vase with dragon pattern (Yuan Dynasty)
卵白釉龙纹双戟尊	〈陶瓷〉egg-white glazed zun with double halberd handle and dragon pattern (Yuan Dynasty)
卵白釉龙纹玉壶春瓶	〈陶瓷〉egg-white glazed Yuhuchun vase with dragon pattern
卵白釉菩萨塑像	〈陶瓷〉egg-white glaze Buddha statue (Yuan Dynasty)
卵青釉	〈陶瓷〉egg and spinach glaze
乱罚款	arbitrary fines; quotas and fines; unjustified fines
乱收费	arbitrary charges
乱摊派	arbitrary requisition of donations
轮机长	chief engineer officer
论文崇拜	worship of research paper
论文答辩	thesis/dissertation (oral) defense
论文导师	supervisor

论资排辈	to assign priority according to seniority
罗布麻茶	Apocynum venetum tea
罗布麻叶	〈中医药〉(of Latin) Foliun Apocyni Veneti; Dogbane Leaf
罗定豆豉鸡	〈饮食〉Luoding Braised Chicken in Black Bean Sauce
罗汉肚	〈饮食〉Pork Tripe Stuffed with Meat
罗汉果	〈中医药〉(of Latin) Fructus Momordicae; Grosvenor Momordica Fruit
罗裙	skirt of thin silk
罗天益	Luo Tianyi (1220—1290, a medical scientist in the Yuan Dynasty)
罗田县胜利烈士陵园	Martyrs Cemetery at Victory Town in Luotian County (Hubei)
罗纹针织物	rib knit fabric
萝卜包	〈饮食〉Steamed Bun Stuffed with Turnip
萝卜煲排骨汤	〈饮食〉Pork Ribs with Turnip Soup
萝卜炒干腊肉	〈饮食〉Stir-Fried Preserved Pork with Turnip
萝卜干腊肉	〈饮食〉Stir-Fried Preserved Pork with Dried Radish
萝卜干毛豆	〈饮食〉Pickled Turnip with Green Soy Bean
萝卜糕	〈饮食〉Fried Turnip Patty
萝卜牛腩煲	〈饮食〉Stewed Beef Brisket and Turnip in Clay Pot
萝卜丝鲫鱼汤	〈饮食〉Crucian Carp Soup with Shredded Turnips
萝卜丝酥饼	〈饮食〉Pan-Fried Turnip Pancake
萝酥饼	〈饮食〉Turnip Pancake; Turnip Puff
螺髻	(of hairstyle) luo bun; spiral-shaped coil bun
裸辞	naked resignation (without finding another job)
裸官	naked official (whose spouse and children reside abroad)
裸婚	naked wedding; bare marriage; down-to-earth marriage (a simple way of getting married without purchasing a house or car)

裸考	naked exam (meaning no one can get any additional points because of one's other talents or performance)
络石藤	〈中医药〉(of Latin) Caulis Trachelospermi; Chinese Starjasmine Stem
络穴	〈中医药〉collateral acupoints; network acupoints

M

麻布	linen; flax; gunny (cloth)
麻点釉	〈陶瓷〉sesame spot glaze
麻纺服装	hemp spun garment; linen garment
麻沸散	〈中医药〉Mafei San; Powder for Anesthesia
麻姑茶	Magu green tea
麻花	〈饮食〉Mahua; Fried Dough Twists
麻黄	〈中医药〉(of Latin) Herba Ephedrae; (Chinese) Ephedra; Ephedra Herb
麻黄附子甘草汤	〈中医药〉Mahuang Fuzi Gancao Tang; Ephedra, Aconite, and Licorice Decoction
麻黄附子细辛甘草汤	〈中医药〉Mahuang Fuzi Xixin Gancao Tang; Ephedra, Aconite, Asarum and Licorice Decoction
麻黄附子细辛汤	〈中医药〉Mahuang Fuzi Xixin Tang; Ephedra, Aconite and Asarum Decoction
麻黄根	〈中医药〉(of Latin) Radix Ephedrae; Ephedra Root
麻黄汤	〈中医药〉Mahuang Tang; Ephedra Decoction
麻黄杏仁甘草石膏汤	〈中医药〉Mahuang Xingren Gancao Shigao Tang; Decoction of Ephedra, Almond, liquorice and Gypsum
麻将	mahjong; mah-jong
麻酱拌面	〈饮食〉Cold Noodles with Sesame Paste
麻酱布袋鸡	〈饮食〉Crisp Wrapped Chicken with Sesame Paste
麻酱冬笋	〈饮食〉Bamboo Shoots with Sesame Paste
麻酱海参	〈饮食〉Sea Cucumbers with Sesame Paste
麻酱花卷	〈饮食〉Huajuan with Sesame Paste; Steamed Twisted Rolls with Sesame Paste

麻酱面	〈饮食〉Sesame Paste Noodles; Noodles with Sesame Paste
麻酱笋条	〈饮食〉Shredded Lettuce with Sesame Paste
麻酱糖饼	〈饮食〉Sweet Pancake with Sesame Paste
麻酱鱼肚	〈饮食〉Stir-Fried Fish Maws with Sesame Paste
麻辣鹌鹑脯	〈饮食〉Spicy-Braised Quail Breast
麻辣豆腐	〈饮食〉Spicy Hot Tofu; Fried Bean-Curd with Hot Pepper
麻辣肚丝	〈饮食〉Shredded Pork Tripe with Chili Sauce
麻辣耳丝	〈饮食〉Shredded Pig Ears with Chili Sauce
麻辣海参片	〈饮食〉Braised Sea Cucumber Slices with Chili Sauce
麻辣鸡	〈饮食〉Chicken with Chili and Wild Pepper Sauce
麻辣鹿筋	〈饮食〉Spicy-Braised Venison Tendon
麻辣面	〈饮食〉Spicy Hot Noodles
麻辣牛肚	〈饮食〉Spicy Beef Tripe; Spicy Marinated Beef Tripe
麻辣牛筋	〈饮食〉Spicy Beef Tendon; Beef Tendon with Chili Sauce
麻辣牛展	〈饮食〉Spicy Sliced Beef; Sliced Beef with Chili Sauce
麻辣汤	spicy and hot soup
麻辣烫	〈饮食〉Malatang; Spicy Hot Pot
麻辣响螺片	〈饮食〉Stir-Fried Sliced Sea Whelks in Hot and Spicy Sauce
麻辣鸭膀丝	〈饮食〉Shredded Duck Wings with Chili Sauce; Shredded Spicy Duck Wings
麻辣野鸭	〈饮食〉Stir-Fried Wild Duck with Sesame and Pepper Sauce
麻辣玉兔腿	〈饮食〉Stir-Fried Rabbit Legs with Hot Spicy Sauce
麻辣蘸酱	〈饮食〉spicy dipping sauce
麻婆豆腐	〈饮食〉Mapo Tofu; Stir-Fried Tofu in Hot Spicy Sauce

麻婆龙虾仔	〈饮食〉Mapo Baby Lobster; Braised Baby Lobster in Chili Sauce
麻蓉大包	〈饮食〉Steamed Bun Stuffed with Sesame Paste and Black Sesame
麻纱底衫	linen undergarment
麻薯	〈饮食〉Deep-Fried Glutinous Rice Cake Stuffed with Bean Paste
麻团	〈饮食〉Fried Glutinous Rice Balls with Sesame
麻油	→芝麻油
麻子仁丸	〈中医药〉Maziren Wan; Pill of Fructus Cannabis; Hemp Seed Pill
麻醉医师	anaesthetist; anaesthesiologist
马边云雾茶	Mabian Cloud and Mist tea
马鞭草	〈中医药〉(of Latin) Herba Verbenae; European Verbena Herb
马齿苋	〈中医药〉(of Latin) Herba Portulacae; Purslane Herb
马到成功	to achieve immediate victory; to win instant success
马兜铃	〈中医药〉(of Latin) Fructus Aristolochiae; Dutchmanspipe Fruit
马[短]褂	〈服饰〉riding jacket; mandarin jacket; Chinese jacket (worn over a gown)
马甲	〈服饰〉vestcoat; vest →坎肩
马鲛鱼	〈饮食〉Pan-Fried Mackerel
马拉盏炒菜	〈饮食〉Stir-Fried Vegetables with Shrimp Paste
马拉盏炒鱿鱼	〈饮食〉Stir-Fried Squid with Shrimp Paste
马铃薯笋焖鸡	〈饮食〉Stewed Chicken with Potato and Bamboo Shoots
马路新闻	hearsay; gossip
马面(褶)裙	horse-face shaped skirt
马奶酒	〈蒙古族〉kumiss; horse milk wine
马年	Year of Horse (one of the 12 Zodiac Years)
马屁精	flatterer; boot-licker; apple-polisher

马钱子	〈中医药〉(of Latin) Semen Strychni; Nux Vomica
马蹄西米花生糊	〈饮食〉Creamy Peanut and Water Chestnut Kernel Soup
马蹄鲜虾肠粉	〈饮食〉Steamed Rice Rolls with Shrimps and Water Chestnuts
马蹄袖	〈服饰〉horse-hoof sleeve; horse-hoof-shaped cuff (in the Qing Dynasty)
马蹄尊	〈陶瓷〉horse-hoof-shaped zun
马尾帽	〈瑶族〉horse-tail cap
马应龙麝香痔疮膏	〈中医药〉Mayinglong Shexiang Zhichuang Gao; Mayinglong Musk Hemorrhoids Cream/Ointment
蚂蚁上树	〈饮食〉Stir-Fried Vermicelli with Spicy Minced Pork
买方市场	buyer's market
买一送一	two-for-one offer; to buy one and get one free
麦冬	〈中医药〉(of Latin) Radix Ophiopogonis; Dwarf Lilyturf Tuber
麦粒灸	〈中医药〉wheat-grain size cone moxibustion; moxibustion with seed-sized moxa cone
麦门冬汤	〈中医药〉Maimendong Tang; Ophiopogon Decoction
麦片粥	〈饮食〉Oatmeal Porridge
麦芽	(of Latin) Fructus Hordei Germinatus; Barley Sprout; Wheat Germ
麦芽香	〈茶〉malty aroma
卖场经理	store manager
脉痹	→热[脉]痹
脉道不利	〈中医药〉unsmoothness of vessels
《脉经》	〈中医药〉*Maijing*; *Pulse Classic*; *The Pulse Canon* (by Wang Shuhe in the Western Jin Dynasty)
脉静	〈中医药〉tranquil pulse; calm pulse
脉逆四时	〈中医药〉incongruence of pulse with four seasons
脉象	〈中医药〉pulse manifestation; pulse condition; pulse pattern

脉象浮紧	〈中医药〉floating and tense pulse
脉象细弱	〈中医药〉thin and weak pulse
脉应四时	〈中医药〉congruence of pulse with four seasons
馒头	〈饮食〉Steamed Bread; Steamed Bun
馒头窑	〈陶瓷〉dome kiln; kiln in the shape of steamed bun
满汉全席	Manchu-Han imperial feast (full and formal banquet combining Manchurian and Chinese delicacies)
满山红	〈中医药〉(of Latin) Folium Rhododendri Daurici; Dahurian Rhododendron Leaf
满堂红	an all-round success; to be successful in every endeavor
满意度	degree of satisfaction
蔓荆子	〈中医药〉(of Latin) Fructus Viticis; Shrub Chastetree Fruit; Vitex Fruit
漫游费	roaming fees
漫游服务	roaming service
慢性病	〈防疫〉chronic disease; chronic ailment
芒果止咳片	〈中医药〉Mangguo Zhike Pian; Mango Cough-Checking Tablet
芒硝	〈中医药〉(of Latin) Natrii Sulfas; Mirabilite
芒针疗法	〈中医药〉elongated needle therapy; long needle therapy
盲流	blind floaters; influx laborers aimlessly flowing from rural areas into large cities
蟒袍	〈服饰〉long robe embroidered with python
猫腻儿	illegal deal; underhanded activity; something-fishy
猫爪草	〈中医药〉(of Latin) Radix Ranunculi Ternati; Cat-claw Buttercup Root
毛茶[条]	crude tea
毛冬青	〈中医药〉(of Latin) Radix Ilicis Pubescentis; Hairy Holly Root

毛家[氏]红烧肉	〈饮食〉Braised Pork in Mao's Family Style
毛呢服装	woolen garment
毛皮袄	〈服饰〉coat with fur lining
毛圈针织物	terry knitted fabric
毛式中山装	〈服饰〉Mao-style suit; Mao tunic suit
毛粘混纺	wool-rayon blending
毛装	〈服饰〉maozhuang; Mao suit →毛式中山装
矛盾统一	〈中医药〉contradictory and unity
茅台	→贵州茅台
牦牛肉干	〈饮食〉Yak Jerky; Dried Yak Meat
卯发	maofa; juvenile's chignon (hairstyle for children or maids)
贸易财务主管	trade finance executive
贸易主管	trading supervisor
贸易专员	trading specialist
没有硝烟的战争	〈防疫〉a war without smoke
玫瑰红茶	rose black tea
玫瑰花	〈中医药〉(of Latin) Flos Rosae Rugosae; Rose Flower
玫瑰酒	rose liquor
眉茶	mee tea; eyebrow-like green tea
眉冲	〈中医药〉Meichong acupoint; Eyebrow Ascension (BL3)
梅菜扣肉	〈饮食〉Steamed Braised-Pork with Preserved Vegetables
梅菜蒸扣肉	〈饮食〉Steamed Pork with Preserved Vegetables in Casserole
梅花	〈中医药〉(of Latin) Flos Mume; Plum Flower
梅花针	〈中医药〉plum-blossom needle; percussopunctator
梅酱拌鸡片	〈饮食〉Chicken Slices with Plum Sauce
梅龙茶	Meilong Green tea
梅樱小炒皇	〈饮食〉Stir-Fried Squid with Shredded Pork and Leek

梅汁蹄膀	〈饮食〉Braised Pork Knuckles with Jam Sauce
梅子脆皮鸡	〈饮食〉Crispy Chicken with Plums
梅子青釉	〈陶瓷〉plum green glaze
湄潭翠芽	〈茶〉Meitan Cuiya tea; Meitan Green Bud tea
媒婆	〈旧〉woman matchmaker
《霉疮秘录》	〈中医药〉*Meichuang Milu*; *Secret Record for Syphilis* (by Chen Sicheng in the Ming Dynasty)
美国红腰豆扣鲍片	〈饮食〉Braised Sliced Abalone with American Kidney Beans
美极葱香鸡脆骨	〈饮食〉Stir-Fried Chicken Gristle with Scallion in Maggi Sauce
美极酱肉虾饭	〈饮食〉Rice with Shrimps in Maggie Sauce
美极掌中宝	〈饮食〉Stir-Fried Chicken Paws in Maggi Sauce
美甲师	manicurist; nail technician
美人醉釉	→孩儿脸[美人醉]釉
美容顾问	beauty advisor; beauty consultant
美容师	beautician; plastic surgeon
美容助理	beautician assistant
美食节	gourmet festival; food festival
美食夜市	cuisine night market
美术编辑	art editor; artistic editor
美术设计师	graphic designer
美术指导	art director; art direction
美团	Meituan (a mobile application for group buying)
美味多菌汤	〈饮食〉Chef's Special Mushroom Soup
美味牛筋	〈饮食〉Tasty Beef Tendon
美味烟鲳鱼	〈饮食〉Smoked Pomfret with Piquant Sauce
美味烟香鸡	〈饮食〉Smoked Chicken with Chilli Sauce
镁橄榄石瓷	〈陶瓷〉forsterite porcelain
镁质瓷	〈陶瓷〉magnesia ceramic; magnesia porcelain
门第	family status; pedigree
焖	〈饮食〉to simmer/stew (in a covered pot over a slow fire); braised; stewed; simmered
焖鸡腿	〈饮食〉Braised Chicken Thighs; Stewed Chicken Drumsticks

焖辣子鸡腿		〈饮食〉Stewed Chicken Drumsticks with Fresh Chilli
焖竹节鸭		〈饮食〉Braised Stuffed Duck with Bamboo Shoots and Mushrooms
蒙自年糕		〈饮食〉Mengzi Rice Cake (a special local product in Yunnan)
礞石滚痰丸		〈中医药〉Mengshi Guntan Wan; Chlorite/Mica Phlegm-Rolling Pill; Pill of Chlorite-Schist for Expelling Phlegm
蒙顶黄芽		〈茶〉Mengding Huangya tea; Mengding Yellow Bud tea
蒙古刀		Mongolian knife
蒙古帽		Mongolian hat
蒙古袍		Mongolian gown
蒙古王		〈酒〉Mongolian King
蒙古族刺绣		Mongolian embroidery
猕猴桃根		〈中医药〉(of Latin) Radix Actinidiae Chinensis; Yang Tao Actinidia Root
米		〈饮食〉Plain Rice; Steamed Rice
米醋海蜇		〈饮食〉Jellyfish with Vinegar
米粉		〈饮食〉Rice Noodles; Rice Vermicelli
米粉扣肉		〈饮食〉Steamed Sliced Pork Belly with Ground Glutinous Rice
米粉排骨		〈饮食〉Steamed Spare Ribs with Ground Glutinous Rice
米粉肉		〈饮食〉Steamed Pork with Ground Glutinous Rice
米粉条		〈饮食〉Rice-Flour Noodles; Rice Vermicelli
米粉蒸牛肉		〈饮食〉Steamed Beef with Glutinous Rice Flour
米粉蒸肉		〈饮食〉Steamed Pork Slices with Ground Glutinous Rice
米黄色釉		〈陶瓷〉beige glaze; cream glaze
米酱炒蛏肉		〈饮食〉Stir-Fried Fresh Clam with Seasoning Sauce
米酒		rice wine
米汤		〈饮食〉Rice Soup; Thin Rice Gruel

米汤豆苗	〈饮食〉Pea Sprouts in Rice Soup
米香型风格	〈酒〉rice flavor type; rice fragrance
米熏鸡	〈饮食〉Rice-Smoked Chicken
泌尿外科医师	urological surgeon; urologist surgeon
《秘传眼科龙木论》	〈中医药〉*Michuan Yanke Longmu Lun*; *Nagajuna's Secret Treatise on Ophthalmology*; *Nagajuna's Ophthalmology Secretly Handed Down* (written between the Song and Yuan Dynasties)
秘书长	secretary-general; chief secretary
秘戏钱	〈古〉coin with sex pattern
秘制鸳鸯鸡	〈饮食〉Braised Chickens like Mandarin Duck
密蒙花	〈中医药〉(of Latin) Flos Buddlejae; Pale Butterfly-bush Flower
密切跟踪	〈防疫〉to closely monitor the epidemic
密切接触者	〈防疫〉close contact
密陀僧	〈中医药〉(of Latin) Lithargyum; Litharge
幂离	〈服饰〉mi black silk head-covering
蜜豆百合炒鱼菘	〈饮食〉Stir-Fried Fish Floss with Sweetened Beans and Lily Bulbs
蜜炼川贝枇杷润嗓含片	〈中医药〉Milian Chuanbei Pipa Runsang Hanpian; Cordyceps Fritillaria Loquat Voice-Moistening Tablet
蜜糖龟苓膏	〈饮食〉Guiling Jelly (Chinese Herbal Jelly, Served with Honey)
蜜糖子姜鸡	〈饮食〉Honey-Stewed Chicken with Ginger Shoots
蜜桃水晶丸	〈饮食〉Deep-Fried Shrimp Balls with Peach Sauce
蜜月旅行	honeymoon trip
蜜汁叉烧	〈饮食〉Honey-Stewed Barbecued Pork
蜜汁叉烧酥	〈饮食〉Honeyed Barbecue Pork Puff; Barbecued Pork Buns
蜜汁煎鸭胸	〈饮食〉Pan-Fried Duck Breast with Honey Sauce
蜜汁金枣	〈饮食〉Honeydew Gold Dates
蜜汁烧小肉排	〈饮食〉Stewed Spare Ribs in Honey Sauce
蜜汁烟熏鸭肉卷	〈饮食〉Smoked Duck Rolls with Honey Sauce

蜜制	〈中医药〉stir-fried with honey
绵绵冰	〈饮食〉Mein Mein Ice
棉袄	〈服饰〉cotton-padded jacket; cotton-wadded coat
棉布服装	cotton clothes; cotton garment
棉大戟	〈中医药〉(of Latin) Radix Stellerae; Cotton Root of Beijing Euphorbia
棉大衣	padded cotton overcoat
棉缎	sateen
棉缎帽	cotton wadded satin cap
棉花糖	cotton candy; marshmallow
棉甲	〈服饰〉(of ancient times) cotton armor
棉裤	cotton wadded trousers; cotton-padded trousers; cotton trousers
棉类服装	cotton garment
棉毛裤	cotton trousers
棉毛衫	cotton jersey
棉袍	cotton wadded robe
免费师范教育	free normal education; tuition-free education in normal university
免费师范生	free normal student; tuition-free normal college student
免费中等职业教育	free tuition for secondary vocational education
免税商店	duty-free shop
免税商品	tax-free commodities
免验放行	to pass without examination
冕	〈古〉top hat; royal crown
冕板	〈服饰〉plate on the crown-top; coronal plate
冕旒	king's crown with tassels; ceremonious hat for the emperor and high officials
冕圈	circle of solar corona
面部识别	facial recognition; face recognition
面茶	〈饮食〉Seasoned Millet Mush
面点师	pastry cook; baker
面颊	〈中医药〉Mianjia acupoint; Cheek (LO5, 6i)

面筋百叶	〈饮食〉Stewed Wheat Gluten Puff and Bean Curd Sheets
面料采购员	fabric purchaser
面料开发员	fabric developer
面目一新	to take on an entirely new look
面色苍白	〈中医药〉pale complexion
面色淡白	〈中医药〉pale white complexion
面色红润	〈中医药〉rosy cheeks; ruddy complexion
面色晦暗	〈中医药〉dim (facial) complexion
面色黧黑	〈中医药〉darkish facial complexion
面色青紫	〈中医药〉greenish or purple facial complexion
面色萎黄	〈中医药〉sallow facial complexion
面色无华	〈中医药〉lusterless facial complexion
面拖牡蛎	〈饮食〉Oyster Fritters
面衣	〈古〉ace-covering veil (for dead people in the Wei Jin Southern and Northern Dynasties)
面釉	〈陶瓷〉overglaze; cover glaze
面鱼儿烧鸭	〈饮食〉Braised Duck with Fish-Like Dough
面子工程	face job; face-saving project; prestige project; vanity project
面子消费	face consumption (not for practical needs, but merely to show off and gratify the owners' vanity)
苗绣	Miao embroidery
苗药	〈中医药〉Miao herbal medicine
描金云龙纹直颈瓶	〈陶瓷〉straight-necked vase with gold drawing cloud and dragon pattern
秒杀	seckilling; instant kill; flash sale
妙姿减肥胶囊	〈中医药〉Miaozi Jianfei Jiaonang; Miaozi Slimming Capsule
灭活疫苗	〈防疫〉inactivated vaccine
民办高校	private higher learning institution
民办教师	citizen-managed teacher
民办教育	non-government funded education
民办[私立]教育	non-government funded education; private education

民办学校	non-governmental school; non-publicly funded school
民兵战士	militia fighter
民法通则	general provisions of the civil law
民工	migrant laborer; migrant worker
民工潮	farmers' frenzied hunt for work in cities; farmer-worker booming
民工荒	migrant worker shortage
民工流	migrant worker stream
民间文化遗产	folk cultural heritage
民间协商	consultation on a non-governmental basis
民间艺人	folk artisan
民间资本	private capital
民盟	→中国民主同盟
民权葡萄酒	Minquan grape wine
民事审判庭	civil tribunal
民事诉讼	civil procedure
民俗服	folk costume →民族服装
民俗学家	expert on folklore; folklorist
民谣歌手	balladeer; folk singer
民意测验	opinion poll; opinion survey
民营企业	individually-run enterprise
民约	social contract; regulation and non-governmental agreement
民主活动家	Chinese democracy activist
民主监督	democratic supervision
民族服装	ethnic costume →民俗服
民族凝聚力	national cohesion
民族医学	ethno medicine
民族医药	〈中医药〉folk medicines of ethnic minorities
民族意识	national consciousness
民族优越感	ethnocentrism; national superiority complex
闽菜	〈饮食〉Min Cuisine; Fujian Cuisine
闽煎黄鱼	〈饮食〉Fujian Fried Yellow Croaker

闽龙陶瓷	〈陶瓷〉Minlong ceramics
名利双收	to gain in both fame and wealth
名人效应	celebrity charm
《名医类案》	〈中医药〉*Mingyi Leian*; *Classified Case Histories of Famous Physicians*; *Classified Case Records of Celebrated Physicians* (by Jiang Guan in the Ming Dynasty)
名誉董事长	honorary chairman
名誉顾问	honorary adviser
名誉会长	honorary president
名誉教授	honorary professor; emeritus professor
明党参	〈中医药〉(of Latin) Radix Changii; Medicinal Changium Root
明裥袋	box pleated pocket
明炉串肉片	〈饮食〉Grilled Pork Brochettes with Ketchup
明炉烧鸭	〈饮食〉Barbecued Duck with Sweet Paste
明炉鱼卷	〈饮食〉Baked Fish Rolls with Lard
明码标价	to sell at expressly marked price; to mark the price clearly; to mark clearly the price of the commodity
明码标价制度	to mark clearly the prices of the commodities; to sell at expressly marked price
明目地黄丸	〈中医药〉Mingmu Dihuang Wan; Rehmannia Bolus for Improving Eyesight; Eye-Brightening Rehmannia Pill
明目上清丸	〈中医药〉Mingmu Shangqing Wan; Eye Brightener Clear-Raising Pill; Eyesight-Improving and Upper-Heat-Removing Bolus
明虾鸡酥卷	〈饮食〉Prawn and Chicken Shortcake Rolls
明星效应	celebrity effect
明月红松鸡	〈饮食〉Braised Chicken Drumsticks (Shaped as a Moonlight Scene)
冥器	mingqi; funerary object
命门	〈中医药〉mingmen; vital gate; gate of vitality
命门火衰	〈中医药〉decline of the vital gate fire

命门火衰证	〈中医药〉pattern of debilitation of the life gate fire
命门之火	〈中医药〉vital gate fire; fire from life gate
模范教师	model teacher
模具工程师	tooling engineer
模拟测试	mock test; simulated exam
模拟招聘会	mock interview
摩罗丹	〈中医药〉Mo Luo Dan; Stomach-Harmonizing and Spleen-Fortifying Elixir
磨背式货贝	〈币〉flatten-back cypraea/monetaria moneta (issued since the Shang Dynasty)
磨郭五铢	five-zhu coin with inner frame ground off (issued in the Western Han Dynasty)
磨砂玻璃影	〈防疫〉ground-glass opacities
磨洋工	to dawdle along; linger over one's work
蘑菇鲍脯	〈饮食〉Braised Abalone with Fresh Mushrooms
蘑菇煎蛋卷	〈饮食〉Mushroom Omelette
蘑菇芥菜	〈饮食〉Stir-Fried Mushrooms and Leaf Mustard with Chicken Fat
蘑菇面	〈饮食〉Noodles with Mushroom
蘑菇牛肉乳蛋派	〈饮食〉Beef and Mushroom Pie
魔芋烧鸭	〈饮食〉Braised Duck with Shredded Konjak
抹茶	matcha; tea powder
抹茶单碗点茶法	individual bowl matcha-whisking method
抹茶罐	matcha pot; powder tea canister
抹茶小杯点茶法	small cup matcha-whisking method
抹胸	〈服饰〉boob tube top; stomacher
末班车时间	final vehicle hour
没药	〈中医药〉(of Latin) Commiphora Myrrha; Myrrh
茉莉花茶	jasmine tea
莫来石瓷	〈陶瓷〉mullite porcelain
墨地三彩	〈陶瓷〉tri-colored porcelain with china-ink; dark ground tri-colored porcelain
墨旱莲	〈中医药〉(of Latin) Herba Ecliptae; Yerbadetajo Herb

墨江云针	〈茶〉Mojiang Cloud Needle
默哀三分钟	to observe three minutes of silence to mourn the deceased
母系氏族社会	matriarchal clan society
母婴传播	mother-baby transmission (mother-to-child HIV transmission)
牡丹皮	〈中医药〉(of Latin) Cortex Moutan Radicis; Tree Peony Bark
牡丹头髻	(of hairstyle) peony-shaped high bun
牡丹香烟	Mudan cigarettes; Peony cigarettes
牡丹珠圆鸡	〈饮食〉Chicken and Crab Roe with Shrimp Balls
牡荆叶	〈中医药〉(of Latin) Folium Viticis Negundo; Hemp-leaf Negundo Chastetree Leaf
牡蛎	〈中医药〉(of Latin) Concha Ostreae; Oyster Shell
牡蛎煎	〈饮食〉Oyster Omelette
牡蛎汤	〈饮食〉Oyster Soup
牡蛎细面	〈饮食〉Oyster Thin Noodles; Thin Noodles with Oyster
亩	(of area measurement unit) mu (equal to 666.6m^2)
拇指平推法	〈中医药〉horizontal pushing with the thumb; thumb flat-pushing manipulation
木鳖子	〈中医药〉(of Latin) Semen Momordicae; Cochinchina Momordica Seed
木耳炒山药	〈饮食〉Stir-Fried Chinese Yam with Black Fungi
木耳过油肉	〈饮食〉Quick-Fried Boiled Pork with Black Fungus
木耳肉片	〈饮食〉Stir-Fried Sliced Pork with Black Fungus
木瓜	〈中医药〉(of Latin) Fructus Chaenomelis; Common Floweringqince Fruit
木瓜炖百合	〈饮食〉Stewed Papaya with Lily Bulbs
木瓜炖翅	〈饮食〉Shark's Fin Soup with Papaya
木瓜炖官燕	〈饮食〉Braised Bird's Nest with Papaya
木瓜海虎翅	〈饮食〉Supreme Shark's Fins Soup with Papaya

木瓜丸	〈中医药〉Mugua Wan; Chaenomeles Fruit Pill
木瓜腰豆煮海参	〈饮食〉Braised Sea Cucumbers with Kidney Beans and Papaya
木蝴蝶	〈中医药〉(of Latin) Semen Oroxyli; Indian Trumpet Flower Seed
木槿花	〈中医药〉(of Latin) Flos Hibisci; Rose-of-Sharon Flower
木棉花	〈中医药〉(of Latin) Bombax Malabaricum; Common Bombax Flower
木偶戏演员	puppet actor; puppeteer
木通	〈中医药〉(of Latin) Caulis Akebiae; Akebia Stem
木屐	〈旧〉wood slippers; wooden shoes
木香	〈中医药〉(of Latin) Radix Aucklandiae; Common Aucklandia Root
木香槟榔丸	〈中医药〉Muxiang Binlang Wan; Aplotaxis Auriculata Compound Pill; Costusroot and Areca Pill
木香顺气丸	〈中医药〉Muxiang Shunqi Wan; Aplotaxis Carminative Pill; Sausurean Qi-Smoothing Pill
木贼	〈中医药〉(of Latin) Herba Equiseti Hiemalis; Common Scouring Rush Herb
目无法纪	to defy the law (or standards of discipline)
幕后操纵	to pull strings behind the scenes; wire-pulling
幕墙工程师	curtain wall engineer

N

拿…开涮	to make sb. the laughingstock; to make a fool of sb.
拿腔拿调	to speak affectedly
拿手好戏	(of idiom) masterpiece; something in which one is an expert; to have subject at one's fingers
纳干法	〈中医药〉→纳甲法
纳谷不香	〈中医药〉poor appetite; loss of appetite; no pleasure in eating
纳甲法	〈中医药〉day-prescription of points; heavenly stem-prescription of point selection; day-prescription of acupoints
纳税人	tax payer; tax bearer
纳税申报制度	tax declaration system
纳支法	〈中医药〉→纳子法
纳子法	〈中医药〉hour-prescription of points; earthly branch-prescription of point selection; hour-prescription of acupoints
奶黄包	〈饮食〉Baozi Stuffed with Creamy Custard
奶黄糯米糍	〈饮食〉Glutinous Rice Balls Stuffed with Cream Custard
奶油烩鹧鸪条	〈饮食〉Fricassée Partridge Strip in Cream Sauce
奶油焗龙虾	〈饮食〉Baked Lobster with Fresh Cream
奶油咖喱鸡	〈饮食〉Curry Chicken with Fresh Cream
奶油妈妈	milky mom (referring to mothers who, after the maternity leave, go back to work but keeping feeding their babies with their own milk)
奶油鱼唇	〈饮食〉Stir-Fried Fish Lips with Cream Sauce

奶油鱼肚	〈饮食〉Stir-Fried Fish Maws with Cream Sauce
耐热瓷器	〈陶瓷〉refractory porcelain
耐用消费品	durable consumer goods; consumer durables
男宝胶囊	〈中医药〉Nanbao Jiaonang; Men's Treasure Capsule
男耕女织	men tilling the farm and women weaving; men ploughing and women weaving
男女同工同酬	equal pay for equal work irrespective of sex
男权主义思想	male chauvinism
男人婆	macho woman; tomboy
男式服装	men's wear; men's clothes
男助产士	accoucheur; man-midwife
南安石亭绿	〈茶〉Nan'an Stone Pavilion Green tea
南昌米粉	〈饮食〉Nanchang Rice Noodles
南淡北咸	〈饮食〉light southern cuisine and salty northern cuisine; light flavor in the south and salty in the north
南瓜饼	〈饮食〉Deep-Fried Pumpkin Pancake; Pumpkin Pancake
南瓜黄焖栗子鸡	〈饮食〉Braised Chestnut Kernels Chicken in Pumpkin Tureen
南瓜酥	〈饮食〉Pumpkin Puff; Crunchy Pumpkin Crisps
南瓜团子	〈饮食〉Pumpkin Dumplings
南瓜香芋蒸排骨	〈饮食〉Steamed Spare Ribs with Pumpkin and Taro
南瓜芋头煲	〈饮食〉Stewed Taro with Pumpkin in Casserole
南瓜汁百合	〈饮食〉Lily Bulb in Squash Sauce
南瓜粥	〈饮食〉Pumpkin Congee
南煎肝	〈饮食〉Soft Stir-Fried Pork Liver with Soy Sauce, Sugar and Water Chestnut Powder
南京板鸭	〈饮食〉Nanjing Pressed Duck; Steamed Nanjing Duck Cutlets
南京黄釉	〈陶瓷〉Nankin yellow glaze
南京香烟	Nanjing cigarettes

南京雨花茶	Nanjing Yuhua Green tea
南乳粗斋煲	〈饮食〉Braised Assorted Vegetables with Marinated Tofu
南乳碎炸鸡	〈饮食〉Deep-Fried Chicken Cubes with Preserved Tofu
南乳汁肉	〈饮食〉Braised Pork with Pickled Bean Curd Sauce
南沙参	〈中医药〉(of Latin) Radix Adenophorae; Fourleaf Ladybell Root
南山白毛茶	Nanshan Baimao tea; Nanshan White Fuzz Bud tea
南宋官窑	〈陶瓷〉guan/official kiln of the Southern Song Dynasty
南天仙子	〈中医药〉(of Latin) Semen Hygrophilae; Southern Henbane Seed
南五味子	〈中医药〉(of Latin) Fructus Schisandrae Sphenantherae; Southern Schisandra Berry
南洋双喜香烟	Nanyang Double Happiness cigarettes
南岳云雾茶	Nanyue Cloud and Mist tea
《难经》	〈中医药〉*Nanjing*; *Classic of Difficult Issues*; *Classic of Questioning* (written before the Eastern Han Dynasty)
脑得生片	〈中医药〉Naodesheng Pian; Life-Regaining of Brain Tablet
脑干	〈中医药〉Naogan acupoint; Brain Stem (AT3, 4i)
脑户	〈中医药〉Naohu acupint; Back of the Head; Brain's Door (GV17)
脑空	〈中医药〉Naokong acupoint; Brain Hollow (GB19)
脑力宝丸	〈中医药〉Naolibao Wan; Brain Treasure Pill
脑灵素胶囊	〈中医药〉Naolingsu Jiaonang; Brain Working Element Capsule
脑体倒挂	limbs before brains (referring to the phenomenon that some talent-intensive jobs are paid less than labor-intensive ones)
脑子进水	bubble brain (meaning someone who is being stupid or confused)

闹洞房	bridal chamber pranks; rough horseplay at weddings
闹情绪	to be disgruntled; to be in a fit of pique
臑会	〈中医药〉Naohui acupoint; Upper Arm Convergence (SJ13)
臑俞	〈中医药〉Naoshu acupoint; Upper Arm Transport (SI10)
内鼻	〈中医药〉Neibi acupoint; Internal Nose (TG4)
内闭外脱	〈中医药〉internal block and outward desertion
内补黄芪汤	〈中医药〉Neibu Huangqi Tang; Astragalus Root Decoction for Tonifying the Internal
内耳	〈中医药〉Neier acupoint; Internal Ear (LO6)
内防反弹	〈防疫〉to prevent a resurgence of the outbreak at home; to guard against a rebound in indigenous cases
内防扩散	〈防疫〉to prevent coronavirus spreading within local regions
内关	〈中医药〉Neiguan acupoint; Inner Pass (PC6)
内踝尖	〈中医药〉Neihuai Jian acupoint; Tip of the Inner Ankle Bone (EX-LE8)
内科医生	physician; internist
内伤脾胃,百病由生	〈中医药〉internal impairment of the spleen and stomach causes various diseases; internal injury to the spleen and stomach leads to all kinds of diseases
内生五邪	〈中医药〉five endogenous pathogenic factors; five internal pernicious influences
内湿	〈中医药〉endogenous dampness; internal dampness
内束腰	〈古服饰〉inner girdling
内庭	〈中医药〉Neiting acupoint; Inner Court (ST44)
内膝眼	〈中医药〉Nei Xiyan acupoint; Inner Eye of the Knee (EX-LE4)

内消瘰疬丸	〈中医药〉Neixiao Luoli Wan; Scrofula Internal Dispersion Pill
内衣裤	underwear; underclothes
内衣外穿	lingerie look; underwear fashion
内迎香	〈中医药〉Nei Yingxiang acupoint; Inner Fragrance Access; Inner Welcome Fragrance (EX-HN9)
内治法	〈中医药〉internal treatment; internal therapy
嫩黄光亮	〈茶〉tender yellow bright
嫩绿	〈茶〉tender green
嫩爽	〈茶〉tender and brisk
嫩香	〈茶〉tender aroma
嫩匀	〈茶〉tender and even
泥封	→封泥
泥浆釉	〈陶瓷〉slip glaze; clay glaze
泥钧釉	→广[泥]钧釉
泥疗法	〈中医药〉mud therapy; pelotherapy
泥炉烤羊肉	〈饮食〉Roasted Mutton in Mud Oven
泥釉彩饰法	〈陶瓷〉clay glazed ornament
麑裘	〈服饰〉white coat made of fawn's fur
逆行者	〈防疫〉countermarching person; people who brave coronavirus risk or a dangerous situation
年表	chronology; chronological table
年糕	〈饮食〉Nian Gao; Rice Cake; New Year's Cake
年鉴	yearbook; almanac
年历	annual calendar; single-page calendar
年利润	annual return; annual profit
年龄结构	age structure
年谱	a chronicle of sb.'s life
年清族	yearly spend-all (who spend virtually all their savings within a year)
年午饭	Lunar New Year's lunch
年夜饭	Chinese New Year's Eve dinner; family reunion dinner on Chinese New Year's Eve
鲇鱼烧茄子	〈饮食〉Braised Cat Fish and Eggplant

黏食	〈饮食〉Glutinous Snack
捻襟坎肩	〈旧〉waistcoat with lapel on the right (popular in the Qing Dynasty)
捻转	〈中医药〉twirling method; twirling of needle
酿菜心	〈饮食〉Stuffed Green Cabbage/Choy Sum
酿大乌参	〈饮食〉Stuffed Black Sea Slugs; Stuffed Black Sea Cucumbers
酿鸽蛋	〈饮食〉Stewed Stuffed Pigeon Eggs
酿黄瓜	〈饮食〉Stuffed Cucumber; Braised Cucumber with Pork Filling
酿黄瓜条	〈饮食〉Pickled Cucumber Strips
酿面筋	〈饮食〉Stuffed Wheat Gluten in Bean Curd Sheet Soup
酿排鸡翼	〈饮食〉Stewed Stuffed Chicken Wings
酿皮	〈饮食〉Niangpi (a typical Qinghai snack)
酿青椒	〈饮食〉Stuffed Green Pepper
鸟兽纹瓦当	(of building) eaves tile with bird and animal pattern
尿毒清颗粒	〈中医药〉Niaoduqing Keli; Uremic Clearance Granule
尿液	〈中医药〉urine
捏撮进针法	〈中医药〉insertion of the needle by pinching up the skin
宁德核电站	Ningde nuclear power plant (Fujian)
宁泌泰胶囊	〈中医药〉Ningmitai Jiaonang; Excretion-Calming Peace Capsule
宁神补心片	〈中医药〉Ningshen Buxin Pian; Spirit-Calming and Heart-Tonifying Tablet
宁心开窍	〈中医药〉to calm heart for resuscitation
柠檬鸡	〈饮食〉Stir-Fried Chicken with Lemon
柠檬鸡球	〈饮食〉Stir-Fried Chicken Balls with Lemon; Lemon Chicken Balls
柠檬牛肉	〈饮食〉Lemon Beef; Stir-Fried Beef with Lemon
柠檬虾球	〈饮食〉Lemon Prawn Balls; Prawn Balls with Lemon

柠汁生炸鸡	〈饮食〉Deep-Fried Chicken with Lemon Juice
凝固釉	〈陶瓷〉solidified glaze
凝聚起战胜疫情的强大合力	〈防疫〉to form strong synergies to beat the pandemic
牛蒡汤	〈中医药〉Niubang Tang; Burdock Soup; Burdock Root Decoction
牛蒡子	〈中医药〉(of Latin) Fructus Arctii; Great Burdock Achene; burdock-seed
牛肝菌红烧豆腐	〈饮食〉Braised Tofu with Boletus in Brown Sauce
牛黄	〈中医药〉(of Latin) Calculus Bovis; Cow-Bezor; Bovine Bezoar
牛黄降压胶囊	〈中医药〉Niuhuang Jiangya Jiaonang; Cow-Bezoar Capsule for Lowering Blood Pressure
牛黄解毒片	〈中医药〉Niuhuang Jiedu Pian; Bezoar Antidotal Tablet; Bovine Bezoar Toxin-Resolving Tablet
牛黄清心丸	〈中医药〉Niuhuang Qingxin Wan; Bezoar Sedative Pill; Bolus of Cow-Bezoar for Clearing Heart-Fire
牛黄上清丸	〈中医药〉Niuhuang Shangqing Wan; Bovine Bezoar Upper-Heat-Clearing Pill
牛黄蛇胆川贝液	〈中医药〉Niuhuang Shedan Chuanbei Ye; Mixture of Bezoar, Snack Bile and Fritillary
牛黄至宝丸	〈中医药〉Niuhuang Zhibao Wan; Bezoar Supreme Jewel Pill
牛栏山经典二锅头	〈酒〉Niulanshan Classic Erguotou (500ml 52°)
牛奶甜酒	milk liqueur; posset
牛腩煲	〈饮食〉Stewed Beef Brisket in Casserole
牛腩面	〈饮食〉Soup Noodles with Beef Brisket
牛肉炒年糕	〈饮食〉Stir-Fried Rice Cakes with Beef
牛肉炖土豆	〈饮食〉Braised Beef with Potatoes
牛肉盖饭	〈饮食〉Steamed Rice with Beef; Rice Topped with Beef
牛肉锅贴	〈饮食〉Guotie Stuffed with Beef
牛肉烧麦	〈饮食〉Beef Shaomai; Shaomai Stuffed with Beef
牛肉蔬菜炒面	〈饮食〉Stir-Fried Noodles with Beef and Vegetable

牛肉汤	〈饮食〉Beef Soup; Beef Broth
牛肉粥	〈饮食〉Minced Beef Congee
牛膝	〈中医药〉(of Latin) Radix Achyranthis Bidentatae; Twotoothed Achyranthes Root
牛血红釉	〈陶瓷〉ox-blood glaze
牛杂烩	〈饮食〉Cooked Chopped Beef Offal; Stewed Chopped Entrails of Ox
扭达	〈土族〉niuda (a headwear)
扭秧歌	to do the yangko dance
扭转病例增加的趋势	〈防疫〉to reverse the trend of an increasing number of cases
纽扣绊	〈服饰〉cotton strip-sewed button loop
纽扣结	〈服饰〉cotton cord-knitted button
农村合作医疗	rural cooperative medical service
农村户口	rural hukou; rural household registration; rural registered permanent residence
农村寄宿制学校	boarding schools in rural areas
农村劳动力转移培训	job training for farm laborers looking for urban employment
农村剩余劳动力	surplus rural labor/laborers
农村信用社	rural credit cooperatives
农村养老金制度	rural pension system
农二代	the second generation of migrant workers
农副产品供应	〈防疫〉supply of agricultural products
农副产品流通	〈防疫〉circulation of agricultural products
农副产品生产	〈防疫〉production of agricultural products
农机具补贴	subsidies for agricultural machinery and tools
农机下乡	to bring agricultural machinery to the countryside
农技站	agro-technical station
农家乐	happy farmhouse; farmer's home inn
农经员	agricultural management personnel
农科员	agricultural science personnel
农历新年	lunar New Year
农民工	off-farm worker; rural migrant worker; farmer-turned migrant worker

农民工子女	children of rural migrant worker in cities
农民人均纯收入	rural per capita net income
农民意识	peasant mentality; farmer consciousness; rural mentality
农特产	special agricultural product
农畜产品卖难问题	difficulties in selling their produce and livestock
农药残留物	pesticide residue; residue of agricultural chemicals
农业产业化经营	industrialized operation of agriculture; industrialized agricultural operation
农业技术推广研究员	researcher for agricultural technology promotion
农业技术员	agricultural technician; agro-technician
农业生态学	agricultural ecology
农业生物工程	agro-biological engineering
农业税	agricultural tax
农艺师	agronomist; agrotechnician
《农政全书》	〈中医药〉*Nongzheng Quan Shu*; *Agricultural Policy Book*; *A Complete Treatise on Agriculture* (by Xu Guangqi in the Ming Dynasty)
农转非	rural residents becoming urban residents
浓醇	〈茶〉strong, tasteful and mellow
浓厚	〈茶〉strong and irritative
浓涩	〈茶〉irritative and astringency
浓缩当归丸	〈中医药〉Nongsuo Danggui Wan; Enrichment Angelica Pill
浓缩煎剂	〈中医药〉concentrated decoction; condensed decoction
浓缩浸膏	〈中医药〉condensed extract; concentrated extract
浓缩丸	〈中医药〉concentrated pill; condensed pill
浓汤鸡煲翅	〈饮食〉Braised Shark's Fins in Chicken Broth
浓汤金华四宝蔬	〈饮食〉Braised Four Kinds of Vegetables in Broth
浓汤娃娃菜	〈饮食〉Braised Baby Cabbage in Broth
浓汤鱼唇	〈饮食〉Braised Fish Lips in Thick Soup
浓汤鱼肚羹	〈饮食〉Fish Maw Thick Soup; Steamed Fish Maw Porridge

浓汤鱼肚烩散翅	〈饮食〉Stewed Shark's Fins in Fish Maw Soup
浓香型(风格)	〈酒〉strong aromatic-flavor style; Luzhou-flavor liquor
浓郁	〈茶〉strong and lingering flavor
浓汁鲍丝翅	〈饮食〉Braised Shark's Fins and Abalone in Heavy Gravy
浓汁三鲜鱼翅	〈饮食〉Three Delicacies and Shark's Fin Soup; Shark Fin Soup with Three Delicacies
浓汁四宝鱼翅	〈饮食〉Four Delicacies and Shark's Fin Soup; Shark Fin Soup with Four Delicacies
浓汁鱼肚	〈饮食〉Braised Fish Maws with Chicken Broth
女宝胶囊	〈中医药〉Nübao Jiaonang; Women's Treasure Capsule
女衬衫	blouse; shirtwaist
女儿红	〈酒〉Nü'er Hong; Maiden Rose
女权运动	movement for women's rights
女式服装	women's wear; women's clothes
女性烟民	female smoker
女贞子	〈中医药〉(of Latin) Fructus Ligustri Lucidi; Ligustrum Fruit; Glossy Privet Fruit
暖巢管家	housekeeper for the old (a new model of providing old-age care services); empty-nest servant
暖肝煎	〈中医药〉Nuangan Jian; Liver-Warming Brew
暖肝散寒	〈中医药〉to warm liver for dispelling cold
暖宫散寒	〈中医药〉to warm uterus/womb for dispelling cold
暖帽	warm hat; winter official hat (used in the Qing Dynasty)
暖通工程师	heating ventilation and air conditioning (HVAC) engineer
糯米饭	〈饮食〉Sticky Rice; Glutinous Rice
糯米糕	〈饮食〉Glutinous Rice Cake
糯米酒	glutinous rice wine
糯米卷	〈饮食〉Glutinous Rice Rolls
糯米鸭	〈饮食〉Steamed Duck Stuffed with Glutinous Rice

O

藕粉 〈饮食〉Lotus Root Starch
藕节 〈中医药〉(of Latin) Nodus Nelumbinis Rhizomatis; Lotus Rhizome Node

P

爬格子	to engage in writing
拍板	to have the final say (or last word); to make a decision
拍马屁	to apple polish; to lick sb.'s shoes/boots; to fawn on
拍拖	to have a date with sb.; to go on a date with sb.
拍胸脯	to strike one's chest to guarantee sth.
排版设计师	layout designer
排毒养颜胶囊	〈中医药〉Paidu Yangyan Jiaonang; Toxin-Expelling Cosmetics Capsule
排骨拉面	〈饮食〉Hand-Pulled Noodle Soup with Spare Ribs
排骨面	〈饮食〉Soup Noodles with Spare Ribs
排石颗粒	〈中医药〉Paishi Keli; Urinary Calculus-Expelling Granule
排头兵	bellwether; vanguard
牌坊	memorial archway
牌位	memorial tablet (with the name of the deceased inscribed on and placed in an honored position)
派出所	local police station
派出医疗小组协助抗疫	〈防疫〉to send medical teams to help combat the coronavirus
攀高枝	to put oneself under the patronage of a higher-up
攀亲	to establish friendly relationship with other units or organizations; to claim ties of blood or acquaintance
盘桓髻	(of hairstyle) panhuan bun; twisted and rolled bun

盘扣[纽]	〈服饰〉knot button; cotton cord-knitted button; Chinese frog
膀胱湿热	〈中医药〉dampness-heat of bladder; bladder dampness-heat
膀胱湿热证	〈中医药〉bladder damp-heat pattern; pattern of dampness-heat of bladder
膀胱俞	〈中医药〉Pangguangshu acupoint; Bladder Transport (BL28)
膀胱虚寒	〈中医药〉deficient cold of bladder; bladder deficiency cold
膀胱虚寒证	〈中医药〉bladder vacuity cold pattern; pattern of deficient cold of bladder
胖大海	〈中医药〉(of Latin) Semen Sterculiae Lychnophorae; Boat-Fruited Sterculia Seed
胖大海含片	〈中医药〉Pangdahai (Tangguo) Hanpian; Sterculia Throat Lozenge Tablet
抛家髻	(of hairstyle) paojia bun; throwing shape bun
狍皮大袍	〈服饰〉gown made of roe deer leather
狍皮服饰	costume made of roe deer leather
狍头帽	hat made of roe deer scalp
狍头皮帽	〈鄂伦春族〉fur hat in the shape of roe deer head
袍衫	long gown
跑红	to have good luck; (of a performer) to be popular
跑龙套	to play an insignificant role/a bit role; to be a general handyman
跑堂儿	〈旧〉errand runner; to be a waiter (in a wineshop, small restaurant etc.)
跑腿	to run errands
泡吧	to kill time in a bar
泡菜什锦	〈饮食〉Assorted Pickled Vegetables
泡菜坛子	〈饮食〉pickle jar; pickle pot
泡菜鱼翅羹	〈饮食〉Shark's Fin Soup with Pickles
泡茶	to make tea; to brew tea; tea-brewing
泡茶法	tea-brewing method

泡茶巾	tea-brewing cloth
泡茶器	tea-brewing utensil; tea-brewing ware
泡饭	〈饮食〉Rice Soaked with Water; Rice in Soup
泡椒炒牛蛙	〈饮食〉Stir-Fried Bullfrog with Pickled Peppers
泡椒凤爪	〈饮食〉Chicken Paws with Pickled Peppers
泡椒甲鱼	〈饮食〉Turtle with Pickled Peppers
泡椒山鸡片	〈饮食〉Stir-Fried Pheasant Slices with Pickled Pepper
泡椒鸭丝	〈饮食〉Shredded Duck with Pickled Peppers
泡萝卜炒肉丝	〈饮食〉Stir-Fried Pork Slices with Pickled Turnip
泡沫经济	bubble economy
泡妞	to chase after the girls
泡润	〈中医药〉soaking moistening
泡腾片	〈中医药〉effervescent tablet
炮灰	cannon fodder
炮制[炙]	〈中医药〉processing; processing of medicinals
醅	〈酒〉unstrained liquor
陪伴服务	escort services
陪床	to look after a patient
陪酒女郎	barmaid; tavern-maid
培菌糟	〈酒〉distilland after inoculation and cultivation
培训部	training department
培训部主任	training officer; head/director of the training department
培训策划	training planner
培训督导[主管]	training supervisor
培训顾问	training adviser; training consultant
培训讲师	training instructor
培训经理	training manager
培训文员	training clerk
培训协调员	training coordinator
培训专员	training specialist
培养费	training expense
帔	〈古服饰〉short embroidered cape (worn by noble ladies)

佩巾	〈服饰〉pendant long ribbon (tied on the left side of the waist of ancient women when they were going out)
佩兰	〈中医药〉(of Latin) Herba Eupatorii; Fortune Eupatorium Herb
配套政策	supporting policies
配伍	〈中医药〉combination; compatibility of medicines; to combine agents in a formula
配伍禁忌	〈中医药〉prohibited combination; incompatibility of drugs in a prescription
配穴法	〈中医药〉acupoint combination; acupoint association
配音演员	dubber; dubbing actor; voice actor
喷雾疗法	〈中医药〉spraying therapy
盆栽	potted plant; pot culture
烹饪	to fry quickly in hot oil and stir in sauce
朋友圈	Wechat moments; circle of friends
棚户区	shanty town; rundown urban area
硼釉	〈陶瓷〉boracic glaze
碰钉子	to bump one's head against a nail; to get snubbed; to receive serious rebuff
碰头会	brief meeting; confrontation meeting
批发采购员	wholesale buyer
批条子	to approve by writing a slip of paper; to grant requests made by subordinate units
坯粉	〈陶瓷〉body refuse
坯裂	〈陶瓷〉crack on pottery body
坯泡	〈陶瓷〉biscuit blister; blistering of body
坯体	〈陶瓷〉clay body
坯窑	〈陶瓷〉biscuit kiln
披领	〈服饰〉tippet-collar (for official ornament in the Qing Dynasty)
皮弁服	〈古〉robes with deer leather crown (as the imperial uniform of emperors)

皮蛋	〈饮食〉Preserved Egg →松花蛋
皮蛋豆腐	〈饮食〉Tofu with Preserved Eggs
皮蛋瘦肉粥	〈饮食〉Congee with Minced Pork and Preserved Eggs
皮肤科医师	dermatologist
皮肤针	〈中医药〉cutaneous needle; dermal needle
皮肤针疗法	〈中医药〉cutaneous needle therapy; dermal needle therapy
皮甲	〈古〉leather armor
皮内针	〈中医药〉intradermal needle
皮内针疗法	〈中医药〉intradermal needle therapy
皮影戏	shadow play; shadow puppetry (leather-silhouette show)
皮影戏演员	shadow play performer
皮制大袍	〈服饰〉leather gown; leather robe
枇杷叶	〈中医药〉(of Latin) Folium Eriobotryae; Loquat Leaf
铍针	〈中医药〉stiletto needle
啤酒肚	general's belly; beer belly →将军肚
啤酒鸡	〈饮食〉Stewed Chicken in Beer
琵琶襟	〈服饰〉(of a top garment) pipa-shaped front lapel (in the Qing Dynasty)
琵琶襟旗袍	cheongsam with pipa-shaped lapel
琵琶虾仁	〈饮食〉Pipa-Shaped Shelled Shrimps
琵琶尊[瓶]	〈陶瓷〉pipa-shaped vase
脾不统血	〈中医药〉blood control failure; spleen failing to govern blood
脾不统血证	〈中医药〉pattern of spleen failing to control blood
脾肺气虚证	〈中医药〉pattern of spleen-lung qi vacuity/deficiency
脾气下陷	〈中医药〉falling of spleen-qi; spleen-qi falling
脾气虚	〈中医药〉spleen-qi deficiency; deficiency of spleen-qi
脾肾阳虚	〈中医药〉yang-deficiency of the spleen and kidney; spleen-kidney yang deficiency

脾肾阳虚证	〈中医药〉pattern of spleen-kidney yang vacuity/deficiency
脾失健运	〈中医药〉dysfunction of spleen in transportation; spleen failing in transportation
脾为生痰之源	〈中医药〉spleen being the source of phlegm formation
脾胃辨证	〈中医药〉pattern identification of the spleen and stomach; spleen and stomach differentiation pattern
脾胃不和证	〈中医药〉pattern of incoordination between the spleen and stomach
《脾胃论》	〈中医药〉Piwei Lun; Treatise on the Spleen and Stomach; On the Spleen and Stomach (by Li Gao in the Jin Dynasty)
脾胃气虚证	〈中医药〉pattern of spleen-stomach qi vacuity/deficiency
脾胃湿热	〈中医药〉dampness-heat of the spleen and stomach; spleen-stomach dampness-heat
脾胃湿热证	〈中医药〉pattern of spleen and stomach damp-heat; spleen-stomach damp-heat pattern
脾胃虚寒	〈中医药〉deficiency cold of the spleen and stomach; spleen-stomach deficiency cold
脾胃虚寒证	〈中医药〉pattern of deficiency cold of the spleen and stomach; pattern of spleen-stomach vacuity cold
脾胃虚弱	〈中医药〉deficiency/weakness of the spleen and stomach
脾胃阴虚	〈中医药〉yin-deficiency of the spleen and stomach; spleen-stomach yin deficiency
脾胃阴虚证	〈中医药〉pattern of spleen-stomach yin deficiency; pattern of yin vacuity of the spleen and stomach
脾喜燥恶湿	〈中医药〉spleen preferring dryness to dampness; spleen being more adaptable to dryness than dampness

脾虚不固证	〈中医药〉pattern of unconsolidation due to spleen deficiency
脾虚气陷证	〈中医药〉spleen vacuity and qi falling pattern; pattern of qi declining due to spleen deficiency
脾虚生风	〈中医药〉spleen deficiency causing wind; spleen vacuity engendering wind
脾虚生痰	〈中医药〉spleen deficiency generating phlegm
脾虚湿困	〈中医药〉dampness-retention due to spleen deficiency
脾虚湿困证	〈中医药〉pattern of dampness stagnancy due to spleen deficiency
脾虚湿热证	〈中医药〉pattern of dampness-heat due to spleen deficiency; pattern of spleen vacuity with damp-heat
脾虚食积证	〈中医药〉pattern of food retention due to spleen deficiency; pattern of spleen vacuity with food accumulation
脾虚水泛证	〈中医药〉pattern of water diffusion due to spleen deficiency; pattern of spleen vacuity with water flood
脾虚水肿	〈中医药〉edema due to spleen deficiency
脾虚痰湿证	〈中医药〉pattern of phlegm-dampness due to spleen deficiency; pattern of spleen vacuity with phlegm-damp
脾虚证	〈中医药〉pattern of spleen deficiency; spleen vacuity pattern
脾阳	〈中医药〉spleen-yang
脾阳不振	〈中医药〉inactivation of spleen-yang
脾阳虚	〈中医药〉spleen-yang deficiency; deficiency of spleen-yang
脾阳虚水泛证	〈中医药〉pattern of water diffusion due to spleen-yang deficiency
脾阳虚证	〈中医药〉pattern of spleen-yang deficiency; spleen-yang vacuity pattern

脾阴虚	〈中医药〉spleen-yin deficiency; deficiency of spleen yin
脾阴虚证	〈中医药〉pattern of spleen-yin deficiency; spleen-yin vacuity pattern
脾主肌肉	〈中医药〉spleen governing/controlling muscles
痞根	〈中医药〉Pigen acupoint; Glomus Root (EX-B4)
偏方	folk remedy; folk prescription; traditional popular prescription
偏瘫复原丸	〈中医药〉Piantan Fuyuan Wan; Hemiplegia-Restoring Pill
片酬	remuneration for a movie actor or actress
片刀	〈古〉slicer; slicing knife (a kind of weapon)
片儿川面	〈饮食〉Pian Er Chuan Noodles; Noodles with Preserved Vegetables
片儿警	section-policeman (responsible for registration of residents, public security, etc. in a certain area)
片姜黄	〈中医药〉(of Latin) Rhizoma Wenyujin Concisa; Wenyujin Concise Rhizome; Sliced Turmeric
骗汇、逃汇、套汇	to obtain foreign currency and false pretenses, and not turn over foreign currency owed to the government and illegal arbitrage
骗税	tax fraud; tax cheating; tax rebate cheat
缥瓷	〈陶瓷〉faint colored porcelain; pale green porcelain
飘香手撕鸡	〈饮食〉Poached Sliced Chicken
飘逸杯	〈茶〉Piaoyi tea pot (Taiwan high quality tea set) →茶道杯
票贩子	ticket scalper; ticket tout
票房大卖	box office hit
票房毒药	box office flop
票房冠军	box office champion
票务代理	ticket agent
票友	(of Peking Opera) amateur performer; amateur actors

拼爹	competition of family background
贫富悬殊	wide gap between the rich and the poor
贫困地区农民	farmers in poor areas
贫困线	poverty line
品茗［茶］	to sip tea (to judge its quality); to sample tea
品茗杯	〈茶〉tea-sipping cup; fragrance-smelling cup
品牌产品	branded product
品牌效应	brand effect
品牌主管	brand supervisor
品牌专员	brand specialist
品色衣	color-graded official costume (different colors indicating different official's ranks)
品学兼优的学生	student of good morality and scholarship
乒乓球协会	table tennis association
平贝母	〈中医药〉Fritillaria ussuriensis Bulbus; Fritillaria Bulb
平补平泻	〈中医药〉neutral supplementation and draining; even reinforcing-reducing method
平刺	〈中医药〉transverse insertion; horizontal insertion of the needle
平伏	〈茶〉flat and even
平肝和胃	〈中医药〉to soothe the liver and harmonize the stomach
平肝降逆	〈中医药〉to suppress hyperactive liver for descending/lowering adverse qi
平肝潜阳	〈中医药〉to pacify the liver to subdue yang; to suppress hyperactive liver for subsiding yang
平肝息风	〈中医药〉to suppress hyperactive liver for calming endogenous wind
平肝止血	〈中医药〉to soothe the liver to stop bleeding; to calm the liver to stop bleeding
平滑	〈茶〉flat and smooth
平髻	〈古〉(of hairstyle) flat bun; flat chignon
平巾［上］帻	〈古服饰〉flat turban-hat

平凉酥饼	〈饮食〉Pingliang Style Pancake
平脉	〈中医药〉normal pulse
平面设计师	graphic artist; graphic designer
平面设计主管	graphic design supervisor
平面设计总监	graphic design director
平面制作经理	print production manager
平桥豆腐	〈饮食〉Tofu Boiled in Chicken and Carp Broth
平日门票	standard day ticket
平日优惠票	standard day special ticket/admission
平水珠茶	Pingshui Pearl tea
平调寒热	〈中医药〉to mildly regulate cold and heat; to balance regulation of cold and heat
平胃散	〈中医药〉Pingwei San; Peptic Powder; Stomach-Calming Powder
平纹布	single jersey; plain cloth
平熄内风剂	〈中医药〉formula for calming down internal wind
平阳黄汤	〈茶〉Pingyang Yellow Soup
平展	〈茶〉flat leaf side
平正	〈茶〉with little tea aroma but have no offensive odor
评估总监	chief valuation officer; CVO
评职称	professional evaluation
苹果咖喱鸡	〈饮食〉Curry Chicken with Apple
屏风	folding screen; floor screen
瓶状窑	〈陶瓷〉bottle-shaped kiln
泼冷水	to throw cold water on sth.; to dampen the enthusiasm of for sth.
破格	to break old conventions (in selecting or appointing talented people)
破张	〈茶〉broken leaves
魄户	〈中医药〉Pohu; Corporeal Soul Door (BL42)
葡萄紫釉	〈陶瓷〉grape purple glaze
葡汁鸡	〈饮食〉Braised Chicken with Port Wine
蒲公英	〈中医药〉(of Latin) Herba Taraxaci; Dandelion

蒲公英颗粒	〈中医药〉Pugongying Keli; Dandelion Soluble Preparation
蒲公英片	〈中医药〉Pugongying Pian; Dandelion Tablet
普洱茶	Pu'er tea
普洱茶砖	brick Pu'er tea
普洱紧压茶	Pu'er pressed tea
普洱生茶	raw Pu'er tea
普洱熟茶	fermented Pu'er tea
普及初等教育	to make primary education universal; to achieve universal primary education
普及九年制义务教育	to make nine-year compulsory education universal
普济禅院	Kun Iam Temple (Macao)
《普济方》	〈中医药〉*Puji Fang*; *Prescriptions for Universal Relief* (by Zhu Xiao et al. in the Ming Dynasty)
普济消毒饮	〈中医药〉Puji Xiaodu Yin; Universal Salvation Toxin-Dispersing Beverage
普通高等教育	regular higher education
普通高校	regular institutions of higher learning
普通话等级考试	national Mandarin test
普陀佛茶	Putuo Buddha tea
普选制	general election system
氆氇	〈藏族〉Tibet wool (woolen fabric for making blankets, garments, etc.)
氆氇长袍	〈藏族〉Tibet wool robe
氆氇筒裙	〈藏族〉Tibet wool tight/tube skirt

Q

七宝美髯丹	〈中医药〉Qibao Meiran Dan; Seven-Jewel Beard-Blackening Elixir
七彩菊	〈中医药〉(of Latin) Helichrysum bracteatum; Bracteantha Bracteata; Colorful Chrysanthemum
七彩袖	〈土族〉seven-colored sleeve
七境堂绿茶	Qijingtang Green tea
七厘散	〈中医药〉Qili San; Anti-Bruise Powder
七年之痒	(of a marriage) seven-year itch
七匹狼香烟	Qipi Lang cigarettes; Septwolves cigarettes
七情内伤	〈中医药〉internal damage due to seven emotions; internal injury due to emotional disorder
七情所伤	〈中医药〉to be damaged by excess of seven emotions
七星披肩	〈纳西族〉sheepskin shawl with seven stars
七星针	〈中医药〉seven-star needle
七叶莲	〈中医药〉(of Latin) Schefflera Arboricola Hayata; Scandent Schefflera Stem and Leaf; Taiwan Schefflera
七制香附丸	〈中医药〉Qizhi Xiangfu Wan; Sevenfold Processed Cyperus Pill
妻管严	hen-pecked husband
期货操盘手	futures operator; futures trader
期货经纪人	future broker
期门	〈中医药〉Qimen acupoint; Cycle Door (LR13)
期望寿命	life expectancy
期望值	expectation; expectancy

欺上瞒下	to deceive one's superiors and subordinates; to conceal from higher authority and deceive lower authority
漆器	lacquer work; lacquer ware
齐法化	〈币〉knife-shaped coin (issued in the Warring States period) →三字刀
齐胸襦裙	〈古〉chest-covering served skirt (peculiar to the Sui, Tang and Five Dynasties)
祁红熏子鸡	〈饮食〉Smoked Spring Chicken with Tea Flavor
祁门茶	Keemun tea
祁门红茶	Keemun black tea
祁门香	〈茶〉Keemun aroma
岐伯	Qibo (believed as the ancestor of traditional Chinese medicine)
岐山臊子面	〈饮食〉Qishan Noodles Topped with Minced Pork
奇方	〈中医药〉odd-numbered formula; odd-ingredient prescription
奇经八脉	〈中医药〉eight extraordinary channels/meridians
奇经纳卦法	〈中医药〉→灵龟八法
奇瑞汽车	Chery automobile
奇异果炒花枝	〈饮食〉Stir-Fried Sliced Cuttlefish with Kiwi Fruit
歧视性的限制	discriminatory restrictions
脐带血库	(umbilical) cord blood bank →生命银行
棋子烤鸡卷	〈饮食〉Roasted Crispy Chicken Rolls (Shaped as a Chess)
旗舰店	flagship store
旗袍	〈服饰〉chi-pao; cheongsam; Chinese style close-fitting skirt
旗袍裙	Chinese style close-fitting skirt; Chinese style straight skirt
旗鞋	→花盆底鞋
旗装	Manchu clothes; women's dress of Manchu ethnic group

麒麟鸡	〈饮食〉Steamed Sliced Chicken with Mushrooms and Vegetables
企划指导	planning director
企划总监	planning supervisor
企事业单位	enterprise and public institution
企业策划人员	business planning staff
企业法律顾问	corporate legal counsel
企业法律顾问执业资格证书	enterprise counsel qualification certificate
企业年金	enterprise annuity; supplementary pension
杞菊地黄丸	〈中医药〉Qiju Dihuang Wan; Lycium Berry, Chrysanthemum and Rehmannia Pill
启动重大突发公共卫生事件一级响应	〈防疫〉to activate the first-level public health emergency response
启发式教学	heuristic education; heuristic teaching
起跑线	starting line for a race (usually used for children's education)
起绒针织物	knitted fleece; napped jersey
气闭	〈中医药〉qi blockage; qi block
气闭证	〈中医药〉pattern of qi blockade; qi block pattern
气不摄血	〈中医药〉qi failing to control blood; failure of qi to check the blood
气不摄血证	〈中医药〉pattern of qi failing to contain the blood
气功	〈中医药〉qigong; a system of deep breathing exercises
气海俞	〈中医药〉Qihaishu acupoint; Sea of Qi Transport (BL24)
气户	〈中医药〉Qihu acupoint; Qi Door (ST13)
气化不利	〈中医药〉disturbance of qi transformation; dysfunction of qi in transformation
气机不利	〈中医药〉disorder of qi movement; disturbance of visceral function
气机调畅	〈中医药〉smooth activity of qi; harmonious functional activities of qi

气机郁滞不畅	〈中医药〉stagnation of qi activity
气厥	〈中医药〉coma with qi disorder; syncope due to disorder of vital energy
气逆	〈中医药〉reversed flow of qi; adverseness of qi; circulation of vital energy in the wrong direction
气逆证	〈中医药〉qi counter-flow pattern; pattern of reversed qi flow
气溶胶传播	〈防疫〉aerosol transmission
气上冲心	〈中医药〉reflux of qi to the heart; qi surging upward to the heart
气随津脱	〈中医药〉exhaustion of qi due to loss of body fluid
气随血脱	〈中医药〉exhaustion of qi due to hemorrhea; qi desertion due to blood depletion
气随液脱	〈中医药〉depletion of fluid involving qi desertion; exhaustion of qi due to depletion of body fluid
气脱证	〈中医药〉qi desertion pattern; pattern of qi desertion
气陷证	〈中医药〉qi falling pattern; pattern of qi declination
气象卫星	meteorological satellite
气虚不摄	〈中医药〉failure of keeping fluid due to qi deficiency; qi deficiency failing to control
气虚发热证	〈中医药〉pattern of fever due to qi deficiency
气虚外感证	〈中医药〉pattern of exogenous disease due to qi depletion
气虚血瘀	〈中医药〉blood stasis due to qi deficiency; blood stagnation due to qi vacuity
气虚血瘀证	〈中医药〉pattern of blood stasis due to qi deficiency
气虚证	〈中医药〉qi vacuity pattern; pattern of qi deficiency
气虚中满	〈中医药〉flatulence caused by qi deficiency; abdominal distension with qi deficiency
气穴	〈中医药〉Qixue acupoint; Qi Cavity (KI13)
气血功能紊乱	〈中医药〉dysfunction of qi and blood
气血津液	〈中医药〉qi-blood and fluid

气血两虚证	〈中医药〉pattern of both qi and blood deficiency
气血凝滞	〈中医药〉stagnation of qi and blood
气血生化之源	〈中医药〉source of the production and transformation of qi and blood
气血失调	〈中医药〉disorder/disharmony of qi and blood
气血双补剂	〈中医药〉formula for benefiting both qi and blood
气血运行	〈中医药〉qi-blood circulation; flow of qi and blood
气阴两虚	〈中医药〉deficiency of both qi and yin; dual deficiency of qi and yin
气阴两虚证	〈中医药〉pattern of both qi and yin deficiency
气郁	〈中医药〉stagnation of qi; obstruction of the circulation of vital energy
气郁化火	〈中医药〉qi depression transformed into fire; stagnated qi turned into fire
气郁化火证	〈中医药〉pattern of qi depression transformed into fire
气郁化热	〈中医药〉qi stagnation transformed into heat; qi depression turned into heat
气滞	〈中医药〉stagnation of qi; stagnated vital energy; stagnancy of the circulation of vital energy
气滞耳窍证	〈中医药〉pattern of qi stagnation in the ear
气滞津停	〈中医药〉retention of fluid due to stagnation of qi
气滞湿阻证	〈中医药〉pattern of damp retention due to qi stagnation
气滞胃痛颗粒	〈中医药〉Qizhi Weitong Keli; Granule for Promoting Qi and Relieving Stomach Pain
气滞血瘀	〈中医药〉qi stagnation and blood stasis; stagnation of qi and blood stasis
气滞血瘀证	〈中医药〉pattern of qi stagnation and blood stasis →游走性舌炎
气滞腰痛	〈中医药〉lumbago due to qi stagnation; qi stagnation lumbar pain
气滞证	〈中医药〉qi stagnation pattern; pattern of qi stagnation

汽车工程师	automotive engineer
汽车共享业务	car-sharing business
汽车图书馆	mobile library
汽车限购	car purchase restriction
汽车修理工	automobile mechanic; garageman
汽车修理师	automobile mechanical technician
汽锅虫草炖老鸭	〈饮食〉Stewed Duck with Aweto in Steam Pot
汽锅鸡	〈饮食〉Steamed Chicken in Casserole
汽锅鸡翅	〈饮食〉Steamed Chicken Wings in Casserole
掐头去尾	〈酒〉cutting-out both ends of the distillate
千柏鼻炎片	〈中医药〉Qianbai Biyan Pian; Rhinitis Tablet of Climbing Groundsel and Spikemoss
千层酥烤鲜贝	〈饮食〉Baked Scallops Mille Feuille
千岛玉叶	〈茶〉Thousand Island Jade Leaf
《千金翼方》	〈中医药〉*Qianjin Yi Fang*; *Supplement to Invaluable Formulary for Ready Reference*; *A Supplement to the Essential Recipes for Emergent Use* (by Sun Simiao in the Tang Dynasty)
千金子	〈中医药〉(of Latin) Semen Euphorbiae; Caper Euphorbia Seed
千里光	〈中医药〉(of Latin) Herba Senecionis Scandentis; Climbing Groundsel
千年健	〈中医药〉(of Latin) Rhizoma Homalomenae; Obscured Homalomena Rhizome; Homa Lomena Root
千山白酒	Qianshan white liquor
千禧婴儿	millennium infant; millennium baby
牵牛子	〈中医药〉(of Latin) Semen Pharbitidis; Pharbitis Seed
牵线搭桥	to act as a go-between
牵正散	〈中医药〉Qianzheng San; Pull Aright Powder
铅硼釉	〈陶瓷〉lead borate glaze
前峰雪莲	〈茶〉Qianfeng White Bud tea
前谷	〈中医药〉Qiangu acupoint; Front Valley (SI2)

前胡	〈中医药〉(of Latin) Radix Peucedani; Hogfennel Root
前襟	front part of a Chinese robe or jacket
前列回春胶囊	〈中医药〉Qianlie Huichun Jiaonang; Prostate Rejuvenating Capsule
前列康普乐安片	〈中医药〉Qianlie Kang Pule'an Pian; Prostate Recovery Tablet
前列通片	〈中医药〉Qianlietong Pian; Prostate Unobstruction Tablet; Prostate-Freeing Tablet
前列消胶囊	〈中医药〉Qianliexiao Jiaonang; Prostatitis Disappearing Capsule
前台接待	front desk clerk
前台组长	front desk supervisor
前厅部	front office department
前厅接待	front office receptionist
前厅经理	front office manager
前厅文员	front office clerk
前沿技术研究	frontier technology research; cutting-edge technology research
前沿科技	frontier technology; cutting-edge technology
前沿科学	front-line science; cutting-edge science
前沿性交叉性研究	pioneering and interdisciplinary research
前沿学科	front-line subject; frontier discipline
前圆后连袖	split raglan sleeve
钱	〈旧〉(of weight unit) qian (equal to 5grams, or to about 3.72 grams for old system)
钱袋子	fund sources; money bags
钱文钱	〈古〉coin with money inscription
乾隆粉彩百花觚	〈陶瓷〉famille-rose goblet with floral pattern (Qing Qianlong period)
乾隆青瓷鸡熏	〈陶瓷〉celadon chicken-shaped incense burner (Qing Qianlong period)
乾隆通宝	〈币〉coin with characters Qianlong tongbao (square-holed copper coin of Qianlong period)

潜伏期	〈防疫〉incubation; latent period
潜规则	default rule; unwritten rules; unspoken rules
潜意识	subconsciousness
黔春酒	Guizhou Spring liquor
芡实	〈中医药〉(of Latin) Semen Euryales; Gordon Euryale Seed
茜草	〈中医药〉(of Latin) Radix Rubiae; Madder Root
嵌花	〈陶瓷〉applique; intarsia
羌活	〈中医药〉(of Latin) Rhizoma et Radix Notopterygii; Incised Notopterygium Rhizome
羌活胜湿汤	〈中医药〉Qianghuo Shengshi Tang; Notopterygium Dampness-Overcoming Decoction
强电工	strong current worker
强骨胶囊	〈中医药〉Qianggu Jiaonang; Bone-Strengthening Capsule
强骨生血口服液	〈中医药〉Qianggu Shengxue Koufuye; Bone-Strengthening and Blood-Engendering Oral Liquid
强化班	intensive training class
强化公共卫生法治保障	〈防疫〉to strengthen the legal framework of public health
强间	〈中医药〉Qiangjian acupoint; Unyielding Space (GV18)
强筋壮骨	〈中医药〉to strengthen tendons and bones; to invigorate sinew and bone
强力枇杷露	〈中医药〉Qiangli Pipa Lu; Strong Loquot Leaf Syrup
强力天麻杜仲胶囊	〈中医药〉Qiangli Tianma Duzhong Jiaonang; Powerful Strength Gastrodia Eucommia Capsule
强强联手	win-win co-operation; one-two punch
强弱电领班	strong and weak current captain
抢得先机	to take the preemptive opportunities; to get a head start
抢购	panic buying; scare buying
抢红灯	to run a red light; to jump the lights

襁褓	swaddling clothes; swaddling bands
炝腰花泡菜	〈饮食〉Stir-Fried Boiled Kidney with Pickled Vegetables
炝糟鸡丝	〈饮食〉Stir-Fried Shredded Chicken with Red Rice Wine Sauce
侨胞	overseas Chinese; countrymen residing abroad; compatriot from the overseas
侨商	overseas Chinese merchant/businessman
荞麦馒头	〈饮食〉Buckwheat Mantou; Mantou with Buckwheat Flour
荞麦面条	〈饮食〉Buckwheat Flour Noodles
桥梁工程师	bridge system engineer; BSE
巧拌海茸	〈饮食〉Mixed Seaweed
巧克力松饼	〈饮食〉Chocolate Muffins; Chocolate Waffle
翘楚	top figure; top performer
翘尾巴	to stick one's tail up; to be cocky/arrogant
切菜板	〈饮食〉chopping board
切断传播途径	〈防疫〉to cut off the channels of transmission
切脉	〈中医药〉to feel the pulse →号脉
切身利益	vital interests; immediate interests
茄丁肉酱手擀面	〈饮食〉Handmade Noodles with Diced Eggplant and Minced Pork in Sauce
茄皮紫釉	〈陶瓷〉aubergine glaze
茄汁炒牛肉片	〈饮食〉Stir-Fried Sliced Beef with Tomato Sauce
茄汁挂炉牛肉	〈饮食〉Barbecued Beef with Tomato Sauce
茄汁煎酿鸡翼	〈饮食〉Pan-Fried Chicken Wings with Tomato Sauce
茄汁明虾球	〈饮食〉Stir-Fried Prawn Balls with Tomato Sauce
茄汁牛蒡鸡块	〈饮食〉Fried Chicken Drumsticks with Burdock and Tomato Sauce
茄汁石斑块	〈饮食〉Deep-Fried Garoupa Slices with Tomato Sauce
茄汁虾仁	〈饮食〉Stir-Fried Shelled Shrimps with Tomato Sauce

茄汁鸭块汤	〈饮食〉Duck Soup with Tomato Sauce
茄汁鱼片	〈饮食〉Fried Fish Slices with Tomato Sauce
茄汁鱼球	〈饮食〉Fried Fish Balls with Tomato Sauce
茄子肉丁打卤面	〈饮食〉Noodles with Eggplant and Diced Pork
侵吞公款	to embezzle public funds; embezzlement of public funds
芹菜炒肉丝	〈饮食〉Stir-Fried Shredded Pork with Celery
芹菜炒香干	〈饮食〉Stir-Fried Dried Tofu Slices with Celery
芹香木耳	〈饮食〉Stir-Fried Black Fungi with Celery
秦巴雾毫	〈茶〉Qin Ba Mist Bud tea
秦半两	〈币〉banliang coin of the Qin State
秦将军陶俑	〈陶瓷〉pottery figurine of a Qin general
秦艽	〈中医药〉(of Latin) Radix Gentianae Macrophyllae; Largeleaf Gentian Root
秦皮	〈中医药〉(of Latin) Cortex Fraxini; Ash Bark
秦山核电站	Qinshan nuclear power plant (Zhejiang)
秦俑坑军阵队列	battle formation array in the Terracotta Warriors
禽流感	〈防疫〉bird flu; avian influenza
勤工俭学	part-work and part-study system; to study under a work-study program
勤洗手	〈防疫〉to wash your hands frequently
勤政廉政建设	to keep government functionaries honest and industrious
噙化	〈中医药〉administered under tongue
青白瓷	〈陶瓷〉greenish white porcelain; bluish white porcelain
青白瓷刻花瓶	〈陶瓷〉bluish-white vase with carved flowers
青白瓷四大天王塑像	〈陶瓷〉Four Heavenly Kings' statue of bluish white porcelain (Yuan Dynasty)
青白瓷印花把壶	〈陶瓷〉celadon and Blanc de Chine vessel with handle and impressed decoration
青饼	〈茶〉pile cake Pu'er
青城雪芽	〈茶〉Qingcheng Xueya tea; Qingcheng Snow Bud
青春崇拜	youth worship; cult of youth

青春饭	(of a job) youth occupation; professions for young persons only
青瓷	〈陶瓷〉celadon (porcelain); blue china
青瓷鼎	〈陶瓷〉celadon cauldron; celadon tripod
青瓷对书俑	〈陶瓷〉celadon proof reading figurine
青瓷对坐俑	〈陶瓷〉celadon figurines sitting opposite each other
青瓷凤首龙柄壶	〈陶瓷〉celadon ewer with phoenix headed cover and dragon-shaped handle
青瓷凤首尊	〈陶瓷〉celadon phoenix-head jar
青瓷盖碗	〈陶瓷〉celadon bowl with cover
青瓷谷仓	〈陶瓷〉celadon model of granary
青瓷谷仓罐	〈陶瓷〉celadon granary jar
青瓷罐	〈陶瓷〉celadon porcelain jar
青瓷褐斑香炉	〈陶瓷〉celadon incense burner with brown spots
青瓷鸡首壶	〈陶瓷〉celadon pot with chicken-head spout
青瓷鸡首龙柄盘口壶	〈陶瓷〉celadon plate-mouthed pot with chicken-head spout and dragon-shaped handle
青瓷加彩蛙形双系罐	〈陶瓷〉celadon colored frog-shaped jar with two ears
青瓷井	〈陶瓷〉celadon model of well
青瓷莲花瓶	〈陶瓷〉celadon vase with lotus pattern
青瓷莲花托碗	〈陶瓷〉celadon bowl on a stand with lotus pattern
青瓷莲花尊	〈陶瓷〉celadon jar in the shape of lotus
青瓷盆	〈陶瓷〉celadon basin
青瓷辟邪水注	〈陶瓷〉celadon water dropper in the shape of fabulous animal
青瓷骑狮俑	〈陶瓷〉celadon figurine of man riding on lion
青瓷棋盘	〈陶瓷〉celadon porcelain chessboard
青瓷狮子水壶	〈陶瓷〉celadon lion-shaped water dropper
青瓷双系双纽盖罐	〈陶瓷〉celadon lidded jug with double ears and knobs
青瓷四耳罐	〈陶瓷〉four-eared celadon jar
青瓷四系罐	〈陶瓷〉celadon jar with four ears
青瓷唾壶	〈陶瓷〉celadon porcelain spittoon

青瓷卧羊	〈陶瓷〉celadon porcelain ram
青瓷香熏	〈陶瓷〉celadon incense burner
青瓷象首八系壶	〈陶瓷〉celadon pot with elephant-head spout and eight ears
青瓷熊灯	〈陶瓷〉celadon bear-shaped lamp
青瓷羊形器	〈陶瓷〉celadon ram-shaped wine vessel
青瓷羊形水注	〈陶瓷〉celadon ram-shaped water dropper
青瓷仰覆莲花瓷尊	〈陶瓷〉celadon lotus zun with the other one downwards on the top
青瓷膺首壶	〈陶瓷〉celadon pot with eagle-head pattern
青瓷釉	〈陶瓷〉celadon glaze
青瓷盂	〈陶瓷〉celadon porcelain spittoon
青瓷鱼形水丞	〈陶瓷〉celadon fish-shaped water dropper
青岛白葡萄酒	Tsingtao/Qingdao white wine
青岛啤酒	Tsingtao beer
青岛生[扎]啤	〈酒〉Tsingtao draught beer
青豆炒牛肉粒	〈饮食〉Stir-Fried Diced Beef with Green Beans
青豆炒肉丁	〈饮食〉Stir-Fried Diced Pork with Green Peas
青豆虾仁	〈饮食〉Stir-Fried Shelled Shrimps with Green Peas
青风藤	〈中医药〉(of Latin) Caulis Sinomenii; Ovientvine Stem
青瓜鸡丁	〈饮食〉Stir-Fried Diced Chicken with Cucumber
青瓜肉松煮鱼肚	〈饮食〉Boiled Fish Maw with Minced Pork and Cucumber
青果	〈中医药〉(of Latin) Fructus Canarii; Chinese White Olive
青果领	shawl collar; shawl lapel
青蒿	〈中医药〉(of Latin) Herba Artemisiae Annuae; Sweet Wormwood Herb
青蒿鳖甲汤	〈中医药〉Qinghao Biejia Tang; Sweet Wormwood and Turtle Shell Decoction
青蒿素	〈中医药〉Artemisininum; Arteannuin; Qinghao Su
青花暗刻花卉龙纹高足杯	〈陶瓷〉blue and white stem cup with covert-engraved floral dragon pattern (Yuan Dynasty)

青花八棱壶	〈陶瓷〉blue and white octagonal ewer
青花八棱龙纹瓶	〈陶瓷〉blue and white octagonal vase with dragon pattern
青花八棱云龙瓶	〈陶瓷〉blue and white octagonal vase with cloud and dragon pattern
青花八仙过海图碗	〈陶瓷〉blue and white bowl with a pattern of Eight Immortals crossing the sea (Qing Qianlong period)
青花八仙葫芦瓶	〈陶瓷〉blue and white gourd-shaped vase with Eight Immortals pattern (Ming Zhengde period)
青花八仙人物纹碗	〈陶瓷〉blue and white bowl with Eight Immortals pattern (Qing Guangxu period)
青花拔白莲草鱼纹碗	〈陶瓷〉blue and white bowl with lotus and fish pattern (Ming Xuande period)
青花扁瓶	〈陶瓷〉blue and white flat bottle (Ming Xuande period)
青花缠枝花卉大碗	〈陶瓷〉large blue and white bowl with interlaced branches and flowers pattern (Ming Hongwu period)
青花缠枝花卉莲纹折沿盆	〈陶瓷〉blue and white edge-folded basin with interlaced branches, flowers and lotuses pattern (Ming Yongle period)
青花缠枝花卉葡萄纹折沿大盘	〈陶瓷〉large blue and white edge-folded plate with interlaced branches, flowers and grapes pattern (Ming Yongle period)
青花缠枝花卉纹高足杯	〈陶瓷〉blue and white stem cup with interlaced branches and flowers pattern (Ming Xuande period)
青花缠枝花卉纹罐	〈陶瓷〉blue and white jar with interlocked branches and flower pattern (Ming Yongle period)
青花缠枝花卉纹碗	〈陶瓷〉blue and white bowl with floral pattern of interlocked branches (Ming Yongle period)
青花缠枝花纹碗	〈陶瓷〉blue and white bowl with interlocked branches and flowers pattern
青花缠枝莲花瓠	〈陶瓷〉blue and white goblet with interlocked branches and lotus pattern (Ming Zhengde period)

青花缠枝莲龙纹盘	〈陶瓷〉blue and white plate with interlocked branches of lotus and dragon pattern (Ming Chenghua period)
青花缠枝莲纹大碗	〈陶瓷〉large blue-and-white bowl with interlaced branches and lotuses pattern (Ming Xuande period)
青花缠枝莲纹双耳尊	〈陶瓷〉blue and white amphora zun with interlaced branches and lotuses pattern (Qing Qianlong period)
青花缠枝牡丹纹大碗	〈陶瓷〉large blue and white bowl with interlaced branches and peony pattern
青花缠枝如意花卉卧足碗	〈陶瓷〉blue and white flat-bottom bowl with interlaced branches and auspicious floral pattern (Ming Xuande period)
青花缠枝寿字纹大罐	〈陶瓷〉large blue and white jar with interlaced branches and 寿-character pattern (Ming Jiajing period)
青花瓷	〈陶瓷〉blue and white porcelain
青花带托盏	〈陶瓷〉blue and white small cup with saucer
青花刀马人物图凤尾尊	〈陶瓷〉blue and white phoenix tail zun with knights and horses pattern (Qing Kangxi period)
青花番莲鱼篓尊	〈陶瓷〉blue and white zun with lotus pattern and in the shape of fish basket (Ming Yongle period)
青花梵文莲瓣洗	〈陶瓷〉blue and white writing-brush washer in the shape of lotus petals and with Sanskrit words
青花凤穿花执壶	〈陶瓷〉blue and white jug with phoenix amidst flowers pattern
青花凤凰花卉纹八棱玉壶春瓶	〈陶瓷〉blue and white octagonal Yuhuchun vase with phoenix and flower pattern (Yuan Dynasty)
青花凤凰花卉纹高足杯	〈陶瓷〉blue and white stem cup with phoenix and flower pattern (Ming Chenghua period)
青花凤凰花卉纹罐	〈陶瓷〉blue and white jar with phoenix and flower pattern (Ming Jiajing period)
青花凤首扁壶	〈陶瓷〉blue and white flask with a phoenix head spout

青花凤首壶	〈陶瓷〉blue and white pot with phoenix-headed spout (Yuan Dynasty)
青花凤纹摇铃尊	〈陶瓷〉blue and white bell zun with phoenix pattern (Qing Kangxi period)
青花高士赏花图玉壶春瓶	〈陶瓷〉blue and white Yuhuchun vase with a pattern of hermit admiring the beauty of flowers (Yuan Dynasty)
青花勾莲纹盘	〈陶瓷〉blue and white plate with interlaced lotuses pattern (Qing Qianlong period)
青花海水缠枝花卉纹罐	〈陶瓷〉blue and white jar with seawater and interlaced branches floral-pattern (Yuan Dynasty)
青花海水瑞兽纹长颈瓶	〈陶瓷〉blue and white long-necked vase with seawater and lucky animal pattern (Qing Kangxi period)
青花鹤鹿纹凤尾尊	〈陶瓷〉blue and white phoenix tail zun with crane and deer pattern
青花红彩高足碗	〈陶瓷〉celadon red-glazed stem bowl (Ming Xuande period)
青花红彩碗	〈陶瓷〉blue and white bowl with red decoration (Ming Xuande period)
青花红釉花卉纹瓷盖罐	〈陶瓷〉blue and white lidded jug with red-glazed floral pattern
青花花卉大盖罐	〈陶瓷〉large blue and white lidded jar with floral pattern
青花花卉回纹大罐	〈陶瓷〉large blue and white jar with floral pattern (Ming Zhengde period)
青花花卉纹杯	〈陶瓷〉blue and white cup with floral pattern (Yuan Dynasty)
青花花卉纹葵口大盘	〈陶瓷〉large blue and white sunflower-mouthed plate with floral pattern (Yuan Dynasty)
青花花卉纹盘	〈陶瓷〉blue and white plate with floral pattern (Qing Qianlong period)
青花花卉纹碗	〈陶瓷〉blue and white bowl with floral pattern (Ming Hongwu period)

青花花卉纹玉壶春瓶	〈陶瓷〉blue and white Yuhuchun vase with floral pattern (Yuan Dynasty)
青花花鸟龙纹水呈	〈陶瓷〉blue and white water jug with flower, bird and dragon pattern (Yuan Dynasty)
青花花鸟纹盘	〈陶瓷〉blue and white plate with flowers and birds pattern (Yuan Dynasty)
青花吉祥如意盘	〈陶瓷〉blue and white plate with auspiciousness characters patterns (Qing Qianlong period)
青花教子莲花纹大盘	〈陶瓷〉large blue and white plate with children's instruction and lotus pattern (Ming Jiajing period)
青花九桃盘	〈陶瓷〉blue and white plate with nine peaches pattern (Qing Qianlong period)
青花开窗人物仙鹤纹凤尾尊	〈陶瓷〉blue and white phoenix tail zun with window-people and cranes pattern (Qing Kangxi period)
青花开光葡萄折枝花卉菱口折沿大盘	〈陶瓷〉large blue and white edge-folded plate with grapes and floral pattern (Ming Yongle period)
青花莲池鸳鸯纹八棱罐	〈陶瓷〉blue and white octagonal jar with a pattern of mandarin ducks in lotus pond
青花莲池鸳鸯纹盘	〈陶瓷〉blue and white plate with a pattern of mandarin ducks in lotus pond
青花莲塘大碗	〈陶瓷〉blue and white big bowl with lotus pattern (Ming Zhengde period)
青花莲托八宝纹盉壶	〈陶瓷〉blue and white pot with lotus and eight treasures pattern (Qing Qianlong period)
青花莲纹梅瓶	〈陶瓷〉blue and white plum vase with lotus pattern (Yuan Dynasty)
青花灵芝纹杯	〈陶瓷〉blue and white cup with ganoderma pattern (Ming Jiajing period)
青花刘海戏蟾纹梅瓶	〈陶瓷〉blue and white plum vase with Liuhai playing with toad pattern (Qing Kangxi period)
青花龙穿花纹瓶	〈陶瓷〉blue and white vase with dragon amidst flowers pattern (Qing Kangxi period)
青花龙凤纹高足杯	〈陶瓷〉blue and white stem cup with dragon and phoenix pattern (Ming Yongle period)

青花龙纹盖罐	〈陶瓷〉blue and white lidded jar with dragon pattern (Yuan Dynasty)
青花龙纹盖盒	〈陶瓷〉blue and white lidded box with dragon pattern (Ming Wanli period)
青花龙纹高足杯	〈陶瓷〉blue and white stem cup with dragon pattern (Yuan Dynasty)
青花龙纹高足盘	〈陶瓷〉blue and white high-foot plate with dragon pattern (Qing Kangxi period)
青花龙纹罐	〈陶瓷〉blue and white jar with dragon pattern (Yuan Dynasty)
青花龙纹梅瓶	〈陶瓷〉blue and white plum vase with dragon pattern (Yuan Dynasty)
青花龙纹玉壶春瓶	〈陶瓷〉blue and white Yuhuchun vase with dragon pattern (Yuan Dynasty)
青花牡丹纹梅瓶	〈陶瓷〉blue and white plum vase with peony pattern
青花牡丹纹折沿大盘	〈陶瓷〉large blue and white plate with folded edge and peony pattern (Ming Yongle period)
青花枇杷带纹瓷盘	〈陶瓷〉blue and white porcelain plate with loquat and floral pattern
青花葡萄纹花口大盘	〈陶瓷〉large blue and white flower-edged plate with grape pattern (Ming Xuande period)
青花麒麟博古纹胆瓶	〈陶瓷〉blue and white slender-necked vase with ancient Kylin pattern
青花麒麟花卉纹花觚	〈陶瓷〉blue and white floral wine vessel with Kylin pattern (Qing Kangxi period)
青花鹊纹橄榄式瓶	〈陶瓷〉blue and white olive-shaped vase with magpie pattern
青花群仙祝寿大葫芦瓶	〈陶瓷〉large blue and white gourd vase with a pattern of immortals in birthday celebration (Ming Jiajing period)
青花人物罐	〈陶瓷〉blue and white jar with figural depiction pattern (Ming Blank period)
青花人物花草纹扁壶	〈陶瓷〉blue and white flat jug with figural depiction and flowers pattern (Ming Yongle period)

青花人物花卉纹花觚	〈陶瓷〉blue and white floral wine vessel with figural depiction pattern (Qing Kangxi period)
青花人物双层碗	〈陶瓷〉blue and white double-layer bowl with figural depiction pattern
青花人物纹笔筒	〈陶瓷〉blue and white brush pot with figural depiction pattern (Ming Chongzhen period)
青花人物纹无挡尊	〈陶瓷〉blue and white tubular zun with figural depiction pattern (Ming Zhengde period)
青花人物象腿瓶	〈陶瓷〉blue and white elephant-leg shaped vase with figural depiction pattern (Ming Chongzhen period)
青花人物玉壶春瓶	〈陶瓷〉blue and white Yuhuchun vase with figural depiction pattern
青花三友盘	〈陶瓷〉blue and white plate with bamboo, pine tree, and plum blossom pattern (Qing Qianlong period)
青花山水盖罐	〈陶瓷〉blue and white lidded jar with landscape pattern (Qing Qianlong period)
青花山水麒麟纹粥罐	〈陶瓷〉blue and white porridge jar with landscape and Kylin pattern (Qing Kangxi period)
青花山水人物盘	〈陶瓷〉blue and white plate with landscape and figural depiction pattern (Ming Tianqi period)
青花山水人物纹棒槌瓶	〈陶瓷〉blue and white mallet-shaped vase with landscape and figural depiction pattern (Qing Kangxi period)
青花狮绣球墩	〈陶瓷〉blue and white porcelain stool with lion and silk balls pattern (Ming Zhengde period)
青花寿字纹凤尾尊	〈陶瓷〉blue and white phoenix tail zun with 寿-character pattern (Qing Kangxi period)
青花寿字纹观音瓶	〈陶瓷〉blue and white Guanyin vase with 寿-character pattern (Qing Kangxi period)
青花双龙盒	〈陶瓷〉blue and white box with two dragons pattern (Qing Qianlong period)

青花双葡萄耳花鸟纹瓶	〈陶瓷〉blue and white two-grape-eared vase with flowers and birds pattern
青花双鱼莲花池纹碟	〈陶瓷〉blue and white plate with a pattern of two fish swimming in lotus pond
青花四足云鹤纹爵盘	〈陶瓷〉blue and white four-footed plate with clouds and cranes pattern (Qing Qianlong period)
青花松梅竹纹大盘	〈陶瓷〉large blue and white plate with pine-plum-bamboo pattern (Ming Xuande period)
青花松梅竹纹香炉	〈陶瓷〉blue and white incense burner with pine-plum-bamboo pattern (Ming Yongle period)
青花松竹梅纹盖罐	〈陶瓷〉blue and white lidded jug with pine-bamboo-plum pattern
青花饕餮纹花觚	〈陶瓷〉blue and white floral wine vessel with gluttony-monster pattern (Qing Kangxi period)
青花桃竹纹瓶	〈陶瓷〉blue and white vase with peach and bamboo pattern
青花童子拜观音图插屏	〈陶瓷〉blue and white table screen with boy worshipping Guanyin (Ming Chenghua period)
青花团花纹摇铃尊	〈陶瓷〉blue and white bell zun with flower pattern (Qing Kangxi period)
青花文王访贤纹葫芦瓶	〈陶瓷〉blue and white gourd vase with a pattern of King Zhou's visit to virtuous woman (Qing Kangxi period)
青花五彩八仙香筒	〈陶瓷〉blue and white incense holder with eight colorful Immortals (Ming Zhengde period)
青花五彩海马八宝纹罐	〈陶瓷〉blue and white multicolored jar with seahorse and eight-treasure pattern (Qing Kangxi period)
青花五彩荷花纹蒜头瓶	〈陶瓷〉blue and white garlic shaped vase with multicolored lotus pattern (Ming Wanli period)
青花五彩花鸟纹高颈对瓶	〈陶瓷〉paired blue and white multicolored, long-necked vase with flowers and birds pattern
青花五彩菊花湖石图碗	〈陶瓷〉blue and white multicolored bowl with chrysanthemum and lake stone pattern (Ming Wanli period)

青花五彩镂空龙纹五峰笔山	〈陶瓷〉blue and white multicolored brush-rest with hollow-engraved dragon pattern (Ming Wanli period)
青花五彩蟠螭纹绶带葫芦瓶	〈陶瓷〉Blue and white gourd vase with multicolored dragon-like animal and ribbon pattern
青花象耳瓶	〈陶瓷〉blue and white vase with elephant-shaped ears
青花一把莲纹瓷桌	〈陶瓷〉blue and white porcelain table with single lotus pattern (Ming Xuande period)
青花婴戏龙纹盘	〈陶瓷〉blue and white plate with playing-boys and dragon pattern (Ming Wanli period)
青花婴戏图纹盖罐	〈陶瓷〉blue and white lidded jar with playing-boys pattern (Qing Kangxi period)
青花婴戏纹盒	〈陶瓷〉blue and white box with playing-boys pattern (Ming Wanli period)
青花釉里红八仙人物碗	〈陶瓷〉blue and white underglaze red bowl with eight Immortals pattern (Qing Kangxi period)
青花釉里红八仙纹平底盂	〈陶瓷〉blue and white underglaze red flat-bottom jug with eight Immortals pattern (Qing Qianlong period)
青花釉里红盖罐	〈陶瓷〉blue and white underglaze red jar with cover
青花釉里红花蝶纹直颈瓶	〈陶瓷〉blue and white underglaze red vase with straight neck and flowers and butterflies pattern (Qing Qianlong period)
青花釉里红花卉纹碗	〈陶瓷〉blue and white underglaze red bowl with floral pattern (Qing Kangxi period)
青花釉里红龙纹高足杯	〈陶瓷〉blue and white underglaze red stem cup with dragon pattern (Yuan Dynasty)
青花釉里红镂塑盖罐	〈陶瓷〉blue and white underglaze red lidded jar with hollow engraving pattern
青花釉里红松竹梅盖瓶	〈陶瓷〉blue and white underglaze red lidded vase with pine-bamboo-plum pattern
青花鱼藻纹盖盒	〈陶瓷〉blue and white lidded box with fish and algae pattern (Yuan Dynasty)

青花鱼藻纹梅瓶	〈陶瓷〉blue and white plum vase with fish and algae pattern (Yuan Dynasty)
青花鱼藻纹盘	〈陶瓷〉blue and white plate with fish and algae pattern (Yuan Dynasty)
青花鸳鸯莲花纹兽耳盖罐	〈陶瓷〉blue and white animal-eared lidded jar with mandarin duck and lotus pattern (Yuan Dynasty)
青花鸳鸯莲花纹执壶	〈陶瓷〉blue and white jug with mandarin duck and lotus pattern (Yuan Dynasty)
青花云海龙纹大盘	〈陶瓷〉large blue and white plate with cloud sea and dragon pattern (Ming Yongle period)
青花云龙罐	〈陶瓷〉blue and white pot with cloud and dragon pattern
青花云龙纹扁瓶	〈陶瓷〉blue and white flask with cloud and dragon pattern
青花云龙纹大罐	〈陶瓷〉large blue and white jug with cloud and dragon pattern (Ming Xuande period)
青花云龙纹盘	〈陶瓷〉blue and white plate with cloud and dragon pattern (Ming Wanli period)
青花渣斗	〈陶瓷〉blue and white porcelain spittoon (Qing Qianlong period)
青花折枝花卉纹小罐	〈陶瓷〉blue and white jar with branches and floral pattern (Ming Chenghua period)
青椒炒鸡片	〈饮食〉Stir-Fried Chicken Slices with Green Pepper
青椒炒牛肉	〈饮食〉Stir-Fried Beef with Green Pepper
青椒炒肉片	〈饮食〉Stir-Fried Pork Slices with Green Pepper
青椒炒肉丝	〈饮食〉Stir-Fried Shredded Pork with Green Pepper
青椒夹肉	〈饮食〉Steamed Green Pepper Stuffed with Minced Pork
青椒里脊片	〈饮食〉Stir-Fried Pork Fillet with Green Pepper
青椒牛肉蛋炒饭	〈饮食〉Stir-Fried Rice with Eggs, Beef and Green Pepper

青椒鲥鱼	〈饮食〉Braised Shad with Green Pepper
青椒汁炒牛柳	〈饮食〉Stir-Fried Beef Fillets with Green Pepper and Corn Sauce
青稞酒	highland barley wine
青灵	〈中医药〉Qingling acupoint; Cyan Spirit; Green-Blue Spirit (HT2)
青罗裳	green light clothes
青毛皮袄	〈服饰〉slightly thin cyan fur-lined jacket
青木香	〈中医药〉(of Latin) Radix Aristolochiae; Slender Dutchmanspipe Root
青年标兵	model youth; youth pacemaker
青年才俊	young talent; wonder boy
青年突击手	youth shock worker
青年压力管理服务中心	youth stress management service center
青年志愿者协会	youth volunteers association
青年装[服]	young men's jacket →五四青年学生服
青袍	〈古服饰〉cyan gown
青皮	〈中医药〉(of Latin) Pericarpium Citri Reticulatae Viride; Green Tangerine Peel
青铜贝币	〈古〉bronze money cowrie (issued in the Warring States period)
青铜器	bronze ware; bronze artifact →吉金
青铜色陶器	〈陶瓷〉bronzed pottery; gunmetal earthenware
青沱	〈茶〉aged cake Pu'er
青豌豆肉丁	〈饮食〉Stir-Fried Diced Pork with Green Peas
青葙子	〈中医药〉(of Latin) Semen Celosiae; Feather Cockscomb Seed
青叶胆	〈中医药〉(of Latin) Herba Swertiae Mileensis; Mile Swertia Herb
青叶豆腐	〈饮食〉Steamed Tofu with Green Vegetables
青釉瓷谷仓	〈陶瓷〉celadon porcelain model of granary
青釉瓷器	〈陶瓷〉celadon glazed porcelain
青釉瓷鱼篓尊	〈陶瓷〉green-glazed zun in the shape of a bamboo fish basket

青釉釉里红堆塑龙蒜头瓶	〈陶瓷〉green glaze garlic shaped vase with heaped underglaze-red dragon (Ming Jiajing period)
青元烩鲜虾	〈饮食〉Braised Prawns with Peas and Asparagus
青藏铁路	Qinghai-Tibet Railway
轻轨列车	light rail train
轻剂	〈中医药〉light formula
轻身消胖丸	〈中医药〉Qingshen Xiaopang Wan; Slimming Figure and Fat-Reducing Pill
轻症患者	〈防疫〉patient with mild symptoms
轻质瓷	〈陶瓷〉light china; lightweight ceramics
氢氧治疗仪	〈防疫〉oxy-hydrogen breathing machine
倾国倾城	drop-dead gorgeous (one's beauty is such as to overthrow cities and ruin states)
清半夏	〈中医药〉(of Latin) Rhizoma Pinelliae Preparata; Purified Pinellia Tuber
清仓处理	clearance sale
清仓拍卖	rummage sale
清茶	green tea; tea served without refreshment
清炒	〈饮食〉to plain-fry; to simple-fry; plain-fried; simple-fried
清炒鲍贝	〈饮食〉Plain-Fried Abalone and Scallops
清炒贝仁	〈饮食〉Plain-Fried Scallops
清炒菠菜	〈饮食〉Plain-Fried Spinach
清炒大龙虾	〈饮食〉Plain-Fried Lobster with Leek, Wine and White Pepper
清炒豆尖	〈饮食〉Plain-Fried Bean Sprouts
清炒海蛙	〈饮食〉Plain-Fried Rana Cancrivora
清炒荷兰豆	〈饮食〉Plain-Fried Snow Peas
清炒红菜薹	〈饮食〉Plain-Fried Chinese Kale
清炒鸡米	〈饮食〉Plain-Fried Minced Chicken and Water Chestnuts
清炒鸡丝	〈饮食〉Plain-Fried Chicken Shreds
清炒芥蓝	〈饮食〉Plain-Fried Chinese Broccoli
清炒鳝糊	〈饮食〉Stir-Fried Shredded Eel; Sautéed Mashed Eel

清炒时菜	〈饮食〉Stir-Fried/Plain-Fried Seasonal Vegetables
清炒时蔬	〈饮食〉Stir-Fried Seasonal Vegetables
清炒丝瓜	〈饮食〉Plain-Fried Sponge Gourd
清炒西兰花	〈饮食〉Plain-Fried Broccoli
清炒虾仁	〈饮食〉Plain-Fried Shelled Shrimps; Stir-Fried Shelled Prawns
清炒蟹粉	〈饮食〉Plain/Stir-Fried Crab Meat
清纯	〈茶〉clean and pure
清醇	〈茶〉clean and mellow
清淡型香烟	light cigarette
清炖淮山枸杞鸡	〈饮食〉Stewed Chicken with Chinese Yam Wolfberries
清炖甲鱼	〈饮食〉Braised Turtle in Clear Soup
清炖甲鱼汤	〈饮食〉Stewed Turtle in Clear Soup; Stewed Turtle in Broth
清炖鹿肉	〈饮食〉Braised Venison in Clear Soup
清炖牛尾	〈饮食〉Stewed Oxtail in Clear Soup
清炖狮子头	〈饮食〉Stewed/Steamed Minced Pork Balls
清炖水鱼	〈饮食〉Steamed Turtle with Ham in Clear Soup
清炖羊肉	〈饮食〉Stewed Lamb in Clear Soup
清肺润燥	〈中医药〉to clear lung-heat and moisten dryness
清肝明目	〈中医药〉to remove liver-fire for improving eyesight
清肝泻火	〈中医药〉to clear liver-fire; to clear the liver and drain fire
清高	〈茶〉clean and high
清骨散	〈中医药〉Qinggu San; Bone-Clearing Powder
清喉利咽颗粒	〈中医药〉Qinghou Liyan Keli; Throat-Clearing and Pharynx-Disinhibiting Granule
清化暑湿	〈中医药〉to clear summer heat and dissipate dampness
清黄	〈茶〉clear and yellow
清烩海参	〈饮食〉Braised Sea Cucumbers

清烩鸭块	〈饮食〉Plain-Stewed Diced Duck with Ham, Mushrooms and Bamboo Shoots
清火栀麦片	〈中医药〉Qinghuo Zhimai Pian; Fire-Clearing Gardenia Ophiopogon Tablet
清洁服务人员	housekeeping staff
清洁能源	clean energy
清开灵口服液	〈中医药〉Qingkailing Koufuye; Qingkailing Oral Liquid
清开灵注射液	〈中医药〉Qingkailing Zhusheye; Clearing-Opening-Magic Injection
清冷渊	〈中医药〉Qingleng Yuan acupoint; Clear Cold Abyss (TE11)
清里泄热	〈中医药〉to clear heat in the interior; to clear the interior for releasing heat
清利三焦	〈中医药〉to clear heat-dampness of sanjiao
清凉油	〈中医药〉Qingliang You; Cooling Balm; Menthocamphorate
清淋颗粒	〈中医药〉Qinglin Keli; Strangury Clearing Granule
清络饮	〈中医药〉Qingluo Yin; Channels-Clearing Beverage; Decoction for Clearing Away Heat in Lung Collateral
清脑降压片	〈中医药〉Qingnao Jiangya Pian; Brain-Clearing and Hypertension-Reducing Tablet
清内热	〈中医药〉to clear/reduce internal heat
清气分热剂	〈中医药〉formula for clearing heat at the qi level
清气化痰丸	〈中医药〉Qingqi Huatan Wan; Qi-Clearing and Phlegm-Transforming Pill; Bolus for Clearing Heat and Phlegm
清热暗疮片	〈中医药〉Qingre Anchuang Pian; Heat-Clearing Acne Tablet
清热导滞	〈中医药〉to clear heat and remove food stagnation
清热法	〈中医药〉antipyretic method; heat-clearing method

清热攻下	〈中医药〉to clear heat and purgation; to clear heat and offensively precipitate
清热化痰	〈中医药〉to remove/clear heat and dissipate phlegm
清热剂	〈中医药〉heat-clearing formula
清热解毒	〈中医药〉to clear heat and remove toxin/toxicity
清热解毒剂	〈中医药〉heat-clearing and toxin-resolving formula
清热解毒口服液	〈中医药〉Qingre Jiedu Koufuye; Heat-Clearing and Toxin-Resolving Oral Liquid
清热解暑剂	〈中医药〉formula for clearing summer heat and resolving heat evil
清热利湿	〈中医药〉to clear heat and promote diuresis; to clear heat and disinhibit dampness
清热凉血	〈中医药〉to clear heat and cool blood; to remove pathogenic heat from blood
清热凉血药	〈中医药〉heat-clearing blood-cooling medicine
清热排脓	〈中医药〉to clear heat for discharging pus; to eliminate pus by clearing away the heat
清热祛湿剂	〈中医药〉formula for clearing heat and eliminating dampness
清热润燥	〈中医药〉to clear heat and moisten dryness
清热生津	〈中医药〉to clear heat and promote fluid production
清热通淋片	〈中医药〉Qingre Tonglin Pian; Heat-Clearing and Strangury-Opening Tablet
清热息风	〈中医药〉to clear heat for calming endogenous wind
清热消肿	〈中医药〉to clear heat for detumescence; to clear heat to disperse swelling
清热泻肺	〈中医药〉to clear heat and purge lung; to clear away heat from the lung
清热泻火	〈中医药〉to clear heat and reduce pathogenic fire
清润化痰剂	〈中医药〉formula for resolving phlegm with clear-moistening drugs
清散郁热	〈中医药〉to clear and disperse stagnant heat

清式山楂蜜饯	〈饮食〉Qing-Style Candied Hawthorn Berries
清暑益气汤	〈中医药〉Qingshu Yiqi Tang; Decoction for Clearing Summer Heat and Nourishing Qi
清水衙门	work unit which has no outside income; public institution with limited funds and resources; government office free from corruption
清算公司	clearing corporation; liquidation company
清算人员	settlement clerk
清算银行	clearing bank
清汤干贝鲜蘑	〈饮食〉Stewed Dried Scallops and Fresh Mushrooms in Clear Soup
清汤火腿鲍鱼	〈饮食〉Ham and Abalone Clear Soup
清汤柳叶燕菜	〈饮食〉Stewed Swiftlet Nest with Ham and Pegeon Eggs in Clear Soup
清汤牛肉河粉	〈饮食〉Rice Noodle Soup with Beef; Rice Noodles with Beef in Clear Soup
清汤三鲜	〈饮食〉Three Delicacies Soup
清汤四宝	〈饮食〉Four Delicacies Soup
清汤蟹肉	〈饮食〉Chicken Broth with Crab Meat; Crab Meat in Broth
清汤鸭舌羊肚菌	〈饮食〉Duck Tongue and Morel Soup
清汤鸭四宝	〈饮食〉Soup of Four Delicacies of Duck
清汤燕窝	〈饮食〉Braised Bird's Nest in Clear Soup
清汤鱼册	〈饮食〉Wrinkled Fish and Pork Ball Soup
清汤鱼翅	〈饮食〉Shark's Fins in Clear Soup
清汤鱼肚	〈饮食〉Fish Maws in Clear Soup
清汤珍珠鸡	〈饮食〉Chicken Balls in Clear Soup (Shaped as a Pearl)
清汤竹荪丸	〈饮食〉Bamboo Funus Balls in Clear Soup
清甜	〈茶〉clear/brisk and sweet
清胃散	〈中医药〉Qingwei San; Powder for Clearing Stomach-Heat; Stomach-Heat Clearing Powder
清胃泄热	〈中医药〉to clear stomach and purge heat

清瘟败毒散	〈中医药〉Qingwen Baidu San; Antipyretic and Antitoxic Powder; Scourge-Clearing and Toxin-Vanquishing Powder
清溪玉芽	〈茶〉Qingxi Yuya tea; Clear Stream Jade Bud tea
清鲜	〈茶〉aromatic and fresh
清香黄金糕	〈饮食〉Fried Sponge Cake
清香苦苣	〈饮食〉Boiled Endive with Sauce; Common Sowthistle Herb with Sauce
清香型(风格)	〈酒〉delicate fragrance; Fen-flavor liquor
清泄虚热	〈中医药〉to clear deficiency heat; to clear and discharge deficiency-heat
清泻肠热	〈中医药〉to clear intestinal heat; to clear and drain intestinal heat
清泻肝胆	〈中医药〉to purge the liver and gallbladder; to clear and drain liver and gallbladder heat and fire
清心泻火	〈中医药〉to clear heart-fire; to clear heart and drain fire
清心斋肠粉	〈饮食〉Steamed Rice Rolls with Vegetables
清虚热剂	〈中医药〉formula for clearing asthenic fever
清宣润燥	〈中医药〉to disperse lung-qi and moisten dryness
清宣郁热	〈中医药〉to clear stagnated heat; to clear and diffuse depressed heat
清咽丸	〈中医药〉Qingyan Wan; Throat-Clearing Pill
清营凉血剂	〈中医药〉formula for clearing nutrient level and cooling blood
清营汤	〈中医药〉Qingying Tang; Construction-Clearing Decoction
清脏腑热剂	〈中医药〉formula for clearing heat in the viscera
清燥救肺汤	〈中医药〉Qingzao Jiufei Tang; Decoction for Relieving Dryness of the Lung; Dryness-Clearing and Lung-Rescuing Decoction
清燥润肺合剂	〈中医药〉Qingzao Runfei Heji; Dryness-Clearing and Lung-Moistening Mixture
清炸鸡胪	〈饮食〉Fried Chicken Gizzards

清炸猪里脊	〈饮食〉Deep-Fried Pork Fillets/Tenderloin
清真北大寺	Muslim North Temple (Hebei, Shandong)
清真食品	halal food; Muslim food
清蒸八宝甲鱼	〈饮食〉Steamed Soft-Shelled Turtle with Eight Delicacies
清蒸白鳝	〈饮食〉Steamed White Eel
清蒸白鱼	〈饮食〉Steamed White Fish with Cooking Wine and Pepper
清蒸鳊鱼	〈饮食〉Steamed Bream Fish
清蒸草鱼	〈饮食〉Steamed Grass Carp
清蒸大闸蟹	〈饮食〉Steamed Hairy Crab/Chinese Mitten Crab
清蒸冬菇鸡	〈饮食〉Steamed Chicken with Dried Mushrooms in Clear Soup
清蒸多宝鱼	〈饮食〉Steamed Turbot Fish
清蒸桂花鱼	〈饮食〉Steamed Mandarin Fish
清蒸红花蟹	〈饮食〉Steamed Spotted Sea Crab
清蒸滑鸡	〈饮食〉Steamed Chopped Chicken in Clear Soup
清蒸黄河鲤	〈饮食〉Steamed Yellow River Carp
清蒸火腿鸡片	〈饮食〉Steamed Sliced Chicken with Ham in Clear Soup
清蒸甲鱼	〈饮食〉Steamed Turtle
清蒸炉鸭块	〈饮食〉Steamed Barbecued Duck Cubes
清蒸鲈鱼	〈饮食〉Steamed Perch/Weever
清蒸鲈鱼腩	〈饮食〉Steamed Perch-Flank
清蒸全鸡	〈饮食〉Steamed Whole Chicken in Clear Soup
清蒸全鸭	〈饮食〉Steamed Whole Duck with Onion and Ginger
清蒸全鱼	〈饮食〉Steamed Whole Fish
清蒸肉蟹	〈饮食〉Steamed Hard-Shell Crab
清蒸石斑鱼	〈饮食〉Steamed Sea Garoupa
清蒸蒜蓉带子	〈饮食〉Steamed Scallops with Minced Garlic →蒜蓉蒸带子
清蒸童子鸡	〈饮食〉Steamed Spring Chicken in Clear Soup
清蒸武昌鱼	〈饮食〉Steamed Wuchang Fish

清蒸鲜鱼	〈饮食〉Steamed Fresh Fish with Ginger, Chive and Soy Sauce
清蒸羊肉	〈饮食〉Steamed Mutton in Clear Soup
清蒸阳澄湖蟹	〈饮食〉Streamed Yangcheng Lake Crab
清蒸游水石斑	〈饮食〉Steam Live Rock Cod
清蒸糟青鱼	〈饮食〉Steamed Black Carp with Distilled Grains
清蒸猪脑	〈饮食〉Steamed Pig Brains with Ginger and Green Scallion
清正廉明	to be honest and clean
蜻蜓头	〈茶〉dragonfly head (leaves curl up like dragonfly's head)
情报信息分析人员	market intelligence analyst
情感消费	emotional consumption
情歌	love ballads
情侣装	his-and-hers clothes; couple clothes
情商	emotion quotient; EQ
情同手足	to be bound together like brothers and sisters; to be as close as brothers
情有独钟	to show special preference (favor) to sb./sth.
请客送礼	to invite guests and give them gifts; to give feasts and present gifts; to fete guests and distribute gifts
磬折刀	〈币〉curved clasp knife (issued in the Yan State) →方折刀
邛窑绿釉省油灯	〈陶瓷〉green glaze oil saving lamp of Qiong Kiln
秋梨润肺膏	〈中医药〉Qiuli Runfei Gao; Cordyceps Fritillaria Cough-Stopping Gel
秋燥症	〈中医药〉autumn-dryness disease
求实精神	matter-of-fact attitude
求同存异	to seek common ground while putting aside differences; to agree to disagree
求职信	application letter; cover letter
球形乌龙	〈茶〉pelleted Oolong
裘革服装	fur or leather garment

区域公共卫生应急联络机制	〈防疫〉regional emergency liaison mechanism
区域经理	regional manager
区域客户经理	regional account/customer manager
区域销售代表	regional sales representative
区域销售经理	regional sales manager
区域销售总监	regional sales director
曲池	〈中医药〉Quchi acupoint; Pool at the Bend/Crook (LI 11)
曲骨	〈中医药〉Qugu acupoint; Curved Bone (RN2)
曲襟旗袍	cheongsam with curved lapel
曲裾	〈古服饰〉quju; curving-front robe
曲母	〈酒〉ripe starter for inoculation
曲坯	〈酒〉raw starter brick before incubation
曲泉	〈中医药〉Ququan acupoint; Spring at the Bend (LR8)
曲泽	〈中医药〉Quze acupoint; Marsh at the Bend/Crook (PC3)
驱虫法	〈中医药〉worm-expelling method; intestinal parasites expelling method
驱虫攻下	〈中医药〉to expel intestinal parasites by purgation
驱虫剂	〈中医药〉worm-expelling formula; anti-helminthic formula
祛虫消积	〈中医药〉to remove parasites to eliminate accumulation
祛风化痰	〈中医药〉to dispel pathogenic wind and eliminate phlegm
祛风解痉	〈中医药〉to dispel/expel pathogenic wind for resolving convulsion
祛风明目	〈中医药〉to dispel pathogenic wind for improving eyesight
祛风散寒	〈中医药〉to eliminate/expel pathogenic wind for dispersing cold

祛风燥湿	〈中医药〉to dispel pathogenic wind and remove dampness
祛风止痛胶囊	〈中医药〉Qufeng Zhitong Jiaonang; Wind-Expelling the Pain-Stopping Capsule
祛湿法	〈中医药〉dampness eliminating method
祛湿剂	〈中医药〉dampness-dispelling formula; desiccating formula
祛湿宣痹	〈中医药〉to remove dampness and dredge channel blockage
祛暑解表	〈中医药〉to dispel summer heat to relieve superficies/exterior syndrome
祛痰法	〈中医药〉phlegm-dispelling method; phlegm expelling method
祛痰化浊	〈中医药〉to eliminate/expel phlegm and resolve turbidity; to remove the phlegm and turbid urine
祛痰剂	〈中医药〉phlegm-dispelling formula; phlegm-expelling formula
祛痰宣痹	〈中医药〉to eliminate/expel phlegm and dredge channel blockage
祛痰止咳药	〈中医药〉phlegm dispelling and cough suppressing medicine; herbs for eliminating phlegm and stopping cough
祛邪扶正	〈中医药〉to eliminate pathogen and strengthen vital qi
祛瘀散结胶囊	〈中医药〉Quyu Sanjie Jiaonang; Stasis-Dispelling and Bind-Dissipating Capsule
祛瘀生新	〈中医药〉to dispel stasis to promote regeneration; to remove blood stasis for promoting tissue regeneration
祛风湿药	〈中医药〉wind-damp expelling medicine; herbs for expelling wind and dampness
渠道销售经理	sales channel manager
瞿麦	〈中医药〉(of Latin) Herba Dianthi; Lilac Pink Herb
取餐区	〈防疫〉serving area

取缔非法收入	to ban unlawful incomes; to ban illegal earnings
取消大型集会	〈防疫〉to cancel mass gatherings
取信于民	to attain the people's trust; to win the people's confidence
去毒生肌	〈中医药〉detoxication and granulation promotion; to eliminate toxin and engender flesh
去腐生肌	〈中医药〉to eliminate necrotic tissues and promote granulation; to eliminate putridity and engender flesh
去腐生肌散	〈中医药〉Qufu Shengji San; Powder for Eliminating Putridity and Engendering Flesh
去腐消肿	〈中医药〉to eliminate slough and reduce the swelling; to eliminate necrotic tissues and detumescence
圈外人士	people out of the loop; out-group
权术	trickery in politics; political trickery; art of politics
全草	〈中医药〉whole herb
全发酵茶	complete fermentation tea
全国哀悼日	〈防疫〉national day of mourning
全国计算机等级考试	National Computer Rank Examination; NCRE
全国计算机等级证书	National Computer Rank Examination Certificate
全国教科规划办	→全国教育科学规划领导小组办公室
全国教育科学规划	national education sciences planning/program
全国教育科学规划领导小组办公室	National Office for Education Sciences Planning
全国精子库	national sperm bank
全国居民消费价格指数	〈防疫〉consumer price index; CPI
全国数学建模比赛	national mathematical modeling contest
全国学联	→中华全国学生联合会
全国哲学社会科学规划办公室	National Planning Office of Philosophy and Social Science
全国重点文物保护单位	national priority cultural relic protection site; major historical and cultural site protected at the national level

全家福	family picture; family photograph; family portrait
全聚德集团	Quanjude Group
全聚德烤鸭	〈饮食〉Quanjude Roast Duck
全力以赴	all-out efforts; to pull out all the stops
全面禁烟	carpet smoking ban
全面小康社会	a well-off society in an all-round way; a moderately prosperous society in all aspects
全面战略伙伴关系	comprehensive strategic partnership
全民健身计划纲要	outline of the nationwide body-building plan
全民健身运动	extensive mass fitness program; nationwide fitness campaign
全能冠军	all-around winner
全盘否定	totally repudiate; to throw the baby out with the bathwater
全球变暖	global warming
全球定位系统	global positioning system; GPS
全球防范工作监测委员会	〈防疫〉Global Preparedness Monitoring Board; GPMB
全球公共卫生安全	〈防疫〉global public health security
全球公共卫生高级别会议	〈防疫〉high-level meeting on international public health security
全球公共卫生治理	〈防疫〉global public health governance
全球海上安全救助系统	global marine defense safe system; GMDSS
全球卫星导航系统	Global Navigation Satellite System; GNSS
全天候飞机	all-weather aircraft
全天麻胶囊	〈中医药〉Quan Tianma Jiaonang; Tall Gastrodia Capsule
全托	full-time nursery; boarding nursery
全蝎	〈中医药〉(of Latin) Scorpio; dried body of Scorpion
全心全意为人民服务	to serve the people wholeheartedly; to serve the people heart and soul
全兴大曲酒	Quanxing Daqu liquor; Quanxing twice fully-fermented liquor

全脂奶	whole milk; full fat milk
拳参	〈中医药〉(of Latin) Rhizoma Bistortae; Bistort Rhizome
拳头产品	competitive product; knockout product; blockbuster
券商	securities trader
缺斤少两	to give less quantity to consumers; to give short weight
缺襟袍	robe short of right lapel →行袍
缺釉	〈陶瓷〉glaze deficiency
雀啄灸	〈中医药〉pecking sparrow moxibustion; sparrow-pecking moxibustion
确诊病例	〈防疫〉confirmed patient; confirmed case
鹊桥会	match-making party
榷酤	quegu; liquor monopoly system
榷酒	〈古〉quejiu system →榷酤
裙带关系	nepotism; networking through petticoat influence
裙裤	culotte; pantskirt; divided skirt
群防群控	〈防疫〉to strengthen society-wide efforts to prevent and control the epidemic
群聚环境	〈防疫〉congregate setting
群聊	group chat; multi-user chat
群言堂	to allow everybody to air his view; to let all people have their say; to rule by the voice of the many
群众来信	letter from the mass; complaint correspondence from the public

R

然谷	〈中医药〉Rangu acupoint; Blazing Valley; Burning Valley (K12)
扰乱治安	to disturb public order; to disturb the peace; breach of peace
绕襟深衣	long clothes with detour lapel
绕圈子	to take a circuitous route; to beat around the bush
热[脉]痹	〈中医药〉pyretic arthralgia; arthralgia due to heat-toxicity; heat impediment
热炽津伤	〈中医药〉injury of fluid due to exuberant heat
热毒闭肺证	〈中医药〉pattern of heat-toxin blocking lung
热毒攻喉证	〈中医药〉pattern of heat-toxin attacking/invading throat
热毒攻舌证	〈中医药〉pattern of heat-toxin invading tongue
热毒内陷证	〈中医药〉pattern of heat toxin falling inward
热毒伤阴证	〈中医药〉pattern of yin damaged by heat toxicity
热敷疗法	〈中医药〉hot compress therapy; hot pack therapy
热干面	〈饮食〉Hot Dry Noodles; Hot Noodles with Sesame Paste
热极生风	〈中医药〉wind generation due to extreme heat; intense heat engendering wind
热极生寒	〈中医药〉cold generation due to extreme heat; intense heat engendering cold
热结	〈中医药〉heat bind; heat accumulation
热结膀胱	〈中医药〉heat binding in the bladder
热厥	〈中医药〉heat syncope; cold limbs due to excessive heat

热扰心神证	〈中医药〉pattern of heat harassing the heart-mind
热扰胸膈证	〈中医药〉pattern of heat harassing the chest and diaphragm
热入下焦证	〈中医药〉pattern of heat invading lower energizer
热入血室证	〈中医药〉pattern of heat invading blood chamber
热伤肺络证	〈中医药〉pattern of heat damaging the network vessels of the lung
热伤神明	〈中医药〉mental disorder due to heat; mental disorder caused by heat-evil
热胜则肿	〈中医药〉swelling caused by predominant heat; excessive heat bringing about swelling
热盛耗伤津液	〈中医药〉depletion of the body fluid due to excessive heat
热盛伤津证	〈中医药〉pattern of fluid depletion due to intense heat
热痰证	〈中医药〉heat-phlegm pattern; pattern of pyretic cough
热烫伤目	〈中医药〉eye injured by overheat; eye impaired by excessive heat
热线电话	telephone hotline
热邪	〈中医药〉heat evil; heat pathogen; pathogenic heat
热郁	〈中医药〉heat stagnation; heat depression
热者寒之	〈中医药〉to treat heat with cold; to treat heat syndrome with cold natured drugs
热重于湿证	〈中医药〉dampness-heat pattern with predominant heat; pattern of heat predominating over dampness
人才储备	reserve of talents; talent pool
人才交流	talent exchange; intellectual exchange
人才库	talent pool; talent bank; brain bank
人才流动	flow of talent; mobility of talented personnel
人才流失	brain drain; outflow of talent
人才强国战略	strategy of reinvigorating China through human resource development

人才市场	personnel market
人才战	competition for talented people; war for talent
人才中介	talent intermediary
人传人	〈防疫〉person-to-person transmission; human-to-human transmission
人大代表	deputy to the National People's Congress; deputy to the NPC
人丹	〈中医药〉Rendan; Rendan Mini-Pill
人防工程	civil air-defense project
人浮于事	overstaffed; to have more hands than needed
人格障碍	personality disorders
人工降雨	artificial rain; cloud seeding
人工老窖	〈酒〉artificial old fermentation pit
人工智能	artificial intelligence; AI
人海战术	huge-crowd strategy
人机交互	human-computer interaction
人际交往	human communication; interpersonal relationship
人际泡沫	interpersonal bubble
人均可支配收入	per capita disposable income
人均住房	per capita housing; living space per capita
人均资源量	per capita quantity of the resources
人口出生率	birth rate
人口负增长	negative population growth
人口老龄化	aging of population; population aging
人口流动	population flow
人口普查	population census; national census
人口素质	quality of population
人口自然增长	natural growth of the population
人来疯	(of a child) to be more mischievous than usual in the presence of guests; to get hyped before crowd
人类免疫缺陷病毒	〈防疫〉Human Immunodeficiency Virus; HIV
人力车	〈旧〉rickshaw; jinrikisha; two-wheeled vehicle drawn by man

人力资源	human resources; manpower resources
人力资源部	human resources division/department
人力资源部经理	human resources manager
人力资源部总监	director of human resources
人力资源从业资格证书	qualification of human resources practitioner
人力资源管理	human resources management
人力资源系统分析员	human resources information system analyst
人力资源协调员	human resources coordinator
人力资源信息系统专员	human resources information system specialist
人力资源招聘人员	human resources recruiter
人力资源总裁	president of human resources
人力资源总监	human resources director; director of human resources; HRD
人脸识别	facial recognition
人脸识别系统	facial recognition system
人民币	renminbi (RMB); Chinese Yuan (CNY)
人民币升值	appreciation of the RMB (Renminbi)
人民币债券	yuan-denominated bonds; renminbi bonds
人民法庭庭长	chief judge of the people's tribunal
人民调解	mediation by the people; people's mediation
人民调解委员会	people's mediation committee
人情债	debt of gratitude; obligation to sb. for their help
人肉搜索	human flesh search; cyber manhunt (the phenomenon of distributed researching using Internet media such as blogs and forums)
人身意外保险	personal accident insurance
人参	〈中医药〉(of Latin) Radix Ginseng; Ginseng
人参茶	ginseng tea
人参炖鸡	〈饮食〉Stewed Chicken with Ginseng
人参蛤蚧精	〈中医药〉Renshen Gejie Jing; Ginseng Gecko Extractum
人参健脾丸	〈中医药〉Renshen Jianpi Wan; Ginseng Bolus for Tonifying the Spleen
人参酒	ginseng liquor

人参灵芝大补酒	ginseng glossy ganoderma tonic wine
人参乌龙茶	ginseng Oolong tea
人参养荣丸	〈中医药〉Renshen Yangrong Wan; Ginseng Tonic Bolus
人参叶	〈中医药〉(of Latin) Folium Ginseng; Ginseng Leaf
人参再造丸	〈中医药〉Renshen Zaizao Wan; Ginseng Recreating Bolus
人事部	personnel department
人事部经理	personnel manager
人事副理	assistant personnel manager
人事培训经理	personnel and training manager
人事调动	personnel transfer
人事文员	human resources staff
人事主管	human resources supervisor
人事专员	human resources specialist
人事总监	chief human resources officer; human resources director
人寿保险	life insurance
人寿保险精算师	life insurance actuary
人性化服务	people-oriented service
人性化管理	human-based management
人迎	〈中医药〉Renying acupoint; Man's Prognosis (ST9)
人员价值分析员	human resources benefits analyst
人造毛皮服装	artificial fur and leather garment
人中	〈中医药〉Renzhong acupoint; Philtrum; Middle of Upper Lip (GV26) →水沟
《仁斋直指方》	〈中医药〉*Renzhai Zhi Zhi Fang*; *Effective Recipes from Renzhai House* (by Yang Shiying in the Southern Song Dynasty)
忍冬藤	〈中医药〉(of Latin) Caulis Lonicerae; Honeysuckle Stem
认购登记制度	subscription registration system
认证工程师	certification engineer
认证审核员	certification auditor

任脉	〈中医药〉controlling channel; regulating vessel
妊娠恶阻	〈中医药〉malign obstruction in pregnancy; permicious vomiting with pregnancy
妊娠风疹	〈中医药〉gestational rubella; rubella during pregnancy
日常基本生活物资	〈防疫〉daily necessities
日托	day care for kids; day nursery; daytime childcare
日用陶瓷	〈陶瓷〉porcelain for daily use
日语能力考试	Japanese language proficiency test
日照绿茶	Rizhao Green tea
日铸雪芽	〈茶〉Rizhu Snow-Bud Green tea
戎服	〈古〉military uniform
荣誉称号	title of honor
绒大衣	plush topcoat
融资经理	treasury manager
融资主管	treasury supervisor
融资专员	treasury specialist
柔肝息风	〈中医药〉to soften the liver for calming endogenous wind
揉面	〈饮食〉to knead dough; to dough
揉捻法	〈中医药〉massaging and twisting manipulation
肉饼蒸蛋	〈饮食〉Custard with Minced Pork; Steamed Eggs with Minced Pork
肉苁蓉	〈中医药〉(of Latin) Herba Cistanches; Desertliving Cistanche
肉丁	〈饮食〉diced meat; meat dices
肉丁炸酱	〈饮食〉Diced Pork with Bean Paste
肉豆蔻	〈中医药〉(of Latin) Semen Myristicae; Nutmeg
肉羹汤	〈饮食〉Pork Thick Soup
肉桂	〈中医药〉(of Latin) Cortex Cinnamomi; Cassia Bark
肉夹馍	〈饮食〉Rou Jia Mo (finely chopped pork stuffed in toasted wheat flour flat bread); Marinated Meat in Baked Bun

肉酱炒米粉	〈饮食〉Stir-Fried Rice Noodles with Minced Pork Meat
肉酱豆腐	〈饮食〉Braised Tofu with Minced Meat
肉卷	〈饮食〉Grilled Bun with Minced Pork Stuffing
肉末	〈饮食〉minced meat; chopped meat
肉末冬菜包	〈饮食〉Steamed Bun Stuffed with Pork and Preserved Vegetables
肉末鸡蛋	〈饮食〉Omelette with Minced Pork
肉末烧饼	〈饮食〉Sesame Seed Cake Stuffed with Minced Pork
肉末雪菜	〈饮食〉Stir-Fried Preserved Vegetables with Minced Pork
肉末粥	〈饮食〉Porridge with Chopped Pork
肉片	〈饮食〉meat slice; sliced meat
肉片焖海参	〈饮食〉Braised Sea Cucumbers with Pork Slices
肉片汤	〈饮食〉Soup with Meat Slices; Sliced Meat Soup
肉片鱼羹	〈饮食〉Sliced Meat with Fish Paste in Broth
肉丝	〈饮食〉shredded meat; meat shred
肉丝拌面	〈饮食〉Noodles with Shredded Pork
肉丝炒饭	〈饮食〉Stir-Fried Rice with Shredded Pork
肉丝炒面	〈饮食〉Stir-Fried Noodles with Shredded Meat
肉丝黄豆汤	〈饮食〉Soy Bean and Shredded Pork Soup
肉丝烩饭	〈饮食〉Stewed Rice with Shredded Pork
肉丝汤面	〈饮食〉Noodle Soup with Shredded Meat
肉丝炸春卷	〈饮食〉Fried Spring Rolls Stuffed with Shredded Pork
肉松松饼	〈饮食〉Shredded Pork Puff; Minced Pork Pancake
肉碎蒸滑蛋	〈饮食〉Steamed Egg Custard with Minced Pork
肉丸	〈饮食〉meat ball; meatball
肉馅	〈饮食〉meat filling; meat stuffing
肉圆	〈饮食〉→肉丸
肉圆粉丝汤	〈饮食〉Pork Balls Soup with Bean Vermicelli
如意冬笋	〈饮食〉Stir-Fried Bamboo Shoots with Pea Sprouts and Shrimps

如意金黄散	〈中医药〉Ruyi Jinhuang San; Agreeable Golden Yellow Powder
如意襟旗袍	〈服饰〉cheongsam with ruyi pattern lapel
儒巾	〈古〉scholar's headscarve
《儒门事亲》	〈中医药〉*Rumen Shi Qin*; *Confucians' Duties for Parents* (by Zhang Zihe in the Jin Dynasty)
濡养肌肤	〈中医药〉to moisten and nourish the skin
汝窑	〈陶瓷〉Ru Kiln (one of the five famous kilns in the Song Dynasty)
乳白釉	〈陶瓷〉opaline glaze
乳根	〈中医药〉Rugen acupoint; Breast Root (ST18)
乳光釉	〈陶瓷〉opalescence glaze
乳康片	〈中医药〉Rukang Pian; Breast Recovering Tablet
乳癖消胶囊	〈中医药〉Rupixiao Jiaonang; Breast Masses Clearing Capsule
乳癖消片	〈中医药〉Rupixiao Pian; Mammary Aggregation Dispersing Tablet
乳茸莲香鸡	〈饮食〉Steamed Chicken Stuffed with Lotus Seeds and Cream Sauce
乳中	〈中医药〉Ruzhong acupoint; Breast Center (ST17)
乳猪片	〈饮食〉Sliced Suckling Pig
乳猪拼盘	〈饮食〉Roasted Suckling Pig
入党积极分子	applicant for party membership
入党申请书	Party membership application
入境口岸	〈防疫〉port of entry
入境旅游	inbound tourism
入境旅游市场	inbound tourism market
入境人员闭环管理	〈防疫〉to ensure a seamless and hermetic process for managing the quarantine and monitoring of travelers arriving in China
入殓	(of funeral) to lay/put a dead body in a coffin; to encoffin
入药部分	〈中医药〉medicine part of herbs; the part used for medical purpose

入园难	kindergarten crunch; problems concerning access to preschool education
软瓷	〈陶瓷〉soft porcelain
软膏剂	〈中医药〉ointment; unguentum
软坚散结	〈中医药〉to soften hardness and dissipate binds; to soften and resolve hardness; to soften hardness and dissipate stagnation
软件测试工程师	software testing engineer
软件工程师	software engineer
软件架构师	software architect
软件用户界面工程师	software user interface engineer
软件用户界面设计师	software user interface designer
软胶囊剂	〈中医药〉soft capsule; soft gelatin capsule
软熘草鱼	〈饮食〉Soft-Fricassée Grass Carp
软熘肥肠	〈饮食〉Quick-Fried Pork Intestines with Brown Sauce
软性技能	soft skills such as communication and cooperation skills in addition to professional know-how
软炸鸽蛋	〈饮食〉Soft-Fried Pigeon Eggs
软炸里脊肉	〈饮食〉Soft-Fried Pork Fillets/Tenderloin
软炸石斑鱼片	〈饮食〉Soft-Fried Garoupa Slices with Cornstarch and Ketchup
软炸童子鸡	〈饮食〉Soft-Fried Spring Chicken
软炸虾仁	〈饮食〉Soft-Fried Shelled Shrimp with Eggs
软炸鱼片	〈饮食〉Soft-Fried Sliced Fish
软炸猪肝	〈饮食〉Soft-Fried Pigs Liver
蕤仁	〈中医药〉(of Latin) Nux Prinsepiae; Hedge Prinsepia Nut
芮仁	〈中医药〉(of Latin) Semen Prinsepiae; Prinsepia Seed
瑞雪兆丰年	(of idiom) a fall of seasonal snow gives promise of a fruitful year; a timely snow promises a good harvest

《瑞竹堂经验方》	〈中医药〉 Ruizhutang Jingyan Fang; Empirical Recipes from Auspicious Bamboo Hall; Empirical Formulas from the Auspicious Bamboo Hall (by Shatu Musu in the Yuan Dynasty)
闰年	leap year; intercalary year
闰月	leap month; intercalary month (in the lunar calendar)
润肠丸	〈中医药〉 Runchang Wan; Intestine-Moistening Pill
润肺化痰	〈中医药〉to moisten the lung for removing phlegm
润肺止咳	〈中医药〉to moisten the lung to suppress cough; to moisten the lung for arresting cough
润下剂	〈中医药〉lubricant laxative formula; moistened cathartic formula
润燥法	〈中医药〉dryness-moistening method
润燥化痰	〈中医药〉to moisten dryness to resolve phlegm; to moisten dryness for removing phlegm
润燥通便	〈中医药〉to moisten dryness for relaxing bowels
弱电工	weak current worker
弱脉	〈中医药〉weak pulse; feeble pulse
弱势群体	disadvantaged groups

S

撒账钱	〈古〉coin-shaped castings used in wedding ceremonies (usually with blessing words)
塞鼻疗法	〈中医药〉nose-plugging therapy
塞耳疗法	〈中医药〉ear-plugging therapy
三八妇女红旗手	"March 8th Red Banner" outstanding woman pacemaker
三宝酒	three treasures liquor (with ginseng, deer antler and male mink organ)
三杯鸡	〈饮食〉Stewed Chicken with Three Cups Sauce
三鞭补酒	tonic tincture of three male animal organs
三彩骆驼载乐俑	〈陶瓷〉tri-color glazed camel carrying musicians
三彩牛肉丝	〈饮食〉Stir-Fried Shredded Beef with Vegetables
三彩女侍俑	〈陶瓷〉tri-color glazed figurine of a maid
三彩女俑	〈陶瓷〉tri-color glazed female figurine
三彩女坐俑	〈陶瓷〉tri-color glazed sitting lady figurine
三彩三足盖碗	〈陶瓷〉tri-color tripod jar with cover
三彩陶骆驼	〈陶瓷〉tri-color glazed pottery camel
三彩陶马	〈陶瓷〉tri-color glazed pottery horse
三彩啸马	〈陶瓷〉tri-color glazed neighing horse
三彩印花碟	〈陶瓷〉tri-colored plate with printed floral pattern
三彩印花盘	〈陶瓷〉tri-colored tray with printed floral pattern
三成分瓷器	〈陶瓷〉triaxial porcelain
三寸金莲	three-inch "golden lotuses"; woman's bound feet; lotus shoes for bound feet (in the feudal age)
三等功	third-class merits

三丁包子	〈饮食〉Steamed Bun Stuffed with Three Sorts of Diced Meat
三高农业	agriculture of three highs; "three highs" agriculture (high yield, high quality and high efficiency)
三好学生	Three Goods Student (good in morality, study and health); Triple-A Outstanding Student; Merit Student
三黄膏	〈中医药〉Sanhuang Gao; Three Yellow Plaster; Golden Cypress, Golden Thread and Scutellaria Plaster
三黄片	〈中医药〉Sanhuang Pian; Three Yellow Tablet; Rheum Officinale, Berberine Chloride and Scutellaria Tablet
三裥裙	tri-pleated skirt
三焦	〈中医药〉Sanjiao acupoint; Triple Burner; Triple Energizers (CO17)
三焦辨证	〈中医药〉triple burner pattern identification; pattern differentiation of triple energizer
三焦俞	〈中医药〉Sanjiaoshu acupoint; Triple Burner/Energy Transport (BL22)
三角恋爱	love triangle (love between two men and a woman or two women and a man)
三金片	〈中医药〉Sanjin Pian; Three Gold Tablet
三九胃泰胶囊	〈中医药〉Sanjiu Weitai Jiaonang; Three-9 Stomachache Calming Capsule
三棱	〈中医药〉(of Latin) Rhizoma Sparganii; Common Burreed Rhizome; Sparganium Root
三棱针	〈中医药〉three-edged needle
三棱针疗法	〈中医药〉three-edged acupuncture; three-edged needle therapy
三鹿奶粉丑闻	Sanlu milk powder scandal
三年制高中教育	three-year high school education
三炮台香烟	San Paotai cigarettes; Three Castles cigarettes

三七	〈中医药〉(of Latin) Radix Notoginseng; Pseudo-Ginseng; Notoginseng
三七花	〈中医药〉(of Latin) Flos Notoginseng; Notoginseng Flower
三七化痔丸	〈中医药〉Sanqi Huazhi Wan; Notoginseng Hemorrhoid-Desolving Pill
三七片	〈中医药〉Sanqi Pian; Pseudo-ginseng Tablet
三七伤药片	〈中医药〉Sanqi Shangyao Pian; Pseudo-ginseng Tablet for Invigorating Blood Circulation and Dissolving Intumescence
三仁汤	〈中医药〉Sanren Tang; Three Kernels Decoction
三色鲍鱼菇	〈饮食〉Stir-Fried Abalones, Mushrooms and Vegetables
三色中卷	〈饮食〉Squid Rolls Stuffed with Bean, Ham and Egg Yolk
三蛇胆川贝糖浆	〈中医药〉Sanshedan Chuanbei Tangjiang; Three Snake-Gallbladder and Sichuan-Fritillaria Syrup
三蛇龙虎会	〈饮食〉Fricassée Three Kinds of Snakes with Civet and Hen Meat
三丝翅羹	〈饮食〉Braised Ham, Mushroom and Bamboo Shoot in Shark's Fin Soup
三丝春卷	〈饮食〉Spring Rolls Stuffed with Three Delicacies
三丝木耳	〈饮食〉Black Fungi with Cucumber and Vermicelli
三维电影	three-dimensional movie
三维动画片	three-dimensional animation
三文鱼刺身	〈饮食〉Salmon Sashimi; Raw Salmon Fish
三无人员	"sanwu" people (people without identification papers, a normal residence permit and a source of income)
三物备急丸	〈中医药〉Sanwu Beiji Wan; Three Agents Emergency Pill
三峡移民	migrants from Three Gorges area
三鲜包子	〈饮食〉Steamed Bun Stuffed with Three-Delicacy Stuffing

三鲜豆腐	〈饮食〉Stir-Fried Tofu with Three Delicacies
三鲜锅贴	〈饮食〉Pan-Fried Jiaozi Stuffed with Pork, Eggs and Vegetables; Three-Delicacy Guotie
三鲜焦炒面	〈饮食〉Stir-Fried Noodles with Pork, Eggs and Vegetables
三鲜水煎包	〈饮食〉Pan-Fried Baozi Stuffed with Three-Delicacy Stuffing
三鲜水饺	〈饮食〉Jiaozi/Dumplings Stuffed with Three-Delicacy Stuffing
三鲜汤	〈饮食〉Soup with Fish, Shrimps and Pork Balls
三鲜汤面	〈饮食〉Noodle Soup with Shredded Seafood
三鲜小笼包	〈饮食〉Baozi Stuffed with Three-Delicacy Stuffing
三鲜鱼肚	〈饮食〉Stewed Fish Maws with Balls of Shelled Shrimps, Fish and Minced Pork
三鲜蒸饺	〈饮食〉Steamed Jiaozi Stuffed with Three-Delicacy Stuffing
三线城市	third-tier city
三星金六福	〈酒〉Three-Star Jinliufu liquor
三阳络	〈中医药〉Sanyangluo acupoint; Three Yang Collaterals (TE8)
《三因极一病证方论》	〈中医药〉*Sanyin Ji Yi Bingzheng Fang Lun*; *Treatise on Three Categories of Pathogenic Factors* (by Chen Yan in the Song Dynasty)
三阴交	〈中医药〉Sanyinjiao acupoint; Crossroad of Three Yins (SP6)
三子强肾胶囊	〈中医药〉Sanzi Qiangshen Jiaonang; Sanzi Kidney-Strengthening Capsule
三子养亲汤	〈中医药〉Sanzi Yangqin Tang; Three-Seed Filial Devotion Decoction
三字刀	〈币〉knife coin with three-characters →齐法化
散户	private investor; retail investor
散客	individual traveler
散脉	〈中医药〉scattered pulse; dissipated pulse
馓子	〈饮食〉Sanzi; Deep-Fried Dough Twists

散发病例	〈防疫〉sporadic cases
散风活络丸	〈中医药〉Sanfeng Huoluo Wan; Wind-Dissipating and Channels-Invigorating Pill
散寒除湿	〈中医药〉to dispel cold and remove dampness; to dissipate cold and eliminate dampness
散寒化饮	〈中医药〉to dispel cold and resolve fluid retention; to dissipate cold and resolve rheum
散伙饭	farewell dinner; farewell party
桑白皮	〈中医药〉(of Latin) Cortex Mori; White Mulberry Root-bark
桑寄生	〈中医药〉(of Latin) Herba Taxilli; Chinese Taxillus Herb
桑姜感冒片	〈中医药〉Sangjiang Ganmao Pian; Mulberry Ginger Common Cold Tablet
桑姜感冒注射液	〈中医药〉Sangjiang Ganmao Zhusheye; Mulberry-Ginger Common Cold Injection
桑菊饮	〈中医药〉Sangju Yin; Mulberry Leaf and Chrysanthemum Beverage
桑落酒	Sangluo liquor
桑麻	〈中医药〉Sangma
桑拿天	sauna(-like) weather; sauna days
桑椹子	〈中医药〉(of Latin) Fructus Mori; Mulberry Fruit
桑杏汤	〈中医药〉Sangxing Tang; Mulberry Leaf and Apricot Kernel Decoction
桑叶	〈中医药〉(of Latin) Folium Mori; Mulberry Leaf
桑枝	〈中医药〉(of Latin) Ramulus Mori; Mulberry Twig
扫除文盲	to eliminate illiteracy
扫黄打非	to eliminate pornography and illegal publications
扫黄运动	anti-porn campaign
扫码支付	code scanning payment
色釉	〈陶瓷〉colored glaze
色釉瓷	〈陶瓷〉color glazed porcelain
色釉金彩	〈陶瓷〉color glaze with gold
涩肠固脱剂	〈中医药〉formula for astringing the intestine and arresting proptosis

涩肠止泻	〈中医药〉to astringe the intestines and check diarrhea; to relieve diarrhea with astringents
涩精止遗	〈中医药〉to astringe essence to stop seminal emission; to astringe essence for checking (seminal) emission and enuresis
涩精止遗剂	〈中医药〉formula for astringing spermatorrhea
涩脉	〈中医药〉uneven pulse; rough pulse
森林覆盖率	forest coverage; percentage of forest cover
杀虫消疳	〈中医药〉to eliminate parasites for curing malnutrition
杀鸡用牛刀	to break a butterfly on the wheel
杀青	〈茶〉water removing; deactivation of enzymes
杀手锏	sudden thrust of the mace (one's trump or master card)
沙茶炒鸡丝	〈饮食〉Stir-Fried Shredded Chicken with Green Pepper and Satay Paste
沙茶酱烤鸭	〈饮食〉Barbecued/Roast Duck with Satay Paste
沙茶烤排骨	〈饮食〉Baked Pork Chop with Satay Paste
沙茶焖海参	〈饮食〉Braised Sea Cucumbers with Satay Paste
沙茶面	〈饮食〉Shacha Noodles; Noodles with Satay Sauce
沙茶牛肉串	〈饮食〉Beef Brochette with Satay Paste
沙茶牛松饭	〈饮食〉Stir-Fried Rice with Minced Beef and Satay Sauce
沙茶鱼头煲	〈饮食〉Braised Fish Head with Satay Sauce in Casserole
沙尘暴	sandstorm; dust storm
沙葱炒鸡蛋	〈饮食〉Scrambled Eggs with Golden Onion
沙棘	〈中医药〉(of Latin) Fructus Hippophae; Seabuckthorn Fruit
沙姜焗软鸡	〈饮食〉Steamed Chicken with Ginger and Salt
沙漠化	desertification
沙苑子	〈中医药〉(of Latin) Semen Astragali Complanati; Flatstem Milkvetch Seed
砂锅	earthenware pot; casserole

砂锅白菜粉丝	〈饮食〉Stewed Chinese Cabbage and Vermicelli in Pottery Pot
砂锅炒翅	〈饮食〉Stir-Fried Shark's Fins in Casserole
砂锅豉香鳝	〈饮食〉Braised Eel with Black Bean Sauce in Casserole
砂锅豆腐	〈饮食〉Stewed Tofu in Pottery Pot
砂锅肚丝翅	〈饮食〉Braised Shredded Fish Maw and Shark's Fins in Casserole
砂锅富豪焖饭	〈饮食〉Steamed Rice with Diced Abalone and Scallops
砂锅菇丝翅	〈饮食〉Braised Shark's Fins with Shredded Mushrooms in Casserole
砂锅海带炖排骨	〈饮食〉Stewed Spare Ribs with Kelp in Casserole
砂锅海米豆腐	〈饮食〉Stewed Tofu and Dried Shrimps in Pottery Pot
砂锅滑鸡	〈饮食〉Stewed Chicken and Vegetables in Casserole
砂锅鸡	〈饮食〉Stewed Chicken in Casserole
砂锅鸡煲翅	〈饮食〉Braised Shark's Fins with Chicken Soup in Casserole
砂锅鸡肉丸子	〈饮食〉Stewed Chicken Meat Balls in Pottery Pot
砂锅烤鸡	〈饮食〉Roasted/Grilled Chicken in Casserole
砂锅栗子鸡	〈饮食〉Stewed Chicken with Chestnut Kernels in Casserole
砂锅萝卜羊排	〈饮食〉Stewed Lamb Chops and Turnip in Pottery Pot
砂锅牛尾	〈饮食〉Braised Cattle Tail in Terrine
砂锅排骨土豆	〈饮食〉Stewed Spare Ribs with Potatoes in Casserole
砂锅裙边翅	〈饮食〉Braised Shark's Fins and Shredded Turtle Rim in Casserole
砂锅三菇	〈饮食〉Stewed Three Kinds of Mushrooms in Pottery Pot
砂锅三菌	〈饮食〉Braised Assorted Mushrooms in Casserole

砂锅狮子头	〈饮食〉Stewed Meatballs in Earthen-Pot
砂锅丸子	〈饮食〉Boiled Meat Balls in Casserole
砂锅小排翅	〈饮食〉Stewed Small Shark's Fins in Pottery Pot
砂锅油豆腐鸡	〈饮食〉Stewed Chicken with Fried Bean Curd in Casserole
砂锅鱼	〈饮食〉Braised Fish in Casserole
砂锅鱼肚	〈饮食〉Stewed Fish Maws in Pottery Pot
砂锅鱼头	〈饮食〉Braised Fish Head in Casserole
砂锅鱼头豆腐	〈饮食〉Stewed Fish Head with Tofu in Pottery Pot
砂金釉	→金星[砂金]釉
砂仁	〈中医药〉(of Latin) Fructus Amomi Villosi; Villous Amomum Fruit
砂质灰色陶器	〈陶瓷〉sandy grey pottery
砂质黏土壶	〈陶瓷〉sandy clay pot
煞住歪风	to put an end to the unhealthy practice
傻帽	blockhead; simpleton; foolishness; to exude foolishness
山城血旺	〈饮食〉Stir-Fried Eel with Duck Blood Curd
山慈菇	〈中医药〉(of Latin) Pseudobulbus Cremastrae seu Pleiones; Cremastra Appendiculata; Indian Iphigenia Bulb
山东菜	〈饮食〉→鲁菜
山东海参	〈饮食〉Shandong Style Sea Slugs; Shandong Sea Cucumber Soup
山东老酒	Shandong aged liquor
山豆根	〈中医药〉(of Latin) Radix Sophorae Tonkinensis; Bushy Sphora Root
山菌金针肉卷	〈饮食〉Mushroom and Pork Rolls
山麦冬	〈中医药〉(of Latin) Radix Liriopes; Liriope Platyphylla Root
山柰	〈中医药〉(of Latin) Rhizoma Kaempferiae; Resurrection Lily Rhizome
山笋香菇包	〈饮食〉Steamed Bun Stuffed with Bamboo Shoots and Savory Mushrooms

山岩翠绿	〈茶〉Mountain Rock Jade Green tea
山羊绒	〈服饰〉Cashmere wool; goat wool
山药	〈中医药〉(of Latin) Rhizoma Dioscoreae; Common Yam Rhizome
山药炒牛肉片	〈饮食〉Stir-Fried Sliced Beef with Chinese Yam
山药牛肉片	〈饮食〉Stir-Fried Sliced Beef with Yam
山药烧海参	〈饮食〉Braised Sea Cucumbers with Chinese Yam
山野菜	〈饮食〉Edible Wild Vegetables
山楂	〈中医药〉(of Latin) Fructus Crataegi; Hawthorn Fruit
山寨	copycat; cheap copy; knockoff
山珍菌皇汤	〈饮食〉Fungus and Mushroom Soup
山茱萸	〈中医药〉(of Latin) Fructus Corni; Dogwood Fruit
山茱萸酒	dogwood liquor
山竹牛肉球	〈饮食〉Steamed Beef Balls with Bean Curd Sheets
珊瑚笋尖	〈饮食〉Sweet and Sour Bamboo Shoots
珊瑚釉粉彩牡丹纹瓷瓶	〈陶瓷〉coral-glazed vase with pastel peony pattern
闪罐	〈中医药〉quick cupping; successive flash cupping
闪火法	〈中医药〉flash-fire cupping method; fire twinkling method
疝气治疗带	〈中医药〉Shanqi Zhiliao Dai; Hernia Treating Belt
鳝血疗法	〈中医药〉eel-blood therapy
鳝鱼面	〈饮食〉Eel Noodles
《伤寒论》	〈中医药〉*Shanghan Lun*; *Treatise on Cold Damage Diseases*; *Treatise on Cold Pathogenic Diseases* (by Zhang Zhongjing in the Eastern Han Dynasty)
《伤寒明理论》	〈中医药〉*Shanghan Mingli Lun*; *Concise Exposition on Cold Pathogenic Diseases*; *Concise Exposition Exogenous on Febrile Diseases* (by Cheng Wuji in the Jin Dynasty)
伤寒学派	〈医疗〉school of febrile diseases by cold injury
《伤寒杂病论》	〈中医药〉*Shanghan Zabing Lun*; *On Cold Damage and Miscellaneous Diseases*; *Treatise on Cold Pathogenic and Miscellaneous Diseases* (by Zhang Zhongjing in the Eastern Han Dynasty)

伤科跌打丸	〈中医药〉Shangke Dieda Wan; Traumatic Injury Pill
伤湿止痛膏	〈中医药〉Shangshi Zhitong Gao; Dampness Damage Pain-Relieving Plaster
商场部	shopping arcade department
商场部经理	shop manager
商场营业员	shop assistant
商场组长[主管]	retail shop supervisor
商代白陶豆	〈陶瓷〉Shang Dynasty white pottery stem bowl (usually with a cover)
商店经理助理	assistant store manager
商行	〈旧〉commercial house; commercial firm
商会	chamber of commerce
商陆	〈中医药〉(of Latin) Radix Phytolaccae; Pokeberry Root
商品房	commercial residential building
商品房空置	vacancy problem in commercial housing; commercial housing vacancy; unoccupied commercial dwellings
商务出境	outbound tour for commercial affairs
商务旅游	business travel
商务日语能力考试	business Japanese proficiency test
商务英语证书	business English certificate
商务中心	business center
商务主管	business supervisor
商务专员	business specialist
商务总监	chief business officer (CBO)
商业博览会	business expo
商业步行街	commercial pedestrian street; pedestrian mall
商业炒作	commercial speculation
商业道德	business ethics
商业登记证	business registration certificate
商业发票	commercial invoice
商业顾问	business consultant; business advisor

商业养老保险	commercial endowment/pension insurance
商业艺术家	commercial artist
觞	〈古〉shang; drinking vessel; wine cup
赏钱	cumshaw; gratuity; tip
赏月航班	moon-viewing flight
上臂三角肌内注射	〈防疫〉deltoid intramuscular injection in upper arm
上耳根	〈中医药〉Shang'ergen acupoint; Upper Ear Root (R1)
上关	〈中医药〉Shangguan acupoints; Upper Pass (GB3)
上海菜煨面	〈饮食〉Shanghai Noodles with Vegetables
上海大众艺术中心	Shanghai Mass Art Center
上海国际金融中心	Shanghai International Financial Center; SIFC
上海红双喜	Red Double Happiness cigarettes (Shanghai)
上海虹桥国际机场	Shanghai Hongqiao International Airport
上海虹桥火车站	Shanghai Hongqiao Railway Station
上海辣酱面	〈饮食〉Shanghai Noodles with Chili Soy Bean Paste
上海浦东国际机场	Shanghai Pudong International Airport
上海世博会	Shanghai World Expo; World Expo in Shanghai (in 2010)
上海酸辣汤	〈饮食〉Shanghai Hot and Sour Soup
上海特奥会	Shanghai Special Olympics
上寒下热证	〈中医药〉pattern of upper cold and lower heat; upper body cold and lower body heat pattern
上红榜	to be listed on red list (honor roll)
上呼吸道感染	〈防疫〉upper respiratory tract infection; URTI
上火	〈中医药〉to suffer from excessive internal heat; excessive internal heat
上焦	〈中医药〉upper warmer/burner; upper energizer
上焦湿热	〈中医药〉dampness heat in upper energizer; upper burner dampness-heat
上焦湿热证	〈中医药〉upper burner damp-heat pattern; pattern of dampness-heat in upper energizer

上焦穴	〈中医药〉Shangjiao acupoints; Upper Burner/Energizer points
上梁钱	〈古〉coin placed on the beams (by the ancients when building houses)
上门服务	door-to-door service
上门推销员	door-to-door salesman; huckster
上清丸	〈中医药〉Shangqing Wan; Upper-Heat-Removing Bolus; Upper-Body-Clearing Pill
上饶白眉	〈茶〉Shangrao White Mee tea
上热下寒证	〈中医药〉pattern of upper heat and lower cold; upper body heat and lower body cold pattern
上山下乡	(of educated urban youth) to go and work in the countryside or mountain areas
上盛下虚	〈中医药〉upper body exuberance and lower body deficiency; excess heat in upper and deficiency in lower
上盛下虚证	〈中医药〉pattern of excess heat in upper and deficiency in lower body
上素炒鸽脯	〈饮食〉Stir-Fried Pigeon Breast with Vegetables
上汤鸡毛菜	〈饮食〉Braised Green Vegetables in Broth
上汤芥菜胆	〈饮食〉Braised Chinese Mustard Green in Chicken Soup
上汤芥蓝	〈饮食〉Braised Chinese Broccoli in Broth
上汤浸时蔬	〈饮食〉Braised Seasonal Vegetables in Broth
上汤焗龙虾	〈饮食〉Braised Lobster in Chicken Soup
上汤龙虾捞面	〈饮食〉Lobster Lo Mein; Lobster Noodles in Soup
上汤水饺	〈饮食〉Dumpling Soup; Dumplings in Soup
上汤云吞	〈饮食〉Wonton Soup; Wonton in Soup
上下配穴法	〈中医药〉superior-inferior point combination/association
上香	to burn joss-stick; to go to a temple to pray
上新台阶	to reach a new level; to reach a higher stage of development

上虚下实	〈中医药〉upper body deficiency and lower body repletion deficiency in the upper and excess in the lower
上学难,上学贵	difficulty and high cost of receiving an education
上迎香	〈中医药〉Shang Yingxiang acupoint; Upper Fragrance Access; Upper Welcome Fragrance (EX-HN8)
烧饼	〈饮食〉Clay Oven Cake; Sesame Seed Cake
烧二冬	〈饮食〉Braised Winter Mushrooms and Bamboo Shoots
烧凤眼鸡肝	〈饮食〉Barbecued Chicken Livers (Shaped as a Phoenix Eye)
烧海参裙边	〈饮食〉Braised Sea Cucumbers and Turtle Rim
烧椒皮蛋	〈饮食〉Preserved Eggs with Chili
烧酒	Chinese samshu; liquor; spirit
烧烤厨师领班	grillardin
烧烤鲈鱼片	〈饮食〉Char-Grilled Perch Fillet
烧麦[卖]	〈饮食〉Shaomai; Steamed Pork Dumplings with the Top Opened
烧青衣鱼头	〈饮食〉Braised Green Wrasse Head
烧三鲜	〈饮食〉Braised Sliced Abalone, Fish Maw and Chicken
烧蚀疗法	〈中医药〉burning-eroding therapy
烧味厨师	grill chef; BBQ cook
烧虾球海参	〈饮食〉Stewed Sea Cucumbers and Shrimp Balls
烧羊肉	〈饮食〉Stewed Mutton with Brown Sauce
烧汁鳗鱼条	〈饮食〉Stir-Fried Eel in Spicy Sauce
烧汁香煎鸽脯	〈饮食〉Pan-Fried Pigeon Breast with Gravy
芍药	〈中医药〉(of Latin) Paeonia Lactiflora; Chinese Herbaceous Peony
芍药汤	〈中医药〉Shaoyao Tang; Peony Decoction
少先队	→中国少年先锋队
绍圣元宝	〈币〉coin with characters shaosheng yuanbao (issued in the Northern Song Dynasty)

绍兴花雕	〈酒〉Shaoxing Huadiao Medium Sweet
绍兴米酒	Shaoxing rice wine
绍兴善酿酒	Shaoxing shanniang rice wine →双套酒
赊店老酒	Shedian aged liquor
舌象	〈中医药〉tongue manifestation; tongue picture
舌诊	〈中医药〉tongue inspection; tongue diagnosis
蛇床子	〈中医药〉(of Latin) Fructus Cnidii; Common Cnidium Fruit
蛇胆川贝枇杷膏	〈中医药〉Shedan Chuanbei Pipa Gao; Snake Gallbladder, Sichuan Fritillaria and Loquat Paste
蛇胆川贝液	〈中医药〉Shedan Chuanbei Ye; Snake-Gallbladder and Sichuan Fritillaria Liquid
蛇羹	〈饮食〉Snake Soup; Soup with Snake Meat
蛇莓	〈中医药〉(of Latin) Herba Duchesnea Indica; Indian Mock Strawberry
蛇皮绿釉	〈陶瓷〉green snake-skin glaze
蛇皮釉	〈陶瓷〉snake-skin glaze
蛇头	snakehead; human smuggler; people smuggler (people who organize stowaway)
蛇蜕	〈中医药〉(of Latin) Periostracum Serpentis; Snake Slough
蛇油护手霜	〈中医药〉Sheyou Hushou Shuang; Snake Oil Hand-Protecting Cream
舍近求远	to reject what is near at hand and seek what is far away
设备工程师	facility engineer; equipment engineer
设备经理	facility manager
设备维护经理	equipment maintenance manager
设计总监	design director
社会保险机构	social security institution
社会保障基金	social security funds
社会保障支出	expenditure for social security
社会保障制度	social security system
社会福利彩票	social welfare lottery ticket

社会工作先进个人	advanced individual of social work
社会工作者	social worker
社会公德教育	education of social morality
社会公众利益	interests of the general public
社会化服务体系	socialized service system; social service system
社会活动	social/public activities
社会集资	to pool resources in public; to collect money; to raise social funds
社会力量办学	running of schools by non-governmental sectors
社会热点问题	hot spot; social hot issue
社会实践	social practice
社会事业	social undertakings
社会投资	nongovernmental investment
社会效益	social effect; social benefit
社会信用体系	social credit system
社会舆论	public opinion
社会治安情况	public security situation
社会主义初级阶段	primary stage of socialism
社会主义价值观	socialist value outlook
社会主义精神文明建设	socialist ideological and ethical progress
社会主义市场经济	socialist market economy
社会主义先进文化	advanced socialist culture
社会主义政治文明建设	construction of socialist political civilization
社会总产值	total social output value
社会总供给	total social supply
社会总需求	total social demand
社科院	→中国社会科学院
社区传播	〈防疫〉community spread
社区服务	community services
社区感染	〈防疫〉community infection; community-acquired infection
社区疫情防控	〈防疫〉community-based epidemic prevention and control
社团艺术节	community festival

射干	〈中医药〉(of Latin) Rhizoma Belamcandae; Belamcanda Root
射干汤	〈中医药〉Shegan Tang; Blackberry Lily Rhizome Decoction
射频工程师	radio frequency engineer
涉外经济	foreign-related business
摄法	〈中医药〉pressing-kneading around the inserted needle
麝香	〈中医药〉(of Latin) Moschus; Chinese Musk
麝香保心丸	〈中医药〉Shexiang Baoxin Wan; Musk Heart-Protecting Pills
麝香祛痛气雾剂	〈中医药〉Shexiang Qutong Qiwuji; Moschus Analgesic Aerosol
麝香痔疮栓	〈中医药〉Shexiang Zhichuang Shuan; Musk Hemorrhoid Suppository
麝香壮骨膏	〈中医药〉Shexiang Zhuanggu Gao; Musk Plaster for Rheumatoid
麝香追风膏	〈中医药〉Shexiang Zhuifeng Gao; Moschus Rheumatalgia-Relieving Plaster; Musk Wind-Expelling Plaster
申脉	〈中医药〉Shenmai acupoint; Extending Vessel (BL62)
申通快递	STO Express
伸筋草	〈中医药〉(of Latin) Herba Lycopodii; Common Clubmoss Herb
伸筋活络丸	〈中医药〉Shenjin Huoluo Wan; Muscles-Stretching and Network Vessels-Quickening Pill
身份证	ID card; identification card
身外之物	worldly possessions
身柱	〈中医药〉Shenzhu acupoint; Body Pillar (GV12)
参附汤	〈中医药〉Shenfu Tang; Decoction of Ginseng and Prepared Aconite
参苓白术散	〈中医药〉Shenling Baizhu San; Ginseng, Poria and Atractylodes Macrocephalae Powder

参麦注射液	〈中医药〉Shenmai Zhusheye; Ginseng-Ophiopogon Injection
参芪降糖宁胶囊	〈中医药〉Shenqi Jiangtangning Jiaonang; Ginseng Astragalus Blood-Sugar Lowering Capsule
参杞补酒	lycium-ginseng tonic wine
参杞炖老鸭	〈饮食〉Stewed Duck with Ginseng and Chinese Wolfberries
参茸固本片	〈中医药〉Shenrong Guben Pian; Red Ginseng and Velvet Deerhorn Root-Securing Tablet
参茸药酒	ginseng antler medical/medicated liquor
参苏饮	〈中医药〉Shensu Yin; Ginseng and Perilla Beverage
绅带	〈古〉scholar-official's silk belt; scholar-bureaucrat's belt with decoration
深度游	in-depth travel
深海载人潜水器	manned deep-sea submersible
深衣	〈古〉ancient Chinese long robe; one piece garment (a combination of upper and low garments)
神灯照疗法	〈中医药〉lamp lighting up therapy
神经外科医师	neurosurgeon
神经系统	〈防疫〉nervous system
神门	〈中医药〉Shenmen acupoint; Spirit Gate (HT7)
《神农本草经》	〈中医药〉*Shennong Bencao Jing*; *Shen Nong's Herbal Classic*; *Shennong's Classic of Materia Medica* (the earliest existing Chinese medicine work written before the Western Han Dynasty)
《神农本草经集注》	〈中医药〉*Shennong Bencao Jing Jizhu*; *Variorum of Shennong's Classic of Materia Medica*; *Variorum of the Divine Husbandman's Herbal Foundation Canon* (by Tao Hongjing in Liang of the Northern and Southern Dynasties)
神农绿茶	Shennong Green tea
神曲	〈中医药〉(of Latin) Massa Medicata Fermentata; Medicated Leaven

神阙	〈中医药〉Shenque acupoint; Spirit Sinus (RN8)
神舟五号载人飞船	manned spacecraft Shenzhou V
审计部	audit department
审计经理	audit manager
审计师	auditor; senior auditor
审计员	staff auditor; auditing clerk
审计长	auditor general
审计主管	audit supervisor
《审视瑶函》	〈中医药〉*Shenshi Yao Han*; *Compendium of Ophthalmology*; *Precious Book of Ophthalmology* (by Fu Renyu in the Ming Dynasty)
肾宝糖浆	〈中医药〉Shenbao Tangjiang; Kidney-Protecting Syrup
肾不纳气	〈中医药〉failure of the kidney in holding qi; kidney dysfunction in qi holding
肾及膀胱辨证	〈中医药〉kidney and bladder pattern identification
肾精不足	〈中医药〉insufficiency of kidney essence
肾精亏虚证	〈中医药〉pattern of kidney essence deficiency
肾开窍于耳	〈中医药〉kidney opening at the ears
肾气[下元]不固	〈中医药〉non-consolidation of kidney qi; insecurity of kidney qi
肾气不固证	〈中医药〉pattern of kidney-qi unconsolidation
肾气丸	〈中医药〉Shenqi Wan; Kidney-Qi Tonifying Pill; Bolus for Tonifying the Kidney-Qi
肾气虚	〈中医药〉deficiency of kidney qi; kidney qi deficiency
肾气虚证	〈中医药〉pattern of kidney-qi deficiency; kidney-qi vacuity pattern
肾俞	〈中医药〉Shenshu acupoint; Kidney Transport (BL23)
肾为先天之本	〈中医药〉kidney being congenital origin
肾虚寒湿证	〈中医药〉pattern of cold-dampness due to kidney deficiency; pattern of kidney vacuity and cold-damp

肾虚水泛	〈中医药〉asthenia renal edema; edema due to kidney deficiency; water diffusion due to kidney deficiency
肾虚髓亏证	〈中医药〉pattern of marrow depletion due to kidney deficiency; pattern of kidney vacuity and marrow depletion
肾炎舒胶囊	〈中医药〉Shenyanshu Jiaonang; Nephritis Recovery Tablet
肾炎四味片	〈中医药〉Shenyan Siwei Pian; Four Ingredients Nephritis Tablet
肾阳式微	〈中医药〉declination of kidney yang
肾阳虚	〈中医药〉deficiency of kidney-yang; kidney-yang deficiency
肾阳虚水泛证	〈中医药〉pattern of water diffusion due to kidney-yang deficiency
肾阳虚证	〈中医药〉pattern of kidney-yang deficiency; kidney-yang vacuity pattern
肾阴不足	〈中医药〉insufficiency of kidney-yin
肾阴虚	〈中医药〉deficiency of kidney-yin; kidney-yin deficiency
肾阴虚火旺证	〈中医药〉pattern of fire hyperactivity due to kidney-yin deficiency
肾阴虚证	〈中医药〉pattern of kidney-yin deficiency; kidney yin vacuity pattern
肾阴阳两虚证	〈中医药〉pattern of both kidney yin and yang deficiency
肾之府	〈中医药〉house of the kidney; residence of the kidney
肾主纳气	〈中医药〉kidney governing inspiration; kidney controlling respiratory qi
肾主水液	〈中医药〉kidney governing water (metabolism)
渗湿化痰	〈中医药〉to eliminate dampness and resolve phlegm; to percolate dampness and eliminate phlegm

渗湿利水	〈中医药〉to eliminate dampness and diuresis; to percolate dampness and disinhibit water
升级换代	(of products) updating and upgrading
升麻	〈中医药〉(of Latin) Rhizoma Cimicifugae; Cimicifuga Root
升麻葛根汤	〈中医药〉Shengma Gegen Tang; Cimicifuge and Pueraria Decoction
升学率	enrolment rate; admission rate
生煸枸杞	〈饮食〉Stir-Fried Chinese Wolfberries
生煸毛豆	〈饮食〉Stir-Fried Fresh Green Soy Beans
生煸四季豆	〈饮食〉Stir-Fried String Beans
生煸苋菜	〈饮食〉Stir-Fried Amaranth with Garlic
生菜牛肉炒饭	〈饮食〉Stir-Fried Rice with Beef and Lettuce
生产部部长助理	assistant of production director
生产部经理	production manager
生产大队	〈旧〉production brigade
生产督导	production superintendent
生产计划协调员	production planning coordinator
生产领班	production team leader
生产线主管	production line supervisor
生产总监	production director
生炒芙蓉蟹	〈饮食〉Stir-Fried Crab in Shell and Egg Whites
生炒海蚌	〈饮食〉Stir-Fried Sea Clam
生炒鸡丝	〈饮食〉Stir-Fried Shredded Chicken with Bamboo Shoots
生炒鸡翼球	〈饮食〉Stir-Fried Chicken Wing Balls
生炒鳗片	〈饮食〉Stir-Fried Eel Slices
生炒乳鸽松	〈饮食〉Stir-Fried Minced Pigeon with Lettuce
生炒水鸭片	〈饮食〉Stir-Fried Wild Duck Slices with Green Pepper
生炒田鸡	〈饮食〉Stir-Fried Frog Legs with Ginger Sprouts
生辰八字	date of birth and the eight characters of a horoscope
生氽牛肉片	〈饮食〉Poached Beef Fillets; Sliced Beef in Casserole

生地黄	〈中医药〉(of Latin) Radix Rehmaniae Recens; Unprocessed Rehmannia Root
生滚海鲜粥	〈饮食〉Seafood Congee; Poached Seafood Congee
生化汤	〈中医药〉Shenghua Tang; Blood-Nourishing and Stasis-Dissolving Decoction
生活必需品	〈防疫〉necessities of life; daily necessities
生活补助	living subsidies
生活津贴	living allowance; subsistence allowance
生肌定痛	〈中医药〉to promote granulation and relieve pain
生肌收口	〈中医药〉to promote tissue regeneration and close wound; to promote granulation and wound healing
生肌玉红膏	〈中医药〉Shengji Yuhong Gao; Flesh-Engendering Jade and Red Plaster
生计问题	bread-and-butter issue; livelihood
生煎包	〈饮食〉Pan-Fried Baozi Stuffed with Pork
生煎番茄饼	〈饮食〉Pan-Fried Cake Stuffed with Tomato
生煎锅贴	〈饮食〉Pan-Fried Guotie Stuffed with Pork
生煎金华腿	〈饮食〉Pan-Fried Jinhua Ham with Shrimps
生煎里脊肉	〈饮食〉Pan-Fried Pork Fillets/Tenderloin
生煎柳肉	〈饮食〉Pan-Fried Pork Fillets with Sea Kale (Shaped as a Coin)
生煎馒头	〈饮食〉Pan-Fried Mantou; Pan-Fried Steamed Bun
生煎牛柳	〈饮食〉Pan-Fried Beef Fillets
生姜	〈中医药〉(of Latin) Rhizoma Zingiberis Recens; Fresh Ginger
生津安神	〈中医药〉to promote the production of body fluid and tranquilize the mind
生焗海参煲	〈饮食〉Braised Sea Cucumbers in Casserole
生脉散	〈中医药〉Shengmai San; Pulse-Engendering Powder
生脉饮	〈中医药〉Shengmai Yin; Pulse-Activating Decoction
生脉注射液	〈中医药〉Shengmai Zhusheye; Pulse-Activating Injection

生焖大虾	〈饮食〉Braised Prawns with Tomato Sauce
生焖鸽子青椒	〈饮食〉Braised Pigeon with Green Peppers
生焖明虾	〈饮食〉Braised Prawns in Shell
生命银行	life bank (for keeping the donated organs and remains of dead persons for medical use) →脐带血库
生命重于泰山	〈防疫〉saving lives is of paramount importance
生坯	〈陶瓷〉green body; green ware
生啤酒	draught beer
生漆	raw lacquer; Chinese lacquer
生巧烧海参	〈饮食〉Stewed Sea Slugs with Finless Eel
生晒参	〈中医药〉(of Latin) Radix Ginseng; Dried Fresh Ginseng
生丝	tsatlee; raw silk
生态环境部应急办	〈防疫〉Emergency Management Office of the Ministry of Ecology and Environment
生态活动	eco-activity
生态建筑	ecological construction
生态林	ecological forest
生态旅游	ecotourism; eco-travel
生态农业	ecological agriculture; environmental-friendly agriculture
生态系统	ecological system; ecosystem
生态效益	ecological benefit
生余牛肉片	〈饮食〉Poached Beef Fillets; Sliced Beef in Soup
生物识别	biological recognition
生物识别数据	biometric data
生鲜食品加工员	raw food processor
生肖动物	zodiac animal; zodiac sign
生腌百合南瓜	〈饮食〉Marinated Lily Bulbs and Pumpkin
生意兴隆	to wish a brisk business; to wish one's business success
生源地助学贷款	student-origin-based loan; locally-granted student loan
生蒸龙虾	〈饮食〉Steamed Lobster with Mustard Sauce

省试	〈古〉metropolitan examination
《圣济经》	〈中医药〉*Sheng Ji Jing*; *Classic of Holy Benevolence*; *Sages' Salvation Canon* (by Zhao Ji in the Song Dynasty)
《圣济总录》	〈中医药〉*Shengji Zonglu*; *General Records of Holy Universal Relief*; *General Medical Collection of Royal Benevolence* (by Zhao Ji in the Song Dynasty)
失透釉	〈陶瓷〉devitrification glaze
失笑散	〈中医药〉Shixiao San; Blood-Nourishing and Stasis-Dissolving Powder
师德	teachers' code of morality; teachers' professional ethics
师德标兵	virtue pacesetter; teachers' ethics pacesetter
师范生免费教育	student majoring in education exempted from paying tuition; free education for students in teacher education program
师兄弟	(senior and junior) fellow apprentice; fellow apprentice of one and the same master
诗歌创作比赛	poetry creation contest
狮口银芽	〈茶〉Shikou Silver Bud tea
狮子头面	〈饮食〉Noodles with Pork Balls
施工工程师	construction engineer; operating engineer
施釉陶器	〈陶瓷〉slipware
湿毒蕴结证	〈中医药〉pattern of accumulated dampness-toxin
湿敷疗法	〈中医药〉moisten compress therapy; hydropathic compress therapy
湿货市场	〈防疫〉wet market
湿热犯耳证	〈中医药〉pattern of dampness-heat invading the ears
湿热浸淫证	〈中医药〉pattern of excessive dampness-heat; damp-heat spreading pattern
湿热弥漫三焦证	〈中医药〉pattern of dampness-heat spreading in the triple energizer

湿热下注证	〈中医药〉pattern of dampness-heat pouring downward
湿热泄泻	〈中医药〉diarrhea due to damp-heat
湿热壅滞证	〈中医药〉pattern of stagnant and jamming dampness-heat
湿热瘀阻证	〈中医药〉pattern of damp-heat stasis obstruction
湿热蕴结证	〈中医药〉pattern of accumulated dampness-heat
湿热蕴脾	〈中医药〉dampness-heat stagnating in the spleen
湿热蕴脾证	〈中医药〉pattern of dampness-heat brewing in the spleen
湿热蒸舌证	〈中医药〉pattern of dampness-heat steaming the tongue
湿热阻络证	〈中医药〉pattern of dampness-heat obstructing the collaterals/the network vessels
湿痰证	〈中医药〉pattern of dampness-phlegm; damp-phlegm pattern
湿邪犯肺	〈中医药〉invasion of the lung by pathogenic dampness
湿邪困脾	〈中医药〉impediment of the spleen by pathogenic dampness
湿壅鼻窍证	〈中医药〉pattern of dampness invading the nose; pattern of dryness damaging the nasal orifice
湿重于热证	〈中医药〉dampness-heat pattern with predominant dampness; pattern of dampness predominating over heat
湿阻证	〈中医药〉dampness retention pattern; damp obstruction pattern
十八反	〈中医药〉eighteen clashes; antagonism in the eighteen medicinal herbs; eighteen incompatible medicaments
十八街麻花	〈饮食〉Eighteenth Street Deep-Fried Dough Twists
十菜炒牛肉	〈饮食〉Stir-Fried Beef with Bean Sprouts (a tenth course plus Chinese chives (jiu cai) which sounds like nine courses)

十滴水	〈中医药〉Shidishui Tincture; Rheo-camphoradin; Drop Bubble (a popular medicine for summer ailments)
十二刺	〈中医药〉twelve techniques of needling
十二段锦	〈武术〉twelve-sectioned exercises; twelve-routine exercises
十二经别	〈中医药〉twelve divergent channels/meridians; branches of twelve regular channels
十二经筋	〈中医药〉musculature of twelve meridians; tendons of twelve channels
十二经脉[正经]	〈中医药〉twelve (regular) channels/meridians
十二生肖	12 zodiac animals (corresponding to the 12 Terrestrial Branches); Chinese zodiac signs; Chinese zodiacs
十佳社团	top ten outstanding associations
十佳新秀奖	top ten outstanding rising stars award
十九畏	〈中医药〉nineteen incompatibilities; nineteen medicaments of mutual antagonism
十全大补丸	〈中医药〉Shiquan Dabu Wan; Perfect Major Supplementation Pill; Bolus of Ten Powerful Tonics
十三科	〈中医药〉thirteen branches of medicine; thirteen departments of medicine in the Yuan and Ming Dynasties
十四经	〈中医药〉fourteen channels; fourteen meridians
《十四经发挥》	〈中医药〉*Shisijing Fahui*; *Elucidation of the Fourteen Channels*; *Elaboration of the Fourteen Meridians* (by Hua Shou in the Yuan Dynasty)
十香返生丸	〈中医药〉Shixiang Fansheng Wan; Ten Fragrances Life-Reviving Pill
十香醉烤鸡	〈饮食〉Roasted Chicken with Ten Spices
十宣	〈中医药〉Shixuan acupoint; Ten Finger-Tips; Ten Diffusing points (EX-UE11)
十字花绣[挑花]	→挑花[织]
十字髻	(of hairstyle) cross bun

十字绣	cross-stitch (embroidery); cross embroidery
什菜鸡	〈饮食〉Stir-Fried Chicken with Mixed Vegetables
什果杏仁豆腐	〈饮食〉Tofu with Chilled Almond and Fresh Fruits
什烩干贝	〈饮食〉Stewed Dried Scallops with Assorted Vegetables
什烩肉	〈饮食〉Roast Pork with Mixed Vegetables
什烩虾	〈饮食〉Braised Shrimps with Mixed Vegetables
什锦扒牛肉	〈饮食〉Stewed Beef with Mixed Vegetables
什锦炒饭	〈饮食〉Stir-Fried Rice with Meat and Vegetables
什锦炒面	〈饮食〉Stir-Fried Noodles with Meat and Vegetables
什锦炒蔬	〈饮食〉Stir-Fried Mixed Vegetables
什锦冬瓜粒泡饭	〈饮食〉Rice with White Gourd and Assorted Meat in Soup
什锦瓜丁汤	〈饮食〉Assorted Meat Soup with Diced White Gourd
什锦肉炒饭	〈饮食〉Stir-Fried Rice with Mixed Meat
什锦水果松饼	〈饮食〉Assorted Fruit Muffin
什锦汤面	〈饮食〉Noodle Soup with Meat and Vegetables
什锦甜食	〈饮食〉Traditional Assorted Sweets
什锦小吃	〈饮食〉Assorted Cold Foods
什菌炒红烧肉	〈饮食〉Stir-Fried Red-Cooked Pork with Assorted Mushrooms
什菌炒双脆	〈饮食〉Stir-Fried Chicken Gizzard and Pork Tripe with Assorted Mushrooms
什笙上素	〈饮食〉Bamboo Vegetables
石菖蒲	〈中医药〉(of Latin) Rhizoma Acori Tatarinowii; Grassleaf Sweetflag Rhizome
石耳豆腐汤	〈饮食〉Stone Fungi and Bean Curd Soup
石关	〈中医药〉Shiguan acupoint; Stone Pass (KI18)
石斛	〈中医药〉(of Latin) Herba Dendrobii; Dendrobium Stem
石斛明目丸	〈中医药〉Shihu Mingmu Wan; Dendrobium Eye Brightener Pill

石斛夜光丸	〈中医药〉Shihu Yeguang Wan; Dendrobium Night Light Pill
石灰釉	〈陶瓷〉lime glaze →钙釉
石甲	〈古〉stone armor
石决明	〈中医药〉(of Latin) Concha Haliotidis; Abalone Shell
石淋通冲剂	〈中医药〉Shilintong Chongji; Stone and Strangury Opening Soluble Preparation
石榴皮	〈中医药〉(of Latin) Pericarpium Granati; Pomegranate Rind
石磨	stone mill
石楠藤	〈中医药〉Caulis Photinia serrulata; Photinia Stem
石烹肥牛	〈饮食〉Grilled Beef with Chili on a Stone Plate
石屏烧豆腐	〈饮食〉Braised Shiping Tofu/Bean Curd
石狮香烟	Shishi cigarettes; Stone Lion cigarettes
石韦	〈中医药〉(of Latin) Folium Pyrrosiae; Shearer's Pyrrosia Leaf
石油工程师	petroleum engineer
石油天然气技术人员	petroleum and natural gas technician
石鱼炒蛋	〈饮食〉Quick-Fried Lushan Fish with Eggs
时菜斑球	〈饮食〉Stir-Fried Rock Cod with Seasonal Vegetables
时菜炒鸽脯	〈饮食〉Stir-Fried Sliced Pigeon Breast with Seasonal Vegetables
时菜炒鱼片	〈饮食〉Stir-Fried Sliced Fish with Seasonal Vegetables
时菜鹌蛋	〈饮食〉Stir-Fried Quail Eggs with Seasonal Vegetables
时菜炖蟹肉	〈饮食〉Stewed Crab Meat with Seasonal Vegetables
时菜鸡	〈饮食〉Stir-Fried Chicken with Seasonal Vegetables
时菜排骨	〈饮食〉Stir-Fried Spareribs with Seasonal Vegetables

时菜鲜鱿	〈饮食〉Stir-Fried Squid with Seasonal Vegetables
时蔬炒鸡片	〈饮食〉Stir-Fried Sliced Chicken with Seasonal Vegetables
时蔬炒牛肉	〈饮食〉Stir-Fried Beef with Seasonal Vegetables
时装调配师	fashion coordinator
识别和追踪	〈防疫〉to identify and track
实地调查	field survey; field investigation
实干家	doer; man of action (a person who is earnest and down-to-earth in his work)
实寒证	〈中医药〉excessive cold pattern; substantive cold pattern
实脉	〈中医药〉replete pulse; forceful pulse
实名举报	real-name reporting; real-name complaint
实名认证	real-name authentication
实名制	real-name system
实名制注册	real-name registration
实脾散	〈中医药〉Shipi San; Powder for Reinforcing the Spleen
实热证	〈中医药〉excessive heat pattern; substantive heat pattern
实时到账	real-time account settlement
实时发布	〈防疫〉real-time update
实习护士	intern nurse
实习生[期]	internship
实习医师	intern doctor
实行动态调整	〈防疫〉to make dynamic adjustments
实行封闭式管控	〈防疫〉to exercise management by sealing off entities
实验技师	lab technician
实验室负责人	lab administrator
实验室工程师	lab engineer
实验员	laboratory technician
实者[则]泻之	〈中医药〉to treat excess syndrome by purgation therapy/with purgative method

食窦	〈中医药〉Shidou acupoint; Food Cavity; Food Hole (SP17)
食粉	baking soda
食疗	〈中医药〉dietary therapy; food therapy
《食疗本草》	〈中医药〉*Shiliao Bencao*; *Dietetic Materia Medica*; *Materia Medica for Dietotherapy* (by Meng Shen in the Tang Dynasty, supplemented by Zhang Ding)
食疗技师	dietary technician
食品安全	food safety
食品保管员	storeroom keeper of food and beverage
食品服务经理	food service manager
食品检查员	food inspector
《食医心鉴》	〈中医药〉*Shiyi Xin Jian*; *Heart Mirror of Dietotherapy*; *Heart Mirror of Diet Therapy* (by Zan Yin in the Tang Dynasty)
食滞胃肠证	〈中医药〉pattern of food stagnating in the stomach
炻瓷	〈陶瓷〉stoneware
史国公药酒	〈中医药〉Shiguogong Yaojiu; Shiguogong Medicinal Wine
使君子	〈中医药〉(of Latin) Fructus Quisqualis; Rangooncreeper Fruit
使用存量资金	〈防疫〉to tap into unallocated funds
使用消毒剂	〈防疫〉to use disinfection
士大夫	〈古〉scholar-bureaucrat; scholar-official; literati and officialdom (in feudal China)
世博餐饮中心	Expo dining center
世博会纪念品	Expo-themed souvenir
世博急救中心	Expo first-aid center
世界卫生组织	〈防疫〉World Health Organization; WHO
世界无烟日	World No-Tobacco Day
世界针灸学会联合会	World Federation of Acupuncture-Moxibustion Societies
世卫组织驻华代表处	〈防疫〉WHO China Representative Office

《世医得效方》	〈中医药〉Shiyi Dexiao Fang; Effective Formulae Handed down for Generations; Effective Formula from a Family Tradition (by Wei Yilin in the Yuan Dynasty)
市场部部长	marketing department director
市场部部长助理	director assistant of marketing department
市场调查分析员	market research analyst
市场调研部经理	marketing research manager; marketing representative manager
市场调研人员	market research officer
市场分析员	market analyst
市场开发部经理	marketing development manager
市场企划经理	marketing planning manager
市场企划主管	marketing planning supervisor
市场企划专员	marketing planning specialist
市场通路经理	trade marketing manager
市场通路主管	trade marketing supervisor
市场通路专员	trade marketing specialist
市场行政总监	executive marketing director
市场营销部	sales and marketing division
市场营销职业证书	certificate in marketing
市场营销总监	director of sales and marketing; marketing and sales director
市场[营销]总监	marketing director; chief marketing officer; CMO
事件处理员	event-handling clerk
事业编制人员	staffing of government affiliated institution
试剂	〈防疫〉reagent
试剂盒	〈防疫〉testing kit
视频开发工程师	video development engineer
柿蒂	〈中医药〉(of Latin) Calyx Kaki; Persimmon Calyx
适时下调响应级别	〈防疫〉to downgrade the emergency response level in due course
适应公众获取信息渠道的变化	〈防疫〉to meet people's evolving ways of acquiring information

室内公共场所全面禁烟	complete ban on indoor public smoking
室内空气流通	〈防疫〉indoor ventilation
室内设计师	interior designer
室内外装潢设计	design for decorating the indoor and outdoor
室内外装潢设计师	interior/indoor and outdoor decoration designer
室内维修工	indoor maintenance worker
收发督导员	shipping expediter; receiving expediter
收益管理经理	revenue manager
收银主管	cashier supervisor
收治率	〈防疫〉patient admission rate
手工水饺	〈饮食〉Hand-Made Jiaozi; Hand-Made Boiled Dumplings
手机支付交易	mobile payment transaction
手扒羊排	〈饮食〉Grilled Lamb Chops
手扒[抓]羊肉	〈饮食〉Hand-Grabbed Mutton; Mutton Eaten with Hands
手三里	〈中医药〉Shousanli acupoint; Arm Three Li (LI10)
手三阳经	〈中医药〉three yang channels/meridians of the hand
手三阴经	〈中医药〉three yin channels/meridians of the hand
手撕龙虾	〈饮食〉Hand-Shredded Boiled Lobster with Worcestershire Sauce
手五里	〈中医药〉Shouwuli acupoint; Arm Five Li (LI13)
手掌参	〈中医药〉(of Latin) Rhizoma Gymnadeniae; Gymnadenia Tuber
手抓琵琶骨	〈饮食〉Hand-Held Braised Spare Ribs
手足厥冷	〈中医药〉cold hands and feet; reversal cold of the extremities
手足口病	〈防疫〉hand-foot-mouth disease; HFMD
手足心汗	〈中医药〉sweating from the palms and soles
手足心热	〈中医药〉feverishness in the palms and soles; heat in the centers of the palms and soles
首日封	(of stamp issuance) first-day cover

首饰盒	casket; jewelry box; jewel case
首乌藤	〈中医药〉(of Latin) Caulis Polygoni Multiflori; Tuber Fleeceflower Stem
首乌丸	〈中医药〉Shouwu Wan; Flowery Knotweed Fill
首席安全官	chief security officer; CSO
首席财务官	chief financial officer; CFO
首席代表	chief representative
首席技术官	chief technology officer; CTO
首席检察官助理	assistant attorney general
首席谈判官	chief negotiation officer; CNO
首席信息官	chief information officer; CIO
首席营运官	chief operating office; COO
首席战略官	chief strategy officer; CSO
首席政府关系官	chief government officer; CGO
首席知识官	chief knowledge officer; CKO
首席执行官	chief executive officer; CEO
寿眉茶	Shou Mee White tea
寿面	→长寿面
《寿世保元》	〈中医药〉*Shoushi Baoyuan*; *Longevity and Life Preservation*; *Prolonging Life and Preserving the Origin* (by Gong Tingxian in the Ming Dynasty)
寿桃馒头	〈饮食〉Peach-Shaped Mantou
售后服务专员	after-sales service specialist
售卖经理	vending manager
兽医技术员	veterinary technician
兽医师	veterinarian
绶带	Ribbon (attached to an official seal or a medal)
瘦身顾问	slimming counselor; weight loss counselor
枢府瓷	〈陶瓷〉Shufu porcelain
枢府窑印花龙纹白瓷碗	〈陶瓷〉Shufu Kiln white porcelain bowl with printed dragon pattern
枢府釉镂塑花卉纹高足杯	〈陶瓷〉egg-white glazed stem cup with hollow engraved floral pattern (Yuan Dynasty)
枢府釉镂塑人物花卉纹高足杯	〈陶瓷〉egg-white glazed stem cup with hollow engraving figures and flower pattern (Yuan Dynasty)

枢府釉双兽耳双环瓶	〈陶瓷〉egg-white glazed vase with two animal ears and rings (Yuan Dynasty)
淑女班	fair maiden class
舒城兰花	〈茶〉Shucheng Orchid-Flavor tea
舒[疏]肝和胃	〈中医药〉to soothe the liver to harmonize the stomach; to disperse stagnated liver-qi for regulating the stomach
舒肝和胃丸	〈中医药〉Shugan Hewei Wan; Liver-Soothing and Stomach-Pacifying Pill
舒筋活络	〈中医药〉to relax sinews and activate collaterals; to relieve rigidity of muscles and activate collaterals; to relax tendons and activate collaterals
舒眠胶囊	〈中医药〉Shumian Jiaonang; Sleeping Pleasure Capsule
舒张进针法	〈中医药〉skin-spreading needle insertion; to insert the needle by stretching the skin with finger
疏风透疹	〈中医药〉to dispel wind for promoting eruption
疏风泄热	〈中医药〉to disperse wind and discharge heat; to dispel wind and reduce heat
疏肝解郁	〈中医药〉to disperse stagnated liver-qi for relieving qi stagnation
疏肝利胆	〈中医药〉to disperse stagnated liver-qi for promoting bile flow; to course the liver to disinhibit the gallbladder
疏散风邪	〈中医药〉to dispel wind pathogens; to course and dissipate wind evil
疏散外风剂	〈中医药〉formula for dispersing external wind
输入(性)病例	〈防疫〉imported case
输穴	〈中医药〉Shu-Stream acupoints; Transport points
蔬菜炒饭	〈饮食〉Stir-Fried Rice with Vegetables
蔬菜炒鸡球	〈饮食〉Stir-Fried Chicken Balls with Vegetables
蔬菜炒面	〈饮食〉Stir-Fried Noodles with Vegetables
蔬菜炒肉丝	〈饮食〉Stir-Fried Shredded Pork with Vegetables
蔬菜厨师领班	entremetier

蔬菜春卷	〈饮食〉Spring Rolls Stuffed with Vegetables
蔬菜干豆汤	〈饮食〉Hearty Lentil Soup; Vegetable and Dried Bean Soup
蔬菜海鲜汤	〈饮食〉Seafood and Vegetable Soup
蔬菜鸡什汤	〈饮食〉Chicken Giblets Soup with Vegetables
蔬菜面	〈饮食〉Noodles with Vegetables
蔬菜上汤鸡	〈饮食〉Steamed Chicken with Vegetables in Clear Soup
熟地黄	〈中医药〉(of Latin) Radix Rehmanniae Preparata; Prepared Rehmannia Root
熟火乌龙	〈茶〉roasted Oolong; roast Oolong
熟闷味	〈茶〉stewed taste
熟狍子皮	〈服饰〉dressed roe deer skin; roe deer leather
熟普洱	〈茶〉fermented Pu'er
熟食加工员	cooked food assistant
暑伤肺络证	〈中医药〉pattern of summer heat damaging the lung collaterals
暑伤津气证	〈中医药〉pattern of summer heat damaging fluid and qi
暑湿袭表证	〈中医药〉pattern of summer heat-dampness attacking the exterior
暑邪	〈中医药〉summer-heat pathogen; pathogenic summer-heat
蜀锦	Sichuan brocade; Sichuan figured satin
薯仔煲冬菇汤	〈饮食〉Potato and Savory Mushroom Soup
术士冠	〈古〉warlock's hat; ancient astronomer's hat
树花炖土鸡	〈饮食〉Stewed Home Chicken with Tree Flowers
俞府	〈中医药〉Shufu acupoint; Transport House (KI27)
俞募配穴法	〈中医药〉combination of transport and alarm points; combination of front and back transport points
腧穴	〈中医药〉→输穴
数据库分析师	database analyst
数据库工程师	database engineer

数据库管理员	database administrator
数据录入员	data-entry clerk
数据通信工程师	data communication engineer
数控工程师	computerized numerical control engineer; CNC engineer
数字化健康证明	〈防疫〉digital health certificate
数字医疗服务	〈防疫〉digital medical service
刷脸支付	face scanning payment
摔跤服	〈蒙古族〉wrestling costume
涮羊肉	〈饮食〉Instant-Boiled Sliced Mutton; Sliced Mutton Rinsed in Hot Pot
双刀髻	(of hairstyle) double-knife-shaped bun
双冬炒鸭肉	〈饮食〉Stir-Fried Duck Meat with Snow Peas and Mushrooms
双冬辣鸡球	〈饮食〉Stir-Fried Chicken Balls with Mushrooms and Bamboo Shoots
双冬牛肉	〈饮食〉Beef with Mushrooms and Bamboo Shoots
双冬烧茄子	〈饮食〉Braised Eggplants with Winter Mushrooms and Bamboo Shoots
双肺浸润性病灶	〈防疫〉infiltration in both lungs
双沟大曲	〈酒〉Shuanggou Daqu liquor
双菇鲜带子	〈饮食〉Stir-Fried Fresh Scallops with Mushrooms
双挂髻	(of hairstyle) double hanging circlet bun
双环髻	(of hairstyle) double-looped bun; dual looped chignon
双黄连口服液	〈中医药〉Shuanghuanglian Koufuye; Lonicera, Scutellaria and Forsythia Mixture
双黄连注射液	〈中医药〉Shuanghuanglian Zhushe Ye; Double Coptis Injection
双髻	(of hairstyle) double bun; dual chignon
双襟	〈服饰〉double lapel clothes; double-front lapel costume
双梁鞋	double ridge-line shoes

双龙柄白瓷盘口壶	〈陶瓷〉white porcelain pot with plate-mouth and twin dragon handle
双龙银针	〈茶〉Shuanglong Silver Needle tea
双轮酒	double fermented liquor
双罗纹针织物	interlock fabric
双螺髻	(of hairstyle) double-bunch bun; dual-spiraled chignon
双面针织物	double knit fabric
双片锅巴	〈饮食〉Stir-Fried Sliced Pork and Liver with Fried Rice Crust
双平髻	(of hairstyle) double flat bun
双嵌线袋	double welt pocket
双色鸡粥	〈饮食〉Bicolored Chicken Broth; Chicken and Pork Porridge
双手进针法	〈中医药〉double-handed needle insertion; needle-inserting with both hands
双绶	〈服饰〉double ribbon
双梳栉经编针织物	two-bar fabric
双套酒	shuangtao yellow rice wine →绍兴善酿酒
双丸汤面	〈饮食〉Noodle Soup with Fish and Shrimp Balls
双味鸡球	〈饮食〉Stir-Fried Chicken Balls with Two Tastes
双味软炸鲜贝	〈饮食〉Soft-Fried Scallops in Two Tastes
双虾海参煲	〈饮食〉Braised Sea Cucumbers and Shrimps in Casserole
双仙采灵芝	〈饮食〉Stir-Fried Mushrooms with Broccoli
双鲜扒鸡腿菇	〈饮食〉Braised Mushrooms and Vegetables
双向收费	two-way charges
双象耳观音瓶	〈陶瓷〉Guanyin vase with two elephant ears (Ming Hongwu period)
双效筋骨通	〈中医药〉Shuangxiao Jingu Tong; Double Effective for Removing Pains
双斜襟旗袍	〈服饰〉cheongsam with bi-oblique lapels
双丫髻	(of hairstyle) two-side bun for maidservant

"双一流"大学建设	"Double First-Class" Initiative/Project; construction of first-class universities and first-class disciplines
双蒸酒	double distilled liquor
爽口西芹	〈饮食〉Crispy Celery; Scalded Celery
水车	(of agriculture) Chinese waterwheel; water mill (driven by flowing water for irrigation and grinding)
水道	〈中医药〉Shuidao acupoint; Waterways; Water Passage (ST28)
水电工程师	hydroelectric engineer
水分	〈中医药〉Shuifen acupoint; Water Diffluence; Water Distributary (CV9)
水沟	〈中医药〉Shuigou acupoint; Water Drain (GV26) →人中
水果酥	〈饮食〉Fresh Fruit Puff Pastry; Fresh Fruit Pudding
水果味香烟	fruit-flavored cigarette
水红花子	〈中医药〉(of Latin) Fructus Polygoni Orientalis; Pirnce-Feather Fruit
水火不济	〈中医药〉water-fire imbalance; discordance between water and fire
水火相克	〈中医药〉contradiction between water and fire; mutual restriction between water and fire
水货	smuggled goods; unauthorized commodities
水激馍	〈饮食〉Swashed Steamed Bun
水煎	〈中医药〉to decoct with water
水饺	〈饮食〉Boiled Jiaozi; Boiled Dumplings
水晶鹅肝	〈饮食〉Goose Liver Aspic
水晶桂鱼	〈饮食〉Boiled Mandarin Fish with Crystal Sauce
水晶饺	〈饮食〉Pyramid Dumplings; Crystal-Stuffed Dumplings
水晶萝卜	〈饮食〉Sliced Turnip with Sauce
水晶蹄膀	〈饮食〉Cold Pork Knuckles in Jelly

水晶鸭舌	〈饮食〉Duck Tongue Aspic
水晶鱼冻	〈饮食〉Fish Aspic; Crystal Fish Jelly
水晶肘	〈饮食〉Stewed Pig Hocks in Sauce
水井坊酒	Shuijingfang liquor
水酒	watery wine (said by the host to refer to the wine for treating guests)
水利工程师	water conservancy engineer
水疗技师	spa technician
水疗游泳接待	spa and pool receptionist
水蜜丸	〈中医药〉water-honeyed pill
水牛角	〈中医药〉(of Latin) Cornu Bubali; Buffalo Horn
水气凌心证	〈中医药〉pattern of pathogenic water attacking the heart; pattern of pathogenic water intimidating the heart
水泉	〈中医药〉Shuiquan acupoint; Water Spring (KI5)
水生木	〈中医药〉water generating/engendering wood
水湿内停证	〈中医药〉pattern of internal fluid-dampness stagnation
水田衣	paddy-field costume; split-joint dress; patchwork outer vestment (popular in the Ming and Qing Dynasties, especially for Buddhist monk) →百衲衣
水突	〈中医药〉Shuitu acupoint; Water Prominence (ST10)
水土不服	〈中医药〉to be not acclimatized; failure to acclimatize to a new environment
水洗领班	laundry captain
水烟袋	hookah; water (tobacco) pipe
水针疗法	〈中医药〉hydro-acupuncture therapy; fluid injection therapy
水蛭	〈中医药〉(of Latin) Hirudo seu Whitmania; Leech
水煮草鱼	〈饮食〉Boiled Grass Carp in Hot Chili Oil
水煮鹿里脊	〈饮食〉Boiled Venison Tenderloin in Hot Chili Oil
水煮萝卜丝	〈饮食〉Poached Shredded Turnip
水煮牛肉	〈饮食〉Poached Sliced Beef with Hot Chili Oil

水煮鲜鱿	〈饮食〉Fresh Squid in Hot Chili Oil
水煮鱼	〈饮食〉Sliced Fish in Hot Chili Oil
税务会计	tax accountant
税务检查员	tax inspector
税务员	tax collector
税务主管	tax supervisor
税务专员	tax executive; tax commissioner
税制改革	tax/taxation system reform
睡眠卡	inactive bank card
睡衣裤	pyjamas; sleepwear
顺丰速运	SF Express
顺价销售	to sell sth. at profitable price; to sell sth. at a profit
硕博连读	successive postgraduate and doctoral programs of study
司仪	emcee; master of ceremonies; event host
丝绸	silk; silk fabric; silk cloth
丝绸服装	silk garment; silk dress
丝绸之路	Silk Road; Silk Route
丝绸之路城市	Silk Road city
丝绸之路经济带	Silk Road Economic Belt
丝绸之路精神	Silk Road spirit
丝绸之路论坛	Silk Road forum
丝绸之路探险	(of a game) A Silk Road Adventure (Yusuf Turk, 2015)
丝绸之路项目	Silk Road project
丝绸之路研究	Silk Road research
丝瓜络	〈中医药〉(of Latin) Retinervus Luffae Fructus; Luffa Vegetable Sponge
丝路	→丝绸之路
丝路方舟	Silk Road Ark
丝路基金	Silk Road Fund
丝绵袄	padded silk jacket; silk refuse wadded jacket
丝－棉混纺布料	silk and cotton blended fabric
丝苗白饭	〈饮食〉Steamed Rice

丝绒大衣	plush coat
丝绒裤	plush trousers
丝绒衣	plush shirt
私立教育	→民办[私立]教育
私募股权基金	private equity fund
私人秘书	private secretary
私人企业家精神	private entrepreneurship
私塾	〈旧〉sishu; old-style private school; home school with a private tutor
思虑伤脾	〈中医药〉worry impairing the spleen; excessive contemplation hurting the spleen
思想道德教育	ideological and moral education
思想道德体系	ideological and moral system
思想教育运动	ideological education movement
思想品行	ideological morality
思想政治工作	ideological and political work
思想政治建设	ideological and political development
思则气结	〈中医药〉pensiveness leading to qi stagnation; anxiety making qi depressed
死亡病例数	〈防疫〉number of deaths
死亡率	〈防疫〉mortality rate
死要面子	to be dead determined to save face; to try to preserve one's fall at all costs
四宝豆腐羹	〈饮食〉Steamed Tofu Soup
四宝菌烧素鸡	〈饮食〉Braised Deep-Fried Tofu with Mushrooms
四宝烤麸	〈饮食〉Marinated Steamed Gluten with Peanuts and Black Fungi
四川菜	〈饮食〉→川菜
四川炒鸡球	〈饮食〉Sichuan Stir-Fried Chicken Balls
四川炒虾球	〈饮食〉Sichuan Stir-Fried Shrimp Balls
四川炒鲜鱿	〈饮食〉Sichuan Stir-Fried Fresh Squid
四川辣子鸡	〈饮食〉Sichuan Stir-Fried Diced Chicken with Chili and Pepper
四川凉面	〈饮食〉Sichuan Cold Noodles

四川泡菜	〈饮食〉Sichuan Pickles; Szechwan-Style Pickled Vegetables
四川藏茶	Sichuan Tibetan tea
四川藏洋	〈币〉(of the late Qing Dynasty) Sichuan silver dollar (the earliest portrait coin in China)
四大菜系	〈饮食〉four major Chinese cuisines (Sichuan Cuisine, Shandong Cuisine, Huaiyang Cuisine and Cantonese Cuisine)
四大古典小说	four classical Chinese novels (including Romance of the Three Kingdoms, Dream of the Red Chamber, Journey to the West and Water Margin)
四方平定巾	〈服饰〉square flat soft hat; scarf hat with four corners (popular in the early Ming Dynasty)
四合院	quadrangle dwelling (a courtyard with houses on all sides)
四君子汤	〈中医药〉Sijunzi Tang; Decoction of Four-Noble Drugs; Ginseng, Atractylodes, Poria and Licorice Decoction
四棱小花帽	〈维吾尔族〉four-tile like hat with floral pattern → 尕巴
四连冠	four straight/consecutive championships; four championships on the run
四满	〈中医药〉Siman acupoint; Fourfold Fullness (KI14) →髓府, 髓中
四妙勇安汤	〈中医药〉Simiao Yong'an Tang; Four Wonderous Herb-Decoction for Fast Pain-Relieving
四磨汤口服液	〈中医药〉Simotang Koufuye; Four-Milled-Ingredient Decoction Oral Liquid
四逆散	〈中医药〉Sini San; Counterflow Cold Powder; Powder for Regulating the Liver and Spleen
四逆汤	〈中医药〉Sini Tang; Counterflow Cold Decoction; Decoction for Treating Yang Exhaustion
四人帮	〈旧〉Gang of Four (during the period of Cultural Revolution)

四神丸	〈中医药〉Sishen Wan; Four Spirits Pill; Pill of Four Ingredients with Magical Effect
四世同堂	four generations under one roof
四喜丸子	〈饮食〉Four-Joy Meatballs; Braised Pork Balls in Gravy Sauce
四喜鸭茸饺	〈饮食〉Duck Meat Jiaozi/Dumplings with Four-Delicacy Stuffing
四鲜丸子	〈饮食〉Steamed Pork Quenelles with Garnish; Four-Delicacy Balls
四诊	〈中医药〉four diagnostic methods; four methods of diagnosis (observation, auscultation and olfaction, interrogation, and pulse feeling and palpation)
四诊合参	〈中医药〉correlation of all four examinations; comprehensive analysis of data gained by four diagnostic methods
四铢半两	〈币〉four zhu half tael issued in the Han Dynasty)
松菇银鳕鱼	〈饮食〉Braised Codfish with Mushrooms
松花蛋	〈饮食〉Preserved Duck Eggs →皮蛋
松节	〈中医药〉Oleum Terebinthinae; Knotty Pine Wood
松卷绿茶	curled green tea
松罗茶	Sunglo tea
松仁小肚	〈饮食〉Braised Pork Tripe with Pine Kernels
松仁玉米	〈饮食〉Stir-Fried Sweetcorn with Pine Kernels
松茸烩鱼翅	〈饮食〉Braised Shark's Fins with Matsutake
松茸扒鹅肝	〈饮食〉Pan-Fried Goose Liver with Matsutake
松茸裙边	〈饮食〉Braised Turtle Rim with Mushrooms
松鼠桂[鳜]鱼	〈饮食〉Squirrel-Shaped Mandarin Fish with Sweet and Sour Sauce
松鼠黄鱼	〈饮食〉Squirrel-Shaped Deep-Fried Yellow Croaker with Sweet and Sour Sauce
松田青豆	〈饮食〉Boiled Songtian Green Beans
松烟香	〈茶〉pine smoky flavor
松阳银猴	〈茶〉Songyang Silver Monkey tea

松子叉烧酥	〈饮食〉Barbecued Pork Pastry with Pine Kernels
松子桂[鳜]鱼	〈饮食〉Fried Mandarin Fish with Pine Kernels
松子黄鱼	〈饮食〉Fried Yellow-Fin Tuna with Pine Kernels; Fried Yellow Croaker with Pine Kernels
松子金黄鸭	〈饮食〉Braised Duck with Pine Kernels (Golden Color)
松子肉	〈饮食〉Braised Pork Breast Stuffed with Pine Kernels
松子[仁]香菇	〈饮食〉Braised Dry Mushrooms with Pine Kernels
宋河粮液	〈酒〉Songhe grain liquor
宋锦	Song brocade
送货上门	home/doorstep delivery service; delivery at customers' doorsteps
苏菜	〈饮食〉Su Cuisine; Jiangsu Cuisine
苏合香丸	〈中医药〉Suhexiang Wan; Storax Pill; Resina Liquidambaris Orientalis Bolus
苏绣	→苏州刺绣
苏烟香烟	Suyan cigarettes
苏州刺绣	Suzhou embroidery
苏子降气汤	〈中医药〉Suzi Jiangqi Tang; Perilla Fruit Qi-Downbearing Decoction
酥饼	〈饮食〉Crisp Savarin with Sesame; Flaky Pastry
酥海带	〈饮食〉Crispy Kelp; Crispy Seaweed
酥鲫鱼	〈饮食〉Crispy Crucian Carp with Kelp, Carrots and Water Chestnuts
酥皮蛋黄莲蓉包	〈饮食〉Crisp Yolk and Lotus Seeds Mousse Coulibiac
酥皮牛柳	〈饮食〉Crispy Beef Fillets; Crispy Beef Tenderloin
酥香鹌鹑	〈饮食〉Crispy-Braised Quail with Sesame
酥油饼	〈饮食〉Crispy Pancake; Crisp Fried Cake
酥油糌粑	〈饮食〉Ghee Zanba (one of the staple traditional foods of Tibetan farmers)
酥炸	〈饮食〉to crispy-fry; crispy-fried
酥炸春花肉	〈饮食〉Crispy-Fried Pork Croquettes

酥炸大虾	〈饮食〉Deep-Fried Prawns
酥炸蛤卷	〈饮食〉Deep-Fried Crispy Mussel Rolls
酥炸鸡胸	〈饮食〉Deep-Fried Crispy Chicken Breast
酥炸山菌	〈饮食〉Quick-Fried Wild Mushrooms
酥炸生蚝	〈饮食〉Crispy-Fried Oysters
酥炸鲜鱿	〈饮食〉Crispy-Fried Squids; Deep-Fried Squid
酥炸羊腩	〈饮食〉Crispy-Fried Lamb Brisket
酥炸鱼条	〈饮食〉Crispy-Fried Sliced Garoupa
素包子	〈饮食〉Baozi with Vegetable Stuffing; Steamed Bun Stuffed with Vegetables
素饼	〈饮食〉Vegetable Patties; Vegetarian Cakes
素彩瓷	〈陶瓷〉plain porcelain
素菜豆腐	〈饮食〉Stir-Fried Tofu with Mixed Vegetables
素菜馆	〈饮食〉vegetarian restaurant
素菜汤	〈饮食〉Vegetable Soup; Vegetable Rice Soup
素菜汤面	〈饮食〉Noodle Soup with Vegetables
素炒面	〈饮食〉Stir-Fried Noodles with Vegetables
素炒年糕	〈饮食〉Stir-Fried Rice Cake with Vegetables
素春卷	〈饮食〉Vegetarian Spring Rolls; Fried Veggie Egg Rolls
素瓷	〈陶瓷〉unglazed porcelain; biscuit porcelain
素咕噜肉	〈饮食〉Vegetarian Gulurou; Sweet and Sour Diced Carrots and Bamboo Shoots
素烩四味	〈饮食〉Stewed Four Kinds of Vegetables
素胚[坯]	〈陶瓷〉biscuit; low bisque
素扒酿竹荪	〈饮食〉Braised Bamboo Fungi Stuffed Vegetables
素三彩缠枝莲纹狮钮冲天耳三足香炉	〈陶瓷〉plain-tricolored tripod incense burner with twisted branches, lotus pattern and upward lion-ear (Qing Kangxi period)
素三彩刀马人物纹凤尾尊	〈陶瓷〉plain-tricolored phoenix tail zun with knight and horse pattern (Qing Kangxi period)
素三彩观音像	〈陶瓷〉plain-tricolored Guanyin statue (Ming Dynasty)
素三彩花鸟纹盖罐	〈陶瓷〉plain-tricolored lidded jar with flowers and birds pattern (Qing Kangxi period)

素烧	〈陶瓷〉biscuit firing; biscuiting
素烧窑	〈陶瓷〉biscuit firing kiln
素什锦	〈饮食〉Stir-Fried Assorted/Mixed Vegetables
《素问》	〈中医药〉(of *Yellow Emperor Internal Classic*) *Suwen*; *Plain Questions*; *Elementary Questions* (written in the Warring States period, revised by Wang Bing in the Tang Dynasty)
素香粉丝	〈饮食〉Fried Vermicelli with Hot Bean Sauce
素鸭	〈饮食〉Vegetarian Duck; Marinated Bean Curd Skin Rolls
素煮干丝	〈饮食〉Stewed Shredded Dried Bean Curd Slices
速递服务	express delivery service
速记打字员	shorthand typist
速溶茶	instant tea
速效救心丸	〈中医药〉Suxiao Jiuxin Wan; Quick-Acting Pill for Heart Resurrection; Speedy Heart-Rescuing Pill
宿舍管理员	dormitory keeper
宿舍长	head of the dormitory
粟米瑶柱羹	〈饮食〉Corn Soup with Dry Scallops
粟米鱼羹	〈饮食〉Sweetcorn and Fish Soup; Garoupa and Millet Soup
酸菜	〈饮食〉Pickled Chinese Cabbage
酸菜肚丝汤	〈饮食〉Pickled Cabbage and Shredded Pork Tripe Soup
酸菜粉丝	〈饮食〉Stir-Fried Pickled Cabbage and Vermicelli
酸菜龙抄手	〈饮食〉Wonton Soup with Preserved Vegetable
酸菜鱼	〈饮食〉Boiled Fish with Pickled Cabbage and Chili
酸黄瓜	〈饮食〉Pickled Cucumber
酸辣炒姬菇	〈饮食〉Stir-Fried Mushrooms with Hot and Sour Sauce
酸辣炒木耳	〈饮食〉Stir-Fried Black Fungi with Hot and Sour Sauce
酸辣粉	〈饮食〉Potato Vermicelli/Noodles in Hot and Sour Soup

酸辣瓜条	〈饮食〉Cucumber Strips with Hot and Sour Sauce
酸辣海参乌鱼蛋汤	〈饮食〉Hot and Sour Cuttlefish Roe Soup with Sea Cucumber
酸辣蕨根粉	〈饮食〉Fern Root Noodles with Hot and Sour Sauce
酸辣鲇鱼	〈饮食〉Hot and Sour Catfish with Garlic, Ginger and Coriander
酸辣鳝丝	〈饮食〉Hot and Sour Shredded Eel
酸辣汤	〈饮食〉Hot and Sour Soup
酸辣汤水饺	〈饮食〉Jiaozi/Dumplings in Hot and Sour Soup
酸辣乌鱼蛋汤	〈饮食〉Hot and Sour Cuttlefish Roe Soup
酸辣鱿鱼羹	〈饮食〉Hot and Sour Squid Soup
酸辣鱼唇	〈饮食〉Stir-Fried Fish Lips in Vinegar-Pepper Sauce
酸辣玉米面	〈饮食〉Corn Noodles with Sour and Hot Sauce
酸梅焖鸭	〈饮食〉Braised Duck in Sour Plum Sauce
酸汤鳜鱼	〈饮食〉Boiled Mandarin Fish in Sour Soup
酸甜咕噜虾	〈饮食〉Sweet and Sour Shrimps; Shrimps with Sweet and Sour Sauce
酸甜咕噜鱼	〈饮食〉Sweet and Sour Fish; Deep-Fried Crispy Diced Fish with Tomato Sauce
酸甜明炉烧鸭	〈饮食〉Roast Duck with Sweet and Sour Sauce
酸甜炸春卷	〈饮食〉Deep-Fried Spring Rolls with Sweet and Sour Sauce
酸甜猪肝	〈饮食〉Stir-Fried Sliced Pork Liver with Sweet and Sour Sauce
酸枣仁	〈中医药〉(of Latin) Semen Ziziphi Spinosae; Spine Date Seed; Spiny Jujube Kernel
酸枣仁汤	〈中医药〉Suanzaoren Tang; Spina Date Seed Decoction
蒜泥白肉	〈饮食〉Sliced Boiled Pork with Garlic Sauce
蒜泥鸽片	〈饮食〉Sliced Pigeon in Grated Garlic
蒜蓉	〈饮食〉minced garlic
蒜蓉豆苗	〈饮食〉Stir-Fried Pea Sprouts with Minced Garlic

蒜蓉芥蓝	〈饮食〉Stir-Fried Chinese Broccoli with Minced Garlic
蒜蓉海带丝	〈饮食〉Sliced Kelp with Garlic Sauce
蒜蓉牛柳条	〈饮食〉Beef Fillets with Garlic Sauce
蒜蓉时蔬	〈饮食〉Stir-Fried Seasonal Vegetables with Minced Garlic
蒜蓉西兰花	〈饮食〉Stir-Fried Broccoli with Minced Garlic
蒜蓉腰片	〈饮食〉Stir-Fried Pork Kidney Slices with Mashed Garlic
蒜蓉蒸带子	〈饮食〉Steamed Scallops with Minced Garlic; Steamed Scallops in Garlic Sauce →清蒸蒜蓉带子
蒜蓉蒸龙虾	〈饮食〉Steamed Lobster with Minced Garlic
蒜蓉蒸扇贝	〈饮食〉Steamed Scallop in Shell with Minced Garlic
蒜蓉蒸虾	〈饮食〉Steamed Prawns with Minced Garlic
蒜头烧黄鳝	〈饮食〉Braised Finless Eel with Garlic
蒜香烩肥肠	〈饮食〉Braised Pork Intestines with Mashed Garlic
蒜香椒盐肉排	〈饮食〉Deep-Fried Spare Ribs with Minced Garlic and Spicy Salt
蒜香鳗片	〈饮食〉Stir-Fried Eel Slices with Garlic
蒜香排骨饭	〈饮食〉Rice with Spare Ribs with Garlic
蒜香炸虾卷	〈饮食〉Deep-Fried Shrimp Rolls with Garlic
蒜汁鹅胗	〈饮食〉Goose Gizzards in Garlic Sauce
蒜汁煎灌肠	〈饮食〉Pan-Fried Starch Sausage with Garlic Sauce
算命先生	fortune-teller
算盘	abacus; counting frame
隋唐大运河	Sui-Tang Grand Canal; Grand Canal of the Sui and Tang Dynasties
随访和复诊	〈防疫〉follow-up and subsequent visits
随礼[份子]	to give presents in returns
随云髻	(of hairstyle) scrolling cloud-shaped bun
髓府	〈中医药〉Suifu acupoint; House of Marrow (KI14) →四满,髓中

髓海	〈中医药〉Suihai acupoint; Sea of Marrow (KI14) →四满,髓府
髓亏证	〈中医药〉pattern of marrow deficiency; marrow depletion pattern
髓中	〈中医药〉Suizhong acupoint; Central Marrow (KI14) →四满,髓府
遂昌银猴	〈茶〉Suichang Silver Monkey tea
碎辫子	fine crushing braids; crochet braids (a hairstyle popular among women in pastoral areas)
碎茶	broken tea
碎肉炒鹌蛋	〈饮食〉Stir-Fried Quail Eggs with Minced Pork
碎形红茶	shredded black tea
碎形小袋茶	shredded-tea bag
隧道工程师	tunnel engineer
穗城片皮鹅	〈饮食〉Guangzhou Barbecued Goose Slices
孙冶方经济科学奖	Sun Yefang Economic Science Prize
笋炒鸡片	〈饮食〉Stir-Fried Chicken Slices with Bamboo Shoots; Stir-Fried Sliced Chicken with Bamboo Shoots
笋炒鸡脯	〈饮食〉Stir-Fried Chicken Breast with Bamboo Shoots
笋炒鸡丝	〈饮食〉Stir-Fried Shredded Chicken with Bamboo Shoots
笋干焖腩肉	〈饮食〉Braised Tenderloin (Pork) with Dried Bamboo Shoots
笋菇炒鸡丁	〈饮食〉Stir-Fried Diced Chicken with Bamboo Shoots and Mushrooms
笋尖炒虾球	〈饮食〉Stir-Fried Prawn Balls with Bamboo Shoots
笋尖鲜虾饺	〈饮食〉Jiaozi/Dumplings Stuffed with Shrimp and Bamboo Shoots
娑罗子	〈中医药〉(of Latin) Semen Aesculi; Buckeye Seed
梭式窑	〈陶瓷〉shuttle kiln; drawer kiln
梭织服装	woven garment

蓑衣	〈旧〉coir raincoat; straw rain cape; palm-bark rain cape
缩釉	〈陶瓷〉glaze crawling
锁阳	〈中医药〉(of Latin) Herba Cynomori; Songaria Cynomorium Herb
锁阳固精丸	〈中医药〉Suoyang Gujing Wan; Cynomorium Essence-Securing Pill

T

台式蛋黄肉	〈饮食〉Steamed Pork with Salted Egg Yolk in Taiwan Style
台式卤肉饭	〈饮食〉Taiwan Rice with Stewed Pork
台湾当局	Taiwan authorities
台湾高山茶	Taiwan high mountain tea
台湾高山乌龙	〈茶〉Taiwan high mountain Oolong tea
台湾流行音乐	Taiwanese popular music
台湾肉羹	〈饮食〉Taiwan Shredded Pork and Squid Soup
台湾同胞	Taiwan compatriots
台湾乌龙茶	Taiwan Oolong tea
台柱子	mainstay; pillar backbone
抬杠	to argue for the sake of arguing; to bicker
太白	〈中医药〉Taibai acupoint; Supreme White (SP3)
太白酒	Taibai liquor
太冲	〈中医药〉Taichong acupoint; Supreme Surge (LR3)
太极拳	Taiji quan; Tai Chi boxing; hexagram boxing
太极素菜羹	〈饮食〉Thick Vegetable Soup; Mixed Vegetable Soup
太空飞行员	taikonaut
太空行走	spacewalk
太空站	space station
太平猴魁	〈茶〉Taiping Kowkui; Taiping Houkui green tea

《太平惠民和剂局方》	〈中医药〉Taiping Huimin Heji Ju Fang; Prescriptions of the Bureau of Taiping People's Welfare Pharmacy; Formulary of Peaceful Benevolent Dispensary (by Bureau of Taiping People's Welfare Pharmacy and revised by Chen Shiwen in the Song Dynasty)
《太平圣惠方》	〈中医药〉Taiping Shenghui Fang; Peaceful Holy Benevolent Prescriptions; Taiping Holy Prescriptions for Universal Relief (by Wang Huaiyin et al. in the Northern Song Dynasty)
太平天国钱币	coins of the Taiping Heavenly Kingdom
太平天国运动	Movement of the Taiping Heavenly Kingdom (1851—1864)
太平通宝	〈币〉coin with characters taiping tongbao (the first coin inscribed with imperial or reign title in the Northern Song Dynasty)
《太素》	〈中医药〉(of Yellow Emperor Internal Classic) Grand Simplicity; Comprehensive Notes (by Yang Shangshan in the Sui Dynasty)
太溪	〈中医药〉Taixi acupoint; Supreme Stream (KI3)
太阳能汽车	solar cell plate; solar car
太阳穴	〈中医药〉Taiyang acupoint; Supreme Yang; Temple (EX-HN5)
太阳浴	insolation; sun bathing
太乙	〈中医药〉Taiyi acupoint; Supreme Unity (ST23)
太乙神针	〈中医药〉Taiyi moxa stick moxibustion; Taiyi miraculous moxa moxibustion/roll
太渊	〈中医药〉Taiyuan acupoint; Supreme Abyss (LU9)
太子党	taizidang; offspring of party elders; crown prince party
太子参	〈中医药〉(of Latin) Radix Pseudostellariae; Heterophylly Falsestarwort Root
泰和通宝	〈币〉coin with characters taihe tongbao (issued in the Jin Dynasty)

泰和重宝	〈币〉coin with characters taihe zhongbao (issued in the Jin Dynasty)
泰式豆腐	〈饮食〉Braised Tofu in Thai Sauce
贪多嚼不烂	to bite off more than one can chew
贪图享受	love of pleasure and comfort; to covet enjoyment; to indulge in leisure and pleasure
贪污腐化	corruption degeneration
摊饭酒	tanfan rice wine
摊牌	to put/lay one's card on the table; showdown
坛子	jar; earthen jar; bombonne
坛子肉	〈饮食〉Diced Pork in Pot; Braised Pork in Crock
弹法	〈中医药〉flicking manipulation; needle-handle flicking
弹花机	cotton fluffer
弹花匠	craftsman who makes cotton quilt
弹性工资	flexible pay
弹性就业	flexible employment
痰火闭窍证	〈中医药〉pattern of phlegm-fire blocking the orifices
痰火扰神证	〈中医药〉pattern of phlegm-fire disturbing mind; pattern of phlegmatic fire harassing the spirit
痰火扰心	〈中医药〉harassment of heart by phlegm-fire
痰凝胞宫证	〈中医药〉pattern of phlegm congealing in the uterus
痰气互结证	〈中医药〉pattern of phlegm and qi intermingled with each other; pattern of phlegm-qi binding together
痰热动风证	〈中医药〉pattern of stirring wind due to phlegma-heat; pattern of phlegm-heat stirring wind
痰热犯鼻证	〈中医药〉pattern of phlegm-heat invading the nose
痰热结胸证	〈中医药〉pattern of phlegm-heat congealing in the chest
痰热内闭证	〈中医药〉pattern of phlegm-heat blocking internally

痰热内扰证	〈中医药〉pattern of phlegm-heat attacking internally
痰热壅肺证	〈中医药〉pattern of phlegm-heat congesting the lung
痰湿泛耳证	〈中医药〉pattern of phlegm-dampness flooting the ears
痰湿阻络证	〈中医药〉pattern of phlegm-dampness blocking collaterals/the network vessels
痰食互结证	〈中医药〉pattern of dyspepsia and phlegm blockage; pattern of dyspeptic food intermingled with phlegm blockade
痰饮	〈中医药〉phlegmatic-fluid retention; phlegm and retained fluid
痰瘀互结证	〈中医药〉pattern of phlegm and blood stasis intermingled with each other
痰瘀阻肺证	〈中医药〉pattern of phlegm and blood stasis obstructing lung
痰浊阻肺	〈中医药〉obstruction of lung by turbid phlegm
痰浊阻肺证	〈中医药〉pattern of turbid phlegm obstructing lung
痰阻心脉证	〈中医药〉pattern of phlegm blocking heart vessel
檀香	〈中医药〉Santalum Album; Sandalwood
坦赞铁路	Tazara Railway; Tanzam Railway; Tanzania-Zambia Railway
探亲	to (return to) visit one's family; to go to visit one's relatives
探亲假	family reunion leave; home leave; travel on home leave
探月车	lunar roving vehicle; lunar rover
探月工程	lunar exploration program/project; lunar probe program/projcct
汤包	〈饮食〉Juicy Baozi; Steamed Baozi Stuffed with Minced Meat and Gravy
汤沟特曲	〈酒〉Tanggou Special Yeast spirit

汤酱草头	〈饮食〉Stir-Fried Wrinkled Skin of Pork with Alfalfa
《汤头歌诀》	〈中医药〉*Tangtou Gejue*; *Decoctions in Rhymes*; *Recipes in Rhymes* (by Wang Ang in the Qing Dynasty)
《汤液本草》	〈中医药〉*Tangye Bencao*; *Materia Medica for Decoctions*; *Herbal Foundation for Decoctions* (by Wang Haogu in the Yuan Dynasty)
汤圆	〈饮食〉Tangyuan; Ground Glutinous Rice Balls with Sweet Stuffing
《唐本草》	〈中医药〉*Tang Bencao*; *Tang Material Medica* (written in the Tang Dynasty, around AD 659, the first book about medicine in the world)
唐代科举制度	imperial examination system of the Tang Dynasty
唐国通宝	〈币〉coin with characters tangguo tongbao (state titled money, issued in the Southern Tang)
唐人街	Chinatown; Chinese quarter
唐三彩	〈陶瓷〉tri-colored glazed pottery of the Tang Dynasty
唐三彩飞鸟云纹三足盘	〈陶瓷〉tri-colored tripod plate with flying bird and cloud pattern (Tang Dynasty period)
唐三彩黑马俑	〈陶瓷〉tri-colored black horse figurine (Tang Dynasty period)
唐三彩壶	〈陶瓷〉Tang tri-colored pot
唐三彩五足盆式炉	〈陶瓷〉tri-colored incense burner in basin shape with five-legs (Tang Dynasty period)
唐三彩鸭形杯	〈陶瓷〉tri-color glazed duck-shaped cup (Tang Dynasty period)
唐三彩鸳鸯踩莲枕	〈陶瓷〉tri-colored pillow with mandarin ducks and lotus pattern (Tang Dynasty period)
唐三彩鸳鸯形壶	〈陶瓷〉tri-colored pot in the shape of mandarin duck (Tang Dynasty period)
唐宋煎茶道	steamed tea ceremony of the Tang Song Dynasties
搪瓷	〈陶瓷〉enamel; porcelain enamel

糖拌西红柿	〈饮食〉Tomato Slices with Sugar
糖醋白菜墩	〈饮食〉Chinese Cabbage with Sweet and Sour Flavor
糖醋豆苗	〈饮食〉Stir-Fried Pea Sprouts with Sweet and Sour Sauce
糖醋古老肉	〈饮食〉Fried Pork Slices with Sweet and Sour Sauce
糖醋果肉	〈饮食〉Pork Croquettes with Sweet and Sour Sauce
糖醋黄鱼	〈饮食〉Sweet and Sour Yellow Croaker; Braised Yellow Croaker with Sweet and Sour Sauce
糖醋鸡块	〈饮食〉Stir-Fried Chicken with Sweet and Sour Sauce
糖醋鸡条	〈饮食〉Stir-Fried Sliced Chicken with Sweet and Sour Sauce
糖醋里脊	〈饮食〉Stir-Fried Pork Fillets with Sweet and Sour Sauce
糖醋鲤鱼	〈饮食〉Stewed Fried Carp with Sweet and Sour Sauce
糖醋排骨	〈饮食〉Stir-Fried Pork Chop with Sweet and Sour Sauce
糖醋茄饼	〈饮食〉Stuffed Eggplant with Sweet and Sour Sauce
糖醋全鱼	〈饮食〉Deep-Fried Whole Fish with Sweet and Sour Sauce
糖醋山药	〈饮食〉Stir-Fried Chinese Yam with Sweet and Sour Sauce
糖醋鱿鱼	〈饮食〉Sweet and Sour Squid; Stir-Fried Crispy Squid with Sweet and Sour Sauce
糖醋鱼片	〈饮食〉Stir-Fried Crispy Fish Slices with Sweet and Sour Sauce
糖葫芦	→冰糖葫芦
糖化发酵剂	〈酒〉sacchariferous and fermentative agent; saccharifying ferment

糖脉康颗粒	〈中医药〉Tangmaikang Keli; Sugar Vessel Comfort Granule
糖尿病	〈防疫〉diabetes; diabetes mellitus
糖人	sugar figurine
糖蒜	〈饮食〉Pickled Sweet Garlic
洮南香酒	Taonan hsiang chiew; Taonan liquor
桃红葡萄酒	rose wine; pink wine; chiaretto
桃花汤	〈中医药〉Taohua Tang; Peach Blossom Decoction
桃仁	〈中医药〉(of Latin) Semen Persicae; Peach Seed
桃山白酒	Taoshan bei chiew; Taoshan liquor
陶瓷	〈陶瓷〉pottery and porcelain; ceramics
陶瓷素烧坯	〈陶瓷〉biscuit; unglazed ware
陶对书俑	〈陶瓷〉pottery proof reading figurine
陶量	〈陶瓷〉pottery volume measure
陶皿	〈陶瓷〉earthenware bowl
陶女坐俑	〈陶瓷〉pottery seated lady figurine
陶器	〈陶瓷〉earthenware; pottery ware
陶射手俑	〈陶瓷〉pottery bowman figurine
陶土	〈陶瓷〉pottery clay; syderolite (main raw material for preparing china/porcelain clay)
陶武士俑	〈陶瓷〉pottery warrior figurine
陶熏器	〈陶瓷〉pottery censer
陶冶情操	to cultivate one's taste/temperament
陶艺	〈陶瓷〉porcelain art
陶针疗法	〈中医药〉pottery needle therapy
淘宝电子商务平台	Taobao e-commerce platform
淘宝店	Taobao store; Taobao shop
淘宝供货商市场	Taobao vendor market
淘宝卖家	Taobao seller
淘宝网店	Taobao online shop; online shop on Taobao
淘港族	mainland bargain-hunters in Hong Kong
讨债公司	debt collection company; collection agency
套餐服务	set menu; package service
套购	fraudulent purchase; arbitrage; to illegally buy-up (state-controlled commodity for resale)

套话	empty conventional talk; set expressions for the writing of articles or letters; trite remarks
套汇	arbitrage; to illegally obtain foreign exchange
套近乎	to cotton (up) to sb.; to curry favor with sb.
套裤	leggings; leggin; overalls
套鞋	galoshes; overshoes; overboots
特别黄鱼羹	〈饮食〉Yellow Croaker and Clams Potage
特定传染病	〈防疫〉specific infectious disease
特级教师	teacher of special grade; special-grade teacher
特快专递	express mail service
特派记者	accredited correspondent
特聘	to specially engage/invite sb.; to be specially invited
特曲酒	tequ chiew; special yeast spirit
特色菜	〈饮食〉special dish; specialty
特色产品	special product
特色潮州烧鹅	〈饮食〉Chaozhou Specially Braised Goose
特事特办	to handle special cases with special methods
特殊教育	special education; special needs education; education for those with special learning needs
特香型风格	〈酒〉special flavor style
特效药	〈防疫〉specific medicine
特型演员	typecast actor
特许金融分析师	certified financial analyst; CFA
特许商品	franchised good; licensed product
特许市场营销师	certified marketing manager
特邀代表	specially invited representative/delegate
特异性抗体	〈防疫〉specific antibody
特约编辑	contributing editor
特约记者	special correspondent
特约评论员	special (guest) commentator
特诊室	〈防疫〉special service department
特种兵	special forces
特种部队	special forces; special troops

特种国债	special treasury bond
特种教育家	special-needs educator
特种债券	special bond
腾冲蜜饯	〈饮食〉Tengchong Style Preserved Fruits
踢皮球	to kick the ball to each other; to pass the buck to each other (mutually shirking responsibilities)
提高救治水平	〈防疫〉to improve the quality of medical treatment
提高免疫力	〈防疫〉to strengthen immune system
提高社会参与度	to enhance/encourage mass participation
提高收治率	〈防疫〉to improve the admission rate
提高治愈率	〈防疫〉to improve the cure rate
提供抗疫物资	〈防疫〉to offer supplies in support of the fight against the pandemic
提花针织物	jacquard knitted fabric
提捏进针法	〈中医药〉skin-pinching needle insertion; pinch-and-lift needle insertion; insertion of the needle by pinching up the skin
体彩	→体育彩票
体温检测	〈防疫〉to check body temperature; body temperature monitoring
体温检测热像仪	〈防疫〉thermal imaging camera for temperature monitoring
体温筛查	〈防疫〉temperature screening
体温异常	〈防疫〉abnormal body temperature
体系工程师	system engineer
体系审核员	system auditor
体育彩票	sports lottery
体育产业	sports industry
体育道德风尚奖	physical education ethic award
体育健康服务	sports health service
体育委员	commissary in charge of sports
体育运动教练	sports coach
体制创新	institutional innovation
替班厨师	tournant; relief cook

替身演员	stunt man/woman; stand-in; body double
天朝	〈古〉celestial empire; Chinese empire
天池	〈中医药〉Tianchi acupoint; Celestial Pool (P1)
天池茗毫	〈茶〉Tianchi Minghao tea; Tianchi Tender tea
天地香烟	Tian Di cigarettes; Heaven and Earth cigarettes
天帝	(of Chinese legend) Emperor/Lord of Heaven; Celestial Ruler; Supreme God
天冬	〈中医药〉(of Latin) Radix Asparagi; Cochinchinese Asparagus Root
天府	〈中医药〉Tianfu acupoint; Celestial Storehouse (LU3)
天赋人权	natural rights; man's natural right; innate rights of man
天宫空间站	Tiangong space station
天宫太空实验室	Tiangong space laboratory
天河2号	Tianhe-2; Milkyway-2 (a supercomputer)
天花粉	〈中医药〉(of Latin) Radix Trichosanthis; Snake-gourd Root
天井	〈中医药〉Tianjing acupoint; Heaven Well (SJ10)
天葵子	〈中医药〉(of Latin) Radix Semiaquilegiae; Muskroot-like Semiaquilgia Root
天髎	〈中医药〉Tianliao acupoint; Heavenly Crevice (SJ15)
天麻	〈中医药〉(of Latin) Rhizoma Gastrodiae; Tall Gastrodia Tuber
天麻炖乳鸽	〈饮食〉Stewed Pigeon with Gastrodia Tuber
天麻钩藤饮	〈中医药〉Tianma Gouteng Yin; Gastrodia and Uncaria Decoction/Beverage
天麻头风灵胶囊	〈中医药〉Tianma Toufengling Jiaonang; Gastrodia Headache-Relieving Capsule
天麻丸	〈中医药〉Tianma Wan; Gastrodia Pill; Gastrodia Tuber Bolus
天猫	Tmall (online shopping mall)
天猫网上商城	online marketplace Tmall

天目釉	〈陶瓷〉temmoku glaze
天南星	〈中医药〉(of Latin) Rhizoma Arisaematis; Jackinthepulpit Tuber
天启青花罗汉炉	〈陶瓷〉blue and white porcelain censer with Arhat pattern (Ming Tianqi period)
天泉	〈中医药〉Tianquan acupoint; Celestial Spring; Heavenly Spring (PC2)
天然药物	〈中医药〉natural medicine
天山绿茶	Tianshan green tea
天枢	〈中医药〉Tianshu acupoint; Celestial Pivot; Heavenly Pivot (ST25)
天顺青花人物梅瓶	〈陶瓷〉blue and white plum vase with portraiture pattern of Tianshun's reign
天顺青花鸳鸯荷莲梅瓶	〈陶瓷〉blue and white plum vase with a pattern of mandarin ducks, lotus flowers and lotus seeds (Ming Tianshun's period)
天台乌药散	〈中医药〉Tiantai Wuyao San; Tiantai Lindera Powder
天突	〈中医药〉Tiantu acupoint; Heavenly Prominence; Celestial Chimney (CV22)
天王补心丹	〈中医药〉Tianwang Buxin Dan; Cardiotonic Bolus; Celestial Emperor Heart-Supplementing Elixir
天溪	〈中医药〉Tianxi acupoint; Celestial Stream; Heavenly Stream (SP18)
天仙藤	〈中医药〉(of Latin) Herba Aristolochiae; Dutchmanspipe Vine
天仙子	〈中医药〉(of Latin) Semen Hyoscyami; Henbane Seed
天牖	〈中医药〉Tianyou acupoint; Sky Window; Heavenly Window (TE16)
天舟一号货运飞船	Tianzhou-1 Cargo Spacecraft
天竹黄	〈中医药〉(of Latin) Concretio Silicea Bambusae; Tabasheer
天柱	〈中医药〉Tianzhu acupoint; Heavenly Pillar (BL10)

天柱剑毫	〈茶〉Tianzhu Sword Bud tea
田七	〈中医药〉(of Latin) Radix Notoginseng; Pseudo-Ginseng →三七
田七痛经胶囊	〈中医药〉Tianqi Tongjing Jiaonang; Notoginseng Dysmenorrhea Capsule
田七镇痛膏	〈中医药〉Tianqi Zhentong Gao; Notoginseng Pain-Relieving Plaster
甜酒	sweet wine
甜浓	〈茶〉sweet and heavy
甜烧饼	〈饮食〉Sweet Sesame (Seed) Pancake
甜爽	〈茶〉sweet and brisk
甜酸鸡	〈饮食〉Sweet and Sour Chicken; Stir-Fried Chicken with Sweet and Sour Flavor
甜酸鸡腿肉	〈饮食〉Stir-Fried Chicken Drumsticks with Sweet and Sour Flavor
甜酸石斑鱼	〈饮食〉Sweet and Sour Garoupa; Deep-Fried Garoupa with Sweet and Sour Sauce
甜香	〈茶〉sweet aroma
填仓酒	Tiancang wine (served on the 15th day of the 1st lunar month)
填鸭式教学	cramming method of teaching; to spoon-feed
挑大梁	to shoulder a heavy responsibility or a demanding task; to be the mainstay
条形绿茶	twisted green tea
条形乌龙	〈茶〉twisted Oolong
调和肝脾	〈中医药〉to harmonize the liver and spleen; to regulate the function of the liver and spleen
调和气血	〈中医药〉to harmonize the qi and blood; to regulate the movement of the qi and blood
调和药	〈中医药〉harmonizing drug
调和诸药	〈中医药〉to moderate the property of herbs
调减市内公交	〈防疫〉to reduce the frequency of bus services in the city
调节收入	to readjust income distribution
调理肠胃	〈中医药〉to coordinate intestines and stomach

调理阴阳	〈中医药〉to coordinate yin and yang
调味茶	spiced tea
调香和调味	〈酒〉blending flavor and taste
挑刺法	〈中医药〉piercing method; pricking blood therapy
挑花[织]	〈服饰〉cross-stitch work
跳梁小丑	contemptible scoundrel; buffoon
跳棋	Chinese checkers; Chinese draughts
跳水木耳	〈饮食〉Black Fungi with Pickled Capsicum
贴布花裙	appliqued skirt
贴袋	patch pocket
贴花	〈服饰〉applique; transfer-decoration
贴花刺绣	applique embroidery; broderie suisse; elysee work
贴牌生产商	Original Equipment Manufacturer; OEM
铁板串烧牛肉	〈饮食〉Beef Kebabs Served on a Sizzling Iron Plate
铁板葱烧豆腐	〈饮食〉Sizzling Tofu with Scallion; Tofu with Scallion Served on a Sizzling Iron Plate
铁板豆豉鸡	〈饮食〉Sizzling Chicken in Black Bean Sauce; Chicken with Black Bean Sauce Served on a Sizzling Iron Plate
铁板酱爆带子	〈饮食〉Grilled Scallops with Chili and Vegetables Served on a Sizzling Iron Plate
铁板酱鲜鱿	〈饮食〉Pan-Fried Fresh Squid with Soy Sauce Served on a Sizzling Iron Plate
铁板咖喱酱烧骨	〈饮食〉Sizzling Spare Ribs with Curry Sauce
铁板木瓜牛仔骨	〈饮食〉Calf Ribs with Papaya Served on a Sizzling Iron Plate
铁板牛肉	〈饮食〉Beef Steak Served on a Sizzling Iron Plate
铁板沙爹鳝球	〈饮食〉Sizzling Eel Balls with Satay Sauce; Pan-Fried Eel Balls with Satay Sauce Served on a Sizzling Iron Plate
铁板什锦肉扒	〈饮食〉Assorted Meats Served on a Sizzling Iron Plate
铁板掌中宝	〈饮食〉Sizzling Chicken Paws; Chicken Paws Served on a Sizzling Iron Plate

铁饭碗	(of job) iron rice bowl; secure job
铁哥们儿	faithful pal; buddy; sworn friend
铁观音	〈茶〉Tie Guanyin tea; Iron Mercy Goddess tea (one of the ten famous teas in China)
铁锅牛柳	〈饮食〉Braised Beef Fillets in Iron Pot
铁甲	〈古〉cuirass; iron armor
铁交椅	iron (lifetime) post; guaranteed leading post
铁扒	〈饮食〉to grill; to broil
铁扒牛排	〈饮食〉Grilled Beef Steak; Grilled Rump Steak
铁扒什锦	〈饮食〉Grilled Assorted/Mixed Vegetables
铁器时代	iron age; age of iron
听宫	〈中医药〉Tinggong acupoint; Auditory Palace (SI19)
听会	〈中医药〉Tinghui acupoint; Auditory Convergence (GB2)
廷对	〈古〉final imperial examination; to respond to the emperor's queries at court
停薪留职	to retain one's position with one's salary suspended; to obtain the job but suspend the salary
停运长途汽车	〈防疫〉to halt long-distance buses
停止接待群体性聚餐	〈防疫〉to stop hosting group dinners and banquets
停止堂食	〈防疫〉to stop providing dine-in service
葶苈子	〈中医药〉(of Latin) Semen Lepidii; Semen Descurainiae; Pepperweed Seed; Tansymustard Seed
通便灵胶囊	〈中医药〉Tongbianling Jiaonang; Bowel Loosening Capsule
通才	versatile person
通草	〈中医药〉(of Latin) Medulla Tetrapanacis; Ricepaperplant Pith
通道式公共汽车	→铰接[通道]式公共汽车
通风制曲	〈酒〉to produce raw starter by blowing wind
通腑泄热	〈中医药〉to purge the bowels and discharge heat
通关一体化	integrated customs clearance

通化葡萄酒	Tonghua grape wine
通络下乳	〈中医药〉to dredge collateral for promoting lactation
通脉颗粒	〈中医药〉Tongmai Keli; Vessel Freeing Granule
通票	through ticket
通窍鼻炎片	〈中医药〉Tongqiao Biyan Pian; Orifice-Opening Rhinitis Tablet
通窍耳聋丸	〈中医药〉Tongqiao Erlong Wan; Orifice-Opening Deafness Pill
通天冠	tongtian crown (a hat worn by the emperor in the Song and Ming Dynasties)
通天岩茶	Tongtian rock tea
通信技术工程师	communication engineer
通宣理肺丸	〈中医药〉Tongxuan Lifei Wan; Diffusion-Freeing and Lung-Rectifying Pill
通胀预期	inflation expectations
同病异治	〈中医药〉different treatments for the same disease; to treat the same disease with different methods
同步卫星	geostationary satellite
同等学力	to have the same educational level (as that of the regular school or class); equivalent education level
同等学力申请硕士学位统考	general examination for applicants with education background equivalent to college graduates for master's degree
同名经配穴法	〈中医药〉combination of acupoints of the namesake channels/meridians
同情用药	〈防疫〉compassionate use of a drug (using a drug not yet approved under the compassionate use program)
同仁大活络丸	〈中医药〉Tongren Dahuoluo Wan; Tongren Major Network-Channel-Quickening Pill
同仁堂	Tong Ren Tang; Tongren Drugstore
同声传译员	simultaneous interpreter

同乡会	association of fellow-provincials
同治通宝	〈币〉coin with characters tongzhi tongbao (issued in the Qing Dynasty)
同舟共济	〈防疫〉to strengthen solidarity
铜(仿)贝	〈币〉bronzed shell (the earliest metal currency in China)
铜官窑黄釉褐蓝彩双系罐	〈陶瓷〉Tong Guan Kiln yellow glaze pot with two ears and brown and blue pattern
铜官窑黄釉褐蓝彩执壶	〈陶瓷〉Tong Guan Kiln yellow glazed ewer with brown and blue pattern
铜官窑题诗执壶	〈陶瓷〉Tong Guan Kiln jug with poem inscription
铜胎掐丝珐琅	〈陶瓷〉filigree enamel with copper body
铜香炉	bronze incense burner
铜元	〈旧〉(of currency) tongyuan; copper coin (in the Qing Dynasty)
瞳子髎	〈中医药〉Tongziliao acupoint; Pupil Crevice (GB1)
统保	all risk insurance
统筹安排	comprehensive arrangement
统筹安排轮休	〈防疫〉to better schedule rotating shifts
统筹兼顾	to make overall plans and take all factors into consideration
统筹推进疫情防控和脱贫攻坚	〈防疫〉to coordinate epidemic control with poverty alleviation
统筹疫情防控和经济社会发展	〈防疫〉to coordinate epidemic prevention and control with economic and social development
统计员	junior statistician; statistical clerk
统一应急物资保障体系	〈防疫〉unified emergency supply system
统一战线	united front
筒裙	pailform skirt; straight skirt; tight skirt →直[筒]裙
筒仔米糕	〈饮食〉Rice Tube Pudding; Rice Tube Cake
痛风定胶囊	〈中医药〉Tongfengding Jiaonang; Pain-Wind Stabilizing Capsule
痛泻要方	〈中医药〉Tongxie Yaofang; Pain and Diarrhea Formula

偷工减料	to use inferior materials and turn out sub-standard products; to cut corners; to stint on both labor and materials
偷税漏税	tax evasion; to defraud the revenue
头春茶	first season tea; early spring tea
头寸紧	credit crunch; fund shortage
头寸松	loose money; credit ease
头风痛胶囊	〈中医药〉Toufengtong Jiaonang; Wind Headache Capsule
头号种子选手	No.1 seed player; top seed player
头巾	head-covering; kerchief; turban
头临泣	〈中医药〉Toulinqi acupoint; Head Overlooking Tears (GB15)
头泡茶	first infusion of tea
头皮针	scalp acupuncture; scalp vein set
头皮针疗法	〈中医药〉scalp acupuncture therapy
头窍阴	〈中医药〉Touqiaoyin acupoint; Head Portal Yin (GB11)
头饰	headwear; headdress
投机商号	(of a stock) bucket shop
投机投资性购房	purchase of homes for speculation or investment purposes
投诉热线	complaint hotline; dial-a-cheat confidential hotline
投诉中心	complaint center
投诉专员	complaints commissioner
投资代表	investment representative
投资顾问	investment advisor
投资精算师	investment actuary
投资热点	popular investment spot; investment hot spot
投资项目经理	investment manager
投资者关系经理	investor relation manager
投资咨询师	investment counselor
透过现象看本质	to see through the appearance to perceive the essence

透辉石瓷	〈陶瓷〉diopside porcelain
透明釉	〈陶瓷〉transparent glaze
透脓散	〈中医药〉Tounong San; Pus-Outthrusting Powder; Power for Promoting Pus Discharge
透脓生肌	〈中医药〉to promote pus drainage and granulation
透心凉	bitterly disappointed
凸雕	〈陶瓷〉rilievi; embossment
突出才能奖	model student of outstanding capacity; awards for students with outstanding talent
突出贡献奖	prize for the outstanding contribution; outstanding contribution award
突出重点	〈防疫〉to focus on key issues
突发公共卫生事件	〈防疫〉public health emergency
突击队	shock brigade; commando
突破性技术	breakthrough technology
屠苏酒	Tusu liquor (served on the 1st day of the 1st lunar month for averting pestilence)
土贝母	〈中医药〉(of Latin) Rhizoma Bolbostematis; Paniculate Bolbostemma
土鳖虫	〈中医药〉(of Latin) Eupolyphaga seu Steleophaga; Ground Beetle
土(特)产	local specialty; local and special product
土地承包期	land contract period
土地担保协调员	field assurance coordinator
土地登记代理人	land registration agent
土地公	(of a legend) land god; God of the Earth
土地家庭承包制	household-based land contract system
土地沙化	desertification; desert encroachment
土地酸化	acidification
土地征收征用制度	land expropriation and requisition system
土豆饼	〈饮食〉(Mashed) Potato Pancake
土豆炒牛柳条	〈饮食〉Stir-Fried Beef Fillets with Potatoes
土茯苓	〈中医药〉(of Latin) Rhizoma Smilacis Glabrae; Glabrous Greenbrier Rhizome

土茯苓炖山龟	〈饮食〉Stewed Turtle with Sarsaparilla
土豪	tuhao; rich local tyrant; local despot
土建[木]工程师	structural engineer; civil engineer
土锦	〈土家族〉Tu brocade; silk weaved fabric
土荆皮	〈中医药〉(of Latin) Cortex Pseudolaricis; Golden Larch Bark
土井	earthen well
土老帽	clodhopper; country bumpkin
土楼	tulou; earth building; earthen building
土木工程技师	civil engineering technician
土木香	〈中医药〉(of Latin) Radix Inulae; Inula Root
土牛膝	〈中医药〉(of Latin) Radix et Rhizome Achyranthes; Native Achyranthes (Root)
土特产	native product; local special product; local speciality
吐槽	to disclose one's secret; trash talk; debunk
吐苦水	to pour out one's grievance; to whine
菟丝子	〈中医药〉(of Latin) Semen Cuscutae; Dodder Seed
团队建设奖	prize for the team contribution; teamwork award
团购	group purchase; group buying
团购经理	group purchase manager
团购业务员	group purchase salesman
团购主管	group purchase supervisor
团扇	circular fan; moon-shaped fan →宫扇, 纨扇
团委会	Youth League Committee
团委会书记	secretary of the Youth League Committee
团圆	family reunion (for husband and wife, parents and children, etc.)
团支部书记	League branch secretary; secretary of the Youth League Branch Committee
团支书	→团支部书记
褖[缘]衣	〈古〉ceremonial robe or dress for queen
推出更多外汇便利化业务	〈防疫〉to offer more services to facilitate foreign exchange transactions

推罐	→走[推]罐
推广分时段就餐	〈防疫〉to allow consumers to dine at staggered times
推广科研成果	to turn laboratory achievements into commercial/mass production; commercialization of laboratory achievements
推广系统有效的防控指南	〈防疫〉to promote control and treatment protocols that are systematic and effective
推进城镇化	to carry out urbanization
推进疫情防控的好经验好做法	〈防疫〉to promote best practices in prevention and control from across the country
推拿	〈中医药〉tuina; massage therapy; Chinese traditional manipulation
推拿法	〈中医药〉pushing and grasping manipulation
推拿师	massage therapist
推拿手法	〈中医药〉massage manipulation; manipulations for tuina; manipulating technique
推销经理	promotion manager
腿裙甲	〈古〉leg skirt armor
腿汁扒芥菜	〈饮食〉Braised Leaf Mustard with Ham Gravy
退耕还林	to convert restore/return cultivated land to forests
退耕还林还草	grain for green; to return farmland to forests or grassland
退耕还林还牧	to convert/restore the land for forestry and pasture; to return cultivated land back to pasture
退居二线	to take a back seat; to retire from leading post
退烧药	〈防疫〉febrifuge; antipyretic
退休金	pension; retirement benefits
退役军人	ex-servicemen; veteran; retired serviceman; former military man
屯溪绿茶	Twaikay tea; Tunxi green tea
屯溪腌鲜鳜鱼	〈饮食〉Tunxi Pickled Fresh Mandarin Fish
囤积居奇	to store up goods to make a good bargain; to corner the market; hoarding and profiteering

囤积食物	〈防疫〉to stock up on food
托里排脓	〈中医药〉to expel pathogens by strengthening vital qi and expelling pus
托您吉言	thank you for your blessings; thanks to your kind words
托人情	to ask an influential figure to help arrange sth.
拖拉作风	procrastination style; dilatory style of work; to be dilatory in work
拖油瓶	children from the preceding marriage (who are now living with stepmothers or stepfathers); (of a woman) to remarry with children from her previous husband
脱产培训	off-job training
脱产学习	to study on day release; to be released from regular work for study
脱汗	〈中医药〉desertion sweating; sweating in shock; sweating in critical stage
脱盲	to cast off illiteracy; to eradicate illiteracy
脱毛膏	〈中医药〉Tuomao Gao; Depilatory Paste/Cream
脱销	(of commodity) to be out of stock
脱脂奶	skimmed milk
沱牌曲酒	Tuopai yeast liquor
驼绒	〈服饰〉camel's hair; camel hair cloth
拓展部经理	marketing manager

W

挖墙脚	to pull the rug (out) from under sb.'s feet; to undermine the foundation of sth.; to cut the ground from under sb.'s feet
瓦当	patterned tile-end; eave tile with a pattern (shielding of the front end of the roof tile covering eaves)
瓦罐	〈陶瓷〉earthen jar; earthenware pitcher
瓦罐煨汤	〈饮食〉Stewed Soup with Crock
瓦楞子	〈中医药〉(of Latin) Concha Arcae; Ark Shell; Blood Clam Shell
歪才	talent for intrigue or deviousness; talent in a field other than mainstream professions; genius that is often regarded as a professional misfit
歪风邪气	unhealthy practices and evil phenomena
外鼻	〈中医药〉Waibi acupoint; External Nose (TG1; TG2)
外部环境	external environment
外地滞留人员安全有序返乡	〈防疫〉people stranded in other places return home in a safe and orderly manner
外防输出	〈防疫〉to prevent coronavirus spreading beyond local boundaries
外防输入	〈防疫〉to guard against coronavirus spreading from abroad
外感发热	〈中医药〉external contraction heat; exogenous fever
外感咳嗽	〈中医药〉externally contracted cough; exogenous cough

外感六淫	〈中医药〉diseases caused by exogenous pathogenic factor
外感热病	〈中医药〉heat disease caused by exogenous pathogenic factor
外关	〈中医药〉Waiguan acupoint; Outer Pass (TE5)
外国人居留证	residence permit for foreigner; foreigner's residence certificate/permit
外国人永久居留证	foreigner's permanent residence card; alien permanent residence permit
外踝尖穴	〈中医药〉Waihuaijian acupoint; Tip of the Outer Ankle (EX-LE9)
外汇比价	exchange ratio
外汇波动	foreign-exchange fluctuation
外汇部核算员	foreign exchange settlement clerk
外汇部职员	foreign exchange clerk
外汇储备	foreign exchange reserve; forex reserve
外汇管制	foreign exchange control
外汇经纪人	foreign exchange broker
外汇平衡	balance of foreign exchange
外汇(兑换)券	〈旧〉foreign exchange certificate; FEC
外汇外流	outflow of foreign exchange
外汇主管	foreign exchange supervisor
外酱釉里霁青暗云龙纹高足碗	〈陶瓷〉brown glaze stem bowl with inner celadon and covert cloud and dragon pattern (Ming Hongwu period)
外景拍摄	location shooting; filming on location
外科处置	〈防疫〉surgical treatment
《外科精要》	〈中医药〉*Waike Jingyao*; *Essentials of External Medicine*; *Essence of External Diseases* (by Chen Ziming in the Southern Song Dynasty)
外科医生	surgeon; chirurgeon
《外科正宗》	〈中医药〉*Waike Zhengzong*; *Orthodox Manual of External Medicine/Diseases* (by Chen Shigong in the Ming Dynasty)

《外科证治全生集》	〈中医药〉*Waike Zhengzhi Quansheng Ji*; *Life-Saving Manual of Diagnosis and Treatment of External Diseases*; *Life-For-All Compendium of External Medicine, Patterns and Treatment* (by Wang Hongxu in the Qing Dynasty)
外联部	public relations department
外卖店	takeaway; take-out restaurant
外卖服务	〈防疫〉takeout services
外贸经理	foreign trade manager
外贸主管	foreign trade supervisor
外贸自营权	right to engage in foreign trade
外派	to send sb. to units or organizations in other areas or to a foreign country
外勤工作	field operation
《外台秘要方》	〈中医药〉*Waitai Miyao Fang*; *Arcane Essentials from the Imperial Library*; *Medical Secrets from the Royal Library* (by Wang Tao in the Tang Dynasty)
外销部经理	export sales manager
外袖	→大[外]袖
外用膏剂	〈中医药〉medicinal extract for exterior application
外语教师	foreign language teacher
外源性感染	〈防疫〉exogenous infection
外燥证	〈中医药〉exogenous dryness pattern; external dryness pattern
外治法	〈中医药〉external treatment; external therapy
外资企业	foreign investment enterprise; wholly foreign-owned enterprise
弯针	〈中医药〉bending of the needle; bent needle
豌豆炒辣牛肉	〈饮食〉Stir-Fried Beef and Green Peas with Spicy Sauce
豌豆糕	〈饮食〉Steamed Pea Flour Cake
豌豆黄	〈饮食〉Pea Flour Cake (a traditional snack of Beijing)

豌豆烩鸡丝	〈饮食〉Braised Shredded Chicken with Peas
丸子汤	〈饮食〉Soup with Meat Balls; Pork Balls Soup
纨扇	round silk fan; flat and round fan with framed gauze →团扇, 宫扇
完带汤	〈中医药〉Wandai Tang; Discharge-Ceasing Decoction
完谷不化	〈中医药〉diarrhea with undigested food; undigested food in stool
完善信息发布机制	〈防疫〉to improve the information release mechanism
玩不转	to be beyond one's ability; to be unable to manage
挽词	elegiac words; elegy
挽歌	dirge; elegy; requiem; lament
挽联	elegiac couplets
晚蚕沙	〈中医药〉(of Latin) Faeces Bombycis; Silkworm Droppings
晚会主持人	host on the entertainment/evening party
晚香玉炒鸡丝	〈饮食〉Stir-Fried Shredded Chicken with Tuberose
碗糕	〈饮食〉Salty Rice Pudding
《万病回春》	〈中医药〉*Wanbing Huichun*; *Recovery from All Ailments*; *Curative Measures for All Diseases* (by Gong Tingxian in the Ming Dynasty)
万金油	〈中医药〉Wanjin You; Tiger Balm (for treating headaches, scalds and other ailments)
万历通宝	〈币〉coin with characters Wanli tongbao (issued in the Ming Dynasty)
《万密斋医学全书》	〈中医药〉*Wan Mizhai Yixue Quanshu*; *Wan Mizhai's Complete Medical Book* (by Wan Mizhai in the Ming Dynasty)
万人计划	Ten-Thousand Talents Program
万通筋骨片	〈中医药〉Wantong Jingu Pian; Ten Thousands Tendons and Bones Opening Tablet

万元户	〈旧〉ten-thousand-yuan household; household with ten thousand yuan (earlier affluent people in China in the late 1970s)
尪痹冲剂	〈中医药〉Wangbi Chongji; Lame Impediment Granule
亡阳	〈中医药〉yang depletion; yang exhaustion
亡阳证	〈中医药〉yang depletion pattern; yang exhaustion pattern
亡阴	〈中医药〉yin depletion; yin exhaustion
亡阴证	〈中医药〉yin depletion pattern; yin exhaustion pattern
王不留行	〈中医药〉(of Latin) Semen Vaccariae; Cowherb Seed
王朝干白	〈酒〉Dynasty dry white wine
王朝干红	〈酒〉Dynasty dry red wine
王朝红葡萄酒	Dynasty red wine
王朝葡萄酒	Dynasty wine
王府酥鱼	〈饮食〉Deep-Fried Crispy Fish with Soy Sauce
王老吉广东凉茶颗粒	〈中医药〉Wanglaoji Guangdong Liangcha Keli; Wanglaoji Cool Tea Granule
王爷	〈古〉wangye; his (or your) royal highness
网店	→网上商店
网店店主	online store owner
网格化管理	grid-based Management; latticed management; digital management for a matrix of urban communities
网恋	cyber romance; virtual romance; internet relationship
网络拜年	online new year greeting
网络版权产业	network copyright industry
网络出版	online publishing
网络犯罪	cyber crime; network crime
网络工程师	network engineer
网络构架师	network architect

网络购票系统	online ticket booking/purchasing system; online booking system
网络管理经理	manager of network administration
网络管理员	webmaster; network administrator
网络规划设计师	network planning designer
网络祭扫服务	〈防疫〉online tomb-sweeping services
网络经济	cyber economy; internet economy
网络蓝军	Online Blue Army
网络零售商	online retailer
网络软件开发工程师	Internet software engineer
网络摄像机	web cam; IP camera (internet protocol camera)
网络审查	Internet censorship
网络售票	web sales of ticket; Internet ticket sales
网络文学	net literature; online literature
网络信息安全	online information security
网络信息安全工程师	network information security engineer
网络舆情	Internet public opinion
网络主管	network director
网上报名	online registration
网上订餐	online food/meal ordering/booking
网上购票系统	online ticket booking/purchasing system; online booking system
网上购物	shopping online
网上购物狂欢节	online shopping carnival
网上交易平台	online trading platform
网上金融服务	Internet financial service
网上就业服务	〈防疫〉online recruitment services
网上跨境贸易	cross-border online trade
网上零售平台	online retail platform
网上商城	online shopping mall
网上商店	online store; online shop; e-shop
网上社区	online community
网上食物配送	online food delivery
网上世博会	Expo (Shanghai) online

网上书店	online bookstore
网上丝绸之路	online Silk Road
网上限时抢购	online flash sale
网上行政	online administration
网上银行	online bank
网上支付	online payment
网页设计大赛	web page design competition
网瘾	Internet addiction
网油包鸡肝	〈饮食〉Frittered Paupiette of Chicken Livers with Lard
网游监护	online guardianship
网约车服务	online car-hailing service; online ride-hailing service
网约车平台	online car-hailing platform; online ride-hailing platform
网站编辑	web editor; website editor
网站架构设计师	web architecture designer
网站维护工程师	web maintenance engineer
网站营运经理	web operations manager
网站营运主管	web operations supervisor
网站营运专员	web operations specialist
往返票	round-trip ticket
忘我精神	spirit of self-sacrifice
旺销季节	peak sales period; peak selling period
望络脉	〈中医药〉inspection of the collateral/the network vessels
望诊	〈中医药〉visual examination; inspection of illness symptom (including the patient's complexion, tongue, expression, behavior, etc.)
望子成龙	to hold high hopes for one's child
危房[楼]	dilapidated house; building in a state of disrepair
危房改造	dilapidated housing renovation; to renovate dilapidated housing
危改	→危房改造

危机感	crisis awareness; sense of emergency
危险建筑物［楼房］	dangerous building; decrepit house
威灵仙	〈中医药〉(of Latin) Radix Clematidis; Chinese Clematis Root
微博	Weibo; micro-blog
微博账号	Weibo account; micro-blog account
微脉	〈中医药〉faint pulse
微笑服务	service with a smile
微信公众号	public Wechat account
微信钱包	WeChat wallet
微信群	WeChat group
微信消息	WeChat message
微信用户	WeChat user
微信账号	WeChat account
微信支付	WeChat pay
微型企业	micro-sized enterprise
煨	〈饮食〉to cook over a slow fire; to braise; to stew
煨氽里脊黄瓜	〈饮食〉Pork Fillet and Cucumber Soup; Poached Tenderloin Slices and Cucumber Soup
煨氽羊肉片黄瓜	〈饮食〉Stewed Poached Lamb Slices and Cucumber
煨昆仑豆腐	〈饮食〉Stewed Bean Curd and Fish Mousse Potage
违法分包	illegal subcontracting
违法占用土地	illegal appropriation of farmland
违反合同	breach of contract
违约罚金	penalty for breach of contracts; default fine
围刺法	〈中医药〉encircling needling
围垦造田	to enclose tideland for cultivation; to reclaim land from marshes
围棋	weiqi; go game (a game played with black and white pieces on a board of 361 crosses) →弈
围着锅［灶］台转	to be tied to the kitchen sink
唯利是图	to be bent solely on profit; to put profit first; mercenary

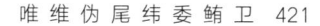

唯论文论	paper-centric
维护市场公平竞争	to protect fair competition in the market
维权	to protect rights; to safeguard rights
维修工程师	maintenance engineer
维修机械师	maintenance technician
伪军	〈旧〉puppet troop
伪君子	hypocrite; a wolf in sheep's clothing
尾巴工程	tail construction (project with a small part remaining unfinished for a long time)
纬编针织物	weft-knitted fabric
纬帽	weft hat; brimless cap (a summer hat of the Qing Dynasty)
纬平针织物	plain knit fabric
委陵菜	〈中医药〉(of Latin) Potentillae Chinensis; Chinese Silverweed
委培	to consign the training of personnel to a certain school
委阳	〈中医药〉Weiyang acupoint; Bend Yang; Gathered Yang (BL39)
委中	〈中医药〉Weizhong acupoint; Bend-Center; Gathered Brume (BL40)
鲔鱼松饼	〈饮食〉Tuna Pancake; Tuna Muffin
卫气不固	〈中医药〉defensive qi instability; defensive-energy failing to protect the body
卫生瓷器	〈陶瓷〉sanitary porcelain
卫生机构	〈防疫〉health institution
卫生检疫	〈防疫〉health quarantine
卫生系统	〈防疫〉health system
卫生员	health worker; (of an army) corpsman
卫星导航	satellite navigation
卫星导航产业	satellite navigation industry
卫星电视	satellite television
卫星电视频道	satellite TV channel
卫星电视台	satellite TV station

卫星镇	satellite town
为…筹资	to pool resources for sb./sth.
为国争光	to win honors for one's country
为世界公共卫生事业做贡献	〈防疫〉to contribute to safeguarding global public health
未病先防	〈中医药〉to take preventive measures before the occurrence of disease
未发酵茶	non-fermented tea
未来学家	futurologist; futurist
味美思酒	Vermouth wine
畏恶风寒	〈中医药〉aversion to wind and cold
畏寒喜热	〈中医药〉aversion to cold and preference for heat
胃不和	〈中医药〉discomfort in stomach; disharmony of stomach
胃仓	〈中医药〉Weicang acupoint; Stomach Granary (BL50)
胃寒肠热	〈中医药〉stomach cold and intestinal heat
胃火炽盛	〈中医药〉exuberance of stomach fire; intense stomach fire
胃火炽盛证	〈中医药〉pattern of exuberant/intense stomach fire
胃火燔龈证	〈中医药〉pattern of stomach fire inflaming gums
胃津	〈中医药〉stomach fluid
胃康灵胶囊	〈中医药〉Weikangling Jiaonang; Stomach Recovery Capsule
胃乃安胶囊	〈中医药〉Weinai'an Jiaonang; Stomach Peace Capsule
胃内泛酸	〈中医药〉acid regurgitation; acid upflow in the stomach
胃气不降	〈中医药〉failure of stomach-qi to descend; non-down bearing of stomach-qi
胃气上逆	〈中医药〉adverse rising of stomach-qi; abnormal flow of stomach-qi
胃气上逆证	〈中医药〉pattern of stomach-qi ascending counterflow

胃气虚	〈中医药〉deficiency of stomach-qi; stomach-qi deficiency
胃气虚证	〈中医药〉stomach-qi deficiency pattern; pattern of stomach-qi vacuity
胃热肠寒	〈中医药〉stomach heat and intestinal cold
胃热消谷	〈中医药〉stomach heat with swift digestion; stomach heat accelerating digestion
胃俞	〈中医药〉Weishu acupoint; Stomach Transport (BL21)
胃苏颗粒冲剂	〈中医药〉Weisu Keli; Granule for Harmonizing Stomach-Qi and Alleviating Pain
胃疼宁片	〈中医药〉Weitengning Pian; Stomachache Calmness Tablet
胃脘下俞	〈中医药〉Weiwan Xiashu acupoint; Lower Transport of Stomach Duct (EX-B3)
胃喜润恶燥	〈中医药〉stomach preferring moistness to dryness; stomach being more adaptable to moistness than dryness
胃虚	〈中医药〉gastric asthenia; stomach deficiency
胃益胶囊	〈中医药〉Weiyi Jiaonang; Stomach Benefiting/Tonifying Capsule
胃阴虚	〈中医药〉deficiency of stomach-yin; stomach-yin deficiency
胃阴虚证	〈中医药〉stomach-yin deficiency pattern; pattern of stomach-yin vacuity
胃燥津伤证	〈中医药〉pattern of fluid injury due to stomach dryness
胃主受纳	〈中医药〉stomach governing intake (of food and drink)
慰安站	〈旧〉comfort station (for invading Japanese troops)
温饱工程	Adequate Food and Clothing Program
《温病条辨》	〈中医药〉*Wenbing Tiaobian*; *Systematized Identification of Warm (Pathogen) Diseases*; *Detailed Analysis of Epidemic Warm Diseases* (by Wu Tang in the Qing Dynasty)

温病学	〈中医药〉study on warm disease; science of epidemic febrile disease
温病学派	〈中医药〉school of warm diseases; sect of epidemic febrile diseases
温补脾胃	〈中医药〉to warm and tonify the spleen and stomach; to warmly invigorate the spleen and stomach
温补脾阳	〈中医药〉to warmly invigorate spleen yang; to warm and supplement spleen yang
温补肾阳	〈中医药〉to warmly invigorate/recuperate kidney yang; to warm and supplement kidney yang
温补心肺	〈中医药〉to warmly invigorate the heart and lung; to warm and supplement the heart and lung
温补心阳	〈中医药〉to warmly invigorate heart yang; to warm and supplement heart yang
温胆汤	〈中医药〉Wendan Tang; Gallbladder-Warming Decoction
温肺散寒	〈中医药〉to warm the lung for dispelling cold
温和灸	〈中医药〉gentle moxibustion; mild-warm moxibustion
温化寒痰	〈中医药〉to warm and transform cold-phlegm; to warmly resolve cold-phlegm
温化水湿剂	〈中医药〉formula for warmly resolving watery dampness
温经活血	〈中医药〉to warm channel to activate blood circulation
温经散寒	〈中医药〉to warm channel for dispelling cold; to warm meridians to dissipate cold
温经散寒剂	〈中医药〉formula for warming the channel and dispersing cold
温经汤	〈中医药〉Wenjing Tang; Menses-Warming Decoction; Decoction for Warming Channels
温经止血	〈中医药〉to warm channel for stopping/arresting bleeding

温灸器灸	〈中医药〉moxa burner moxibustion; moxibustion with moxibustioner
温酒	to keep the wine warm; to heat wine; to warm wine
温酒煮茶	to heat wine and brew a pot of tea
温开剂	〈中医药〉warm formula for resuscitation
温里法	〈中医药〉interior-warming method
温里剂	〈中医药〉cold-dispelling formula; interior-warming formula
温脾汤	〈中医药〉Wenpi Tang; Spleen-Warming Decoction; Decoction for Warming the Spleen
温清并用	〈中医药〉to use warming and heat-clearing simultaneously
温肾健脾	〈中医药〉to warm the kidney and fortify/strengthen the spleen
温肾散寒	〈中医药〉to warm the kidney for dispelling cold
温通小肠	〈中医药〉to warmly dredge the small intestine
温胃散寒	〈中医药〉to warm the stomach for dispelling cold
温胃舒颗粒	〈中医药〉Wenweishu Keli; Stomach-Warming Comfortability Granule
温下剂	〈中医药〉warm-purgative formula; warm-cathartic formula
温阳行气	〈中医药〉to warm yang for activating qi-flowing
温阳化饮	〈中医药〉to warm yang for resolving fluid retention
温阳利水	〈中医药〉to warm yang for diuresis; to warm yang and disinhibit water
温阳散寒	〈中医药〉to warm yang for dispelling cold
温阳通便	〈中医药〉to warm yang for relaxing bowels
温阳益气	〈中医药〉to warm yang for benefiting qi
温养脏腑	〈中医药〉to warm and nourish the viscera
《温疫论》	〈中医药〉*Wenyi Lun*; *Treatise on Pestilence*; *On Plague Diseases* (by Wu Youxing in the Ming Dynasty)

温燥化痰剂	〈中医药〉formula for resolving phlegm with warm drugs
温燥证	〈中医药〉warm-dryness pattern
温针灸	〈中医药〉warm needling; acupuncture with needle warmed by moxa
温中散寒	〈中医药〉to warm the middle energizer to dissipate cold; to warm spleen and stomach for dispelling cold
温中散寒剂	〈中医药〉formula for warming the interior and dispersing cold
瘟毒下注证	〈中医药〉pattern of virulent heat invading downward
瘟疫	〈中医药〉pestilence; epidemic infectious disease
文案	official documents and correspondence; copywriting
文案指导	copywriter director
文本短信服务	Short Message Service; SMS
文档工程师	document engineer
文工团	song and dance ensemble; art troupe; cultural trope
文化产业	culture industry
文化冲击	culture shock
文化底蕴	cultural deposits
文化旅游	culture-oriented travel
文化渗透	cultural infiltration
文化体制改革	cultural restructuring; reform of cultural administrative system
文化之旅	cultural tour
文化专员	culture specialist; cultural attaché
文君酒	Wenjun liquor
文君嫩绿	〈茶〉Wenjun Tender Green tea
文明礼貌月	Ethics and Courtesy Month
文明社区	model community; civilized community
文明行车	courteous driving

文凭主义	credentialism; diplomaism
文体委员	recreation & sports secretary
文物保护	protection of cultural relics; preservation of historical relics
文言文	classical Chinese; classical Chinese language (the literary language used in ancient China and preserved today for formal occasion or conspicuous display)
文娱委员	commissary in charge of entertainment
文字处理操作员	word-processing operator
闻诊	〈中医药〉listening and smelling examination; auscultation and olfaction inspection
稳心颗粒	〈中医药〉Wenxin Keli; Heart-Calming Granule
问责风暴	accountability furor; liability storm
窝里斗	internecine struggle; infighting
窝窝头	steamed corn bun; steamed bread of corn
渥堆普洱	〈茶〉pile-fermented Pu'er
乌鸡白凤丸	〈中医药〉Wuji Baifeng Wan; White Phoenix Bolus of Black-Bone Chicken; Black Chicken and White Phoenix Pill
乌角巾	→东坡[乌角]巾
乌龙茶	Oolong tea
乌龙面	〈饮食〉Seafood Noodles
乌梅	〈中医药〉(of Latin) Fructus Mume; Smoked Plum
乌梅丸	〈中医药〉Wumei Wan; Fructus Mume Pill
乌纱帽	black gauze cap (referring to an official position)
乌梢蛇	〈中医药〉(of Latin) Zaocys; Black-Tail Snake
乌蛇止痒丸	〈中医药〉Wushe Zhiyang Wan; Black Snake Itching-Stopping Pill
乌头	〈中医药〉(of Latin) Radix Aconiti; Rhizome of Chinese Monkshood
乌药	〈中医药〉(of Latin) Radix Linderae; Combined Spicebush Root

乌鱼蛋汤	〈饮食〉Cuttlefish Roe Soup with Ginger Juice and White Pepper
污水处理	〈防疫〉sewage disposal
污水处理工程师	sewage treatment engineer
屋顶花园	roof garden
无本地新增病例	〈防疫〉to report no domestic cases; to record no locally transmitted infections
无偿献血	blood donation without compensation
无尘粉笔	dust-free chalk; dustless chalk
无党派人士	non-party personage; independent politician; non-partisan politician
无风不起浪	there are no waves without wind; there's no smoke without fire
无公害蔬菜	green vegetable; pollution-free vegetable
无领满襟衣	〈土家族〉collarless jacket with full front lapel
无人机	→无人驾驶飞机
无人驾驶飞机	unmanned aerial vehicle; push-button plane; pilotless aircraft
无人售票	self-service ticketing; one-man operation; driver-only operation
无土栽培	soilless cultivation; aeroponics or hydroponics
无为而治	to govern by doing nothing that is against nature; to govern by non-interference
无息贷款	interest-free loan
无锡毫茶	Wuxi Green Pekoe
无现金支付	cashless payment
无现金支付平台	cashless payment platform
无线通信工程师	wireless communication engineer
无线支付	wireless payment
无形资产	intangible assets
无性生殖法	asexual reproduction; agamogenesis
无袖旗袍	sleeveless cheongsam
无烟奥运	smoke-free Olympics
无烟工业	smokeless industry

无烟环境	smoke-free environment
无烟区	no-smoking area
无釉陶	〈陶瓷〉unglazed pottery
无症状病例	〈防疫〉asymptomatic case
无症状的潜伏期	〈防疫〉silent/asymptomatic incubation period
无症状感染者	〈防疫〉asymptomatic case; asymptomatic inflection of COVID-19 patient
无症状感染者精准防控	〈防疫〉targeted management of asymptomatic cases
无症状携带者	〈防疫〉asymptomatic virus carrier
无中生有	to make/create sth. out of nothing; ex nihilo
吴茱萸	〈中医药〉(of Latin) Fructus Evodiae; Medicinal Evodia Fruit
吴茱萸汤	〈中医药〉Wuzhuyu Tang; Evodia Decoction
蜈蚣	〈中医药〉(of Latin) Scolopendra; Centipede
五保户	household enjoying the five guarantees (childless and infirm old persons who are guarateed food, clothing, medical care, housing and burial expenses)
五倍子	〈中医药〉(of Latin) Galla Chinensis; Chinese Gall
五彩福禄寿人物观音瓶	〈陶瓷〉multicolored Guanyin vase with Fortune-Longevity Immortals pattern (Qing Kangxi period)
五彩胡人献宝纹玉壶春瓶	〈陶瓷〉multicolored Yuhuchun vase with a pattern of Huns presenting treasures (Qing Kangxi period)
五彩花卉龙纹花觚	〈陶瓷〉multicolored wine vessel with dragon and floral pattern (Ming Wanli period)
五彩花鸟纹瓶	〈陶瓷〉polychrome vase with flower and bird pattern (Qing Kangxi period)
五彩酱鹅肝	〈饮食〉Goose Livers with White Gourd
五彩龙凤海水花卉纹觚	〈陶瓷〉multicolored wine vessel with dragon, phoenix and seawater floral pattern (Ming Wanli period)
五彩龙纹棒槌瓶	〈陶瓷〉multicolored mallet-shaped vase with dragon pattern (Qing Kangxi period)

五彩镂空云凤纹瓷瓶	〈陶瓷〉polychrome hollow engraving vase with cloud and phoenix pattern
五彩盆	〈陶瓷〉polychrome basin; colorful pot
五彩人物盘	〈陶瓷〉multicolored plate with figural depiction pattern (Qing Kangxi period)
五彩人物长颈瓶	〈陶瓷〉multicolored long-necked vase with figural depiction pattern (Qing Kangxi period)
五彩诗文花卉纹盘	〈陶瓷〉multicolored plate with verse and floral pattern (Ming Tianqi period)
五彩四妃十六子纹罐	〈陶瓷〉multicolored jar with four concubines and sixteen sons pattern (Qing Kangxi period)
五彩燕窝	〈饮食〉Bird's Nest in Five Colors
五彩鱼藻纹盖罐	〈陶瓷〉polychrome lidded jar with fish and seaweed pattern (Ming Jiajing period)
五彩鸳鸯莲池蒜头瓶	〈陶瓷〉polychrome garlic-shaped vase with a pattern of mandarin ducks in lotus pond (Ming Wanli period)
五彩云凤纹葫芦瓶	〈陶瓷〉polychrome gourd-shaped vase with cloud and phoenix pattern (Ming Wanli period)
五彩云龙纹大盘	〈陶瓷〉large multicolored plate with clouds and dragons pattern (Qing Kangxi period)
五刺	〈中医药〉five needling methods; five techniques of needling
五大官窑	〈陶瓷〉five great kilns (including Jun Kiln, Ru Kiln, Guan Kiln, Ding Kiln and Ge Kiln in the Song Dynasty)
五福化毒丸	〈中医药〉Wufu Huadu Wan; Five Happinesses Toxin-Transforming Pill
五谷虫	〈中医药〉(of Latin) Larva Chrysomyiae ; Screwworm
五花肉炖萝卜皮	〈饮食〉Braised Streaky Pork with Turnip Peel
五积散	〈中医药〉Wuji San; Five-Accumulation Powder
五加草虫口服液	〈中医药〉Wujia Caochong Koufuye; Wilsonii and Pilose Antler Blood Oral Liquid

五加皮	〈中医药〉(of Latin) Cortex Acanthopanax Radicis; Acanthopanax Bark
五加皮(药)酒	〈中医药〉Wu-Chia-Pee Liquor; Cortex Periplocae Liquor
五粮液酒	Wuliangye liquor
五灵脂	〈中医药〉(of Latin) Faeces Togopteri; Flying Squirrel's Droppings
五苓散	〈中医药〉Wuling San; Poria Five Powder
五熘鲩鱼[草鱼]	〈饮食〉Poached Grass Carp with Sweet-Sour Sauce
五柳菜	〈饮食〉Five-Color Pickles; Five Kinds of Salted Shredded Vegetables with Sugar in Rice Vinegar
五柳料	〈饮食〉five-color aromatics
五皮饮	〈中医药〉Wupi Yin; Five-Peel Beverage
五禽戏	five-animal exercises; five mimic-animal exercises (imitating the movements of tiger, deer, bear, ape and bird)
五仁大包	〈饮食〉Steamed Bun Stuffed with Semen Juglandis, Almond, Pine Kernel, Peanut and Guaren
五仁润肠丸	〈中医药〉Wuren Runchang Wan; Five Seeds Pill for Smoothing Intestines
五色带	〈中医药〉five-colored vaginal discharge
五山盖米茶	Wugaishan Rice tea
《五十二病方》	〈中医药〉*52 Bing Fang*; *Prescriptions for Fifty-two Diseases* (unearthed medical book from Mawangdui Tombs of the Han Dynasty)
五枢	〈中医药〉Wushu acupoint; Fifth Pivot (GB27)
五输配穴法	〈中医药〉five-shu acupoints combination/association combination of five-transport acupoints
五输穴	〈中医药〉Wushu acupoint; Five Transport Points
五丝白菜卷	〈饮食〉Braised Chinese Cabbage Rolls with Five Kinds of Shredded Vegetables
五四青年学生服	May 4th youth student uniform →青年装[服]
五味豆腐	〈饮食〉Five-Flavored Tofu; Multi-Flavored Tofu
五味九孔	〈饮食〉Fresh Abalone in Spicy Sauce

五味酒	punch wine
五味牛腱	〈饮食〉Multi-Spiced Beef Shank
五味消毒饮	〈中医药〉Wuwei Xiaodu Yin; Five-Ingredient Toxin-Dispersing Beverage; Antiphlogistic Decoction of Five Drugs
五味子	〈中医药〉(of Latin) Fructus Schisandrae Chinensis; Chinese Magnoliavine Fruit
五味子糖浆	〈中医药〉Wuweizi Tangjiang; Schisandra Fruit Syrup
五香茶叶蛋	〈饮食〉Tea Flavored Boiled Eggs
五香脆鳝	〈饮食〉Stir-Fried Shredded Eel with Spicy Sauce
五香大排	〈饮食〉Spiced Pork Ribs
五香鸡	〈饮食〉Spiced Chicken; Multi-Flavored Chicken
五香牛肉	〈饮食〉Spiced Beef; Spicy Roast Beef
五香树菇	〈饮食〉Spiced Tea Tree Mushrooms
五香水鸭	〈饮食〉Braised Spiced Wild Duck Served with Bean Curd Cake
五香兔肉	〈饮食〉Spicy-Braised Hare Slices
五香熏干	〈饮食〉Spiced Smoked Dried Tofu
五香熏鱼	〈饮食〉Spiced Smoked Fish
五香芸豆	〈饮食〉Spiced Kidney Beans
五心	〈中医药〉five centers (palms, soles and chest)
五心烦热	〈中医药〉feverish sensation over the five centers; dysphoria with feverish sensation in chest, palms and soles
五行	〈中医药〉five elements; five phases (water, fire, wood, metal, soil)
五行相乘	〈中医药〉overwhelming among the five phases; over-restriction among five phases
五行相克	〈中医药〉mutual restriction among five elements; generation-inhibition in five elements
五行相生	〈中医药〉mutual generation among five elements
五行相侮	〈中医药〉rebellion/counter-restriction among five phases

五行学说	〈中医药〉theory of five elements; five phases theory
五叶神香烟	Wuye Shen cigarettes; Five Leaves cigarettes
五铢(钱)	〈币〉wuzhu coin; five-zhu coin (issued in the Han Dynasty)
五子衍宗丸	〈中医药〉Wuzi Yanzong Wan; Five-Seed Progeny Pill
武打片	kung fu film; martial arts movie; Chinese swordplay movie
武大郎烧[炊]饼	〈饮食〉Wu Dalang Sesame (Seed) Pancake
武冠	〈古〉crown/hat of military official
武陵酒	Wuling liquor
武侠小说	tales of roving knights; martial arts novel; kung fu novel
武夷茶	Bohea tea
武夷岩茶	Wuyi rock tea; Mt. Wuyi's cliff-grown tea
舞蹈编剧	choreographer
舞台监督	stage manager
舞台主任	stage performance supervisor
舞台总监	stage performance director
舞厅服务员	stage attendant
务工人员安全返岗	〈防疫〉migrant workers return to their posts in security
务虚会	theory-discussing meeting
物流经理	logistics manager
物流师职业资格证书	certificate of international logistics specialist
物流主管	logistics supervisor
物流总监	logistics director
物美价廉	to be affordable but of very high quality; reliable and affordable; nice and cheap
物业公司	property management company
物业顾问	property consultant; property advisor
物业管理	estate management; property management
物业管理经理	property management manager

物业管理师	property manager
物业维修人员	property maintenance personnel/staff
物质鼓励	material encouragement
物质文明	material progress; material civilization
物资平衡	balance in the supply and demand of goods and materials

X

夕阳产业	sunset industry
西餐部	western restaurant department
西餐部经理	western restaurant manager
西餐厨师长	chef of western kitchen; western chef
西电东送	to transmit the electricity from western areas to East China; West-East power transmission project
西凤酒	Hsi Feng chiew; Xifeng liquor
西瓜霜润喉片	〈中医药〉Xiguashuang Runhou Pian; Watermelon Frost Lozenge
西汉半两	〈币〉banliang coin/half a tael of the Western Han Dynasty
西汉早期青瓷俑	〈陶瓷〉celadon figurine of the Early Western Han Dynasty
西河柳	〈中医药〉(of Latin) Cacumen Tamaricis; Chinese Tamarisk Twig
西红花	〈中医药〉(of Latin) Stigma Croci; Saffron
西红柿炒蛋	〈饮食〉Scrambled Eggs with Tomato
西红柿鸡蛋汤	〈饮食〉Tomato and Egg Soup with Onion and Ketchup
西湖绸伞	West Lake silk umbrella
西湖醋鱼	〈饮食〉Steamed Grass Carp in Vinegar Gravy; West Lake Fish in Vinegar Gravy
西湖龙井	〈茶〉West Lake Longjing tea
西湖牛肉羹	〈饮食〉West Lake Beef Soup; West Lake Beef Chowder
西兰花炒鸡片	〈饮食〉Stir-Fried Chicken Slices with Broccoli

西兰花炒牛柳	〈饮食〉Stir-Fried Beef Fillets with Broccoli
西兰花炒鳕鱼球	〈饮食〉Stir-Fried Codfish Balls with Broccoli
西兰卡普	〈服饰〉(of Tujia ethnic group) Xilan Kapu brocade
西柠百花鲜鱿	〈饮食〉Deep-Fried Squid with Minced Shrimps in Lemon Sauce
西气东输	to transmit natural gas from western areas to East China; West-East natural gas transmission project
西芹百合	〈饮食〉Stir-Fried Lily Bulbs and Celery
西芹腰果鸡球	〈饮食〉Stir-Fried Chicken Balls with Celery and Cashew Kernels
西蜀豆花	〈饮食〉Braised Tofu with Peanuts and Pickles
西夏王冰白	〈酒〉Xixia King ice white wine
西夏王干红	〈酒〉Xixia King dry red wine
西夏王葡萄酒	Xixia King wine
西夏王世纪	〈酒〉Xixia King red wine
西洋菜街	Sai Yeung Choi Street (Hong Kong); West Ocean Vegetable Street
西洋参	〈中医药〉(of Latin) Radix Panacis Quinquefolii; American Ginseng
西柚汁	〈饮食〉grapefruit juice
吸二手烟	second hand smoking
吸烟所致疾病	tobacco-related disease
息风定痫	〈中医药〉to arrest epilepsy by calming endogenous wind
息风解痉	〈中医药〉to relieve spasm by calming endogenous wind
息事宁人	to patch up a quarrel and reconcile the parties concerned; to pour oil on troubled waters
稀露鱼肚	〈饮食〉Stewed Fish Maws in Chicken Broth
犀角地黄汤	〈中医药〉Xijiao Dihuang Tang; Rhinoceros Horn and Rehmannia Decoction
锡釉陶	〈陶瓷〉majolica; faience
溪布街	Xibu Street (folk shopping boutique street of west Hu'nan)

溪黄草	〈中医药〉Herba Rabdosiae Serrae; Linearstripe Rabdosia Herb
熙春茶	hyson tea; young hyson
豨莶草	〈中医药〉(of Latin) Herba Siegesbeckiae; Siegesbeckia Herb
膝关	〈中医药〉Xiguan acupoint; Knee Joint (LR7)
膝内	〈中医药〉Xinei acupoint; Inner Knee (EX-LE3)
膝眼	〈中医药〉Xiyan acupoint; Knee Eyes (EX-LE5)
膝阳关	〈中医药〉Xiyangguan acupoint; Knee Yang Joint (GB33)
习酒	Xijiu liquor
洗儿钱	〈古〉money gifted by relatives and friends to new babies
洗耳疗法	〈中医药〉ear-washing therapy
洗脑	brainwashing; brainwash
洗手液	〈防疫〉hand sanitizer; liquid soap
洗衣房经理	laundry manager
洗衣房主管	laundry supervisor
《洗冤录》	〈中医药〉*Xiyuan Lu*; *Records for Washing Away Wrong Cases/Injustice* (by Song Ci in the Southern Song Dynasty)
喜酒	wedding wine; wedding banquet
喜怒伤气	〈中医药〉excessive joy and anger impairing qi
喜忧参半	mingled hope and fear; bittersweet; mixed blessing
喜则气缓	〈中医药〉excessive joy leading to qi loose
喜洲粑粑	〈饮食〉Xizhou Crisp Pie
喜字饼	〈饮食〉Steamed Bun Stuffed with Jujube Paste (patterned with a Chinese character Xi)
戏剧总监	theatrical director
戏衣	stage costume; traditional opera clothes/clothing
系统操作员	system operator
系统程序员	system programmer
系统工程师	system engineer

系统集成工程师	system integration engineer
系统架构设计师	system architecture designer
系主任	(of a university) head/chair/chairman of the department
细瓷	〈陶瓷〉fine china; porcelain of superior quality
细脉	〈中医药〉thready pulse; fine pulse
细嫩	〈茶〉fine and tender
细纹丝帛	fine silk (product)
细小	〈茶〉fine and small
细辛	〈中医药〉(of Latin) Herba Asari; Manchurian Wildginger
细圆	〈茶〉fine and round
细直	〈茶〉fine and straight
虾炒面	〈饮食〉Stir-Fried Noodles with Shrimps
虾酱炒鸡蛋	〈饮食〉Scrambled Eggs with Shrimp Paste
虾龙糊	〈饮食〉Prawns in Thick Soup; Stir-Fried Shrimp Paste in Lobster Sauce
虾米粉丝煲	〈饮食〉Stewed Bean Vermicelli with Dried Shrimps in Clay Pot
虾片	〈饮食〉Prawn Crackers
虾球	〈饮食〉Shrimp Balls
虾球清汤面	〈饮食〉Noodle Soup with Shrimp Balls; Noodles with Shrimp Balls in Clear Soup
虾仁炒饭	〈饮食〉Stir-Fried Rice with Shrimps
虾仁扒豆腐	〈饮食〉Stewed Shelled Shrimps with Bean Curd
虾仁跑蛋	〈饮食〉Omelette with Shelled Shrimps
虾仁水饺	〈饮食〉Jiaozi/Dumplings Stuffed with Shrimps and Vegetables
虾仁汤面	〈饮食〉Noodle Soup with Shrimps; Noodles with Shrimps in Soup
虾仁鱼翅	〈饮食〉Braised Shark's Fins with Shelled Shrimps
虾仁鱼肚	〈饮食〉Stir-Fried Fish Maws with Shelled Shrimps
虾肉炒年糕	〈饮食〉Stir-Fried Rice Cakes with Shrimps
虾圆玉子豆腐	〈饮食〉Steamed Tofu and Shrimps

虾仔烧海参		〈饮食〉Braised Sea Cucumbers with Shrimp Roe
虾枣鱼丸豆腐煲		〈饮食〉Stewed Seafood and Tofu in Casserole
虾子大乌参		〈饮食〉Braised Black Sea Slugs with Shrimp Roe
虾子冬笋		〈饮食〉Stir-Fried Winter Bamboo Shoots with Shrimp Roe
虾子姜葱捞面		〈饮食〉Noodles with Ginger and Green Onion
虾子烧素		〈饮食〉Braised Shrimps with Vegetables
虾子蹄筋		〈饮食〉Braised Shrimp Roe with Pork Tendon
虾子鱼肚		〈饮食〉Stewed Fish Maws with Shrimp Roe
虾籽炒豆腐		〈饮食〉Stir-Fried Tofu with Shrimp Roe
峡州碧峰		〈茶〉Xiazhou Bifeng Bud tea
霞帔		〈古服饰〉xiapi; shawl (a scarf over ceremonial robe for noble ladies); embroidered vest
下不为例		not to be taken as a precedent; not to be repeated
下耳根		〈中医药〉Xia'ergen acupoint; Lower Ear Root (R3)
下关		〈中医药〉Xiaguan acupoint; Lower Pass/Joint (ST7)
下合穴		〈中医药〉Xiahe acupoint; Lower Joint of the Six Bowels; Lower Confluent Acupoint
下焦		〈中医药〉lower warmer/burner; lower energizer
下焦湿热		〈中医药〉dampness-heat in lower burner; lower energizer dampness-heat
下焦湿热证		〈中医药〉pattern of dampness-heat in lower energizer
下焦穴		〈中医药〉Xiajiao acupoints; Lower Burner/Energizer points
下巨虚		〈中医药〉Xiajuxu acupoint; Lower Great Hollow (ST39)
下马酒		〈蒙古族〉down horse wine
下损及上		〈中医药〉deficiency transmitted from lower body to upper body
下脘		〈中医药〉Xiawan acupoint; Lower Stomach Duct (CV10)
下乡		〈旧〉to go down to the countryside; to rusticate
下元不固		→肾气「下元」不固

夏布	grass cloth; grass linen
夏朝冠	summer crown (used in the Qing Dynasty)
夏枯草	〈中医药〉(of Latin) Spica Prunellae; Common Self-heal Fruit-Spike
夏天无	〈中医药〉(of Latin) Rhizoma Corydalis Decumbentis; Decumbent Corydalis Tuber
夏威夷木瓜炖翅	〈饮食〉Stewed Shark's Fin with Hawaiian Papaya
仙方活命饮	〈中医药〉Xianfang Huoming Yin; Immortal Formula Life-Giving Beverage; Fairy Decoction for Treating Cutaneoius Infections
仙鹤草	〈中医药〉(of Latin) Herba Agrimoniae; Hairyvein Agrimonia Herb
仙茅	〈中医药〉(of Latin) Rhizoma Curculigins; Common Curculigo Rhizome
仙女牌香烟	Xiannü cigarettes; Victory cigarettes
仙人掌茶	cactus-like green tea
先富带后富	the rich first pushing those being rich later
先积累后消费	accumulation before consumption
先进班集体	advanced class
先进个人	advanced individual; outstanding student
先进工作者	advanced worker
先天之精	〈中医药〉prenatal essence; congenital essence; innate essence
先下手为强	to catch the ball before the bound
鲜纯	〈茶〉fresh and pure
鲜醇	〈茶〉fresh and mellow
鲜菇炒大虾	〈饮食〉Stir-Fried Prawns with Fresh Mushrooms
鲜菇炒牛肉	〈饮食〉Stir-Fried Beef with Fresh Mushrooms
鲜菇炒虾球	〈饮食〉Stir-Fried Shrimp Balls with Fresh Mushrooms
鲜菇烩鸭舌	〈饮食〉Stewed Duck Tongue with Fresh Mushrooms
鲜菇扒菜胆	〈饮食〉Braised Vegetables with Mushrooms

鲜果馅汤圆	〈饮食〉Fruit-Stuffed Tangyuan; Glutinous Rice Balls Stuffed with Fruit
鲜果香槟骨	〈饮食〉Spare Ribs with Champagne and Fresh Fruit
鲜果玉带虾	〈饮食〉Stir-Fried Shrimps and Scallops with Fresh Fruit
鲜活商品	fresh goods
鲜菌鱼头汤	〈饮食〉Fish Head Soup with Fresh Mushrooms
鲜莲鸡丁	〈饮食〉Stir-Fried Diced Chicken with Lotus Seeds
鲜莲鸭羹	〈饮食〉Duck and Lotus Seeds Soup
鲜灵	〈茶〉fresh lovely
鲜蘑包公鸡	〈饮食〉Braised Chicken with Fresh Mushrooms
鲜蘑炒蜜豆	〈饮食〉Stir-Fried Mushrooms and Sweetened Kidney Beans
鲜奶馒头	〈饮食〉Milk Mantou; Steamed Bun made with Milk
鲜嫩	〈茶〉fresh and tender
鲜柠檬烤鸡	〈饮食〉Baked/Roasted Capon with Fresh Lemon
鲜浓	〈茶〉fresh and heavy
鲜藕夹心肉	〈饮食〉Frittered Lotus Root with Pork Meat Stuffing
鲜人参煲老鸭	〈饮食〉Stewed Duck with Fresh Ginseng
鲜人参炖土鸡	〈饮食〉Braised Chicken with Fresh Ginseng
鲜肉水饺	〈饮食〉Jiaozi/Dumplings Stuffed with Minced Pork
鲜肉云吞面	〈饮食〉Noodle Soup with Pork Wonton
鲜爽	〈茶〉fresh and brisk
鲜甜	〈茶〉fresh and sweet
鲜豌豆炒河虾仁	〈饮食〉Stir-Fried Shelled Shrimps with Fresh Beans
鲜虾炒饭	〈饮食〉Stir-Fried Rice with Fresh Shrimps
鲜虾春卷	〈饮食〉Spring Rolls Stuffed with Shrimps
鲜虾烧麦仔	〈饮食〉Shaomai Stuffed with Shrimps
鲜虾生肉包	〈饮食〉Steamed Bun Stuffed with Shrimp and Pork

鲜虾西芹	〈饮食〉Stir-Fried Shrimps with Celery
鲜虾小馄饨	〈饮食〉Shrimp Wonton Soup
弦脉	〈中医药〉stringlike pulse; taut pulse; wiry pulse
咸菜大鳝煲	〈饮食〉Stewed Eel with Preserved Vegetables in Casserole
咸蛋黄炒肉蟹	〈饮食〉Stir-Fried Hard-Shell Crab with Salted Egg Yolk
咸蛋肉饼	〈饮食〉Steamed Minced Pork with Salted Duck Eggs
咸丰通宝	〈币〉coin with characters Xianfeng tongbao (in the Qing Dynasty)
咸丰元宝	〈币〉coin with characters Xianfeng yuanbao (in the Qing Dynasty)
咸花生	〈饮食〉Salted Peanuts; Boiled Peanuts with Salt
咸肉炒饭	〈饮食〉Stir-Fried Rice with Bacon
咸水大虾	〈饮食〉Boiled Prawns with Salt; Salted Prawns
咸水虾	〈饮食〉Boiled Shrimps with Salt; Salted Shrimps
咸水鸭	〈饮食〉Boiled Duck with Salt; Salted Duck
咸水鸭肝	〈饮食〉Boiled Duck Liver with Salt; Salted Duck Liver
咸水羊肉	〈饮食〉Boiled Mutton with Salt; Salted Mutton
咸鸭蛋	〈饮食〉Salted Duck Eggs
咸鱼鸡粒炒饭	〈饮食〉Stir-Fried Rice with Salted Fish and Chicken Cubes
咸鱼鸡粒豆腐煲	〈饮食〉Stewed Tofu with Salted Fish and Diced Chicken in Clay Pot
咸鱼蒸肉饼	〈饮食〉Steamed Pork Meat Pies with Salted Fish Cutlet
嫌贫爱富	to despise the poor and curry favor with the rich
苋菜黄鱼羹	〈饮食〉Amaranth and Yellow Croaker Potage
现场表演	on-the-spot demonstration; live-demonstration
现场应用工程师	field application engineer; FAE
现场直播	live broadcast
现代思潮	modern schools of thought

现代远程教育	modern distance education
现代中药产业化	modern production/industrialization of traditional Chinese medicines
现代综合运输体系	modern integrated transportation system
现钱关子	〈币〉guanzi banknote (issued by the government for merchants to exchange cash in the Southern Song Dynasty)
现身说法	(of Buddhism) power that enables the Buddha to appear in various human forms to give advice to people; to use one's own experience as an object lesson
线上登记失业	〈防疫〉online registration of unemployment
线上零售商	online retailer
线上申领失业保险金	〈防疫〉online application for unemployment security insurance
线上职业技能培训	〈防疫〉online vocational training
陷谷	〈中医药〉Xiangu acupoint; Sunken Valley (ST43)
馅饼	〈饮食〉Stuffed Biscuits; Pie Stuffed with Meat
腺病毒载体疫苗	〈防疫〉adenovirus vector vaccine
乡村小豆腐	〈饮食〉Stir-Fried Tofu with Vegetables
相关性基础疾病	〈防疫〉related primary disease
相火妄动证	〈中医药〉pattern of ministerial fire hyperactivity
相兼脉	〈中医药〉concurrent pulse; combined pulse
相克	〈中医药〉mutual restriction; restriction or checking relation (among five elements)
相亲	blind date (a meeting between a male and female for the purpose of matrimony)
相杀	〈中医药〉mutual detoxication; to counteract the toxicity of another drug
相生	〈中医药〉mutual generation; interpromoting relation (among five elements)
相生相克	〈中医药〉mutual generation and restriction; mutual promotion and restraint among five elements
香薄	〈茶〉thin aroma

香草蒜茸炒鲜蘑	〈饮食〉Stir-Fried Fresh Mushrooms with Minced Garlic and Vanilla
香肠炖排骨	〈饮食〉Stewed Spare Ribs with Sausages
香橙炖官燕	〈饮食〉Braised Bird's Nest in Orange Sauce
香吃茶树菇	〈饮食〉Spicy Tea Tree Mushrooms
香豉牛肉片	〈饮食〉Stir-Fried Sliced Beef and Preserved Beans
香椿炒鸭胗	〈饮食〉Stir-Fried Duck Gizzard with Chinese Toon
香椿豆腐	〈饮食〉Tofu with Chinese Toon
香椿煎蛋	〈饮食〉Fried Eggs with Chopped Chinese Toon Leaves
香葱白果虾	〈饮食〉Stir-Fried Shrimps with Gingko and Scallion
香葱排骨	〈饮食〉Fried Pork Chop with Chive
香葱酥鱼	〈饮食〉Crispy Crucian Carp in Scallion Oil
香醋蟹粉	〈饮食〉Stir-Fried Crab Meat with Vinegar and Parsley
香脆贴饼子	〈饮食〉Crispy Baked Corn Cake
香丹注射液	〈中医药〉Xiangdan Zhusheye; Fragrant Salvia Injection
香雕绍兴酒	Xiangdiao Shaoxing Medium Sweet
香浮	〈茶〉weak aroma
香附子	〈中医药〉(of Latin) Rhizoma Cyperi; Nutgrass Galingale Rhizome; Cyperus Root
香港脚	〈中医药〉athlete's foot (contagious skin infection caused by the ringworm fungi)
香菇炒蟹肉	〈饮食〉Stir-Fried Crab Meat with Savory Mushrooms
香菇鸡肉包	〈饮食〉Steamed Bun Stuffed with Chicken and Savory Mushrooms
香菇鸡丝面	〈饮食〉Noodle Soup with Shredded Chicken and Savory Mushrooms
香菇鸡丝粥	〈饮食〉Congee with Black Mushrooms and Shredded Chicken
香菇牛肉饭	〈饮食〉Rice with Beef and Savory Mushrooms

香菇排骨饭	〈饮食〉	Rice with Spare Ribs and Savory Mushrooms
香菇雪耳烩竹虾	〈饮食〉	Stewed Shrimps with Savory Mushrooms and White Fungi
香菇油菜水饺	〈饮食〉	Jiaozi/Dumplings Stuffed with Mushrooms and Cabbage
香滑鲈鱼球	〈饮食〉	Stir-Fried Perch Balls with Starch and Sugar
香滑芋茸包	〈饮食〉	Steamed Bun Stuffed with Taro
香滑芝麻糊	〈饮食〉	Cream Sesame Paste; Sweetened Sesame Cream
香加皮	〈中医药〉	(of Latin) Cortex Periplocae; Chinese Silkvine Root-Bark
香煎菜肉锅贴	〈饮食〉	Guotie Stuffed with Vegetables and Pork
香煎鹅肝	〈饮食〉	Pan-Fried Goose Livers
香煎腐皮卷	〈饮食〉	Pan-Fried Tofu Sheet Rolls Stuffed with Shrimps
香煎黄金糕	〈饮食〉	Pan-Fried Sponge Cakes
香煎鲫鱼	〈饮食〉	Pan-Fried Crucian Fish with Pepper, Ginger and Celery
香煎韭菜饺	〈饮食〉	Pan-Fried Jiaozi/Dumplings Stuffed with Chinese Chives
香煎萝卜糕	〈饮食〉	Pan-Fried Turnip Cake with Bacon
香煎咸鱼	〈饮食〉	Pan-Fried Salted Fish with Ginger and Chili Sauce
香煎银鳕鱼	〈饮食〉	Pan-Fried Codfish with Soy Sauce
香酱爆鸭丝	〈饮食〉	Stir-Fried Shredded Duck with Soy Sauce
香蕉锅炸	〈饮食〉	Fried Banana Patters
香辣炒板鸭	〈饮食〉	Stir-Fried Pressed Duck with Hot Spicy Sauce
香辣脆鳝	〈饮食〉	Deep-Fried Eel with Chili and Pepper
香辣肚块	〈饮食〉	Stir-Fried Pork Tripe Cubes with Chili
香辣芙蓉鱼	〈饮食〉	Spicy Sliced Fish with Egg White
香辣手撕茄子	〈饮食〉	Hand-Shredded Eggplant with Chili Sauce

香辣虾	〈饮食〉Stir-Fried Shrimps with Hot and Spicy Sauce
香辣(炒)蟹	〈饮食〉Stir-Fried Crab with Hot and Spicy Sauce
香辣猪扒	〈饮食〉Grilled Pork with Spicy Sauce
香连片	〈中医药〉Xianglian Pian; Aucklandia-Coptis Tablet; Costusroot and Coptis Tablet
香连丸	〈中医药〉Xianglian Wan; Aucklandia-Coptis Pill; Costusroot and Coptis Pill
香露炖童鸡	〈饮食〉Braised Spring Chicken in Casserole
香芒烧茄子	〈饮食〉Braised Eggplants with Mango
香蜜橙花骨	〈饮食〉Stir-Fried Spare Ribs in Orange Sauce
香囊	sachet; perfume satchel; incent bag
香浓牛尾汤	〈饮食〉Savory Oxtail Soup
香扒春鸡	〈饮食〉Grilled Spring Chicken; Marinated Chargrilled Spring Chicken
香茜带子饺	〈饮食〉Jiaozi/Dumplings Stuffed with Scallop, Prawn and Coriander
香茜鱼片汤	〈饮食〉Fish Fillets and Coriander Soup
香芹茶干	〈饮食〉Stir-Fried Dried Tofu with Parsley
香薷	〈中医药〉(of Latin) Herba Moslae; Chinese Mosla
香薷草	〈中医药〉Herba Elsholtziae; Elsholtzia
香砂六君丸	〈中医药〉Xiangsha Liujun Wan; Pill of Costus and Amomum with Six Noble Ingredients
香砂六君子丸	〈中医药〉Xiangsha Liujunzi Wan; Six Ingredients Pill with Costusroot and Amomum
香砂养胃丸	〈中医药〉Xiangsha Yangwei Wan; Stomachic Pill with Cyperus and Amomum; Costusroot and Amomum Stomach-Nourishing Pill
香烧鱿鱼	〈饮食〉Braised Squid with Chives, Onions and Cucumbers
香酥鹅	〈饮食〉Crisp Spiced Goose
香酥鸡	〈饮食〉Crispy Deep-Fried Chicken; Savoury and Crispy Chicken
香酥鸡腿	〈饮食〉Fried Crispy Chicken Drumsticks

香酥韭菜盒	〈饮食〉Crispy Dumplings Stuffed with Chinese Chives
香酥萝卜丸子	〈饮食〉Crisp Radish Balls
香酥麻饼	〈饮食〉Crispy Sesame Pancake; Sesame Pastry
香酥鸭荷叶夹	〈饮食〉Deep-Fried Duck Wrapped in Lotus Leaf
香酥鸭子	〈饮食〉Deep-Fried Spiced Crisp Duck
香荽鸭翼	〈饮食〉Stir-Fried Duck Wings with Coriander
香烟打火机	cigarette lighter
香油苦瓜	〈饮食〉Marinated Bitter Melon with Sesame Oil
香油鳝糊	〈饮食〉Braised Shredded Eel with Sesame Oil
香芋黑椒炒牛柳条	〈饮食〉Stir-Fried Beef Fillets with Black Pepper and Taro
香芋烩牛肉	〈饮食〉Braised Beef with Taro
香芋枣排	〈饮食〉Taro and Chinese Date Cake
香橼	〈中医药〉(of Latin) Fructus Citri; Citron Fruit
香糟焗龙虾	〈饮食〉Baked Lobster in Rice Wine Sauce
香糟熘鱼片	〈饮食〉Stir-Fried Sliced Fish in Rice Wine Sauce
香糟鸭卷	〈饮食〉Marinated Duck Rolls with Rice Wine
厢房	wing room; adjacent accommodation
湘菜	〈饮食〉Xiang Cuisine; Hunan Cuisine
湘泉酒	Xiangquan liquor
湘味回锅肉	〈饮食〉Stir-Fried Pork with Pepper in Hunan Style
湘绣	Hu'nan embroidery
祥云髻	〈古〉(of hairstyle) lucky cloud-shaped bun
享乐主义	hedonism
响铃海参	〈饮食〉Stewed Sweet and Sour Sea Slugs with Bamboo Shoots, Mushrooms and Peppers
响螺烧梅花参	〈饮食〉Braised Sea Cucumbers with Sea Whelks
向钱看	money-oriented; to follow the money
向疫情全面宣战	〈防疫〉to declare an all-out war on the epidemic
项目策划人员	project planner
项目工程师	project engineer
项目估算师	project estimator
项目经理	project manager

项目立项	to approve and initiate a project
项目评价	project evaluation
项目申报	project application
项目协调人员	project coordinator
项目预算	project budget
项目执行人员	project specialist; project executive
项目主管	project supervisor
项目总监	project supervisor; project development director
巷弄	lanes and alleys
象棋云雾	〈茶〉Xiangqi Cloud and Mist tea
逍遥散	〈中医药〉Xiaoyao San; Free Wanderer Powder
逍遥丸	〈中医药〉Xiaoyao Wan; Leisurely Liver-Soothing and Spleen Strengthening Pill
消博会	→中国国际日用消费品博览会
消导积滞	〈中医药〉to promote digestion and remove food retention
消毒剂[液]	〈防疫〉disinfectant; antiseptic solution
消毒湿巾	〈防疫〉disinfectant wipe; antiseptic wipe
消毒通风	〈防疫〉disinfection and ventilation
消毒员	sanitation worker; disinfection worker
消防安全工程师	fire protective engineer
消防安全主管	fire prevention supervisor
消费品价格指数	consumer price index
消费期望	consumer expectations
消费时代	consumption era; consumption times
消费税	consumption tax
消费信贷	consumer credit services
消费者购买力	consumer purchasing power
消费者委员会	consumer council
消费者协会	consumers' association
消风散	〈中医药〉Xiaofeng San; Wind-Dispersing Powder
消谷善饥	〈中医药〉rapid digestion of food with polyorexia; swift digestion with rapid hungering
消化系统	〈防疫〉digestive system

消咳喘糖浆	〈中医药〉Xiaokechuan Tangjiang; Syrup for Dispersing Cough with Dyspnea
消痞化积	〈中医药〉to relieve oppression and masses
消食化滞	〈中医药〉to promote digestion and transform stagnation; to resolve food stagnation
消食剂	〈中医药〉digestant formula; digestive formula
消食贴	〈中医药〉Xiaoshi Tie; Baby's Food-Dispersing Sticker
消栓通络片	〈中医药〉Xiaoshuan Tongluo Pian; Embolism-Eliminating and Meridian-Opening Tablet
消委会	→消费者委员会
消息灵通人士	well-informed sources
消炎利胆片	〈中医药〉Xiaoyan Lidan Pian; Inflammation-Resolving and Gall-Bladder-Excreting Tablet
消痈散疖	〈中医药〉to disperse abscesses and boils; to resolve carbuncle and expulse boil
消痔栓	〈中医药〉Xiaozhi Suan; Hemorrhoid-Eliminating Suppository
消痔丸	〈中医药〉Xiaozhi Wan; Hemorrhoid-Dispersing Pill
消肿生肌	〈中医药〉to disperse swelling and engender flesh; to reduce swelling and promote granulation
销售部	sales department
销售部联络员	sales coordinator
销售策略	marketing strategy
销售代表	sales representative
销售副总裁	vice-president of sales
销售工程师	sales engineer
销售计划员	sales planning staff
销售监管	sales supervisor
销售经理	sales manager; sales department manager
销售渠道	distribution channel; access to market
销售热线	sales hotline
销售支持经理	sales support manager

销售中心主任	sales center supervisor
销售主管	sales executive; sales supervisor; director of sales
销售助理	sales assistant
销售总监	director of sales; sales director
小便不通	〈中医药〉urinary obstruction; urinary stoppage
小便黄赤	〈中医药〉deep-colored urine; reddish yellow urine
小便频数	〈中医药〉frequent micturition; frequent urination
小便清长	〈中医药〉clear urine in large amounts; clear abundant urine
小布岩茶	Xiaobu rock tea
小柴胡颗粒	〈中医药〉Xiaochaihu Keli; Minor Bupleurum Granule
小柴胡汤	〈中医药〉Xiao Chaihu Tang; Minor Bupleurum Decoction
小肠实热	〈中医药〉excessive heat of small intestine; sthenia-heat of small intestine
小肠实热证	〈中医药〉pattern of small intestine excessive heat
小肠俞	〈中医药〉Xiaochangshu acupoint; Small Intestine Transport (BL27)
小肠虚寒	〈中医药〉deficiency and cold of small intestine; hypofunction of small intestine with cold manifestation
小炒黑山羊	〈饮食〉Stir-Fried Sliced Lamb with Pepper and Parsley
小炒腊牛肉	〈饮食〉Stir-Fried Preserved Beef with Leek and Pepper
小吃店	snack bar; snack shop
小吃街	snack street; food court
小吃摊	food stand; snack stand
小葱拌豆腐	〈饮食〉Bean Curd Mixed with Chopped Spring Onion
小道消息	hearsay; grapevine; word on the street
小恩小惠	fringe benefit; petty favors; small acts of kindness
小儿肺热咳喘口服液	〈中医药〉Xiao'er Feire Kechuan Koufuye; Pediatric Lung Heat and Cough-Panting Oral Solution

小儿腹泻宁糖浆	〈中医药〉Xiao'er Fuxiening Tangjiang; Children's Diarrhea Calmness Syrup
小儿肝炎颗粒	〈中医药〉Xiao'er Ganyan Keli; Children's Hepatitis Granule
小儿感冒颗粒	〈中医药〉Xiao'er Ganmao Keli; Children's Anti-cold Granule
小儿化痰止咳颗粒	〈中医药〉Xiao'er Huatan Zhike Keli; Children's Phlegm-Dissolving and Cough-Relieving Granule
小儿回春丹	〈中医药〉Xiao'er Huichun Dan; Children's Restorative Granule; Children's Return-of-Spring Elixir
小儿健脾颗粒	〈中医药〉Xiao'er Jianpi Keli; Infants' Spleen-Fortifying Granule
小儿咳喘灵颗粒	〈中医药〉Xiao'er Kechuanling Keli; Infants' Cough-Panting Granule
小儿清热止咳口服液	〈中医药〉Xiao'er Qingre Zhike Koufuye; Children Heat-Clearing and Cough-Suppressing Oral Liquid
小儿清咽颗粒	〈中医药〉Xiao'er Qingyan Keli; Infants' Throat-Clearing Granule
小儿推拿	〈中医药〉infantile massage; massage for child diseases
小儿脱证	〈中医药〉Infantile desertion pattern
《小儿药证直诀》	〈中医药〉*Xiao'er Yaozheng Zhijue*; *Key to Therapeutics of Children's Diseases*; *Key to Diagnosis and Treatment of Children's Diseases* (by Qian Yi in the Song Dynasty)
小儿止咳糖浆	〈中医药〉Xiao'er Zhike Tangjiang; Children Cough-Suppressing Syrup
小儿至宝丸	〈中医药〉Xiao'er Zhibao Wan; Children Jewel Pill
小而全	small but all-inclusive; small but complete
小方脉	〈古中医〉infantile pulse; medical department for children; pediatric department
小骨空	〈中医药〉Xiaogukong; Little Finger Bone Hollow (EX-UE6)

小红书	Little Red Book
小糊涂仙	〈酒〉Xiao Hutuxian; Tipsy spirit
小皇帝	little-emperor (the only child of a family who is spoiled by his or her parents and grandparents)
小黄瓜蘸酱	〈饮食〉Baby Cucumbers with Soybean Paste
小茴香	〈中医药〉(of Latin) Fructus Foeniculi; Fennel
小活络丹	〈中医药〉Xiao Huoluo Dan; Minor Network-Quickening Elixir; Small Bolus for Activating Channels and Collaterals
小蓟	〈中医药〉(of Latin) Herba Cirsii; Field Thistle Herb
小蓟饮子	〈中医药〉Xiaoji Yinzi; Small Cephalanoploris Decoction
小建中汤	〈中医药〉Xiao Jianzhong Tang; Minor Center-Fortifying Decoction
小脚女人	〈旧〉woman with bound feet; a timid and conservative woman
小金丹	〈中医药〉Xiao Jindan; Minor Gold Elixir; Antiphlogistic Bolus
小金库	private coffer; self-concerned exchequer
小金丸	〈中医药〉Xiao Jinwan; Minor Gold Pill; Antiphlogistic Pill
小康	xiaokang; (comparatively) well-off; moderate prosperity
小康家庭	well-off family; moderately prosperous family; comfortably-off family
小康社会	xiaokang society; well-off society; moderately prosperous society
小康生活	better-off life; to be moderately better off; fairly comfortable life
小康水平	well-off standard of living; level of being well-off; comfortable level of living
小康之家	well-off family; comfortably-off family; well-to-do family
小孔式货贝	〈币〉pinhole cowrie; punctured cowrie (issued in the Shang Dynasty)

小笼包	〈饮食〉Small Meat-Stuffed Steamed Bun; Steamed Baozi Stuffed with Juicy Meat
小笼葱油花卷	〈饮食〉Huajuan with Scallion Oil; Steamed Twisted Rolls with Scallion Oil
小笼汤包	〈饮食〉Steamed Bun/Baozi Stuffed with Juicy Pork
小米饭	〈饮食〉Cooked Millet; Steamed Millet
小米金瓜粥	〈饮食〉Millet Congee with Pumpkin
小米粥	〈饮食〉Millet Porridge; Millet Gruel
小排量汽车	small-displacement vehicle; low-emission vehicle
小青龙汤	〈中医药〉Xiao Qinglong Tang; Minor Green-Blue Dragon Decoction
小曲	〈酒〉ball shaped rice starter (for alcoholic fermentation); rice yeast for making liquor
小曲酒	Xiaoqu liquor; Chinese yeast liquor →酒药
小人	villain; a base person; vile character
小商品城	small commodity market; commodity city
小时工	hourly worker
小绶	〈古服饰〉lesser ribbon of jewels
小笋烧牛肉	〈饮食〉Braised Beef with Bamboo Shoots
小续命汤	〈中医药〉Xiao Xuming Tang; Minor Life-Prolonging Decoction
小学高级教师	senior primary school teacher
小鸭酥	〈饮食〉Duckling-Shaped Crispy Puff
小叶种	〈茶〉small-leaf variety
小意思	small token of one's appreciation; small token of kindly feelings; a mere trifle; not worth mentioning
小种红茶	Souchong black tea
孝顺	to show filial obedience; filial piety
孝悌	filial piety and fraternal duty; to love and respect one's elder brother; to do one's duty as a younger brother
孝子	dutiful son; submissive and obedient son

校董事会董事长	chairman of the board of trustees
校园歌曲	campus song; school tunes
校园十杰	ten prominent youths on campus; top ten youths on campus
校园数字化	campus digitalization
校园文化	campus culture; school culture
校长	(of a university) president; (of a middle/primary school) principal, headmaster
歇止脉	〈中医药〉pausing pulse; stopped pulse
协警	auxiliary police
邪气	〈中医药〉pathogenic qi; pathogenic factor
邪气内陷	〈中医药〉internal invasion of pathogenic factor
邪气盛	〈中医药〉excess of pathogenic qi
邪热入里	〈中医药〉interior invasion of pathogenic heat
邪正盛衰	〈中医药〉exuberance and debilitation of vital qi and pathogen
斜刺	〈中医药〉oblique insertion; oblique insertion of the needle
斜襟旗袍	cheongsam with oblique lapel
斜襟衣	Chinese garment with middle-right front lapel
斜裙	a-line skirt; bias skirt
斜纹布	bombazine; drill weave
写手	hack; scribbler (one who writes for money's sake)
泄剂	〈中医药〉purgative prescription; purgative formula; discharging formula
泻白散	〈中医药〉Xiebai San; White-Draining Powder; Lung-Heat Expelling Powder
泻而不藏	〈中医药〉excretion without storage
泻肺逐饮	〈中医药〉to eliminate pathogens from the lung for expelling fluid retention
泻停封胶囊	〈中医药〉Xietingfeng Jiaonang; Diarrhea Stopping Capsule
泻下不爽	〈中医药〉non-smooth diarrhea; ungratifying diarrhea

泻下剂	〈中医药〉purgative formula; formula for purgation
泻下逐水	〈中医药〉to expel water by purgation; to remove water retention by purgation
泻叶	〈中医药〉Folium Sennae; Senna Leaf
亵衣	〈旧〉close-fitting underwear; close-fitting underclothes
谢幕	to answer/respond a curtain call; to acknowledge the applause
薤白	〈中医药〉(of Latin) Bulbus Allii Macrostemonis; Longstamen Onion Bulb
蟹粉豆腐	〈饮食〉Stewed Crab Meat and Tofu/Bean Curd
蟹粉烧卖	〈饮食〉Shaomai Stuffed with Pork and Crab Meat
蟹粉狮子头	〈饮食〉Crab Meat and Minced Pork Ball in Casserole
蟹粉蹄筋	〈饮食〉Braised Crab Meat with Pork Tendons
蟹黄金钩翅	〈饮食〉Braised Shark's Fins with Crab Roe
蟹黄扒鱼翅	〈饮食〉Braised Shark's Fins and Crab Ovum
蟹黄扒珍珠笋	〈饮食〉Braised New Sweetcorn and Crab Roe
蟹黄汤包	〈饮食〉Baozi Stuffed with Juicy Crab Roe
蟹黄虾仁	〈饮食〉Stir-Fried Shelled Shrimps with Crab Roe
蟹黄一品锅	〈饮食〉Stewed Tofu with Crab Roe
蟹黄鱼翅	〈饮食〉Shark's Fins in Crab Ovum
蟹黄鱼翅羹	〈饮食〉Stewed Shark's Fin with Crab Roe
蟹黄珍珠羹	〈饮食〉Crab Roe and Crab Meat Balls Soup
蟹里藏珠	〈饮食〉Stir-Fried Crab Meat with Pigeon Eggs
蟹肉豆腐羹	〈饮食〉Tofu and Crab Meat Soup
蟹肉炖狮子头	〈饮食〉Stewed Pork Meat Balls with Crab Meat
蟹肉芙蓉蛋	〈饮食〉Steamed Egg White with Crab Meat in Sauce
蟹肉烩苋菜	〈饮食〉Stewed Amaranth with Crab Meat
蟹肉烩鱼唇	〈饮食〉Stewed Fish Lips with Crab Meat
蟹肉扒鲜草菇	〈饮食〉Stewed Crab Meat and Grass Mushrooms
蟹肉烧茄子	〈饮食〉Braised Eggplants with Crab Meat
蟹肉水饺	〈饮食〉Jiaozi/Dumplings Stuffed with Pork and Crab Meat

蟹肉丝瓜	〈饮食〉Stir-Fried Sponge Gourd with Crab Meat
蟹肉粟米羹	〈饮食〉Sweetcorn Soup with Crab Meat
蟹肉鱼翅	〈饮食〉Braised Sharks Fins with Minced Crab Meat
蟹肉鱼肚	〈饮食〉Stewed Fish Maw with Crab Meat
蟹汤红焖狮子头	〈饮食〉Steamed Pork Ball with Crab Soup
心肺气虚	〈中医药〉qi deficiency of heart and lung; heart-lung qi deficiency
心肺气虚证	〈中医药〉pattern of heart-lung qi deficiency; heart-lung qi vacuity pattern
心肝火旺	〈中医药〉hyperactivity of heart-liver fire; exuberance of heart and liver fire
心肝血虚	〈中医药〉blood deficiency of heart and liver; heart-liver blood deficiency
心火炽盛证	〈中医药〉pattern of heart fire exuberance; intense heart fire pattern
心火亢盛	〈中医药〉exuberance of heart fire; hyperactivity of heart fire
心火上炎	〈中医药〉flaring up of heart fire; heart fire flaming upward
心火上炎证	〈中医药〉pattern of heart fire flaming upward; heart-fire flaming pattern
心及小肠辨证	〈中医药〉pattern differentiation of heart and small intestine
心悸[慌]	〈中医药〉heart palpitations; cardiopalmus
心开窍于舌	〈中医药〉heart opening at the tongue
心理创伤	〈防疫〉psychological trauma
心理发展部	psychological development department
心理辅导教师资格证书	psychological counseling teacher certificate
心理素质	psychological quality
心理治疗	psychotherapy; psychological treatment
心理咨询	psychological consulting
心理咨询教师	school psychologist
心脉痹阻证	〈中医药〉pattern of heart vessel blockage; heart vessel obstruction pattern

心脉通片	〈中医药〉Xinmaitong Pian; Repatency Tablet of Heart and Vessels
心脉瘀阻	〈中医药〉blood stasis in the heart vessels; stasis obstruction of the heart vessels
心脑清软胶囊	〈中医药〉Xinnaoqing Ruanjiaonang; Heart Brain Clearing Soft Capsule
心脾两虚	〈中医药〉deficiency of both heart and spleen; heart-spleen deficiency
心脾两虚证	〈中医药〉pattern of both heart and spleen deficiency; pattern of dual vacuity of the heart and spleen
心气充沛	〈中医药〉abundance of heart-qi
心气虚	〈中医药〉deficiency of heart-qi; heart-qi deficiency
心气虚血瘀证	〈中医药〉pattern of heart-qi deficiency and blood stasis; heart-qi vacuity and blood stasis pattern
心气血两虚证	〈中医药〉pattern of both heart-qi and blood deficiency; pattern of dual vacuity of heart-qi and blood
心气阴两虚证	〈中医药〉pattern of both heart-qi and yin deficiency; pattern of dual vacuity of heart qi and yin
心肾不交	〈中医药〉heart-kidney imbalance; disharmony between heart and kidney
心肾不交证	〈中医药〉pattern of disharmony between the heart and kidney; pattern of non-interaction of the heart and kidney
心肾相交	〈中医药〉heart and kidney interaction; harmony/coordination between heart and kidney
心肾阳虚	〈中医药〉yang deficiency of heart and kidney; heart-kidney yang deficiency
心肾阳虚证	〈中医药〉pattern of yang deficiency of heart and kidney; heart-kidney yang vacuity pattern
心肾阴虚证	〈中医药〉pattern of heart-kidney yin deficiency; heart-kidney yin vacuity pattern
心俞	〈中医药〉Xinshu acupoint; Heart Transport (BL15)

心想事成	may all your wish come true; to get what you want
心心相印	to have mutual affinity; to have heart-to-heart communion
心虚胆怯证	〈中医药〉pattern of timidity due to deficiency of heart qi
心血管病	〈防疫〉cardiovascular disease
心血虚证	〈中医药〉pattern of heart blood deficiency; heart blood vacuity pattern
心血瘀阻	〈中医药〉stagnant blockade of heart blood; heart blood stasis/obstruction
心阳暴脱证	〈中医药〉pattern of heart-yang fulminant desertion
心阳不振	〈中医药〉devitalization of heart-yang; heart-yang hypoactivity
心阳虚证	〈中医药〉pattern of heart-yang deficiency; heart yang vacuity pattern
心阴不足	〈中医药〉asthenic cardio-yin; insufficiency of heart-yin
心阴虚证	〈中医药〉pattern of heart-yin deficiency; heart yin vacuity pattern
心阴阳两虚证	〈中医药〉pattern of both heart yin and yang deficiency
心照不宣	to have a tacit understanding; to give tacit consent; tacit understanding
辛凉解表	〈中医药〉to release the exterior with pungent-cool; to resolve exterior syndrome with pungent and cool natured drugs
辛凉解表剂	〈中医药〉cool acrid superficies-resolving formula; formula for relieving superficies syndrome with pungent and cool natured drugs
辛凉清热	〈中医药〉to clear heat with pungent and cool-natured drugs; to clear heat with coolness and acridity

辛温解表	〈中医药〉to release the exterior with pungent-warm; to relieve exterior syndrome with pungent and warm-natured drugs
辛温解表剂	〈中医药〉warm acrid superficies-resolving formula; formula for relieving superficies syndrome with pungent and warm natured drugs
辛温解表药	〈中医药〉warm acrid superficies-resolving medicine; Chinese bitter-warm-property sudorific drugs; warm-pungent diaphoretic drug
辛温开窍	〈中医药〉to induce resuscitation with pungent and warm-natured drugs
辛夷	〈中医药〉(of Latin) Flos Magnoliae; Biond Magnolia Flower
新茶	neocha; fresh tea
新长征突击手	pace-setter in the new Long March
新冠病毒的主要传染源	〈防疫〉major source of the spread of novel coronavirus
新冠病毒检测为阳/阴性	〈防疫〉to test positive/negative for the coronavirus
新冠病毒溯源	〈防疫〉COVID-19 origins-tracing
新冠肺炎	〈防疫〉→新型冠状病毒肺炎
新冠经济	〈防疫〉coronanomics
新冠恐惧	〈防疫〉coronaphobia
新冠偏执	〈防疫〉coronoia
新冠娃娃	〈防疫〉corona-baby
新冠疫苗	〈防疫〉COVID-19 vaccine
新冠疫情	〈防疫〉COVID-19 epidemic; COVID-19 outbreak
新冠疫区	〈防疫〉COVID-19 affected area
新冠重症	〈防疫〉critical condition; severe case of COVID-19
新华人寿保险	New China Life Insurance
新华社	→新华通讯社
新华通讯社	Xinhua News Agency
新江羽绒茶	Xinjiang Down Green tea
新疆红钱	Xinjiang red coin (issued in the Qing Dynasty)

新浪微博	Sina Weibo; Sina Microblog
新娘礼服	wedding gown; bridal gown
新农合	→新型农村合作医疗保险
新农合医疗	→新型农村合作医疗保险
新儒家学者	neo-Confucian scholar
新时代最可爱的人	〈防疫〉the most admirable people in the new era
新闻门户	news portal
新闻主播	news anchor; news presenter
新新人类	new human being; X generation
新兴市场	emerging market
新型冠状病毒	〈防疫〉novel coronavirus
新型冠状病毒成功分离	〈防疫〉successful isolation of a novel coronavirus
新型冠状病毒传播	〈防疫〉transmission of a novel coronavirus
新型冠状病毒肺炎	〈防疫〉COVID-19 pneumonia
新型农村合作医疗保险	new rural cooperative medical insurance
《新修本草》	〈中医药〉*Xinxiu Bencao*; *Newly Revised Materia Medica* (also known as *Tang Materia Medica*) (by Su Jing et al. in the Tang Dynasty)
新增病例数	〈防疫〉number of new cases
《新针灸学》	〈中医药〉*New Art of Acupuncture and Moxibustion* (by Zhu Lian in 1951)
囟会	〈中医药〉Xinhui acupoint; Fontanel Meeting (GV22)
信贷分析人员	loan officer; credit officer
信贷经理	credit manager
信丰萝卜饺	〈饮食〉Xinfeng Jiaozi/Dumplings Stuffed with Turnip, Pork and Fish
信件中心管理员	mail room supervisor
信息安全工程师	information security engineer
信息反馈员	information feedback staff
信息分析员	information analyst
信息服务主管	director of information service
信息高地	information highland
信息管理员	information manager; information system clerk

信息技术工程师	information technology engineer
信息技术经理	information technology manager
信息技术主管	information technology supervisor
信息技术专员	information technology specialist
信息检索	information retrieval
信息经济	information economy
信息流	information flow
信息时代	information era
信息系统项目管理师	information system project manager
信阳毛尖	〈茶〉Xinyang Maojian tea; Xinyang Tippy tea
信仰危机	crisis of belief; crisis in moral conviction; crisis of faith
信用分析师	credit analyst
信用管理员	credit clerk; credit controller; credit administrator
信用文化	credit culture
兴我中华演讲比赛	speech competition on revitalizing China
星级饭店	star grade hotel
星探	talent scout; casting director
星洲炒米粉	〈饮食〉Singapore Stir-Fried Rice Noodles
邢窑	〈陶瓷〉Xing Kiln (in the Sui-Five Dynasties period)
行贿受贿	to offer and take bribes; to give or receive bribes; to commit or accept bribery
行袍	〈服饰〉official's outdoor robe (used in the Qing Dynasty) →缺襟袍
行气降逆	〈中医药〉to move qi and downbear counterflow; to activate qi for lowering adverse qi
行气利水	〈中医药〉to activate qi to excrete water; to promote the circulation of qi for inducing diuresis
行气消瘀	〈中医药〉to activate qi to resolve stagnation; to promote the qi circulation for dispersing stasis
行为模式	behavior pattern; behavior model
行[运]针	〈中医药〉needle manipulation; to manipulate needle

行[运]针手法	〈中医药〉needling manipulation; needle manipulation technique
行政部主任	director of administration department
行政副总裁	vice-president of administration
行政管家	executive housekeeper
行政经理	administration manager; office manager
行政人员	administration staff; administrator
行政事业性收费	administrative fees
行政主厨	executive chef
行政主管	administrative director; administrative supervisor
行政助理	administration assistant; executive assistant
行政专员	administrative specialist; administration officer
行政总裁	→首席执行官
行政总厨	executive chef; administrative chef
行政总监	administrative director; executive director
行走的传染源	〈防疫〉mobile source of infection
形象工程	vanity project; image project
醒脾养儿颗粒	〈中医药〉Xingpi Yang'er Keli; Spleen-Awakening Baby-Nourishing Granule
杏花村汾酒	Xinghua Village Fen liquor
杏片炸鱼条	〈饮食〉Deep-Fried Fish Fillets with Almonds
杏仁百花脆皮鸡	〈饮食〉Crispy Chicken with Shrimp Paste and Almonds
杏仁炒南瓜	〈饮食〉Stir-Fried Pumpkin with Almonds
杏仁豆腐	〈饮食〉Almond Junket; Almond Curd in Syrup
杏仁止咳糖浆	〈中医药〉Xingren Zhike Tangjiang; Compound Almond Syrup
杏苏散	〈中医药〉Xingsu San; Apricot Kernel and Perilla Powder
杏香橙花鸡脯	〈饮食〉Stir-Fried Chicken Breast with Almonds in Orange Dressing
杏汁炖官燕	〈饮食〉Double-Boiled Superior Bird's Nest with Almond Juice
杏汁芦荟木瓜	〈饮食〉Papaya with Aloe and Almond Juice

性别比例失衡	gender imbalance; sex-ratio imbalance
性别歧视	sexual/gender discrimination
性骚扰	sexual harassment; sexual disturbance
性状鉴定	〈中医药〉macroscopical identification
芎菊上清丸	〈中医药〉Xiongju Shangqing Wan; Ligusticum-Chrysanthemum Upper-Heat-Removing Bolus
芎香通脉丸	〈中医药〉Xiongxiang Tongmai Wan; Ligusticum Odoratum Vessels-Freeing Pill
胸甲	〈古〉cuirass; chest armor
胸闷	〈防疫〉chest distress; chest oppression
胸乡	〈中医药〉Xiongxiang acupoint; Chest Village (SP19)
胸胁苦满	〈中医药〉fullness and discomfort in the chest and hypochondrium; fullness in the chest and rib-side
胸椎	〈中医药〉Xiongzhui acupoint; Thoracic Vertebrae (AH11)
雄黄酒	〈中医药〉realgar wine; wine mixed with arsenic sulphide drunk
熊胆痔灵膏	〈中医药〉Xiongdan Zhiling Gao; Bear's Gall Ointment for Hemorrhoid
熊猫香烟	Xiongmao cigarettes; Panda cigarettes
休舱	〈防疫〉to close temporary treatment center
休车日	alternate no-car day; car free day
休闲阅读	light reading; read for pleasure
绣花	embroidery; to do embroidery; to embroider
绣花丝线	embroidery floss
绣花鞋	embroidered satin shoe
绣花衣	embroidered clothes; embroidered clothing
绣花枕头	pillow with pretty embroidered case outside but stuffed with straw; glittering appearance outside and rubbish inside; many a fine dish has nothing on it
绣袍	〈服饰〉embroidered gown; embroidered robe
绣球干贝	〈饮食〉Fried Scallops in Silk Ball Shape
绣线	embroidery thread

虚寒证	〈中医药〉deficiency-cold pattern
虚汗停颗粒	〈中医药〉Xuhanting Keli; Debility Sweat-Stopping Granule
虚火上浮证	〈中医药〉pattern of deficiency fire flaring up; up-flaming vacuity heat pattern
虚火上炎证	〈中医药〉pattern of deficiency-fire flaring up; up-flaming vacuity-fire pattern
虚火灼龈证	〈中医药〉pattern of deficiency-fire inflaming the gums; pattern of vacuity-fire scorching the gums
虚脉	〈中医药〉feeble pulse; deficient pulse
虚拟存款	window-dressing deposits
虚拟市场	virtual market
虚拟现实	virtual reality
虚拟银行	virtual bank
虚实辨证	〈中医药〉pattern differentiation of excess and deficiency; vacuity-repletion pattern identification
虚实夹杂证	〈中医药〉pattern of deficiency and excess intermingled with each other; vacuity-repletion complex pattern
虚阳上浮	〈中医药〉deficient yang with upper manifestation; up-floating of asthenia yang
虚则补之	〈中医药〉to tonify deficiency; to treat deficiency with tonification
需求工程师	requirement engineer
徐长卿	〈中医药〉(of Latin) Radix Cynanchi Paniculati; Paniculate Swallowwort Root
《徐灵胎医学全书》	〈中医药〉*Xu Lingtai Yixue Quanshu*; *Xu Lingtai's Complete Medical Book* (by Xu Lingtai in the Qing Dynasty)
畜牧技术员	livestock technician
畜牧师	livestock specialist; animal husbandry specialist
续断	〈中医药〉(of Latin) Radix Dipsaci; Himalayan Teasel Root

《续名医类案》	〈中医药〉*Xu Mingyi Lei'an*; *Supplement to Classified Case Records of Celebrated Physicians* (by Wei Zhixiu in the Qing Dynasty)
蓄势而发	to accumulate strength for a take-off; to be poised for sth.
宣德青花花卉水注	〈陶瓷〉blue and white water dropper with floral pattern (Ming Xuande period)
宣德青花夔龙纹罐	〈陶瓷〉blue and white jar with kui-dragon pattern (Ming Xuande period)
宣德青花鸟食罐	〈陶瓷〉blue and white bird feeder jar (Ming Xuande period)
宣德青花五彩莲池鸳鸯纹碗	〈陶瓷〉blue and white bowl with polychrome lotus pond and mandarin ducks pattern (Ming Xunde period)
宣德青花竹石芭蕉瓷瓶	〈陶瓷〉blue and white vase with bamboo-stone-plantain pattern (Ming Xuande periond)
宣肺化痰	〈中医药〉to diffuse the lung for resolving phlegm; to disperse lung-qi for dissipating phlegm
宣肺降逆	〈中医药〉to disperse lung-qi for lowering adverse qi; to diffuse the lung to downbear counterflow
宣肺平喘	〈中医药〉to diffuse the lung to calm panting; to disperse lung-qi to stop asthma
宣剂	〈中医药〉diffusing formula; dispersing prescription
玄米茶	brown rice green tea; kirara rice tea
玄明粉	〈中医药〉(of Latin) Natrii Sulfas Exsiccatus; Refined Mirabilite
玄参	〈中医药〉(of Latin) Radix Scrophulariae; Figwort Root
玄孙女	great-great-granddaughter
玄孙子	great-great-grandson
悬起灸	〈中医药〉over-skin moxibustion; suspension moxibustion
悬枢	〈中医药〉Xuanshu acupoint; Suspended Pivot (GV5)

悬钟	〈中医药〉Xuanzhong; Suspended Bell; Hanging Bell (GB39)
旋覆花	〈中医药〉(of Latin) Flos Inulae; Inula Flower
炫富	to flaunt the considerable wealth; to show off one's prosperity
穴位	〈中医药〉point; acupoint; acupuncture point
穴位注射疗法	〈中医药〉acupoint-injection therapy; acupuncture point injection therapy
学部委员	academic commissioner; member of the Chinese Academy of Sciences
学部主任	chairman of an academician committee
学而优则仕	(of a Confucian slogan for education) a good scholar can become an official; he who excels in study can follow an official career
学分制	academic credit system
学科带头人	pace-setter in scientific research; academic leader
学雷锋活动	"Learning from Lei Feng" activity
学历教育	education with record of formal schooling
学前教育	preschool education
学区房	school estate; school district housing
学生处	students' affair division; department of student affairs
学生会	student union
学生会主席	president of the student union
学生社团	students' association
学生营养改善计划	Nutrition Improvement Program for Compulsory Education Students
学生月票	student monthly ticket
学术部干事	a member of the academic department
学术超人	superman-scholar; academic superman
学术委员会	academic board; academic committee
学术委员会副主任	vice chairman of scientific board/committee
学术委员会委员	member of academic board/committee
学术委员会主任	chairman of scientific board/committee

学位制	academic degree system
学习标兵	student pacemaker; model student
学习委员	study secretary
学习优秀生	model student of academic records
学校注册主任	school registrar
学业技能	academic skills
学有所教	all the people enjoy their rights to education
噱头	gimmick; stunt
雪菜	〈饮食〉Potherb Mustard; Preserved Vegetable
雪菜百贝	〈饮食〉Stir-Fried Bean Curd Sheets and Salted Vegetables
雪菜拌花生	〈饮食〉Deep-Fried Peanuts and Red-in-Snow
雪菜包	〈饮食〉Steamed Bun Stuffed with Preserved Vegetables
雪菜炒豆瓣	〈饮食〉Stir-Fried Beans with Preserved Vegetables
雪菜炒豆皮	〈饮食〉Stir-Fried Bean Curd Sheets with Potherb Mustard
雪菜炒肉丝	〈饮食〉Stir-Fried Shredded Pork with Potherb Mustard
雪菜大汤黄鱼	〈饮食〉Stewed Yellow Croaker with Potherb Mustard and Bamboo Shoots
雪菜墨鱼丝	〈饮食〉Stir-Fried Shredded Cuttlefish with Potherb Mustard
雪菜肉丝	〈饮食〉Shredded Pork with Salted Potherb Mustard
雪菜肉松拉面	〈饮食〉Hand-Pulled Noodle Soup with Minced Pork and Preserved Vegetables
雪菜虾仁豆腐	〈饮食〉Stir-Fried Tofu with Shrimps and Potherb Mustard
雪菜野鸭汤	〈饮食〉Wild Duck and Slated Vegetable Soup
雪豆炒牛肉	〈饮食〉Stir-Fried Beef with Snow Peas
雪豆鸡	〈饮食〉Stir-Fried Chicken with Snow Peas
雪豆马蹄	〈饮食〉Stir-Fried Snow Peas with Water Chestnuts

雪豆虾	〈饮食〉Stir-Fried Shrimps with Snow Peas
雪耳木瓜煲排骨	〈饮食〉White Fungi, Pawpaw and Spare Ribs Soup
雪峰毛尖	〈茶〉Xuefeng Maojian tea; Xuefeng Tippy tea
雪蛤海皇羹	〈饮食〉Snow Clam and Scallop Soup
雪红鱼唇	〈饮食〉Stewed Fish Lips with Minced Ham
雪花鸡腿	〈饮食〉Deep-Fried Chicken Drumsticks (Shaped as a Snowflake)
雪花鱼翅	〈饮食〉Shark's Fins with Egg Whites
雪梨炖百合	〈饮食〉Snow Pear and Lily Bulb Soup; Stewed Snow Pears with Lily Bulb
雪梨官燕	〈饮食〉Braised Bird's Nest with Snow Pear
雪莲止痛贴	〈中医药〉Xuelian Zhitong Tie; Snow Lotus Pain-killing Plaster
雪球干贝	〈饮食〉Stewed Dried Scallops and White Radish Balls
雪水云绿	〈茶〉Snow Cloud Green tea
雪笋花枝片	〈饮食〉Stir-Fried Sliced Cuttlefish with Bamboo Shoots
血府逐瘀汤	〈中医药〉Xuefu Zhuyu Tang; Blood-House Stasis-Expelling Decoction
血寒证	〈中医药〉pattern of cold in blood; blood cold pattern
血浆治疗	〈防疫〉infusions of blood plasma
血竭	〈中医药〉(of Latin) Sanguis Draconis; Dragon's Blood
血清诊断	〈防疫〉serodiagnosis; serum diagnosis
血热肠燥证	〈中医药〉pattern of intestinal dryness due to blood heat
血热动风证	〈中医药〉pattern of stirring wind due to blood heat
血随气逆	〈中医药〉bleeding due to qi reversed flow; blood flowing counter-flow with qi
血脱证	〈中医药〉pattern of blood depletion; blood desertion pattern

血虚肠燥证	〈中医药〉pattern of intestinal dryness due to blood deficiency
血虚动风证	〈中医药〉pattern of stirring wind due to blood deficiency
血虚风燥证	〈中医药〉pattern of wind and dryness due to blood deficiency
血虚寒凝证	〈中医药〉pattern of coagulated cold due to blood deficiency
血虚津亏证	〈中医药〉pattern of blood deficiency and depleted fluid
血虚生风	〈中医药〉blood deficiency generating/engendering wind
血虚证	〈中医药〉pattern of blood deficiency; blood vacuity pattern
血瘀耳窍证	〈中医药〉pattern of blood stasis in the ear orifice
血瘀气滞证	〈中医药〉pattern of blood stasis and qi-stagnation
血瘀舌下证	〈中医药〉pattern of blood stasis under the tongue; sublingual blood stasis pattern
血瘀证	〈中医药〉pattern of blood stasis; blood stasis pattern
血余炭	〈中医药〉(of Latin) Crinis Carbonisatus; Carbonized Hair
《血证论》	〈中医药〉*Xuezheng Lun*; *On Blood Syndromes*; *On Blood Pathoconditions* (by Tang Zonghai in the Qing Dynasty)
熏花红茶	scented black tea
熏花绿茶	scented green tea
熏花茉莉	〈茶〉scented jasmine
熏花普洱	〈茶〉scented Pu'er tea
熏花乌龙	〈茶〉scented Oolong tea
熏黄鱼	〈饮食〉Smoked Yellow Croaker with Lettuce and Onion
熏鸡	〈饮食〉Smoked Chicken
熏马哈鱼	〈饮食〉Smoked Salmon

熏洗疗法	〈中医药〉fuming-washing therapy; fumigation and washing therapy
熏鸭腰	〈饮食〉Smoked Duck Kernel with Pea Sprouts
熏鱼	〈饮食〉Smoked Fish
熏蒸疗法	〈中医药〉fumigating therapy; fumigation and steaming therapy
薰花花茶	scented flower tea
薰衣草祛疤凝胶	〈中医药〉Xunyicao Quba Ningjiao; Lavender Scar Removing Gel
巡回医疗	medical tour; mobile clinic visits
巡回展览	exhibition tour
巡回招聘	milk round
浔阳鱼片	〈饮食〉Xunyang Braised Fish Slices
驯兽师	wild animal trainer
徇私枉法	to bend the law for personal gain
徇私舞弊	to bend the law for personal gain and engage in fraud

Y

压岁[祟]钱	lucky money; New Year lucky money (given to children as a Chinese New Year gift)
鸦胆子	〈中医药〉(of Latin) Fructus Bruceae; Java Brucea Fruit
鸭蛋青瓷	〈陶瓷〉duck-egg porcelain; pale blue china
鸭肝汤	〈饮食〉Duck Liver Soup with Fresh Mushrooms and Ginger Slices
鸭羹粥	〈饮食〉Glutinous Rice in Duck Broth
鸭骨菜汤	〈饮食〉Duck Bone Soup with Vegetables
鸭黄焗南瓜	〈饮食〉Braised Pumpkin with Salted Duck Yolk
鸭架汤	〈饮食〉Roast Duck Bone Soup with Onion, Ginger and Wine
鸭茸奶油蘑菇汤	〈饮食〉Minced Duck Meat Soup with Mushrooms and Butter
鸭肉面	〈饮食〉Noodles with Duck
鸭丝春卷	〈饮食〉Spring Rolls Stuffed with Shredded Duck
鸭丝火腿汤面	〈饮食〉Noodle Soup with Shredded Duck and Ham
鸭丝上汤米粉	〈饮食〉Rice Noodle Soup with Shredded Duck
鸭汤醋椒鱼	〈饮食〉Braised Mandarin Fish with Chili Pepper in Duck Bone Soup
鸭汤馄饨	〈饮食〉Wonton in Duck Soup
鸭溪窖酒	Yaxijiao liquor; Yaxi Cellar liquor
鸭油萝卜丝酥	〈饮食〉Pan-Fried Turnip Cake with Duck Oil
鸭掌汤	〈饮食〉Duck Web Soup with Yams, Chopped Carrots and Green Onions

鸭汁炆鱼唇	〈饮食〉Stewed Fish Lips with Duck Sauce
鸭跖草	〈中医药〉(of Latin) Herba Commelinae; Dayflower Herb
牙科保健员	dental hygienist
牙科技师	dental technician
牙科医生	dentist; dental surgeon
牙科助理	dental assistant
芽菜回锅肉	〈饮食〉Stir-Fried Sliced Pork with Scallion and Bean Sprouts
芽菜扣肉	〈饮食〉Steamed Pork Slices with Bean Sprouts
芽叶连枝	〈茶〉whole shoot
哑门	〈中医药〉Yamen acupoint; Mute's Gate; Acupuncture Point at the Back of the Head (GV15)
雅安黑茶	Ya'an dark tea
雅安黄茶	Ya'an yellow tea
雅令	〈酒〉drinking game verses →筹令
亚麻纤维混纺	flax fiber blending
亚麻子	〈中医药〉(of Latin) Semen Lini; Flax Seed
咽炎片	〈中医药〉Yanyan Pian; Throat-Inflammation Tablet
胭脂	Chinese rouge
胭脂红釉盘	〈陶瓷〉rouge-red glazed tray
烟草公司	tobacco company
烟草广告	tobacco advertising
烟草流行	tobacco epidemic
烟草消费	tobacco consumption
烟草专卖	tobacco monopoly
烟草专卖局	tobacco monopoly bureau
烟草专卖行政管理部门	administrative department for tobacco monopoly
烟草专卖制度	tobacco monopolization system
烟斗	cigarette holder
烟丝	pipe tobacco
烟台白葡萄酒	Yantai white wine
烟台红葡萄酒	Yantai red wine
烟熏红茶	smoked black tea

烟熏味	〈茶〉smoke taste; smoky flavor
烟瘾	smoking addiction; craving for tobacco
腌	〈饮食〉to pickle; to salt; pickled; salted
腌氽	〈饮食〉Corned Pork and Black Carp Soup
腌缸	〈陶瓷〉curing tank
腌牛肉	〈饮食〉Salted Beef; Corned Beef
腌三文鱼	〈饮食〉Marinated Salmon
腌雪里蕻	〈饮食〉Pickled Potherb Mustard
腌渍调料	〈饮食〉marinade; pickling sauce
燕京啤酒	Yanjing beer
燕京生［扎］啤	Yanjing draught beer
燕京无醇啤酒	Yanjing non-alcoholic beer
延长春节假期	〈防疫〉to extend the Chinese New Year holiday
延迟开学	〈防疫〉to postpone the reopening of schools
延丹益心胶囊	〈中医药〉Yandan Yixin Jiaonang; Corydalis Salvia Heart-Benefiting Capsule
延胡索	〈中医药〉(of Latin) Rhizoma Corydalis; Corydalis Tuber
延年益寿	(of idiom) to prolong life; to extend one's years
严禁疲劳驾车	prohibition of fatigue driving; drowsy driving prohibited
严控堂食	〈防疫〉to strictly control dine-in service
严厉打击涉疫违法犯罪	〈防疫〉to take firm action against epidemic-related crimes
严重急性呼吸道感染	〈防疫〉severe acute respiratory infection; SARI
严重急性呼吸综合征［非典］	〈防疫〉severe acute respiratory syndrome; SARS
炎可宁片	〈中医药〉Yankening Pian; Inflammation-Reducing Tablet
研发工程师	research and development engineer
研究发展技术员	research and development technician
研究实习员	research assistant
研究所所长	director of research institute
研究团队	research team

研究型大学	research-oriented university
研究员	research fellow
研究总监	chief research officer (CRO)
研讨会协调员	symposium coordinator
盐菜肚片汤	〈饮食〉Pork Tripe Slices and Pickled Vegetable Soup
盐煎肉	〈饮食〉Fried Pork Slices with Salted Pepper
盐井[矿]	salt well; salt mine; brine pit
盐焗鸡	〈饮食〉Salt Baked Chicken; Baked Chicken in Salt
盐烤荷叶鸭	〈饮食〉Salt-Baked Duck Wrapped in Lotus Leaf
盐烤信丰鸡	〈饮食〉Baked Xinfeng Chicken in Salt
盐水菜心	〈饮食〉Salt Green Tender/Choy Sum
盐水鹅肉	〈饮食〉Goose Slices in Salted Spicy Sauce
盐水肝	〈饮食〉Boiled Livers with Salt; Salted Livers
盐水鸡	〈饮食〉Boiled Chicken with Salt; Salted Chicken
盐水虾	〈饮食〉Boiled Shrimps with Shell in Salted Water
盐水虾肉	〈饮食〉Salted Shrimp Meat; Poached Salted Shrimps without Shell
盐水鸭	〈饮食〉Boiled Duck with Salt; Poached Chilled Duck with Pepper Corn
盐酥生中虾	〈饮食〉Baked Crispy Prawns with Salt
眼保健按摩	health massage for eyes
眼红	green-eyed; to be jealous; to be envious
眼镜袋	glasses pocket
眼科医生	oculist; eye-doctor; ophthalmologist
演讲比赛	oratorical contest; speech competition
宴会销售代表	catering sales representative
宴会销售经理	catering sales manager
宴会销售文员	catering sales staff
宴会销售主管	catering sales executive
验方	〈中医药〉experiential effective recipe
《验方新编》	〈中医药〉*Yanfang Xinbian*; *New Compilation of Effective Recipes*; *New Compilation of Empirical Formulas* (by Bao Xiang'ao in the Qing Dynasty)

验光师	optometrist; optician
雁荡毛峰	〈茶〉Yandang Maofeng tea; Yandang Tippy tea
燕尾服	swallow-tailed coat
燕窝炖鹌鹑蛋	〈饮食〉Stewed Quail Eggs with Bird's Nest
燕窝鸽蛋	〈饮食〉Stewed Pigeon Eggs with Bird's Nest
燕窝汤	〈饮食〉Soup of Edible Bird's Nest; Bird's Nest Soup
燕窝椰子炖鸡	〈饮食〉Stewed Chicken with Swiftlet Nest and Coconut
燕子领	swallow collar; wing collar
央视	→中央电视台
央视春节联欢晚会	CCTV Spring Festival Gala; CCTV Chinese New Year Gala
央视青年歌手大奖赛	CCTV Young Singers Competition; CCTV Young Singers Grand Prix
央视新闻	CCTV news
央视元宵晚会	CCTV Lantern Festival Gala
秧歌(舞)	yangko; yangko dance (popular in Northern China)
扬州菜	〈饮食〉Yangzhou cuisine
扬州炒饭	〈饮食〉Yangzhou Stir-Fried Rice
羊肚菌爆虾球	〈饮食〉Stir-Fried Shrimp Balls with Sponge Mushrooms
羊羔美酒	Yanggao good liquor
羊肉串	〈饮食〉Mutton Kebab; Barbecue Sliced Mutton
羊肉蘑菇片	〈饮食〉Lamb Cooked with Sliced Mushroom
羊肉泡馍	〈饮食〉Yangrou Paomo; Wheaten Cake Soaked in Lamb Soup; Mutton and Cake Pieces in Soup
羊肉汤	〈饮食〉Mutton Soup; Lamb Soup
羊蝎子	〈饮食〉Lamb Spine Hot Pot with Tempeh, Pepper and Chili
羊油酒	mutton fat wine
羊杂烩	〈饮食〉Fricassée Chopped Entrails of Sheep
羊杂碎汤	〈饮食〉Sheep Entrails Soup

阳池	〈中医药〉Yangchi acupoint; Yang Pool (SJ4)
阳春面	〈饮食〉Plain Noodle Soup; Plain Noodles
阳谷	〈中医药〉Yanggu acupoint; Yang Valley (SI5)
阳光产业	sunshine industry
阳和汤	〈中医药〉Yanghe Tang; Yang Harmonizing Decoction
阳交	〈中医药〉Yangjiao acupoint; Yang Intersection (GB35)
阳陵泉	〈中医药〉Yangling Quan acupoint; Yang Mount Spring (GB34)
阳明病证	〈中医药〉yang brightness disease pattern; pattern of yang heat hyperactivity
阳明腑证	〈中医药〉yang brightness bowel pattern; pattern of yang heat hyperactivity in the abdomen
阳明经证	〈中医药〉yang brightness channel pattern; pattern of yang heat hyperactivity in the meridians
阳气暴脱证	〈中医药〉pattern of yang-qi fulminant desertion; sudden yang exhaustion pattern
阳气不振	〈中医药〉inactivation of yang-qi
阳气衰退	〈中医药〉declination of yang-qi
阳胜生外热	〈中医药〉exuberance of yang leading to exterior heat
阳盛	〈中医药〉overabundance of yang; yang excessiveness
阳损及阴	〈中医药〉depletion of yang affecting yin; impairment of yang involving yin
阳损及阴证	〈中医药〉pattern of detriment to yang affecting yin; pattern of yang deficiency involving yin
阳亡阴竭证	〈中医药〉pattern of yang depletion with yin exhaustion
阳溪	〈中医药〉Yangxi acupoint; Yang Creek (LI5)
阳虚发热	〈中医药〉fever due to yang deficiency
阳虚寒凝证	〈中医药〉pattern of yang deficiency and coagulated cold; yang vacuity and exuberant cold pattern

阳虚气滞证	〈中医药〉pattern of yang deficiency and qi stagnation; yang vacuity and qi stagnation pattern
阳虚生寒	〈中医药〉cold manifestation due to yang deficiency
阳虚水泛证	〈中医药〉pattern of water overflowing due to yang deficiency; yang vacuity and water overflowing pattern
阳虚痰凝证	〈中医药〉pattern of yang deficiency and coagulated phlegm; yang vacuity and phlegm congealing pattern
阳虚外感证	〈中医药〉pattern of exogenous disease due to yang deficiency
阳虚血瘀证	〈中医药〉pattern of yang deficiency and blood stasis; yang vacuity and blood stasis pattern
阳虚则寒	〈中医药〉yang deficiency leading to cold
阳虚证	〈中医药〉yang deficiency pattern; yang vacuity pattern
《疡科心得集》	〈中医药〉*Yangke Xinde Ji*; *Experience Gained in Treating External Diseases*; *Sores Branch Collected Heart-Perceptions* (by Gao Bingjun in the Qing Dynasty)
疡医	〈古〉royal surgeon
洋葱牛柳丝	〈饮食〉Stir-Fried Shredded Beef Fillets with Onion
洋葱牛肉丝	〈饮食〉Stir-Fried Shredded Beef with Onions
洋葱煮鱼	〈饮食〉Boiled Fish with Onion
洋河大曲酒	Yanghe Daqu liquor; Yanghe twice fully-fermented liquor
洋金花	〈中医药〉(of Latin) Flos Daturae; Datura Flower
洋参炖甲鱼	〈饮食〉Stewed Turtle with American Ginseng
仰韶低度白酒	Yangshao low-alcohol liquor
仰钟杯	→铃铛杯
养儿防老	to rear children for old age; to bring up children for the purpose of being looked after in old age; to bring up sons to support parents in their old age
养老保险	endowment insurance; pension

养生	〈中医药〉health preserving; health maintenance
养生防病	〈中医药〉to cultivate health to prevent disease
养胃舒胶囊	〈中医药〉Yangweishu Jiaonang; Stomach-Nourishing Capsule
养血安神	〈中医药〉to nourish blood for tranquillization; to nourish blood for tranquilizing mind
养血安神丸	〈中医药〉Yangxue Anshen Wan; Blood Nourishing and Tranquillization Pill
养血当归糖浆	〈中医药〉Yangxue Danggui Tangjiang; Blood-Nourishing Tangkuei Syrup
养血明目	〈中医药〉to nourish blood for improving eyesight
养血清脑颗粒	〈中医药〉Yangxue Qingnao Keli; Blood-Nourishing and Brain-Clearing Granule
养血荣发颗粒	〈中医药〉Yangxue Rongfa Keli; Blood-Nourishing and Hair-Flourishing Granule
养血柔肝	〈中医药〉to tonify blood and nourish the liver
养血生发胶囊	〈中医药〉Yangxue Shengfa Jiaonang; Blood-Nourishing and Hair-Growing Capsule
养血生肌	〈中医药〉to nourish blood and promote granulation
养血调经	〈中医药〉to nourish blood for regulating menstruation
养阴清肺膏	〈中医药〉Yangyin Qingfei Gao; Yin-Nourishing and Lung-Clearing Syrup
养阴清肺汤	〈中医药〉Yangyin Qingfei Tang; Decoction for Nourishing Yin and Clearing the Lung-Heat
养阴清热	〈中医药〉to nourish yin and clear away heat
养阴生肌	〈中医药〉to nourish yin and promote granulation
养殖部主管	director of cultivation department
氧化铝瓷	〈陶瓷〉alumina porcelain
氧化镁瓷	〈陶瓷〉magnesium oxide ceramic
腰骶椎	〈中医药〉Yaodizhui acupoint; Lumbosacral Vertebrae (AH9)

腰豆西芹炒鱼松	〈饮食〉Stir-Fried Minced Fish with Celery and Kidney Beans
腰果炒牛肉粒	〈饮食〉Stir-Fried Diced Beef with Cashew Kernels
腰果鸡丁	〈饮食〉Stir-Fried Diced Chicken with Cashew Kernels
腰果鸡球	〈饮食〉Stir-Fried Chicken Balls and Cashew Kernels
腰果肉丁	〈饮食〉Diced Pork with Cashew Kernels
腰果鲜虾仁	〈饮食〉Stir-Fried Shelled Fresh Shrimp with Cashew Kernels
腰俞	〈中医药〉Yaoshu acupoint; Lumbar Transport (DU2)
腰痛宁胶囊	〈中医药〉Yaotongning Jiaonang; Lumbago-Calming Capsule
腰眼	〈中医药〉Yaoyan acupoint; Lumbar Eyes (EX-B7)
腰阳关	〈中医药〉Yaoyangguan acupoint; Lumbar Yang Gate (GV3)
窑洞	yaodong; cave dwelling (in Shaanxi-Gansu-Ningxia region)
摇钱树	money tree (a legendary tree that sheds coins when shaken); cash cow; money-spinner
遥控飞机	remote control aircraft; telecontrolled aircraft; push-button plane
瑶斑布	〈瑶族〉batik calico
瑶柱灌汤饺	〈饮食〉Jiaozi/Dumplings Stuffed with Juicy Scallop
瑶柱烩裙边	〈饮食〉Braised Turtle Rim with Scallops
瑶柱鸡丝烩生翅	〈饮食〉Braised Shark's Fins with Shredded Chicken and Scallops
药斑布	medicinal herb stained blue cloth
药材	〈中医药〉medicinal material; crude drug; crude mcdicinc
药兜疗法	〈中医药〉medicinal bag therapy
药膏疗法	〈中医药〉medicinal paste therapy; ointment therapy

药剂师	druggist; chemist; pharmacist
药酒	medicinal liquor; medicated wine
药库主任	pharmacy store director
药品集中采购	〈防疫〉centralized procurement of drugs
药品技师	pharmacy technician
药品检验员	drug inspector
药品市场推广经理	pharmaceutical marketing manager
药品市场推广主管	pharmaceutical marketing supervisor
药品市场推广专员	pharmaceutical marketing specialist
药品注册师	pharmaceutical registration officer
药膳	〈中医药〉Chinese medicinal diet
药栓疗法	〈中医药〉medicinal suppository therapy
药王	〈中医药〉god of medicine
药物采制	〈中医药〉collection and preparation of herbs
药物毒性	〈中医药〉toxicity of medicinal herbs
药物灸	〈中医药〉medicinal blister-causing moxibustion; medicinal moxibustion
药物饮片	〈中医药〉processed herb; medicinal herbs prepared in ready-to-use form
药线疗法	〈中医药〉medicated thread therapy
药香型酒	medicinal-flavor liquor
药学师	pharmacist; pharmacy technician
药引	〈中医药〉guiding drug; medicinal usher
药引子	〈中医药〉yaoyinzi; medicinal usher (efficacy-enhancer added to medicine)
药用植物	〈中医药〉medicinal plant
药用植物学	〈中医药〉pharmaceutical botany
药浴疗法	〈中医药〉medicinal bath therapy
药熨疗法	〈中医药〉hot medicinal compress therapy
药枕疗法	〈中医药〉medicinal pillow therapy
要面子	to save face; to be keen on face-saving
耀窑刻花葫芦形执壶	〈陶瓷〉Yao Kiln gourd-shaped ewer with carved flower pattern
耀窑刻花青釉三足带盖罐	〈陶瓷〉Yao Kiln celadon tripod lidded jar with carved flower pattern

耀窑刻花三足瓷炉	〈陶瓷〉Yao Kiln tripod porcelain burner with carved flower pattern
耀州窑	〈陶瓷〉Yaozhou Kiln
耀州窑青瓷刻花梅瓶	〈陶瓷〉Yaozhou Kiln celadon plum vase with carved flower pattern
耀州窑青瓷刻花碗	〈陶瓷〉Yaozhou Kiln celadon bowl with carved flower pattern
椰丝糯米糍	〈饮食〉Glutinous Rice Balls Stuffed with Coconut
椰油咖喱鸡	〈饮食〉Curry Chicken with Coconut Oil
椰汁炖雪蛤	〈饮食〉Stewed Clam in Coconut Milk
椰汁西米露	〈饮食〉Sweet Sago Cream with Coconut Milk; Coconut Tapioca
野菊花	〈中医药〉(of Latin) Flos Chrysanthemi Indici; Wild Chrysanthemum Flower
野菌鹅肝	〈饮食〉Pan-Fried Goose Livers with Wild Mushrooms
野菌烧豆腐	〈饮食〉Braised Tofu with Mushrooms
野木瓜注射液	〈中医药〉Yemugua Zhusheye; Wild Chaenomele Injection
野山红炒木耳	〈饮食〉Stir-Fried Black Fungi with Red Peppers
野山椒炒牛肉丝	〈饮食〉Stir-Fried Shredded Beef with Wild Pepper
野山参	〈中医药〉(of Latin) Radix Ginseng Indici; Wild Ginseng
野山珍鲈鱼	〈饮食〉Perch with Wild Mushrooms
野生菌烩乌鱼片	〈饮食〉Stewed Cuttlefish Fillets/Slices with Wild Mushrooms
野鸭饭	〈饮食〉Stir-Fried Rice with Diced Wild Duck
业务部门经理	(of a bank) corporate banking manager
业务部门主管	(of a bank) corporate banking supervisor
业务跟单经理	merchandiser manager
业务客户经理	(of a bank) corporate banking account manager
业务拓展主管	business development supervisor
业务拓展专员	business development specialist
业务拓展总监	business development dircctor

业务主管	steward supervisor; business supervisor
业务主任	business controller
叶缘垂卷	〈茶〉leaf side roll down
夜大学	〈旧〉evening university; after-hours university
夜猫子	night owl; night people (who go to bed late)
夜明砂	〈中医药〉(of Latin) Feaces Vespertilio; Bat's Droppings
夜审计员	night auditor
夜市	night market
液门	〈中医药〉Yemen acupoint; Fluid Gate (SJ2)
液脱证	〈中医药〉pattern of turbid fluid exhaustion; humor desertion pattern
一次性杯子	sanitary cup; disposable cup
一次性筷子	throwaway chopsticks; disposable chopsticks
一次性手套	〈防疫〉disposable gloves
一次性用品	disposable goods
一帆风顺	to be plain/clear sailing; wish you every success
一夫法	〈中医药〉finger-breadth cun; 4-finger-breadth measurement
一贯煎	〈中医药〉Yiguan Jian; All-the-Way through Brew
一棍子打死	knock sb. down at one stroke; to finish sb. off with a single blow; to completely negate
一级应急响应	〈防疫〉the first-level emergency response
一客一用一消毒	〈防疫〉disinfection after each serving
一路平安[顺风]	to wish a good journey; to speed sb. on their way
一米线	〈防疫〉one meter spacing in line; to wait in line at an interval of one meter
一票通用制度	universal ticket system
一品梅香烟	Yipin Mei cigarettes; First Class Plum cigarettes
一品什锦汤面	〈饮食〉Noodle Soup with Assorted Vegetables
一品蒜花鸡	〈饮食〉Deep-Fried Chicken with Garlic
一人一方案	〈防疫〉personalized treatment plan for each patient
一人一团队	〈防疫〉dedicated team for each patient

一色衣[服]	〈古〉uni-color overall clothes →质孙服
一窝蜂	to rush to do sth. like a swarm of bees
一线城市	first-tier city
一线医护人员	〈防疫〉frontline health workers
一线员工	worker at the production line; front-line worker
一心二叶	〈茶〉one-tip two-leaf
一心三叶	〈茶〉one-tip three-leaf
一心四叶	〈茶〉one-tip four-leaf
一心一叶	〈茶〉one-tip one-leaf
一站式服务窗口	one-stop service window
一指禅推法	〈中医药〉one-finger scrubbing; pushing manipulation with one finger
一字领口	boat neckline; slit neckline; off neckline
伊犁酒	Yili liquor
衣裳连属制	〈服饰〉one-piece dress system
《医方集解》	〈中医药〉*Yifang Jijie*; *Medical Formulas Gathered and Explained*; *Collected Exegesis of Recipes* (by Wang Ang in the Qing Dynasty)
医防结合	〈防疫〉to emphasize on both prevention and treatment
《医贯》	〈中医药〉*Yiguan*; *Thorough Knowledge of Medicine*; *Key Link of Medicine* (by Zhao Xianke in the Ming Dynasty)
医护助理	nursing assistant
医疗保险	medical insurance
医疗从业者	〈防疫〉medical practitioner; healthcare professional
医疗废物处置能力	〈防疫〉medical waste disposal capacity
医疗废物日产日清	〈防疫〉to ensure that medical waste is treated on a daily basis
医疗改革	health care reform
医疗合作制度	medical assistance system
医疗机构	〈防疫〉medical institution
医疗挤兑	〈防疫〉medical resources panic squeeze

医疗人员	〈防疫〉medical personnel; health workforce; health workers
医疗物资	〈防疫〉medical supplies
医疗物资紧缺	〈防疫〉shortage of medical supplies
医疗销售代表	medical sales representative
医疗援助	〈防疫〉medical assistance
医疗主任	clinical director; manager in health care
《医林改错》	〈中医药〉Yilin Gaicuo; Correction of Errors in Medical Classics; Correction of the Errors of Medical Works (by Wang Qingren in the Qing Dynasty)
医务人员科学防护和培训	〈防疫〉scientific prevention and proper training for medical workers
《医学纲目》	〈中医药〉Yixue Gangmu; Compendium of Medicine (by Lou Ying in the Ming Dynasty)
医学观察	〈防疫〉medical watch; medical observation
医学检[巡]查	〈防疫〉medical inspection
医药技术人员	medical technician
医药技术研发管理人员	management staff of pharmaceutical technology research and development
医药技术研发人员	specialist of pharmaceutical technology research and development
医药销售代表	pharmaceutical sales representative
医药销售经理	medical sales manager
医药销售主管	pharmaceutical sales supervisor
医用口罩	〈防疫〉surgical mask; medical facemask
医院/院内感染	〈防疫〉nosocomial infection; hospital-acquired infection
医院管理人员	hospital administrator
医院管理员	hospital supervisor
《医宗金鉴》	〈中医药〉Yizong Jinjian; Golden Mirror of Medicine (by Wu Qian in the Qing Dynasty)
依法防治	〈防疫〉law-based measures in the prevention and control of the epidemic
依法治国	to manage state affairs according to law; to run state affairs according to law; to rule by law

移动电话漫游	mobile phone roaming
移动电话双向收费	two-way charges for cellular phones
移动通信工程师	mobile communication engineer
移动支付	mobile payment
移动支付交易	mobile payment transaction
移动支付平台	mobile payment platform
疑似病例	〈防疫〉suspected patient; presumptive case
疑似病例筛查	〈防疫〉screening of suspected patients
疑似病例追踪	〈防疫〉tracing of suspected patients
乙肝扶正胶囊	〈中医药〉Yigan Fuzheng Jiaonang; Hepatitis-B Rightness-Supporting Capsule
乙肝解毒胶囊	〈中医药〉Yigan Jiedu Jiaonang; Hepatitis-B Toxin-Resolving Capsule
乙肝宁冲剂［颗粒］	〈中医药〉Yiganning Chongji/Keli; Hepatitis B Halting Granule
乙肝宁颗粒	〈中医药〉Yiganning Keli; Hepatitis-B Calmness Granule
乙类传染病	〈防疫〉category B infectious diseases
以…为龙头	with sth. as the leading role
以讹传讹	to incorrectly relay an erroneous message
以空间换取时间	to trade space for time
以权谋私	to seek private gain through power
以人为本	people oriented; to put people foremost
以市场为导向	market-oriented
义教	voluntary teaching
义盛永熏鸡	〈饮食〉Yishengyong Smoked Chicken
义务兵役制	compulsory military service; conscription
义务教育	compulsory education
义演	benefit performance; charity performance; fund-raising performance
义诊	(of a doctor) to give volunteer medical consultation
艺考	→艺术高考
艺术高考	Art College Entrance Examination
艺术教师	art instructor; art teacher

艺术团	art troupe
艺术总监	art director; chief artistic officer; CAO
议价商品	commodity with negotiated price; bargain commodity
异病同治	〈中医药〉like treatment of unlike disease; the same treatment for different diseases; to treat different diseases with the same therapeutic principle
抑制新冠病毒传播	〈防疫〉to curb the spread of the novel coronavirus
抑制需求	to depress demand; to take hold on consumption
译审	review translator; senior translator
易感人群	〈防疫〉susceptible population; vulnerable population
易黄汤	〈中医药〉Yihuang Tang; Yellow-Transforming Decoction
弈	Chinese chess game; to play Chinese chess →围棋
疫毒内闭证	〈中医药〉pattern of epidemic toxin internal block; internal-epidemic toxin blockage pattern
疫毒侵袭证	〈中医药〉pattern of epidemic toxin invasion
疫苗临床试验	〈防疫〉clinical trial of vaccines
疫苗上市使用	〈防疫〉application of vaccines
疫苗研发	〈防疫〉vaccine development
疫情暴发	〈防疫〉epidemic outbreak of disease
疫情防控	〈防疫〉epidemic prevention and control
疫情防控措施	〈防疫〉epidemic prevention and control measures
疫情防控国家重点医疗物资保障调度平台	〈防疫〉national distribution center/platform for major anti-epidemic medical supplies
疫情防控重点地区	〈防疫〉key regions in epidemic prevention and control effort
疫情峰值	〈防疫〉epidemic peak
疫情高发区	〈防疫〉severely-hit areas; regions with high infection rates
疫情监测	〈防疫〉epidemic monitoring
疫情就是命令	〈防疫〉the epidemic is an order

疫情可防可控	〈防疫〉an epidemic that can be prevented and controlled
疫情瞒报	〈防疫〉to underreport epidemic situation
疫情重灾区	〈防疫〉epicenter of the outbreak/epidemic
益肺胶囊	〈中医药〉Yifei Jiaonang; Lung Benefiting Capsule
益肺止咳胶囊	〈中医药〉Yifei Zhike Keli; Lung-Boosting and Cough-Suppressing Capsule
益火消阴	〈中医药〉to boost source of fire for eliminating abundance of yin
益母草	〈中医药〉(of Latin) Herba Leonuri; Motherwort Herb
益母草膏	〈中医药〉Yimucao Gao; Semifluid Motherwort Extract Paste
益母草颗粒	〈中医药〉Yimucao Keli; Motherwort Granule
益脑胶囊	〈中医药〉Yinao Jiaonang; Brain-Enriching Capsule
益气安神	〈中医药〉to benefit qi for tranquillization; to boost qi for relieving uneasiness of mind
益气固表	〈中医药〉to invigorate qi for consolidating superficies/exterior
益气活血	〈中医药〉to benefit qi for activating blood circulation; to boost qi and quicken the blood flow
益气健脾	〈中医药〉to tonify qi and nourish the spleen
益气解表	〈中医药〉to benefit qi for relieving superficies/exterior syndrome; to boost qi to resolve the exterior
益气生津	〈中医药〉to benefit qi for promoting production of fluid; to boost qi and engender liquid
益气生血	〈中医药〉to benefit qi for promoting production of blood; to boost qi and engender flood
益气滋阴	〈中医药〉to benefit qi for nourishing yin; to boost qi for enriching yin
益肾灵颗粒	〈中医药〉Yishenling Keli; Kidney-Boosting Effectiveness Granule

益胃汤	〈中医药〉Yiwei Tang; Stomach-Boosting Decoction
益元散	〈中医药〉Yiyuan San; Origin-Boosting Powder
益智仁	〈中医药〉(of Latin) Fructus Alpiniae Oxyphyllae; Sharp-Leaf Glangal Fruit; Bitter Cardamon
益中生血胶囊	〈中医药〉Yizhong Shengxue Jiaonang; Middle-Warmer Benefiting and Blood Engendering Capsule
意见簿	visitors' book; customers' book; book for comments and criticism
意外风险	emergency risk; unknown risk
薏苡仁	〈中医药〉(of Latin) Semen Coicis; Coix Seed
因材施教	to teach students according to their aptitude
因果报应	retribution for one's sin; karmic retribution
阴谷	〈中医药〉Yingu acupoint; Yin Valley (KI10)
阴交	〈中医药〉Yinjiao acupoint; Yin Intersection (RN7)
阴竭阳脱	〈中医药〉depletion of yin and yang desertion; yin exhaustion and yang collapse
阴竭阳脱证	〈中医药〉pattern of yin depletion with yang exhaustion
阴廉	〈中医药〉Yinlian acupoint; Yin Corner (LR11)
阴陵泉	〈中医药〉Yinlingquan acupoint; Yin Mound Spring (SP9)
阴胜则阳病	〈中医药〉excess of yin leading to deficiency of yang; predominance of yin inducing disorder of yang
阴盛阳衰证	〈中医药〉pattern of yang deficiency due to yin excess
阴损及阳	〈中医药〉depletion of yin affecting yang; yin deficiency involving yang
阴损及阳证	〈中医药〉pattern of yin depletion affecting yang
阴邪	〈中医药〉yin pathogen
阴虚	〈中医药〉yin deficiency
阴虚肠燥证	〈中医药〉pattern of intestine dryness due to yin deficiency

阴虚齿燥证	〈中医药〉pattern of teeth dryness due to yin deficiency
阴虚动风证	〈中医药〉pattern of stirring wind due to yin deficiency
阴虚动血证	〈中医药〉pattern of stirring blood due to yin deficiency
阴虚发热	〈中医药〉fever due to yin deficiency
阴虚肺燥证	〈中医药〉pattern of lung dryness due to yin deficiency
阴虚火旺	〈中医药〉hyperactivity of fire due to yin deficiency
阴虚火旺证	〈中医药〉pattern of fire hyperactivity due to yin deficiency
阴虚津亏证	〈中医药〉pattern of yin deficiency and fluid depletion
阴虚内热证	〈中医药〉pattern of endogenous heat due to yin deficiency
阴虚生内热	〈中医药〉interior heat due to yin deficiency
阴虚湿热证	〈中医药〉pattern of yin deficiency and dampness-heat
阴虚外感证	〈中医药〉pattern of exogenous disease due to yin deficiency
阴虚血热证	〈中医药〉pattern of yin deficiency and blood heat
阴虚血瘀证	〈中医药〉pattern of yin deficiency and blood stasis
阴虚血燥证	〈中医药〉pattern of yin deficiency and blood dryness
阴虚阳亢	〈中医药〉hyperactivity of yang and deficiency of yin
阴虚阳亢证	〈中医药〉pattern of yang hyperactivity due to yin deficiency
阴虚证	〈中医药〉yin deficiency pattern
阴阳辨证	〈中医药〉pattern differentiation of yin-yang
阴阳并补剂	〈中医药〉formula for benefiting both yin and yang
阴阳互损	〈中医药〉inter-impairment between yin and yang; mutual depletion of yin and yang

阴阳俱损	〈中医药〉simultaneous depletion of yin and yang
阴阳两虚	〈中医药〉deficiency of both yin and yang; yin-yang deficiency
阴阳两虚证	〈中医药〉pattern of deficiency of both yin and yang
阴阳失调	〈中医药〉yin-yang disharmony; imbalance of yin and yang
阴阳学说	〈中医药〉theory of yin and yang; yin-yang theory
茵陈	〈中医药〉(of Latin) Herba Artemisiae Scopariae; Virgate Wormwood Herb
茵陈蒿汤	〈中医药〉Yinchenhao Tang; Herbae Artemisiae Capillariae Decoction; Oriental Wormwood Decoction
茵陈五苓散	〈中医药〉Yinchen Wuling San; Five Substances Powder with Poria Plus Virgate Wormwood
茵栀黄注射液	〈中医药〉Yinzhihuang Zhusheye; Capillaries-Gardenia-Scutellaria Injection
音频点播	audio-on-demand
音乐教师	music teacher
音乐疗法	music therapy
姻亲	kinsmen by affinity; relationship by marriage
姻亲关系	relationship by affinity; relation by marriage
姻缘	Yinyuan (the happy fate which brings lovers together); prefixed/predestined fate of marriage; predestined marriage
殷豉炒肉蟹	〈饮食〉Stir-Fried Hard-Shell Crab with Black Bean Sauce
殷豉炒珍宝蟹	〈饮食〉Stir-Fried Jumbo Crab with Black Bean Sauce
殷门	〈中医药〉Yinmen acupoint; Gate of Abundance (BL37)
银白鱼肚	〈饮食〉Stewed Fish Maw with Mung Bean Sprouts
银背扣	〈侗族〉silver buckles on the back
银柴胡	〈中医药〉(of Latin) Radix Stellariae; Starwort Root

银锭	〈古〉silver ingot; sycee (silver ingots formerly used as a medium of exchange)
银耳海棠蛋汤	〈饮食〉Pigeon Eggs and White Fungi Soup
银根紧缩	credit squeeze; monetary stringency
银行出纳	bank clerk; bank cashier
银行存单	deposit receipt
银行存折	bankbook; passbook
银行代收费	deposit payment at bank
银行高级职员	banking executive
银行汇款单	bank money order; remittance sheet/bill
银角子	cob money (a common name of silver coins since the end of Qing Dynasty)
银绿	〈茶〉silvery green
银帽	silver cap
银泡	〈景颇族〉silver bubble (women's unique shoulder pendant)
银翘解毒颗粒	〈中医药〉Yinqiao Jiedu Keli; Forsythia Granule; Fructus Forsythiae Antidotal Granule
银翘散	〈中医药〉Yinqiao San; Lonicera and Forsythia Powder
银饰	silver ornament; silver jewellery; silverwork
银项圈	silver necklace
银杏百合炒虾球	〈饮食〉Stir-Fried Shrimp Balls with Lily Bulbs and Ginkgo
银杏炒百合	〈饮食〉Stir-Fried Lily Bulbs with Gingko Kernels
银杏果	〈中医药〉(of Latin) Semen Ginkgo Biloba; Gindgo Nut
银杏鸡花	〈饮食〉Diced Chicken with Gingko
银杏叶	〈中医药〉(of Latin) Folium Ginkgo; Ginkgo Leaf
银芽炒鲍丝	〈饮食〉Stir-Fried Shredded Abalone with Bean Sprouts
银芽炒牛肉	〈饮食〉Stir-Fried Beef and Bean Sprouts
银芽炒虾松	〈饮食〉Stir-Fried Minced Shrimps with Bean Sprouts

银芽干炒牛河	〈饮食〉Stir-Fried Rice Noodles with Beef and Bean Sprouts
银芽肉丝	〈饮食〉Stir-Fried Shredded Pork with Bean Sprouts
银芽肉丝炒面	〈饮食〉Stir-Fried Noodles with Shredded Pork and Bean Sprouts
银元	〈旧〉silver coin →大洋
银簪	silver hairpin
银针	〈中医药〉acupuncture needle; silver needle
银针白毫	〈茶〉white tip silver needle
银针绿茶	silver needle green tea
银制头饰	silver head ornament
淫羊藿	〈中医药〉(of Latin) Herba Epimedii; Epimedium Herb
龈交	〈中医药〉Yinjiao acupoint; Gum Intersection (DU28)
引经药	〈中医药〉channel ushering drug
引流疗法	〈中医药〉drainage therapy
饮留胃肠证	〈中医药〉pattern of fluid retention retaining in stomach and intestines
《饮膳正要》	〈中医药〉*Yinshan Zhengyao*; *Principles of Correct Diet* (by Hu Sihui in the Yuan Dynasty)
饮食不节	〈中医药〉imbalanced diet; improper diet; dietary irregularities
饮食禁忌	〈中医药〉dietetic contraindication
饮食劳倦	〈中医药〉improper diet and overstrain
饮食疗法	〈中医药〉dietotherapy; dietary treatment; food therapy
饮食所伤	〈中医药〉injury due to diet
饮食调理	〈中医药〉dietetic regulation
饮食中药	〈中医药〉dietary Chinese medicine
饮停胸胁证	〈中医药〉pattern of fluid retention in chest and hypochondrium
饮溢四肢证	〈中医药〉pattern of fluid retention overflowing in limbs

隐性感染	〈防疫〉covert infection; silent infection; inapparent infection; subclinical infection
隐性就业	unregistered employment
隐性失业	recessive unemployment
隐性收入	invisible income; off-payroll income; side money
瘾君子	drug addict; drug fanatic; narcotic addict
印绶	〈古〉seal with silk ribbon; official seal
印刷机械机长	printing machine operator
印刷排版师	printing typesetter
印刷制版师	computer-to-plate (CTP) technician
印堂	〈中医药〉Yintang acupoint; Hall of Impression (GV29)
应届毕业生	the year's graduates; new graduates; recent graduates
英德红茶	Yingde black tea
英德绿茶	Yingde green tea
英山云雾茶	Yingshan Cloud Mist tea
英语培训中心	English training center
英语专业八级	Test for English Major Grade 8 Certificate; TEM8
英语专业四级	Test for English Major Grade 4 Certificate; TEM4
婴儿安全岛	baby safety island (for protecting the right to live of abandoned babies)
婴儿服装	baby clothes; infant's wear
罂粟壳	〈中医药〉(of Latin) Pericarpium Papaveris; Poppy Capsule
缨枪	〈古〉red-tassel spear
缨子	〈服饰〉hat tassel; cap tassel
璎珞	〈佛〉keyura; pearl and jade necklace; jade-like stone
樱桃白雪鸡	〈饮食〉Steamed Chicken Drumsticks and Pork with Red Cherries
樱桃萝卜蘸酱	〈饮食〉Radish with Soy Bean Paste
樱桃肉	〈饮食〉Braised Sweet and Sour Pork (Shaped as a Cherry)

樱桃汁煎鸭胸	〈饮食〉Pan-Fried Duck Breast with Cherry Sauce
迎宾酒	Yingbin chiew; welcome drink
迎宾员	usher; hostess
迎香	〈中医药〉Yingxiang acupoint; Fragrance Access; Welcome Fragrance (LI20)
迎新晚会	welcome party for the freshmen
盈江黄酒	Yingjiang yellow rice wine
盈亏责任制	system of responsibility for profit or loss
营销分析助理	marketing analyst assistant
营销顾问	marketing consultant
营销经理	marketing manager
营销助理	marketing assistant
营养师	nutritionist; dietician
营业部大堂经理	lobby manager of sales department
营业(部)经理	business manager; sales manager; operational manager
郢爰	〈币〉yingyuan coin; gold coin of Chu (the earliest gold coin in China)
影青缠枝卷叶纹瓷瓶	〈陶瓷〉misty blue porcelain vase with interlaced branches and leaves pattern
影青观音	〈陶瓷〉misty blue porcelain Goddess of Mercy
影青广寒宫瓷枕	〈陶瓷〉misty blue porcelain pillow in the shape of moon palace
影青酒壶	〈陶瓷〉yingqing (misty blue) porcelain wine pot
影青莲瓣温酒碗	〈陶瓷〉misty blue warming bowl with lotus-petal pattern
影青人物梅瓶	〈陶瓷〉blue and white plum vase with portraiture pattern
影青釉里红鸳鸯花纹罐	〈陶瓷〉misty blue underglaze red jar with mandarin ducks and lotus flower pattern
影视策划人员	film and television planner
影视制作人员	film and television producer
应变措施	emergency measures; contingency measures
应急模式	〈防疫〉emergency mode

应急医院	〈防疫〉makeshift hospital
应用工程师	application engineer
应用软件程序员	application programmer
硬瓷	〈陶瓷〉hard porcelain
硬件工程师	hardware engineer
拥军优属	to support the army and give preferential treatment to the families of servicemen and martyrs
雍正瓷器	〈陶瓷〉enamel/porcelain of the Emperor Yongzheng's reigning period (in the Qing Dynasty)
雍正斗彩花卉尊	〈陶瓷〉clashing color zun with floral pattern (Qing Yongzheng period)
永和窑剪纸贴花三凤纹碗	〈陶瓷〉Yonghe Kiln bowl with three-decal-phoenix applique pattern
永乐青花无挡尊	〈陶瓷〉blue and white tubular zun (Ming Yongle period)
泳池服务员	pool attendant
涌泉	〈中医药〉Yongquan acupoint; Gushing Spring (KI1)
涌吐法	〈中医药〉emesis method
涌吐剂	〈中医药〉emetic formula; emetic prescription
用户界面顾问	user interface consultant
用户界面设计师	user interface designer
用药不当	〈中医药〉inappropriate use of medicines
用药禁忌	〈中医药〉contraindication in using herbs
优酷	(of video platform) Youku
优良学风班	class of good style study
优先免费通行	〈防疫〉priority and toll-free access
优秀毕业生	outstanding graduates
优秀辩手	excellent debate
优秀工作者	excellent staff
优秀共青团员	excellent league member
优秀会员	excellent member
优秀教师	excellent teacher
优秀节目奖	best program award

优秀青年志愿者	outstanding young volunteer
优秀团干	outstanding league cadres
优秀团体奖	excellent group award
优秀团员	→优秀共青团员
优秀学生干部	excellent student cadre
优秀员工	outstanding employee; employee of the month/year
优秀指导教师奖	excellent guide teacher award
优秀志愿者	outstanding volunteer
优秀组织奖	outstanding organization award
幽门	〈中医药〉Youmen acupoint; Pylorus (KI12)
幽香	〈茶〉gentle flowery flavor
油爆干贝	〈饮食〉Stir-Fried Dried Scallops with Choice Vegetables
油爆里脊丁	〈饮食〉Stir-Fried Diced Pork Fillet with Scallion
油爆鳝片	〈饮食〉Quick-Fried Sliced Eel with Sea Kale
油爆鱿鱼	〈饮食〉Quick-Fried Squid with Sea Kale
油葱香酥	〈饮食〉Fragrant Scallion Cakes
油豆腐	〈饮食〉Oily Tofu; Fried Bean Curd Puff
油豆腐粉丝汤	〈饮食〉Fried Tofu and Vermicelli Soup
油煎鹌鹑	〈饮食〉Pan-Fried Quail with Bamboo Shoots
油煎蛋皮肉卷	〈饮食〉Pan-Fried Egg Rolls Stuffed with Minced Pork
油酱毛蟹	〈饮食〉Braised River Crab with Soy Bean Paste
油浸多宝鱼	〈饮食〉Tender-Fried Marinated Turbot Fish
油浸鳜鱼	〈饮食〉Tender-Fried Marinated Mandarin Fish
油浸鲤鱼	〈饮食〉Tender-Fried Marinated Carp
油浸鲈鱼	〈饮食〉Tender-Fried Marinated Perch
油浸石斑鱼	〈饮食〉Tender-Fried Marinated Grouper
油浸娃娃菜	〈饮食〉Braised Baby Cabbage with Soy Sauce
油淋鸡	〈饮食〉Scalded Chicken with Boiling Oil
油焖大虾	〈饮食〉Braised Prawns in Oil; Stewed Prawns with Tomato Sauce
油面筋酿肉	〈饮食〉Stewed Dried Wheat Gluten with Pork Stuffing

油泡料	〈饮食〉pre-frying ingredients
油泡石斑球	〈饮食〉Tender-Fried Marinated Grouper Meat Balls
油泡虾球	〈饮食〉Crystal Prawn Balls
油泡小牛肉	〈饮食〉Roasted Beef with Shredded Scallion and Ginger in Oil
油泼全鸡	〈饮食〉Fried Spring Chicken with Chive and Parsley
油条	〈饮食〉Fried Bread Stick; Deep-Fried Twisted Dough Stick
油盐水浸时蔬	〈饮食〉Braised Seasonal Vegetables with Sauce
油炸	〈饮食〉to deep-fry; deep fried
油炸臭豆腐	〈饮食〉Deep-Fried Fermented Tofu
油炸凤尾鱼	〈饮食〉Deep-Fried Anchovy; Boquerones Fritos
油炸软米糕	〈饮食〉Fried Millet Cake with Sugar
油炸豌豆粉	〈饮食〉Deep-Fried Pea Flour Noodles
油炸虾丸	〈饮食〉Deep-Fried Shrimp Balls
鱿鱼丝	〈饮食〉Shredded Squid
鱿鱼汤	〈饮食〉Squid Soup
游戏开发工程师	game development engineer
游学	(overseas) study tour; to study away from home
游走性舌炎	〈中医药〉migratory glossitis; glossitis areata exfoliativa
有盖贴袋	patch pocket with flap
有个奔头	to have sth. to look forward to
有害垃圾	〈防疫〉hazardous waste
有路子	to have friends in high places; to have resources to draw upon
有线传输工程师	wired transmission engineer
有效性和安全性研究	〈防疫〉safety and efficacy studies
有序安全的国际人员流动	〈防疫〉orderly and safe flow of people between countries
有序复工	〈防疫〉to resume production in an orderly manner

有氧治疗师	respiratory therapist
有针对性减税降费政策	〈防疫〉targeted tax and fee breaks
右归丸	〈中医药〉Yougui Wan; Right-Restoring (Life Gate) Pill; Kidney Yang-Reinforcing Bolus
右归饮	〈中医药〉Yougui Yin; Right-Restoring (Life Gate) Beverage; Kidney Yang-Reinforcing Drink
右衽	〈服饰〉right-lapel Han robe
《幼幼集成》	〈中医药〉*Youyou Jicheng*; *Compendium of Pediatrics*; *Complete Work on Children's Diseases* (by Chen Fuzheng in the Qing Dynasty)
《幼幼新书》	〈中医药〉*Youyou Xinshu*; *New Book of Pediatrics* (by Liu Fang et al. in the Southern Song Dynasty)
釉里红杯	〈陶瓷〉underglaze-red cup (Ming Yongle period)
釉里红缠枝花卉菱口盏托	〈陶瓷〉copper-red cup stand with interlocked branches and floral pattern (Ming Hongwu period)
釉里红缠枝玉壶春瓶	〈陶瓷〉underglaze red Yuhuchun vase with interlaced branches pattern
釉里红瓷瓶	〈陶瓷〉underglaze red porcelain jar
釉里红高足杯	〈陶瓷〉underglaze-red stem cup (Yuan Dynasty)
釉里红海兽蒜头瓶	〈陶瓷〉underglaze red garlic-head vase with sea mammals pattern (Qing Qianlong period)
釉里红花卉龙纹盘	〈陶瓷〉underglaze-red plate with floral and dragon pattern (Yuan Dynasty)
釉里红花卉纹四系扁壶	〈陶瓷〉underglaze-red four-eared flat jug with floral pattern (Ming Hongwu period)
釉里红菊纹玉壶春瓶	〈陶瓷〉underglaze-red Yuhuchun vase with red chrysanthemum pattern (Yuan Dynasty)
釉里红龙纹罐	〈陶瓷〉underglaze red jar with dragon pattern
釉里红牡丹纹碗	〈陶瓷〉underglaze red bowl with peony pattern
釉里红菩萨塑像	〈陶瓷〉underglaze red Buddha statue (Yuan Dynasty)
釉里红三鱼碗	〈陶瓷〉underglaze red bowl with three fish pattern (Ming Xuan period)

釉里红松梅竹纹四系扁壶	〈陶瓷〉underglaze-red four-eared flat jug with pine-plum-bamboo pattern (Yuan Dynasty)
釉里红松梅竹纹玉壶春瓶	〈陶瓷〉underglaze-red Yuhuchun vase with pine-plum-bamboo pattern (Ming Hongwu period)
釉里红松竹梅罐	〈陶瓷〉underglaze red jar with pine-bamboo-plum pattern
釉里红鱼莲纹盖罐	〈陶瓷〉underglaze-red lidded jar with fish and lotus pattern (Ming Xuande period)
釉料	〈陶瓷〉glaze; glaze material
釉泡	〈陶瓷〉glaze bubble
釉上彩	〈陶瓷〉overglazed color figure; on-glazed
釉烧窑	〈陶瓷〉glost kiln; glost burning kiln
釉下彩	〈陶瓷〉underglaze color; under glazed
釉下彩龙纹瓷壶	〈陶瓷〉underglaze porcelain ewer with dragon pattern
瘀热入络证	〈中医药〉pattern of stagnant-heat invading collaterals/the network vessels
瘀血致泻	〈中医药〉disease caused by blood stasis
瘀血阻络	〈中医药〉obstruction of the collaterals by blood stasis
瘀血阻络证	〈中医药〉pattern of static blood blocking the collaterals; pattern of stagnant blood obstructing the collaterals
瘀阻胞宫证	〈中医药〉pattern of static blood blockade in uterus; pattern of stasis obstructing the uterus
瘀阻胞脉证	〈中医药〉pattern of stasis obstructing uterine vessels pattern of static blood blocking in uterine vessel
瘀阻脑络证	〈中医药〉pattern of stasis obstructing the network vessels of the brain; pattern of blood stasis blocking the brain
瘀阻胃络证	〈中医药〉pattern of stasis in stomach collaterals/the network vessels

瘀阻咽喉证	〈中医药〉pattern of static blood stagnated in throat
余毒未清证	〈中医药〉residual toxin pattern; pattern of remained toxin/toxicity
余热未清证	〈中医药〉lingering heat pattern; residual heat pattern
鱼菜厨师领班	poissionier
鱼翅汤	〈饮食〉Shark Fin Soup; Soup with Shark Fins
鱼唇羹	〈饮食〉Thickened Fish Snout Soup
鱼袋	〈古〉fish-shaped bag (for distinguishing officials' identity)
鱼肚鸡片汤	〈饮食〉Codfish Maw Soup with Sliced Chicken
鱼肚粟米羹	〈饮食〉Fish Maw in Sweetcorn Soup
鱼腐扒菜胆	〈饮食〉Braised Green Vegetables with Fish Curd
鱼际	〈中医药〉Yuji acupoint; Fish Border (LU10)
鱼露白肉	〈饮食〉Sliced Boiled Pork in Anchovy Sauce
鱼米之乡	abundant place; land abundant in fish and rice; land of fish and rice
鱼片浓汤	〈饮食〉Fish Fillet Soup with Lily and Pepper
鱼生虾米粥	〈饮食〉Sliced Fish and Dried Shrimps Broth
鱼酥	〈饮食〉Deep-Fried Crispy Fish; Fried Fish Crackers
鱼头砂锅	〈饮食〉Stewed Fish Head in Pottery Pot
鱼丸烧海参	〈饮食〉Stewed Sea Cucumbers with Fish Balls
鱼丸汤	〈饮食〉Fish Ball Soup
鱼香炒鳝丝	〈饮食〉Stir-Fried Shredded Eel with Fish Flavor
鱼香大虾肉	〈饮食〉Stir-Fried Prawn Meat with Fish Flavor
鱼香干贝	〈饮食〉Stir-Fried Dried Scallops with Fish Flavor
鱼香鸡片	〈饮食〉Stir-Fried Chicken Slices with Fish Flavor
鱼香芥蓝	〈饮食〉Stir-Fried Chinese Broccoli with Fish Flavor
鱼香里脊丝	〈饮食〉Stir-Fried Fillet Shreds in Spicy Garlic Sauce
鱼香明虾球	〈饮食〉Stir-Fried Prawn Balls with Fish Flavor

鱼香牛肉丝	〈饮食〉Fish Flavored Beef Slices; Stir-Fried Beef Slices with Spicy Garlic Sauce
鱼香茄子	〈饮食〉Stir-Fried Eggplants with Fish Flavor
鱼香茄子煲	〈饮食〉Stewed Eggplant with Spicy Garlic Sauce in Casserole
鱼香肉丝	〈饮食〉Stir-Fried Pork Shreds with Spicy Garlic Sauce
鱼香丝瓜煲	〈饮食〉Stewed Sponge Gourd with Spicy Garlic Sauce in Casserole
鱼香碎米鸡	〈饮食〉Stir-Fried Diced Chicken with Fish Flavor
鱼腥草	〈中医药〉(of Latin) Houttuynia Cordata; Heartleaf Houttuynia Herb
鱼腥草拌米线	〈饮食〉Special Herbal Rice Noodles
竽	〈乐〉yu (ancient 36-reed windpipe)
娱乐服务员	entertainment waiter
娱乐领班	entertainment service supervisor
娱乐市场	entertainment market
娱乐业	entertainment industry
渔业场长	head of fishing industry; head of fishery
瑜伽教练	yoga coach; yoga instructor
舆论监督	supervision by public opinions; media's supervision
褕翟[狄]	〈服饰〉yuzhai; queen's ceremonial robe
羽绒服	down garment; down coat/jacket
羽绒裤	down wadded trousers; down pants
雨前茶	yu-chien tea (made from bud tips before Grain Rain)
雨衣	raincoat; waterproof
语文出版社	Language & Culture Press
语言病理学家	speech pathologist; speech-language pathologists
语音开发工程师	audio development engineer
玉冰烧	〈酒〉Yubing Shao; Jade Ice Shochu
玉带干贝酥	〈饮食〉Fried Scallops with Crispy Taro Strips and Vegetables

玉带钩	jade belt hook
玉带芦笋汤	〈饮食〉Scallop and Asparagus Soup
玉蝠饺	〈饮食〉Steamed Shrimps and Pork Rissole
玉环干贝	〈饮食〉Stuffed Cucumbers with Scallops (Shaped as a Ring)
玉兰山鸡片	〈饮食〉Stir-Fried Pheasant Slices with Lily Flower
玉兰酥香肉	〈饮食〉Fried Pork and Walnut Kernels (in the shape of an orchid)
玉米羹	〈饮食〉Sweetcorn Soup; Mealie Soup
玉米鸡茸浓汤	〈饮食〉Sweetcorn and Minced Chicken Soup
玉米面馒头	〈饮食〉Mantou/Steamed Bun with Corn Flour
玉米须	〈中医药〉(of Latin) Stigma Maydis; Corn Stigma; Corn Silk
玉女煎	〈中医药〉Yunü Jian; Gypsum Decoction
玉屏风颗粒	〈中医药〉Yupingfeng Keli; Jade Screen Granule
玉屏风散	〈中医药〉Yupingfeng San; Jade Wind-Barrier Powder
玉搔头	(of headwear) jade hairpin; emerald hairpin
玉树地震	Yushu earthquake (on the 14th April, 2010)
玉笋炒酸菜	〈饮食〉Stir-Fried Pickled Cabbage with Bamboo Shoots
玉溪香烟	Yuxi cigarettes
玉叶清火胶囊	〈中医药〉Yuye Qinghuo Jiaonang; Jade Leaf Fire-Clearing Capsule
玉叶清火片	〈中医药〉Yuye Qinghuo Pian; Jade Leaf Fire-Clearing Tablet
玉液	〈酒〉jade wine; good wine
玉簪	→玉搔头
玉簪明虾球	〈饮食〉Stir-Fried Prawn Balls with Vegetables and Scallops
玉珠大乌参	〈饮食〉Braised Black Sea Slug and Pigeon Eggs
玉竹	〈中医药〉(of Latin) Rhizoma Polygonati Odorati; Fragrant Solomonseal Rhizome
芋艿鸡骨酱	〈饮食〉Stewed Chinese Eddo and Diced Chicken Drumstick in Bean Sauce

芋艿肉骨酱	〈饮食〉Stewed Pork Chops with Chinese Eddo
芋茸香酥鸭	〈饮食〉Crispy Boneless Duck with Taro Puree
芋丝炸春卷	〈饮食〉Deep-Fried Taro Spring Rolls
芋头饼	〈饮食〉Deep-Fried Taro Pancake
芋头排骨汤	〈饮食〉Spare Ribs with Taro Soup
芋头蒸排骨	〈饮食〉Steamed Spare Ribs with Taro
郁多罗僧	〈佛〉Uttarasanga (the upper garment of monk's vestment)
郁金	〈中医药〉(of Latin) Radix Curcumae; Turmeric Root Tuber
郁李仁	〈中医药〉(of Latin) Semen Pruni; Chinese Dwarf Cherry Seed
浴衣	bathrobe; bath gown
预备党员	probationary party member
预订部	reservation department
预订部经理	reservation manager
预订部文员	reservation clerk
预订部主管	reservation supervisor
预订部组长	reservation group leader
预防措施	〈防疫〉preventive measure
预算分析师	budget analyst
预算内投资结构	〈防疫〉structure of investment from the government budget
预算员	budgeteer; budgeting specialist; budget officer
预算执行者	budget executive
预约服务	reservation service
预约进站	〈防疫〉to make reservations at subway stations
预知子	〈中医药〉(of Latin) Fructus Akebiae; Akebia Fruit
御姐	mature and domineering woman
鸳鸯锅	〈饮食〉Two-Flavor Hot Pot
冤大头	a person deceived on account of his generosity; to be taken for a ride
元	yuan (China's standard unit of currency)
元宝	〈币〉shoe-shaped gold/silver ingot; sycee

元宝髻	(of hairstyle) ingot-shaped bun; sycee-shaped bun
元代杂技俑	〈陶瓷〉acrobatic figurines of the Yuan Dynasty
元胡止痛胶囊	〈中医药〉Yuanhu Zhitong Jiaonang; Corydalis Pain-Stopping Capsule
元胡止痛片	〈中医药〉Yuanhu Zhitong Pill; Tablet of Corydalis Tuber for Alleviating Pain
元宵	〈饮食〉Yuanxiao; Glutinous Rice Balls for Lantern Festival
元贞通宝	〈币〉coin with characters Yuanzhen tongbao (issued in the Yuan Dynasty)
元贞元宝	〈币〉coin with characters Yuanzhen yuanbao (issued in the Yuan Dynasty)
芫爆鹌鹑脯	〈饮食〉Stir-Fried Quail Breast with Coriander
芫爆鸡片	〈饮食〉Stir-Fried Chicken Slices with Coriander; Stir-Fried Sliced Chicken with Coriander
芫爆里脊丝	〈饮食〉Stir-Fried Shredded Pork Fillet with Coriander
芫爆鳝鱼片	〈饮食〉Stir-Fried Sliced Eel with Coriander
芫爆素鳝	〈饮食〉Stir-Fried Savory Mushrooms with Coriander
芫花	〈中医药〉(of Latin) Flos Genkwa; Lilac Daphne Flower Bud
芫荽子	〈中医药〉(of Latin) Fructus Coriandri; Coriander Seed
园艺设计师	landscape architect; horticultural designer
员工代表	workers' representative; staff representative
员工顾问	personnel consultant
员工关系部	staffing relationship department
员工关系代表	employer relations representative
员工事务长	staff purser
员针	〈中医药〉rounded needle
袁大头	〈币〉Yuandatou's silver coin (issued in the period of the Republic China)
原笼糯米蒸蟹	〈饮食〉Steamed Crab with Glutinous Rice Served in Bamboo Steamer

原络配穴法	〈中医药〉primary-collateral acupoint combination; source and network points combination
原始青瓷炫纹尊	〈陶瓷〉proto-celadon zun with string pattern
原形绿茶	lightly rubbed green tea
原穴	〈中医药〉source point; Yuan-primary Point
原汁鸡球	〈饮食〉Stir-Fried Chicken Balls in Natural Gravy
原汁鸡虾片	〈饮食〉Stir-Fried Chicken Breast and Prawn Slices in Natural Gravy
原盅椰子炖鸡	〈饮食〉Steamed Chicken in Coconut Juice
圆饺	〈饮食〉Round Jiaozi; Round Dumplings
圆襟旗袍	cheongsam with round lapel
圆利针	〈中医药〉round-sharp needle
圆领	round collar; shawl lapel
圆领大袖衫	shirt with round collar and large sleeves; round-necked robe with large sleeves
圆领口	round neckline
圆领袍	〈服饰〉round-collar robe (a casual shirt in gown-style in the Sui and Tang Dynasties)
圆领缺胯袍	round collar robe with lateral splits; round-necked robe with flank slits
圆首刀	〈币〉round head knife (issued in the Warring States period)
圆通速递	YTO Express
圆袖	set-in sleeve
圆窑	〈陶瓷〉circular kiln; round kiln
圆整	〈茶〉round and normal
圆直	〈茶〉roundy and straight
圆珠绿茶	pearled green tea
圆足布	〈币〉bronze spade coin with round-feet (issued in the Warring States period)
鼋鱼酒	yuanyu chiew; soft-shelled turtle liquor
缘分	to be preordained to come together (as if by predestination); predestined relationship
远安黄茶	Yuan'an yellow tea

远部取穴	〈中医药〉distant acupoint selection
远程办公	〈防疫〉telecommuting; teleworking; remote office work
远红外肩周炎痛贴	〈中医药〉Yuan Hongwai Jianzhouyan Tong Tie; Far Infrared Ray Plaster for Shoulder Periarthritis
远红外腰痛贴	〈中医药〉Yuan Hongwai Yaotong Tie; Far Infrared Ray Plaster for Lumbago
远近配穴法	〈中医药〉distal-proximal acupoint combination
远志	〈中医药〉(of Latin) Radix Polygalae; Thinleaf Milkwort Root
院士	academician
院长	(of a court) president; (of a university) dean, director of the faculty; (of a hospital) director
月饼模	moon cake mold
月季花	〈中医药〉(of Latin) Flos Rosae Chinensis; Chinese Rose Flower
月嫂	maternity matron; doula
月子中心	confinement center; maternity hotel
乐舞陶俑	〈陶瓷〉pottery music dance figurine
岳西翠兰	〈茶〉Yuexi Cuilan tea; Yuexi Jade Green tea
越鞠保和丸	〈中医药〉Yueju Baohe Wan; Depression-Overcoming and Harmony-Preserving Pill
越鞠丸	〈中医药〉Yueju Wan; Depression-Overcoming Pill
越窑青瓷带托茶杯	〈陶瓷〉Yue Kiln celadon teacup with saucer
越窑青瓷瓜体盖罐	〈陶瓷〉Yue Kiln celadon lidded jar in the shape of a melon
越窑青瓷海棠杯	〈陶瓷〉celadon begonia-shaped cup of Yue Kiln
越窑青瓷莲花形盅	〈陶瓷〉Yue Kiln celadon lotus-shaped cup
越窑青瓷莲形罐	〈陶瓷〉Yue Kiln celadon jar in the shape of lotus
越窑青瓷水注	〈陶瓷〉Yue Kiln celadon water dropper
越窑青瓷执熏	〈陶瓷〉Yue Kiln celadon censer
粤菜	〈饮食〉Cantonese Cuisine
粤式点心	Cantonese dim sum
晕针	〈中医药〉faint during acupuncture treatment; fainting on acupuncture

云安全	cloud security; security of cloud computing
云办公软件	〈防疫〉cloud-based office tool
云贝母	〈中医药〉(of Latin) Bulbus Fritillariae Cirrhosae; Yunnan Fritillary Bulb
云服务业务	cloud service business
云海白毫	〈茶〉Cloud Sea Pekoe
云计算技术	cloud computing technology
云计算市场	cloud computing market
云肩	〈服饰〉cappa; shoulder adornment; shawl
云南白毫	〈茶〉Yunnan Pekoe
云南白药	〈中医药〉Yunnan Baiyao; Yunnan Notoginseng Powder
云南白药膏	〈中医药〉Yunnan Baiyao Gao; Yunnan Notoginseng Plaster
云南白药胶囊	〈中医药〉Yunnan Baiyao Jiaonang; Yunnan Notoginseng Capsule
云南红葡萄酒	Yunnan red wine
云腿穿鸡翼	〈饮食〉Ham Brochette in Chicken Wings
云腿骨香炒鸽片	〈饮食〉Stir-Fried Sliced Pigeon with Ham
云腿鸡片	〈饮食〉Stir-Fried Chicken Slices and Ham
云腿芥菜胆	〈饮食〉Stir-Fried Mustard Green with Ham
云纹瓦当	(of building) tile end with cloud design, eave tile with could pattern
云雾茶	cloud and mist tea
云雾毛尖	〈茶〉cloud and mist tippy tea
云选会	〈防疫〉cloud job fair
芸豆焖猪尾	〈饮食〉Braised Pigtails with French Beans
运输经理	traffic manager; transport manager
运输协调员	traffic coordinator
运输主管	transport supervisor
运营总监	director of operations
运针	→行[运]针手法
运针手法	→行[运]针
韵达速递	Yunda Express

Z

扎染布	bandhnu tie-dyed cloth
扎缬	→扎染布
咂酒	zajiu wine; sucking-up wine (usu. provided on the 1st day of the 10th lunar month for the year festival of Qiang and Miao people)
杂技陶俑	〈陶瓷〉pottery acrobat figurine
杂锦云吞汤	〈饮食〉Combination Wonton Soup
杂裾垂髾服	〈古〉silk folded gown with long ornamental ribbons and large hanging sleeves (used in the Wei Jin Southern and Northern Dynasties)
杂碎	〈饮食〉Lamb Chop Suey
砸牌子	to ruin reputation
灾后重建	post-disaster reconstruction
再生环保纸	recycled paper
再造散	〈中医药〉Zaizao San; Rehabilitation Powder; Renewal Powder
在斗争一线考察识别干部	〈防疫〉to put officials to the test on the frontline
在全社会弘扬真善美	to promote high moral standards throughout society
在线贷款人	online lender
在线教育	〈防疫〉online education
在线问诊	〈防疫〉online medical inquiry
在线直播	〈防疫〉live streaming
在职博士生	on-the-job doctorate
在职培训	in-job training

糌粑	〈藏族〉Zanba; fried and cooked highland barley flour (a traditional staple food of Tibetan ethnic group)
簪	〈首饰〉ornamental hairpin; clasping stick for the hair
暂缓或减少留学人员等双向流动	〈防疫〉to postpone or reduce the two-way flow of overseas students
暂停海外团队旅行	〈防疫〉to suspend overseas group tours
暂住证	temporary residence card; temporary residence permit
赞助费	sponsorship fee
脏腑辨证	〈中医药〉bowel and visceral pattern identification
脏腑兼病辨证	〈中医药〉pattern differentiation of concurrent visceral manifestation; bowel and visceral pattern identification
藏袍	Tibetan robe
藏漂族	Tibet drifter; drifter in Tibet
藏青果喉片	〈中医药〉Zangqingguo Tablet; Myrobalan Throat Lozenge
藏药	〈中医药〉Tibetan medicine; Tibetan drug; Tibetan herbs
藏医	〈中医药〉Tibetan medicine; Tibetan doctor
糟白肉	〈饮食〉Cold Pork Slices Marinated in Wine Essence
糟蛋烩鱼唇	〈饮食〉Stewed Fish Lips and Eggs Preserved in Distillers' Grains
糟烩虾仁	〈饮食〉Braised Shelled Shrimps in Rice Wine Sauce
糟熘鳜鱼	〈饮食〉Stir-Fried Mandarin Fish with Rice Wine Sauce
糟熘三白	〈饮食〉Stir-Fried Three White Slices (Chicken, Fish and Bamboo Shoots) with Rice Wine
糟熘鳕鱼	〈饮食〉Stir-Fried Codfish Fillets with Rice Wine Sauce

糟熘鱼片	〈饮食〉Stir-Fried Fish Slices with Rice Wine Sauce
糟片鸭	〈饮食〉Sliced Duck with Red Rice Wine Paste; Frittered Duck Slices with Sea Kale
糟香毛豆	〈饮食〉Green Soy Beans in Rice Wine Sauce
糟醉鸡	〈饮食〉Liquor-Soaked Chicken
早茶	morning tea
早发现早隔离	〈防疫〉early detection and early isolation
早市	morning session; morning market/fair
枣泥方圊	〈饮食〉Steamed Mini Jujube Dumplings
枣生栗子鸡	〈饮食〉Stewed Chicken with Jujubes, Peanuts and Chestnut Kernels
皂角刺	〈中医药〉(of Latin) Spina Gleditsiae; Chinese Honeylocust Spine
皂石瓷	〈陶瓷〉soapstone porcelain
皂衣	〈古〉black robe (for lower government officials)
灶台	stove; kitchen range; cooking bench
灶王爷	Kitchen God
造船工程师	naval architect
造福子孙	to bring benefits to our posterity
造假账	falsified accounts; to cook the books
造价工程师	cost engineer; pricing engineer
造林运动	afforestation drive; afforestation campaign
造型师	image designer; stylist; styling designer
噪声治理	noise abatement
燥裂苔	〈中医药〉dry and cracked fur
燥气伤肺	〈中医药〉dry qi impairing lung; impairment of the lung by dryness
燥热伤肺	〈中医药〉injury of the lung by dryness-heat
燥伤鼻窍证	〈中医药〉pattern of dryness invading the nose; pattern of dryness damaging the nasal orifice
燥湿化痰	〈中医药〉to dry dampness for resolving phlegm; to dry the wetness-evil to eliminate phlegm
燥湿健脾	〈中医药〉to dry dampness for fortifying the spleen; to dry dampness and strengthen the spleen

燥湿敛疮	〈中医药〉to eliminate dampness and astringe sores
燥痰证	〈中医药〉dry-phlegm pattern; dryness phlegm pattern
燥邪犯肺证	〈中医药〉pattern of dryness invading the lung; pattern of dryness evil infringing the lung
泽兰	〈中医药〉(of Latin) Herba Lycopi; Hirsute Shiny Bugleweed Herb
泽泻	〈中医药〉(of Latin) Rhizoma Alismatis; Oriental Waterplantain Rhizome
曾孙	great-grandson
曾孙女	great-granddaughter
增强收治能力	〈防疫〉to raise the hospital admission capacity
增强现实技术	augmented reality
缯帛	silk fabrics (generic name of silk)
甑	〈古〉pottery food steamer; earthen utensil for steaming rice
甑箄	(of cooking utensil) sieve tray; perforated plate of still
甑桶	〈酒〉retort barrel; steaming bucket
扎啤	draught beer
轧花机	cotton gin; cotton ginning machine
炸鹌鹑	〈饮食〉Deep-Fried Quail with Tomato Sauce
炸八块鸡	〈饮食〉Deep-Fried Chicken Chunks
炸炒脆鹿柳	〈饮食〉Deep-Fried Crispy Venison Fillets
炸大虾	〈饮食〉Deep-Fried Prawns; Fried Jumbo Shrimps
炸凤尾明虾	〈饮食〉Deep-Fried Prawns in the Shape of Phoenix
炸凤尾虾	〈饮食〉Deep-Fried Phoenix Tail Shrimps
炸糕	〈饮食〉Deep-Fried Rice Cakes
炸鳜鱼	〈饮食〉Deep-Fried Mandarin Fish with Tomato, Onion and Ginger
炸花生米	〈饮食〉Deep-Fried Peanuts with Salt
炸鸡卷	〈饮食〉Deep-Fried Chicken Rolls

炸鸡肉串	〈饮食〉Deep-Fried Chicken Shashlik
炸鸡胗肝	〈饮食〉Deep-Fried Chicken Gizzards
炸酱面	〈饮食〉Noodles with Chopped Meat in Fried Bean Sauce; Noodles with Soya Bean Paste
炸酱肉丁	〈饮食〉Fried Pork Dices with Soybean Paste
炸金钱大虾	〈饮食〉Deep-Fried Prawns in the Shape of Golden Coin
炸金钱蟹盒	〈饮食〉Fried Crab Meat (Shaped as a Box)
炸麻球	〈饮食〉Deep-Fried Glutinous Rice Balls with Sesame
炸馒头	〈饮食〉Deep-Fried Mantou; Deep-Fried Steamed Bun
炸明虾	〈饮食〉Deep-Fried King Prawns with Pepper Salt
炸南瓜饼	〈饮食〉Deep-Fried Pumpkin Cake
炸烹大虾	〈饮食〉Deep-Fried Jumbo Prawns with Sauce
炸烹虾球	〈饮食〉Quick-Fried Prawn Meat with Sauce
炸烹鲜贝	〈饮食〉Quick-Fried Scallops with Sauce
炸肉茄盒	〈饮食〉Deep-Fried Eggplant with Pork Stuffing
炸肉茄夹	〈饮食〉Fried Eggplant with Meat Stuffing; Fried Eggplant Stuffed with Meat
炸田鸡腿	〈饮食〉Deep-Fried Frog Legs
炸丸子	〈饮食〉Fried Pork Balls with Bread Crumbs and Onions
炸五丝筒全蝎	〈饮食〉Deep-Fried Rolls with Five Shreds Filling and Scorpion
炸虾饼	〈饮食〉Deep-Fried Prawn/Shrimp Cutlets
炸虾串	〈饮食〉Deep-Fried Prawn Shashlik
炸虾球	〈饮食〉Deep-Fried Prawn/Shrimp Balls
炸虾托	〈饮食〉Deep-Fried Prawn Canape
炸羊肉串	〈饮食〉Fried Lamb Shashlik/Kebabs
炸腰花	〈饮食〉Fried Pigs Kidney with Egg and Starch
炸油饼	〈饮食〉Deep-Fried Pancake; Deep-Fried Dough Cake
炸云吞	〈饮食〉Deep-Fried Wonton
炸芝麻肉	〈饮食〉Fried Pork Fillet with Sesame

炸猪排	〈饮食〉Deep-Fried Spare Ribs with Onions and Carrots
炸猪肉串	〈饮食〉Pork Shashlik with Five-Spice and Cumin Powder
炸竹笋脆虾	〈饮食〉Deep-Fried Prawns with Bamboo Shoots
炸子鸡	〈饮食〉Deep-Fried Spring Chicken with Worcestershire Sauce
榨菜炒牛肉	〈饮食〉Stir-Fried Beef with Pickled Vegetables
榨菜粉丝汤	〈饮食〉Hot Pickled Tuber Mustard Soup with Bean Noodles
榨菜肉丝	〈饮食〉Stir-Fried Shredded Pork with Hot Pickled Tuber Mustard
榨菜肉丝面	〈饮食〉Noodle Soup with Preserved Vegetables and Shredded Pork
榨菜肉丝汤	〈饮食〉Shredded Pork Soup with Hot Pickled Tuber Mustard
榨菜汤	〈饮食〉Hot Pickled Tuber Mustard Soup
斋饭	〈饮食〉Vegetarian Meals; food given to monks
宅男宅女	indoorbody; indoorsy
窄袍	narrow imperial robe (for the emperor in the Song Dynasty)
沾…光	to benefit from association with sb. or sth.
毡顶皮帽	fur hat with felt top
毡帽	felt hat; felt cap; trilby
毡袜	felt socks; woollen stockings
盏	〈陶瓷〉zhan; small cup; bowl-shaped
盏托	→茶船
展脚幞头	〈服饰〉futou headwear with straight flaps (for officials in the Ming Dynasty)
展衣	〈古〉formal gown (one of the six dresses of ancient empress)
占着茅坑不拉屎	(of idiom) to be a dog in the manger; just marking time
战略总监	strategy director

战胜疫情	〈防疫〉to prevail over the epidemic; to beat the epidemic; to win the battle against the epidemic
战胜疫情的中坚力量	〈防疫〉core forces in victory over the epidemic
蘸水牛肉	〈饮食〉Boiled Beef with Sauce
张掖腊羊肉	〈饮食〉Zhangye Bacon Mutton
张掖香饭	〈饮食〉Zhangye Stewed Rice with Various Fixing Stuff
章鱼炖鹧鸪	〈饮食〉Steamed Partridge and Octopus
掌上明珠	pearl in the palm; apple of one's eye
障眼明片	〈中医药〉Zhangyanming Pian; Screened Eyes Brightening Tablet
招标师	tenderer
招募顾问	employment consultant
招聘会	job fair
招聘网站	recruitment site
招聘协调人	recruitment coordinator
招聘主管	recruitment supervisor; staffing supervisor
招聘专员	recruiter; recruitment specialist
爪篱	long handled cullender
爪切法	〈中医药〉nail-pressing-aided needle inserting
爪切进针法	〈中医药〉nail-press needle insertion
赵刀	〈币〉knife-shaped coin of the Zhao State
照海	〈中医药〉Zhaohai acupoint; Shining Sea (KI6)
照明工程师	lighting engineer
折叠花边	Pleated frill
折叠屏风	folding screen
折扇	folding fan
折腾	to be restless; to do sth. over and over again; torment
蜇皮炒鸡丝	〈饮食〉Stir-Fried Chicken Shreds with Jellyfish
赭色砂质粘土	〈陶瓷〉ocherous sandy clay
赭色粘土陶器	〈陶瓷〉terra sigillata; ochre clay pottery
浙贝母	〈中医药〉(of Latin) Bulbus Fritillariae Thunbergii; Zhejiang Fritillaria Bulb; Thunberbg Fritillary Bulb
浙菜	〈饮食〉Zhe Cuisine; Zhejiang Cuisine

浙江菜	〈饮食〉→浙菜
贞节崇拜	〈古〉chastity cult (traditional consciousness and custom for women)
贞芪扶正冲剂[颗粒]	〈中医药〉Zhenqi Fuzheng Chongji/Keli; Astragalus Membranaceus-Ligustrum Lucidum Tonic Capsule
针刺补泻	〈中医药〉acupuncture reinforcement-reduction manipulation; reinforcing and reducing techniques of acupuncture therapy
针刺角度	〈中医药〉angle of needle insertion; needling angle
针刺疗法	〈中医药〉acupuncture therapy
针刺麻醉	〈中医药〉acupuncture anesthesia
针刺深度	〈中医药〉depth of needling; needling depth
针刺手法	〈中医药〉acupuncture manipulation; needle manipulation
针刺镇[止]痛	〈中医药〉acupuncture analgesia; to alleviate pain with acupuncture
针感	〈中医药〉needle sensation; needling sensation
针罐法	〈中医药〉needling associated/combined with cupping
针灸	〈中医药〉zhenjiu; acupuncture and moxibustion
针灸处方	〈中医药〉acupuncture and moxibustion prescription; acu-moxibustion prescription
《针灸大成》	〈中医药〉*Zhenjiu Dacheng*; *Complete Compendium of Acupuncture and Moxibustion* (by Yang Jizhou in the Ming Dynasty)
《针灸甲乙经》	〈中医药〉*Zhenjiu Jiayi Jing*; *A-B Classic of Acupuncture and Moxibustion*; *Systematized Canon of Acupuncture and Moxibustion* (by HuangFu Mi in the Jin Dynasty)
针灸科	〈中医药〉department of acupuncture and moxibustion
针灸疗法	〈中医药〉acumoxatrerapy; acupuncture-moxibustion therapy

针灸推拿学	〈中医药〉Acupuncture and Moxibustion and Tuina of Chinese medicine
针灸穴位	〈中医药〉acupressure-moxibustion point
针灸学	〈中医药〉science of acupuncture and moxibustion of traditional Chinese medicine
针灸诊所	acupuncture clinic
针灸治疗学	〈中医药〉therapeutics of acupuncture and moxibustion
针首刀	〈古〉knife-shaped coin with sharp and long head (used in the Spring and Autumn period and Warring Sates period)
针织服装	knitted garment
珍宝炒带子	〈饮食〉Stir-Fried Scallops with Cashew Kernels
珍菌滑炒肉	〈饮食〉Stir-Fried Pork with Mushrooms
珍鹿香烟	Zhen Lu cigarettes; Treasure Deer cigarettes
珍珠明目滴眼液	〈中医药〉Zhenzhu Mingmu Di Yan Ye; Pearl Bright Eye Drops
珍珠母	〈中医药〉(of Latin) Concha Margaritifera; Mother-of-Pearl; Nacre
珍珠釉	〈陶瓷〉pearl glaze
真寒假热证	〈中医药〉pattern of true cold disease with false heat manifestation
真热假寒证	〈中医药〉pattern of true heat disease with false cold manifestation
真人养脏汤	〈中医药〉Zhenren Yangzang Tang; True Man Viscus-Nourishing Decoction
真实假虚证	〈中医药〉pattern of true excessive disease with false deficient manifestation
真丝	real silk; pure silk
真武汤	〈中医药〉Zhenwu Tang; True Warrior Decoction; Decoction for Strengthening the Spleen-Yang
真虚假实证	〈中医药〉pattern of true deficient disease with false excessive manifestation
诊断器具	〈防疫〉diagnostic tool; diagnostic kit

震颤法	〈中医药〉trembling method; needle-body trembling
镇江黑醋	Zhenjiang black vinegar
镇库钱	〈古〉coin with treasury inscription
镇脑宁胶囊	〈中医药〉Zhennaoning Jiaonang; Brain-Conquering Calmness Capsule
征文比赛	essay competition
蒸	〈饮食〉to steam; steamed
蒸肠粉	〈饮食〉Steamed Rice (Flour) Rolls
蒸芙蓉鸡球	〈饮食〉Steamed Chicken Balls with Egg Whites
蒸锅	steamer; a pot for steaming food
蒸饺	〈饮食〉Steamed Jiaozi; Steamed Dumplings
蒸金钱片塘虱	〈饮食〉Steamed Catfish with Ginger, Chive and Soy Sauce
蒸笼	food steamer (usu. made of bamboo); bamboo steamer
蒸酿冬笋	〈饮食〉Steamed Stuffed Bamboo Shoots
蒸牛肉丸	〈饮食〉Steamed Beef Balls
蒸汽吸入疗法	〈中医药〉atmotherapy; steam-inhaling therapy
蒸青绿茶	steamed green tea
蒸山水豆腐	〈饮食〉Steamed Tofu with Pepper, Onion and Coriander
蒸鱼料	〈饮食〉aromatics for steaming fish
整复疗法	〈中医药〉reduction therapy (for tendon and bone injury)
整形工程师	plastic engineer
正常舌象	〈中医药〉normal tongue picture; normal tongue manifestation
正德青花婴戏碗	〈陶瓷〉blue and white porcelain bowl with playing boys pattern (Ming Zhengde period)
正德通宝	〈币〉coin with characters Zhengde tongbao (issued in the late Ming and Qing Dynasties)
正骨科	〈中医药〉department of bone orthopedics

正骨手法	〈中医药〉bone-righting manipulation; manipulation of bone-setting
正骨水	〈中医药〉Zhenggu Shui; Bone-Setting Liquor
正骨推拿	〈中医药〉massage for bone-setting
正骨医生	osteopathist; chiropractor
正隆元宝	〈币〉coin with characters Zhenglong yuanbao (issued in the Jin Dynasty)
正能量	positive energy
正气	1 uprightness; righteousness; healthy atmosphere 2〈中医药〉vital qi (energy); healthy qi; body resistance
正清灵芝胶囊	〈中医药〉Zhengqing Lingzhi Jiaonang; Zhengqing Ganoderma Capsule
正山小种红茶	Lapsang Souchong black tea
正式党员	full Party member; full member of the Party
正统青花孔雀牡丹纹罐	〈陶瓷〉blue and white jar with peacock and peony pattern (Ming Zhengtong period)
正统中国文化	orthodox Chinese culture
正邪相争	〈中医药〉struggle between vital qi and pathogen
正虚邪恋证	〈中医药〉pattern of lingering pathogen due to deficient vital qi
正虚邪实	〈中医药〉asthenia of healthy qi and sthenia of pathogenic factors; deficiency of vital qi and excess of pathogenic factors
正元胶囊	〈中医药〉Zhengyuan Jiaonang; Origin-Rectifying Capsule
正治法	〈中医药〉routine treatment; straight treatment; orthodox treatment
正宗中餐	〈饮食〉authentic Chinese food
证候错杂	〈中医药〉intermingling pattern; complex pattern
证券从业资格证书	certificate of securities qualification
证券分析师	securities analyst; bond analyst
证券交易员	bond trader; securities trader

《证治准绳》	〈中医药〉Zhengzhi Zhunsheng; Level-Lines of Pattern Identification and Treatment; Standards for Diagnosis and Treatment (by Wang Kentang in the Ming Dynasty)
政治辅导员	political instructor; political advisor
政治思想教育	political and ideological education
挣工分	〈旧〉to earn workpoints
支付宝	Alipay
支付宝服务	Alipay service
支沟	〈中医药〉Zhigou acupoint; Branch Canal (TE6)
支竹羊腩煲	〈饮食〉Stewed Lamb Brisket with Dry Tofu in Clay Pot; Lamb and Tofu Sheets in Casserole
支竹羊肉煲	〈饮食〉Stewed Lambs with Bean Curd Sheets in Casserole
汁卤	〈饮食〉to stew in gravy; gravy-stewed
汁烧鸡肉	〈饮食〉Stewed Chicken in Sauce
芝麻叉烧酥	〈饮食〉Barbecued Pork Pastry with Sesame
芝麻大饼	〈饮食〉Pan-Fried Sesame Pancake
芝麻豆腐	〈饮食〉Sesame Tofu; Sesame Bean Curd
芝麻锅炸	〈饮食〉Sesame Fritters; Deep-Fried Sesame Pudding
芝麻鸡	〈饮食〉Boiled Chicken with Sesame and Spicy Sauce
芝麻酱拌腰片	〈饮食〉Sliced Pork Kidney with Sesame Paste
芝麻金珠肉	〈饮食〉Fried Pork Balls with Sesame Sauce
芝麻凉卷	〈饮食〉Sesame Rolls
芝麻牛肉	〈饮食〉Stir-Fried Beef with Sesame
芝麻球	〈饮食〉Glutinous Rice Sesame Balls
芝麻香型风格	〈酒〉sesame-flavor style
芝麻油	〈饮食〉sesame oil
芝麻芋条	〈饮食〉Deep-Fried Taro Sticks with Sesame
芝麻肘子	〈饮食〉Braised Pork Knuckles with Sesame
芝士南瓜面	〈饮食〉Noodles with Cheese and Pumpkin
知柏地黄丸	〈中医药〉Zhibai Dihuang Wan; Anemarrhena, Phellodendron and Rehmannia Pill
知母	〈中医药〉(of Latin) Rhizoma Anemarrhenae; Common Anemarrhena Rhizome

知青	→知识青年
知识产权顾问	intellectual property advisor
知识产权专员	intellectual property specialist
知识风采比赛	knowledge competition
知识青年	educated youth (during the period of Cultural Revolution)
织带	braid; mesh belt; narrow goods
织花腰带	waistband with floral pattern
织锦	brocade; tapestry; picture-weaving in silk
栀子豉汤	〈中医药〉Zhizichi Tang; Gardeniae and Fermented Soybean Decoction
栀子仁	〈中医药〉(of Latin) Fructus Gardeniae; Gardenia Fruit; Cape Jasmine Fruit
执法人员	law enforcement official/officer
执壶	〈陶瓷〉jug; pitcher
执行编辑	managing editor; executive editor
执行创意总监	executive creative director; ECD
执行董事	executive director
执行副总裁	executive vice president
执行秘书	executive secretary
执行主席	executive chairman; presiding chairman
执行总裁	executive president
执业药师	licensed pharmacist
执业中药师	licensed pharmacist of Chinese medicine
直百五铢	〈币〉hundred five zhu coin (equal to the value of 100 five zhu coin in the Three Kingdoms)
直播	live stream; live telecast; live broadcast; (of agriculture) direct seeding
直播平台	live-streaming platform
直刺	〈中医药〉perpendicular insertion; perpendicular insertion of the needle
直刀	straight knife
直裰	〈服饰〉(of ancient times) monk's and priest's robe
直接灸	〈中医药〉direct moxibustion
直襟旗袍	cheongsam with straight lapel

直裾	〈服饰〉straight-front robe; straight lapel (in the Han Dynasty)
直裾深衣	〈服饰〉straight-front long full body garment (in the Han Dynasty)
直[筒]裙	straight skirt →筒裙
直身	〈服饰〉scholar robe (popular in the Ming Dynasty)
值班工程师	duty engineer; shift engineer
职称	professional title
职高	→职业高中
职前培训	pre-employment training
职业暴露	〈防疫〉occupational exposure
职业道德教育	education in professional ethics
职业服	business suit; professional garments
职业高中	vocational high school
职业公共实训基地	public vocational training base
职业顾问	vocational counselor
职业技能训练	job skill training
职业技术教育	vocational and technical education
职业教师	professional teacher
职业教育培训制度	the system of vocational education and training
职业教育体系	vocational education system
职业介绍所	employment agency; career service center; labor exchange
职业经理人	professional manager
职业经理人招聘	recruitment of professional manager
职业目标	career objective
职业年金	occupational pension; occupational annuity
职业培训	job training; vocational training
职业培训和就业服务	vocational training and employment service
职业培训体系	vocational training system
职业院校	vocational school; vocational college
职业治疗师	occupational therapist
职业资格证书	vocational qualification certificate; professional certificate

植树运动	afforestation campaign; tree planting drive
《植物名实图考》	〈中医药〉Zhiwu Mingshi Tukao; Treatise on the Names, Facts and Illustrations of Plants; Textual Research on Reality and Titles of Plants (by Wu Qixun in the Qing Dynasty)
植物扒鹅掌	〈饮食〉Stewed Goose Webs and Vegetables
止痉散	〈中医药〉Zhijing San; Spasmolytic Powder
止嗽散	〈中医药〉Zhisou San; Cough-Stopping Powder
止痛化癥胶囊	〈中医药〉Zhitong Huazheng Jiaonang; Pain-Relieving Lump-Resolving Capsule
止血剂	〈中医药〉blood-stanching formula
纸包风味羊排	〈饮食〉Fried Lamb Chops Wrapped in Foil
纸包鸡	〈饮食〉Chicken Wrapped in Glassine; Deep-Fried Chicken in Tin Foil
纸包(炸)鸡	〈饮食〉Deep-Fried Chicken Wrapped in Tin Foil
纸包鸡片	〈饮食〉Stir-Fried Chicken Slices in Rice Paper/Tin Foil
纸槌瓶	〈陶瓷〉paper-mallet shaped vase
纸甲	〈古〉paper-padded armor
指寸定位法	〈中医药〉location of point by finger cun; finger-cun measurement
指导顾问	guidance counselor
指导教师	tutor; instructor; faculty adviser
指定日优惠票	designated/peak day special ticket
指切进针法	〈中医药〉finger-press needle insertion; insertion of the needle aided with finger pressure
指纹识别	fingerprint identification
指压推拿	〈中医药〉finger-pressing massage
指针疗法	〈中医药〉finger-pressure therapy; acupressure
枳具子	〈中医药〉(of Latin) Semen Hovenia Acerba; Honey Tree Fruit
枳壳	〈中医药〉(of Latin) Fructus Aurantii; Orange Fruit
枳实	〈中医药〉(of Latin) Fructus Aurantii Immaturus; Immature Orange Fruit

枳实导滞丸	〈中医药〉Zhishi Daozhi Wan; Unripe Bitter Orange Stagnation-Abducting Pill
枳实消痞丸	〈中医药〉Zhishi Xiaopi Wan; Unripe Bitter Orange and Glomus-Dispersing Pill; Pill of Immature Bitter Orange for Relieving Stuffiness
枳术丸	〈中医药〉Zhizhu Wan; Aurantii Immaturi and Atractylodis Pill
至宝丹	〈中医药〉Zhibao Dan; Supreme Jewel Elixir
至道元宝	〈币〉coin with characters zhidao yuanbao (issued in the Song Dynasty)
至阳	〈中医药〉Zhiyang acupoint; Supreme Yang; Extremity of Yang (GV9)
至阴	〈中医药〉Zhiyin acupoint; Supreme Yin; Extremity of Yin (BL67)
制服部经理	uniform manager
制服部职员	uniform room staff
制服部组长	uniform room team leader
制假售假	production and sale of counterfeit goods/products
制片人	producer; production manager
制片协调员	production coordinator
制售假冒伪劣商品	to manufacture and market counterfeit and substandard goods; to produce and sell counterfeit and shoddy goods
制造工程师	manufacturing engineer
制造业经理	manufacturing manager
制作编辑	production editor
质检部	quality inspection department
质检部经理	quality control manager; quality assessment manager
质控总监	chief quality control officer; CQO
质量改进工程师	quality improvement engineer
质量工程师	quality engineer; quality assurance engineer
质量管理工程师	quality control engineer
质量管理检查员	quality control inspector

质量管理经理	quality control manager
质量管理[控制]主管	quality control supervisor
质量检测技术员	quality testing technician
质量检验师	quality examiner; quality inspector
质量检验员	quality inspector; QC inspector
质孙服	〈古〉Mongol overall garment (originated form Yuan Dynasty) →一色衣[服]
炙甘草	〈中医药〉(of Latin) Radix Glycyrrhizae Preparata; Prepared Liquorice Root
炙甘草汤	〈中医药〉Zhigancao Tang; Fried Glycyrrhizae Decoction
治风化痰剂	〈中医药〉formula for resolving phlegm with arresting wind
治风剂	〈中医药〉wind-dispelling formula; formula for wind disorder
治未病	〈中医药〉preventive treatment of disease; to treat disease before it arises
治愈病例	〈防疫〉cured case; recovered case
治愈率	〈防疫〉recovery rate; cure rate
致病机理	〈防疫〉pathogenesis; pathogenic mechanism
致病性	〈防疫〉pathogenicity; virulence
致病源	〈防疫〉pathogen; etiology
致死率	〈防疫〉fatality rate; death/mortality rate
智慧医疗	〈防疫〉smart medical care
智力引进	to recruit/introduce (foreign) talents
智能仓库	intelligent warehouse; smart warehouse
智能车	intelligent car; smart car; intelligent vehicle
智能储物柜	smart lock box; intelligent locker; smart cabinet
智能电饭煲	intelligent/smart electric rice cooker
智能电网	smart power grid; intelligent grid
智能轨道快运系统	Autonomous Rail Rapid Transit; ART
智能机器	intelligent machine; smart machine
智能技术	intelligence technology
智能家居	smart home; home automation

智能交通系统	intelligent transportation system; ITS
智能马桶	intelligent closestool; smart toilet
智能农业服务仓库	intelligent/smart agricultural service warehouse
智能设备	intelligent device; smart device
智能手机操作系统	smart phone operating system
智能锁	smart lock; intelligent lock
智能物流网络	smart logistics network
智能移动	smart mobility
智能语音交互	intelligent speech interaction
智能自行车	smart bike; intelligent bicycle
滞针	〈中医药〉stuck needle; stucking of needle
觯	〈酒〉zhi; bronze drinking vessel
中保协	→中国保险行业协会
中餐	〈饮食〉Chinese food
中餐部	Chinese restaurant department
中餐部[厅]经理	Chinese restaurant manager
中餐厨师长	Chinese chef; Chinese kitchen chef; Chinese master chef
中餐馆	〈饮食〉Chinese restaurant
中餐具	〈饮食〉Chinese dinner set/service; Chinese tableware/cutlery
中草药	〈中医药〉Chinese herbal medicine; Chinese medicinal herb
中草药配方	〈中医药〉Chinese herbal remedy; prescription of Chinese herb medicine; traditional herbal prescription
中超(联赛)	China Super League; CSL →中国足球协会超级联赛
中超冠军	(of football) champion of China Football Association Super League; CSL champion
中成药	〈中医药〉Chinese patent medicine; traditional Chinese patent medicines and simple preparations; proprietary Chinese medicine; ready-prepared Chinese medicine

中冲	〈中医药〉Zhongchong acupoint; Central Hub (on the radial side of the middle finger) (PC9)
中等职业教育	secondary vocational education
中等职业学校	secondary vocational school; trade school
中东呼吸综合征	〈防疫〉Middle East respiratory syndrome; MERS
中风险地区	〈防疫〉medium-risk region
中府	〈中医药〉Zhongfu acupoint; Central House (LU1)
中高协	→中国高尔夫球协会
中国八大菜系	〈饮食〉Eight Major Chinese Cuisines; Chinese Eight Cuisines (including Sichuan Cuisine, Shandong Cuisine, Cantonese Cuisine, Jiangsu Cuisine, Fujian Cuisine, Zhejiang Cuisine, Hu'nan Cuisine and Hui Cuisine)
中国白瓷	〈陶瓷〉Chinese white porcelain; Chinese whiteware; Chinese ceramics
中国白酒	Chinese baijiu; Chinese (white) liquor/spirit
中国白酒文化	Chinese baijiu culture; Chinese liquor culture
中国半导体行业协会	China Semiconductor Industry Association; CSIA
中国棒球协会	Chinese Baseball Association; CBA
中国棒协	→中国棒球协会
中国保险公司	Chinese insurance company; insurance company of China
中国保险行业协会	Insurance Association of China; IAC
中国编辑学会	China Society of Editors
中国财富排名	China Fortune Ranking
中国菜	〈饮食〉Chinese cuisine
中国餐馆综合征	〈中医药〉Chinese restaurant syndrome
中国残疾人联合会	China Disabled Persons' Federation; CDPF
中国残联	→中国残疾人联合会
中国茶	Chinese tea
中国茶文化	Chinese tea culture
中国茶叶博物馆	China National Tea Museum (Zhejiang)
中国超级联赛俱乐部	Chinese super league club
中国成语大会	(of a TV program) Chinese Idiom Congress (CCTV)

中国城市人口	China's urban population
中国城镇居民登记	China's urban resident register
中国出境旅游	Chinese outbound tourism
中国出境旅游市场	China outbound tourism market
中国出境游客	Chinese outbound tourist/traveler
中国出口产品	Chinese export product
中国传统成人礼	traditional Chinese adult ceremony; traditional Chinese coming-of-age ceremony
中国传统佛教风俗	traditional Chinese Buddhist custom
中国传统服装	traditional Chinese costume
中国传统画	traditional Chinese painting
中国传统婚俗	traditional Chinese wedding custom
中国传统建筑风格	traditional Chinese architectural style
中国传统教育体系	traditional Chinese educational system
中国传统民乐	traditional Chinese folk music
中国传统烹调法	traditional Chinese cooking method
中国传统水墨画	traditional Chinese ink painting
中国传统小吃	traditional Chinese snack
中国传统养生文化	traditional Chinese healthcare culture
中国传统医学	traditional Chinese medicine
中国传统饮食	traditional Chinese food
中国传统园林艺术	traditional Chinese garden art
中国传统乐器	traditional Chinese musical instrument
中国春节	China's Spring Festival; Chinese Spring Festival (on the 1st day of the 1st lunar month)
中国辞书学会	China Association for Lexicography
中国慈善联合会	China Charity Alliance; CCA
中国大奖赛	Chinese Grand Prix
中国大陆旅客	traveler/tourist from Chinese mainland
中国大陆企业	Chinese mainland enterprise/business
中国大陆人	Chinese mainland resident; people from mainland of China
中国大妈	Chinese dama (used by US media to poke fun at middle-aged Chinese women for purchasing large amounts of gold)

中国大熊猫保护研究中心	China Conservation and Research Center for Giant Pandas
中国大众文化	Chinese mass/popular culture
中国灯笼	Chinese lantern
中国电信	China Telecom
中国电影节	Chinese Film Festival
中国电影周	Chinese Film Week
中国独生子女政策	China's one child policy; Chinese one-child policy
中国方言译员	Chinese dialect translator
中国访问学者	Chinese visiting scholar; Chinese academic visitor
中国风格	Sinicism; Chinoiserie; Chinese style
中国风味	China's taste; Chinese taste
中国佛教僧侣	Chinese Buddhist monk
中国佛教神话	Chinese Buddhist myth
中国佛学院	Buddhist Academy of China
中国扶贫基金会	China Foundation for Poverty Alleviation
中国福利彩票	China welfare lottery
中国富豪榜	China Rich List; List of Chinese by net worth
中国高等教育	China higher education
中国高尔夫球协会	China Golf Association; CGA
中国高考	China Gaokao; National College Entrance Examination; NCEE
中国高铁	China Railway High-Speed (CRH); Chinese High-Speed Rail (HSR); High-Speed Rail (HSR) in China
中国革命传统	Chinese revolutionary tradition
中国革命人物	Chinese revolutionary figure
中国革命战争	Chinese revolutionary war
中国工商银行	Industrial and Commercial Bank of China; ICBC
中国工协	→中国工业协会
中国工业协会	Chinese Industrial Association; CIA
中国工艺美术馆	China National Arts and Crafts Museum (Beijing)
中国公民	Chinese citizen
中国公民社会	Chinese civil society

中国公益慈善项目交流展示会	China Charity Fair; CCF
中国功夫	Chinese kung fu; Chinese Kungfu
中国功夫大师	Chinese kung fu master
中国功夫文化	Chinese kung fu culture
中国古典园林	Chinese classical garden
中国古谚语	ancient Chinese proverb
中国关爱基金会	China Care Foundation
中国广场舞	Chinese square dance; Chinese dancercise in a square or park
中国国宝	China's national treasure; Chinese national treasure
中国国道	China national highways
中国国歌	Chinese national anthem (March of the Volunteers)
中国国际服装服饰博览会	China International Fashion Fair; CHIC
中国国际旅行社	China International Travel Service
中国国际日用消费品博览会	China International Consumer Goods Fair; CICGF
中国国际商会	China Chamber of International Commerce
中国国际时装周	China Fashion Week (in March or October)
中国国际形象	China's international image; Chinese international image
中国国家博物馆	National Museum of China (Beijing)
中国国家电视台	China's state broadcaster; Chinese state broadcaster
中国国家旅游局	China National Tourist Administration
中国国家形象宣传片	(of a documentary) China National Publicity Film; China's National Image Promotion/Publicity (State Council Information Office, 2011)
中国国民性格	Chinese national character
中国国庆日	Chinese National Day (on the 1st October)
中国航海博物馆	China Maritime Museum (Shanghai)
中国黑醋	Chinese black vinegar

中国红茶	Chinese black tea
中国红歌会	(of a TV program) China Red Song Show (Jiangxi TV, 2006)
中国红十字会	Red Cross Society of China
中国红十字基金会	Chinese Red Cross Foundation; CRCF
中国黄山国际旅游节	China Huangshan International Tourism Festival
中国黄页	Chinese yellow page (B2B business/commercial website)
中国机械工业联合会	China Machinery Industry Federation; CMIF
中国疾病预防控制中心	〈防疫〉Chinese Center for Disease Control and Prevention; China CDC
中国家用电器协会	China Household Electrical Appliances Association; CHEAA
中国建设银行	China Construction Bank; CCB
中国教育年鉴	China Education Yearbook
中国教育体制[制度]	Chinese education/educational system; education system in China
中国教育委员会	Chinese Education Committee; CEC
中国景德镇国际陶瓷博览会	China Jingdezhen International Ceramic Fair
中国军民关系	Chinese civil-military relation
中国科学院院士	academician of Chinese Academy of Sciences
中国科学院院长	president of Chinese Academy of Sciences
中国孔子基金会	China Confucius Foundation
中国孔子学院总部	China Confucius Institute Headquarters
中国快递协会	China Express Association; CEA
中国联通	China Unicom
中国流行歌曲	Chinese pop song
中国流行歌手	Chinese pop singer
中国流行文化	Chinese pop culture
中国龙	Chinese loong; Chinese dragon
中国旅游产业博览会	China Tourism Industry Exposition
中国旅游饭店业协会	China Tourist Hotel Association; CTHA
中国旅游协会	China Tourism Association; CTA

中国旅游业	Chinese tourism; tourism industry of China
中国绿色债券市场	China's green bond market
中国美食节	Chinese Food Festival
中国门球协会	Chinese Gateball Association; CGA
中国门协	→中国门球协会
中国民歌	Chinese folk song
中国民间故事	Chinese folk tale
中国民间文学	Chinese folk literature
中国民间艺术节	Chinese Folk Art Festival (in October)
中国民间音乐	Chinese folk music
中国民生银行	China Minsheng Bank
中国民俗文化	Chinese folk culture
中国民主同盟	China Democratic League
中国民族电影	Chinese national film; Chinese national cinema
中国民族室内乐	China national chamber music
中国民族特色	Chinese national characteristic
中国民族医药学会	China Medical Association of Minorities; CMAM
中国农业博物馆	China Agricultural Museum (Beijing)
中国农业银行	Agricultural Bank of China; ABC
中国烹饪	Chinese culinary; Chinese cuisine
中国烹饪传统	Chinese culinary tradition
中国烹饪协会	China Cuisine Association, CCA
中国烹协	→中国烹饪协会
中国平安保险	Ping An Insurance of China
中国普洱茶节	China Puer Tea Festival (in April)
中国漆工艺	Chinese lacquer art; Chinese lacquering technology
中国棋盘游戏	Chinese board game
中国旗袍文化	Chinese cheongsam culture
中国青年节	Chinese Youth Day (on the 4th May)
中国青少年艺术节	China Youth Arts Festival
中国屈原诗歌奖	Chinese Qu Yuan Poetry Awards
中国人民保险	People's Insurance Company of China, PICC
中国人寿保险	China Life Insurance
中国日报	China Daily
中国肉类协会	China Meat Association; CMA

中国肉协	→中国肉类协会
中国商业联合会	China General Chamber of Commerce; CGCC
中国商业协会	Chinese Business Association
中国少年先锋队	Young Pioneers of China; Chinese Young Pioneers; CYP
中国社会福利基金会	China Social Welfare Foundation; CSWF
中国社会科学院	Chinese Academy of Social Sciences; CASS
中国神话	Chinese mythology
中国时代剧	Chinese period drama
中国时装周	China fashion week
中国食品工业协会	China National Food Industry Association; CNFIA
中国食协	→中国食品工业协会
中国史学	Chinese historiography; Chinese science of history; Chinese historical science
中国史学会	Association of Chinese Historians; ACH
中国事务助理	China affair assistant
中国授权展	China Licensing Expo; CLE
中国兽医协会	Chinese Veterinary Medical Association; CVMA
中国书法家协会	Chinese Calligraphers Association; CCA
中国丝绸	China silk
中国丝绸博物馆	China National Silk Museum (Zhejiang)
中国丝绸艺术展	Chinese silk art exhibition
中国四大银行	China's four largest banks
中国太平洋保险	China Pacific Insurance Company; CPIC
中国探月工程	Chinese Lunar Exploration Program; CLEP →嫦娥工程
中国陶瓷	〈陶瓷〉China Ceramics; Chinese pottery and porcelain
中国特色世界一流大学	world-class universities with Chinese characteristics
中国体育彩票	China sports lottery
中国田径协会	Chinese Athletics Association
中国铁路快递	China railway express
中国网红	Chinese wanghong; China's online star/celebrity

中国文化观	Chinese cultural perspective; concepts of Chinese culture
中国文化遗产	China cultural heritage; Chinese cultural heritage/legacy
中国文化展	Chinese culture exhibition/show
中国文化中心	China Cultural Center
中国文物	Chinese cultural relic
中国文物保护基金会	China Foundation for Cultural Heritage Conservation; CFCHC
中国文学	Chinese literature
中国武术协会	Chinese Wushu Association; CWA
中国消费者协会	China Consumers Association
中国消协	→中国消费者协会
中国新年	Chinese New Year →中国春节
中国性学会	China Sexology Association
中国烟草产业	Chinese tobacco industry
中国烟草总公司	China National Tobacco Corporation; CNTC
中国研究生入学考试	National Entrance Examination for Postgraduate; NEEP
中国养生酒	China nutritious liquor
《中国药典》	〈中医药〉*Chinese Pharmacopoeia*; *Pharmacopoeia of People's Republic of China* (by the State Pharmacopoeia Commission of PR China, the first edition in 1953, as the Legal Technical Standards for State Supervision and Administration of Drug Quality)
中国野生动物保护协会	China Wildlife Conservation Association; CWCA
中国伊斯兰教协会	China Islamic Association
中国伊协	→中国伊斯兰教协会
中国医学史	Chinese medical history; history of Chinese medicine
中国医药学	〈中医药〉Chinese medicine and pharmacology; science of traditional Chinese medicine
中国医院协会	Chinese Hospital Association; CHA
中国移动	China Mobile

中国艺术家协会	China Artist Association; CAA
中国艺术节	China Art Festival
中国艺协	→中国艺术家协会
中国银行	Bank of China; BOC
中国银联	China UnionPay
中国饮食文化	Chinese culinary culture; Chinese food culture
中国印	(of Beijing Olympics) Chinese Seal
中国营养学会	Chinese Nutrition Society; CNS
中国邮政	China Post
中国油画	Chinese oil painting
中国游客	Chinese tourist
中国语言服务业大会	China Language Service Industry Conference
中国语言文学系	department of Chinese language and literature
中国语言文字	Chinese language and characters
中国语言学会	Chinese Linguistics Society
中国元素	Chinese element
中国元宵节	Chinese Lantern Festival (on the 15th day of the 1st lunar month)
中国针灸学会	China Association of Acupuncture-Moxibustion; CAAM
中国证券业协会	Securities Association of China
中国证券指数	China securities index
中国政府奖学金	Chinese Government Scholarship; China Scholarship Council (CSC) Scholarship
中国执业药师协会	China Licensed Pharmacist Association; CLPA
中国执业药师在线	Chinese Licensed Pharmacist Online
中国职业经理人	Chinese professional manager
中国职业经理人资格认证	certificate of Chinese professional manager
中国指数研究院	China Index Academy (Hong Kong)
中国智能物流骨干网	China Smart Logistics Network; CSN
中国中西医结合学会	Chinese Association of Integrative Medicine; CAIM
中国中药协会	China Association of Traditional Chinese Medicine; CATCM
中国绉	(of textile) China crepe

中国自行车协会	China Bicycle Association
中国总商会	Chinese General Chamber of Commerce; CGCC
中国足球俱乐部	Chinese Football Club
中国足球协会	Chinese Football Association; CFA
中国足球协会超级联赛	Chinese Football Association Super League; CSL →中超(联赛)
中华传统美德	traditional Chinese virtues
中华传统美食文化	traditional Chinese food culture
中华慈善总会	China Charity Federation
中华儿女	all sons and daughters of the Chinese nation
中华老字号	China time-honored brand; China long-standing shop
中华民族自豪感	Chinese national sense of pride
中华全国工商业联合会	All-China Federation of Industry and Commerce; ACFIC
中华全国归国华侨联合会	All-China Federation of Returned Overseas Chinese; ACFROC
中华全国律师协会	All-China Lawyers Association
中华全国青年联合会	All-China Youths' Federation; ACYF
中华全国体育总会	All-China Sports Federation; ACSF
中华全国新闻工作者协会	All-China Journalists' Association; ACJA
中华全国学生联合会	All-China Students' Federation; ACSF
中华全国总工会	All-China Federation of Trade Unions
中华社会救助基金会	China Social Assistance Foundation
中华投资者俱乐部	China Investors Club
中华万年历	Chinese Lunar Calendar
中华香烟	Chungwa cigarettes; Chinese cigarettes
中华孝道	China's filial piety
中华医学会	Chinese Medical Association
中华中医药学会	China Association of Chinese Medicine; CACM
中级会计职称	medium-level accountant
中级涉外秘书证	intermediate foreign secretary certificate
中级职称	intermediate professional title
中极	〈中医药〉Zhongji acupoint; Central Pole; Middle Pole (CV3)

中间宿主	〈防疫〉intermediate host
中焦	〈中医药〉middle warmer/burner; middle energizer
中焦湿热	〈中医药〉dampness-heat in middle energizer
中焦湿热证	〈中医药〉pattern of dampness-heat in middle energizer
中焦实热证	〈中医药〉pattern of excessive heat in middle energizer
中焦穴	〈中医药〉Zhongjiao acupoints; Middle Burner/Energizer points
中考	senior high school entrance exam; entrance examination for secondary school
中髎	〈中医药〉Zhongliao acupoint; Central Bone Hole; Middle Crevice (BL33)
中膂俞	〈中医药〉Zhonglüshu acupoint; Central Backbone Transport (BL29)
中满	〈中医药〉abdominal distension; abdominal flatulence
中南海香烟	Zhongnanhai cigarettes
中气	〈中医药〉qi of middle-burner; middle-jiao energy; qi from the spleen and stomach
中秋节	Mid-Autumn Festival (on the 15th day of the 8th lunar month)
中泉	〈中医药〉Zhongquan acupoint; Middle Spring (EX-UE3)
中山服领	Zhongshan coat collar
中山米酒	Zhongshan rice wine
中山装	Sun Yat-sen uniform; Chinese tunic suit
中式大衣	Chinese-style coat; Eastern style coat
中式风格	Chinese-style; China Style
中式服装	Chinese-style clothing; Chinese costume
中式裤	Chinese-style trousers
中式快餐	〈饮食〉Chinese fast food; Chinese-style fast food
中式领	mandarin collar

中式牛柳	〈饮食〉Chinese-Style Beef Fillets; Beef Fillets with Tomato Sauce
中式牛排	〈饮食〉Chinese-Style Beef Steak with Tomato Sauce
中式上衣	Chinese-style coat
中式晚宴	Chinese-style dinner party
中(国)式英语	Chinglish
中式粥	Chinese-style congee
中枢	〈中医药〉Zhongshu acupoint; Central Pivot (GV7)
中庭	〈中医药〉Zhongting acupoint; Central Atrium; Central Courtyard (CV16)
中通快递	ZTO Express
中统元宝交钞	〈币〉Zhongtong paper-printed money (issued in the late Yuan Dynasty, the earlist paper money in ancient China)
中外合资大学	Sino-foreign joint venture university
中晚籼稻	middle-season and late indica rice
中脘	〈中医药〉Zhongwan acupoint; Central Venter; Middle Cavity (CV12)
中温曲	〈酒〉medium temperature raw starter
中文课程	Chinese course
中文媒介	Chinese medium
中文拼音	Chinese pinyin
中文搜索引擎	Chinese search engine
中文系	→中国语言文学系
中文信息处理系统	Chinese information processing system
中西医结合	integration of traditional Chinese and western medicine
中西医结合[并用]	〈防疫〉combined use of TCM and Western medicine
中西医结合医学	Chinese and Western Integrative Medicine
中小型商品房	small and medium sized commodity housing/building
中学高级教师	senior secondary school teacher
中央电视台	China Central Television; CCTV

中央歌剧院	China National Opera House (Beijing)
中药	〈中医药〉traditional Chinese medicine; Chinese materia medica; Chinese herbal medicine
中药本草	〈中医药〉Chinese material medica
中药材	〈中医药〉traditional Chinese medicinal material; Chinese medicinal crop; Chinese herbal material
中药产品	〈中医药〉traditional Chinese medicine product
中药成分	〈中医药〉traditional Chinese medicine ingredient; TCM ingredient
中药处方	〈中医药〉traditional Chinese medicine prescription
中药店	〈中医药〉traditional Chinese medicine shop
中药房	〈中医药〉traditional Chinese medicine pharmacy/dispensary
中药复方	〈中医药〉Chinese herbal compound
中药化学	chemistry of Chinese materia medica; Chinese pharmaceutical chemistry
中药活性成分	Chinese herbal active constituent
中药鉴别学	identification of Chinese materia medica
中药库	〈中医药〉traditional Chinese medicine storehouse
中药理论	〈中医药〉theory of traditional Chinese herbal; Chinese herbal theory
中药凉茶	〈中医药〉Chinese medicine herbal tea
中药疗法	〈中医药〉Chinese herbal therapy
中药麻醉	〈中医药〉Chinese medicine/herbal anesthesia; Chinese traditional medicinal anesthesia
中药炮制学	〈中医药〉science of processing Chinese materia medica; processing of herbal medicinals
中药配方	〈中医药〉traditional Chinese medicine formula
中药配方胶囊	〈中医药〉Chinese herbal formula capsule
中药配方疗法	〈中医药〉Chinese herbal formula treatment
中药配方治疗	〈中医药〉herbal formula treatment
中药师	〈中医药〉traditional Chinese pharmacist; pharmacist of traditional Chinese medicine; Chinese herbalist

中药食材	〈中医药〉traditional Chinese medicine food
中药食物	〈中医药〉traditional Chinese medicine food
中药汤	〈中医药〉traditional Chinese medicine decoction
中药丸	〈中医药〉traditional Chinese medicine pill
中药学	〈中医药〉Chinese materia medica; science of Chinese traditional medicine; traditional Chinese Pharmacology
中药药材	〈中医药〉herbal medicinal material
中药药剂学	〈中医药〉pharmacy of Chinese materia medica; Chinese Pharmaceutics
中药药理学	〈中医药〉pharmacology of Chinese materia medica; pharmacology of traditional Chinese medicine; Chinese medical herbology and pharmacology
中药饮食	〈中医药〉Chinese medicinal diet
中药制剂	〈中医药〉Chinese herbal preparation
中药制剂分析	〈中医药〉analysis of Chinese medicine preparation
中药治疗	〈中医药〉Chinese herbal treatment
中叶种	〈茶〉medium-leaf variety
中医	〈中医药〉traditional Chinese medicine; doctor of traditional Chinese medicine
中医八纲	〈中医药〉eight principles of differentiating diseases (yin and yang, exterior and interior, cold and heat, deficiency and excess)
中医保健养生	〈中医药〉health care on traditional Chinese medicine
中医病理学	〈中医药〉traditional Chinese pathology
中医儿科学	〈中医药〉pediatrics of traditional Chinese medicine
中医耳鼻喉科学	〈中医药〉otorhinolaryngology of traditional Chinese medicine
中医妇产科学	〈中医药〉traditional Chinese and gynecology obstetrics
中医妇科学	〈陶瓷〉gynecology of traditional Chinese medicine

中医肛肠科学	〈中医药〉proctology of traditional Chinese medicine
中医各家学说	〈中医药〉theories of different schools of traditional Chinese medicine
中医护理学	〈中医药〉science of nursery of traditional Chinese medicine; traditional Chinese nursing
中医基础理论	〈中医药〉basic theory of traditional Chinese medicine
中医接骨科	〈中医药〉traditional Chinese bone-setting department
中医康复学	〈中医药〉science of rehabilitation of traditional Chinese medicine; science of traditional Chinese rehabilitation
中医科医生	〈中医药〉traditional Chinese medicine practitioner →中医师
中医理论	〈中医药〉traditional Chinese medicine theory
中医疗法	〈中医药〉traditional Chinese medicine treatment; TCM treatment
中医临床学	〈中医药〉clinical traditional Chinese medicine
中医门诊	〈中医药〉traditional Chinese medicine clinic
中医内科	〈中医药〉internal traditional Chinese medicine
中医内治八法	〈中医药〉eight methods for traditional Chinese internal medicine (diaphoresis, ejection, precipitation, harmonization, warming, heat-clearing, dispersion and tonification)
中医皮肤科学	〈中医药〉dermatology of traditional Chinese medicine
中医器械	〈中医药〉equipment used in traditional Chinese medicine
中医伤科学	〈中医药〉traditional Chinese traumatology
中医生理学	〈中医药〉traditional Chinese physiology
中医师	〈中医药〉doctor of traditional Chinese medicine →中医科医生
中医食疗	〈中医药〉Chinese dietary therapy

中医术语	〈中医药〉traditional Chinese medicine term
中医推拿学	〈中医药〉science of tuina of traditional Chinese medicine; traditional Chinese tuina
中医外科学	〈中医药〉surgery of traditional Chinese medicine
中医文化	〈中医药〉traditional Chinese medicine culture
中医学	〈中医药〉traditional Chinese medical science; traditional Chinese medicine; TCM theory
中医学会	association of traditional Chinese medicine
中医学校	Chinese medicine school
中医学院	institute of traditional Chinese medicine
中医眼科学	〈中医药〉ophthalmology of traditional Chinese medicine
中医养生学	〈中医药〉science of health preservation on traditional Chinese medicine; traditional Chinese life nurturing
中医药	〈中医药〉traditional Chinese medicine and pharmacy
中医药方	〈中医药〉traditional Chinese medicine prescription
中医医院	〈中医药〉hospital of traditional Chinese medicine
中医饮食疗法	〈中医药〉dietary therapy of traditional Chinese medicine
中医院	〈中医药〉traditional Chinese medicine hospital; hospital/institute of traditional Chinese medicine
中医哲学	〈中医药〉traditional Chinese medicine philosophy
中医诊断学	〈中医药〉diagnostics of traditional Chinese medicine
中医诊法	〈中医药〉diagnostic method of traditional Chinese medicine
中医诊所	〈中医药〉Chinese medicine clinic
中医治疗	〈中医药〉traditional Chinese medicine treatment; TCM treatment
中医治疗学	〈中医药〉traditional Chinese therapeutics

中原野战军	〈旧〉Central Plains Field Army (one of the main forces of the Chinese People's Liberation Army during the War of Liberation)
中指同身寸	〈中医药〉middle finger cun; middle finger as identical unit; proportional unit of the middle finger
中渚	〈中医药〉Zhongzhu acupoint; Central Islet (TE3)
忠靖服	〈服饰〉zhongjing official robe (a uniform for government officials in the Ming Dynasty)
忠靖冠	〈服饰〉zhongjing official hat (a headwear for government officials in the Ming Dynasty)
终身雇佣制	lifetime employment
终身职务制	life-long tenure
终生职业	lifetime career
终止劳动合同	termination of labor contract; to terminate labor contract
钟楼香烟	Zhonglou cigarettes; Bell Tower cigarettes
中风	〈中医药〉apoplexy; stroke; wind-stroke pattern
中风回春丸	〈中医药〉Zhongfeng Huichun Wan; Apoplexy Rejuvenating Pill
中签	(of a stock) to be the lucky number; to win a ballot
中签率	(of a stock) lot winning rate; success rate
重大传染病防治	〈防疫〉prevention and control of major infectious/communicable diseases; to prevent and control major endemics
重大动物疫病	〈防疫〉major infectious animal disease
重大疾病保险	critical illness insurance
重大疾病保险计划	major/critical illness insurance scheme
重大疾病保障	critical illness insurance; to insure against serious diseases
重大疾病防控	〈防疫〉prevention and control of major diseases; to prevent and control major diseases
重大疾病防控体系	〈防疫〉the system to prevent and control the outbreak of major diseases
重大突发公共卫生安全事件	〈防疫〉major public health and security emergency

重大突发公共卫生事件一级响应	〈防疫〉the first-level public health emergency response
重大疫情防控体制机制	〈防疫〉mechanism for major epidemic prevention and control
重点高中	key high school; elite high school
重感灵片	〈中医药〉Zhongganling Pian; Heavy Cold Tablet
重台履	〈服饰〉zhongtai shoes; thick sole shoes; chopine (used in the Tang Dynasty)
重镇安神	〈中医药〉tranquillization with heavy prescription; to quiet the spirit with heavy calmatives
重症病例	〈防疫〉severe case; case of serious conditions
重症病区	〈防疫〉special ward (for patients with severe conditions)
重症患者	〈防疫〉patient in severe or critical condition
重症监护病房	〈防疫〉intensive care unit (ICU)
重症监护室医师	〈防疫〉intensivist; ICU physician
舟车丸	〈中医药〉Zhouche Wan; Boats and Carts Pill; Pill for Relieving Ascites
周元通宝	〈币〉coin with characters zhouyuan tongbao (during the Five Dynasties and Ten Kingdoms period)
《肘后备急方》	〈中医药〉*Zhouhou Beiji Fang*; *Handbook of Prescriptions for Emergencies*; *Prescriptions for Emergent Reference* (by Ge Hong in the Eastern Jin period)
肘尖	〈中医药〉Zhoujian acupoint; Elbow Tip; Tip of the Elbow (EX-UE1)
肘髎	〈中医药〉Zhouliao acupoint; Elbow Crevice (LI12)
肘子炖冬瓜	〈饮食〉Stewed Pork Knuckles and White Gourd in Casserole
绉	crepe, wrinkle (an ancient silk fabric)
绉缎	crepe satin; crepe-back satin
朱红彩八宝纹炉	〈陶瓷〉scarlet-colored censer with eight Chinese treasures pattern

朱明衣	Zhuming robe; clothes in vermilion (for prince in the Song Dynasty)
朱砂	〈中医药〉(of Latin) Cinnabaris; Cinnabar
朱砂安神丸	〈中医药〉Zhusha Anshen Wan; Cinnabar Sedative Pill
朱衣	〈古〉red official uniform
珠宝设计师	jewelry designer
珠宝玉石质量检验师	gemstone quality examiner
珠茶	gunpowder tea; pinhead tea (a kind of green tea whose leaves look like beads)
珠花旗袍	bead embroidery cheongsam; beaded and embroidered gown
珠子参	〈中医药〉(of Latin) Rhizoma Panacis Majoris; Largeleaf Japanese Ginseng Rhizome
《诸病源候论》	〈中医药〉*Zhu Bingyuan Hou Lun*; *Treatise on the Pathogenesis and Manifestations of All Diseases*; *General Treatise on Causes and Manifestations of All Diseases* (by Chao Yuanfang in the Sui Dynasty)
诸诸滑鸡煲	〈饮食〉Chicken Clay Pot; Stewed Chicken in Clay Pot
铢	〈古〉(of weight unit) ancient Chinese baht (twenty-four bahts equaling to one tael (37.301g) in the old system) →锱
猪肠汤	〈饮食〉Pork Intestine Soup
猪脚面线	〈饮食〉Rice Noodles with Pig Trotter
猪苓汤	〈中医药〉Zhuling Tang; Umbellate Pore Decoction
猪肉白菜水饺	〈饮食〉Jiaozi/Dumplings Stuffed with Pork and Chinese Cabbage
猪肉包子	〈饮食〉Pork-Stuffed Baozi;Steamed Bun Stuffed with Pork
猪肉炒饭	〈饮食〉Stir-Fried Rice with Pork
猪肉炒年糕	〈饮食〉Stir-Fried Rice Cakes with Pork
猪肉大葱水饺	〈饮食〉Jiaozi/Dumplings Stuffed with Pork and Scallion

猪肉炖粉条	〈饮食〉Braised Pork with Vermicelli
猪肉锅贴	〈饮食〉Pork-Stuffed Guotie; Pan-Fried Pork Dumpling
猪肉茴香水饺	〈饮食〉Jiaozi/Dumplings Stuffed with Pork and Fennel
猪肉芹菜水饺	〈饮食〉Jiaozi/Dumplings Stuffed with Pork and Celery
猪肉烧甲鱼	〈饮食〉Braised Turtle with Diced Pork
猪肉西葫芦水饺	〈饮食〉Jiaozi/Dumplings Stuffed with Pork and Marrow
猪肉蒸饺	〈饮食〉Steamed Jiaozi/Dumplings Stuffed with Pork
猪油夹沙八宝饭	〈饮食〉Sweet Rice with Lard and Bean Paste
竹杯	bamboo cup
竹编	bamboo plaiting; bamboo weaving; bamboo-made articles
竹编大师	bamboo-weaving master
竹编织品	bamboo-splint-woven article
竹罐	〈中医药〉bamboo cup; bamboo jar (used in cupping therapy)
竹简	〈古〉bamboo slip; slips of bamboo for writing
竹节参	〈中医药〉(of Latin) Rhizoma Panacis Japonici; Japanese Ginseng
竹筷	bamboo chopsticks
《竹林寺女科》	〈中医药〉*Zhulinsi Nüke*; *Bamboo Forest Temple's Secret on Women's Diseases*; *Bamboo Grove Temple Gynecology* (by Monks of Bamboo Forest Temple in the Qing Dynasty)
竹棉混纺	bamboo-cotton blending
竹签	bamboo stick; bamboo skewer
竹茹	〈中医药〉(of Latin) Caulis Bambusae in Taenia; Bamboo Shavings
竹笙海皇羹	〈饮食〉Bamboo Fungi and Seafood Soup

竹笙笋鸡丝翅	〈饮食〉Braised Shark's Fin Soup with Shredded Chicken and Bamboo Fungus
竹荪炖菜汤	〈饮食〉Bamboo Fungi and Vegetable Soup
竹荪银耳汤	〈饮食〉Bamboo Fungi and White Fungi Soup
竹笋黄鱼汤	〈饮食〉Stewed Yellow Croaker with Bamboo Shoots Soup
竹笋青豆	〈饮食〉Bamboo Shoots and Green Peas
竹笋鸭掌汤	〈饮食〉Duck Webs Soup with Bamboo Shoots
竹筒粉蒸肠	〈饮食〉Steamed Intestines with Ground Glutinous Rice in Bamboo Tube
竹筒腊肉	〈饮食〉Steamed Preserved Pork in Bamboo Tube
竹香鲫鱼	〈饮食〉Deep-Fried Crucian Carp with Bamboo Flavor
竹叶椒	〈中医药〉(of Latin) Zanthoxylum Armatum; Fruit of Chinese Wingleaf Prickyash; Bambooleaf Prickleyash
竹叶青茶	Zhuyeqing tea
竹叶青酒	bamboo leaf green liquor
竹叶石膏汤	〈中医药〉Zhuye Shigao Tang; Lophatherum and Gypsum Decoction
逐水剂	〈中医药〉drastic diuretics formula
主办单位	organizer; sponsor
主宾	the most honorable guest
主管护师	nurse-in-charge
主管技师	medical technologist-in-charge
主管药师	pharmacist-in-charge
主客配穴法	〈中医药〉host-guest points combination/association
主任	(of a center or office) director; chief; head; (of an institution) chairman
主任编辑	senior editor; managing editor
主任播音员	chief announcer
主任工程师	chief engineer; principal engineer
主任护师	senior nurse

主任记者	senior journalist; chief reporter
主任技师	senior medical technologist
主任科员	principal staff member
主任秘书	chief secretary
主任委员	chairman of committee
主任药师	senior pharmacist; senior physician
主任医师	chief physician; senior doctor
主修课程	major subject; major courses
主治医师	attending doctor; attending physician
煮	〈饮食〉to boil; to scald; boiled; scalded →白灼
煮丁丝	〈饮食〉Shredded Bean Curd Sheets; Stewed Shredded Bean Curd Cake
煮鸡蛋	〈饮食〉Boiled Eggs
助理编辑	assistant editor
助理翻译	assistant translator
助理工程师	assistant engineer
助理工艺美术师	assistant craft artist
助理馆员	assistant librarian
助理记者	assistant journalist
助理技术编辑	assistant technical editor
助理检察员	assistant procurator; assistant inspector
助理教练	assistant coach
助理教师[助教]	assistant lecturer; teaching assistant
助理教授	assistant professor
助理经济师	assistant economist
助理审判员	assistant judge; deputy judge
助理实验师	assistant experimentalist
助理兽医	veterinary assistant
助理兽医师	assistant veterinarian
助理调研员	assistant consultant
助理统计师	assistant statistician
助理畜牧师	assistant livestock specialist
助理巡视员	assistant counsel
助理驯兽师	assistant wild animal trainer
助理研究员	assistant research fellow

助理药剂师	assistant pharmacist
助学贷款	student loan
助学行动	activity to assist the impoverished students
助学政策	education assistance policy
助阳解表	〈中医药〉to reinforce yang for relieving exterior syndrome
住房保障机制	housing support mechanism
住房保障基金	housing guarantee fund
住房补贴	rental allowance; housing allowance
住房公积金	housing provident fund; house accumulation fund
住院	to be hospitalized; to be admitted to hospital
住院医师	resident doctor; resident physician
贮酒池	spirit storage pool
注册安全工程师	certified safety engineer
注册采矿/矿物工程师	registered engineer of mining/mineral exploration and design
注册测绘师	registered surveyor
注册城市规划师	registered urban planner
注册电气工程师	registered electrical engineer
注册房地产估价师	certified real estate appraiser
注册公用设备工程师	registered engineer of public utility
注册国际投资分析师	certified international investment analyst
注册核安全工程师	certified nuclear safety engineer
注册化工工程师	registered chemical engineer
注册环保工程师	registered environmental protection engineer
注册机械工程师	registered mechanical engineer
注册计量师	certified metrology engineer
注册监理工程师	registered supervision engineer
注册建筑师	registered architect
注册结构工程师	registered structural engineer
注册金融策划师	certified financial planner
注册金融分析师	certified financial analyst; CFA
注册会计师	certified public accountant; CPA
注册会计师证书	certificate of certified public accountant; CPA certificate

注册设备监理师	registered equipment supervisor
注册石油天然气工程师	registered engineer of petroleum exploration and design
注册事务主管	registrar; regulatory affairs supervisor
注册税务师	registered tax agent
注册土木工程师	registered engineer of civil engineering
注册验船师	registered marine surveyor
注册冶金工程师	registered engineer of metallurgical exploration and design
注册咨询工程师	(of investment) registered consulting engineer
注册资产评估师	(of investment) certified public valuer
注塑技师	injection engineer; injection-molding technician
驻车丸	〈中医药〉Zhuche Wan; Carriage-Halting Pill
驻店经理	resident manager
驻色酒	complexion-retaining wine (served on the Beginning of Summer in ancient times)
柱侯牛腩煲	〈饮食〉Stewed Beef Brisket and Scallops in Casserole
柱侯酱	Chee Hou sauce; Chu Hou sauce
铸币	to mint coins; mintage; coined money
箸	〈旧〉zhu; chopsticks
专访	exclusive interview
专柜彩妆顾问	beauty advisor
专家论证	expert argumentation; to be expounded through peer review
专家咨询制度	expert consulting/advisory system; the system for soliciting opinions from experts
专科学校	technical college; college for professional training; training school
专科医生	medical specialist
专栏作家	columnist; column writer
专利代理商	patent agent
专利复审委员会	Patent Re-examination Board; Board of Patent Appeals and Interferences; BPAI

专利顾问	patent advisor
专利合作条约	Patent Cooperation Treaty; PCT
专利技术	patent technology
专利专员	patent specialist
专卖店	exclusive shop; franchised store; specialty store
专门人才	professional personnel; special talent; trained personnel
专升本	to upgrade from a vocational school to a university one
专项资金	special fund
专业顾问	professional advisor
专业培训师	professional trainer
专业营销	professional marketing
砖茶	brick tea
砖雕	brick carving
转基因大豆	genetically-modified soybean; GM soybean
转基因大豆油	genetically-modified soybean oil; GM soybean oil
转基因生物	genetically modified organisms; GMOs; transgenic organism
转基因食品	genetically modified food; GM food
转基因水稻	genetically modified rice; GM rice
转基因水稻［大米］	genetically-modified rice; GM rice
转基因水稻技术	GM rice technology
转基因作物	genetically modified crop; GM crop
转配股	transferred allotted share
转业	(of an armyman) to be transferred to civilian work
转院	to transfer to another hospital
装嫩	to act young; mutton dressed as lamb
装配技师	assembly technician
壮布	〈壮族〉Zhuang cloth
壮骨关节丸	〈中医药〉Zhuanggu Guanjie Wan; Bone-Joint Strengthening Pill
壮锦	〈壮族〉Zhuang brocade
壮行酒	farewell wine

状元	zhuangyuan (the top scholar in the imperial examination); number one scholar; gaokao top scorer
撞肘礼	〈防疫〉elbow bump greeting
追风透骨丸	〈中医药〉Zhuifeng Tougu Wan; Wind-Expelling and Bones-Outthrusting Pill
追星族	star-struck; star fan; groupie
锥把瓶	〈陶瓷〉awl-shaped handle vase; conical handle bottle
着肤灸	〈中医药〉→直接灸
孜然寸骨	〈饮食〉Stir-Fried Spare Ribs with Cumin
孜然烤牛肉	〈饮食〉Grilled Beef with Cumin
孜然辣汁焖牛腩	〈饮食〉Braised Beef Brisket with Cumin in Chili Sauce
孜然羊肉	〈饮食〉Fried Lamb with Cumin
咨询经理	consulting manager
咨询热线	service hotline; consultation hotline
咨询总监	consulting director; consultant director
资产评估师	public valuer; public assets estimator
资金调拨	transfer of financial resources; bank treasurer
资金主管	fund supervisor; treasury supervisor
资料检索	document retrieval; data retrieval
资深销售中心预订员	senior reservation clerk at sales center
资深研发工程师	senior research and development engineer
缁衣	〈古〉ziyi garment; black silk court dress; black monk and nun clothes
滋补肺阴	〈中医药〉to nourish lung-yin; to enrich lung-yin
滋补脾胃	〈中医药〉to nourish the spleen and stomach
滋补砂锅大虾	〈饮食〉Braised King Prawns in Casserole
滋补肾精	〈中医药〉to nourish/replenish kidney essence
滋补肾阴	〈中医药〉to nourish kidney yin; to enrich kidney-yin
滋补心肺	〈中医药〉to nourish the heart and lung
滋补心阴	〈中医药〉to nourish heart-yin; to enrich heart-yin
滋肝明目	〈中医药〉to nourish the liver for improving eyesight

滋肾养肝	〈中医药〉to enrich the kidney and nourish the liver; to nourish the kidney and liver
滋养脏腑	〈中医药〉to moisten and nourish the viscera
滋阴安神	〈中医药〉to nourish yin for tranquillization
滋阴补血	〈中医药〉to nourish yin and tonify blood
滋阴补阳	〈中医药〉to enrich yin and tonify yang; to nourish yin and tonify yang
滋阴降火	〈中医药〉to nourish yin for lowering fire/inner heat
滋阴解表	〈中医药〉to nourish yin for relieving exterior syndrome
滋阴平肝	〈中医药〉to nourish yin and tranquillize liver yang
滋阴清热	〈中医药〉to nourish yin and clear heat
滋阴柔肝	〈中医药〉to nourish yin for emolliating the liver
滋阴润燥	〈中医药〉to nourish yin for moistening dryness
滋阴疏肝	〈中医药〉to nourish yin and disperse stagnated liver-qi
滋阴息风	〈中医药〉to nourish yin to extinguish wind; to nourish yin for calming endogenous wind
滋阴益胃	〈中医药〉to nourish yin for benefiting the stomach; to enrich yin to boost the stomach
锱	〈古〉(of weight unit) zi (equaling to one quarter of a tael) →铢
子姜炒鸭	〈饮食〉Stir-Fried Duck with Tender Ginger
子姜鸡	〈饮食〉Stir-Fried Chicken with Tender Ginger
子姜牛肉	〈饮食〉Stir-Fried Shredded Beef with Ginger Shoots
子姜肉	〈饮食〉Stir-Fried Shredded Pork with Ginger Shoots
子姜虾	〈饮食〉Stir-Fried Shrimps with Ginger Shoots
子午流注法	〈中医药〉midnight-noon ebb-flow acupoint selection
子虾烧黄瓜	〈饮食〉Stir-Fried Shrimps and Cucumbers
子牙钓鱼台	Bloomer Diaoyu Islands (Shaanxi)

紫菜蛋花汤	〈饮食〉Seaweed and Egg Soup with Dried Shrimp and Chopped Green Onion
紫菜汤	〈饮食〉Seaweed Soup
紫菜虾卷	〈饮食〉Seaweed Rolls Stuffed with Shrimps
紫菜虾米汤	〈饮食〉Dried Shrimps and Red Laver Soup
紫草	〈中医药〉(of Latin) Radix Lithospermi; Radix Amebiae; Gromwell Root
紫河车	〈中医药〉(of Latin) Placenta Hominis; Dried Human Placenta
紫花地丁	〈中医药〉(of Latin) Herba Violae; Tokyo Violet Herb
紫荆皮	〈中医药〉(of Latin) Cortex Kadsurae Radicis; Cercis Bark; Bark of Chinese Redbud
紫袍	purple robe (court dress of senior officials in ancient China)
紫茄卷筒肉	〈饮食〉Stewed Paupiette in Eggplant Rolls
紫砂	〈陶瓷〉purple clay; purple sand; purple granulated
紫砂茶具	〈陶瓷〉purple clay teaware
紫砂壶	〈陶瓷〉purple clay pot
紫砂陶器	〈陶瓷〉purple clay pottery; purple earthenware
紫砂提梁壶	〈陶瓷〉purple clay pot with top handle; purple sand teapot with loop handle
紫梢花	〈中医药〉(of Latin) Spongilla fragilla fragilis Leidy; Freshwater Sponge
紫苏梗	〈中医药〉(of Latin) Caulis Perillae; Perilla Stem
紫苏叶	〈中医药〉(of Latin) Folium Perillae; Perilla Leaf
紫苏子	〈中医药〉(of Latin) Fructus Perillae; Perilla Fruit
紫菀	〈中医药〉(of Latin) Radix Asteris; Tatarian Aster Root
紫雪散	〈中医药〉Zixue San; Anti-pestilence and Fever Powder
紫阳毛尖	〈茶〉Ziyang Maojian tea; Ziyang Tippy tea
自产自销	to market one's own products; to produce and market all by oneself

自动柜员机	automatic teller machine; ATM
自动控制工程师	automatic control engineer
自动售货机	slot machine; vending machine
自动资料检索系统	automatic document retrieval system
自费生	commoner
自驾车营地	recreational vehicle park; self-drive camp
自觉接受医学观察	〈防疫〉to present oneself to medical observation
自考	→高等教育自学考试
自酿啤酒	〈陶瓷〉homebrewing
自我隔离	〈防疫〉to isolate oneself; quarantine oneself; self-isolation
自行研制	self-designed and made
自学	self-learning; to study independently; to study on one's own
自学成才	to become a qualified professional through self-taught way; self-taught; autodidact
自学考试	self-study examination; self-taught examination
自由行	independent traveling; self-service traveling; free walker
宗匠茶	mastery tea
综合测评	comprehensive evaluation of students' performance
综合管理部部长	minister of colligation and management department
综合管理部总务	general affair of colligation and management department
综合素质	comprehensive quality
综合素质优秀学生	excellent student of comprehensive quality
综合性测试	integrative test
综合性非药物性干预措施	〈防疫〉comprehensive non-pharmaceutical intervention
综合业务经理	integrated service manager
综合业务专员	integrated service specialist
棕刷	palm brush

棕釉	〈陶瓷〉brown glaze
总编辑	chief editor; editor-in-chief; managing editor
总裁办主任	director of president office
总裁判	chief arbiter; chief referee
总裁助理	CEO (chief executive officer) assistant; president assistant; general manager assistant
总厨	head cook; head chef
总导演	head director; director in chief
总干事	secretary-general; commissioner
总工程师	chief engineer; head engineer
总监秘书	secretary of director
总建筑师	chief architect; architect-in-charge
总经理秘书	secretary of general manager; executive secretary
总经理室	general manager's office; executive office
总经理行政助理	administrative assistant to general manager
总会计师	chief accountant
总台结账领班	front desk cashier captain
总台收款员	front desk cashier
总务长	dean of general affairs
总账会计	general ledger accountant
总账主管	general ledger supervisor
棕香糯米翅	〈饮食〉Steamed Chicken Wings with Glutinous Rice in Bamboo Leaves
棕子	〈饮食〉zongzi; sticky rice dumpling; traditional Chinese rice-pudding (especially for the Dragon Boat Festival)
走狗	running dog; lackey; stooge; flunky
走[推]罐	〈中医药〉moving cupping; sliding cupping; cup moving
走过场	to go through the motions; to make it a mere formality
走红	to become popular; to be in favor with; to be in vogue
走红运	to be in good luck; to have a spell of good luck
走后门	to get in by the back door; to secure advantages through pull or influence; to pull strings

走俏	to sell well; to enjoy brisk sales
走私贩私	smuggling and sale of smuggled goods
走形式	to go through the motions/formality
走穴	(of actors, singers, etc.) to do moonlighting; to perform for extra income without approval by the unit they belong to
走油蹄膀	〈饮食〉Braised Pig Knuckles with Brown Sauce
租赁企业	leased enterprise
租住公屋	public rental housing
足部按摩	foot massage
足临泣	〈中医药〉Zulinqi acupoint; Foot Governor of Tears; Foot Overlooking Tears (GB41)
足窍阴	〈中医药〉Zuqiaoyin acupoint; Yin Portals of the Foot (GB44)
足三里	〈中医药〉Zusanli acupoint; Leg Three Li (ST36)
足三阳经	〈中医药〉three yang channels/meridians of foot
足通谷	〈中医药〉Zutonggu acupoint; Foot Valley Passage (BL66)
阻断全国本土疫情传播	〈防疫〉to contain domestic coronavirus outbreak
阻止疫情在全球蔓延	〈防疫〉to contain the global spread of the virus
组合基金经理	portfolio manager
组织委员	commissary in charge of organization
祖先崇拜	ancestor worship; veneration of the dead
钻空子	to avail oneself of a loophole; to exploit an advantage
最低生活保障	basic living allowance; basic cost of living allowance; subsistence allowance
最低生活保障标准	subsistence allowance standard
最低生活保障制度	minimum living allowance system; basic living allowance system; subsistence allowance system
最低收购价	a floor price; minimum purchase price
最高级别响应	〈防疫〉top-level response
最佳辩手	best debater
最佳才艺奖	outstanding talent award

最佳创意奖	best creativity award
最佳剧本奖	best script award
最佳口才奖	best eloquence award
最佳气质奖	outstanding quality award
最佳人气奖	best popularity award
最佳台风奖	best stage style award
最佳组织奖	prize for the best organization
最具潜质奖	most potentiality award
醉鸡	〈饮食〉Liquor-Soaked Chicken; Liquor-Saturated Chicken
醉排骨	〈饮食〉Fried Small Pork Chops with Wine Sauce; Drunken Chops
醉蒸黄油蟹	〈饮食〉Steamed Crabs Drunken with Rice Wine
尊	〈古〉zun (a drinking or wine vessel)
尊老爱幼	to respect the old and cherish the young; to respect the elderly and care for the young; to respect the aged and take good care of children
尊老爱幼的家庭美德	family virtues of respecting the elderly and loving the young
尊师重教	to respect teachers and value education; to show respect to teachers and attach great importance to education
遵义毛峰	〈茶〉Zunyi Maofeng tea; Zunyi Tippy tea
左公鸡	〈饮食〉General Tso's Chicken (with Sweet, Spicy and Salty Tastes)
左归丸	〈中医药〉Zuogui Wan; Left-Restoring (Life Gate) Pill; Kidney Yin-Reinforcing Bolus
左归饮	〈中医药〉Zuogui Yin; Left-Restoring (Life Gate) Beverage; Kidney Yin-Reinforcing Drink
左金丸	〈中医药〉Zuojin Wan; Liver-Fire-Purging and Stomach-Regulating Pill
左派思想观念	leftist ideology
左倾知识分子	left-leaning intellectual
左右配穴法	〈中医药〉left-right acupoint combination/association

左宗豆腐	〈饮食〉General Tsuo's Tofu
作业室经理	studio manager
坐骨神经	〈中医药〉Zuogu Shenjing acupoint; Sciatic Nerve (AH6)
坐观成败	to sit on the fence
坐月子	confinement in childbirth; to sit the month; to be confined in childbirth
做好返程人员疫情防控	〈防疫〉to help returnees from infected regions in epidemic prevention and control
做好重点地区疫情防控	〈防疫〉to strengthen epidemic prevention and control in key regions
做好重点防控部位人员的物资保障	〈防疫〉to ensure essential supplies for personnel in key posts of epidemic prevention and control

附录一
《牛津英语大词典》中的汉语借词词表

　　本词表共收词 632 条。全部通过三个渠道从《牛津英语大词典》(在线版)中提取出来的:(1)通过应用界面上的词源统计进行逐条分析;(2)对显示界面的相关义项、释义和内词目进行人工识别;(3)运用自建"涉华英语语言知识库"中的部分相关词汇进行反向查询。英语表达的词形(含大小写)直接取自词典,汉语字/词是通过解读词典中的英语释义后按汉语习惯表达方式反向翻译出来的。借词出现的年份取自该词在收集到的实际用例中出现的时间(不是收录时间)。同一个汉语字词在不同时期会有很多不同的英语书写方法,这里仅提取了部分在历史上比较常用的拼写形式。

英语表达	汉语字词来源	年份
acupuncture point	穴位	1932
add oil (go on)	加油	1964
Amoy	厦门话	1851
baozi	包子	2014
bao-zi	包子	1997
barefoot doctor	赤脚医生	1971
beef tea	牛肉浓汤	1873
bing	茗(茶)	1701
bird's-nest	燕窝(汤)	1599
bohea	武夷茶	1701
bok choy	白菜	1847
bonze	僧人	1577
Boxer rebellion	义和团起义	1899
Boxers	义和团	1899

Boxer uprising	义和团起义	1961
brainwashing	洗脑	1950
brick tea	砖茶	1789
broken tea	碎茶	1870
Buddha-nature	佛性	1872
bush tea	灌木茶	1728
campoi	拣焙茶	1842
Canton china	广式瓷	1881
Canton crepe	广绫	1865
Canton enamel	广彩;广州搪瓷	1910
Cantonese[1]	广州话	1857
Cantonese[2]	广州人	1857
Canton flannel	绒布	1881
Canton matting	广式地垫	1860
capitalist road	资本主义道路	1966
capitalist roader	走资派	1967
Ch'ien Lung	乾隆	1901
cha	茶	1616
chah	茶	1616
cham	可汗	1553
Chan	禅	1876
chen shu	真书	1655
cheongsam	旗袍	1957
cheongsam	长衫	1957
chi (of philosophy)	气	1897
chi gung	气功	1966
chin chin	请请	1795
chipao	旗袍	1955
choi cum	菜心	1939
chop-chop	快快	1834
chop-stick/chopstick	筷子	1699
chopsuey	杂碎	1888
chop-suey v.	炒杂碎	1888
chow[1]	(原产中国的)狗	1889
chow[2]	食物	1856

chow³ (derogatory)	〈俚〉中国人(贬)	1872
chow-chow	松狮狗	1886
chow-chow¹	中国咸菜;杂碎	1795
chow-chow²	什锦菜(的)	1795
chow-chow³	松狮狗	1896
chow mein	炒面	1903
choy sum	菜心	1932
Chün	钧窑瓷	1888
Confucian	孔子的	1837
Confucianism	儒教;孔子学说	1862
Confucianist	儒家;儒教徒	1846
congou	工夫茶	1725
cowslip tea	黄花茶	1723
cultural revolution	文化大革命	1966
cumshaw¹	酬金	1839
cumshaw²	小费;小额贿赂	1839
cumshaw³ v.	给赏钱;送小礼物	1839
daimiate	大名府	1889
daimio	大名	1839
deem sim	点心	1952
dharma talk	(佛)法语	1964
dim sum	点心	1948
ding	鼎	1904
Ding	定窑瓷	2000
Dingyao	定窑	2012
dizi	笛子	1982
dotchin	戥子;戥秤,提秤	1685
doucai	多彩(瓷)	1980
dragon boat	龙舟	1846
dragon fruit	火龙果	1963
East Wind (of mahjong)	东风	1908
egg roll	蛋卷	1938
erhu	二胡	1908
fan-tan (a gambling game)	蕃摊(游戏)	1878
fen (monetary unit)	(货币单位)分	1852

feng-shui	风水	1797
Flowery Empire (originated from hwa kwo)	花国(中国)	1862
Flowery Kingdom (originated from hwa kwo)	花国(中国)	1901
Flowery Land (originated from hwa kwo)	花国(中国)	1847
Flowery Nation (originated from hwa kwo)	花国	1867
foo yong	芙蓉蛋	1928
fooyong	芙蓉蛋	1965
foreign devil	洋鬼子	1804
fo yung	芙蓉蛋	1917
fum	凤(凰)	1820
functional food	功能性食品	1900
fu yung	芙蓉蛋	1972
fu-yung	芙蓉蛋	1945
galingale	高良姜	1000
Gan	赣方言	1943
ganbei	干杯	1940
ganbu	干部	1956
Gang of Four	四人帮	1976
ginseng	人参	1654
goji	枸杞	2002
goldfish	金鱼	1698
gow	(鸦片)膏	1922
grass carp	草鱼	1885
Great Leap Forward	大跃进	1958
gung ho	共好精神的;同心协力的	1942
gung hou	工合	1942
Hakka[1]	客家	1867
Hakka[2]	客家话	1867
Han	汉(朝)	1736
hao	毫	1948
hien	县	1938
hoey (social organisation)	会(社会组织)	1865

ho-ho bird	凤凰	1901
hoisin	海鲜(酱)	1957
hoisin sauce	海鲜酱	1957
Hokkien	闽南话	1832
Honan¹	河南绸	1878
Honan²	河南瓷	1878
hong	(商)行	1726
hsien	县	1837
Hunanese	湖南话	1937
Hundred Flowers	百花齐放	1958
hutung	胡同	1922
hyson	熙春茶	1740
I Ching	易经	1876
inro	印笼	1617
itzebu	四分之一两	1616
jap	偷袭	1957
Jap (colloquial)	日本的;日本人	1880
Japan (obsolete)	日本漆;亮漆	1577
japan¹	亮漆	1688
Japan²	日本	1577
Japanese¹	日本人	1604
Japanese²	日本语	1828
Japaneseness	日本特点	1965
Japanesery	日本装饰品	1885
Japanesque	日本式的	1883
Japanesy	日式的	1890
Japanism	日本精神	1888
Japanization	日本化	1895
Japanize	日本化	1890
japanned leather	黑亮漆皮	1814
japanned peacock	黑亮孔雀	1814
japanner¹	油漆工	1695
Japanner²	(旧)日本人	1614
Japanner³	(旧)日本船	1719
japanning	涂油漆	1688

Japanology	日本学	1888
Japanophile	亲日派	1905
Japlish	日式英语;英日混合语	1960
Japonian[1]	日本人的	1613
Japonian[2]	(旧)日本人的;日本人	1600
Japonica	日本山茶	1819
Japonism	日本风格	1890
jiao (monetary unit)	(货币单位)角	1949
jiaozi	饺子	1978
K'ang-Hsi	康熙	1906
kago	驾笼;滑竿	1857
kaifong	街坊	1857
k'ai shu	楷书	1876
kalgan	喀尔干皮货;张家口皮货	1930
kang	炕	1770
kanji[1]	(日语)汉字库;汉字体系	1920
kanji[2]	日本汉字	1960
kaoliang	高粱酒	1904
kaolin	高岭土	1727
kaolinic	高岭土的	1879
kaolinite	高岭石	1867
kaolinization	使高岭土化	1886
kaolinize	使高岭土化	1874
Keemun	祁门红茶	1892
ketchup	番茄酱	1711
Khotan	和田毯;和阗毯	1871
ki (of philosophy)	气	1736
Kiangsi	江西(苏区)	1937
kiasu	怕输的人;怕失败的人	1978
kirin	麒麟	1727
Ko	哥窑	1882
ko (ancient Chinese weapon)	戈	1923

Ko iú	哥窑	1882
kongsi	公司	1839
Ko ware	哥窑瓷	1882
kowtow/kotow	磕头	1804
Ko yao	哥窑	1882
Kuan	官	1814
Kuan Hua	官话	1814
Kuan ware	官窑	1888
Kuan yao	官窑	1888
Kuan Yin	观音	1906
Kuchaean/Kuchean	龟兹语	1939
kuei (ancient Chinese bronze food-vessel)	簋	1935
kumquat	金橘	1699
kungfu	功夫	1966
Kuomintang	国民党	1912
Kuo-yü	国语	1932
kwai-lo	鬼佬	1969
Kwan	官	1814
Kwan Yin	观音	1832
kylin/kilin	麒麟	1857
labour hero	劳模	1945
lah (modal particle)	啦	1972
Lahu	拉祜人	1900
Langshan (fowl)	狼山鸡	1871
Lapsang Souchong	正山小种红茶（有烟熏味）	1883
Latinxua	拉丁化	1937
lean to one side	一边倒	1956
lei (ancient Chinese wine or water vessel)	罍	1929
lei-wên (decorative patterns on ancient bronzes and potteries)	雷纹	1922
li[1] (a weight unit equaling to one-thousandth part of a liang)	厘	1771
li[2] (ancient Chinese cooking vessel)	鬲	1945

li³ (rites)	礼	1912
li⁴ (unit for itinerary measure)	里	1588
liang/leang (a weight unit)	（重量单位）两	1827
likin (of tax)	厘金(税)	1876
ling	菱(角)	1860
ling chih¹	灵芝	1904
ling chih²	（瓷器上的）靈芝圖案	1915
lion dance	狮子舞	1937
li shu (ancient Chinese calligraphic script)	隶书	1824
Lisu	傈僳族	1896
litchi	荔枝	1588
li ting (ancient Chinese cooking vessel)	鬲鼎	1958
loan to one side	一边倒(外教政策)	1956
Lohan	罗汉	1878
longan	龙眼	1732
Long March	长征	1937
loquat	枇杷	1820
lose face	丢脸	1876
lotus seeds	莲子	1655
lü (of music)	（音）律	1655
Lung-ch'üan	龙泉瓷	1904
Lung-shan	龙山(文化)	1938
Macanese	澳门人	1902
macao	赌博	1778
mafoo	马夫	1863
mah-jong	麻将	1922
Mamenchisaurus	马门溪龙属	1954
mandarin	（旧时）中国政府高级官吏	1604
mandarin hat	官帽	1882
mandarin jacket	马褂	1970
mandarin porcelain	官瓷；中国瓷器	1873
man t'ou	馒头	1955
man-tou/mantou	馒头	1955

Mao collar	中山装式领子	1967
Maoism	毛泽东思想	1950
Mao jacket	中山装;毛装	1972
Mao-style	毛式	1972
Mao suit	中山装;毛装	1973
Mao-t'ai (strong alcoholic drink)	茅台酒	1962
Mao tai/Mao-tai	茅台酒	1973
martial arts	武术	1920
May (the) Fourth	五四(运动)	1930
May (the) Fourth Movement	五四运动	1938
mee^1	米粉	1935
mee^2	面条	1935
mei p'ing	梅瓶	1915
mei ping (porcelain vase with a narrow neck)	梅瓶	1915
meridians (of acupuncture)	(针灸)经络;脉络	
Miao^1	苗语	1834
Miao^2	苗族(人)	1834
Miaotse (pejorative)	苗子(贬)	1810
Middle Empire (originated from Zhōngguó)	中国	1698
Middle Kingdom (originated from Zhōngguó)	中国	1662
mien	面条	1890
Mien (self appellation of Yao people)	勉(瑶族人自称)	1873
milk name	乳名	1836
Min^1	闽语	1902
Min^2	闽	1902
Ming	明(代)	1795
ming	命(运)	1937
ming chi	冥器	1958
Min Yuen	民援	1951
moc-main	木棉	1866
Mohism	墨家学说	1861
money tree	摇钱树	1934

Mongol[1]	蒙古人	1738
Mongol[2]	蒙古语	1738
monthly rose	月季	1964
moogoo gai pan	蘑菇鸡片	1902
moon cake	月饼	1938
Moon Festival	中秋节	1892
moon flask	月瓶(瓷器)	1892
moon flask (of Chinaware)	(抱)月瓶	1945
moon gate	月亮门	1924
moo shu	木须肉	1962
mou	亩	1836
moutan	牡丹	1808
nankeen	南京布	1755
Nanyang	南洋	1946
Nei kuan (of acupuncture point)	(穴位)内关	1959
nien hao	年号	1824
no can do	做不了	1868
North Wind (of mahjong)	(麻将)北风	1969
oolong	乌龙茶	1845
oopack	湖北红茶	1855
oracle bone(s)	甲骨(文)	1915
orange pekoe	橙白毫	1829
P.L.A.	人民解放军	1950
p'an	(青铜)盆	1904
p'o	魄	1850
paiban (of musical instrument)	拍板	1884
pai gow	牌九	1906
pai-hua	白话	1923
pailou	牌楼;牌坊	1836
paitung	白铜	1736
pakapoo (of lottery)	白鸽票	1886
pak choy	(广东)白菜	1847
pak pai (illegal taxi in Hongkong)	白牌车	1972
paktong	白铜	1775
pa-kua	八卦	1875

pan (a percussion instrument)	（快）板	1874
Panchen Lama	班禅喇嘛	1780
pao-chia (system)	保甲	1931
pao tzu	包子	1927
pao-tzu	包子	1944
paper tiger	纸老虎	1836
pearl tea	珍珠奶茶	1838
pékin	北京人	1827
Pekin(g)	北京鸭	1885
Pekin[1]	北京宽条绸	1776
Pekin[2]	北京鸭	1885
Pekinese[1]	北京狗；狮子狗	1902
Pekinese[2]	北京狗的；狮子狗的	1898
Peking[1]	北京鸭	1902
Peking[2]	北京地毯	1904
Peking carpet	北京地毯	1969
Peking crepe	北京条子丝绸	1895
Peking duck	北京鸭	1874
Pekingese[1]	北京话	1849
Pekingese[2]	北京人	1860
Pekingese[3]	北京的	1858
Peking man	北京猿人	1926
Peking opera	京剧	1953
Peking stripe	北京宽条绸	1879
pekoe	白毫茶	1713
pekoe v.	与…白毫茶混合	1892
pela	白蜡	1754
Pelong (Dragon Boat Festival in Taiwan)	白龙船节	1675
pe-tsai	白菜	1788
petuntse	白墩子(高岭土)	1728
pi (shallow ladle with a crooked handle)	匕	1871
pidgin[1]	皮钦语；洋泾浜语	1845
pidgin[2]	事务	1807
pidgin[3]	关注点；专长	1902
pillow book	枕边(禁)书	1906

Pinyin	拼音	1963
pipa	琵琶	1839
plum rains	梅雨	1968
Pong (pejorative)	中国佬(贬)	1910
pongee	茧绸	1711
porcelain tower	琉璃塔	1666
po shan lu	宝山(香)炉	1915
potsticker	锅贴	1968
powder blue	粉蓝彩	1910
Puerh	普洱茶	1893
Pu-Erh/Pu-erh	普洱茶	1880
pung (of mahjong)	碰	1922
Pure Land	净土;极乐世界	1819
putonghua	普通话	1950
qi^1	气	1850
qi^2 (of philosophy)	气	1870
qigong	气功	1996
Qin	秦(代)	1790
qin	琴	1839
Qing	清(代)	1790
Qingdao	青岛啤酒	1979
qinghaosu (of Chinese medicine)	青蒿素	1977
qipao	旗袍	1984
rectification campaign	整风运动	1956
Red Army	红军	1934
red button	红顶子(官员)	1797
Red China	红色中国	1934
red-cooking	红烧(肉)	1956
Red Guard	红卫兵	1966
reform through labour	劳动改造;劳改	1913
reform through labour camp	劳动改造;劳改	1991
reform through labour farm	劳动改造;劳改	1962
reign name	(皇帝的)年号	1871

reign name (the symbolic name adopted by a sovereign in China)	年号	1976
reign title (the symbolic name adopted by a sovereign)	(皇帝的)年号	1898
renminbi	人民币	1957
reorganizationist (of the Kuomintang in 1928—31)	改组派	1930
rice bowl (to earn a living)	饭碗	1828
running dog	走狗	1937
samfu	衫裤	1955
sampan	舢板	1620
samshoo	三烧酒	1697
samshu	三烧酒	1697
Sanfan	三反(运动)	1956
sang	人参	1843
san hsien	三弦	1839
san ts'ai (of chinaware)	三彩	1901
save one's face	保全面子	1898
scorched earth (a translation of Chinese jiāotǔ zhèngcè)	焦土政策	1937
se (a musical instrument)	(25弦琴)瑟	1874
semi-proletariat	半无产阶级	1951
senshaw	(薯莨)绸	1817
sesshin (of Zen Buddhism)	(禅宗)摄心;接心	1922
Shang	商(朝)	1669
shang (equivalent to approximately 15 mu)	垧(约15亩)	1887
Shanghai	浦东鸡;三黄鸡	1853
Shanghailander	上海人	1917
Shanghainese[1]	上海话的	1964
Shanghainese[2]	上海人的	1965
Shanghainese[3]	上海话	1964
shantung	山东绸	1882
Shaolin	少林(派,武术)	1974
Shaoshing	绍兴酒	1961

shark-fin	鱼翅	1793
Shar-Pei	沙皮狗	1976
shen	神	1847
sheng¹	生（角）	1886
sheng² (a musical instrument)	笙	1795
shibuichi	四分一（铜银合金）	1880
Shih Tzu	狮子狗	1921
shihtzu	狮子狗	1921
Shintoism	神道教	1857
Shintoist	神道信徒	1727
Shintoistic	神道的	1893
Shintoize v.	使神道化	1895
silk road	丝绸之路	1931
silk route	丝绸之路	1931
sing-song girl	歌女	1934
sinograph	汉字	1979
sinseh	先生；医生	1972
sinseh	中医师	1972
Six Dynasties	六朝	1934
snakehead	蛇头	1965
so-na	唢呐	1908
Song	宋（朝）	1673
Son of Heaven	天子	1613
souchong	小种茶	1761
South Wind (of mahjong)	南风	1922
soy milk	豆浆	1907
spade-money	铲币	1892
splittism	分裂主义	1962
splittist¹	分裂主义分子	1968
splittist²	分裂主义的	1978
spring roll	春卷	1943
stir-fry	颠炒	1959
struggle meeting	斗争会	1966
suan-pan	算盘	1736
subgum	（素）什锦	1911

Sui	隋(朝)	1738
Sun Yat-senism	三民主义	1927
Sun Yat-sen jacket	中山装	1946
Sun Yat-sen suit	中山装	1942
sweet and sour/sweet-sour	糖醋的	1723
sycee	银锭	1711
Szechuan	四川话	1956
Sze Yap	(广东)四邑话	1948
T'ai Chi	太极拳	1736
t'ien	天	1613
Tachai	大寨(式)	1969
Tachai-type	大寨模式	1977
ta chuan	大篆	1894
tael (a weight unit)	(重量单位)两	1598
taikonaut	太空人	1998
taipan (the manager or head of a firm)	大班	1834
Tai-ping	太平天国(运动)	1853
Taiwanese	台湾人(的);台湾话(的)	1942
tan^1	旦(角)	1886
tan^2 (a gambling game)	番摊	1883
tan^3 (a weight unit)	担	1911
Tang	唐朝	1669
tangpu	(国民党)党部	1941
tangram	七巧板	1864
$Tangut^1$	党项族;西夏人(的)	1598
$Tangut^2$	西夏语(的)	1979
Tangutan	唐古忒	1876
tanka (a religious painting on woven material in Tibetan Buddhism)	唐卡	1925
$Tanka^1$	疍家	1839
$Tanka^2$	疍民	1839
tao	道教	1736
Tao Kuang	道光	1927

taotai	道台	1747
taotie/t'ao t'ieh (the name of a mythical monster, or the design showing its face on ancient Chinese vessels)	饕餮(纹)	1915
taotieh	饕餮;饕餮纹	1915
ta tzu-pao	大字报	1960
te	德	1895
tea¹	茶	1655
tea²	茶饮	1601
tea³ (with qualifying words)	(代修饰词)表示各类茶	1704
tea bag	袋茶	1886
tea bag *v.*	制作袋茶	1969
tea egg	茶叶蛋	1920
teaer	饮茶人	1892
teaey	茶味的	1890
teagarden¹	有茶室的花园;露天茶室	1802
teagarden²	茶园	1882
tea-gardened	(花园)带茶室的	1843
tea-gardener	露天茶室主或侍者	1903
teagardeny	茶园的;茶室的	1862
teaing	饮茶	1845
teaish	像茶的	1836
teaism	茶瘾	1904
tea *v.*	喝茶	1810
Tê-hua	德化瓷	1923
temmoku	天目釉	1880
temple block (of musical instrument)	木鱼	1929
Teochew¹	潮州话	1893
Teochew²	潮州人	1893
Thibet/Tibet	藏毛织品;藏服	
thousand-year egg	皮蛋	1961
thousand-year-old egg	皮蛋	1972
three-anti	三反(运动)	1966

tiao (of ancient monetary unit)	（古货币单位）吊	1883
Tientsin	天津地毯	1904
tile-tea	砖茶	1858
tim sum	点心	1945
ting	亭(子)	1853
Ting	定窑瓷	1888
Ting ware	定窑瓷	1904
Ting-yao	定窑	1857
ti-tzu	笛子	1874
tong (a secret society or fraternal organization especially of Chinese in the U.S.)	堂会(秘密帮会或兄弟会)	1883
to ride a tiger	骑虎难下	1902
tou (ancient Chinese food vessel)	豆	1899
tou ts'ai[1]	多彩的	1960
tou ts'ai[2]	多彩瓷	1953
towcok	豆角	1866
Triad Society	三合会	1821
tribute rice	贡米	1853
ts'ao shu	草书	1876
tsatlee	七里丝	1848
Tsingtao	青岛啤酒	1972
tsu	（氏）族	1939
tsun	尊(中大型酒器)	1958
tsung	琮	1904
tuchun	督军	1917
tui na	推拿	1979
tu-mo (of acupuncture point)	督脉(穴位)	1972
tung	桐油	1889
Tungan	东干人	1875
tung oil	桐油	1881
tung tree	油桐树	1973
tupan	督办	1925
tutang	督堂(总督)	1613
Twankay	屯溪茶	1840

Twankay tea	屯溪茶	1840
tycoon	大亨	1857
typhoon	台风	1588
typhoon v.	刮台风	1953
Tz'u Chou	磁州陶瓷	1910
ve-tsin	味精	1958
walking on or with two legs	两条腿走路	1962
walking on two legs	两条腿走路	1959
wallposter	墙报	1962
wampee	黄皮(果)	1830
Wan-Li	万历瓷	1876
war-lord	军阀	1922
Warring States	战国	1929
Wei	魏(朝)	1894
wei ch'i	围棋	1871
wên jên	文人	1958
wen li (based on a misconception of the Chinese meaning)	文言(误用形成的词)	1887
wen yen	文言	1936
West Wind (of mahjong)	西风	1922
whangee	黄篾竹	1790
White Terror	白色恐怖	1965
Wing Chun	咏春拳	1967
wok	镬;锅	1858
wonk	黄狗	1900
won ton	馄饨	1948
wood ear	木耳	1876
worker-peasant	工农	1937
worker-peasant-soldier	工农兵	1963
work point	工分	1964
Wu	吴语	1908
Wufan	五反运动	1956
wushu	武术	1973
wu ts'ai[1]	五彩釉	1904

wu ts'ai²	五彩瓷器	1964
Wu-wei	无为教	1859
wu-wei	无为	1859
wu-wei (of taoism)	（道教）无为	1859
wuxia	武侠	1936
yamen	衙门	1747
yang	阳	1671
yang ch'in	扬琴	1876
yang-ko	秧歌	1954
Yang-Mills	杨-米尔斯理论	1961
Yang Shao	仰韶文化	1923
Yao	瑶族	1834
Yarkand¹	叶尔羌河	1875
Yarkand² *adj.*	叶尔羌的	1880
yellow jacket	黄马褂	1878
yen¹	元	1874
yen²	（鸦片烟）瘾	1882
yen³	鸦片烟	1926
yen⁴	（日）元	1874
yen⁵ *v.* (to have an intense desire)	犯烟瘾；强烈渴望	1919
Yenan	延安；延安时期的	1949
yen hop	（鸦片）烟斗	1901
yen pock	鸦片丸	1934
yen she	烟屎	1892
yen shee	烟屎	1912
yen siang	（鸦片）烟枪	1882
yen-yen	烟瘾	1886
Yi	彝族（的）	1960
Yi Hsing ware	宜兴瓷器	1915
Yi Hsing yao	宜兴窑瓷	1904
Yin	（商）殷	1846
yin	阴	1671
ying ch'ing	影青瓷	1922
yu (a wine or rice vessel in ancient China)	卣（古代酒器）	1904
Yuan	元朝	1673

yuan[1] (a monetary unit)	元	1921
yuan[2]	院(政府和事业机构)	1928
yuan hsiao	元宵	1945
yüeh (ancient Chinese weapons)	钺	1956
Yüeh[1]	越窑	1887
Yüeh[2]	越窑瓷的	1910
Yüeh[3]	越族	1901
Yüeh[4]	越人	1901
Yüeh[5]	粤语	1954
Yüeh[6]	粤语的	1956
yüeh ch'in	月琴	1839
Yüeh ware	越窑瓷器	1915
yulan	玉兰	1822
yulo[1]	摇橹	1878
yulo[2]	摇橹［动］	1878
yum cha	(港式)饮茶	1936
Yung Chêng	雍正	1925
Yung-ching	雍正	1902
Yunnanese	云南人	1849
zhuyin zimu	注音字母	1938

附录二 《韦氏第三版新国际英语词典》中的汉语借词词表

本词表共收词 613 条,主要取自《韦氏新国际英语词典三版》,少部分来自《梅里亚姆-韦伯斯特》(Merriam-Webster)在线词典。取词方式主要是根据《牛津英语大词典》中的汉语借词和加兰·坎农(Garland Cannon)的"英语中的汉语借词词表",以及其词条之间的参见和相互关联等进行逐条查询获得的。对于一些在源词典中分列出义项的词这里按不同含义分别出条。该词中的汉语和民族地名很多,基本都是汉语拼音形式,本表仅提取了一些在英美文化中比较常用的部分城市或民族名称。这类专名大多注释为名词,但也可以作修饰语用,因此在其后特意加上了"(的)"进行提示。英语表达的词形(含大小写)直接取自源词典,汉字词是按汉语习惯表达方式反向翻译出来的。

英语表达	汉语字词来源
Achang	阿昌族
acupuncture	针灸
ahung	阿訇
Ai-lao	哀牢族
Amoy	厦门(的)
Amoyese[1]	厦门话(的)
Amoyese[2]	厦门人(的)
ang-khak	红曲;植物染料
Anking	安庆的
Anqing	安庆
Anshan	鞍山
apricot plum	杏李;红杏

Atayal	（台湾）泰雅族
bamboo oyster	竹蛏
barefoot doctor	赤脚医生
beef tea	牛肉浓汤
beggar's chicken	叫化鸡
Beijing	北京
Black Miao	黑苗
black pottery	黑陶
Bohea	武夷茶
bok choy	白菜
bonze	僧人
Boxer	义和团成员
brainwashing	洗脑
brick tea	砖茶
bush tea	草茶；灌木茶
cambric tea	红茶牛奶
Canton	广州
Canton china	广式(青花)瓷
Canton crepe	广绫
Canton enamel	广式搪瓷
Cantonese	广州人；广州话
canton flannel	广绒
Canton ginger	广式腌姜
Canton ware	广瓷
Celestial	天朝的；中国的
Celestial Empire	天朝
Celestial Teacher	天师
centipede grass	假俭草；蜈蚣草
ch'an	禅
ch'ang shan	（草药）常山
Ch'ichia	齐家文化(的)
Ch'ing Ming	清明节
Changsha	长沙(的)
Ch'anism	禅宗
Ch'anist	禅宗信徒

Chefoo	芝罘(烟台)
Chekiang	浙江(的)
Chen-chiang	镇江(的)
Chengdu	成都(的)
Ch'eng-tu	成都(的)
Ch'eng-tzu-yai	城子崖(文化)的
cheongsam	旗袍
chiao (a monetary unit)	(货币单位)角
Ch'ien lung	乾隆(的)
Chien ware	津窑瓷
Chien yao	建窑
China ale	麦芽啤酒
China aster	翠菊
China bean	豇豆
China bedbug	锥鼻虫;臭虫
Chinaberry	楝树;苦楝
China blue	中国蓝
China brier	菝葜
China cantharides	中国芫菁
China cinnamon	肉桂
China fir	杉木
China grass	苎麻
China ink	中国墨
China jute	苘麻
China mark	螟蛾
China mink	黄鼬;黄鼠狼
China orange	中国橙
China pink	石竹
China rooster	环颈雄鸡
Chinaroot	菝葜根
China rose	月季
China shot	美人蕉
China silk	中国丝绸
China tea	中国茶
China wax	中国蜡

China wood oil	桐油
chin-chin[1]	你好
chin-chin[2]	请请
chin-chin[3]	再见
Chinchow	锦州(的)
Chinese air plant	火焰兰
Chinese alligator	扬子鳄
Chinese angelica	当归
Chinese anise	八角
Chinese arbor vitae	侧柏
Chinese artichoke	草石蚕;宝塔菜
Chinese azalea	黄杜鹃;闹羊花
Chinese banana	粉蕉
Chinese bean oil	豆油
Chinese bellflower	桔梗
Chinese bezique	中国纸牌
Chinese bladdernut	栾树
Chinese blister fly	横纹芫菁
Chinese block	木鱼
Chinese blue	中国蓝
Chinese boxes	套盒
Chinese bridge	中国桥牌
Chinese bush cherry	郁李
Chinese cabbage	大白菜
Chinese checkers	跳棋
Chinese chestnut	板栗
Chinese cinnamon	桂皮
Chinese cinnamon oil	桂皮油
Chinese civet	果子狸
Chinese cork tree	黄蘖
Chinese crescent	中国弦月
Chinese crested dog	中国冠毛犬
Chinese date[1]	枣树
Chinese date[2]	枣子
Chinese dogskin	中国狗皮草

Chinese drum	中国大鼓
Chinese elm	榔榆
Chinese evergreen	万年青
Chinese export porcelain	中国外销瓷
Chinese fan palm	蒲葵
Chinese fiddle	二胡
Chinese fir	杉木
Chinese fleece vine	花蓼
Chinese forget-me-not	中国毋忘草
Chinese gall	五倍子
Chinese gelatin	明胶
Chinese ginger	高良姜
Chinese gong	锣
Chinese goose	鸿雁
Chinese gooseberry	猕猴桃
Chinese green (a green dye)	中国绿
Chinese hat plant	阳伞花
Chinese hibiscus	朱槿;扶桑
Chinese holly	枸骨;铁冬青
Chinese horn	唢呐
Chinese ink	中国墨
Chinese insect wax	中国石蜡;虫白蜡
Chinese isinglass	明胶
Chinese jujube	大果枣
Chinese jute	苘麻
Chinese lacquer	中国漆
Chinese lantern	纸灯笼
Chinese lantern plant	灯笼草
Chinese lemon	枸橼
Chinese lilac	华丁香;什锦丁香
Chinese lily	淡紫百合
Chinese liver fluke	中华肝吸虫
Chinese matrimony vine	枸杞
Chinese millet	高粱
Chinese money plant	银扇草

Chinese musk	麝香
Chinese mustard	小叶芥;芥菜
Chinese nut	荔枝
Chinese olive	青果;橄榄
Chinese orange	金枣
Chinese parasol tree	梧桐
Chinese parsley	香菜
Chinese pavilion	中国馆
Chinese pear	鸭梨;中国梨
Chinese pea tree	锦鸡儿
Chinese peel	藤
Chinese pheasant	环颈雉鸡
Chinese preserving melon	冬瓜
Chinese primrose	藏报春
Chinese pulsey	狗尾草
Chinese puzzle	中国智力玩具
Chinese quince	木瓜
Chinese red	中国红
Chinese rhubarb	大黄
Chinese rose	月季
Chinese rose beetle	长金龟
Chinese rouge	橘红
Chinese sacred lily	水仙花;中国水仙
Chinese scale	梨圆蚧
Chinese scholar tree	槐树
Chinese silk plant	苎麻
Chinese snow ball	绣球花
Chinese squill	绵枣儿
Chinese stick	墨条
Chinese sumac	天堂树;臭椿
Chinese tallow	乌桕油
Chinese tallow tree	乌桕
Chinese temple block	木鱼
Chinese tree wax	中国树蜡
Chinese trumpet creeper	凌霄花

Chinese vampire	中华大耳蝠
Chinese varnish tree	石栗;油桐树
Chinese vermillion	朱红
Chinese violet	中国紫
Chinese wall	壁垒;理解障碍
Chinese watermelon	冬瓜
Chinese wax	中国蜡
Chinese whist	中国惠斯特牌
Chinese white	中国白(锌白)
Chinese windlass	中国辘轳
Chinese wistaria	紫藤
Chinese witch hazel	白檵木;金缕梅
Chinese wood oil	桐油
Chinese yam	山药
Chinese yellow[1]	雄黄;帝王黄
Chinese yellow[2]	橙黄色;柠檬黄
Ching	清;清朝
ching	经(书)
chingma	苘麻
Chingpaw	景颇族
Chinhsien	锦县(的)
Chongqing	重庆(的)
chop-chop	快点儿
chopstick	筷子
chop suey	杂碎
Choukoutien	周口店文化(的)
chow	吃的东西
chow v.	吃
chow chow	松狮狗
chowchow[1]	蜜饯
chowchow[2]	什锦菜;混合泡菜
chow mein	炒面
Chuang	壮族
Chungchia	仲家族(贵州傣族部落)
Chungking	重庆(的)

Chun ware	钧窑瓷
classifier	量词
clog box	木鱼
comprador	买办
Confucian[1]	儒家
Confucian[2]	儒家(的)
Confucian[3]	儒家学者(的)
Confucianism	儒家学说
Confucianist	儒家
Confucius	孔子
congou	功夫茶
cumshaw	小费
Dandong	丹东
dim sum	点心
Double Ten	双十节
Dragon Boat Festival	端午节
fang shih	方士(方术之士)
fan-tan	番摊(接龙游戏)
fatchoy	发菜
Feast of Lanterns	元宵节
fei ts'ui	翡翠
fen	分
feng huang	凤凰
feng shui	风水
filial piety	孝
Fitzhugh	福州瓷塑
flat peach	蟠桃
Foochow[1]	福州(的)
Foochow[2]	福州话
Foo dog	福狗
foot-binding	缠足
foo yong	芙蓉蛋
foreign devil	洋鬼子
Formosa camphor	樟脑
Formosan pheasant	台湾雉

Fu dog	福狗
Fujian	福建
Fukien	福建(的)
Fu lion	福狮狗
Gaoxiong	高雄(的)
ginseng	人参
golden larch	金钱松
golden monkey	金丝猴
golden pheasant	金鸡
goldfish	金鱼
grass carp	草鱼
grass character	草体字
grass cloth	夏布
grass hand	草书
Guangdong	广东
Guilin	桂林
Guiyang[1]	贵阳(的)
Guiyang[2]	贵阳
gung ho	狂热的
haikwan tael	海关两
Hainanese	海南人
hairy China car damom	阳春砂
haitsai	海菜
Hakka[1]	客家人
Hakka[2]	客家话
Han	汉朝(的)
Hangchow	杭州(的)
Hangzhou	杭州(的)
Hankow	汉口(的)
Heavenly Preceptor	天师
Hei-Miao	黑苗
Henan/Honan	河南
Hengyang	衡阳
hoisin sauce	海鲜酱
Hok-lo	福佬;福建人

Hong	（洋）行
Hong Kong	香港（的）
Hsia	夏朝
Hsi-Fan (of Tibet)	西番
Hsin	信（念）
Hsiung-Nu	匈奴
Hsüan-t'ung	宣统
Hu	胡人
Hubei	湖北
Hunanese[1]	湖南（的）
Hunanese[2]	湖南人
Hupeh	湖北（的）
Hylam[1]	海南话
Hylam[2]	海南人；海南话
hyson	熙春茶
Ipin	宜宾（的）
Jap (disparaging and offensive)	（贬损）日本人（的）
Japan	日本
japan[1]	亮漆
japan[2]	刷油漆
Japanese[1]	日本的
Japanese[2]	日本人
Japanese[3]	日语
Japanesery	日式装饰品
Japanesque	日本式的
Japanesy	日本风格
Japanism	日本民族主义
Japanize	日本化
japanned leather	黑亮漆皮
japanned peacock	黑亮孔雀
japannery	刷漆间
Japanophile	亲日派
Japlish[1]	日式英语
Japlish[2]	英日混合语
Japonian	〈旧〉日本人

Japonica	日本海棠
Japonism	日本风格
jen	仁
Jiangsu	江苏
jiao (a monetary unit)	（货币单位）角
jung	戎
Kaifeng	开封(的)
Kalanchoe	伽蓝菜
kang	炕
Kao-hsiung	高雄(的)
kao liang	高粱(酒)
Kaolin	高岭土
Keelung	基隆(的)
Keemun	祁门红茶
Kiangsu	江苏(的)
Kin	金人
kin[1]	亲族
kin[2]	亲戚；亲属
knife money	刀币
Ko	哥窑
ko-hcmp	葛麻
kowtow	磕头
Kpang Hsi	康熙(的)
Kuan	官窑瓷
Kuan Hua	官话
Kuchean	龟兹语
kumquat	金橘
kung fu	功夫
Kuo-yü	国语
kuping tael	库平两
Kwangtung	广东(的)
Kwangtung ware	广窑瓷器
Kweichow	贵州
Kweilin	桂林(的)
Kweiyang	贵阳(的)

kylin	麒麟
Lanchow	兰州(的)
Lang shan	狼山鸡
Lantian man	蓝田猿人
lao dah	(船)老大
Latinxua	拉丁化
legalist	法家
Li	黎族
li^1	礼
li^2	里
liang	两
likin	厘金
ling^1	菱角
ling^2	鳕鱼
litchi	荔枝
lohan	罗汉
lokao	绿膏；中国绿
long an	龙眼
loquat	枇杷
lung	龙
mafoo	马夫
mah-jong	麻将
mahuang	麻黄
Manchu cherry	毛樱桃；山樱桃
Manchurian crab	毛山荆子
Manchurian dog	满洲犬
Manchurian tiger	东北虎
Manchurian wolf	东北灰狼
mandarin collar	中式领
mandarin duck	鸳鸯
mandarin oil	橘皮油
mandarin orange	柑橘
mandarin porcelain	官瓷
mandarin red	橘红
Maoism	毛泽东思想

Maotai	茅台酒
Miao¹	苗语
Miao²	苗族
Miao-tse	苗子
mi-lu	麋鹿
Min	闽语
Min-chia¹	民家族；民家人
Min-chia²	民家语
Ming	明朝（的）
moon cake	月饼
moon-gate	月洞门
mou	亩
moutan	牡丹
mui-tsai	妹仔
Na-khi	纳西族
Nanchang	南昌（的）
nankeen	南京棉布
nankeen	南京棉布
nankeen cotton	南京棉
nankeen lily	南京百合
Nankeen porcelain	南京青花瓷
nankeens	南京棉布裤
Nankin	南京瓷
Nanking	南京瓷
Nanking cherry	南京樱桃；毛樱桃
nanmu	楠木
Nanning	南宁（的）
Nantung	南通（的）
neo-Confucian	新儒家（的）
Ningpo	宁波（的）
Nung	侬人
oolong	乌龙茶
oopak	湖北红茶
oracle bone	甲骨（文）
pai-hua	白话

pailou	牌楼
pak-a-pu (of lottery)	白鸽票
pakchoi	（小）白菜
paktong	白铜
Paoting	保定（的）
peen-to	扁桃
Peiping	北平（的）
Pekin	北京鸭
Peking	北京（的）
Peking blue	北京蓝
Peking cotoneaster	灰栒子
Peking duck	北京烤鸭
Pekingese[1]	北京话（的）
Pekingese[2]	北京人（的）
Peking man	北京猿人
Peking nightingale	红嘴相思鸟
Pekingology[1]	北京学
Pekingology[2]	中国政策研究
Pekoe	白毫
pela	白蜡
pe-tsai	（大）白菜
petuntse	白墩子；瓷土
phonetic	声旁
phonogram	形声字
pidan	皮蛋
pien niu	犏牛
Pinyin	拼音
pi-pa (a musical instrument)	（乐器）琵琶
pongee	柞丝绸
P'u-i	溥仪
radical	部首
Red Guard	红卫兵
red rice	红曲；植物染料
renminbi	人民币
rice-field eel	黄鳝

ring-necked pheasant	环颈雉
running dog	走狗
Sage-King	圣君
sampan	舢板
samshu	烧酒
sand pear	沙梨
sang	笙
sangley	常来人；商旅（菲律宾华商）
seal character	篆体字
see-low (dice game)	四五六（骰子游戏）
Sekhwan	生番（台湾土著人）
senso	蟾酥
Shandong	山东
Shang	商朝（的）
shanghai	拐骗
Shanghai	上海（的）
Shanghailander	上海人
shan-jen	山人
shantung	山东绸
Shan-tung	山东（的）
shantung straw	山东金丝草帽
Shao-hsing	绍兴（的）
Shaoxing	绍兴
shar-pei	沙皮狗
Shasi	沙市（的）
She	畲族
sheng	升
Shenyang	沈阳
shih tzu	狮子狗；西施犬
shou	寿（字）
shu	恕
silken	丝制的
silking	丝纹
silklike	丝状的
silky	丝滑

singsong girl	歌女
sling	西宁山羊毛
sodoku	鼠咬热
Son of Heaven	天子
Soochow	苏州(的)
souchong	小种红茶
spade money	铲币；布币
suan pan	算盘
subgum	炒什锦
Suchow	徐州(的)
Sung	宋朝(的)
sung lo	松萝茶
Sun Yat-senism	中山主义
Swatow	汕头(的)
sweet orange	甜橙
sycee	银锭
T'ien	天；天命
T'ien T'ai	天台宗
Tai	傣族
Tai Chi	太极拳
Taichung	台中(的)
Tainan	台南(的)
taipan	大班
Taipei	台北(的)
Taiping	太平天国起义者
Taiwan	台湾(的)
Taiyuan	太原(的)
tan	担
Tan	疍家人
Tang	唐朝(的)
tangram	七巧板
T'ang T'ai Tsung	唐太宗(李世民)
Tanka	疍家
tao	道
tao-tieh	(瓷器上的)饕餮纹

Tayal	(台湾)泰雅族
tea	茶
teagarden[1]	茶园
teagarden[2]	茶室
Thian Shan sheep	天山盘羊
Thian Shan stag	天山鹿
thunder god vine	雷公藤
tiao	吊
T'ien	天神
Tientsin	天津(的)
Tientsin jute	天津黄麻
ting	鼎
Ting	定窑
Ting ware	定窑
Ting yao	定窑
tong (a secret society of Chinese in the U. S.)	堂会;兄弟会
tongman	堂会成员
tree ear	木耳
trigram	卦
trumpet lily	卷丹
tsao	枣
tsatlee	辑里生丝
Tsinan	济南(的)
Tsingtao	青岛(的)
tuchun	督军
tu-chung	杜仲
T'u-jen (division of Dai ethnic group)	(傣族)土佬人
T'u-lao	土佬部落
Tung-hu	东胡
tung oil	桐油
tung tree	油桐树
Twankay tea	屯溪茶
typhoon	台风
Tzpu-chou	磁州瓷
urheen	二弦

wampee	黄皮树
wang	（大）王
water pine	水松
Wenchow	温州(的)
wen-li	文言文
wen-yen	文言文
whangee	黄藜竹
wok	镬；锅
wongshy	黄栀
won ton	馄饨
Wu	吴语
Wuchang	武昌(的)
Wuhan	武汉(的)
Wuhu	芜湖(的)
wu shu	武术
Wusih	无锡(的)
wu-ts'ai	五彩
wu wei	无为
Xi'an	西安(的)
Xuzhou	徐州(的)
yang	阳
yangtao	猕猴桃
Yantai	烟台(的)
Yarkand[1]	莎车
Yarkand[2]	叶尔羌河
Yaw Yin	野人(景颇族)
yen[1] (a Japanese monetary unit)	元
yen[2]	瘾
yen[3] v.	强烈希望；渴望
yen-hok	鸦片烟针构
yen-shee	烟屎
Yibin	宜宾
Yi-hsing	宜兴
Yi-hsing ware	宜兴陶器
Yi-hsing yao	宜兴窑

Yin	(商)殷
yin	阴
Yuan	(行政、司法、考试、监察等)院
yuan (a monetary unit)	元
Zhejiang	浙江
Zhenjiang	镇江(的)

附录三　坎农版英语中的汉语借词词表

美国德州 A & M 大学（Texas A & M University）的加兰·坎农（Garland Cannon）于 1988 年在《美国语》（American Speech）第 1 期上发表了《英语中的汉语借词》（Chinese Borrowings in English）一文，他结合相关语料和 8 部英语案头词典对 970 余个汉语借词的形式、意义、来源、分类等进行了阐述，并在附表中列出了其中 790 个词。除几个找不到汉语来源依据的以外，本词表全数引用（排序略有变化），并提供了汉语对应词。英文大小写、词类注释均取自原文，括注是译者所加。由于这些孤立的词没有任何语境可以参考，只能结合相关词典和资料进行分析其含义，翻译中肯定有不准确的地方，仅供参考。

英语表达	中国特色词
Abyssinian tea	阿比西尼亚茶
afternoon tea	下午茶
Amoy	厦门话
Amoy *adj.*	厦门的
Amoyese	厦门人
Analects of Confucius	论语
an hua	暗花
Anking *adj.*	安庆的
Anshan *adj.*	鞍山的
ansu	山杏树
Antung *adj.*	安东的
Appalachian tea	阿巴拉契亚茶
Arabian tea	阿拉伯茶；巧茶
Australian tea	澳洲茶
barefoot doctor	赤脚医生

bear's paw	熊掌
beef tea	牛肉浓汤
beggar's chicken	叫化鸡
Benkulen tea	明古鲁茶
bird's nest	燕窝
bird's nest *adj.*	燕窝的
bird's nest *v.*	采摘燕窝
bird's nest fungus	鸟巢菌
bird's nest soup	燕窝汤
black tea	红茶
Blue Mountain tea	蓝山茶
bohea	武夷茶
bohea *adj.*	武夷茶的
bok choy	白菜
bonze	和尚;僧人
Botany Bay tea	博特尼湾茶
Bourbon tea	波旁茶
Brazilian tea	巴西茶
brick tea	砖茶
broken tea	碎茶
bush tea	灌木茶
cambric tea	牛奶红茶
campoi	拣焙茶
Canada tea	加拿大茶
Canton	广州
Canton *adj.*	广州的
Canton crepe	广绫
Cantonese	广州话
Cantonese *adj.*	广州的
canton flannel	绒布
Canton ginger	广式腌姜
Canton matting	广式地垫
Canton ware	广州彩瓷
capitalist road	资本主义道路
capitalist roader	走资派

Ceylon tea	锡兰茶
Ceylon tea tree	锡兰茶树
Ch'an	禅
Changchun *adj.*	长春的
Changsha *adj.*	长沙的
ch'ang shan	（植物）常山
Ch'anism	禅宗
Ch'anist	禅宗信徒
char	茶
Chefoo *adj.*	芝罘的
Chengtu *adj.*	成都的
Ch'eng-tzu-yai *adj.*	城子崖的
Cheongsam	长衫；旗袍
chiao	角
chiao-tou	藠头
Ch'i-chia	齐家文化（的）
chi'en	乾
Chien *adj.*	建窑瓷的
Ch'ien Lung	乾隆
Chien ware	建窑
ch'ih	赤
chih fu	知府
chih hsien	知县
chin	琴
Ch'in	秦
China tea	中国茶
chin-chin	再见
chin-chin *interj.*	你好
chin-chin *v.*	请干杯
Chinchow *adj.*	锦州的
Chinese Revolution	辛亥革命
ch'ing	清
ching[1]	经书
ching[2]	经书的
Ch'ing[1]	清朝

Ch'ing²	清朝的
chingma	苘麻
Ching Ming	清明
Chingpaw	景颇族
Chinkiang *adj.*	晋江的
chop-chop *interj.*	快快
chop-chop *adv.*	快点儿
Chopstick	筷子
Chopsuey	杂碎
Chou	周
Choukoutien	周口店文化
Choukoutien *adj.*	周口店文化的
chow	腌菜
chow *v.*	吃
chow chow	松狮狗
chow fan	炒饭
chow mein	炒面
choy sum	菜心
Chuang	壮族
chüeh	爵
Chün	钧窑瓷
Chün *adj.*	钧窑瓷的
Ch'un Ch'iu	春秋
Chungking *adj.*	重庆的
Chung Yeung	重阳节
Chung Yung	中庸
Confucian	儒家信徒
Confucian *adj.*	儒家的
Confucianism	孔子学说
Confucius	孔子
congou	功夫茶
cowslip tea	黄花茶
Cultural Revolution	文化大革命
cumshaw	赏钱；小礼物
cumshaw *v.*	感谢

cup of tea	一杯茶
daimiate	大名府
daimio	大名
dairi	大内（天皇的宫廷）
Darjeeling	大吉岭茶
dazibao	大字报
dimsum	点心
ding how	顶好
dragon robes	龙袍
dragon's eyes	龙眼
dragon throne	龙座
drunken shrimp	醉虾
Dzungar	准噶尔
face	面子
fang shih	方士
fan kwai	番鬼
fan-tan	番摊（接龙游戏）
fei ts'ui	翡翠
fen	分
fêng huang	凤凰
Fengkieh *adj.*	奉节的
fêng ling	风铃
fêng shui	风水
fên-ting	粉定（白瓷）
fish ball	鱼丸
Five Classics	五经
Fo	佛
foki	伙计
Foochow	福州话
Foochow *adj.*	福州的
foo yong	芙蓉蛋
foreign devil	洋鬼子
Four Books	四书
Fu	府
Fu dog	福狗

Fung shui	风水
Fushun *adj.*	抚顺的
galingale	高良姜
Gang of Four	四人帮
ginkgo	银杏树
ginkgo nut	银杏果；白果
ginseng	人参
ginseng *adj.*	人参的
ginseng family	人参家族
gow	鸦片膏
Great Leap Forward	大跃进
Great Wall of China	中国长城
green tea	绿茶
gung ho *adj.*	工合的；热心的
gunpowder tea	珠茶
gweilo	鬼佬
haikwan	海关
haikwan tael	海关两
Hainanese	海南人
Hainanese *adj.*	海南的
hairy crab	毛蟹；大闸蟹
haitsai	海菜
Hakka	客家人；客家话
Han	汉朝
Han *adj.*	汉人的
Hangchow *adj.*	杭州的
Hankow *adj.*	汉口的
Hanlin	翰林
hao t'ung	毫铜
Harbin *adj.*	哈尔滨的
hegemony	霸权
Hei-Miao	黑苗
Hengyang *adj.*	衡阳（的）
high tea	傍晚茶
hoey	堂会

hoisin sauce	海鲜酱
Hok-lo	福佬
Honan	河南绸
Hong	(洋)行
Hong Kong *adj.*	香港的
Hong Kong dollar	港币
Hsia	夏朝
hsiao	孝
hsien[1]	县
hsien[2]	贤;仙
hsien shêng	先生
Hsi-Fan	西番
hsin	信
hsing shêng	兴盛
Hsinhua	新华
Hsiung-Nu	匈奴
hsiu ts'ai	秀才
hu	和(牌)
Hu	胡人
Huang Ti	黄帝
hu ch'in	胡琴
hui	回族
Hunanese *adj.*	湖南的
Hunanese[1]	湖南话
Hunanese[2]	湖南人
Hundred Flowers	百花
hutung	胡同
hyson	熙春茶
I-Ching	《易经》
Indian tea	印度茶
India tea	印度茶
inro	印笼
Ipin *adj.*	宜宾的
itzebu	四分之一两
Jap	日本人

Jap *adj.*	日本人的
jap *v.*	偷袭
Japan	〈旧〉日本人
japan	亮漆
japan *v.*	涂黑色光亮漆
Japan + N(N)	（做修饰词）日本
Japan ashberry	日本树莓
Japanee	日本人
Japanese	日本人；日语
Japanese *adj.*	日本的
Japanese + N(N)	（做修饰词）日本（式）
Japanese andromeda	马醉木
Japaneseness	日本特点
Japaneserie	日本风格/特色
Japanesery	日本装饰品
Japanesque *adj.*	日本式的
Japanesy *adj.*	日式的
japanic acid	日本蜡酸
Japanism	日本精神
Japanization	日本化
Japanize *v.*	日本化
japanned leather	黑亮漆皮
japanned peacock	黑亮孔雀
Japanner	油漆工
japanners' brown	油漆干燥剂
japannery	刷漆间
japanning	涂漆
Japano- *comb. form*	（构词成分）日本—
Japanology	日本学
Japanophile	亲日派
Japanophobia	恐日派
Japlish	日式英语
Japlish *adj.*	英日混合语
Japonian *adj.*	日本人的
Japonica	日本海棠

Japonism	日本风格
jen	仁
Jesuits' tea	耶稣会士茶
Ju^1	汝窑瓷器
Ju^2	汝州
Judo	柔道
judoist	柔道
judoka	柔道运动员
judoman	柔道运动员
jujitsu	柔术
jusi	菲律宾丝
kago	驾笼;滑竿
Kaifeng adj.	开封的
kaifong	街坊
k'ai shu	楷书
kaito	街渡
Kalanchoe	伽蓝菜
kalgan	喀拉干皮货
Kalgan adj.	张家口的
kang	炕
K'ang Hsi	康熙
K'ang Hsi adj.	康熙瓷的
kanji	（日语）汉字
kan pei	干杯
Kaohsiung adj.	高雄的
kaoliang	高粱酒
kaolin	高岭土
kaolinic adj.	高岭土的
kaolinite	高岭石
kaolinitic adj.	高岭石的
kaolinization	高岭土化
kaolinize v.	使高岭土化
ketchup	番茄酱
kiang	西藏野驴
Kin	金人

kin[1]	金人家族
kin[2]	亲戚关系
kirin	麒麟
Ko	哥窑
koan-tree	菩提树
ko-hemp	葛麻
kongsi	公司
kowtow	磕头
kowtow *v.*	磕头
ku	觜
kuan	官
Kuan	官窑
Kuan Hua	官话
Kuan Yin	观音
Kuchean	龟兹语
kuei[1]	鬼
kuei[2] (food and ritual vessel)	簋
kuk	局
kumquat	金橘
kung *adj.*	公制的
kung fu	功夫
kung hei fat choy	恭喜发财
Kuomintang	国民党
Kuo-yü	国语
kuping tael	库平两
kwai-lo	鬼佬
Kwangtung ware	广东瓷
Kweilin *adj.*	桂林的
Kweiyang *adj.*	贵阳的
kylin	麒麟
Labrador tea	拉布拉多茶
Laisee	利是
Lanchow *adj*	兰州的
Lantian Man	蓝田猿人
laodah (the skipper of a Chinese craft)	船老大

la pa	腊八
Lapsang *adj.*	拉普山的
Lapsang Souchong	正山小种红茶
lap sap	垃圾
lap sap chung	垃圾虫
lei (ancient Chinese wine or water vessel)	罍
Li	礼
li^1	厘
li^2	里
li^3 (ancient Chinese cooking vessel)	鬲
liang	两
liberty tea	自由茶
likin	厘金(税)
lin	麟
ling lung	灵龙
litchi	荔枝
litchi nut	荔枝果
lokao	绿膏
Lolo (ethnic group)	罗罗族
longan	龙眼
Long March	长征
loquat	枇杷
lotus seeds	莲子
lung	龙
Lung Ch'üan	龙泉瓷
Lu-Wang School	陆王心学
macao	赌博纸牌游戏
Macao *adj.*	澳门(的)
mafoo	马夫
mahjong	麻将
mahjong^1 *v.*	和牌
mahjong^2 *v.*	打麻将
Mao	毛泽东
Maoism	毛泽东思想
maotai	茅台酒

marsh tea	沼泽茶叶
mei p'ing	梅瓶
Mexican tea	墨西哥茶
Miao	苗族人；苗族语
Miao *adj.*	苗族(人/语)的
Middle Kingdom	中国
mien	面(条)
Min^1	闽语
Min^2 *adj.*	闽语的
Ming	明朝
Ming *adj.*	明朝的
Ming tree	盆景树
Mohism	墨家学说
Mohist	墨家
Mohist *adj.*	墨家的
mou	亩
mountain tea	山茶
moutan	牡丹
Mukden *adj.*	奉天的
Mutankiang *adj.*	牡丹江的
nagami kumquat	椭圆金柑
nagami kumquat	拿干米金橘
Nanchang *adj.*	南昌的
nankeen	南京棉布
nankeen bird	土布鸟
nankeen hawk	南京鹰
nankeen lily	南京百合
Nankeen porcelain	南京青花瓷
Nanking *adj.*	南京的
Nanking cherry	南京樱桃；毛樱桃
nanmu	楠木
Nanning *adj.*	南宁的
Nantung *adj.*	南通的
National People's Congress	全国人民代表大会
New Jersey tea	新泽西茶

New Zealand tea tree	新西兰茶树
nien hao	年号
Ningpo *adj.*	宁波的
NPC	全国人民代表大会
oolong	乌龙茶
oracle bone(s)	甲骨(文)
orange pekoe	橙白毫
Oswego tea	奥斯威戈茶
P. L. A.	人民解放军
pai-hua	白话
pai-kau	牌九
pai-lou	牌楼
pai ting	白丁
pai tun tzu	白墩子(瓷土)
pai tzu	白族
pak-a-pu	白鸽票
pak choy	(广东)白菜
pak pai (a car used illegally as a taxi)	白牌
paktong	白铜
p'an	盘
pan (a musical instrument)	(竹)板
Panchen Lama	班禅喇嘛
pao-chia	保甲(制度)
Paoting *adj.*	保定的
pao-tzu	包子
paper tiger	纸老虎
Paraguay tea	巴拉圭茶
Peiping *adj.*	北平的
Peke	京巴狗
peke-faced *adj.*	京巴狗脸的
Pekin	北京鸭
Peking *adj.*	北京话的
Peking blue	北京蓝
Peking cotoneaster	灰栒子
Pekingese	北京人;北京话

Pekingese *adj.*	北京的
Peking man	北京猿人
Peking nightingale	北京夜莺
Pekingology	北京学(中国问题研究)
Peking spaniel	北京猎犬
pekoe	白毫茶
pela	白蜡
People's Republic of China	中华人民共和国
pe-tsai	白菜
pctuntse	白墩子(瓷土)
pien chung	编钟
pien k'ing	汴京
pien niu	犏牛
pien yao	汴窑
pink tea	正式的下午茶
pinyin	(汉语)拼音
pi-pa	琵琶
p'o	魄
pongee	柞丝绸
pung *interj.*	碰了(和了)
pung *v.* (of mahjong)	(麻将)碰(和)
Pure Land	净土;极乐世界
Putonghua	普通话
qi (of philosophy)	气
rectification	整风
Red Guard	红卫兵
Red Guard doctor	红卫兵医生
Red Guardism	红卫兵运动
red rice	红米
reform through labor	劳改
rcnminbi	人民币
reorganizationist	改组派
running dog	走狗
sage tea	鼠尾草茶
saimin	细面

Saint Helena tea	圣赫勒拿茶
samfoo	衫裤
samisen	三弦
sampan	舢板
sampan-wallah	纤夫
samshu	三烧酒
Sanfan	三反（运动）
sang *v.*	收人参
sang¹	笙
sang²	参
Sangley (Chinese trader in the Philippines)	常来人；商旅（在菲律宾经商的华人）
san hsien	三弦
san ts'ai	三彩
sassafras tea	黄樟茶
School of Law	法家
School of Mind	心学
scorched earth *adj.*	焦土政策的
se (a musical instrument)	瑟
semi-proletariat	半无产阶级
seppuku	切腹自杀
sesshin (of Zen Buddhism)	（禅宗）摄心；接心
shaku	笏
shakudo	赤铜
Shang	商（朝）
Shang *adj.*	商朝的
Shanghai	浦东鸡；三黄鸡
Shanghai *adj.*	上海的
Shanghai *v.*	强迫；诱骗
shanghaier	拐骗者
Shanghailander	上海人
Shanghainese¹	上海话
Shanghainese² *adj.*	上海话的
Shanghai tael	上海两

Shang-ti	上帝
shan-jen (ethnic groups in west Yunnan)	山人
shantung	山东绸
shantung straw	金丝草帽
Shaoshing	绍兴酒
Shaoshing *adj.*	绍兴的
shark's fin	鲨鱼翅
shark's fin soup	鱼翅汤
sharpei	沙皮狗
Shasi *adj.*	沙市的
She	畲族
Shen	神
sheng *adj.*	生角的
sheng^1	升
sheng^2	生（角）
sheng^3	笙
shibuichi	四分一（铜银合金）
shibuichi-doshi	四分一铜子
Shih Ching	诗经
Shih Tzu	狮子狗；西施犬
Shinto	神道
Shintoism	神道教
Shintoist	神道信徒
Shintoistic *adj.*	神道的
shippo (ware)	七宝瓷器
shogun	（日本古代的）将军
shogunate	将军职位
shu	恕
Shu Fu porcelain	枢府瓷
Sian *adj.*	西安的
sodoku	鼠咬热
soldiers' tea	士兵茶话会
so-na	唢呐
Son of Heaven	天子
Soochow *adj.*	苏州的

souchong	小种茶
South Sea tea	南海茶
soy	大豆;黄豆
soya	大豆(食物)
soya *adj.*	大豆的
soya bean	大豆
soya-bean oil	大豆油
soyate *adj.*	大豆油酸酯的
soybean	大豆
soy-bean *adj.*	大豆油的
soybean cyst nematode	大豆孢囊线虫病
soybean lecithin	大豆卵磷脂
soybean milk	豆浆
soybean oil	豆油
soybean oil meal	大豆油粕
soy flour	大豆粉
soy frame	酱油瓶架
soymilk	豆浆
splittism	分裂主义
splittist	分裂主义分子
splittist *adj.*	分裂主义的
suan pan	算盘
subgum	什锦
subgum *adj.*	素什锦的
Suchow *adj.*	徐州(的)
Sui	隋(朝)
Sung	宋(朝)
Sung *adj.*	宋朝的
sunglo	松罗(茶)
Sun Yat-sen	中山式的(服装)
Sun Yat-senism	三民主义
Swatow	汕头器
Swatow *adj.*	汕头的
Swatow (ware)	汕头瓷器
sweet tea	甜茶

sycee	银锭
Szechuan *adj.*	四川的
Szechuanese	四川人；四川话
Szechuanese *adj.*	四川人/话的
Sze Yap	四邑话
Sze Yap *adj.*	四邑话的
Tachai *adj.*	大寨的
ta chuan	大篆
t'ai chi	太极拳
T'ai Chi	太极
Taichung *adj.*	台中的
taipan	大班
Taipei	台北（的）
Tai-ping	太平天国运动
tai tai	太太
Taiwan *adj.*	台湾的
Taiwan hemp	台湾大麻
Taiwan Strait	台湾海峡
Taiyuan	太原的
tan^1	担
tan^2	旦（角）
Tang	唐朝
Tang *adj.*	唐代工艺的
tangpu	党部
tangram	七巧板
Tangut	唐古特人；唐古特语
Tanka	蛋家
tao	道
Taoism	道家
Taoist	道士；道教徒
Tao Kuang	道光年代
Tao Kuang *adj.*	道光瓷器
taotai	道台
Tao Te Ching	道德经
taotieh	**饕餮**

taoyin	道尹
tau fu	豆腐
tchouma	筹码
Te	德
tea	茶
tea *adj.*	茶饮的
tea *v.*	喝茶
tea + N(N)	（做修饰词）茶
tea bag	袋茶
teaer	饮茶人
teaette	沏茶勺
teaey *adj.*	茶味的
teagardeny	茶园的；茶室的
tealess	无茶的
Tê-hua	德化瓷
Tê-hua *adj.*	德化瓷的
temmoku	天目釉
Temple of Heaven	天坛
Teochew	潮州话
Teochew *adj.*	潮州的
Theezan tea	雀梅藤茶
three-anti	三反（运动）
tiao (a monetary unit)	（货币单位）吊
T'ien	天
Tien Chu	天主
T'ien t'ai	天台宗
Tientsin	天津的
tile-tea	砖茶
ting	鼎
Ting ware	定窑
Tin Hau	天后
ti tzu	笛子
tong[1] (a secret society of Chinese in the U. S.)	堂会
tong[2] *adj.*	堂会的
tongman	堂会成员

tou (ancient Chinese food vessel)	豆
tou ts'ai	多彩
tou ts'ai *adj.*	多彩的(瓷器)
Triad	三合会
Triad *adj.*	三合会的
tribute rice	贡米
tsao shu	草书
tsatlee	生丝
Tsinan *adj.*	济南的
Tsingtao *adj.*	青岛的
tsingtauite	青岛岩
Tso Chüan	《左传》
Tsu	(氏)族
tsun *adj.*	尊形的
tsun[1]	尊
tsun[2]	兽形杯
Tsung-li Yamen	总理衙门
tsungtu	总督
tuchun	督军
tu-chung	杜仲
T'u-jen	土佬人
T'u-lao	土佬族
tu-mo (acupuncture point)	督脉
tungate	桐油催干剂
tung oil	桐油
tung tree	油桐树
tupan	督办
tutang	督堂(总督)
Twankay tea	屯溪茶
tycoon	大亨
typhoon	台风
typhoon *v.*	刮台风
Tz'u-Chou	磁州瓷
urhcen	二弦;二胡
Wai-Chiao pu	外交部

Wai-wu pu	外务部
walking on two legs[1]	两条腿走路
walking-on-two-legs[2] *adj.*	两条腿走路的
wallposter	墙报
wampee	黄皮(果)
wang	王
Wanhsien *adj.*	万县的
Wan-Li	万历瓷
Wan-Li *adj.*	万历瓷的
warlord	军阀
warlordism	军阀割据
Warring States	战国
Wei	魏朝
Wei *adj.*	魏朝的
wei ch'i	围棋
Wenchow *adj.*	温州的
wen jên	文人
wen-li	文言文
wen-yen	文言文
West Indian tea	西印度茶
whangee	黄藜竹
wild tea	野生茶
winter melon	冬瓜
wok	镬;锅
wonk	黄狗
wonton	馄饨
worker-peasant *adj.*	工农的
work point	工分
Wu	吴语
Wu *adj.*	吴语的
Wuchang *adj.*	武昌的
Wufan	五反运动
Wufan *adj.*	五反的
Wuhan *adj.*	武汉的
Wuhu *adj.*	芜湖的

wu shu	武术
Wusih *adj.*	无锡的
wu-ts'ai	五彩釉
wu wei	无为
wuwei *adj.*	无为的
yamen	衙门
yang	阳
yang ch'in	扬琴
Yangchow *adj.*	扬州的
yang ko	秧歌
Yang-Mills *adj.*	杨-米尔斯理论的
Yang Shao *adj.*	仰韶文化的
yangtao	杨桃
yang-ts'ai	洋彩
Yao	瑶族
Yao *adj.*	瑶族的
Yarkand[1]	叶尔羌河
Yarkand[2] *adj.*	叶尔羌的
Yarkandi[1]	叶尔羌人
Yarkandi[2] *adj.*	叶尔羌人的
yen[1]	鸦片烟
yen[2] (a strong desire or propensity)	（鸦片烟）瘾
yen[3] (a Japanese monetary unit)	元
yen[3] *v.* (to have an intense desire)	犯烟瘾；强烈渴望
Yenan *adj.*	延安时期的
yenbond	日元债券
yen-hok	烟杓
yen-shee	烟屎
yen-yen	烟瘾
yi	驿
Yi	彝族语
Yi *adj.*	彝族的
Yi-hsing ware	宜兴窑
Yin	（商）殷
yin[1]	阴

yin²	印
ying ch'ing	影青瓷
ying ch'ing *adj.*	影青瓷的
Yingkow *adj.*	营口的
yin-yang	阴阳
Yin-Yang School	阴阳家
yu¹	竽
yu² (ancient Chinese wine or rice vessel)	盂
yuan (a monetary unit)	元
Yuan¹	元朝
Yuan²	元代瓷器
yuan hsiao	元宵
yüeh	钺（古代兵器）
Yüeh¹	越窑瓷
Yüeh²	粤人
Yüeh³	粤语
Yüeh¹ *adj.*	越窑瓷的
Yüeh² *adj.*	粤语的
yüeh ch'in	月琴
Yüeh-p'an (a division of the Hsiung-Nu, ancestors of the Avars)	鲜卑族
yulan	玉兰
yulo	摇橹
yulo *v.*	摇橹
yum cha	（港式）饮茶
yum sing	饮胜（干杯）
Yung-chêng *adj.*	雍正瓷的
yün lo	云锣
Yunnanese	云南人
Yunnanese *adj.*	云南人的
Zen	禅

说明：在原词表中，还有 hei jen, jo sun, siomio, Tan, teh ch'i, yveh ch'in 等几个词，由于找不到汉语的来源依据，且坎农的相关文章也无相关线索，无法提供汉语对等词。